THE TERRI
WARS OF THE WEST

ALSO BY JERRY KEENAN

*Wilson's Cavalry Corps: Union Campaigns
in the Western Theatre, October 1864 through Spring 1865*
(McFarland, 1998; softcover 2006)

The Terrible Indian Wars of the West

A History from the Whitman Massacre to Wounded Knee, 1846–1890

Jerry Keenan

McFarland & Company, Inc., Publishers
Jefferson, North Carolina

All photographs are from the Library of Congress.

LIBRARY OF CONGRESS CATALOGUING-IN-PUBLICATION DATA

Names: Keenan, Jerry, author.
Title: The terrible Indian Wars of the West : a history from the Whitman Massacre to Wounded Knee, 1846–1890 / Jerry Keenan.
Other titles: History from the Whitman Massacre to Wounded Knee, 1846–1890
Description: Jefferson, North Carolina : McFarland & Company, Inc., Publishers, 2016 | Includes bibliographical references and index.
Identifiers: LCCN 2015044850 | ISBN 9780786499403 (softcover : acid free paper) ∞
Subjects: LCSH: West (U.S.)—History, Military—19th century. | Indians of North America—Wars.
Classification: LCC E81 .K45 2016 | DDC 355.00978—dc23
LC record available at http://lccn.loc.gov/2015044850

BRITISH LIBRARY CATALOGUING DATA ARE AVAILABLE

© 2016 Jerry Keenan. All rights reserved

No part of this book may be reproduced or transmitted in any form or by any means, electronic or mechanical, including photocopying or recording, or by any information storage and retrieval system, without permission in writing from the publisher.

On the cover a print of *The Custer Fight*, the Battle of the Little Bighorn, showing Native Americans on horseback in foreground, 1903, Charles Marion Russell (Library of Congress)

Printed in the United States of America

McFarland & Company, Inc., Publishers
Box 611, Jefferson, North Carolina 28640
www.mcfarlandpub.com

For Dad
From Number One Cub

Acknowledgments

Writing is a lonely endeavor. Despite that, creation does not occur in a vacuum. In one way or another every author owes a debt of thanks to those innumerable souls who inspired, encouraged, and in countless other ways aided the end result of the author's labors. In my case, I can only humbly acknowledge that legion of scholars and writers whose diligent research immeasurably aided my own effort. To them, a heartfelt thanks. Thanks also to Bob Schram, BookendsDesign for creating the map for this volume.

That said, to my wife Carol I owe my deepest debt; her continued love and support made it all possible.

Table of Contents

Preface	1
Timeline	3
Introduction	7

I—The Pacific Northwest

Prologue: The Oregon Country	15
Death on the Rye Grass: The Whitman Massacre and the Cayuse War, 1847–1855	15
Isaac Stevens	20
"Nits make lice": The Rogue River Wars, 1851–1857	20
The War of 1853	27
The War of 1855	31
The Yakima and Coastal Wars, 1856–1858	39

II—California and Nevada

Prologue: Bloody El Dorado	50
The Mariposa War, 1850–1851	51
The Mendocino War, 1859–1860	57
Nevada's Paiute War, 1860	59
The Owens Valley War, 1862–1863	69
War with the Northern Paiutes: Indian Raids Along the Western Segment of the Overland Trail, 1864–1868	73
Chinese Massacre	75
Crook and the Paiutes	76
Hell with the Fires Gone Out: The Modoc War, 1872–1873	79

III—New Mexico

Prologue: Poco Tiempo	92
Navajo Wars	94
The Missouri Volunteers Arrive	94

The Ugliest Man in the Army	98
Sandoval	98
Colonel Edwin Vose Bull Sumner	100
Fort Defiance	100
Henry Dodge	102
Governor David Meriwether	104
Kit Caron Reports	105
Jornada del Muerto	107
Chandler-Eaton Expedition	110
Colonel Benjamin L.E. Bonneville	111
The Black Jim War	115
Lieutenant Colonel Edward R.S. Canby and Major Henry Hopkins Sibley	123
Manuel Chavez, Navajo Fighter	126
The Arrival of Colonel James Henry Carleton	128
Kit Carson's Expedition to Canyon de Chelly	129
The Long Walk of the Navajo	130

IV—THE CENTRAL PLAINS

Prologue: Pike's Peak or Bust	132
The 1851 Horse Creek Treaty	133
Fort Laramie	133
1853 Overture	135
Grattan Massacre	136
"By God I'm for battle—no peace"	137
Blue Water Expedition	138
Bull Sumner Takes the Field	141
To Colorado	146
Governor John Evans	147
Colonel John Milton Chivington	148
The Hungate Massacre	151
The 3rd Colorado Volunteers	152
Sand Creek	154
The Tappan Commission Investigates	162
The War of 1865	165
Attack on Julesburg	166
Mud Springs and Rush Creek	168
The Connor Expedition	170
Colonel Thomas Moonlight	171
Colonel Nelson Cole, Lieutenant Colonel Samuel Walker and Colonel James H. Kidd	173

The Platte Bridge Fight	175
Connor Attacks Black Bear's Village	178
The Odyssey of Cole and Sawyer	178
Hancock Takes the Field	183
The Kidder Tragedy	198
Custer Is Court-Martialed	199
Philip H. Sheridan	202
The Battle of Beecher Island	203
The Battle of Summit Springs	205

V—THE SOUTHERN PLAINS

Prologue: Llano Estacado	207
Conflict on the Southern Plains	209
The Texas Rangers	209
Captain Randolph B. Marcy	211
The Comanche: Lords of the Southern Plains	213
John Robert Baylor	215
The Battle of the Washita	221
Enter the Quakers	227
The Warren Wagon Train Raid	228
Quanah Parker	230
The Red River (Buffalo) War	232
Adobe Walls	234
Colonel Nelson Appleton Miles	235
The Battle of Palo Duro Canyon	240
The Mexican Border Crisis	244

VI—IOWA, MINNESOTA AND THE NORTHERN PLAINS

Prologue: Little Crow to Sitting Bull	248
Conflict on the Northern Plains: War with the Arickaras	248
Spirit Lake, Iowa, 1857	249
Bloodbath in the Heartland: Minnesota, Summer 1862	251
Sunday, August 17, 1862	251
The Santees	252
Little Crow	254
The Uprising Begins	255
First Attack on New Ulm	256
Attack on Fort Ridgely	259
Second Attack on New Ulm	260
The Battle of Birch Coulee	262

General John Pope Is Appointed Department Commander	264
Fort Abercrombie	265
The Battle of Wood Lake and the End of the Uprising	266
The Release of the Hostages	267
The Hanging of the Condemned Santees	267
The Death of Little Crow	268
The Dakota Campaigns of Sibley and Sully, Summer 1863–1864	269
The Battle of Big Mound	270
The Battle of Dead Buffalo Lake	271
The Battle of Whitestone Hill	274
The Minnesota Brigade	278
The Battle of Killdeer Mountain	280
The Teton Lakota: Lords of the Northern Plains	284
Gold and Fire: Red Cloud's War, 1866–1868	285
The Bozeman Trail	285
Fort Phil Kearny: The Hated Post on the Piney	288
The Fetterman Disaster	290
The Amazing Ride of Portugee Phillips	292
The Hayfield and Wagon Box Fights, August 1867	294
The 1868 Laramie Treaty	298
Massacre on the Marias River, January 23, 1870	300
The Northern Pacific Railroad	300
Custer Meets the Sioux	302
Custer's 1874 Black Hills Expedition	303
The Great Sioux War	310
Reynolds Attacks the Cheyenne on Powder River, March 17, 1876	310
The Battle of the Rosebud, June 17, 1876	314
The Little Bighorn: Custer's Nadir, June 25, 1876	316
The "first scalp for Custer"	324
The Battle of Slim Buttes	326
Mackenzie's Attack on Dull Knife's Village	336
The Wolf Mountain Campaign	340
The End of the Great Sioux War	343
The Surrender and Death of Crazy Horse	346
The Flight of the Nez Perce	348
The Battle of White Bird Canyon	352
Joseph Surrenders	363
Flight of the Northern Cheyennes, 1878–1879	365
Sitting Bull Surrenders, 1881	370

VII—THE INTERMOUNTAIN WEST

Prologue: The Ute Crisis	376
Mormon Troubles	377
Walkara's War	378
Conflict in the Mountains	379
Connor Attacks Bear Hunter's Village	380
Colorado Gold	381
The Blackhawk War	381
The Bannack Uprising, 1878	384
The Ute War and the Meeker Massacre, 1879	387
The Battle of Milk Creek, September 1879	391
The Sheepeater War, 1879	394

VIII—THE DESERT SOUTHWEST

Prologue: West of South and South of West	395
Outposts on the Colorado: Clashes with the Yumas and Mojaves, 1849–1858	396
Apacheria	399
The Apache versus the Spanish	400
The Apache versus Mexico	401
Mangas Coloradas	403
The Norte Americanos	405
John Russell Bartlett and the Mexican Boundary Survey	406
The Acoma Peace Agreement	407
The Butterfield Overland Mail Route	408
Michael Steck	409
War with the Americans: The Bascom Affair	411
Cochise Takes the Offensive	415
Colonel James Henry Carleton	417
The Battle of Apache Pass	418
The Death of Mangas Coloradas	420
The Rise of Cochise	422
The Camp Grant Massacre	427
Crook Arrives in Arizona	428
Thomas Jeffords	430
Howard Meets Cochise	431
Crook's Grand Offensive	433
The Salt River Cave Fight	435
The Death of Cochise	436
John Clum	438

The Emergence of Victorio	439
The Rise of Geronimo	440
The Cibecue (Cibicue) Affair, August 1881	442
The Return of General Crook	447
Emmett Crawford and Charles Gatewood	447
The McComas Murders	448
Tom Horn	453
Crook Meets with Geronimo	455
Miles Replaces Crook	455
Miles Meets with Geronimo	457

Epilogue
Wounded Knee, South Dakota, December 1890	459
Notes	463
Recommended Reading	469
Index	473

Preface

For many years, I have felt the need for an all-encompassing single volume history of the Western Indian wars. It seemed to me that a readable volume focusing on this subject would find a ready audience among readers of Western history and the Indian wars in particular, and accordingly, I set out to fill that need.

My objective was to create a readable narrative history of the Western Indian wars, using a selected body of secondary and some primary sources. It was *not* my objective to unearth new facts; to break new ground. Rather I set out to bring together the most recent works in the field, and from them distill a comprehensive, readable narrative, historically accurate, yet without the minutiae found in more detailed studies of individual campaigns and battles. The book seeks, simply, to tell what happened; what brought on the wars, and how they were prosecuted. For obvious reasons, not every skirmish or encounter is recorded here, but it is hoped that the narrative has succeeded in presenting a reasonably complete and factual picture of the Western Indian wars, one that will appeal to both the general reader of Western Americana as well as scholars.

As any historian will testify Indian accounts of historical events are scarce at best. Indigenous people did not have a written historical tradition, relying instead on accounts passed down from generation to generation, through oral tradition, pictographs, and winter counts. This method of preserving facts lacks the completeness and precision that white historians are fond of using. This is not to say that Indian accounts, where they do exist, lack validity, only that they contain less information and detail. Undoubtedly, some of these inter-tribal accounts survive to the present day among descendants, but remain unknown to historians and writers. I regret that this narrative was unable to include more such accounts. As it stands, I necessarily had to rely on available sources. It is hoped that in the future these unknown oral accounts will see the light of publication, thereby providing us with a fuller and more complete understanding of our common history.

While the nation was reaching for Pacific shores, settlement was the primary reason for expansion, but once that goal had been achieved, commerce, tinctured with more than a trace of imperialism became the motivator that fueled further expansion. This book, however, limits its scope to the period of continental growth; to those clashes of arms between Americans and indigenous peoples that came about as a result of the expansion that took place between the Mississippi River and the Pacific Ocean.

In shaping this narrative of the Western Indian wars, I tried to imagine the events from two diametrically opposed perspectives: that of the Anglo-European eager to seek his (or her) fulfillment in this land of seemingly endless opportunity, and the indigenous people who viewed this strange interloper, at first with curiosity, then with alarm, and finally anger, as he watched his traditional homeland and culture swallowed up by this seemingly inexhaustible tide of white men and their towns, their steel rails, and their fences.

Although I fully recognize the Anglo-European's vision of settling (if that is an appropriate term) the vastness of a land that God had surely intended for civilization, I could not help but feel deep sympathy for the people who lost their land and, most importantly, their culture. Of course they resisted; who among us wouldn't have? It is said that history is written by the victors, but it might be well to recognize and appreciate the price paid by the losers.

Earlier general works that covered some of the same ground, such as Cyrus Townsend Brady's *Indian Fights and Fighters*; Paul Wellman's *Death on Horseback and Death in the Desert,* and Dunn's *Massacres of the Mountains* filled a niche in their particular eras, but all tended to be literary histories and left much to be desired insofar as scholarship was concerned. Since then there have been a broad range of books dealing with specific Indian wars, to say nothing of the various battles and campaigns. These have all provided great illumination, but no overall history of the Western Indian wars has appeared in recent times. Robert M. Utley's two superb studies, *Frontiersmen in Blue* and *Frontier Regulars* do cover the Indian wars of the West, but are essentially a history of the frontier military, while Dee Brown's *Bury My Heart at Wounded Knee* chronicles the story of the Indian struggle from Columbus to Wounded Knee.

This present volume, then, seeks to fill a void by presenting a new inclusive study of the Western Indian wars, one that will enable readers to arrive at a fresh and more enlightened view of these terrible conflicts and, it is hoped, emerge with a deeper understanding of how they developed and the lamentable consequences that resulted. If history is to serve a useful purpose it must be not only to inform us about the past, but to illuminate a path to the future.

Finally, throughout this book I have referred to these conflicts as the "terrible Indian wars," and terrible they were indeed, though not as costly, one might argue, as the Civil War. That great internecine conflict had given the nation a new meaning of suffering, one that was only a prologue to what lay ahead. Casualties on both sides during the Indian wars by contrast did not come close to equaling the horrendous casualty lists of our Civil War, or the conflicts yet to come, but in their own way, the Indian wars were cataclysmic in that they witnessed the annihilation of an entire culture.

Whether the subjugation of the indigenous peoples of the American West was necessary to achieve our so-called "Manifest Destiny," is a question to which there can never be a fully satisfactory answer, but we might ask ourselves if there was not a less costly means to achieve the same end? If we could start over again, would we do things any differently? If at some future date, an earth-like planet was discovered with a less advanced civilization than our own, would we attempt to settle and colonize that planet using the same tactics that Anglo-Europeans used to conquer North America? The answer to such questions lies beyond the scope of this book, but they are questions that need to be addressed.

Timeline

Year	Day/Month	Activity
1823	Summer	U.S. Army's war with the Arickaras
1836		Marcus and Narcissa Whitman establish mission at Waiilatpu
1846	August	General Stephen Watts Kearny arrives in Santa Fe to take possession of New Mexico for U.S.
		Mexican-American War begins
		Beginning of warfare between U.S. and Navajo nation
1847	Fall	Mexican-American War ends
	November	Whitman Massacre at Waiilatpu
1848	January 24	Gold is discovered in California
1849	Summer	War with the Yumas begins
1850	May	California's Mariposa Indian War begins
1851		Beginning of Rogue wars in Oregon; four years of intermittent conflict
	May	End of Mariposa War
	September	U.S. government signs Horse Creek Treaty with Plains Tribes
		U.S. government signs Treaties of Traverse de Sioux and Mendota with Santee Sioux
1852	July 11	Mangas Coloradas signs peace accord at Acoma
	October	End of warfare with Yuma Indians
	August 18	Grattan Massacre
	September 2	Battle of the Blue Water
1855		Isaac Stevens negotiates treaties with tribes of the Pacific Northwest
1856		End of warfare with Rogue Indians
	Autumn	First U.S. troops arrive in southern Arizona
1857	March 8	Spirit Lake, Iowa, massacre
	September 11	Mountain Meadows Massacre
1858		Gold discovered on Cherry Creek in Colorado
		U.S. government signs new treaty with Santee Sioux
	December	End of warfare with Mojave Indians
1859	September	Beginning of California's Mendocino War
	December	End of Mendocino War

Timeline

Year	Day/Month	Activity
1860	May 7	Nevada's Paiute Indian war begins
	Autumn	End of warfare with Paiute Indians
1861	January 27	Apaches raid Ward Ranch; take Felix Ward captive. Incident marks beginning of Bascom Affair
1862		Creation of Bozeman Trail
	February	Start of California's Owens Valley War
	March 31	President Lincoln appoints John Evans Territorial Governor of Colorado
	April	Colonel John Chivington defeats Confederate forces at Glorietta and Apache Pass, New Mexico
		Advance elements of General Carleton's California Column clash with Confederate forces at Picacho Pass, Arizona
	August 17	Minnesota Uprising begins
	September 6	General John Pope appointed to command new Military Dept. of the Northwest
	September 23	Battle of Wood Lake ends Minnesota Uprising
1863	January 17	Mangas Coloradas taken prisoner and killed while ostensibly trying to escape
	May 22	End of Owens Valley War
	Summer	Generals Sibley and Sully lead campaigns into Dakota Territory
	August	Death of Little Crow
	September 3	Battle of Whitestone Hill, Dakota Territory
1864	January	Kit Carson ends Navajo War
	February–April	Navajos make "Long Walk" to *Bosque Redondo*
	June 11	Hungate Massacre in Colorado serves as flash point for action against Indians
	June 27	Governor Evans issues proclamation inviting all friendly Indians to separate from the so-called hostiles and establish residence near near army posts
	July 28	Battle of Kildeer Mtn. Dakota Territory
	November	1st Battle of Adobe Walls
	November 29	Sand Creek Massacre
1865	January 6	Indians launch first of two attacks on Julesburg, Colorado
	February 15	Tappan Commission hears testimony about Sand Creek Massacre
	April	Start of Utah's Blackhawk War
	April 20	Tappan Commission concludes hearings on Sand Creek Massacre
	July 26	Battle of Platte Bridge (Casper, Wyoming)
	August 29	General Connor attacks Arapaho village near Ranchester, Wyoming
	October	Treaty of Little Arkansas between U.S. and Southern Plains tribes
1866	July	Colonel Henry B. Carrington establishes Bozeman Trail forts
	December	Fetterman Disaster
1867	April	General Hancock launches campaign against Southern Cheyennes
	October	Hancock's campaign ends
		Treaty of Medicine Lodge, Kansas
	October 11	Custer found guilty of being AWOL and suspended from rank, command, and pay for one year

Year	Day/Month	Activity
1868	April 29	Treaty of Fort Laramie
	November 27	Battle of the Washita
1869	March	President Grant initiates Peace Policy
1871	April 28	Camp Grant, Arizona, Massacre
	June	General Crook arrives in Arizona to take command of department
1872	October 1	General Howard and guide Tom Jeffords meet with Cochise
	October 12	Cochise and General Howard sign peace agreement
	November 28	Modoc War begins
1873	April 11	General E.R.S. Canby is murdered by Modoc leader Captain Jack during peace talks
	April 18	Colonel Ranald Mackenzie leads troops across Mexican border in pursuit of Indian raiders
	May	End of war with Modocs
	Summer	Northern Pacific survey crews work across Yellowstone Valley
1874	June 8	Cochise dies
	June 27	Second Battle of Adobe Walls
	July–August	Custer explores Black Hills
	September 28	Battle of Palo Duro Canyon
1875	March	General Crook assigned to command Dept. of Platte
	December 31	Indian Bureau issues proclamation calling for all the so-called wild bands to report to their agencies by Dec. 31 or be considered hostile
1876	February	U.S. Army prepares for campaign against hostile bands
	March 17	Colonel J. J. Reynolds attacks village on Powder River in first major battle of Great Sioux War
	June 17	Battle of the Rosebud
	June 25	Battle of the Little Bighorn
	November 25	Colonel Ranald Mackenzie destroys Dull Knife's village on Red Fork of Powder River in Wyoming
1877	May 7	Great Sioux War ends with Colonel Miles's destruction of Lame Deer's village
	June 27	Beginning of Nez Perce War
	September 6	Death of Crazy Horse
	October 5	End of Nez Perce War
1878	January	Start of Bannack Indian War
	May	Nathan Meeker arrives at White River Agency, Colorado
	September 4	End of warfare with Bannack Indians
	September 9	Beginning of Cheyenne flight for freedom from Oklahoma
1879	January	Dull Knife's band of Cheyennes cornered by troops and sent to Pine Ridge and Rosebud reservation
	February	Beginning of warfare with Sheepeater Indians
	September 29	Battle of Milk River and Meeker Massacre
		Beginning of Ute War
	October	Release of hostages taken during Meeker Massacre
		End of Ute War
		End of warfare with Sheepeater Indians.

Year	Day/Month	Activity
1879	Fall	Victorio breaks out of San Carlos and begins series of raids across southwestern New Mexico
1880	October 15	Victorio killed in battle with Mexican troops in Tres Castillos Mtns.
1881	July 19	Sitting Bull surrenders at Fort Buford, North Dakota
	August	Utes consigned to reservations in Utah and southern Colorado
		Cibecue affair
1882	September	General Crook reassigned to command in Arizona
1883		General Sherman proclaims that Indians have been eliminated as an obstacle to settlement of the West
1886	March 25	Crook meets with Geronimo at Cañon de los Embudos. Apaches agree to terms but then resume raiding
	April 11	General Miles replaces Crook as commander of Arizona department
	September 4	Miles meets with Geronimo at Skeleton Canyon
		Apaches surrender
		Geronimo and other Apache leaders sent to Florida
1890	December 15	Death of Sitting Bull
		Ghost Dance craze creates tension at Pine Ridge and Rosebud Agencies
	December 29	Fighting erupts between soldiers and Indians resulting in the final tragedy of the Indian wars

Introduction

Expansion! From its inception, the story of the United States might well be encapsulated in that single word. Even before independence had been won, colonists were pressing west across the Appalachians and the Alleghenies. Nationhood had barely become a reality when the Louisiana Purchase took place, followed by acquisition of east and west Florida; then came Texas, Oregon, and finally California and the Southwest to round out the continental U.S. But it did not end there. Alaska became a territorial possession in 1867, and during the course of the next half century so too did Hawaii, Puerto Rico, the Philippines, and a number of remote Pacific outposts, including Samoa, Guam, Midway and Wake Islands. Of these, only the Philippine archipelago is no longer under U.S. control. And lest we forget, Cuba and Santo Domingo (today's Dominican Republic) came close to flying Old Glory as well.[1]

Lewis and Clark's undertaking marked the official beginning of the nation's westward expansion. Mountain men, traders, and adventurers followed, but the vast territory beyond the Mississippi did not really begin to attract significant numbers of immigrants until the middle of the 19th century. With the discovery of gold in California in 1848, followed soon after by the great overland migrations, the nation's Trans-Mississippi expansion got underway in earnest, and as American presence in the Far West began to exert increasing pressure on the indigenous peoples, the inevitable clashes occurred. These clashes, ranging from minor incidents to major encounters that took place over an incredible variety of terrain with vastly different climate patterns, for nearly half a century, are the subject of this book.

It is hoped that readers will see this narrative as something more than a recounting of battles, campaigns, and troop movements, although these are certainly a part of the story for obvious reasons. But beyond that it is hoped that these events will serve to reveal a larger picture; to show how these wars became part of the terrible legacy of our westward expansion. The West may have been "won," as the old adage goes, but the price was steep. For the victors it was now one nation from coast to coast, while for the vanquished, it meant the destruction of a cultural heritage and great humiliation. It was not simply a one-sided story of determined pioneers forging their way west across a harsh, unforgiving wilderness, but that of strong willed immigrants who were forced to give birth to their dreams of settlement while battling indigenous peoples, equally determined to prevent the loss of their culture and life style. That there were countless instances of brutality, betrayal, suffering, self-sacrifice, and heroism on both sides cannot be denied.

The Indian wars of the American West actually represented the continuation of a struggle that began with the arrival of the first Europeans on the shores of North America.

Conflict followed expansion almost in direct proportion to the advancing path of settlement. It was an ongoing conflict that occurred whenever the latter began moving into an area, upsetting the dynamics of a traditional way of life that had been in place for generations; one that ended only with the subjugation of the various Indian nations involved.

Conflicts between so called civilized powers have generally been defined as wars, with the governments involved issuing official proclamations to the effect that a state of war existed. There have always been and still are, of course, exceptions to this. Military interventions and armed conflicts continue to take place *sans* any official declaration of war, Korea being one example. Whether such a clash merits being called a war is perhaps a moot point, but certainly to those involved in the fighting it deserves to be called nothing less. From a purely semantic perspective it is perhaps unfortunate that our lexicon lacks a comparable term to use when the word "war" to describe a particular conflict seems not quite appropriate. This is particularly true when one speaks of the Indian "wars." Unfortunately, we have no other word than war to describe these clashes with any degree of accuracy.

In the East, conflicts such as King Philip's War and Pontiac's War have been labeled as such for so long that calling them anything else now would seem entirely inappropriate, and in the Trans-Mississippi West the Great Sioux War, the Red River War and arguably perhaps, the Nez Perce War have become similarly defined. Yet both east and west of the Mississippi there were hundreds if not thousands of incidents and clashes between Indians and whites that certainly occurred outside the scope of what might be defined as a legitimate war. Except for the Great Sioux War and, arguably, the Red River War of 1874, they don't really deserve to be called "wars," at least not in the sense that we are accustomed to defining war. Mostly, they involved small units of the regular army or local militia or volunteers, or some combination of the two going out in pursuit of Indian raiders.

Retaliatory acts usually followed these raids. Indians stole (notably livestock), murdered, brutalized, and sometimes took hostages, as in incidents such as the Ward Wagon Train raid near present Boise, Idaho, and whites responded in like fashion with the infamous Sand Creek Massacre in Colorado. It is interesting and instructive to note that Indian-white conflicts in the Trans-Mississippi West resulted in eight incidents large enough in size to be defined as "massacres." Of these, four (The Ward Wagon Train Massacre, The Whitman Massacre, the Minnesota Uprising, and The Meeker Massacre) were committed by Indians, three (The Sand Creek Massacre, The Baker Massacre, and the Camp Grant Massacre were committed by whites. The Mountain Meadows Massacre stands as an 8th such incident in which Indians were erroneously blamed, when in fact the perpetrators were whites disguised as Indians. There were of course many incidents much smaller in size in which both whites and Indians were murdered, that do not qualify as a full blown massacre incident. I might add that by definition a massacre involves the wanton, indiscriminate slaughter of unarmed or helpless civilians. Custer's fight on the Little Bighorn and the Fetterman battle do not, by the above definition, qualify as massacres, even though one side was completely wiped out. The annihilation of a body of soldiers, defenders, etc., does not a massacre make.

It might be well to note that Anglo-Europeans did not introduce warfare to indigenous peoples. Anglo-Europeans certainly did introduce steel, firearms, disease, and alcohol, but warfare was already an established practice long before Europeans reached the shores of North America. Inter-tribal warfare was more than simply a competition in which to gain property and honor. These were merciless conflicts, waged for power, new hunting grounds, and captives. They were wars conducted with savage brutality, as between the Lakota (Sioux) and Pawnee, for example. The federal government sought ways to curb inter-tribal wars, often by building military posts in key locations to prevent clashes between traditional foes, but these enmities were deep-seated and mightily resistant to change.[2]

Inter-tribal wars resulted in a displacement of tribes, with the weaker giving way to the stronger. The pattern is as old as humankind itself. Thus, the Lakota were forced out of the woodlands of Minnesota and Wisconsin by the Ojibwa, and the Kiowas and Crows were pressured out of the Black Hills of South Dakota by the Lakota and Cheyenne. Accordingly, the westward expansion of the United States and its subsequent acquisition of Indian lands would seem then to have followed the normal pattern of history, but it should be remembered that the United States had the resources of the Industrial Revolution to support its expansion, a not insignificant advantage.

The gulf between two such terribly diverse cultures makes the inevitability of conflict, in retrospect at least, seem quite inescapable. A young and growing nation's appetite for land seemed insatiable; it was the land, always the land; what was on it (grass, timber, etc.), or what was under it (mineral resources). To one culture, the land could not be bought, sold, or owned; to the other, newly arrived in this seemingly inexhaustible *terra incognita*, ownership and distribution of land was the cornerstone on which the culture was built. Until well into the 19th century, the United States was a predominantly rural culture and land was the force behind the Nation's drive to expand and settle the continent. Indeed, Americans believed it was their God-given mission to expand and reap the harvest of a rich and bountiful land. It was, as editor John L. O'Sullivan declared in an 1845 issue of the *Democratic Review*, the nation's Manifest Destiny to expand.

Once, the land beyond the Mississippi had been thought of as a good place to shuffle the eastern Indian tribes off to; a kind of pen where they would not interfere with the advance of civilization. After all, early Western explorers such as Stephen Harriman Long and Zebulon Montgomery Pike had declared the Great Plains unfit for agricultural settlement, thereby giving rise to the myth of the Great American Desert, so why not move the Indians there? Time would soon prove the naiveté of that misguided belief.[3]

As the flow of Americans into the West grew and tensions between new arrivals and indigenous peoples increased, it became clear that a solution was needed. In the wake of the Revolution, President Washington and Congress clashed over a new and humane Indian policy. In June 1789 Secretary of War Henry Knox wrote to Washington outlining a visionary approach to dealing with Indians. Knox saw the Indians as original owners of the land and believed they should be paid for surrendering title to it. Subsequently, he proposed a treaty with the Creek Indians that was rejected by a corrupt Georgia legislature who planned to sell millions of acres of Creek land to speculators. Washington and Knox were furious, but it was a herald of things to come.[4]

Notwithstanding the failure of the Knox plan, representatives of the U.S. Government entered into negotiations with various tribes to settle specific differences and ease tensions. The negotiations usually resulted in agreements, officially known as treaties, in which the Indians generally agreed to surrender land in exchange for annuities, beef rations, and perhaps other necessities as stipulated. From the first such effort, with the Delaware Indians at Fort Pitt on September 17, 1778, to the final treaty with the Nez Perce on August 13, 1868, the United States entered into a total of 374 treaties with indigenous tribes, none of which ever proved to be more than a temporary solution.

The decade of the 1840s saw the discovery of gold in California, drawing Argonauts from everywhere to the promised land of quick wealth. California also beckoned to settlers as did the Oregon country. A decade later gold was discovered in Colorado, bringing still more prospectors, settlers, and opportunists. Suddenly it seemed, there was more to the West than Pike, Long, and some easterners had thought. The Indians watched all this no doubt with some curiosity at first and if they were not especially troubled, certainly we might imagine they were just a bit uneasy with this development.

At the outset, the Indians felt less threatened by pilgrims with their lumbering wagons and livestock. Clashes along the Great Overland Trail, if a little more than rare, were certainly less frequent than we have been led to believe. When whites began their westward trek they brought along livestock, which offered a tempting target for Indian raiders, who naturally saw these animals as fair game. Horse thievery was, after all, a way to acquire wealth and prestige. Occasionally such raids led to serious clashes with immigrants, but initially these affairs were not, strictly speaking, a militant reaction on the part of the Indians to white presence in their territory, since the travelers were not yet perceived to be a serious threat.

But the picture was changing. Encouraged by the Homestead Act of 1862 and the completion of the trans-continental railroad in 1869, what had been a stream of travelers became a river. New settlements sprang up in the wake of the steel rails. The West's eco-systems from the Pacific Northwest, to the Desert Southwest, to the Great Plains were heavily impacted as expansion increased. On the Great Plains, the seemingly inexhaustible herds of buffalo were diminishing, partly because of environmental factors such as drought, but also due to relentless hunting by both whites and Indians. The culture of the Plains tribes depended on the buffalo; without it they were doomed. Elsewhere in the West it was a similar picture. The arrival of white prospectors and settlers in the Pacific Northwest seriously impacted the salmon fishing on which the indigenous cultures of that region heavily depended on for survival, even as the Plains tribes depended on the buffalo.

Thomas Jefferson had long supported a voluntary Indian removal policy. Indeed, as early as 1816, Choctaws and Cherokees agreed to relocate across the river to Arkansas Territory, but soon that land, too, was needed. Accordingly, in 1830, with President Andrew Jackson's backing, Congress passed an Indian removal act, forcing the remaining tribes of the southeast and some from the heartland to move west on their infamous "Trail of Tears" march. Not all went willingly. The Sauk and Fox, for example, flatly refused, but resistance proved futile and those who failed to comply were soon effectively destroyed as tribal entities. Eventually, these tribes would be relocated to what became known as Indian Territory (Oklahoma).[5]

Throughout its history of dealing with various Indian tribes, U.S. negotiators persisted in expecting that each tribe must have a head chief who was endowed with the authority to speak for the entire tribe. In a few instances, a particular headman or war leader of great renown—Sitting Bull, Joseph, Cochise—might wield enough power to influence his people, but otherwise tribal structure simply did not provide for a single head of state.

Although the treaty system was viewed as the road to acculturation—the ultimate objective from the U.S. point of view—it left much to be desired at best and at worst was a dismal failure for a complex set of reasons. Treaties were never really backed by the full force of the United States Government and became meaningless when the government could no longer support the agreement it had originally offered, usually because of public pressure to occupy land that had been guaranteed to the Indians by virtue of the treaty.

As a vehicle used primarily for the acquisition of land, treaties favored the whites. Moreover, few Indians who attended these treaty negotiations (and not all did) fully understood what was taking place; what these treaties really meant. And why should the Indians have been expected to grasp the intricacies of a document as complex as a treaty, one usually filled with ambiguous phrasing and legalese A treaty was the white man's instrument, an agreement that usually involved the extinguishment of Indian title to a specific tract of land. Not only was the agreement complicated and difficult to understand, but treaty commissioners did not speak the Indian language and dialects and had to rely on translators to deliver their message. Needless to say there was always something lost in the translation.

Even when a treaty was signed and ratified—which itself might take many months after an agreement was reached—government fulfillment of obligations stipulated in the treaty was slow and erratic, often provoking incidents that had far ranging repercussions, as was the case in the 1862 Minnesota uprising. The treaty system also introduced an opportunity for unscrupulous traders and others to intercept annuity payments for Indian debts incurred while awaiting the transmission of funds owed them as part of the treaty agreement. For the Indians it was indeed a vicious circle; a true Catch-22.

It is important to recognize that treaties with various Indian tribes or bands were not actually agreements between sovereign nations in the same way that a treaty might be signed between, say, the United States and Great Britain. The treaties offered a means to an end; a way for the government to respond to pressures for the settlement of Indian lands. Succinctly put, the position of the United States Government was that Indians should not stand as an obstacle to white settlement and the treaty system seemed to offer a way to remove the Indians in a civilized and dignified manner. Problems arising out of any treaty agreement could always be dealt with at that time. Interestingly, President Andrew Jackson was opposed to the idea of treaties; dealing with Indians as though they were sovereign nations. In his view he thought the idea was wholly impractical.[6]

The signing of a treaty did not, by any means, ensure that issues had been resolved and there would be no further trouble. Treaty-breaking was common to both whites and Indians. When whites wanted land and access to gold fields, they gave little thought to treaty provisions, a notable example being the discovery of gold in the Black Hills of South Dakota, which quickly attracted a horde of prospectors despite the Laramie Treaty of 1868 forbidding whites to enter the Hills.[7]

When Indians presented an impediment to the advance of civilization—a completely unacceptable situation from the white man's perspective—the provisions of any treaty promptly became obsolete and demanded a new arrangement. Through the last half of the 19th century, the U.S. Government struggled desperately to untie this Gordian knot, but in the end, if the Indian problem was eventually resolved it was not through any ingenious statesmanship on the part of government, but rather simply because the Indians were largely and quite simply overwhelmed by the might of a culture with a population and resources far beyond those of the indigenous peoples

By the 1870s humanitarian voices, both in and out of government, compelled the administration of President Ulysses S. Grant to end the treaty system as a method of dealing with the Indians. Henceforth, there would be no more treaties and new agreements with any tribe would require full Congressional approval, rather than just ratification by the Senate.

It should be noted that there were many, both in and out of government circles, who genuinely sought a fair and humane way of dealing with the Indians. Christian missionaries saw Indians as God's children who needed to be brought into the fold. The Society of Friends (Quakers) and other peace policy advocates believed in and fought for fair treatment, while others argued for annihilation. Probably not surprisingly, those who favored harsher treatment were Westerners, many of whom had suffered at the hands of Indian raiders. Reporting to the Secretary of The Interior in 1867, Commissioner of Indian Affairs, Nathaniel G. Taylor suggested:

> We have reached a point in our national history when, it seems to me, there are but two alternatives left us as to what shall be the future of the Indian, namely a swift extermination by the sword, and famine, or preservation by gradual concentration on territorial reserves, and civilization.[8]

It had long been believed that the solution to the Indian problem was acculturation, which meant transforming them from whatever their traditional culture had been to an agrarian lifestyle. Indians needed to be educated, Christianized, and taught to be farmers in the Jeffersonian mold. In the words of Richard Henry Pratt, a former U.S. Army officer and founder of the famous Carlisle Indian School, it was necessary to kill the Indian and save the man.

Again, Commissioner Taylor:

> the Indians can only be saved from extinction by consolidating them as rapidly as it can be peacefully done, on large reservations, from which all whites except government employees shall be excluded, and educating them intellectually and morally, and training them in the arts of civilization, so as to render them at the earliest practicable moment self-supporting, and at the proper time to clothe them with the rights and immunities of citizenship.[9]

Whenever a treaty failed to produce the desired effect—which was frequently—trouble generally followed, compelling the government to resort to military action. Thus, the Army became something of a police force, faced with the mission of pacifying a region that all too often lay well beyond its ability to do so in any real effective way. This was especially so in the post Civil War years when the westward expansion, which had slowed somewhat due to the war, really got underway once the conflict in the east ended. Ironically, with the war over, an immediate downsizing of the army, coupled with the deployment of troops on Reconstruction Duty in the South, meant there were far fewer troops than needed to deal with the Indian problem in the West.

Beyond the Mississippi, the vastness of prairie, plain, and mountains meant war of a varied sort. On the Great Plains, between the Missouri River and the Rockies, and from Canada to Mexico, mobility was a prime requisite. Responding to Indian raids in the West represented a formidable challenge. Cavalry was the key. Here, the *modus operandi* was the mounted trooper on a big, grain-fed horse versus the Indian warrior on a small, wiry, pony that was able to survive on available prairie forage and the bark of cottonwood trees in the winter. The popular conception of Indian warfare in the West is probably best exemplified by this image.

Not to be forgotten, however, is the infantry who deserve more recognition than they have been accorded. Their light has always been dimmed by the brighter glare of the more dashing cavalrymen. But these foot soldiers—walk-a-heaps—as the Lakota called them were a tough, hardy breed who could march farther and were more durable than the cavalry horses. As one reporter who accompanied General George Crook's Big Horn and Yellowstone Expedition in 1876 observed "…man is a hardier animal than the horse and that shank's mare is the very best kind of charger."[10]

To the tribes of the plains and foothills, especially, horses might be likened to the crown jewels. No single item, save possibly a modern rifle, held as much value as a horse. The introduction of the horse to the tribes of the Plains during the 18th century had a profound impact on their way of life. Pursuit of the buffalo was made far easier than ever before. Range of movement increased dramatically. Horses became not only valued assets but targets of opportunity for all tribes. Horses became important as well to tribes dwelling in the mountains or foothills: Nez Perce, Utes, and others who ranged out onto the plains in pursuit of buffalo. Horses impacted the tribes of the Pacific Northwest even as they did the fierce, desert-dwelling Apaches. In short, horses played an important, and in some instances, a pivotal role in the Indian wars of the West, more so than in the eastern conflicts.

Beyond the plains, war took on a distinctly different character, especially in the Pacific Northwest, notably in southwest Oregon, for example, where fighting took place in terrain that often proved much too difficult for horses: steep, brush and timber-choked ravines, sliced by fast flowing streams. It was a wet country, too, and cold. Then there was the land of the Modocs: the lava beds, perhaps the most inhospitable terrain in the West. The desert southwest presented yet another environment of the harshest sort. If southwestern Oregon could be cold and wet, the Arizona desert was its polar opposite, demanding an entirely different kind of toughness and endurance from those who waged war in its arid, furnace heat.[11]

This narrative opens in the Pacific Northwest, where missionaries began to arrive as early as 1836, thereby setting the stage for the Whitman Massacre of 1847 and the Cayuse War that followed in its wake.

The late Bernard De Voto once characterized 1846 as the year of decision for our nation, and as I conceptualized this book that year seemed like an appropriate launching point for my own narrative. Only twice did I deviate from that point: in discussion of 1823 where I offer a brief account of the Arickara War, and again in the years preceding the annexation of Texas to the Union.

By 1846, the United States was a nearly contiguous nation and my goal was to present a history of the Western Indian wars that occurred within the limits of the continental United States. By 1846, the Oregon issue with Great Britain had finally been resolved. Then, two years later, in 1848, the Treaty of Guadalupe Hidalgo added a huge slice of territory to the Union, including California, leaving only a small strip of land comprising the extreme southern portions of present Arizona and New Mexico still to be added, and that acquisition was completed with the Gadsden Purchase in 1853.

Some will hasten to point out that there were hostilities between Indians and Anglo-Europeans in the West long before 1847, as indeed there were. The Spanish, Mexicans, and later, the American settlers who began moving into what became known as Texas in the 1820s all had ongoing clashes with Indians, as did travelers and traders along the Santa Fe Trail, but these did not occur within the then limits of the United States. From 1848, forward, however, all Indian-white conflicts west of the Mississippi, for all intents and purposes, took place on U.S. soil.

Since the various wars or conflicts—I have used both terms interchangeably throughout this narrative—did not occur in any orderly progression; were separated by great distances; were not directly related to each other, and often occurred simultaneously, organization of the material has presented something of a challenge. My solution was to organize the material in a regional framework and within that context, chronologically. It is hoped the reader will find this organizational style to be helpful in following the narrative.

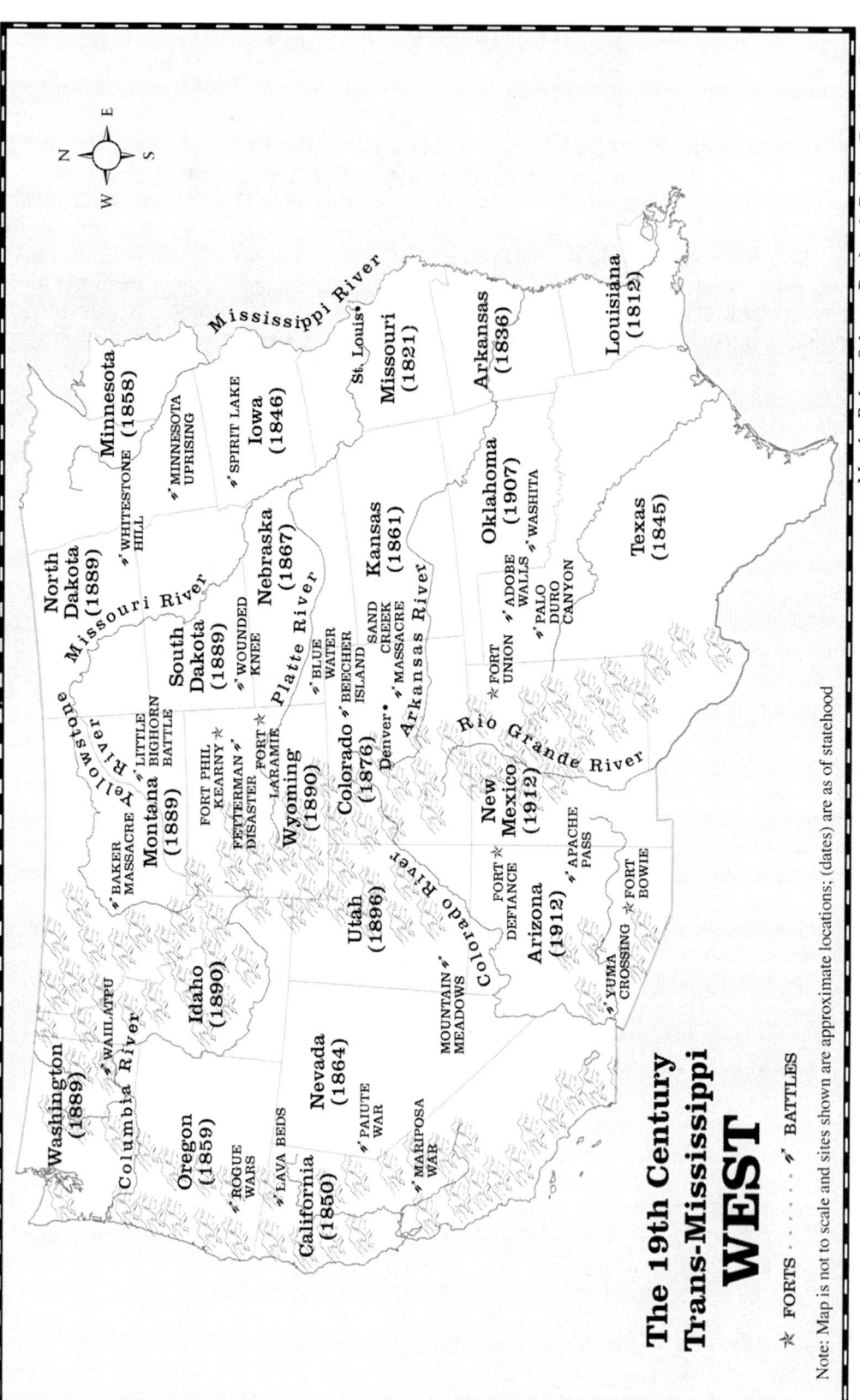

I

The Pacific Northwest

Prologue: The Oregon Country

President Thomas Jefferson's purchase of Louisiana in 1803 provided the first of three key acquisitions that would eventually make up the present Western United States. The Pacific Northwest, today comprised of Washington and Oregon, was known to overland travelers of the mid–19th century as simply Oregon, or the Oregon Country. In 1846 President James K. Polk finalized an agreement with Great Britain that made Oregon a part of the United States. Everything north of the 49th Parallel was conceded to Great Britain, territory south of that line became U.S. territory. Oregon's southern boundary (also California's northern) had previously been established by agreement with Mexico following that nation's independence from Spain in 1821. When the Oregon Territory as such was created in 1848 it consisted of the present states of Idaho, Oregon, Washington, and parts of Montana and Wyoming. The Treaty of Guadalupe Hidalgo, following the end of the Mexican-American War in 1848, together with the Gadsden Purchase (ratified in 1854) completed what we know today as the forty-eight contiguous states.

This Oregon Country, even after losing the territories that later became Washington, Idaho, Montana, and Wyoming, remains a region of giant variations: high deserts in the east and a rugged spine of mountains running north to south through its western sector, all bisected by the mighty Columbia River In the northwest corner one finds a majestic rain forest, and of course, along the western boundary its incomparable coastline. Nowhere else in the Trans-Mississippi West does one find such a spectacular physiographic landscape.

Death on the Rye Grass: The Whitman Massacre and the Cayuse War, 1847–1855

In the late autumn of 1836, a pair of newly wed Presbyterian missionaries, Marcus and Narcissa Prentiss Whitman, established a mission at Waiilatpu, some half a dozen miles west of present day Walla Walla, Washington. The Indians called it (y-ee-la-pu) "Place of the Rye Grass." In visiting the site today one finds a quiet dignity about the place, and yet for a brief moment, on one cold November day more than a century and a half ago, it was a place of unspeakable horror....

The story of Marcus and Narcissa is as tragic as any in the annals of the West. They were young—he was thirty-four, she was twenty-eight—energetic, and possessed a bottomless well of Christian zeal. Marcus was a man of medium height and solidly built. His appearance was rather foreboding, some thought, with an odd mixture of brown and white hair and a somber sort of expression. Narcissa, rescued from the brink of spinsterhood by Marcus, was a tall woman with reddish hair and sandy complexion. Bright-eyed, talented and graceful, she was thought of as an attractive woman. Both Marcus and Narcissa had grown to adulthood in western New York State, shaped by the groundswell of evangelical fervor and anti–Catholicism that swept through northeastern United States during the first half of the 19th century. Given this background it is probably not surprising that the two of them would eventually choose to walk the missionary path.

Marcus had also received a medical degree from Fairfield College and spent four years practicing medicine in Canada before returning to New York where he became an elder in the Presbyterian Church. In 1835, he traveled through the Northwest with a Congregationalist minister named Samuel Parker to select likely sites for missions. Returning to New York, Marcus and Narcissa were married and shortly thereafter set out to fulfill their destiny in the Oregon country.

The missionary group sponsored by the ABCFM (American Board of Commissioners of Foreign Missions) included, in addition to Marcus and Narcissa, a second couple, Henry and Eliza Spalding, William Gray, a handyman (with his own evangelical aspirations), and two Nez Perce Indian lads that Marcus brought back with him from his 1835 reconnaissance with Parker. Interestingly enough, Henry Spalding had been Narcissa's classmate at Franklin Academy and had once sought her hand in marriage, a proposal she rejected.[1]

Arranging to travel with a brigade of fur trappers (parties of trappers were then customarily referred to as brigades) the missionary party journeyed across the Great Plains crossing the Continental Divide at South Pass, Wyoming, on July 4, thereby giving Narcissa and Eliza the distinction of being among the first white women to cross the Rocky Mountains.[2]

The journey was rigorous and demanding, requiring extraordinary courage and stamina. For Narcissa, who had become pregnant en route (speculation has it while they were at Fort Laramie), it must have been an especially trying experience. The trials of such a journey alone would have been difficult enough, but there was ill-feeling between the two missionary couples, probably stemming from Henry's lingering resentment over his earlier rejection by Narcissa. Notwithstanding, on September 1, they finally reached Fort Walla Walla, a Hudson's Bay outpost situated at the junction of the Columbia and Walla Walla Rivers.

After a brief pause, the party traveled down the Columbia to Fort Vancouver, the principal Hudson's Bay outpost in the region, where they anticipated finding information about the best sites to locate a mission. Here they were welcomed by Chief Factor John McLoughlin, one of the most influential figures in the history of the Pacific Northwest. Despite McLoughlin's recommendation that they establish their missions in the Fort Vancouver area, the Whitmans and Spaldings were determined to set up shop in eastern Oregon. Subsequently, it was agreed that the Spaldings would establish a mission at Lapwai (near present day Lewiston, Idaho), a decision that may have been influenced by Narcissa's conclusion that she could no longer tolerate the Spaldings close presence. At Lapwai the Spaldings would administer to the spiritual needs of the Nez Perce. Meanwhile, Marcus and Narcissa would establish a mission at Waiilatpu, where their charges would be the Cayuse Indians, smallest tribe in the region.[3]

Like others imbued with evangelical zeal the Whitmans approached the challenges that faced them without taking into consideration the culture and beliefs of these native people to whom they were determined to bring salvation. There were taboos they failed or simply refused to observe. For example Cayuse men did not perform manual labor, and language of course was always a barrier. It was perhaps not so much an outright dismissal of the beliefs of native people as it was a misplaced conviction in the absolute certitude of their own beliefs.

At Waiilatpu the energetic Whitmans soon established a bustling mission that would eventually embrace living quarters, saw and grist mill, blacksmith shop, and school, together with some 200 acres of cultivated land. In March 1837, the Whitman family was increased by one when Narcissa gave birth to Alice Clarissa, the first white child born in the Pacific Northwest. Sadly, Alice drowned at age two, filling mother and father with inconsolable grief. Narcissa sat with the dead child for three days before giving her body up for burial. To fill the hole in their life, Marcus and Narcissa adopted orphans and immersed themselves ever more deeply into the needs of the mission.

On the face of it, the mission at Waiilatpu appeared to be flourishing. Marcus was indefatigable, planting, building, and administering to the sick, while Narcissa taught school. Waiilatpu had also become a place of respite for new immigrants now flowing into the region. As a center for spiritual salvation, however, the mission was failing to achieve its primary objective, namely Christianizing its charges in the Presbyterian faith. In general, the Indians found Catholicism more to their liking. They could relate to the Catholic icons and rituals, while growing steadily more resentful of the heavy handed brand of Christianity offered by the Protestant missionaries.

Accordingly, in the face of what appeared to be a failed effort, the ABCFM was ready to call it quits and terminate the mission, but Marcus believed in his work and early in 1842 he returned to the East, pled his case and was given a second chance. Reassured, he returned to Waiilatpu filled with new resolve, but lacking a much needed fresh approach toward his charges, who continued to resent his harsh ways. He was always busy—driven might be a better word. He had little time or patience for understanding and the kind of counseling that would likely have brought many Indians into his fold. Indeed, as the months passed his energies were increasingly directed toward providing a place of rest and assistance to newly arrived immigrants. And Narcissa, for her part, although kind enough to the Indians, held herself aloof from them and they regarded her as haughty.

And there was yet another problem. With his medical training, Marcus was continually called on to cure various illnesses, some of which he was able to treat successfully, others not. When an epidemic of measles struck many Indians died, despite Marcus's best efforts. In the Cayuse culture if a "healer" failed to cure the sick person, he faced the penalty of death. Accordingly, Marcus's inability to save many of the stricken Indians did not sit well with the Cayuse.

And so the murmurs and discontent grew and eventually erupted into belligerent acts. In 1842, as a harbinger of things to come, Indians torched the mission mill. Yet, despite such warning signs the Whitmans failed to take precautions against trouble. We shall never know exactly why; perhaps it was simply a refusal to believe they really were in harm's way.

The tragedy so long foretold came to pass on November 29, 1847, a cold and somber sort of day it was, too. That afternoon a Cayuse chief named Tilokaikt approached Marcus requesting medicine. As Marcus was in the process of complying, a second Cayuse named Ta-ma-has struck Marcus in the head with a pipe tomahawk. A struggle ensued, during which Marcus was hit again and again; slashed and mutilated. As soon as the attack on Marcus commenced, other Cayuses joined in. Narcissa was shot in the arm and dragged outside where she was shot repeatedly and beaten. Before it finally ended, several days later, eleven others had been slain, and forty-seven were taken captive. In addition, three others who were being treated at the mission for one kind of illness or another also died from lack of care. As a postscript to their deadly attack, the Indians burned the mission buildings. The rage that the Cayuse felt for wrongs real or imagined had expressed itself in a terrible fury, setting the stage for the first Indian-white war in the Northwest.[4]

In the wake of the tragedy, area residents who were fortunate enough to escape the wrath of the Cayuses fled downriver to the Willamette Valley, spreading word of the terror they had left behind them. Emotions were high. Panic spread. Settlers feared a general uprising of all the tribes. Fortunately for the white settlers in the region, James Douglas, new factor at Fort Vancouver (he had replaced John McLoughlin) enlisted the services of the veteran frontiersman and trader, Pete Skene Ogden to secure the release of the hostages, and by January 2 fifty-one grateful hostages began their down river journey from Fort Walla Walla.

Times were tense along the Columbia ... for both Indians and whites. The Cayuse were the angriest over wrongs inflicted on them by the Protestant missionaries. The Nez Perce, though troubled by the events and having themselves suffered at the hands of Spalding (whose methods were often brutal and harsher by far even than those of Marcus) were more moderate and many remained friendly toward the whites. Those Indians who had been involved in the massacre gloated over their powerful medicine, which in turn attracted others, reinforcing fears among whites of a full blown war. Fear feeds on fear. Wild rumors and accusations blew in the wind. Nativist propaganda charged that Catholic Jesuits were responsible. Indeed, many of the captives who were later ransomed blamed it all on the Papists. Settlers were not alone in their fears. In the aftermath of the tragedy, the mood of the Indians ranged from anger that still simmered, fearing that a white army was going to descend upon them to exact vengeance. Despite the high tension officials of Hudson's Bay Company, together with Jesuits in the area sought to calm feelings and bring about a peaceful solution through negotiations with the Indians.

As it always did on the Western frontier, incidents such as the Whitman Massacre spawned a cry for prompt military action. However, although the Oregon Country was now officially a part of the United States (it was added in 1846), there was as yet no territorial government; no mechanism by which a military force could be created, and no regular army troops were in the region. Not-

Cayuse Indian woman

withstanding, angry, fearful citizens sent a hastily organized regiment under the command of a forty-nine-year-old Baptist minister and Indian-hater named Cornelius Gilliam. Gilliam had reportedly seen action against the Seminoles in Florida and during the Blackhawk War in Iowa and Wisconsin. An early Oregon historian likened him to Oliver Cromwell. To Gilliam's way of thinking, the answer to the Indian problem was extermination. He was not the first man of God to espouse such a philosophy, nor would he be the last.[5]

Towards the end of February, Gilliam with a force numbering about 220 men reached The Dalles, searching for any Cayuses they could find. Governor George Abernathy had hoped that Gilliam and his volunteers would focus their efforts only on capturing those responsible for the massacre and recovering some of the stolen livestock. Indeed the governor so much as ordered Gilliam to avoid unnecessary conflict with any Indians who appeared to be peaceably inclined, but the hour of wrath was at hand and it was a forlorn hope the governor clung to.

Early in March, the volunteers reached Waiilatpu where they buried the remains of those killed in the massacre and erected a small stockade they named Fort Waters. Here, they were met by veteran mountain man, Joe Meek (a relative of President Polk's wife) on his way east to inform the president of the massacre.

Waiilatpu served as a staging point for phase two of Gilliam's operation. Here, the colonel organized a ninety-man force of the best mounted and equipped in his command for an expedition against the Cayuse. Where exactly the Indians might be found remained to be seen.

Gilliam's command set out from Waiilatpu on March 10 and soon found more Indians than he had bargained for. A spirited fight ensued, with the outnumbered volunteers forced back to the Touchet River near present Dayton, where they managed to cross the river and reach Fort Waters at Waiilatpu on the 16th. Fortunately for Gilliam, the Indians seemed satisfied not to pursue.

The fight cost the volunteers one killed and ten wounded. On March 20, Gilliam led a small force back to The Dalles for supplies before continuing on to report to the governor. However, on March 28, while in camp at Well Springs, he died from the accidental discharge of a firearm, an ignominious death for a man who had set out to serve justice for a terrible wrong.

Meanwhile, peace commissioners sought to negotiate a peaceful settlement with the Indians. Whites thought their asking terms seemed more than reasonable: surrender of those responsible for the Waiilatpu massacre. The Cayuses were also to reimburse settlers who had been robbed, or otherwise suffered damages during the uprising. The Cayuses regarded this as unacceptable and elected instead to abandon the area. On this note, the first phase of the Cayuse War ended indecisively with neither side satisfied. Insofar as the whites were concerned there would be no real progress toward reconciliation until the perpetrators of Waiilatpu received their just due.

The tragedy at Waiilatpu, however, did spur the government to action and on August 14, 1848, Congress officially created the Oregon Territory. That same month Congress also created the Willamette Valley Treaty Commission and extended the Indian Trade and Intercourse Act of 1834 to include the new Oregon Territory. The Trade and Intercourse Act essentially prohibited liquor sales to Indians and proclaimed that all officially designated Indian lands were to be governed by tribal authority.[6]

Retribution for Waiilatpu did finally come when early in 1850, a band of Cayuses that had not been involved in the blood-letting sought out the band that had, and after a fight, managed to capture Ta-ma-has who reportedly had been the one to tomahawk Marcus

Whitman. He, along with four others was taken to Oregon City in June, where all five were tried and hanged in a public execution, although some thought only Ta-ma-has ought to have paid for the deed with his life. In any case, it was a preview of the even larger public execution of Indians that would take place in Minnesota a dozen years later.[7]

ISAAC STEVENS

Isaac Ingalls Stevens was probably the single most influential individual in Indian-white relations during the formative years of the Pacific Northwest. Born in 1818, he graduated first in the West Point class of 1839 and later joined the elite Corps of Engineers. He served on General Winfield Scott's staff during the Mexican War, earning brevets for gallantry in three battles. In 1853, Congress divided Oregon Territory into two parts, creating Washington Territory on May 2 with Stevens as governor, a post he would hold for four years. In addition to serving as territorial governor, He was also named Superintendent of Indian Affairs for the territory. He was also a staunch advocate for the transcontinental railroad. Stevens was ambitious to a fault and a shameless promoter of the first order. He behaved as though it was his singular destiny to see to the development of the Pacific Northwest and that meant doing something about the Indians.

For openers, in January 1855, Stevens negotiated treaties with Indians that opened the way for settlement in the Puget Sound area. The following June, Stevens and Joel Palmer, newly appointed Superintendent of Indian Affairs for Oregon Territory convened a great council of tribes of the Columbia River Plateau at Walla Walla. It was one of the larger gatherings of its kind in the West, the end result being a series of treaties with the Walla Walla, Cayuse, Yakima and Nez Perce tribes who surrendered title to a huge portion of their lands in exchange for financial considerations, goods and services. The treaties also stipulated that 600,000 acres would be set aside for them as a reservation that included hunting and fishing rights. A month later, Stevens signed similar treaties with the Flathead and Blackfeet tribes. In these treaties were sowed seeds of discontent. Stevens would live long enough to witness some of the fruits of his treaty-making, but not all. With the outbreak of the Civil War he was appointed brigadier general of volunteers and lost his life at the Battle of Chantilly, Virginia, in 1862.[8]

"Nits make lice": The Rogue River Wars, 1851–1857

From Waiilatpu the scene of Indian-white troubles in the Pacific Northwest shifted west and south to the land of the Rogue River where indigenous people had begun to feel the pressure of white encroachment as early as 1850.

Whereas the terrain of the Columbia River basin was reasonably maneuverable the land of southwestern Oregon was rugged ... and wet, averaging some sixty-five inches of rain annually. Three major river systems course through the region: Umpqua, Coquille, and Rogue, the latter being the most prominent of the triumvirate.

The Rogue River rises among the ermine capped peaks of the Cascade Range and flows in a general westerly course to the Pacific Ocean. En route to its destination, its path is often tortuous as it twists and gropes its way through deep, narrow canyons. This is the land of Crater Lake and towering Mt. McLoughlin (8,495 feet). The north end of the Rogue Valley is bordered by a series of rugged, tumbled hills known as the Umpqua Mountains. To the south looms the high Siskiyous. On the west can be seen the softened profile of the

Coast Range and to the east the mighty Cascades. Roughly, this Rogue country stretches inland from the coast some 180 miles and about 30 miles north of the California line.⁹

Although Spanish, British, Russian, and American vessels all visited the Pacific Northwest coast by the late 18th century, there is no record of any permanent sort of landing, or penetration into the interior of what is now Oregon. By 1800, however, sea otter pelts had begun to attract entrepreneurs of the fur trade, who quickly recognized the northwest coast as prime territory.

By the middle of the 19th century the indigenous people who called this area home consisted of various bands, most of whom spoke a form of Athapascan, although the dialects differed considerably, so much so that many of these bands were able to communicate with each other only with great difficulty.

These bands were political entities unto themselves and dwelled along the area's various river systems. They included Umpquas, Coquilles, Klamaths, Rogues, and Shastas. For whites, tribal identification was confusing and difficult. Sometimes the Indians were referred to by one of these tribal names, but often they were just simply Rogues. To further complicate the identity picture, bands were also known by the name of their head man, who sometimes took a white man's given name for his own, viz. Jo's band or John's band.

There were perhaps as many as 10,000 Rogues in the region when the first Americans began to trickle into the area in the 1840s. The Anglo presence in Oregon began slowly and grew steadily. The staple food of these people throughout the year was fish, especially salmon, but smelt was also popular during the summer run. Now and then, their diet was supplemented by a seal or stranded whale. Camas bulbs and acorns also contributed to the bill of fare.¹⁰

White contact with the Indians of southwest Oregon began about 1827 when a Hudson's Bay fur brigade led by the same Peter Skene Ogden, who would later negotiate for the release of the hostages taken at Waiilatpu, moved into the area. That the Rogues could prove quarrelsome, even then, is evident from the fact that these early traders frequently clashed with them, referring to the Rogues as "rascals" because of their thieving ways. As early as 1828 Unpquas killed fourteen members of mountain man Jed Smith's party in what came to be known as the Umpqua Massacre. Thus, insofar as these early whites were concerned, the epithet Rogue seemed totally appropriate.

Access to the Oregon Territory was via the Oregon-California Trail, which brought immigrants along the Columbia River to Oregon City, at which point the Applegate Cut-off then afforded those who wished to turn south for California an opportunity to do so. Although there was some northbound traffic into Oregon along this route, either way the trail wound through the land of the Rogues, and travelers sometimes clashed with these Indians over stolen livestock and occasionally a killing. Generally, however, the Indians did not feel as threatened by these itinerant travelers as they did by later arrivals that came to stay.

In the territory's early days, permanency came in two forms: settlers who cleared the land, built towns, established homesteads, and prospectors from California who discovered gold in the watercourses of southwestern Oregon, notably along the Rogue River. These permanent settlers upset the dynamics of the region. Food supplies were threatened. Camas roots began to disappear, and game was killed off. Just as elsewhere across the West, a major clash of cultures was inevitable to anyone who cared to look beyond tomorrow.

When President James K. Polk signed a bill creating Oregon Territory in August 1848 he appointed as governor one Joseph Lane, a Southerner and hero of the Mexican War. Lane's term as governor lasted but a year. In 1850 he resigned to try his luck in the California gold fields and was replaced by John Gaines. Lane would later serve as territorial delegate to Congress.

The Rogue wars consisted of a series of clashes that took place on and off over a, roughly, six-year period, punctuated by brief periods of a quasi-peace. As notable battles went, they tended to be loosely connected, mostly gritty little actions, often fought under harsh weather conditions and in difficult terrain between companies of citizen volunteers (and on occasion regular army units) and one or more bands of Rogues. Historians have generally identified two so-called Rogue wars, one in 1853 and a second in 1855. There were, however, serious encounters before and in between that deserve to be viewed as part of the larger picture.

In the spring of 1850, for example, Rogues attacked a mining party returning to the Willamette Valley from California's Gold Hill. Although the miners successfully defended themselves, the Indians did manage to capture the pack train containing, among other things, bags of gold dust. Frustrated, the miners turned to Jo Lane for help. Organizing a party of fifteen men and some friendly Klickitat Indians (enemies of the Rogues) Lane set out to recover the stolen property. In a meeting with Chief Apserkahar's band of Rogues Lane persuaded them to lay down their arms, saying that their rights would be honored if they behaved. After two days of talks—the first recorded discussion between a white American and an Indian in southern Oregon—Apserkahar acquiesced and signed a treaty of sorts. As a result of the interaction between the two men, Apserkahar developed a liking for Lane and took the ex-governor's given name for his own, thus becoming Chief Jo (or Joe).

White settlement in the region was just getting underway, but almost immediately an Indian problem developed. Whites wanted the territory west of the Cascades cleared of Indians, so Lane simply suggested that the Indians to be moved east of the mountains. Congress approved the memorandum as law on June 5 1850, and in October commissioners were appointed to negotiate with the Rogues about surrendering ownership of their land. After a series of meetings lasting several months the commissioners, including new territorial governor John Gaines and new Superintendent of Indian Affairs for Oregon, Anson Dart, signed six treaties with various bands, most of whom were small in number.

It was all for naught, however, as in the interim Congress had decided that such agreements were only valid if negotiated by agents of the Indian Bureau, rather than special commissioners. As territorial Superintendent of Indian Affairs, however, Anson Dart had the necessary authority. Pursuing negotiations alone, by fall he had signed thirteen separate treaties through which the Indians surrendered title to six million acres of land. Treaties did not resolve the Indian problem in Oregon (or anywhere else, for that matter). Whites continued to flow into the area and tensions between Indians and whites mounted.

Also, relevant to these developments, on September 27 1850 Congress passed a Donation Land Law, wherein a person who had lived in Oregon and cultivated land for four years was given a grant of 320 acres, without regard to Indian rights.[11]

In June 1851, a party of nine men in the employ of the Pacific Steamship Line sailed down the Oregon coast and landed at a point twenty-eight miles north of the Rogue River's outlet to the sea. Their mission was two-fold: to establish a port site closer to San Francisco than Astoria on the Columbia River and to construct a road from that point inland to the gold camps. Upon landing, they were confronted by an estimated 400 Rogues. The men constructed a log fortress on a massive rock formation—subsequently known as Battle Rock—a small cannon being the centerpiece of their defense. Following an initial exchange of fire and the deaths of several Indians, a sort of uneasy truce prevailed as the two sides parleyed. The whites pointed out that their ship would be returning soon and at first this seemed an effective deterrent, but when, at length, the *Seagull* failed to show, the defenders decided to try and escape under cover of darkness. Eventually, they were able to reach settlements on the Umpqua River, but the incident stood as a sample of the kind of confrontation to be expected in the future.

Large or small, these early incidents served to inflame feelings on both sides, creating an atmosphere of hate and mistrust. Whites saw Indians not as another culture, but rather as thieves, and murderers, and obstacles to civilization. When Indians committed a depredation it provoked a strong, emotional response from the white populace, just as it had in the aftermath of the Whitman tragedy. Retaliation was the order of the day. The problem was that whites seldom bothered to make a distinction between Indians who were guilty and those who were not. All Indians looked pretty much the same to them. Indians stole and killed; volunteers retaliated, and Indians struck back in what was a self-perpetuating cycle. The regular U.S. Army forces in the region tried to help, but they were spread pitifully thin and were seldom strong enough to make a real difference.

Among other things, the creation of the Oregon Territory brought the first contingent of regular army troops to the region. The First Regiment of Dragoons became the first military unit to reach Oregon, via the Oregon Trail. In October 1849, the regiment established a garrison at Fort Vancouver, site of the old Hudson's Bay post.

They were a tough, boisterous lot, these dragoons, and within the year had become more of a problem for settlers in the Willamette Valley than Indians because of their wild, raucous behavior. Citizens complained and asked, a little prematurely as it turned out, that the regiment be removed and the War Department complied.

In June 1851, Major Philip Kearny (nephew of General Stephen Watts Kearny who had recently marched across the Southwest, captured Santa Fe and moved on to establish an American presence in California) was leading a two-company detachment of dragoons back to Jefferson Barracks, Missouri, by way of California. Kearny, a millionaire and colorful figure in his own right had fought with the French in North Africa, lost an arm in the Mexican War and would later lose his life in the Civil War battle of Chantilly in 1862.

Kearny and his troopers were accompanying a surveying party trying to find a passable route through Umpqua Canyon when he learned that the Rogues, who had been bedeviling locals, were massing near Table Rock, a high mesa not far from present Medford. Acting entirely on his own volition, Kearny decided to chastise the troublesome Rogues. High water delayed his progress, but he finally reached a point about five miles from Table Rock on June 17.

Kearny had hoped to surprise the Rogues, but they discovered his presence before he could strike. Despite having lost the initiative, Kearny attacked anyway. A brisk fight followed in which Captain James Stuart suffered a mortal wound and three enlisted men were also wounded. The Indians were thought to have lost eleven killed and several others wounded. Facing some 300 Rogues, Kearny wisely elected to withdraw and await volunteer reinforcements from Yreka (pronounced Y Reeka), California, some fifty miles distant (not to be confused with the coastal community of Eureka, California).

Meantime, Joseph Lane reentered the picture. He had been looking over some mining property around Yreka before heading off to Washington to assume his new duties as territorial delegate. Learning of Kearny's fight on the 17th he promptly rounded up about forty volunteers and headed for the scene of action, reaching Kearny's camp on the night of the 22nd. The following morning the combined force moved out in search of whatever Rogues they could locate, which turned out to be not many. A few Rogues recognized Lane and sought his intercession, claiming they wanted peace. As a gesture of good faith, the Indians surrendered a party of hostages they had been holding. Lane, however, was in no position to broker any sort of agreement, and Kearny was still under orders to return to Jefferson Barracks. Question was what to do with the hostages? Lane finally agreed to take them to Oregon City.

Word of the trouble had spread and volunteer companies were mustering. Governor Gaines wrote Pres. Millard Fillmore, requesting more federal troops. Under existing territorial law the governor was unable to raise a militia force, so after sending off his request to Washington, Gaines headed down to the Rogue country alone, to see about organizing a company of volunteers. Reaching the Umpqua Valley, he found that most men had already gone off to fight Indians. Nevertheless, he still managed to round up a party of fifteen and hurried off to the troubled area. By the time he arrived, however, Lane had already departed with his hostages.

In due course Gaines located Lane and Kearny and agreed to take charge of the hostages. The governor also managed to open negotiations with the Indians, using as a vehicle an old 1850 treaty wherein the Rogues had promised to return stolen goods and cease their attacks on travelers and miners. In exchange, the Rogues were to be given blankets, pipes and a promise of having their stolen property returned. For the moment there was peace.

By August 1851, the little community of Port Orford had grown to some seventy souls and was becoming increasingly important as a source for cedar lumber. The idea of building a road into the interior remained a high priority, but thus far it had proven an exercise in futility owing to the difficult terrain. Travelers to the interior were forced to rely on Coquille Indians—sometimes friendly, sometimes not—to take them down the Coquille River.

In mid–September 1851, a nine-man party under the leadership of William T'Vault, one of the area's most energetic and successful early explorers, set out from Port Orford to create a road to the interior. However, between terrible terrain and troublesome Indians, they lost their way. Eventually reaching the south fork of the Coquille River they met up with some Coquilles who seemed friendly at first. After taking the party to their village the Coquilles suddenly turned on the white men and a fierce fight ensued. T'Vault and four others managed to escape, leaving behind four dead comrades. "I looked around and, and saw upon the shore the most awful state of confusion [T'Vault remembered]; it appeared to be the screams of thousands, the sound of blows, the groans and shrieks of the dying." The event soon took on the name of the Coquille Massacre.[12]

That same fall of 1851, Alonzo Skinner, the first white man to take advantage of the new Donation Land Law, assumed his duties as the new Indian agent. Skinner, an optimist, told Superintendent Dart that he believed the Indians would remain peaceful if the whites only showed a little tolerance and understanding.

Sovereignty in Oregon also caused the U.S. Army to take the territory into its organizational structure. Early in 1851, Brigadier General Ethan Allen Hitchcock, newly appointed commander of the Pacific Division decided to station detachments in the interior of the new territory as a means of addressing the Indian problem. For openers, Hitchcock directed that a post be built at Port Orford. Accordingly, in September, Lieutenant August V. Kautz arrived at Orford with a detachment of twenty men and orders to construct a new post. Fort Orford (there was now a Fort Orford as well as a Port Orford), however, was poorly situated; it wasn't that far as the crow flies from the Rogue country, but the terrain made passage very difficult and time consuming for an army column trying to reach the area quickly and provide assistance to settlers east of the Coast Range Mountains. Indeed, fighting the Indians was almost a cake walk compared to just reaching the interior from Fort Orford.

In September 1851, Superintendent Dart and agents Josiah Parrish and Henry Harmon Spalding arrived in Port Orford from Portland, arriving about the same time as Lieutenant Kautz. Dart was prepared to make new treaties with the Indians, the object still being to persuade the Rogues to cede lands to the U.S. Unfortunately for Dart, the timing could hardly have been worse, for they reached Orford two days after word of the Coquille Massacre reached the community.

The Coquilles were feeling a bit heady after what they had done to T'Vault's party and were not particularly inclined to negotiate. Dart, accordingly, faced something of a dilemma. How to negotiate with the Indians without appearing to give in to them? He decided to visit the Coquille village to see if he might persuade the Indians to hear him out. It was a brassy sort of thing to do, but Dart took presents and was subsequently able to persuade three of the Coquille leaders to visit his camp for talks. It all went for naught, however. The Coquilles flatly refused to be subjected to white authority.

So, despite the agreement brokered by Governor Gaines and efforts on the part of Dart and others, the situation in southern Oregon remained volatile. During the summer of 1852 Indians committed an estimated thirty-eight murders and many robberies. A military response seemed inevitable. In October, General Hitchcock dispatched three companies of dragoons under Lieutenant Colonel Silas Casey to Fort Orford. Casey's mission was two-fold: first, chastise the Coquilles, second, open a road to the interior that would connect with the Applegate Cut-off.

By early November, Casey's command was able to advance up the Coquille, where, on November 5, they encountered an estimated 150 Indians, who brazenly taunted the soldiers from the opposite shore. During the next two days, the soldiers struggled to build rafts under a heavy, cold downpour. At length, a detachment was able to cross the river, while Casey and the rest of the battalion proceeded upriver along the opposite shore. Going through underbrush, swamps, and canyons would have been bad enough in decent weather, but with continuous drenching rains it was a thoroughly miserable experience. Casey's only success was to burn three abandoned villages while the Rogues fled upriver ahead of them.

Progress it could scarcely be called. Frustrated, Casey sent back to Fort Orford for boats, which took several days to arrive and when they did, were too small to accommodate more than a few soldiers. Moreover, the boats were so crowded that the men would have found it impossible to use their weapons had it been necessary, which fortunately for them it was not. En route, the troops passed more abandoned village sites. On November 21, Lieutenant Thomas Wright took a detachment up the north fork of the Coquille but found nothing. Lieutenant George Stoneman, another future Civil War cavalry leader, meanwhile, took a second detachment in one boat, even as a fourteen-man section moved along the shore following the main branch of the Coquille. Eight miles later, they finally found Indians, who fired on the detachment, prompting Stoneman to order a retreat.

On November 22, scouts finally located the main body of Indians. Casey elected to take his entire force up the main branch of the Coquille. The command was divided into two sections. Two boat loads of five men each rowed upstream, while the others worked their way along the shoreline. About a half mile from the Rogue village, the shore party divided again, with half crossing the river and proceeding along the opposite shore. As the troops in boats approached the village, the Indians opened fire, unaware of the soldiers advancing along the shore. Reaching the village, these men burst forth from the brush and opened fire on the Indians who were taken completely by surprise and fled. Urged on by Casey, the troops pursued, killing fifteen Indians. Two soldiers later died of wounds received.

Mining had been hard on the natives of the region. Many of the streams had become barely fishable, thereby cutting off yet another vital source of food. As well, many Indians were suffering from smallpox, tuberculosis, and measles, diseases introduced by the whites. The miners gave little thought to how their presence disrupted the Indian way of life; gold was all that mattered and so incidents continued.

In December, a new gold strike was found near present Gold Hill on Jackson Creek, bringing another influx of people into the area and giving the Rogues further reason to be discontented. Initially, the small community that sprang up was called Table Rock City and later renamed Jacksonville.

Indian-white relations did not improve much during 1852, either. By the early part of the year, twenty-eight land donation claims had been filed. As the flow of new arrivals into the Rogue River Valley increased, clashes escalated. Prospectors killed Indians, Indians continued to rob and steal, and now and again kill an unfortunate prospector. Although not all Indians were guilty of hostile behavior, most whites were generally mistrustful of any Indian. Nor was it any easier for Indians to know which whites to trust. In July, Agent Skinner, in an effort to calm things down, called for a major conference near Table Rock.

The conference was something of a bust. A few Rogues did put in an appearance, as did a company of volunteers, called the "Avengers," from Yreka led by a man named Elisha Steele who refused to recognize Skinner's authority. Steele and his Avengers had crossed the Siskiyou Mountains in pursuit of some Rogues who were believed to have killed a miner down in California's Shasta Valley. Along the way they captured the son of the head man of one Rogue band. When they reached the conference site, Steele's volunteers suddenly attempted to take the Indians' weapons. Their prisoner panicked and tried to flee but was gunned down by the volunteers. The miners were in a mean mood. As far as they were concerned, the best course of action was to wipe out all the Indians. Parties attacked several villages, killing some women. Those fortunate enough to escape fled into the surrounding hills. For his part, Skinner was discovering the limited range of an agent's influence and authority.

Despite scattered attacks on prospectors and frequent instances of Rogues harassing travelers along the Applegate Trail there was a haphazard sort of peace in the Rogue country throughout what was thought of as a hard fall and winter of 1852–1853.

In the spring of 1853, two events served as the root cause for a renewal of hostilities. First, the U.S. Government authorized the construction of a military road through Umpqua Canyon, an act not designed to win friends among the Rogues. Then, yet another new gold strike exacerbated relations between whites and Indians. Late in 1852, two mixed breed brothers found rich dust among the sands along Whiskey Creek (Run) where the Coquille River flows into the ocean. The claim proved rich and brought a whole new wave of prospectors to the area and soon there were new settlements where nothing but beach and water had previously existed.

In the five years since the creation of Oregon Territory, immigrants continued to flow into the region, which was soon judged too large to govern effectively. Accordingly, in May 1853, Congress divided the territory at the Columbia River, north of which would henceforth be Washington Territory with Isaac Stevens as governor; to the south was Oregon. Yet another noteworthy event of 1853 saw Anson Dart replaced as Superintendent of Indian Affairs by one Joel Palmer. A forty-three-year-old Quaker, Palmer brought some experience to the job, having previously been territorial commissioner of Indian Affairs. A peacemaker and humanitarian, Palmer was to play a pivotal role in Indian-white relations in the harsh climate that was then southern Oregon.

The War of 1853

During the summer of 1853, prospectors suspected that Rogues had killed miners and stolen their gold dust. In reprisal, they hanged a leader named Taylor and executed several others after tying their hands behind their backs. The Rogues of course retaliated by burning every building they could find for a hundred miles between Cow Creek and the Siskiyous, and murdering a number of settlers in the process.

In early August the dead and mutilated body of a man known only as Edwards was found on Bear Creek, leading historian Stephen Dow Beckham to suggest that this may well have been the incident that triggered the war of 1853.[13]

Things continued to get ugly. A party of miners from Jacksonville hanged two Shasta Indians who were most likely innocent of any wrong doing, but as noted, guilt or innocence seldom mattered in these situations. Settlers who lived on Butte Creek, not far from where Edwards was killed, fled to Jacksonville, bringing with them a seven-year-old Indian boy they had grabbed along the way. An angry crowd of miners, said to number about 800, wanted to hang the boy, but were dissuaded from doing so by one Benjamin Dowell, who managed to calm the blood-thirsty group. Victory however proved temporary, for shortly a wild-eyed miner galloped into town, screaming for the extermination of all Indians. "Nits make lice!" Stirred to action, the angry miners quickly hanged the boy alongside the two Shastas. A decade later, the same comment would be echoed during Nevada's Paiute War of 1860 and most famously perhaps, by Colonel John Chivington at a place called Sand Creek, Colorado. The remark, a not uncommon expression in ordinary conversation of the period, took on a particularly ugly connotation when used in the context of Indian–white relations and underscored the anti–Indian bias of many whites.[14]

Jacksonville miners next swooped down on a Shasta village near Ashland, Oregon, while other groups searched the countryside for Indians, paying scant attention to which ones they killed. Meanwhile, a messenger rode hell bent to the nearest army post at Fort Jones in Scott Valley west of Yreka, established a year earlier by a company of the 1st Dragoons. Lieutenant Bradford Alden had but twenty-one men on duty and half of them were sick, but he took the field with a detachment of ten anyway. At Yreka, he enlisted an additional eighty volunteers and headed for Jacksonville, arriving on August 9. Forty-eight hours later, he bivouacked near the old site of Camp Stuart and set about enlisting more volunteers from the surrounding countryside. Even as Alden was assembling his command, other volunteers, operating independently, struck a Rogue village on the Applegate River, and were in turn ambushed themselves. While all this was happening, the Rogues attacked five miners near Willow Springs.

The Applegate River was not the safest of places to be just now if one was a miner, but the area was judged rich in mineral wealth and those who had claims refused to abandon them. As a defensive measure, some gathered at a local trading post and prepared to defend themselves while others sought the questionable safety of a lonely miner's cabin.. Between the two places, there were some seventy miners in all. The Rogues were not dissuaded from attacking fortified positions. Indeed, they struck both positions hard, killing three miners and wounding several others before retiring. The ferocity of the Indian attacks prompted the miners to make a break for Jacksonville, but the Rogues ambushed them and managed to kill one more before the others reached the safety of the town.

Even as the miners along the Applegate were having their problems, Lieutenant Alden had not been idle. He hit upon a plan to trap the Rogues between Table Rock and Evans Creek. Accordingly, on August 16, three companies of volunteers under John Lamerick, James

Goodall, and John Miller took the field. Initially, they had trouble locating any Indians, but one detachment finally found what was thought to be Sam's band on Evans Creek. Word was promptly sent back to bring on the main body. That night Alden's command bivouacked along the creek in a site surrounded by heavy brush and cut by gullies. The site proved a poor choice. Taking advantage of the cover, the Rogues ambushed the camp, killing two men and forcing the volunteers to retreat to a pine tree-covered ridge from where they fought the Indians for three hours until more volunteers arrived from Yreka. Altogether the Rogues killed six volunteers and wounded four others. They also managed to capture some eighteen pack animals loaded with guns, ammunition, and blankets.

Elsewhere, on August 17, Indians attacked other settlers in the valley as well as travelers along the Applegate Trail; one immigrant was killed and five others wounded. Four days later, Jo Lane—this time carrying the rank of general (he had been brevetted major general in the Mexican War)—again visited the valley and took command of all forces at Camp Stuart. Lieutenant Alden's regulars—all ten of them—along with volunteers, placed themselves under the general's command. Lane divided the mixed force into two battalions and took the field on the 22nd. The Rogues, who had been identified as belonging to the bands of Old Jo, John, and Sam, meanwhile, had moved northward toward the Umpqua River. John Ross took one battalion up Evans Creek and into the mountains, while Lane, with Alden's detachment and the companies of Jacob Rhodes and John Miller, moved up the Rogue River to a point near Table Rock.

The two battalions reunited in rugged, heavily timbered country on Evans Creek north of Table Rock. Pursuit was slow and tortuous under the best of conditions which these were not. The Indians chopped down trees to block the trail and set fires that produced smoke and reduced visibility. At daybreak on the 24th, a new trail was discovered and Alden, with Goodall's company, made straight for the camp, believed to be not far ahead, while Rhodes's company moved into what was expected to be a flanking position down a ridge to the left of the main trail.

The original idea had been for Rhodes's men to pour a flanking fire on the Indians, but they were unable to find a suitable spot and instead simply decided to join forces with Alden, so the combined force pushed ahead and when within thirty yards of the Rogue camp opened fire. The Indians were surprised, but reacted quickly and fought back with stubbornness. They were aided, too, by the strength of the position, as their village had wisely been located behind fallen trees. The fight was a hard one, the yelping of village curs mingled with the sounds of gunfire. Captain Pleasant Armstrong was killed and Lieutenant Alden wounded. Presently, however, General Lane arrived and decided to charge the camp head-on, sustaining a shoulder wound in the process. Despite his wound, Lane continued to direct the action until a loss of blood compelled him to be removed to the rear. Once more the Indians asked to parley with Lane, whom they had learned was present.

Despite his wound, Lane met with Joe, Sam, and Jim. It proved a fruitful discussion with both sides agreeing to cease hostilities until formal talks with Superintendent Palmer could be convened at Table Rock. The volunteers remained on the battlefield for two days to bury the four men killed in action. The Indians lost eight killed and another twenty wounded. One volunteer remembered Indians bringing water to wounded soldiers after the fighting had ended. War has a curious way of allowing the better angels of our nature to surface at surprising moments.

Both sides then headed back down the trail together, carrying their wounded, each side more than a little leery of the other. When they reached Table Rock, the canny Indians camped in a virtually inaccessible spot near the top of Table Rock, while Lane's command bivouacked along the river, designating the site Camp Alden.

On the face of it these might have seemed encouraging signs, however, real peace in the valley was far from a reality. Even as Lane's volunteers and the Indians commenced their return journey, another company of volunteers under the command of Captain Elias Owens searched for more Rogues farther downriver. Some of the Grave Creek band were located and induced to surrender, only to suddenly be attacked by the volunteers. Five or six were killed, but others managed to escape and vented their rage by burning cabins in the area. They then ambushed Owens's company at Long's Ferry, killing three of the volunteers, underscoring once again the need for a unified command structure among the volunteer units. As for the Indians, here was yet another illustration of why they were reluctant to trust the whites.

In September Superintendent Palmer and agent Samuel Culver arrived at Camp Alden along with several companies of volunteers. And more federal troops moved into the area as well, though too late to participate in the summer's fighting. Captain Andrew Jackson Smith (future Union Civil War commander) and his dragoons arrived on the scene, having marched through the mountains from Fort Orford. Earlier, Lane and Alden had sent off an urgent message to Governor George Curry—he had replaced Gaines—requesting that arms be furnished to the settlers, who evidently were not as well armed as the Indians. The request was honored. Arms and ammunition were dispatched from Fort Vancouver. Lieutenant Kautz with a detachment of troops and a twelve-pound mountain howitzer also moved into the area.

On a beautiful September morning the 4th day of the month to be exact—Indians and soldiers marched on parade at Camp Alden, preparatory to Lane's treaty presentation. The scene of soldiers and Indians marching together has to be regarded as one of the more unusual events of this or any Indian war. Some of the white principals, including Superintendent Palmer, were garbed in red hunting shirts. Chief Joe, looking more like a visiting missionary, wore a long black robe. The honor guard was a new volunteer company from Crescent City, California, calling themselves the "Crescent City Guards," bearing a flag inscribed "Extermination." How the gathered Indians regarded all this is not known, but since they almost certainly could not read they would have had no idea of the cruel slam represented by the flag.[15]

Formal talks commenced that afternoon. Palmer, Lane, Captain Smith, Agent Culver and Jesse Applegate, were among the most prominent whites in attendance. Smith's dragoons lined up at the foot of Table Rock, scrubbed white belts and polished bayonets glistening in the autumn sun, while Indians gathered on the surrounding hillsides to watch and listen. Tension filled the air and both sides seemed poised to react if necessary. Four days of talks concluded on September 8. The terms called for the Indians to cede more than two million acres of land for $60,000, including $15,000 to settlers for damage claims resulting from Indian raids. The treaty further stipulated that the Indians were to be relocated to a reservation to be established later. The Rogues further agreed to exchange their firearms for blankets and clothing. The treaty was the first in Oregon Territory to be ratified by the U.S. Senate.

The atmosphere was relatively calm until the next day when word came that a company of independent volunteers had killed one of the Grave Creek band and threatened to upend the new treaty, but Lane saved the day by persuading the Indians that the deed had been committed by volunteers not under his authority and to retaliate against Lane and his party would only hurt the Rogues in the long run.

Old Tipsey's band had not been involved in treaty talks as yet, so Lane, his arm still in a sling, in company with an interpreter named Robert Metcalf set out to find his camp, which was finally located on the Applegate River. When the two white men approached, the Indians were prepared to fire, but Metcalf was able to convince them of their peaceful intentions. After some discussion, Tipsey agreed to terms. For the third time, Lane had managed to secure a sort of peace with the Rogues, but again the agreement lacked any sort of permanency. Although an estimated half of the Rogues had signed the treaty, there remained a hard core who refused and were still ready to fight. For example, along the Illinois River [near present day O'Brien], the discovery of rich deposits of gold triggered an Indian attack. A company of volunteers had a tough fight and claimed twelve Indian casualties.

Learning of the trouble, Captain A.J. Smith sent a detachment of troops to the Illinois River Valley, but upon arriving they quickly discovered that the troubled area required more men. When reinforcements arrived on September 22, they pursued the Indians into the Siskiyou Mountains, located the village, killed fifteen Indians, captured horses and destroyed whatever property they could find. Whether these were the guilty Rogues remained open to question, but Smith's troopers suspected they were from out of the area.

The problem with all of these treaties was the shaky foundation on which they were built. Someone, either white or Indian was always ready to break the agreement. There was gold on Indian land that prompted prospectors to ignore the agreements, or there were the white man's horses and mules that were always so tempting to an Indian. The knife cut both ways. And so it was with Lane's 1853 peace agreement. Little brush fire flare-ups kept the kettle simmering.

Early in 1854, a party of white miners massacred a village of Indians on the Coquille River. The sub-agent for the area said the miners had no justification for such an act, but the miners claimed they were only retaliating for Indian thievery and so it went.

Incidents of this sort underscored the need for military posts in the heart of Rogue country. As things stood, Fort Jones was on the other side of the Siskiyous and Fort Orford lay beyond the Coast Range. Consequently, in November, A.J. Smith built Fort Lane a mile below Table Rock. The new post was garrisoned by Captain George Waynefleet Patten, a man of middling height who had lost a thumb and finger in the Mexican-American War. Lieutenant George Crook, who would later rise to the rank of general, serve with distinction in the Civil War and become one of the Army's premier Indian fighters, remembered that Patten's injured hand looked for all the world like the claw of a crawfish. To carry out his assignment, he had four mightily under strength companies totaling one hundred men.

Although there were troublemakers on both sides, there were also examples of Indians and whites working together to confront groups such as the "Avengers" and "Exterminators." When an old Rogue man, a woman, and a baby were murdered by some Avengers, whites and Indians pooled forces to confront them. Subsequently the Avengers were allowed to go free providing they left the country for good. Besides Joel Palmer, an early settler in the region, John Beeson, continued to plead for humane treatment of the Indians, but he was a minority and his position came with a price. "I am afraid Father will have to leave this country [wrote Beeson's son]. Public opinion is so strong against him some would about as leave kill him as an Indian just because he has spoken the truth out boldly against the rascality of this Indian war, or rather butchery of the Indians." Beeson's stand grew increasingly unpopular and in 1856, he was forced to leave the area out of fear for his life.[16]

THE WAR OF 1855

By 1855 relations between the Rogues and the whites had again deteriorated. Harvey Robbins of Linn County, who arrived in Oregon in 1852 and maintained a journal of events, claimed that the War of 1855 was the most savage and sanguinary in the history of Oregon. Historian E.A. Schwartz has called the War of 1855 a "pork barrel" war because it was promoted by politicians to draw Federal funds. This politically motivated effort undermined and overshadowed the good intentions of those in the area who were genuinely interested in establishing peace and a humane reservation system. The politicians who stoked the fires of war were opposed by many in both the Army and the Indian Bureau, all to no avail of course.[17]

An isolated incident ignited another outbreak. The war of 1855 began in May, when a solitary miner was murdered near the Klamath River. Retaliation was swift. Two companies of volunteers formed up immediately and crossed the Siskiyous to the mining community of Kerbyville, from where they went on to murder four Indians. Doctor George Ambrose, the new agent in the area, had suspected trouble might be coming and had removed several Indian families to the reservation on Rogue River, else the volunteers might well have claimed even more lives.

Two months later, drunken Indians who had managed to get their hands on whiskey from irresponsible traders first attacked and killed a miner on Humbug Creek, then set out on a two-day rampage that resulted in the deaths of eleven other miners in the Klamath and Scott River country of northern California. It was *déjà vu*. Volunteer companies were quickly mustered. Lieutenant Henry Judah from Fort Jones brought 100 peaceful Shastas to his post for protection, but all other Indians were fair game for the volunteers. Earlier in the year, when the land lay tight in winter's grip, Judah and a detachment of soldiers known mysteriously as the "forty thieves," in pursuit of the Indians were forced to seek refuge in a cave where the lieutenant warmed himself with copious draughts of whiskey, as did some of the others. Lieutenant George Crook remembered their trail could be followed by drunken soldiers lying in the snow. Although these particular events took place a little to the south of the Rogue territory they were to have an impact on Rogue-white relationship.

Six Rogues, who had left the Table Rock reservation with the agent's permission, just happened to be on the Klamath River when these killings took place. These Indians had been around long enough to know about guilt by location and promptly fled back to their home country. Unfortunately, they had been seen by miners along the Klamath, who of course judged them guilty. Fortunately, not all were so quick to pass judgment. From headquarters, Department of the Pacific, General Wool, writing to the Superintendent of Indian Affairs in San Francisco, reported:

> the inhabitants of (Scott's Valley) had assembled with the avowed purpose of exterminating the unoffending Indians known as the Shasta tribe; but some of the better disposed of the people aiding the commanding officer of Fort Jones, about 100 Indians of all ages and sexes were collected at that post on the military reserve.[18]

In August, a party of volunteers arrived at Fort Lane and asked to have these Indians turned over to them. Captain Smith agreed to have the Indians stand trial in Yreka, but specified that they would be accompanied to that place by a regular army escort, not by volunteers. Angered, the volunteers convened a public hearing on August 5 and agreed that if the Indians were not turned over to them within three days, they would take them by force, but Smith was not about to be intimidated. Agent Ambrose, too, rejected the miners' demand. Interestingly, many locals, including the *Oregon Statesman*, supported the official position in this instance. Faced with this, the miners backed down and returned to California, singing their side of the story to the Yreka *Union*.

Although the majority of Rogues were now on the Table Rock Reservation, Tipsey and some of his followers continued to hide out in the Siskiyous and Cascades, from where they persisted in their thieving and raiding ways. Such acts continued to inflame the miners, so once more the Yreka volunteers took to the field, determined to see the Indians properly punished.

Led by James Lupton, who had commissioned himself major and who had been a packer with the old Mounted Rifles back in '49, marched into Jacksonville in October and, at a public meeting, laid out his plan for extermination of all Indians. The gathering had begun as a church meeting, but it quickly devolved into a forum for attendees to voice their gripes about the Indian problem. Thus, when Lupton presented his plan it was well received, despite the temerity of one man, who dared voice opposition and was quickly scorned and shouted down. Superintendent Joel Palmer recognized the seriousness of the moment for both whites and Indians when he wrote that the "crisis of the destiny of the Indian race in Oregon and Washington Territories is now upon us; and the result of the causes now operating, unless speedily arrested, will be disastrous to the whites, destructive to the Indians, and a heavy reproach upon our national character."[19]

On the night of October 7, the volunteers prepared to carry out their mission. Seven detachments were formed—115 men in all. Lupton himself leading the largest group of 36, attacked Jake's village on Butte Creek, killing everyone they could find. But it wasn't all one-sided. Lupton was mortally wounded and 10 volunteers sustained wounds as well. One newspaper account claimed 40 Indians killed, including 15 women and children. The killing of non-combatants was explained and justified because it was dark and the volunteers were unable to distinguish warriors from non-combatants. While Lupton's boys were attacking Jake's village, the second company of volunteers struck another camp, killing a woman and two boys.

Some in higher authority regarded the situation as out of control. The adjutant general of the territory issued a proclamation by the governor, ordering the disbandment of all unauthorized armed parties.

> Information having been received that armed parties have taken the field in southern Oregon, with the avowed purpose of waging a war of extermination against the Indians in that section of the territory, and have slaughtered, without respect to age or sex, a friendly band of Indians upon their reservation, in despite of the authority of the Indian agent and the commanding officer of the United States troops stationed there, and contrary to the peace of the territory: It is therefore ordered that the commanding officer of the battalions authorized by the proclamation of the governor of the 15th day of October instant, will enforce the disbanding of all armed parties not duly enrolled into the service of the Territory, by virtue of said proclamation.[20]

As usual, the Rogues retaliated, killing an agency employee. Some Rogues, fearful of continued bloodshed, turned themselves into the army at Fort Lane, while those who still had fight in them left the valley to strike elsewhere another day and did so. On October 9, they attacked and burned a ranch near Grant's Pass, killing rancher Jacob Wagner [or Waggner], his daughter and another young woman. Wagner's wife and another wounded daughter fought on from inside their house for several hours. When the Rogues decided they had had enough and left, Mrs. Wagner and her daughter fled into the woods. Later that day, having gotten word of the attack, some twenty miners joined forces with fifty-five dragoons from Fort Lane and rode to the Wagner place, where they found the Wagner women, along with the burned bodies of those killed by the Indians. After burying the bodies, the combined force moved out in pursuit of the Indians. In due course they caught up with the rear guard. A brisk firefight ensued before the elusive Rogues slipped away into the mountains. Elsewhere, there were similar attacks by small bands of Indians, acting independently, though seemingly in concert. Sixteen settlers reportedly died in these attacks.

On the 17th, the combined Rogue bands of George and Limpy had a furious eight-hour fight with forty miners on the Applegate River, but the miners were well positioned behind rocks and as darkness fell, the Rogues were forced to back off, having suffered heavy casualties. But it had been costly for the miners, too, who suffered four killed and eleven wounded. Although the miners won this round, the Rogues were not finished. A week later they struck again, burning cabins and forcing settlers to flee from the valley.

While the Rogue attacks on the Applegate River were being carried out other volunteer units still in the field struck a peaceful village at Looking Glass Prairie, killing five Rogues. The number might have been higher, too, had agent Ambrose not managed to gather some 300 of his charges at Fort Lane where the army provided protection from the exterminators.

Superintendent Joel Palmer, meanwhile, directed his agents to bring their charges to the reservations assigned them back in 1853 and 1854. Palmer was not at all sanguine as to the fate of the Indians. In October 1855 he wrote to Commissioner of Indian Affairs, George Manypenny stating:

> A portion of our own people seem to desire war, and it is greatly to be feared that it has been forced upon us, much against the wish of a large portion of the Indians of that district. But if commenced, whatever may have caused it, I apprehend nothing short of annihilation of these bands will terminate hostilities.[21]

Nor was Palmer the only one who saw such a disastrous outcome. Sub-agent Edward Geary wrote to Palmer, saying "Indiscriminate slaughter of all the Indians is the cry, and probably the general resolve."[22]

Meanwhile, word of the new uprising had spread, prompting many settlers to make for the safety of Jacksonville. Those who refused to abandon their property took steps to make sure their cabins were ready to repel attackers by building log palisades and digging trenches. Sometimes these fortified homesteads were christened with colorful names such as Six-Bit House and Fort Birdseye. The former name was said to have originated from the cost of lodging there.

On October 11, John Ross, acting under the power of a recent resolution by citizens of the area, enlisted 500 men in 9 companies in 3 days. Camp Stuart would be their headquarters, with ammunition and supplies sent up from Yreka and Crescent City. Meanwhile, Governor Curry called for five companies of mounted volunteers to chastise the savage murderers. These three companies—two from Lane County and one from Umpqua—would constitute a northern battalion, part of which operated out of the Eugene City area, while the remainder was at Roseburg. Overall command of the northern battalion was vested in Major William J. Martin, whom the men had elected as their commanding officer. As his battalion prepared to take the field, Martin informed his men that in chastising the enemy you will use your own discretion, provided you take no prisoners.

Harvey Robbins's company—one of the two from Lane County—formed up at Harrisburg, where it elected one, Jonathan Keeney captain, then marched to the vicinity of Eugene City, which place it reached on October 25. Robbins, who probably reflected the attitude of most if not all of these volunteers, said that "Nothing but a severe drubbing will ever quell them [the Rogues]." Robbins's company together with that of Captain Laban Buoy, took the field in earnest on the 25th after having their fervor riled by patriotic speeches.[23]

On October 29, a detachment of thirty men under Lieutenant A.W. Stanard was sent off to deal with Indian troublemakers on Cole's Prairie, while the remainder of the two companies marched on to Roseburg to join the rest of the battalion. About 3 a.m. on the morning of October 30, Stanard's detachment rejoined the company, bringing along ten Indian prisoners. The night had been a rainy one. The volunteers had no tents and local citizens refused to let them use their barns, which of course made the men even angrier at the Rogues. The volunteers not only aimed to give these Rogues a sound thrashing, but also saw them as responsible for the miserable state of affairs in which they now found themselves.

From Fort Vancouver, Washington, Lieutenant John Withers, commanding the post, wrote to Adjutant General, Samuel Cooper in Washington (later to serve in the Confederate Army), suggesting that the causes of the Rogue War differed from those that provoked trouble in Washington Territory "where the motive was altogether political, and sprung from no actual grievance; but its result must of course be the same."[24]

For the northern battalion, the first half of November was devoid of conflict. Mostly, the volunteers were occupied with scouting, escorting pack trains and providing protection for those settlers within their sphere of operation. Cold rain and snow continued to make life miserable, particularly as the men still had no tents. Since it appeared their presence in the area would be at least somewhat permanent, the battalion built a post twenty-five miles south of Roseburg that was named Fort Bailey, although it was little more than a fortified tavern that served as a headquarters of sort.

In the midst of all this, a new surveying party under the command of Lieutenant August Kautz, a familiar face in the area, arrived in late October, after a two-week journey from Fort Orford. Incredibly, Kautz arrived in the middle of a war, but that appeared not to have bothered either him or his men and certainly it does not seem to have occurred to his superior that perhaps this was not the best time to be conducting a surveying expedition.

The hard reality of their situation soon became evident, however, when they stumbled on a party of miners and Indians locked in a deadly fight near the Big Bend of the Rogue. Kautz was not at all prepared for this eventuality and quickly returned to Fort Orford for ammunition and supplies, after which he started out anew. However, within three miles of the Oregon-California Trail they were suddenly ambushed by a war party of Rogues. Kautz, himself, was struck by rifle fire, but his pocket diary absorbed the impact of the bullet. The soldiers managed to extricate themselves from the ambush and reach Fort Lane, losing two men in the process. But most importantly, and quite by accident, Kautz's surveying party had chanced upon the main camp of Rogues, reportedly under the leadership of Tecumtum, aka John, who had become the *de facto* leader of the dissident Rogues.

Kautz wasted no time reporting his discovery to Captain A.J. Smith, who immediately alerted the volunteers at Camp Stuart, then marched with 105 regulars to join forces with John Ross's volunteers. Once united, the combined force, totaling about 250 men, worked its way back to where Kautz had discovered the Indian camp, near Six-Bit House. Up ahead, the volunteers clearly saw Rogues on a ridge. Armed with a mixed bag of weapons, ranging from sabers to pistols and rifles, the volunteers, their dander up, charged ahead wildly. Patiently, the Indians waited and when the volunteers were within range, they were met with a shower of bullets and arrows that sent them scrambling back down the mountainside.

Exchanges of fire continued throughout the day, but the volunteers had learned the folly of direct assault

With the arrival of darkness the troops withdrew to find water for their wounded. Later, a stray shot threw the camp into utter chaos. All seemed certain that the Rogues were attacking and in the confusion that followed, one volunteer was killed and two others were wounded. Sensing perhaps that the volunteers were ripe, the Rogues quietly surrounded the camp and attacked at dawn on November 1. It was unfortunate timing for the Rogues. By the time they struck, order had been restored and the attack was repulsed. Nevertheless, four hours of heavy fighting followed.

The combined force of regulars and volunteers were in a bad way, as supplies were low and there was little water. Given their present reduced circumstances, the mixed force decided to withdraw, and fortunately for them, it was not necessary to fight their way out as the Rogues apparently had also decided to pull back. Accordingly, Smith and Ross made a temporary camp at Grave Creek, to which they gave the name of Camp Allaston. This fight—the Battle of Hungry Hill as it came to be known—was the first real battle of the 1855 war and was a costly one. The volunteers lost seven killed and twenty wounded, while Smith lost four killed and seven wounded. Estimates as to the number of Indians in the fight ranged from 200 to 500, and it was thought that the Rogues lost twenty warriors in the fight. Later, some of the Indians, tired of fighting, placed themselves under the protection of Captain A.J. Smith.

Meanwhile, yet another surveying party, this one under Lieutenant Henry Abbot, reached Six-Bit House just about the time the volunteers were arriving with their wounded. Lieutenant George Crook, recorded his memory of that moment in his autobiography:

> We arrived at a place called Six-Bits House, a wayside inn. We went into camp near it, where later there came a company of southern Oregon Mounted Volunteers raise for the ostensible purpose of operating against hostile Indians, and camped near us. When they unsaddled they threw their saddles, bridles and spurs on one pile. The next morning when they went to saddle up the ones who came first found the best. A perfect pandemonium ensued. I thought I had heard obscenity and blasphemy before, but this beat anything I had ever heard.[25]

The morning of November 17 broke with sunshine and a clear sky for a change. Word reached the volunteers that Indians were burning cabins and homesteads along Jump-Jo Creek. Keeney's company was sent in pursuit. With two barbecued bears in their larder they were provisioned and primed. On Sunday morning, November 18, they had marched some nine miles when they met up with couriers who reported that Captain Robert Williams's company had engaged some thirty to forty Rogues, killing five and putting the rest to flight. Believing the Rogues to have retreated toward Grave Creek, Keeney turned his company about, marched three miles to that point and camped for the night. The following morning—November 20—after sending all the horses, save those of the pack train, back to Fort Leland (yet another stockaded tavern), they proceeded on foot down Grave Creek a distance of twelve miles, through rough country to the Rogue River. Here, Keeney sent a detachment of fifteen men back to hurry along the pack train.

It was a weary bunch of volunteers that greeted the arrival of November 21. They were hungry and tired of climbing mountains. One volunteer recorded that his meal consisted of a little dough wound around a stick and baked over an open fire and a small slice of beef. Thus far, anyway, all their effort had produced no Indians. Keeney sent out a forty-man scouting party to search the surrounding area, and a second twenty-man detachment to climb a high peak and see if any Rogues could be spotted. While on the peak, the men heard gunfire from what was thought to come from Grave Creek. Supposing the pack train was under attack, the detachment hurried back to camp and after a four-mile march met up with the pack train plodding leisurely along. The firing, it was later determined, had belonged to another company, which had a firefight with some Rogues.

On November 22, Keeney's company resumed its march down Grave Creek to Rogue River. Near the creek's junction with the Rogue they found an abandoned Indian village site and put the torch to it. The inhabitants, an estimated thirty to forty squaws and children, fled upon hearing the sound of guns. That evening Buoy's command joined Keeney's company.

Elsewhere in the area, on the 24th, Major Martin with 400 men of the northern battalion, discovered what they believed was an Indian camp some four miles ahead in Rogue River Canyon. Early that afternoon they were joined by Captain Williams' command which was able to confirm that it was indeed an Indian camp.

Forty-eight hours later, the southern battalion came down river to reinforce Martin. A scout, meanwhile, reported that the Rogues were preparing to fight and indeed they had moved up and taken positions along the opposite shore. At this point the Rogue River runs through a deep, narrow canyon. The Indians had the advantage of terrain, which was thickly timbered and largely concealed their positions. After felling trees and building rafts, the volunteers commenced their crossing of the river and promptly drew fire from the Indians. Once on the other side, the volunteers returned fire as best they could and sought wherever cover was available. After seven hours of exchanging fire, the volunteers had lost one man killed. More importantly, nothing had been resolved.

The Indians had managed to give a good enough account of themselves to convince Majors Martin and Bruce that they were outnumbered. Reinforcements were requested, along with more provisions. The standoff continued, with Indians and volunteers firing on each other as targets of opportunity presented themselves. The late fall weather continued to be thoroughly miserable with rain, snow, sleet, and wind. Following a six-inch snowfall on December 1, the two majors decided to return to the settlements. The march commenced on the morning of December 2, the men carrying their lone wounded comrade on a litter across sixteen miles of mountains. Three days later, on December 4, they reached Fort Leland.

The weather discouraged further campaigning and besides, there was now more concern over a lack of supplies than with Indians, with whom there had been no further contact anyway. On Christmas Day, the quartermaster brought around a bucket of brandy for the men to celebrate. By the end of the month the volunteers had returned to Roseburg and Eugene and on February 1 were discharged.

As the autumn deepened, the Rogue attacks had not diminished: miners and settlers continued to be attacked and cabins were burned. Those volunteers still in service moved from Camp Stuart to Fort Vannoy, a cluster of log buildings some four miles west of Grant's Pass so as to be closer to the area where the Rogues seemed to be most active. Units were posted to the north to keep that access open, while others guarded peaceful Indians living along the South Fork of the Umpqua. Still another detachment was at Camp Bailey to guard the road through the Grave Creek Hills.

At this time Ross discharged four companies of volunteers, but then promptly mustered them back in as a brand new battalion in accordance with Governor Curry's orders. With a sizeable number of volunteers now in the field and with plenty of supplies available, Major James Bruce, a colleague and supporter of Lupton, who commanded volunteer units in the southern sector, hatched a plan to track down the Rogues and destroy them in the mountains. In this scheme he was aided by regular army officer, Lieutenant Henry Judah.

Judah took the field on November 21 with a detachment of regulars, plus three companies of volunteers. At Grave Creek Crossing, they turned toward the Rogue River, while two other companies of volunteers moved directly downstream. The intent of the plan was to catch the Rogues between the two forces. It was tough campaigning, moving into the very remote and rugged heart of the Rogue domain. On the 23rd, Judah bivouacked near the confluence of Whiskey Creek and the Rogue River. The following day a march of a dozen miles put them at a place called Little Meadows. Fallen timber and heavy brush made for slow going, but this mountainous terrain also contained many grassy meadows, which at least provided good forage for the horses.

Rogues were suspected of being in the vicinity and that night the winking lights of campfires prompted Judah's men to think that the fires were either from the Rogue camp, or belonged to the other volunteer unit. Later that night, however, the other force of volunteers with whom they were supposed to be operating arrived in Judah's camp with the explanation that the canyon had proved too difficult to get through so they had simply followed Judah's trail. The fires, then, were clearly those of the Indians and word went back to Major Bruce who sent scouts to look over the Indian camp on the 25th. Subsequently, scouts returned and reported a camp with 150 warriors and their families, in a strong position on a sandbar in the narrowest part of the canyon. The south side of their position was thickly forested, while precipitous cliffs covered the north side. The Rogues would prove tough to root out of this position.

Undeterred, the combined force of regulars and volunteers moved out on November 26, with Judah's regulars hauling a howitzer. His total force numbered nearly 150 men, with which he proposed to attack the north end of the Rogue position. En route, however, Judah received a message from Major Bruce (who had some 300 men under his command) to turn back. Bruce had reached the river about three miles below the Indian camp and had begun building rafts to cross the river. However, the noise had alerted the Rogues who promptly opened fire. With little cover to protect them, Bruce's command soon suffered five casualties. Once again, the Rogues had managed to repel another expedition, despite being outnumbered five to one.

Meanwhile, Judah's regulars were running short of provisions. Many of the men were without shoes and blankets and with winter approaching, Judah elected to return to Fort Lane. But these regulars were not the only ones hurting. More than 600 peaceful Indians camped at Fort Lane and along the Umpqua, under their agent's supervision, lacked food, shelter, and many were dying from tuberculosis and measles. Superintendent Palmer did not close a blind eye to their condition. He had located reservation sites along the north central Oregon coast and set about moving his charges to their new home.

On December 1, Palmer wrote to General John Wool, commanding the Department of the Pacific, saying

> The existence of a war of extermination by our citizens against all Indians in southern Oregon, which by recent acts appears to evince a determination to carry it out in violation of all treaty stipulations and the common usage of civilized nations, has induced me to take steps to remove the friendly bands of Indians now assembled at Fort Lane and upon Umpqua reservation, to an encampment of the Yamhill river, distant about sixty miles southwest of Vancouver, and adjoining the coast reservations.[26]

That it was difficult for the volunteers to distinguish between friend and foe is true. Who were the hostiles and who were not compounded the difficulty of campaigning against these Rogues, though in the end it really made little difference to most of the volunteers. While Palmer's charges were suffering and dying at Fort Lane, other Umpquas kept the fires of trouble stoked by attacking the cabins of several settlers, killing their livestock, and putting the torch to homes and outbuildings. In early December, a party of volunteers responding to these attacks located the Indian camp and had a hard fight in which the Umpquas lost two killed and several others wounded. The savagery of the volunteers in their attacks on the Indians prompted Palmer to report to Commissioner Manypenny:

> the brutal outrages committed from time to time upon the Indians within the last three years, have resulted in a concerted movement from north to south among the various bands to carry on a war of extermination against the whites; and it is not at all improbable that the bands in this valley are contributing to swell the ranks of the enemy.[27]

All the while, lest they be forgotten, Lupton's exterminators continued their mission. On Christmas Eve, 1855, two companies under officers Alcorn and Rice struck two villages at roughly the same place where Jake's people had been cut down back in October. The duplicity of some of these volunteers was unbelievable, since both Alcorn and Rice had visited these same villages just twenty-four hours earlier and assured the inhabitants of their friendly intentions. The attack resulted in the deaths of nineteen men and the destruction of dwellings and supplies, leaving the women and children to die of exposure and starvation.

Nor were the exterminators finished. A week later, Rice and a company of volunteers, reinforced by twenty-five infantrymen from Fort Lane, marched to the Applegate River, where Indians were reportedly living in abandoned cabins. Unexpectedly, however, on January 2 1856, they were attacked by Rogues near Jacksonville, who managed to kill one exterminator. Undeterred, Rice pressed on and after a three-day delay, resulting from the loss of a mule carrying one of the howitzers plunging off a cliff, the volunteers and regulars approached the Indian camp and opened fire with cannon on January 5, but the Indians would not be forced out. That night, the Rogues—it was John's band—fled out of harm's way. The volunteers had suffered one casualty, the Rogues three.

Notwithstanding their best efforts, the volunteers were unable to locate any other encampments of Indians. However, on the evening of January 23, a party of volunteers, who had been careless enough not to post a guard, were attacked by some Umpquas who killed two of the volunteers before being driven off.

Joel Palmer, meanwhile, continued his efforts on behalf of Indian removal to the Willamette Valley. Some settlers in that area had objected, uncomfortable with an Indian presence in the valley. Palmer understood this, but believed the anxiety had subsided. Unfortunately, whether he fully appreciated it or not, Palmer had grown increasingly unpopular. Thirty-five members of the territorial legislature wrote to President Franklin Pierce, calling for Palmer's removal on the grounds that he recognized individual Indians who were not legitimate leaders and therefore not authorized to make tribal decisions. Moreover, they argued, while Palmer had represented himself as a Democrat and had received his appointment through the Democratic party, he had since become a member of the Know-Nothing Party and was now bound to that hellish secret political order.

The politicos were in high gear. Not only did they urge Palmer's removal, but they also lobbied for the recall of General Wool because in their estimation he had been unsuccessful in resolving the Indian problem. In truth, though, Wool's problems were not just confined to southern Oregon and the Rogue country. His regulars also had to contend with Indian problems in Washington Territory. As well, there was constant friction between Army regulars and volunteers.

The problem was most of the settlers demanded that the Indians be punished and removed, and insofar as they could see this simply was not happening. Wool, however, despite being contentious and opinionated was a thoroughly capable officer with nearly half a century of service behind him. He believed the Indians deserved better than to be exterminated and his position on this issue made him a politically unpopular commander. In 1856, Oregon territorial legislators had asked the president to have him removed and finally in 1857, then Secretary of War Jefferson Davis did exactly that.

Politics played a key role in the Northwest Indian wars, arguably, more so here than elsewhere in the Trans-Mississippi West. The Know-Nothing Party was alleged to be the driving force behind the move to exterminate the Indians and in this was supported by the *Oregonian*. Yet, in a strange incongruity, the Democrats controlled a majority of seats in the territorial legislature and Lupton, a true hard-liner, was also a Democrat. It was the Know-Nothings who pressured Governor Curry to call up volunteers and on October 8, he complied by raising eight companies of mounted troops. Only General Wool, Superintendent Palmer and a few local citizens such as John Beeson, were the voices crying in the wind. Writing to the adjutant general of the U.S. Army, General Wool pointed out that "In Oregon, as well as in the northern part of California, many whites are for exterminating the Indians. This feeling is engendered by two newspapers that go for extermination, and is more or less possessed by the volunteers, as well as others not enrolled under the banners of Gov. Curry."[28]

Notwithstanding the opposition to his efforts, Palmer got underway with his removal plan in late January 1856 and by the end of February some 500 Rogues from various bands made a trek up the coast to be relocated to the Grande Ronde and Siletz reservations in western Oregon, leaving behind the bones of their ancestors. A few scattered and stubborn survivors remained in the mountains, a pitiful remnant of the presence that once populated this area. In effect the War of the Rogues was at last over, though February 1856 saw one final spurt of conflict. Tecumtum's band had moved down the Rogue River to the coast, hoping to find food and supplies. However, regular army forces coming north from California forced the Rogues to abandon their hopes and surrender. Meanwhile, Colonel Robert Buchanan's regulars together with the volunteers who had been coming on in pursuit attacked the Rogues at Big Meadow and again at the Big Bend of the Rogue.

The Rogue troubles had been expensive. In assessing the cost, the Commission on Indian War Expenses in Oregon and Washington Territories reported in December 1857, that the conflicts in southern Oregon had cost $4, 449,949.33. By comparison, the same war if fought today would have cost in excess of $60,000,000. Perhaps as one historian has suggested, it was more profitable to fight Indians than search for gold. More importantly, however, and incalculable was the suffering and loss of human life, white and Indian alike.

Although the Rogue conflicts were mostly fought by citizen volunteers, the conflicts did serve as a training ground for future army leaders. Of those who served in the Wars of the Rogues E.O.C. Ord, Christopher Augur, August Kautz, A.J. Smith, John Reynolds, Silas Casey, Philip Kearny, George Crook, and George Stoneman would all serve as general officers in the Civil War.

The Yakima and Coastal Wars, 1856–1858

He was called Kamiakin. He was the mixed blood son of a Palouse father and a Yakima mother. Raised among his mother's people, his tribal allegiance was to the Yakima. Kamiakin was born to lead. However, because he was not a full-blood Yakima he was ineligible to be a headman, but his prowess as a warrior and his innate skills as a leader surfaced early and resulted in his becoming the *de facto* leader of the Yakimas. As probably the single most effective war leader against the whites in the wars of the Northwest during the 1850s, Kamiakin deserves a place in the pantheon of other notable Indian leaders.[29]

The Yakimas were one of several Sahaptin-speaking tribes that included Klikitat, Palouse, Umatilla, Walla Walla, and Cayuse. These tribes occupied the territory between the Cascades and the Rockies. Their culture had much in common with the nomadic tribes of the Plains. Horses figured prominently in their way of life, and they frequently made forays onto the Plains in search of buffalo.

During the great Walla Walla treaty council of 1855 convened by Governor Isaac Stevens and Superintendent of Indian Affairs for Oregon, Joel Palmer, the Yakima, Cayuse, Umatilla, and Walla Walla tribes were compelled to cede 6 million acres of their land, partly in reparation for the massacre at Waiilatpu, never mind that only the Cayuse had actually been involved in that tragedy. In truth, the real reason behind Stevens' aggressive maneuvering at this and other treaty councils was to make more land available for the steady influx of new immigrants and a right-of-way for the railroad that Stevens was determined to bring to the region. In return, the tribes were to be paid $200,000 over a six-year period and have a reservation of their own.

Initially, Governor Stevens sought two separate reservations, one for the Nez Perce, Cayuse, Umatilla, and Walla Walla and a second for the Palouse and Yakima tribes. However, the Cayuse, Umatilla, and Walla Walla refused that arrangement, thus compelling Stevens to create a third reservation. As treaties went it was to have significant consequences, now and two decades later when abrogation of this treaty led to the Nez Perce War of 1877.

Although Kamiakin and other tribal leaders had no hand in, and disapproved of the Cayuse action at Waiilatpu, they were no less disturbed by many of the same things that had driven the Cayuse to their killing frenzy. The white man's diseases had taken a fearful toll of all the tribes and Hudson's Bay people fed on that fear by spreading rumors that the Americans were responsible because they wanted Indian land, which of course was true.

Governor Stevens had assured the Indians that this time white miners and settlers would not be allowed to trespass on Indian land. As it always did, however, fresh gold strikes, this time in Colville, Washington Territory—dubbed the El Dorado of the North—and in the Fraser River area of British Columbia attracted prospectors who freely crossed Indian land on their way to the diggings, sometimes stealing Indian horses and abusing Indian women en route.

Although he had reluctantly signed the 1855 treaty, Kamiakin was never comfortable with the agreement, especially when it became clear that white prospectors and newly arrived immigrants ignored the reservation boundaries, and there were rumors as well of Mormon efforts to incite Indian attacks. Interestingly, prior to the treaty white travelers felt relatively safe, but after the treaty was signed it became a different story. Kamiakin, perhaps more than other Indian leaders, feared the threat of white settlers. He sent runners to all tribes, urging them to kill any whites who crossed Indian land.

When a party of prospectors bound for Colville was attacked and several were killed, it brought out red-bearded Andrew J. Bolon, sub-agent for the Yakimas, from The Dalles to parley with Kamiakin. En route he was attacked by four Yakima warriors who slit his throat. Bolon's murder served as a warning to any whites who entered Indian territory. As such, the killing struck the spark that ignited the Yakima War.

As a consequence of Agent Bolon's murder, Major Granville Haller started out from Fort Dalles with two companies of the 4th Infantry and a howitzer; eighty-four men in all. About the same time, Lieutenant William Slaughter left Fort Steilacoom (near present

Tacoma) with a force of fifty men bound for the Yakima Valley. By the time he crossed the Cascades, however, Slaughter found the country swarming with Indians, and decided the prudent course of action was to withdraw to White River. Meanwhile, on October 5, Haller found himself confronted by Kamiakin and several hundred warriors—estimates range from 300 to 500—across Toppenish Creek. A fight ensued with Kamiakin getting the better of it. The Army suffered five killed and seventeen wounded, while Indian casualties numbered two killed and four wounded. Kamiakin's success against Haller attracted more Indians to his cause. Some who had not previously been committed to war, including tribes west of the Cascades and north to Puget Sound felt encouraged enough now to join the resistance. Tension was high from southern Oregon to Washington.

Following the fight, Haller returned to Fort Dalles, where Maj, Gabriel Rains, district commander had requested two companies of volunteers each from Washington and Oregon. Isaac Stevens was still out on his treaty-making mission, so acting governor Charles Mason promptly complied. Oregon was another matter, though as Governor Curry said his volunteers would not serve under a federal officer, so he mustered a regiment of mounted volunteers on his own volition and gave the command to Colonel James Nesmith.

Haller, meanwhile, had managed to assemble a force of 350 men from the 4th Infantry, 1st Dragoons and a pair of howitzers to go with the Washington volunteers. Backed by Governor Mason's authority, Rains assumed the rank of brigadier general for this mission. Despite Governor Curry's claim that his volunteers would not serve under regular army officers, Colonel Nesmith decided to report to Rains anyway. It seemed a formidable enough force, but Lieutenant Phil Sheridan, among others, claimed that Rains was incompetent, an opinion that was subsequently proven accurate. On October 30, Rains left Fort Dalles intending to confront Kamiakin at the Yakima River.

Meanwhile, in support of Rains's effort, Captain Maurice Maloney marched from the Puget Sound area with 100 regulars and a company of volunteers. The idea was to catch the Indians between the two forces, a tactic frequently employed during the Indian wars in the West and one that was seldom as successful as it sounded in the talking stage.

Reaching the Yakima Valley, Rains had several skirmishes, notably at Union Gap on the Yakima River. With 300 warriors, Kamiakin was outnumbered more than two to one, plus Rains had howitzers. The Indians had not previously been exposed to howitzer fire and regarded the guns as evil spirits. Retiring to the northwest the Indians managed to get their non-combatants across the Columbia River near Beverly on a bitterly cold night. Despite a tenacious rear guard action on the part of the Indians, many non-combatants were killed. Nearly surrounded, Kamiakin continued his retreat. Priests from nearby St. Joseph's Mission assisted many of the non-combatants to the safety of the mission. Freed from the burden of protecting the non-combatants, Kamiakin and his warriors were able to evade the pursuing soldiers.

Soldiers found gunpowder buried on the mission grounds and assuming the good fathers were aiding the Indians, they proceeded to burn the mission. The soldiers also discovered a letter supposedly dictated by Kamiakin to Father Charles Pandosy at the mission, suggesting that the Indians might be amenable to donating some of their land to the whites in exchange for not being confined to a reservation.

What if anything Rains made of the letter is not known, but having had no luck in bringing about the decisive battle he sought and with winter approaching, Rains headed back to Fort Dalles. Sheridan, among others, thought the campaign had been a flop and indeed, in the weeks following, there was a flurry of accusations and counter-charges. Captain Maloney's column contributed nothing to the campaign, either, but in his case it was the weather that had proved too tough to overcome. Unable to get through the snow at Naches Pass, he was forced to turn back.

In November, Brigadier General John E. Wool, a small, feisty forty-year veteran and commander of the Army's Pacific Division, arrived at Fort Vancouver prepared to deal with the Yakima crisis. Wool's strategy was to station troops in key locations throughout the troubled area. It sounded good, but the problem was that Wool was responsible for a huge area and had only 700 regulars and 300 Washington volunteers to implement his strategy. More regular troops were needed and he advised General of the Army, Winfield Scott accordingly.

Cooperation between federal troops and state volunteers was practically non-existent. Wool charged that the undisciplined Oregon volunteers made poor soldiers and instigated war by giving the Indians no choice but to fight, a policy he laid at the feet of Governor Curry. Volunteers were conducting their own private war against Indians, which clashed with Wool's operations and put a drain on forage and supply stocks. Wool also managed to ruffle the feathers of Washington Territory Governor Isaac Stevens when he discharged the Washington volunteers and pulled the regulars back to Fort Vancouver for the winter. Stevens responded by accusing Wool of being incapable and demanded that the Secretary of War relieve him of command. Wool was convinced that the two territorial governors exaggerated conditions and thereby turned a small problem into a major one.

General Wool was actually fighting a three-front war. In addition to the interference posed by the Oregon volunteers, he had to contend with the situation in the Yakima Valley and along the Columbia River, but there was unrest up in the Puget Sound region, as well, where a Nesqually chief named Leschi, one of Kamiakin's most devoted apostles, was stirring up trouble, warning that reservations were but a prelude to a complete take-over by white men.

Settlements around Puget Sound would have to be defended by the garrison at Fort Steilacoom and whatever U.S. Naval forces happened to be in the area at any given time. In addition, four companies of Washington volunteers lent their weight to the available forces. Indeed it was a slim line of defense. On December 4, near the junction of the Green and White Rivers, a party of Klikitats attacked a party of the 4th Infantry commanded by Lieutenant William Slaughter, killing four including Slaughter, and wounding another.

Seattle was then a fledgling community of 100, featuring some 30 frame buildings. The citizens, anticipating trouble, built themselves an eight-foot-high stockade and several blockhouses. The army garrisons prepared for trouble and the navy sent the sloop *Decatur*, commanded by Commander Isaac Sterrett, up from Mare Island, California, to reinforce the tiny community. The ship rode at anchor in the harbor. On January 26, 1856, Leschi attacked. Sterrett turned *Decatur's* guns on the attackers and sent 120 sailors and marines ashore to reinforce the community. Some sharp fighting followed, but the combined force of defenders gave as good as they got. Faced with this unexpected resistance, the Indians withdrew as night fell.

The situation around Puget Sound had been chancy for months. In 1855 a party of whites had been massacred by Indians and scarcely a month later volunteers had retaliated with a massacre of Indians, which in turn was followed by another massacre of settlers during a month-long siege. In March, a force of 200 Indians attacked Lieutenant August Kautz's company of the 9th Infantry at White River. Reinforcements were rushed to the area and a second fight followed at Connell's Prairie a week later, but between the naval vessels, the blockhouses, and the army's determination, the Indians grew discouraged from further attacks in the region.

East of the Cascades, Oregon Governor Curry had seen fit to send a force of volunteers under Lieutenant Colonel James Kelly into the Yakima Valley to encourage the non-hostile tribes from going on the warpath. The effort was only mildly successful at best since the recalcitrant bands clearly remained hostile. In early December, while things were active in Puget Sound, these volunteers had a sharp fight with a mixed force of Walla Walla, Cayuse, Umatilla, and Palouse. Both sides finally agreed to parley, but some of the volunteers grabbed Peo-Peo-Mox-Mox (Yellow Serpent), the Walla Walla chief, as a hostage, then shot and killed him, claiming he was attempting to escape. The chief's ears and scalp were later sent downriver to be put on display.

The murder of the Walla Walla leader quickly ended the parleying and any hope Governor Curry may have entertained for reconciliation. Fighting resumed, mostly in the form of skirmishing for several days before the Indians scattered across the Snake River. This was exactly the sort of behavior that General Wool had been talking about when he was openly critical of territorial officials and their volunteers. The volunteers were not without supporters, however. When Governor Stevens learned of the Yakima uprising, he believed Kelly's command had forced the break-up of an Indian coalition.

In March 1856, Lieutenant Colonel Thomas Cornelius, who had replaced Colonel Nesmith, led five companies of Oregon Mounted Volunteers into the Palouse country, but located no Indians. Cornelius who had been a sergeant in the old Oregon Rifles during the Cayuse War now found himself a field grade officer. One thing you had to say for service in the volunteer ranks was that promotions came faster than in the regular army. Then early in April Cornelius learned of a body of Indians near The Dalles, and moved against them. However, at Satus Creek he was attacked, losing one man killed and suffered the loss of his horse herd as well. The Indians led by Kamiakin, among others, were said to have lost one killed and three wounded.

General Wool, meantime, was looking ahead to a warm weather campaign. He now had at hand all ten companies of the new 9th Infantry, commanded by white-haired, thirty-year veteran, Colonel George Wright. A stern Vermonter, Wright would serve as field commander. Wright's second was Lieutenant Colonel Silas Casey, who it will be recalled, had seen action against the Rogues. Casey, too, was an able veteran and, as well, the author of a volume on army tactics. Casey was sent up to Fort Steilacoom with two companies and orders to restore peace in the area. The other eight companies remained at Fort Vancouver until spring when Wright planned to settle the Indian troubles east of the Cascades.

With the advent of spring, General Wool proposed a simultaneous advance into the Yakima and Walla Walla Valleys, but as field commander, Wright exercised his own judgment and elected to march into the Walla Walla Valley first, leaving his supply line vulnerable to Yakima raids. On the morning of March 26, Wright marched out of Fort Dalles with five companies of infantry and a detachment of dragoons, 250 men in all. Their immediate objective was Fort Bennett, another of the hastily established advanced bases near the site of Waiilatpu.

While Wright's column was in motion a force of some 100 Yakima, Klickitat, and Chinook warriors attacked settlements near the Cascades, subsequently took control of the Lower Cascade Landing, and laid siege to a blockhouse on the Middle Cascades. The blockhouse—euphemistically named Fort Rains was garrisoned by Sergeant Matthew Kelley and a detachment of nine men from the 4th Infantry. The siege of Fort Rains turned out to be one of the nastiest in the Pacific Northwest wars.

Meanwhile, word of the siege—overall known as the Battle of the Cascades—managed to reach Fort Dalles and Fort Vancouver. From the latter post, Lieutenant Philip Sheridan (the future Civil War luminary) organized a detachment of forty men and ascended the Columbia River on a steamer. At the same time a messenger was sent off to apprise Wright of the situation. Sheridan soon retook the Lower Cascades Landing and moved against the besieged blockhouse.

By this time Wright, having learned of the crisis, returned to Fort Dalles from where he wasted no time moving his command downriver on a pair of steamers. On March 28 he landed at Upper Cascades, cleared the area and advanced to unite with Sheridan and relieve the blockhouse. Indian casualties were few, but Wright did manage to capture Chenowith of the Chinooks and seven others of whom all but one were subsequently hanged.

At the end of April, Wright finally resumed his campaign. On the 28th he left Fort Dalles with essentially the same force he had started out with a month earlier. Lieutenant Colonel Edward Jevnon Steptoe with three companies of the 9th Infantry was directed to join Wright, but was delayed by high water on the Naches River (near present Yakima) and had to build a bridge to get his command across. Thus, it was not until the end of May that Steptoe was able to unite with the main column, bringing Wright's total force to eleven companies of infantry and supporting artillery.

Two additional companies of the 9th Infantry under Major Robert Garnett had also been directed to march east from Puget Sound to join Wright. A Virginian and former instructor at West Point, Garnett was an austere little man with neatly trimmed beard and mustache, who had fought in the Seminole and Mexican Wars as well as on the Texas frontier and would later serve as a general officer in the Confederate Army.

As military campaigns go this one was something of a bust. Several chiefs approached Wright, expressing a desire for peace, but there was considerable divisiveness among the Indians: some sought peace, but others still harbored plenty of fight. Kamiakin, for example, refused to attend the gathering, but sent Wright his assurances of friendship. The chiefs promised to bring in all the hostiles and surrender within five days. Wright did not take the promise at face value and prepared to resume his campaign. Before doing so, however, he detached Steptoe's three companies to build and garrison Fort Naches (or Na-Chess) in the Yakima Valley.

With the rest of his command, Wright then crossed the Naches River and spent the next two months tramping through Yakima country, finding no sign of trouble. In fact, everywhere he went he found nothing but peaceful Indians harvesting salmon. Wright seems not to have realized it but those Indians still considered hostile had simply moved out of the area, leaving the peaceable bands behind. The others, including Kamiakin and his followers had moved northeast to unite with the Palouse and Spokanes. So, having found no Indians to whip, Wright was back at Fort Dalles by late July, having completed a bloodless campaign. Indeed it was alleged by one participant that there was more walking, talking and less fighting than in any other Indian campaign.

Wright regarded it as senseless to confine the Indians to the small reservations defined by Stevens' treaties where the government would be required to feed and care for them. Better to allow them freedom to roam throughout their traditional homeland and care for their own needs, with a strong military post to monitor their behavior. Accordingly, in August 1856, Major Garnett was directed to establish Fort Simcoe, some sixty miles northeast of Fort Dalles.

Governor Stevens, meanwhile, was furious over the way the war was being prosecuted. As far as he was concerned, Wright seemed more interested in talking than fighting. Stevens was angry, too, that the army failed to station a permanent presence in the Walla Walla

Valley. Strategically, he had long regarded the valley as the key to controlling the Indian problem. Consequently, upon learning that the Oregon volunteers under Colonel Cornelius had returned to The Dalles, Stevens decided to act on his own volition. Forming two volunteer units in Washington Territory who would be answerable only to him, Stevens sent one unit across the Cascades to strike the Yakimas, while the second moved up the Columbia to replace the Oregon volunteers.

After crossing Naches Pass, the western unit marched to Fort Dalles and there joined the Walla Walla column commanded by Lieutenant Colonel Benjamin Franklin Shaw. With some 400 men under his command, Shaw reached the Walla Walla Valley in early July 1859. On the 17th, they encountered a comparable force of Walla Walla, Cayuse, Umatilla, John Day, and Deschute warriors in the Grande Ronde Valley. In the sharp fight that followed the volunteers reportedly killed forty Indians and burned a large village. Pleased, Isaac Stevens boasted that he was responsible for breaking up a large Indian force and having done so, he could now finalize the 1855 treaties.

General Wool, ever mindful of civilian interference, cautioned Wright to watch for Indians on his front and civilian volunteers in his rear. He and Stevens did manage to agree on one thing, though: both thought a military post was needed in the Walla Walla Valley. Accordingly, when Wright returned to Fort Dalles Wool directed him to build such a post and Wright in turn assigned the job to Steptoe. Should Shaw's volunteers still be in the area when he arrived, Steptoe was to order them to leave and if necessary arrest and disarm them.

By September, when Governor Stevens was convening his grand council in the Walla Walla Valley, Steptoe had begun work on what was to be Fort Walla Walla some seven miles from the council site. Stevens felt confident that this would be a trouble free conference and released most of the volunteers. Unfortunately, when Kamiakin showed up it encouraged the Indians present—a mixed gathering of some 4,000—to be less than cooperative. Kamiakin's presence emboldened the others, and suddenly there was tension in the air. Stevens sent word to Steptoe for assistance, but the colonel refused, saying he could spare none of his men who were busy building Fort Walla Walla.

Sensing, suddenly, that his position had become more than a little vulnerable, Stevens called off the conference on September 19 and decided to join Steptoe. However, young warriors, angry and out of patience, attacked the Stevens party en route. When word of this reached Steptoe he detailed a company to man the newly finished blockhouse then moved out to escort the governor's party to the Columbia River.

Charges and counter charges flew back and forth. Stevens accused Steptoe of failing to provide support at the site of the council, which might have discouraged the Indians from acting so belligerently. The governor also accused Wright of conducting a weak campaign, one that encouraged the Indians towards violence. Steptoe and Wright, on the other hand, blamed Stevens for bringing too many Indians together at one time, thereby creating a volatile environment. And not to be left out of the picture, General Wool scolded Wright for not being at the council in person to keep Stevens in check.

The Yakima War, or at least the first stage of it, appeared to be over, though there was no clear victor. The peace, such as it was would have to be preserved by the army, which faced a virtually impossible task, given the current state of affairs. In 1858, the U.S. Army had only about 11,000 men available for field duty in the entire nation, and of these, fewer than a thousand for the entire Pacific Northwest.

Meanwhile, as the new territorial delegate to Congress, the ever ambitious and aggressive Isaac Stevens moved on to Washington to fight for ratification of his treaties. At the same time, Secretary of War Jefferson Davis, tired of the wrangling between the army and civil authorities, replaced General Wool with Brigadier General Newman Clarke. The management of Indian affairs, too, underwent a change in both Oregon and Washington Territories with the appointment of Superintendent James W. Nesmith, a former U.S. Marshall who had led a company of Oregon volunteers in 1855. A die-hard Indian hater and anti-Catholic, Nesmith, while welcomed by others of his ilk, was less than an ideal choice for superintendent.

Trouble persisted in brewing beneath the surface of this illusory peace. General Clarke and Superintendent Nesmith haggled over whether the murderers of Agent Bolon should be found and properly tried, despite the fact that Colonel Wright had assured the Indians that this was a dead issue. Insofar as the military was concerned, either the ratification of the Stevens treaties, or any attempt to punish Bolon's killers would invite big trouble.

In the spring of 1858, Colonel Steptoe decided to launch a dual purpose campaign out of Fort Walla Walla. One phase had as its objective to investigate rumors of Mormons inciting Indians to attack along the Oregon Trail, but as a prelude to that effort, he planned a sweep northeast into Palouse country. Indians in that area had been running off livestock and were otherwise being troublesome. Several bands lived along the Spokane River, of which the Palouse had been the most troublesome while others such as the Spokanes, led by forty-four-year-old Spokane Garry (or Gary) had not participated in the Yakima War at all. Nevertheless, Steptoe reasoned that a show of force might discourage them from changing their mind and prompt the others to think twice about making trouble. As well it would serve to let miners in the Colville diggings know that federal troops were paying attention to things in that part of the territory.

Of the various soldiers who served in the Northwest during the Indian wars of the 1850s, none is perhaps better remembered than Edward Jevnor Steptoe. A black-haired aristocratic Virginian, said to be related to George Washington's brother, Steptoe was a West Point graduate and veteran of the Mexican War, where he was promoted for gallantry in action at the Battle of Cerro Gordo. By this point in his life, Steptoe seems not to have been a well man. One historian has suggested that he may have suffered from Multiple Sclerosis. In any case, Edward Steptoe's performance during the Indian wars of the Northwest proved to be something less than his finest hour.[30]

On May 6 Steptoe marched out of Fort Walla Walla at the head of three companies of the 1st Dragoons, twenty-five foot soldiers and a pair of mountain howitzers, in all just over 150 officers and men. Oddly enough, the men carried little ammunition as the colonel seems not to have anticipated any real trouble. Only one company of dragoons was armed with rifles; the rest of the command carried musketoons, a short, muzzle-loading weapon that was more like a shotgun and had a maximum range of fifty yards.

Steptoe's command crossed the Snake River in canoes provided by friendly Nez Perce under old chief Tammutsa who had taken the Christian name of Timothy. These particular Nez Perce had once been on friendly terms with the Whitmans at Waiilatpu and despite the troubles in the region of late, they remained cordial. Perhaps no other tribe in the Northwest made such an effort to befriend whites as did the Nez Perce.

Reaching the Palouse River about May 16, Steptoe suddenly found himself confronted by an estimated 1,000 warriors from several tribes who had gathered to prevent the soldiers from continuing their advance. Captain Charles Winder described the encounter that occurred around noon. The Indians were "all painted and in their war dress, evidently meditating an attack. At first sight with my glass I count but 70." When Steptoe and a small escort advanced to parley with the Indians, a huge swarm suddenly appeared around the troops.[31]

Steptoe attempted to convince the Indians that his mission was peaceful, but the young hotheads grew threatening and the colonel wisely elected to turn back. The Indians followed, hovering about the column. The next morning, as the column neared near present Rosalia, Washington, the rear guard was attacked and the flanks were also threatened. For a time fighting was fierce. Steptoe finally managed to form a position on a hilltop where the howitzers were used to keep the Indians at bay, though at times it was apparently hand-to-hand. One dragoon, a former French army officer reportedly swung his rifle like a sword while wishing for a saber.

By dark, Steptoe had lost six killed, including two officers, and had twelve wounded on his hands. The men were down to three rounds of ammunition apiece. His remaining officers, including Lieutenant David McMurtrie Gregg, later to serve with distinction as a Civil War general of cavalry, argued a retreat, but Steptoe vowed to remain on the hill and fight to the death. However, after a little deeper reflection and urging from his remaining officers, he decided to accept their recommendation. After burying both the dead and the howitzers, they managed to slip down the hill and past the Indian camps, finally reaching Fort Walla Walla on May 22.

Despite a skillful withdrawal, the Steptoe fight was an embarrassment for the Army and quickly took on overtones of a disaster. Once again ripples of fear swept through the region that a general Indian uprising was underway. The Army responded with alacrity. Units were brought in from as far away as San Diego and Fort Yuma on the Colorado River. Recruits were ordered in from Kentucky. But the commitment could only be temporary of course since the regular army was thinly spread and troops were needed elsewhere. The army was engaged in some twenty-two Indian conflicts during the 1850s, and the year 1857 alone had seen thirty-seven campaigns take the field, not all here in the Northwest, of course, so whatever was going to be done here would have to be done quickly before the reinforcements were needed elsewhere.

By mid–June, General Clarke was at Fort Vancouver planning a new campaign. Wright would move north from Fort Walla Walla, essentially following Steptoe's earlier route through Palouse and Spokane country and around Lake Coeur d'Alene, Idaho. Unlike Steptoe's poorly armed soldiers, some of Wright's men carried the new model 1855 rifle. At the same time Wright took the field, Major Garnett would march east from Fort Simcoe into Spokane country, adding a little more muscle to the campaign. Clarke was determined to punish the Palouses who had attacked Steptoe and murdered some miners back in April. He was also anxious to recover Steptoe's buried howitzer. His orders were clear and firm. They were to attack the Indians vigorously until submission was complete. Kamiakin and Qualchin—son of his wife's uncle, Owhi—were regarded as the prime troublemakers and Clarke wanted them removed from the picture.

As General Clarke's campaign got underway, it was Major Garnett who saw action first. Leaving Fort Simcoe in early August with three companies of the 9th Infantry and one of the 4th, Garnett marched north. On August 15, a fifteen-man detachment under Lieutenant Jesse Allen attacked a Yakima camp on the Yakima River. In the misty dawn light, Allen was accidentally killed by one of his own men, putting a damper on an otherwise successful attack, which resulted in the surrender of seventy Yakimas, some of whom were undoubtedly guilty (depending on one's point of view), but how to tell which ones? The soldiers made it simple: they chose five and promptly executed them.

The following week, Lieutenant George Crook, using Yakima informers, found another five who were judged guilty and these, too, were summarily executed. But thus far, there was neither word nor sign of Kamiakin and Qualchan, both of whom (particularly Kamiakin) the army desperately wanted to get its hands on. Meantime, those Yakimas who were still regarded as hostile had moved east to join up with the Spokanes and by September, Garnett was back at Fort Simcoe.

Meanwhile, Wright had assembled a force of some 600 men, including a two-company battalion of the 9th Infantry under Captain Frederick Dent, brother-in-law of Lieutenant Ulysses Grant (who had recently resigned his army commission) and a pair of mountain howitzers. Wright moved north from Fort Walla Walla in mid–August and established a supply depot at a crossing on the Snake River. He also made an alliance with the Nez Perce to help fight the Yakimas and their allies, in return for which the Nez Perce would be furnished with arms and supplies. Some thirty Nez Perce scouts, clad in bright new uniforms, crossed the Snake on August 27, following a pack train of 400 mules. Lieutenant John Mullan, who would later build a road between the Missouri and Columbia Rivers commanded the scouts.

There was some feeling that the Indians might be emboldened by their recent success over Steptoe and indeed, Wright's overture of a peaceful negotiation delivered through the Coeur d'Alene mission was returned with a warning that any soldiers who crossed the Snake and entered their territory would be killed. And there was reason to be concerned, too. It was a long, cumbersome column of men, wagons, and animals. Lieutenant Mullan thought it would be especially vulnerable to an attack from the rear. The weather was hot and sultry. There was little grass for the horses and a heavy pall of dust blanketed the column.

When his scouts reported a large body of Indians gathering near a group of lakes just west of present day Spokane, Wright prepared to advance. The report suggested a major force, said to include Spokane, Coeur d'Alene, Palouse, and Pend d'Oreilles, If true, this could be the major confrontation the army had been seeking, one that could conceivably write a *finis* to the Indian problem.

Reaching the Great Spokane Plain, scouts reported increasing Indian sign. Grass was fired in an attempt to cut off the army's rear guard from the main body, but attackers were repulsed by Captain Erasmus Keyes, commanding a battalion of artillerymen acting as infantry.

On the morning of September 1, Indians in force appeared on the high ground, seemingly ready to fight. After securing his supply train with two companies of infantry and a howitzer, Wright advanced with the dragoons and the remainder of his infantry, capturing the high ground with little effort. The Indians, who strangely had decided to abandon the high ground, continued to be observed in very great numbers as the troops descended toward a group of four beautiful lakes, surrounded by great pine forests.

"Every spot seemed alive with the wild warriors we had come so far to meet," wrote Lieutenant Lawrence Kipp. "They seemed to cover the country for two miles, moving in the pines, on the edge of the lakes, in the ravines and gullies, and swarming over the plain. Mounted on their fleet hardy horses, the crowd swayed back and forth, brandishing their weapons, shouting their war cries, and keeping up a song of defiance."[32]

Wright judged there at least as many as 400 to 500 that could be seen and more probably out of sight. His opening move was to detach a battalion and supporting howitzer under Captain Dent and sent them against the Indians in the timber. Supported by howitzer fire Dent's command, soon forced the Indians out of the timber and into the open. Meanwhile Wright hoped to draw the main body of Indians closer in order to give his dragoons maneuvering ground. At 600 yards his troops opened fire inflicting several casualties. Against the army's rifles, the bows and arrows and Hudson's Bay trade muskets proved totally inadequate leaving the Indians with the option of retiring or moving in closer. They chose the latter, much to Wright's pleasure..

As the Indians advanced the dragoons charged. For a time the action was heavy, but eventually the Indians were forced back. It could have been a splendid opportunity for Wright to score big, but the horses of his dragoons were too fatigued to pursue. Strangely, almost unbelievably, Wright suffered no casualties. The Indians later reported having suffered sixty killed and many others wounded. For Wright, the first round of the Battle of Spokane Plain (sometimes called Four Lakes) had been a clear tactical victory. Lieutenant Mullan, however, was not especially elated. Although the troops had scored big, the Indians had gotten away; the campaign was not over, and he was critical of Superintendent Nesmith, who seemed to take no interest in the Indian situation here in Washington Territory.

Three days later, on September 5, Wright resumed his campaign across the Spokane Plain. As the column approached a rocky, timbered area, they were confronted by a large body of warriors, 500–700 strong. Advancing, Wright unlimbered his howitzers and shelled the area, dispersing the warriors. One shell-burst blew off a tree limb, reportedly injuring Kamiakin's arm. Working their way through the timber and across ravines, the troops gradually dislodged the Indians who dispersed in small groups. This time, Wright suffered one man wounded. It had been a tough campaign. Both sides were exhausted by two hard fought encounters and within forty-eight hours Wright received word that the Indians were ready to talk peace.

Wright evidently did not put much stock in peace talks, not yet anyway. For another three weeks he continued his campaign up the Spokane River to Lake Coeur d'Alene, then down the Palouse River, at one point slaughtering some 900 Palouse ponies. Finally, on September 17, with Jesuit Father Joseph Joset acting as intermediary, Wright met with some of the leading chiefs, all of whom acquiesced to Wright's authority. A number of warriors, accused of depredations, were selected from the various tribes. Fifteen were hanged and a number of others placed in irons. The ever recalcitrant Kamiakin, however, fled into British Columbia. He would later return to the U.S. and live for a time with the Crows before eventually returning to his home country. By the time he returned, however, the wars in the Northwest were over and the authorities apparently had no further interest in taking any action against the man who had been their most formidable adversary. Kamiakin lived out the remainder of his life quietly farming among the Palouse. Qualchin, however, did not fare so well and was subsequently caught and hanged. Wright returned to Fort Walla Walla on October 5, having brought the Yakima War to a successful conclusion. By 1858, the Yakima tribe had lost 90 percent of its traditional land and was confined to a reservation south of the present city of Yakima.

It took four years, but finally in 1859, Isaac Stevens at long last saw Congressional ratification of his 1855 treaties. With the end of the Yakima War, Indian-white conflict in the Pacific Northwest was largely over. Prior to the Yakima War, citizen volunteers played a dominant, if often clumsy and brutal part, with the U.S. Army regulars reduced to a secondary role. Indeed, in no other Western Indian wars did citizen volunteers play as big a part as in the Pacific Northwest. By the time of the Yakima War, however, the regular Army had become the primary architect of success.

II

California and Nevada

Prologue: Bloody El Dorado

As general statistics go, California consists of 158,693 square miles. Its highest point, Mt. Whitney rises 14,491 feet, with the lowest at a mere 282 feet below sea level in Death Valley. Generally, the state's mountain ranges run north and south, with the Sierras in the east and the Coast Ranges in the west, while in between is a system of valleys. There is as well a great variation in climate, from the southern deserts to the mountainous north. As in the Pacific Northwest, the topography and climate would have a significant effect on the clashes between whites and Indians.

The Portuguese explorer, Juan Rodriguez Cabrillo, touched Southern California in 1542. Spanish seafarers were not far behind, though it would be another 227 years before their numbers amounted to anything. Meanwhile, Sir Francis Drake brought the British colors in 1579. The Russians put in an appearance early in the 19th century, founding the settlement of Fort Ross, north of present day San Francisco, and by the late 18th century American maritime explorers had also moved into the picture.

As they did throughout North America, neither the Spanish nor British had any real interest in colonizing the territories they claimed for their respective crowns. They sought instead to take advantage of the indigenous people and the region's abundant natural resources. Labor to reap the fruit of these resources was to be provided by the Indians. The Spanish plan was implemented in 1769 with the establishment of the Mission San Diego. Twenty others followed eventually comprising a chain of missions extending north from Alta (present San Diego) as far as Yerba Buena, which Americans came eventually to know as San Francisco. Priests of the Franciscan order, under the enterprising Father Junipero Serra, brought the word of God to the Indians, while at the same time developing an agricultural program by taking advantage of native labor in what could be thought of as a feudal type system with odds that definitely favored the Europeans. At one time, an estimated 21,000 Indians toiled in the fields of the good fathers.

South from the Pacific Northwest, California stretches like the western arm of the contiguous United States, with the elbow joint bent at approximately mid-point. From the 42d Parallel in the north to roughly the 32d Parallel at its southern terminus, it is the longest state in the lower forty-eight, with a coastline that stretches nearly 800 miles.

Anglo-Europeans reached California in the 16th century. Portuguese, Spanish, British, and Russians had all left their mark in the century that followed. The discovery of gold at Sutter's Mill in 1849 brought a rush of American prospectors, to be followed in short order by a flood of immigrants who were drawn to the region for pretty much the same reason or reasons that drew settlers across the Mississippi: mineral wealth at first, then land. The introduction of Anglo-European settlers created a disruption of the traditional way of life for indigenous people, and led quickly to oppression and hostilities, with predictable results to the Indian population, which, in the twenty-five years between 1845 and 1870, declined 80 percent. One source suggests that 40 percent of deaths during those years were the result of extermination killings. Only a few survived the wars of the 1850s with their extermination campaigns and the relocation to reservations. As did Native Americans elsewhere on the continent, California Indians found it more difficult to adjust to the American presence than they did the Spanish or British, simply because the former coveted the land itself.

When the first American prospectors arrived in California they found a mixed group of indigenous peoples, with organizations not unlike that in the Pacific Northwest, tending to function more as small independent family groups, rather than larger structured tribal entities. By the time California became part of the Union an estimated 100,000–125,000 Indians resided within its borders. On the whole, California's Indians were among the most poorly developed in all of North America. Among the more important of these groups were the Yurok, Karok, Tolowa, Hupa, Wintun, Shasta, Klamath, and Modoc, whose territory was the watersheds of the Trinity, Klamath, and Pit Rivers. In the vicinity of present Yosemite National Park were the Yosemites, Chowchillas, and Nootchus. Home bases were generally referred to as rancherias as opposed to the more common term, village. Between the start of the gold rush period and the end of the Civil War—1848–1865—there were several clashes that deserve to be called wars, together with numerous small skirmishes. General George Crook, who served as a young lieutenant in California and the Pacific Northwest during the 1850s once observed that there was "scarcely ever a time that there was not one or more wars with the Indians somewhere on the Pacific Coast."[1]

During the years 1847–1852 American settlers moved into California's interior valleys and along the north coast. These arrivals included—in addition to the Argonauts—large numbers of adventurers and opportunists: gamblers, prostitutes, etc., all seeking to cash in on a lucrative situation. Almost immediately and not surprisingly, there were clashes with the indigenous people, more often than not brought on by whites who cared little for Indian rights, and on more than one occasion the Indians gave them cause. It was a sad story already grown old.

California (which gained statehood in 1850) had perhaps the harshest official attitude toward Native Americans of any state in the Union. It was an attitude clearly exemplified by Governor Peter H. Burnett on January 7, 1851, when he declared "That a war of extermination will continue to be waged between the races, until the Indian race becomes extinct must be expected. While we cannot anticipate this result but with painful regret, the inevitable destiny of the race is beyond the power or wisdom of man to avert." And California volunteer militia, in company with groups of miners and ranchers, seemed only to happy to carry out the governor's program of genocide, called "extermination" in the press of the day.[2]

The Mariposa War, 1850–1851

The best known of the California Indian wars occurred in the southern Sierra region, The war also led, ironically, to the discovery and naming of Yosemite National Park. Here could be found the densest Indian population in the state and for good reason. Food supplies were plentiful here, and the area was below the snow line. Unfortunately for the Indians, gold was also plentiful in the many streams, and like Ulysses responding to Circe, gold was the siren that drew prospectors in the rush of '49.[3]

It has been alleged that in one sense at least, the Mariposa War is the story of one man. James D. Savage, one of the earliest white arrivals in the area. Savage had been a member of Fremont's California Battalion, earning a reputation as the worst malcontent in the unit. A muscular, blue-eyed blond who liked to wear red shirts to impress the Indians, Savage was a colorful character who reportedly once hauled a barrel of gold dust through the lobby of a San Francisco hotel. He was said to have been an ignorant man, but also a shrewd one. Well imbued with the entrepreneurial spirit, he established trading posts on the Fresno and Merced Rivers and on Mariposa Creek where he conducted a profitable business with the local Indians, charging an ounce of gold for a pound of bacon and five pounds of flour. If one wanted a shirt, boots, or a hat, the price was a pound of gold. Savage was savvy if nothing else. He learned most of the Indian dialects and married women from several bands, at one time reportedly claiming thirty-three such spouses.

In May 1850, a party of Yosemites attacked Savage's trading post on the Merced River, but were driven off. Whether the attack had been provoked by Savage's treatment of the Indians is unclear, but in any event, fearing a second attack, he abandoned the Merced River post and established a second on Mariposa Creek near Agua Fria. Through one of his wives, Savage then learned of a planned uprising in September. Evidently thinking to head-off the uprising, Savage took the Tularenos chief, Jose Juarez to San Francisco, intending to impress him with the white man's resources: ships, guns, cannons, soldiers, and the like. Both imbibed freely with Juarez drunk most of the time. During an argument, Savage reportedly struck the chief several times, humiliating him, and Juarez had a long memory, as Savage would discover. Notwithstanding, the pair remained in San Francisco long enough to celebrate California's entrance into the Union on October 29. They finally returned to the interior after one of the greatest gambling and spending sprees the city had ever witnessed.

Savage returned to find general unrest among the Indians. A white man had been killed and the Indians no longer seemed interested in using gold to trade, a sign that Savage interpreted as impending trouble and confirmed the earlier rumor of a September uprising. Other whites in the area, however, did not attach any particular significance to these signs. Notwithstanding an effort to smooth things over, Savage parleyed with some of the Indian leaders and learned that they had become increasingly inclined toward driving the whites out of their territory. Juarez in particular, still smarting from Savages's treatment, counseled for war, arguing that the white men cannot use their big guns and ships away from the ocean, so there is nothing to fear. Unable to persuade the Indians as to the error of their thinking, Savage returned to his post on Mariposa Creek and began to organize a force of miners to defend against the attack that seemed certain to come.

Savage wasn't the only one trying to prevent an uprising. Governor Peter Burnett sent U.S. Indian Agent, Colonel Adam Johnston to see if a peaceful solution could not be found. The governor's choice of emissaries was a good one. An able and energetic individual, Johnston's contributions to the overall management of California's Indian affairs would eventually prove to be of singular importance, though in this particular instance he was unable to head off trouble.

On the night of December 17, Johnston and Savage, concerned that the Indians who normally lived in the vicinity of the trading post on Mariposa were nowhere to be seen, prepared to take action. With a party of sixteen men, the two set out, hoping to find the

Indians before they joined up with other bands. The Indians, meanwhile, attacked and destroyed Savage's other trading post at Fresno Crossing, killing three.

After tracking the Indians for some thirty miles, Savage and Johnston caught up with them at dawn on December 18. Both sides faced each other on hills, 400 yards apart. Savage managed to parley with the leader of the malcontents, Chief Baptiste, who admitted they were the ones who destroyed the post on the Fresno River, but claimed to have murdered only one man. Savage tried, unsuccessfully, to persuade them to return to their rancherias, but the Indians refused, explaining that it was easier to survive by stealing from the white men.

Returning to Mariposa Creek on the 19th, Johnston next led a party of thirty-five to investigate the damage done to the post at Fresno Crossing, finding the post looted and burned and three men mutilated. It was the sort of discovery that fueled the fires of anger and retaliation.

Things were heating up. A new and larger force—seventy-five men—under Sheriff James Burney, prepared to take the field. Burney was elected captain, with J.W. Riley and a man known only as Skeane as lieutenants. With Savage as guide, the column left Mariposa on January 7. Four days later, at two a.m. on the 11th, they found a camp, containing an estimated 400–500 Indians near present Oakhurst.

Burney advanced cautiously to within 150 yards, before settling down to await the dawn. However, a lone Indian discovered their presence and sounded the alarm just an hour before daylight. Although he had lost the element of surprise, Burney charged the village anyway and received a warm reception as the Indians returned fire with both bullets and arrows. Counter-attacking, the Indians soon recovered their rancheria. Once more Burney charged, driving the Indians back, but they continued to offer vigorous resistance, firing from behind rocks until a final charge by Burney's volunteers dispersed them. It had been a hard fought action lasting three and a half hours. The volunteers suffered eight casualties, including two mortally wounded. The Indians reportedly suffered forty casualties, although the exact number killed is unknown.

Even as Burney was engaging the Indians, Agent Johnston had journeyed to San Jose to seek assistance from both the state and federal government, but he was swimming upstream. Recently arrived federal peace commissioners, Redick McKee, George W. Barbour, and Oliver Wozencraft, had issued a statement, accusing the state of acting in a belligerent manner toward the Indians, so their position on the matter pretty well ruled out any help from the U.S. Army. On the 9th, Peter Burnett resigned and was replaced as governor by John McDougal. On January 13, Burney wrote to the new governor asking for help. His letter was accompanied by a citizen's petition, which reinforced his request. On the 13th, McDougal authorized the creation of the Mariposa Battalion which would come into being in February with an authorized strength of 200.

In the interim, though, Burney and Savage were anxious to do something right away, and between them they organized a force of 164 miners and settlers to relieve those stationed at Savage's Mariposa post. As well, they planned a punitive expedition of three companies under Captains John Kuykendall, John Boling, and William Dill. The plan called for the first two companies to search for Indians north of Mariposa, while Burney with the third company struck south as far as Visalia.

With Savage acting as a guide, Boling and Kuykendall located a large mixed encampment of Chowchillas, Chookchancies, Nootchu, Honachee, Potencie, Kahwah, and Yosemites on the 17th, probably not far from where Burney had his fight on the 12th. The camp seemed to be under the leadership of Chiefs Jose Rey and Jose Juarez of the Chowchillas.

Savage estimated the camp to contain as many as 500 inhabitants. Boling elected to wait until the next day to launch his attack.

The next morning, Boling and Kuykendall struck hard and fast, driving the Indians from the village, after which they put the torch to it. The fire unexpectedly got out of control, however, forcing the volunteers to fall back in order to protect their own camp. In the ensuing chaos and confusion the Indians managed to escape, having suffered twenty-four casualties, including Chief Jose Rey. The volunteers, meanwhile, took no casualties, and Boling wasted little time proclaiming a solid victory.

If Boling was feeling slightly euphoric over his victory and imagined that the path to subjugation had been clearly marked, politics was about to confuse the situation. The mission of the Mariposa Battalion had been to punish the Indians and exact payment for the damages and suffering they had inflicted on the miners and settlers and satisfaction was still to be had.

A frenzy of sorts seemed to grip the state. The governor, who stated publicly that there were 100,000 warriors in the state, had authorized formation of the battalion, and the state legislature quickly passed bills authorizing a loan of up to half a million dollars to be used to pay officers and soldiers who had served during uprisings. It was understood, however, that the federal government would reimburse the state. In any case, once this became clear, the three peace commissioners, who were woefully ignorant of Indian needs and had very little understanding of native culture, decided it was time for a first-hand look at the situation. Escorted by 106 soldiers under Captain Erasmus Keyes, 3rd Artillery, they left San Francisco on February 7, traveling by steamboat to Stockton, then overland to Mariposa. Hopeful of finding a peaceful solution to the Indian trouble, Governor McDougal sent along his aide, Colonel J. Neely Johnson to make certain that the commissioners understood why a military response was necessary.

On February 15, Colonel Johnson addressed the battalion, telling the volunteers that their objective was to subdue any band of Indians who rejected the treaties offered by the commissioners. The men were reminded that they would be trespassing on Indian land and this ought to be taken into consideration during the course of their campaigning. Johnson's language was undoubtedly couched in a manner to convince the peace commissioners of their honorable intentions. On February 19, control of the battalion became a federal responsibility, which, in effect, meant that active operations against the Indians were prohibited until the peace commissioners tried their hand at treaty-making, a restraint that the volunteers found more than a little irksome.

Through the next two months, the peace commissioners were busy roaming through the area, signing treaties with various tribes at Camp Fremont, a temporary site near present Sequoia National Park. The treaties guaranteed assistance to the tribes in establishing farming communities in the San Joaquin Valley. If the commissioners and any others viewed the treaties with a sense of optimism, Indian Agent Johnston did not. He knew the troubles would continue; that both sides would find ample reason to continue their adversarial behavior toward each other. His prescience went unappreciated.

During this sort of limbo period things had not been entirely quiet. On March 16, Kuykendall's company had a skirmish with Indians at Fine Gold Gulch. The volunteers were itching to do what they had been brought into existence to do so the fight was no doubt welcomed. Shifting the Indians to their new home was an agonizingly slow process or at least Savage thought so and contacted the governor in the hope of getting authority to move. Savage had evidently forgotten that the battalion was under federal authority, but it didn't matter because before the governor could even respond, the peace commissioners granted permission for the battalion to move against the Yosemites (Miwok) and Chowchillas (Yokut), and Nootchus none of whom had apparently made an effort to participate in the treaty talks.

While Kuykendall's company moved south in search of the Chowchillas, Savage, with the companies of Boling and Dill marched to the area around Wawona in terrible weather, plowing through three to five-foot snow drifts, not to mention rain, and sleet storms before finally establishing a base camp. On March 24 Savage advanced on the Nootchus village, which was quickly captured with no resistance. The Indians surrendered immediately and preparations were made to transport them to the new reservation. Savage also dispatched runners to the Yosemite villages to explain the terms of the treaty, hoping to entice them to follow suit.

What response Savage imagined he might get can only be surmised, but on the 25th, Tenieya (Tenaya) chief of the Yosemites arrived in camp to discuss the treaty. The chief was amenable to the terms proposed and told Savage that his people were en route and should arrive soon. By the 27th, however, Savage's patience was exhausted and he took the field with Tenieya and fifty-seven men. Halfway to Yosemite Valley they met up with a party of seventy-two Yosemites, mostly women and children. When asked as to the whereabouts of the warriors, Tenieya said they had gone to join others around Mono Lake, east of Yosemite, near the Nevada line. Savage figured the warriors were still be in the valley, however, and sent a detachment in search of them, but found only deserted camp sites.

On the 29th, Savage started back to Wawona with the non-combatants. Progress was slow with the Indians in tow, and as supplies gave out, Savage left Boling and a detachment to shepherd the Indians to Wawona, while he pushed on ahead to get resupplied. On the night of April 1, Tenieya and 250 of his followers slipped away under cover of darkness.

Surely an interesting and, one might suggest a positive development to emerge from this campaign was the naming of Yosemite National Park. So the story goes, around the campfire on the night of March 27, in the presence of towering granite spires and breathtaking waterfalls, the volunteers engaged in a discussion as to what this lovely valley ought to be named. The Indian name was Ahwahnee, to which several other names were added, one of which, Yosemite, was suggested by Dr. Lafayette Bunnell who thought it might be appropriate to name the area after the Indian inhabitants, although it was actually not the tribal name. A vote was taken and Bunnell's name was selected. Although a few of the men were singularly impressed with the great beauty of the area, others were not, and one is reported to have said later that if he had known the place would become so famous he would have looked at it more closely.

Meantime, Kuykendall's campaign had taken him down into the Tulare Valley. At King's River, his scouts discovered and attacked a large Chowchilla Rancheria on April 9. The Indians "were inclined to give us battle [wrote one of the volunteers]. We at once charged into their camp, routed and killed a number, while others were ridden down and taken prisoner." The volunteers pursued those who fled, but a number managed to escape. A few days later, however, some of the Chowchillas who had eluded capture came into Kuykendall's camp and surrendered.[4]

Notwithstanding the surrender of a few, the Chowchillas (a branch of the Yokut tribe whose regular home was the San Joaquin Valley) needed further attention. Informed that it had been the Chowchillas who had engineered the escape of the Indians captured by the Mariposa Battalion, the peace commissioners authorized Savage to commence operations against them.

During the course of the next several weeks, Savage scoured the country. Scouts found evidence of several Indian fires but little else. Then, on the 25th, a village was located across the San Joaquin River and the volunteers, fired up after a rousing speech by Captain Boling, prepared to cross the river and attack. The Indians, it appeared, were ready to give battle, but by the time the battalion had crossed the river after building some rafts, the Chowchillas had dispersed into the hills. One of the volunteers later described the scene:

> All were anxious to mount the hill, which was about as bad as the one we had come down. It was on a bench in the mountain where the Rancheri was situated. We breasted the hill, our Comp^y on the right, B in the centre & A on the left. There was every chance for the Indians to way lay us as we came up the hill & here we expected to meet them, as rocks & Bushes were in abundance, but they were not to be found & we found the Rancheri deserted. We went up the hill further & came to another just deserted, both of which were soon in flames. At the last Rancheri we found the bones of an Indian burnt, the skull & some other bones remaining. The Capt. sent out scouting parties to examine the trails. We found the trails greatly scattered, the freshest, however, taking over the mountain. Lieut. Smith saw two Indians while examining this trail. As soon as we had taken a bite, we put on our packs & started up the mountain which was ¾ of a mile high & nearly perpendicular, & part of the way over smooth granite. Some of the boys fell as much as 20 ft & we came to two more lately deserted Rancheris which we burnt & camped for the night. We also burnt a large quantity of acorns. Distance 6 miles.[5]

Following an unsuccessful pursuit of the Chowchillas, Savage returned to Mariposa Creek on May 3 where a second campaign was being planned against the Yosemites. This column was to include Boling's B Company, supported by a detachment from C under Lieutenant Gilbert, and a third from A to guard the supply train.

On May 9, Boling moved up the south side of Yosemite Valley, sending his Noot-chu and Po-ho-no-chee Indian scouts, under Lieutenant Reuben Chandler, out in all directions. When his scouts reported a party of Indians trying to escape, Boling ordered the entire column to pursue in an effort to cut off the fleeing quarry. The effort proved nearly fruitless and managed to nab only three Indians, but one of was Chief Tenieya's son. The remainder of the Indians had escaped into a narrow canyon from where they pummeled the pursuing volunteers with rocks, forcing them to turn back.

One of the three prisoners was sent to explain peace terms to Tenieya. The two remaining prisoners attempted to escape, including Tenieya's son who was killed in the process. Chandler and his scouts, meanwhile, managed to capture the chief after a wild chase through the Tenaya canyon. When Tenieya saw the body of his dead son he wept and begged to be shot. Although sympathetic, Boling did not comply. After the capture of Tenieya, Boling marched his command some twenty miles to Tenaya Lake where they surprised a small village of Yosemites. This proved to be the final action of the Mariposa War. After escorting the Yosemites to the reservation, Boling returned to Mariposa Creek.

On July 1, the Mariposa Battalion was mustered out, the only blemish on its record being the court-martial of Captain Kuykendall who was charged with being "un-officer-like." He reportedly was a poor disciplinarian who refused to attack peaceful Indians, certainly a quality that did not endear him to the volunteers who had no qualms about attacking Indians almost anywhere they found them.

Although the Mariposa War, as such, was over, there remained the task of finalizing treaties. Between March 1851 and January 1852, the peace commissioners, sent out by President Fillmore, met with a total of 502 Indian leaders from 139 various bands, consummating eighteen separate agreements or treaties that set aside 11,700 square miles, 7,488,000 acres, or 7.5 percent of the state. On the face of it this seemed like a more than generous settlement. But there was a catch. The treaties had to be ratified by Congress and were subsequently rejected in secret session by the senate because of pressure from the California lobby, which opposed ratification. The lobby argued that the land was too valuable agriculturally and that to set it aside solely for Indian use would do an injustice to the people of the state. No thought seems to have been given to what injustice the Indians had already suffered. Besides, it was pointed out that if the treaties were ratified it would cost the Federal government half a million dollars and Congress being in a parsimonious mood, refused to reimburse the state for the expenses of the Mariposa Battalion. Nor did the Indians ever receive the annuities promised them when they signed the treaties. In 1854, limited funds were finally allocated to settlers as compensation for property damages incurred during the war.

Meanwhile, the war was over but incidents continued. Early in 1852, the government permitted Teneiya and a few followers to return to Yosemite Valley and no one seemed to object until a party of prospectors was suddenly attacked by Indians and fled for their lives, before finally reaching Coarse Gold Creek on the 8th. Twenty-five volunteers were enlisted and sent out to the valley to bury the dead and punish the Indians. The incident roused the state to action.

In June, a detachment of the 2d California Infantry under Lieutenant Treadwell Moore arrived in the area from Fort Miller in the San Joaquin Valley. Guided by Augustus Grey, a former member of the Mariposa Battalion, they entered the valley at night and surprised the Indians, capturing five, including Tenieya. Moore charged the five with murder and ordered them shot, but Tenieya and at least one other managed somehow to escape over Mono Pass, pursued by the soldiers, who failed to catch the elusive Indians, but did stumble on some valuable mineral deposits before returning to Fort Miller. Moore's expedition accomplished little, aside from demonstrating once again how innocent until proven guilty did not seem to apply where Indians were concerned. If nothing else, though, the campaigning of the Mariposa Battalion did focus attention on the great natural beauty of the region.

In July 1852, a small party of whites led by one Walter Harvey murdered several Indians. Savage was outraged and called for an investigation. Subsequently, a council was convened in August. En route, Savage and Harvey met and a fight ensued in which Savage was shot four times and killed. Harvey was never convicted. The story of the elusive Tenieya's fate is unclear. One source claims that he returned to the valley in 1853 and was subsequently killed by some neighboring Mono Indians. Another story claims the old man died on a reservation in the San Joaquin Valley.

The Mendocino War, 1859–1860

Round Valley is located in northern Mendocino County, something like 350 miles northwest of the Mariposa country, in the land of the towering Redwood forests that once extended from thirty miles south of present San Francisco as far north as the Oregon line. The valley was originally inhabited by the Yuki Indian tribe, which, like most others in California suffered greatly with the arrival of the Americans, with whom they soon found themselves in competition for a finite supply of natural resources. As these natural resources dwindled, the Yukis were compelled to seek new means of support, one of which included cattle rustling.

As settlers moved into the area in ever-increasing numbers in the early 1850s, tension between whites and Indians rose. To white settlers, Indians were a source of irritation all the time, and a threat to their livelihood most of the time. When friction developed between whites and Indians, the federal government found itself between a rock and a hard place, with what amounted to contradictory missions: protect the Indians from the whites and vice versa, but the efforts such as they were, accomplished little as raids and counter-raids continued to spill considerable blood.

As the decade of the 1850s advanced, numerous campaigns were carried out against the Indians by volunteers reacting to cattle raids by the Indians. In retaliation, rancherias were burned and Indians were killed wherever they were found. "We would kill on average fifty or sixty Indians on a trip," one volunteer recalled, "…and frequently we would have to turn out two to three times a week." And the Indians struck back, stealing more cattle and murdering whites. Between 1857 and 1858, four whites were killed by Yukis, but in terms of numbers, the Indians could not match the whites. In May 1859, for example, settlers in Round Valley reportedly killed 240 Yukis in retaliation for the killing of a prized stallion. The *Sacramento Union* declared that "Aborigines are melting away as the snows of the mountains in June … they are doomed to extirpation."[6]

Late in 1858, Company F, 6th U.S. Infantry under the command of Lieutenant Edward Dillon took up station in the area and established Fort Wright on the western edge of Round Valley. The presence of regular troops should have served as a balm to white settlers, but in time they came to see the soldiers as being more concerned with Indian rights than with those of the whites.

In 1856, as part of the federal government's efforts to bring about an amicable settlement with the California Indians, Congress authorized establishment of the Mendocino Reservation, part of which was designed for Yuki agricultural use, offering an opportunity for the Indians to develop an agrarian lifestyle. Unfortunately, the arrangement, which probably looked workable on paper, proved a poor idea as the Yukis were forced to share their home with several other tribes (or bands), some of whom spoke a different language, and some of whom were traditional enemies. Indeed, the reservation proved to be a hellhole. The population declined as a result of malnutrition and venereal disease, which, coupled with the abduction of women and children made for intolerable conditions. When agent Simon Storms visited a Yuki camp in 1856 he reported that "a number of squaws and children had been taken away by white men." And Lieutenant Edward Dillon said it was a "common occurrence to have squaws taken by force from this place" (the reservation).[7]

Unscrupulous white men not only abducted Yuki women and children but apparently felt that the reservation provided them with an opportunity to break the law without fear of the consequences to which they would be subjected outside the reservation. Such law enforcement as did exist was handled by the Army which had no authority to arrest a lawbreaker unless he happened to be caught *in flagrante delicto*, a rare occurrence. Settlers complained that the soldiers were more concerned with protecting the rights of the Indians, rather than the settlers. The Army was "just a nuisance and never accomplished any good," complained one settler.[8]

On September 6, 1859, Governor John Weller commissioned Walter Jarboe of Ukiah to take charge of punitive measures against the Yuki. His orders, according to one settler, were to kill all Indians. If the governor was after a hard-liner, he couldn't have made a better choice. Jarboe had a notorious reputation as an Indian killer. His Eel River Rangers had already killed an estimated sixty-two Yukis, including women and children. Weller apparently believed that the Yukis represented a genuine threat that called for tough measures, a stance that was supported by the *San Francisco Bulletin* which declared that "Extermination is the quickest and cheapest remedy." Accordingly, when the Army refused to take action, Weller turned to Jarboe, knowing full well he was, in effect, sanctioning genocide.[9]

In December 1859, Jarboe formed a company of forty volunteers to take the field against the Indians. The first effort was commanded by Lieutenant William Frazier who led a twenty-three-man detachment across Eel River, attacking a Yuki *rancheria* and killing twenty, including women and children. One child and two women were taken prisoner.

Early in 1860 a California joint senate and house committee traveled to Mendocino to investigate the on-going hostilities. The committee convened at the ranch of Agent Storm where they heard the testimony of forty-five witnesses. With few exceptions, the testimony focused on Indian crimes and punishment.

Thirty-eight-year-old William Frazier told how he had been one of a party that raided an Indian village after hearing about cattle being killed by the Indians. "All Indians fled when we came, but one. We shot his head off." Lawrence Battalie testified how a party of whites went to the Nome Cult Farm and picked out twenty Indians who were accused of stealing cattle and commenced executing them. Eight Indians were shot and five were hanged. The remainder managed to escape.[10]

When asked if squaws were killed, H.L. Hall said he knew of a group of squaws who were killed for refusing to travel. Babies, said Hall, were simply put out of their misery and a ten-year-old girl was killed for being stubborn. Another settler stated that after he lost twenty hogs, he went after the Indians and shot three of them. Five others were later tried and hanged on the reservation.

After listening to recitations such as this, the committee members must have been taken aback when William Scott said he never had any trouble with Indians. He always treated them kindly and never lost any cattle to Indian thievery.

Surprisingly perhaps, the committee concluded that whites were to blame for the Indian troubles. More Indians had been killed in Mendocino County in four months of 1860 than had been killed in a century of Spanish and Mexican rule. Here was a damning indictment indeed. But then, perhaps fearful of backlash, the committee went on to accuse the Indians of being a "cowardly lot" and proposed a system of peonage under which Indians would be assigned to ranchers as servants. It was all perfectly legal. Incredibly, in 1850 the state legislature passed a law that provided for the apprenticeship of Indians.

As the decade of the 1860s passed on, the Indian problem in Mendocino County gradually disappeared. Most of the Yukis and other bands in the area who had somehow survived the punitive expeditions by Jarboe and his ilk had been concentrated on the reservation. In a sense, perhaps those who had died at the hands of the volunteers were the fortunate ones.

Nevada's Paiute War, 1860

It was then and still is, one of the most sparsely settled areas in the lower forty-eight. U.S. Highway 50 which crosses the central portion of the region between Ely and Fallon, Nevada, is said by some to be the lonesomest highway in the country. This is a high desert land of alkali, sagebrush, and sand; a land of interminable vastness, where summer days are filled with a furnace like heat and nights can be bone-chilling. In winter, snow often spreads across the stark landscape, lying inert beneath a thin sun.

Once Pony Express riders galloped across this vastness, the thudding hoof beats of their mounts the only sound to break the eerie silence, save for the wind, whose symphonies sweep across this landscape, which geologists eventually included as part of the Great Basin, roughly the region lying between the Rockies and the Sierras. Numerous mountain ranges dissect the Great Basin into a number of small desert valleys, the floors of which contain sagebrush, salt grass and greasewood; juniper and piñon occur in scattered spots on mountain slopes. Jackrabbits and ground squirrels abound here, but deer, mountain lions, antelope and mountain sheep are also to be found in the area.

Two principal Indian tribal entities dwelled here: the Northern Paiutes—sometimes spelled Pah-Ute or Piute and the Washos. The former were the dominant tribe, numbering several thousand, while the latter contained some 500–600 souls, whom the commissioner of Indian Affairs, William P. Dole, described as poor and degraded creatures, living on insects and spontaneous products, and can do little harm to anyone. Although the Washos, shared many characteristics of the Paiutes, there appears to have been tension between the two that occasionally led to fighting, however, due to their numerical superiority, the Paiutes were clearly the victor in such encounters and would be the main adversary of the whites in the war of 1860.

Early explorers and settlers tended to lump together all Indians of the region, be they Paiute or Washo, thereby making accurate identification difficult. The origin of the Paiute tribal name seems to derive from the word *Pah*, meaning water and *Ute* meaning direction, although like all Native Americans they referred to themselves as *Nomo*, or "the people."[11]

A tribe of hunters and gatherers, the Paiutes subsisted on a combination of meat and roots. Before the advent of the whites the various bands enjoyed a generally decent existence, having learned to subsist comfortably off the largesse of this harsh land. On special occasions they came together to hunt and fish, to dance and gather piñon nuts, a staple of their diet.

By the 19th century, the Paiutes seem to have numbered about 5,000, divided into some thirty-one small bands, containing 50–200 souls, under the leadership of elected individuals called captains. However, one prominent leader, Makoi or Movitawara—old Winnemucca—seems to have gained a wider following than the others. In any event, whites soon came to view him as the overarching chief of the Paiutes. In company with his daughter, Sarah—called Princess by the whites—Old Winnemucca traveled throughout the region, which probably accounts for the white perception of his role as a tribal leader. In reality, however, Winnemucca was never a leader of more than his own Pyramid Lake band.

The discovery of gold in California in 1849 brought throngs of white men through northern Nevada. Prospectors and opportunists generally followed the Humboldt River along the emigrant trail, seeking to cross this high desert country as quickly as possible. As the Argonauts worked their way to California, their wagon trains soon became the object of Indian attacks, the lure of the emigrants' livestock being too strong a siren for Indians raiders to resist. As a consequence, posses organized from various trains retaliated killing some thirty Indians that summer of 1849 and by the following summer there was constant skirmishing in the Carson Valley southwest of Lake Tahoe.

During the 1850s a few of the emigrants found western Nevada (then part of Utah Territory in the western half of the Great Basin) to their liking and elected to settle here. Some opened trading posts, such as Mormon station (Genoa), while others settled on lush farm lands along the Humboldt and Carson Rivers.

As the flow of traffic increased, these traders soon developed a lucrative business in providing supplies to the west-bound emigrants. The travelers who trundled west gave little if any thought to the Indian lands over which they passed, nor did it trouble them to take advantage of the plentiful piñon forests for fuel and wagon repairs and the wild game for meat. And why not? For most, anyway, the Almighty endowed the land with these riches for them to use. The arriving whites little understood the delicate balance they were disturbing. The land supported the native peoples, who had learned how to use its resources wisely. To the white newcomers the land may have seemed tough and unyielding, but their arrival disrupted the dynamics of a land more fragile than they realized. In short it was difficult for the area to sustain both life styles.

In 1853, it appeared that serious trouble between the whites and Paiutes was imminent when pioneer Peter Lassen, co-founder of Susanville, California, was killed and the Paiutes charged with the crime, although there is some reason to suspect that Lassen was killed by white men disguised as Indians. However, the situation was gradually defused and then five years later the picture brightened when Old Winnemucca signed a treaty with the whites. The terms of the agreement called for acts of aggression on both sides to be punished. Winnemucca even led his warriors alongside the whites to strike back at some Washos, who were raiding potato fields in Roop County. But there was a down side. When one of Winnemucca's warriors was killed in a skirmish, the Paiutes believed white men were responsible. Whether the killers actually were white men is unclear, but in any event, relations between whites and Paiutes deteriorated.

The winter of 1859–1860 proved especially severe for the Paiutes in the Carson District. In their eyes, the whites had despoiled the land and angered the spirits thereby bringing on hard times. On December 17, the Virginia City *Territorial Enterprise* reported that Washo and Paiutes were freezing and starving. Although sympathetic whites built warming fires and brought food, the Indians rejected the offer, fearing the food was poisoned.

Meanwhile, Brigham Young, concerned about the likelihood of trouble in the region had been urging the Federal government to establish military posts along the Humboldt River and at Mormon Station. Young believed it was the responsibility of the whites to see that peace prevailed. However, with tension continuing to build between North and South, the Federal government failed to see this as a high priority.

By the end of the decade, white settlements in the area had proliferated with farms, ranches, and trading posts scattered throughout the fertile valleys of western Nevada, and in the Honey Lake region just across the California line. Along with this growth, came occasional rumors of emigrant massacres—probably exaggerated—and which, in any event, prompted the military to dispatch small patrols along the California Trail. Despite this deterrent incidents increased through the summer of 1859.

Then in June 1859, silver ore was discovered in Gold Canyon, just below present Virginia City and in short order a brand new rush to riches was on, displacing California as the new goal for Argonauts. Prospectors and opportunists from all over flocked to the region, swelling the population to nearly 5,000. With mounting alarm the Paiutes watched this influx of whites swarming over the land. The Paiutes were no less disturbed by the new Pony Express route which crossed their territory, building relay stations at precious water holes that had previously nourished only the Indians.[12]

In January 1860, Dexter F. Deming, a rancher, was killed on Willow Creek, north of the Honey Lake area. Isaac Roop, provisional head of the new Nevada territory (created in 1859), wasted no time taking action. A detachment of rangers under the command of Captain William Weatherlow and Lieutenant J.W. Tutt were dispatched in pursuit of the killer or killers. Not surprising, at least to the pursuers, the trail led to the Paiute camp. Not wishing to precipitate hostilities unnecessarily and probably mindful that he lacked the military resources to deal with a full scale war, Roop subsequently appointed Weatherlow and one, Thomas J. Harvey as commissioners to negotiate with the Indians for the surrender of the guilty parties. The Paiutes refused to comply. Roop, meanwhile, requested military assistance from army headquarters in California, but was advised that troops were not available and moreover, none could be sent across the Sierras in winter at any rate.

Late in April, the Paiutes convened a big council at Pyramid Lake to air their growing concern with the whites, which included cutting down the area's piñon trees. Old Winnemucca did not propose war outright, though apparently he was not opposed to it, either. In any case, he did demand payment in the amount of $16,000 for the white occupation of Honey Lake Valley. Every other leader present, however, except for Numaga or Young Winnemucca (no relation to Old) favored war. Numaga seems to have had a better grasp of white power, however, and counseled peace, though his words were not well received. The Paiutes had had their fill of the white man's empty rhetoric. Notable among those who favored the warpath was one, Mogoannoga, a half blood Bannack, known to the whites as Captain Soo.

Some ten miles northeast of Bucklands on the California Trail, was Williams Station, a Pony Express stop operated by James O. Williams, along with brothers David, Oscar, and Calvin, and on occasion helpers who were passing through. The station was a prosperous one, selling food, whiskey, and other supplies to hungry and thirsty emigrants who had just crossed a desolate stretch of land known as Forty Mile Desert.

Every war begins with a flash point; an incident that sets off a volatile situation awaiting only the spark. In this case, the incident occurred at Williams Station. Exactly what happened is not entirely clear, but most sources seem to agree that on May 7, 1860, an old Paiute man and woman approached the station where they were taken captive by the Williams brothers and three others who were stopping there: Samuel Sullivan, James Fleming and a man known only as Dutch Phil. According to the victims, the old man was tied up and forced to watch the woman being raped. Back at the Paiute council, Numaga continued to argue against war with the whites, reportedly going on a three-day fast to make his point, all of which was lost, however, when a rider arrived to report of the happenings at Williams Station. Whatever hope Numaga may have entertained for his non-war platform now dissipated like the wind over the high desert. With this news, the council disbanded and the Paiutes prepared for war.

Mogoannaga, who needed little encouragement anyway, promptly set out with a revenge party. Approaching the station unseen, the Paiutes attacked, killing David and Oscar Williams as they stood talking outside the building. Sam Sullivan was shot down as he attempted to flee. Torching the station buildings, the attackers finished off Fleming and Dutch Phil, then rounded up Bloomfield's cattle and headed for Pyramid Lake.

Williams Station was not the only point of reckoning on this day, for even as the raiders retaliated for the indignities—real or imagined—inflicted against them at the station, seven settlers were killed at Honey Lake, sixty miles distant and two others died on the Truckee River, although whether this was part of Mogoannaga's plan or was carried out by another war party is unclear.

Word of the raid on Williams Station reached Bucklands via James Williams, the sole surviving brother, who had been away and returned on May 8th to find his brothers dead and the station burned. From Bucklands, riders carried the news to Gold Hill, Virginia City, and on to California. Reports of the raid were already beginning to assume larger than real proportions. A dozen were said to have been killed at Williams Station and James Williams himself claimed that some 500 well armed and mounted Paiutes chased him into the desert.

As word of the raid worked its way through the white communities, messengers were quickly dispatched to warn prospectors and isolated ranchers. Reactions among the whites varied widely. Some were concerned, but went about their business in the usual way. Others ventured out to the site of the raid, looked things over and decided this was an isolated incident and no cause for genuine alarm. A third group, and the one that was to have the strongest reaction, saw this as an opportunity to go Indian hunting; have a little adventure; kill a few Indians and capture some horses.

Newspaper stories, however, suggested that the war scare was exaggerated. Those responsible should certainly be apprehended and punished, one editorial argued, but this should be carried out by properly organized companies not a loose collection of Indian adventurers out for a bit of glory. Notwithstanding, angry citizens demanded a pound of flesh, even as cooler heads argued against hasty action, unfortunately without success.

The *Territorial Enterprise* did not approve of the action, seeing no sense in men living in communities such as Carson and Virginia City, which were largely safe from Indian attack, "running around and scaring every female in the country, and, by their acts, justly entitle themselves to the right to wear petticoats for the rest of their days." While stating that the guilty parties ought to be caught and punished by a properly organized force, the *Enterprise* argued that it was ridiculous to send out a group such as Ormsby's equipped with nothing more than a "few boxes of sardines and a loaf or two of bread to fight Indians who are likely one hundred miles away from here at this time."[13]

In any event, a force of some 100 miners from Carson City, Virginia City, Gold Hill, and Genoa headed out for the Paiute camp reported to be near Pyramid Lake. The avengers, if we may think of them as such, were organized and led by Major William Ormsby, one of Carson City's founding fathers. The excited volunteers predicted they would kill a few Indians and have themselves a time. Like other such posses before and after them, these volunteers had little regard for the fighting ability of Indians, a notion from which they were soon to be painfully disabused. The volunteers camped the night of May 9 at Bucklands, where Sam Bucklands himself decided to join them, perhaps motivated by the fact that they were full of whiskey and determined to avenge wrongs. After all, the blood was clearly up and retribution was the order of the day. At any rate, the next day they reached Williams Station or what remained of it and buried the remains of the men killed in the raid.

Evidently convinced that more men were needed, Ormsby, on May 10, sent back a request for reinforcements and supplies. Accordingly, on the 12th, a party under the leadership of Judge John Cradlebaugh arrived, saying they had seen no Indian sign en route and elected to return, feeling the mission was pointless. The remainder of the volunteers, some seventy in number, continued on, bivouacking the night of May 11 near present Wadsworth. The Indian trail was, apparently, easy to follow as the raiders had strewn behind them, various articles taken in the raid.

The volunteers buoyed by liquor and the prospect of a high old time, the last thing of concern to them was the opposition they might face. No one thought of these Indians as a foe to be reckoned with.

With spirits high, Ormsby's volunteers left camp on the morning of May 12, moving north along the rim of a fifty-foot gorge, through which ran the Truckee River. In view of subsequent developments, it seems clear that although the volunteers had thus far seen no Indians they almost certainly had been under Paiute observation for some time. To the east of Ormsby's advance, about two miles from the southern end of Pyramid Lake, mountainous terrain dropped down almost to the river. At this point, the trail, along which Ormsby's men were advancing, gradually descended onto the sagebrush covered bottom land. On ahead could be seen a grove of cottonwood trees.

The first indication of Indians nearby came in the waning afternoon light when the leading elements of Ormsby's command spotted perhaps two dozen Paiutes on a low rise of ground just ahead. The sight apparently galvanized the volunteers, who promptly surged forward, totally unaware of the main body of Paiutes out of sight around the bend of the river. On they came, with abandon, followed by the main body. The Indians, for their part, commenced to withdraw behind a barrage of arrows. As more Paiutes entered the fray from the main encampment around the Big Bend of the Truckee, they gradually extended their flanks like the great horns of the Zuli impis in South Africa. In short order, Ormsby's volunteers found themselves nearly surrounded. Suddenly these volunteers found themselves in a tight fix, imperiled it seems by these very Indians whose fighting ability they had scorned just a few days earlier.

Despite Ormsby's best efforts to rally his command, chaos set in. Just that quickly it had become every man for himself. Those who could tried to flee. About a mile from the fighting, where the nearby hills reached nearly to the water's edge, a small pass led through the hills and, largely surrounded as they were, served as the only avenue of escape, since the river could not be forded in this area.

Ormsby, astride a mule was wounded in the mouth and the arm. Realizing he could no longer function as a commander, he turned command over to Captain R.G. Watkins. Then, when his saddle slipped, slamming him to the ground, Ormsby was soon surrounded by angry Paiutes. Reportedly, he begged for his life from the Indians, some of whom had been friends in days past, but the Paiutes, it seems were not in a forgiving mood this day. Finishing the major off, they pushed his body into a ditch.

The withdrawal had quickly degenerated into a rout as men pushed and shoved in an effort to escape. Many fell before the relentless pursuit of the Paiutes. Describing the scene later, one of the Paiutes recalled, "White men all cry a heap; got no gun, throw 'um away, too; no want to fight any more now; all big scare; just like cattle, run, run, cry, cry, heap cry, same as papoose; no want Injun to kill 'um any more."[14]

Some forty-six volunteers died in the initial attack and another two dozen perished during the rout, bringing the total to more than two-thirds of Ormsby's entire force. Those who avoided the Paiute wrath, did so by hiding among the cottonwoods and brush that had earlier concealed the Indians. By darkness these thoroughly chastened survivors made their way back to safety. The Battle of Pyramid Lake, if indeed, it justifies being called a battle, was a tragedy that ought never to have happened, and like so many similar incidents it had its genesis in arrogance and stupidity. Newspaper rhetoric was quick to paint a stirring picture, calling it the bloodiest battle since Braddock's defeat in 1755.

According to one reporter, the Paiute leader Minnemocker directed the battle flawlessly, standing on a rise of ground, issuing orders like a Native American Napoleon. He was, reportedly, "dressed in splendid style, with white cap and plume, a red and white sash flung over his shoulder."[15]

By May 15 survivors began to trickle in to Bucklands, among them, one Bart Riley who volunteered to carry Pony Express dispatches to Smith's Creek, some ninety miles east when the regular rider refused to go, owing to potential danger from the Paiutes. Riley carried the dispatches to Smith's Creek and back with no difficulty, only to sustain a mortal wound from the accidental discharge of a friend's gun the following day, dying twenty-four hours later.

If the attack on Williams Station failed to trigger a general alarm among the populace, the Ormsby debacle certainly did. Fright if not outright panic took hold in the settlements. Women and children were hustled into the strongest stone buildings. Miners and ranchers rushed to the settlements from the countryside for safety. No longer did there appear to be any question about the intent of the Paiutes. A few prospectors, who had just crossed the Sierras in search of gold, decided the color was better in California and turned back. In Carson City, the Penrod Hotel was turned into a fort. Wooden cannons were built in Silver City for defense of the community, although what function they were expected to serve is not clear. Perhaps it was hoped the Paiutes would believe them to be real. Not surprisingly, there were wildly exaggerated estimates of Indian numbers, ranging as high as 3,000. Captain Watkins estimated the Indian strength at 600.

Meanwhile, acting Governor Roop requested help from the Federal authorities in California. A regiment of cavalry was reported to be stationed at Honey Lake, and assistant Indian agent Warren Wasson, was ostensibly armed with a telegram from the commanding officer at San Francisco, authorizing these troops to be used in defense against the Paiutes. Captain Joseph Stewart, commanding at Fort Alcatraz was ordered to put down the uprising and soon was en route to the troubled area with some 200 Federal troops. Along the way, the Carson Valley Expedition, as it was known, was augmented by 165 volunteer infantry from Downieville. By May 20, Stewart's command was in Carson City, where he received a telegram ordering him not to engage the enemy until he knew the strength of the Paiutes.

Mobilization didn't stop with the arrival of the Stewart column, however. Yet a second expedition was organized, this one under the command of a former Texas Ranger, Colonel John Coffee "Jack" Hays, who arguably was the quintessential Texas Ranger. Small of stature but big in fighting ability, he had served with distinction on the Texas frontier and in the Mexican War. As historian Robert Utley says, Hays was "Modest, quiet, and soft-spoken, thoughtful, a man of few words either spoken or written, he had no need to boast: his actions told all." If a steady hand was needed to command this expedition, a better man could scarcely have been found.[16] Including Stewart's California troops, Hays's command, formed as the Washoe Regiment, numbered about 800 men, including Stewart's Federals. Lieutenant Colonel Saunders stood as Hays's second in command, with Dan Hungerford the ranking major. The regiment itself was composed of eight companies of infantry and six of cavalry, each with its own colorful and distinctive soubriquet, including Spy Company, Sierra Guards, Carson Rangers, Nevada Rifles, San Juan Rifles, Truckee Rangers, Virginia Rifles, Silver City Guards, and Highland Rangers. All seem to have been well armed, too, with rifled muskets and plenty of ammunition.

The regiment had some difficulty procuring supplies but finally on May 24, buoyed on by cheers from the citizens, Hays and his men marched from Virginia City down Gold Cañon, bivouacking that first night at Miller's Ranch, below Dayton, then known as Chinatown. Commissary stores followed the next day, but the poor quality produced griping among the troops, as it always does.

On the 26th the expedition pushed on to Reed's Station, from which point scout Michael Bushy was dispatched with instructions to see if any Indians were in the immediate vicinity. A veteran scout, Bushy had fought Indians in Washington and Oregon and could be depended on to provide the intelligence Hays needed. Unfortunately, he was not seen alive again.

On the night of the 27th, the column bivouacked near the lower crossing of the Truckee River, where the body of one of Ormsby's unfortunate command was discovered and presumably buried. Progress was slow; another four days march produced but eight miles farther down the Truckee and still no contact with the Paiutes. Indeed, the only casualty thus far was the death of a man killed by the accidental discharge of a rifle. They were in enemy country, though; no doubt of that and Hays, unwilling to risk another disaster, proceeded with great caution.

Meanwhile, as the Hays column was proceeding down the Truckee, Captain Thomas Condon and assistant agent Warren Wasson had persuaded eight men to head north of Carson and occupy a small pass just west of the south end of Pyramid Lake. If defeated by Hays, as was expected, the Paiutes would almost certainly use this pass to reach the Honey Lake area, so it was of more than passing importance that it be guarded and held. Accordingly, on May 31, the defenders were reinforced by a detachment from Honey Lake, bringing Condon's total force to a slightly more respectable thirty-four. Condon's position was somewhat precarious. His little command would be in a dangerous situation should Hays be turned back. Despite lousy weather, Condon pressed on, reaching a point near the south end of Pyramid Lake, where they found the charred grisly remains of seven California prospectors, missing since mid–May.

Even as Condon's detachment was in motion, on the morning of June 2, an eighty-man detail from Hays's column—forty each from the companies of Captains E.F. Storey and J.F. Hagan—was sent on a scout down the Truckee River in search of the Paiute village. Orders emphasized reconnaissance only; a fight was to be avoided because topography favored the Indians. On the west, a high rise of land provided a lookout post to observe the advance of the soldiers. This high ground would also help to insure against any flanking movement on one side, while the Truckee afforded the same protection on the other side. Thus, the Paiutes needed to be concerned only about the open, treeless ground to their immediate front. To further complicate any movement against the Paiutes, recent rains had created a maze of gullies that deepened as one approached the river. Some distance from the high rise of ground stood a 200-foot-high rocky butte. South of the butte the land lay flat and level, while to the north ran a continuous succession of gullies that ended in a narrow pass between the Truckee and the high ground.

Proceeding cautiously Storey and Hagan found more remains of Ormsby's unfortunate command. Presently, though, the volunteers began to take fire from Indians positioned on the rocky butte and soon found themselves facing a Paiute line of battle that reached from the river all the way to the high rise of ground, with warriors concealed behind sagebrush and large rocks.

The two captains elected to send part of their command against the rocky butte, while awaiting the arrival of Hays and the main body. Accordingly, the volunteers advanced and managed to secure the butte, but were taking punishing fire from the direction of the river as well as from the high rise of ground. Fortunately, the main body arrived directly, deploying as skirmishers. And so at last, the battle was fully joined. According to one source, Storey, voice filled with emotion over the death of a friend, was a gallant figure on the field. He was backed by the Virginia Rifles, now in the forefront of the action.

With the arrival of the main body, the regulars advanced as skirmishers, followed by the cavalry, dismounted, their horses held by every fifth trooper. Perhaps recalling the fate of Ormsby's command, Hays wisely held back a reserve of 200.

Despite superiority in weapons, the whites were able to advance only slowly against spirited resistance. Paiutes seemed everywhere, painted for battle, taking advantage of every rock, clump of sagebrush, and fissure. Time and again the whites charged the rocky butte, but the tenacity of the Indian resistance stymied Hays's men until darkness, when overwhelming pressure finally forced them from their places of concealment and into flight.

Fatally shot through the lungs, Storey remained alive, though barely so. Hays suffered two others killed and three wounded. As was usually the case, Indian casualty figures varied wildly. A spy with the Paiutes claimed the Indians lost 160 killed and many more wounded.

Another estimate claimed 46 killed and reportedly seventy bodies were later found concealed in cliffs. The Paiutes themselves acknowledged 4 killed and 7 wounded, which was probably the most realistic set of numbers.

On Monday, June 4, Hays resumed his advance to Pyramid Lake, leaving behind Captain Joseph Vargo and Company J from Sacramento to look after the wounded. Hasty earthworks were erected here and named Camp Storey in honor of the deceased captain, who had finally succumbed to his wounds, along with James Cameron and A.H. Phelps.

Although the Battle of Truckee had been a tactical success for Hays, the advance proceeded with caution on the 5th as they moved north, here and there, continuing to find and bury corpses from the Ormsby party. A range of mountains running north along the eastern flank of Pyramid Lake separated the lake from a second body of water known as Mud Lake. Hays chose the route along the eastern base of the mountains. At the mouth of a canyon running upward into the mountains, the command halted. A party of five, including Sam Bucklands, Ben Webster, S.C. Springer, and William Allen were sent on ahead as scouts under the command of Captain Robert Lyon. As they approached the wide end of the canyon, the party was fired on by Paiutes lying in ambush, killing Allen. The other four scouts escaped, and when Lyon reported to Hays what had happened to Hays and requested permission to take a detail and recover Allen's body, Hays informed the captain that they would all go. After detailing horse-holders, Hays dismounted his cavalry and moved forward on foot, slowly, not knowing the Indians' strength. Arriving on the scene, Hays found the Pyramid Lake camp deserted and the Indians who had ambushed the point guard, having long since disappeared. Allen's body was duly recovered, however, and proved to be the last fatality of the expedition.

Hays had expected to remain in the field until June 7, but with the victory at Truckee and the dispersal of the Paiutes there seemed little need to maintain a field force and besides, it was difficult to supply a force of this size, so the column returned to Carson, turned in their weapons and held services for dead comrades, including Allen and Captain Storey. Later, Major Ormsby's remains were also retrieved and brought to Carson for proper burial. Captain Stewart's eighty-one-man company of regulars was left behind at Pyramid Lake to create a set of earthworks, to be named Fort Haven, in honor of General Haven of California who had volunteered to serve as a private in Hays's command.

Ironically, Stewart had meanwhile received a telegram from headquarters, congratulating him on the victory at Truckee, despite the fact that he had not been in command. The telegram also included orders for him to fall back to Carson River when the Fort Haven earthworks were finished. The California troops were anxious to return home, but for five long weeks they labored under a broiling sun until the earthworks were finished. Finally, specific orders arrived authorizing Stewart to abandon Fort Haven and build a new post on the Carson River to be garrisoned by two companies of infantry and one of dragoons, plus his artillery. With little imagination, one can visualize how Stewart's men must have felt upon receiving word that the earthworks they had labored were now to be abandoned. Accordingly, on July 18 Stewart marched south and selected a new site near Bucklands Station on the big bend of Carson River, which would eventually become Fort Churchill.

The site was a good one, too. Sam Bucklands had already established a ranch and trading post here in 1859. As well, the location had served as a change station for the Pony Express in the spring of 1860. In any case, by July 23, Stewart's entire command had arrived and Stewart promptly sent off a letter to the Department of California, suggesting that the new post be named in honor of General Sylvester Churchill. The suggestion was passed on to Washington, where the War Department approved the name on August 25.

Although the Hays expedition had disbanded following the victory at Truckee it by no means indicated that the Indian troubles were at an end. Some small forces yet remained in the field. Including Stewart's command, a force of some thirty men under a Captain William Weatherlow from the Honey Lake country had been scouting the mountainous country west and north of Pyramid Lake. From here, he dispatched a letter to Acting Governor Roop, reporting that he had not seen an Indian, but had been over the ground where Ormsby's command was cut to pieces. Perhaps it was the experience of being over this ground that gave rise to his arrogance when he claimed that with fifty men he could clean out all the Indians in the region. Many others had and would continue to make a similar claim, without having to support it.

But as said, notwithstanding Hay's victory at Truckee, there was plenty of Indian scare to be had. When word of the outbreak first reached Colonel Philip St. George Cooke, commanding Camp Floyd at Salt Lake City, it came in the form of requests to station soldiers along the Pony Express route to protect emigrant trains, which were frequently under attack. Indeed, throughout the summer and fall, Paiutes harassed Pony Express stations, burning buildings and killing the operators. And more than one Pony Express rider lost his life to the Paiutes. In June, Indian raids caused the owners, Russell, Majors & Waddell to cancel service between Salt Lake City and Carson City. Fortunately, the arrival of Federal troops enabled the company to restore service by July, but the delay cost them $75,000. Remote stations beyond the protective reach of the military continued to be hit hard through the summer.

Notwithstanding the raids of that summer of 1860, Indian agent Frederick Dodge, assisted by Warren Wasson, whom Captain Stewart had hired to help Dodge, managed to persuade many of the Paiutes to return to the Pyramid Lake area. Many, however, retained a hostile attitude, so Dodge had his work cut out for him. Fortunately, he found allies in Numaga and Oderkeo, respected leaders who favored peace. By the end of July, Dodge directed Wasson to establish firm boundaries for a Pyramid Lake reservation, with intruders forbidden to enter. A second reservation was later established at Walker Lake to the south. The Paiutes were encouraged to put up adobe buildings, cut hay, and otherwise engage in peaceful pursuits. In December, every male Indian was given a hickory shirt and blue coveralls, while the women received calico, needles and thread.

For all intents and purposes, the Paiute War seemed to have run its course. But not quite yet. In the spring of 1861, some 1,500 Paiutes assembled at the mouth of Walker River, drawn in it seems by a man named Wahe who claimed to be second chief of all the Paiutes, claiming to be a brother of old Winnemucca, though actually he was in fact half Bannack and half Paiute. His message—not new by any means—was that he was a spirit chief and could not be harmed by bullets. Being a superstitious people, the Paiutes were persuaded to believe that any disobedience of his orders would result in a cruel death.

As the movement, if such it may be called, gained momentum, Warren Wasson learned of the goings-on from a young Paiute interpreter. The plan called for all arms and ammunition at the agency to be seized, after which groups of eight to ten Paiutes would approach Fort Churchill and after gaining entry as peaceful Indians, intended to slaughter the garrison. Armed with this information, Wasson boldly approached the Paiute encampment, which he soon learned contained Bannacks from Idaho and Oregon, as well as Paiutes from other distant camps. Persuasive himself, Wasson managed to defuse the planned uprising through skillful negotiation. Humiliated, Wahe fled to Oregon, returning two years later when he was killed by two Paiutes who had come to see him as a fraud.

On March 12, 1861, full territorial status was conferred on Nevada, who appointed

James W. Nye governor in July. Congress also decreed that the duties of the territorial governor would include supervision of the Indians within his territory. As whites continued to move into the country, the Paiutes old way of life faded away, although they were now receiving more clothing and food than they had in the past. So the time for war in western Nevada, which had begun with a glorious Indian victory had, in the months that followed, gradually dissipated and the majority of Paiutes began the long walk down the white man's road toward acculturation.

The Owens Valley War, 1862–1863

To the east of the Maricopa country, sandwiched between the Sierras on the west and the Inyo Range on the east, lies the Owens Valley, westernmost of some 150 desert basins comprising the Great Basin. The valley stretches from the smaller Cosco Range south of present Owens Lake (a dry bed today), 100 miles to the great bend in the Owens River north of present Bishop, California. It is a beautiful, high lonesome valley, flanked by towering, ermine-capped peaks. Like Arizona's Monument Valley, filmmakers have found Owens Valley a perfect setting for Old West films and others such as *High Sierra* starring Humphrey Bogart.

In the mid–19th century, the valley was an important corridor for travel between Southern California, Salt Lake City and the Nevada mining districts. It also served as an important axis for military traffic.

Owens Valley had been home to the Mono Paiute Indians for many years. Related by language to the Shoshonean tribal groups, the Paiutes were root gatherers and farmers, subsisting on Piñon pine nuts, wild hyacinth and yellow nut grass tubers which they cultivated by building an extensive irrigation system with ditches. Theirs was a hunting culture as well. Deer, Big Horn sheep, fish, and small game rounded out their diet. Like the other California tribes, the Paiutes had no real tribal organization, being, rather, a loose community of families who lived near each other. Although not especially war-like, there were occasional territorial disputes that arose over trespassing on pine nut territory.

The valley seems to have been named for mountain man Richard Owens who spent time in the area during the 1830s, though hardly long enough to have earned naming rights it would seem. During the early 1860s, settlers began to move into the area, in steady if not large numbers. L.R. Ketcham brought cattle to the valley in 1859. Two years later Allen Van Fleet, another rancher, settled near present day Bishop, named for Samuel Bishop, yet another rancher who brought cattle and horses from Fort Tejon, near Bakersfield. About the same time, Charles Putnam built a stone trading post near present day Independence in the shadow of Mt. Whitney. Putnam's trading post was to be a key location during hostilities with the Paiutes.[17]

Early on, the Paiutes seem to have found the white man's cattle a target too tempting to resist and cattle theft soon proved a source of trouble. In 1859, Captain John Wynn "Blackjack" Davidson, a veteran of the Mexican War and later the Civil and Indian wars took Companies B and K, 1st Dragoons from Fort Tejon to Owens Valley in search of stolen livestock.

It turned out to be a pleasant sort of assignment. Davidson found Owens Valley a peaceful place and opined that the Indians ought to be placed on a reservation here and protected by the federal government, with the understanding that they not interfere with white travel through the valley. He was opposed to whites being allowed to settle on the reservation. However, the idea of a reservation in Owens Valley was opposed by those agents and commissioners who regarded the area as not being able to support all the Indians they envisioned relocating here. The winters of the late 1850s and early 1860s were severe and hard on the Paiutes both in Owens Valley and their brethren in Nevada. The cattle brought into the valley by Ketcham, Bishop and others liked to forage on Indian crops—hyacinth and nut grass. Since the cattle were eating their crops, Indians reasoned they had a right to kill the cattle. When a rancher named Al Thompson caught an Indian butchering a steer he killed him. The Paiutes retaliated, killing a man named Yank Crossen who had the misfortune to be traveling through the valley.

Although tensions were high neither side seemed anxious for an all-out war. Besides, the Paiutes were mostly armed with bows and arrows so it would be a real mismatch in any serious clash of arms. In any case, a peace conference was convened at the St. Francis Ranch on January 31, 1862. Both sides agreed that since each had suffered a man killed things were even. The Indians promised not to bother cattle, providing the ranchers controlled where they grazed. The only dissident voice in the gathering was that of Joaquin Jim of the Southern Mono Paiutes who refused to comply with this informal agreement and was soon back raiding.

In February, Jim and his band interrupted one north-bound cattle drive near St. Francis Ranch that sent Jesse Summers and his partner scurrying back to Putnam's Trading Post for help. Rounding up fifteen men they returned to St. Francis Ranch where they found Joaquin and his band. Oddly, nothing in the way of a fight seems to have ensued and an uneventful night was passed, though not we might imagine, without some edginess. In the morning, Jim was gone and the cattle drive resumed. The next night, however, the ranchers lost 200 head which persuaded them to turn back to Owens Valley.

During the next few days there were scattered clashes between ranchers and Paiutes over stolen cattle. Four Indians were reportedly killed, but more importantly, the Paiutes appeared to be growing bolder. While ranchers convened a second meeting at Putnam's, Paiutes attacked a cabin near Hot Springs. The occupant of the cabin, a man named Taylor is said to have killed ten Paiutes before the Indians forced him out by setting fire to his cabin and killing him as he emerged.

Things were ratcheting-up. On March 20, ranchers raided a Paiute camp north of Owens Lake, killing eleven Indians and destroying much food. Three settlers were wounded in the fracas. And so there was no longer a rumor of war. The Paiutes sent word to other bands, hoping to garner support, but the Nevada Paiutes had recently been subjugated and were warned by their leaders not become involved in the Owens Valley conflict.

There was a complicating issue as well. An Aurora, Nevada, firm had agreed to sell firearms to the Paiutes because they believed the settlers in Owens Valley had cheated them in cattle sales. One valley settler traveled to Aurora to buy ammunition but was turned down. Insofar as this particular Nevada merchant was concerned, the Paiutes could kill all the settlers in Owens Valley.

Growing ever more concerned, the settlers petitioned military authorities in Los Angeles and at Fort Tejon for assistance, and the Army complied. In March 1862, Lieutenant Colonel George Evans was ordered to lead an expedition to Owens Valley. The column, consisting of three companies of the 2d California Volunteer Cavalry, was outfitted with 40 days' rations and 100 rounds of ammunition per man.

In the meantime, the settlers were not holding their breath waiting for the Army. They gathered their cattle together thirty miles north of Owens Lake and sent out cries for help to Aurora, Nevada, and Visalia, California. Not all those in Aurora, it might be pointed out were against the Owens Valley settlers. On March 28, John Kellogg, a former army captain, arrived from Aurora with a party of eighteen volunteers, while from Visalia came twenty-two more under a man named Mayfield, whose first name appears to have been lost to history. The addition of locals to the volunteer ranks gave Mayfield—reportedly a former army colonel—a force of sixty men, with which he advanced some fifty miles up the Valley.

Evans and his horsemen arrived at Putnam's on April 4, just in time to drive off a party of thirty Indians who were attacking the post. The next day Evans advanced up the valley, leaving a seven-man detachment to guard the trading post.

Meanwhile, Colonel Mayfield's volunteers found a large body of Indians—as many as 500, it was reported—in the mountains. Undaunted, Mayfield elected to attack. Dividing his command into two sections, the volunteers attacked. A lively skirmish followed that resulted in one man being killed, but that's all it took to discourage the volunteers who panicked and retreated to their camp with the Indians in pursuit. Taking up a defensive position in an Indian irrigation ditch, the volunteers managed to keep the attackers at bay. That night, a man by the name of Scott, the sheriff of Mono County was killed while lighting his pipe; three others died as well. Under cover of darkness, the remaining volunteers managed to escape, having suffered the loss of horses and supplies, to say nothing of a little dignity. The next morning they met up with Evans and his cavalry and bivouacked that night thirty miles north of Putnam's, where they discovered the bodies of two other men killed by Indians.

As things were heating up in Owens Valley, Warren Wasson, acting Indian agent for Nevada had been in touch with Nevada Governor James Nye. Wasson, who was fearful that hostilities in California would escalate and spill over into Nevada, was encouraging a peace mission to Owens Valley. Nye agreed and in turn contacted General George Wright commanding the Department of Pacific. Wright ordered Captain Edwin Rowe, commanding Fort Churchill, Nevada, to provide a peacekeeping detail.

Accordingly, on April 4, even as Evans was approaching Putnam's, Lieutenant Herman Noble, 2d California Cavalry joined Agent Wasson near Aurora, Nevada, and proceeded toward Owens Valley. Meantime, on April 7, Colonel Evans prepared to resume his advance up the valley. In addition to his own command he had Mayfield's volunteers, now reduced to forty and who apparently had recovered some of their elan. Then shortly, they were joined by Noble's column and the combined force advanced up the valley to the site where Mayfield had had his fight, though the Indians had long since moved on. Given this set up, it is a little difficult to envision exactly what sort of peacekeeping mission Wasson and Noble had in mind: perhaps a preemptive strike that would discourage the Paiutes from taking the hostilities into Nevada.

On April 8, Evans's scouts reported a large gathering of Indians near Bishop Creek, but as the soldiers advanced through falling snow, the Indians dispersed. That night their fires were seen in a nearby canyon. The next day, a patrol following an Indian trail up the canyon was attacked with one man killed and another wounded. Evans brought the main body forward, dismounted his men and prepared to attack on foot.

One section of forty men under Lieutenants Noble and Oliver moved up the left side of the canyon, while Evans and Lieutenant George French took another forty up the opposite side. Mayfield and four of his volunteers joined Noble while the remainder waited at the mouth of the canyon. Noble's detachment was able to penetrate the canyon far enough to recover the body of Trooper Christopher Gillespie who had been killed the preceding day, but took heavy fire from the Indians in doing so. Mayfield was killed, forcing Evans and Noble to withdraw a mile and a half down the valley and establish a stronger position. To

Evans and his men it must have assuredly seemed that they were facing a large body of warriors. However, Agent Wasson, who had been observing the fight from a nearby high point, counted but twenty-five Indians and these he imagined probably constituted a rear guard.

On April 10, with provisions exhausted, Evans elected to return to Camp Latham. Noble and his men would accompany them as far as Putnam's, before returning to Aurora. The settlers wanted a military presence left in the valley, but Evans, lacking authority to comply, offered settlers the option of remaining or going to Latham (near present Culver City). A few settlers chose to stay, but most decided to drive their livestock—some 4,000 cattle and 2,500 sheep—to the safety of Camp Latham, which place Evans reached on the 28th. In his report, Evans recommended that a military post be established in Owens Valley to protect the settlers there, and to provide protection for Nevada-bound travelers.

Meanwhile, General George Wright at Department Headquarters in San Francisco had heard—more than occasionally—from the settlers in Owens Valley about their need for protection. Throughout May and June 1862, miners and stockmen were attacked on numerous occasions. This, supported by Evans's report, prompted Wright to direct Colonel Ferris Forman, the new commanding officer at Latham, to establish a post in the valley. Accordingly, Evans soon found himself en route to Owens Valley once again.

On June 14, Evans with 200 men of Companies D, G, and I, 2d California Volunteer Cavalry left Latham, accompanied by forty-six wagons. The idea was to haul enough supplies for sixty days, but the post at Latham could only supply enough for eighteen days. Once he arrived in the valley, Evans spent a week pursuing the Indians, trying to coax them into a fight but to no avail.

On July 4th Evans finally established Camp Independence in honor of the holiday and set about building a permanent post. Until their new home was finished, the men lived in caves on the hillside. Meanwhile, Evans received word that Agent Wasson and Captain Rowe, 2d Cavalry had made a treaty with Indian leaders in the area. A parley was set up between Evans, Wasson, Rowe, and Big George, a fearsome Paiute war chief, who vowed that he was tired of fighting and only wished to be friends with the whites. Anxious for closure, Wasson made promises Evans believed would not be kept, and that if the troops were withdrawn, the raids would resume.Notwithstanding Evans's doubts, the Department of the Pacific supported Wasson's treaty, which called for the Indians to return all stolen property, including hostages. Word was sent out to convene a gathering at Camp Independence where a treaty was signed on October 6. Afterwards, one company of cavalry remained in the area while the rest of Evans's command returned to Camp Latham. Captain George was held at Camp Independence as insurance that the treaty would hold up.

Things were calm enough for a few months, but then in March Captain George suddenly slipped away. Captain James Ropes, now the camp commander issued a warning to area settlers, then sent for reinforcements, which arrived in due course from Visalia in the person of First Lieutenant S.R. Davis at the head of forty-four men.

On March 11, an Army patrol of six men encountered some 200 Paiutes in an area known as Black Rocks. A fight followed, with one soldier killed and four others, including the commander, Lieutenant Dougherty, wounded, but the patrol managed to make its way back to Camp Independence. Evans had been right. Three days later, Captain Ropes with a force of twenty-seven and a few civilians attempted to track down the Indians, who had melted away as they usually did.

On March 19, settlers reported a party of thirty to forty Indians killing livestock in the Alabama Hills [so named because the early settlers were from Alabama]. An army column took the field and chased the Indians down to Owens Lake, reportedly killing most of them. One soldier was wounded.

On April 4, Captain Herman Noble, who had received a promotion, arrived at Camp Independence with Company E, 2d California Volunteers Cavalry, increasing the garrison's strength to two full companies. On the 9th, leading a force of 120 men together with 36 civilians, Ropes took the field in search of Indians, finding a band of some 200 near Big Pine Creek. The fight was a stiff one, but insofar as could be determined, there were no Indian casualties, while two soldiers were wounded.

In late April, Captain Moses McLaughlin arrived at Camp Independence as the new post commander, bringing with him Company D, 2d California Cavalry. As for the Indians, their situation was becoming desperate. Soldiers seemed to always be in pursuit of them, destroying food stores, and constantly keeping the Paiutes on the move. Not only that, but many of the firearms the Indians possessed had become unserviceable due to lack of maintenance. Ammunition was scarce as well, all of which reduced the Indians' capacity to resist.

On May 22, Captain George turned himself in, saying he wanted to talk peace. It was a familiar refrain, but this time he was accompanied by some 400 followers who gave up their weapons. Two months later, on July 22, 900 Indians were escorted to the San Sebastian Reservation near Fort Tejon. For all intents and purposes the Owens Valley War was over. Joaquin Jim and his band continued to launch scattered attacks until 1864 when most of them were hunted down and killed. The Owens Valley War had last a little more than two years, during which time an estimated 60 whites and 200 Indians lost their lives.

War with the Northern Paiutes: Indian Raids along the Western Segment of the Overland Trail, 1864–1868

The discovery of gold in Idaho Territory in the early 1860s resulted in the creation of the Orofino and Owyhee Mining Districts. As it did here and elsewhere throughout the West the incursion of prospectors to these areas, coupled with an increasing flow of immigrant settlers into Oregon and California led inevitably to Indian-white clashes. Travelers along the Oregon/California Trail found travel west of Fort Hall (near present Pocatello) to be particularly hazardous. In the dozen years between 1850 and 1862 a number of wagon trains were attacked, the most notable of which were the Ward, Shepherd, and Utter-Van Ornum trains. Not a few travelers lost their lives in these attacks and the bodies of many were horribly mutilated. Mostly, these raids were carried out by Northern Paiutes, commonly called Snakes. Although their brethren in Central Nevada and California's Owens Valley had been more or less pacified, the Snakes made life in general a risky proposition for whites in the region where southwestern Idaho, northern Nevada, southeastern Oregon, and northeastern California come together.

The increased flow of immigrant traffic into this region led to a demand for improved routes of travel and of course protection from the indigenous people who threatened travelers. Both tasks required army detachments to implement them, but until the end of the Civil War there were few regular army units available to carry out these missions. As had been the case elsewhere during this period, state and/or territorial volunteer units and local companies of hastily organized rangers were called on to deal with Indian raiders, certainly the more pressing of the two needs.

The particular area of depredations fell within the jurisdiction of two U.S. Army military departments: California and Columbia. However, the Civil War in the East had siphoned off nearly all of the regular army units and thus left the job of dealing with the Indian problem to volunteer units from Oregon and Nevada that took the field regularly in an effort to resolve the problem, though to little avail. As an example of the penurious state of affairs in the region, the entire District of Oregon was garrisoned by only a few detachments of the 9th U.S. Infantry. A few companies of Oregon Volunteer Cavalry were patrolling along the Snake River. In July 1863, three companies of the 1st Washington Territorial Infantry commanded by a man with the rather quaint name of Major Pinkney Lugenbeel, established Fort Boise.

General Patrick Connor's smashing defeat of the Shoshoni village of Bear Hunter near Preston, Utah, in January 1863 and the eventual subjugation of a band of Western Shoshonis know as Gosiutes, by volunteers and rangers led to a series of treaties signed with the several tribes occupying the region. These agreements coupled with the establishment of military outposts throughout the region were thought to have finally brought about peace. Such optimism, however, failed to take into account the recalcitrant Snakes.

The October 1864 treaty, for which J.W. Huntington, Superintendent of Indian Affairs for Oregon, was the prime mover, relocated the Klamaths, Modocs, and Northern Paiutes to the Klamath Lake Reservation. A year earlier Fort Klamath had been established to supervise these tribes, although it was thought by some to have been built in a bad location. Huntington's treaty at first established a sort of peace with the Klamaths and Modocs, but the Snakes, particularly Paulina's band of Walpapi raided freight convoys, stagecoaches, ranches, and prospectors, as well as their traditional enemies the Klamaths and Modocs, which was one reason these latter tribes agreed to the treaty since they saw it as a means of protection from the Snakes.

Then, in the fall of 1864, following a minor clash on a creek that later came to be called Paulina Creek, Paulina decided he'd had enough and asked for peace. The fact that his wife and child had been taken captive no doubt encouraged him to walk the peace road. Huntington agreed, providing that Paulina ceased his raiding ways. Although there had been no significant battlefield victories over the Indians, they had been hounded to the point that the situation in southeastern Oregon had quieted notably. Meanwhile, the scene shifted to southwestern Idaho, where, early in 1865, often during brutal winter weather conditions, both rangers and volunteers engaged in several fights with raiding Bannack Indians (Northern Paiutes who had become allied with the Shoshonis through marriage) who had been stealing sheep, burning ranches and attacking travelers.

The end of the Civil War released more regular Army troops for duty in the. In the fall of 1865, the 14th Infantry and 1st Cavalry reached Fort Boise. On Feb. 24, 1866, Major General Fred Steele was appointed to command the Department of Columbia and two companies of the 14th Infantry were relocated to Camp Lyon to relieve the Oregon volunteers. The changes continued. On March 20, 1866, Major Louis Marshall arrived at Ft. Boise.

The arrival of regular troops had little impact on the Indian frame of mind. Raids continued and so did criticism from the local press. In view of this, Major General Henry Halleck, recently appointed commander of the Department of Pacific, decided it would be a good idea to get a first-hand impression of situation and visited Ft. Churchill, Camp Lyon and Fort Boise. Halleck also met with some of the Paiutes and listened to their grievances, as well as locals who begged for more military aid. Although Halleck impressed both the Indians and whites alike, he was not himself persuaded that the situation was as bad as it was made out to be.

These regular soldiers had not long to wait before being called on to respond to Indian depredations on the Owyhee River. On February 23, a mixed force of Oregon volunteers (they were still available to take the field) and the 14th Infantry had a fierce fight on Dry Creek. Not satisfied that enough was being done, rangers from Boise City set out on expedition to clean out Indians from along Snake River. When Governor Caleb Lyon learned what was afoot, however, he quickly clamped down and forbade the expedition, much to the chagrin of the rangers.

Chinese Massacre

In May 1866, a large Paiute war party attacked the stage line along the Humboldt Route and the ferry at Owyhee River Crossing. May was a busy month for the Paiute raiders as well as travelers. Near the Idaho/Nevada line, a party of Chinese immigrants who had started out from Virginia City (Nevada) bound for the silver mines in Idaho was attacked and massacred. The men were reportedly innocently walking along the road, posing about as much threat as school children. A few of the men carried pistols, but otherwise most were armed with nothing more than sluice forks, umbrellas, and bamboo poles. Chinese immigrants were to feel the wrath of Indian raiders on other occasions as well.

Idaho Indian warriors, probably Bannack.

Near the end of May Major Marshall, arriving at Camp Lyon learned of the Chinese massacre and promptly dispatched Lieutenant Silas Pepoon and forty-nine men to investigate. Arriving on the scene, Pepoon found several bodies, which he and his men buried. It was, however, too late to pursue the raiders, so Pepoon returned to Camp Lyon.

Marshall wasted no time, taking up the pursuit of a large war party he believed to be responsible for the Chinese massacre, and he found them, too, at a place called Three Forks on Owyhee River and it was indeed a good size war party, estimated at perhaps 300 warriors who were strongly positioned on cliffs above river. Battle was joined and lasted for several hours. Even with a howitzer for support, Marshall was unable to dislodge Paiutes.

Frustrated, Marshall decided on a flanking movement. He sent half of his command along with the howitzer to cross the river on a raft, which promptly sank, taking the howitzer with it; the men, however, managed to escape drowning. By now, darkness had set in leaving Marshall in a bad spot with a divided command. Fortunately for him the Indians chose not to attack. In the morning, Marshall's men built a second raft, but once on other side Marshall and his men were still confronted the prospect of climbing some pretty steep cliffs to get at the Indians who were in commanding position and able to fire down on troops. After losing one man, Marshall finally decided to withdraw and on June 1, Marshall returned to Camp Lyon.

In July, frustrated civilians organized yet another expedition, this one under Isaac Jennings, a Civil War veteran. Some of the Chinese figured they had a score to settle, too, and offered to join up, but were turned down. On July 2, Jennings attacked a party of Paiutes at the junction of the Owyhee and South Fork, but as a tactician Jennings left something to be desired, for the Indians soon had him surrounded and trapped in a box canyon. A couple of the volunteers scrambled on their mounts and rode for help sixty miles away. Jennings's call for assistance resulted in the arrival of some 200 well armed miners, but by the time they reached the scene the Indians had vanished.

Raids continued through the summer. At times it seemed like a three-cornered game, with the Indian raiders chased back and forth between southeastern Oregon, northern California, and northwest Nevada. For those dissatisfied with the results of the volunteers, the regulars fared little better, not so much because of their fighting qualities or lack thereof, but rather because there were simply too few of them to make an appreciable difference, and General Halleck had done little to improve conditions. But Halleck was now gone, having been replaced by Major General Frederick Steele and that fall, the Oregon legislature turned to Steele for military aid, hoping he would be more receptive to their pleadings than Halleck had been, but he was not.

As a consequence of continuing civilian outcry and media pressure, the Army set out to intensify its efforts against Indian raiders with fall and winter campaigns. Accordingly, the fall and winter of 1866–1867 saw an increase in both raids and corresponding reprisals in northern Nevada and southeastern Oregon. On October 26, for example, a fifty-man force under Lieutenant John Small, guided by three Klamath Indian scouts, attacked a Paiute camp at Lake Abert, Oregon. After a three-hour fight the Indians withdrew and the troops torched the village.

In November, that ever-troublesome old warrior, Paulina, who apparently found the peace road too difficult to travel, planned to attack those peaceable Indians residing on the Klamath Reservation in retaliation for the Klamath Indians who had served as scouts for Lieutenant Small. Word of Paulina's intent reached Captain Franklin Sprague commanding the garrison at Fort Klamath, but he lacked the troop strength to both defend the reservation and pursue the Indians.

Fortunately, a company of Oregon Volunteer Infantry still awaiting their discharge were available to confront Paulina who was subsequently turned back with a loss of thirteen warriors. The volunteers suffered two wounded. Although Paulina had been stifled, depredations continued: cattle theft, murders, attacks on stage lines, all of which in turn produced retaliation against any Indians found, guilty or not.

Crook and the Paiutes

It is hard to imagine one man making a meaningful change in this troubled region, but that is essentially what happened with the arrival George Crook, who arrived in December1866. Now a Civil War veteran and Lieutenant Colonel of the 23rd Infantry, Crook was given the unenviable task of subduing the Snakes. A tough, taciturn, no-nonsense officer not much given to dash and flourish, Crook, it will be recalled, had seen action in the Rogue wars before moving on to distinguish himself in the Civil War rising to the rank of brevet major general of volunteers. Further distinction awaited him in the post Civil War West against Apaches and Sioux, but that was yet to come. A tenacious campaigner, Crook was perhaps the most humane of the Army's Indian fighting field commanders. An avid sportsman, Crook was perhaps most at home when in the field. Probably no other officer in the U.S. Army knew how to live in the field as did George Crook, whose mess was always well supplied with trout. One officer remembered that there was no better fly fisher in the country than Colonel Crook. He was to develop a reputation for fair treatment of those Indians he had subdued. At the moment, however, he proposed to de-fang the troublesome Snakes.

Crook's experience in the Pacific Northwest provided a valuable training ground for waging war against the Indians. He came to see that mule pack trains were a more efficient way to haul supplies than cumbersome wagons. Here in the Northwest, he also developed and refined his idea of using friendly Indians as scouts, an idea he was to use later against the Sioux and Apaches. He recognized as well the value of enlisting the services of able frontiersmen such as Archie McIntosh, Al Sieber, and Frank Grouard.

The idea of using friendly Indians was a controversial issue at the time. There was a precedent for it. Indian scouts had been employed as early as 1853 in Oregon Territory against the Rogues and Governor Stevens used Nez Perce scouts in Washington Territory in 1855. That Crook seemed to have figured out how to use Indian scouts to the best advantage was expressed by one newspaper reporter who observed Crook's campaign against the Snakes first hand and wrote that he believed Crook understood Indian character better than any man in the army.

Upon his arrival at Fort Boise, Crook quickly learned that, in his own words, "Hostile Indians were all over that country, dealing death and destruction everywhere they wished." Soon after his arrival the old District of Boise in the Department of Columbia was disbanded and a new District of the Owyhee was created with Crook in command.[18]

Crook wasted no time getting started, taking the field with a company of the 1st Cavalry. At the outset, he intended to be gone about a week; that turned into more than two years. He said, "I got interested after the Indians and did not return there [Ft. Boise] again for over two years."[19]

As a means of better organizing available troops for responding to the Indian problem, there was a rearrangement of command responsibility. As of January 5, 1867, Crook was named commander of the District of Owyhee, which included Camps Winthrop, Warner, and C.F. Smith, in southeastern Oregon, as well as Camp Lyon and Fort Boise in Idaho. His sphere of responsibility also extended to Camps McDermitt and Winfield Scott, although being in Nevada they were technically outside the District of Owyhee. In August, Fort Klamath and Camps Watson and Bidwell would be under his command as well.

The Warm Springs scouts Crook enlisted were signed on in October 1866. They were given the same pay as a cavalryman and would be allowed to keep any livestock recovered from the Paiutes, save for those animals which carried a U.S. brand which the Paiutes had stolen from the army.

In command of the Warm Springs scouts—namely Wascos and Deschutes—was Dr. William "Billy" McKay resident physician at the reservation. McKay was assisted by John Darragh, who had formerly served as interpreter at the reservation. McKay had a broad frontier heritage. He was the grandson of Alexander McKay who had gone down on the *Tonquin* [see Rogue wars] and was the son of a famous guide. He was also the step grandson of John McLoughlin and had served as interpreter for Governor Isaac Stevens in 1855. Later, during the Modoc troubles in 1872–1873, McKay was once again invited to take charge of a group of Indian scouts, but after the Snake campaign he had no interest in the job and recommended his half brother, Donald McKay who did serve during Modoc War.

Crook's 1867 campaign got underway on July 22. Companies F, H, M, 1st Cavalry and a detachment of Company D 23rd Infantry (mounted) Left Camp C.F. Smith in southern Oregon bound for Camp Warner, about 100 miles to the west. After crossing Steen's Mountain the column was joined at Camp Warner by the Warm Springs scouts and immediately set out in pursuit of Indians who had been helping themselves to the camp's livestock, with little to fear since there were no mounted troops available to pursue them until Crook arrived. In the words of one observer, Camp Smith was a lively place too, overlooking White Horse Valley. Several hundred horses and mules had recently been driven here from Chico, California, bringing the total number of livestock to something in excess of a thousand. Small wonder the place appealed to Indian raiders.

By mid–September, Crook had experienced difficulty locating Indian bands so he divided his command. Companies F and M plus some of the scouts went to the north, while H, D and the 23rd Infantry, together with the remainder of the scouts and Crook himself worked to the south. A mix of rain and snow for several days made for uncomfortable campaigning, but lousy weather seldom deterred George Crook. As the month progressed, they crossed into California and at last managed to find some Indian sign. On the 22nd, one of the white scouts, a man named Isaac Wilson, dubbed Dad by the soldiers, located a large party of Indians, but inexplicably and in direct disobedience of orders opened fire, alerting the Indians. Angry, Crook fired him, but that was not nearly enough to satisfy some of the soldiers who prepared to lynch the scout and he was only rescued at the last minute by an officer of the 23rd Infantry.

During his two-year tenure in command of the Owyhee District, Crook conducted a number of scouting forays through southwestern Idaho, into Oregon's Klamath Lake country and up the Malheur and Owyhee River courses, pursuing Snake and Pit River raiders through fair weather and foul, mostly the latter. At one point Crook said their beards were a "mass of ice." But doggedly the troops pursued through what Crook called "Dunder and Blixen country," fighting six separate engagements, the most dramatic of which was "The Battle of Infernal Caverns," a lava rock fortress where a mixed band of Snakes, Pit River Indians and a few Modocs had taken refuge and had to be rooted out.[20]

Reporter Joseph Wasson described the setting:

> To begin with those promontories and surroundings constitute a most remarkable fortress of natural engineering, and the sagacity of the Indians in selecting it is only equaled by their ingenuity in completing its defensive character in the building of those bird-nest bastions and guarding every approach and parapet with breastworks of suitable dimensions. There are natural shelves, fissures, and caverns in ten acres inclusive and surrounding that, thoroughly known, ten thousand men could be stowed out of sight in fifteen minutes, and five hundred men unacquainted with the place could never capture five well posted, armed, and supplied to stand a siege within.
>
> From the top of the ridge, the ground slopes at an angle of forty-five degrees [Wrote Lieutenant Richard Eskridge of the 23rd Infantry], down to the base of the nearest promontory, the sides of which are so steep as to necessitate the use of hands in climbing up.[21]

Eskridge also described Crook's skill as a marksman:

> In retiring, they [the Indians] were exposed to the keen eye of the colonel, who stood on top of the ridge directing the movements of both companies; two sharp reports of his deadly rifle were heard over our heads, two bodies fell with a dull thud to the rocks at our feet, both companies rushed in with a yell, and the place was ours.

The extraordinary difficulty of the terrain would stand as a predecessor to conditions the Army would experience in its war against the Modocs a few years hence. With the advent of darkness, the "besieged devils turned loose with their Paiute toothpicks" (arrows), wrote Joseph Wasson. "Til midnight thunder and lightning added a peculiar interest to the scene; vivid flashes of the latter lending an infernal coloring to the black basin and wall to the west."[22]

In July 1868, Weawea (or Weahwewa) led the Kidutokado band of Snakes. Weawea had more or less replaced Paulina, who had been killed in the Battle of Little Trout Creek in April 1867, decided his people had had enough and asked for peace. Accordingly, in July some 800 Snakes surrendered to Crook at Fort Harney where they agreed to remove to the Klamath Reservation on the Malheur River. Crook's persistency had paid off. In 1870 he was reassigned to the Department of Arizona where his career would reach its zenith.

The war with the Snakes had been a long, strung-out guerrilla war of attrition. Major battles were few but of tough little engagements there were many; more than 100 between 1864 and 1868. Historian Gregory Michno calls it the "Deadliest Indian war in the West" and points out that it caused more casualties—Indian and white—than any of the Western Indian wars.[23]

Hell with the Fires Gone Out: The Modoc War, 1872–1873

I'm Captain Jack of the Lava Beds
I'm "Cock o' the walk" and chief of the reds.
I kin "lift the ha'r" and scalp the heads
Of the whole United States Army[24]

Some 400 crow-flight miles to the north and nearly a decade after the troubles between whites and the Paiutes in Owens Valley had finally ended, the last of the major Indian-white clashes in California took place amongst the lava-strewn ravines and outcroppings of the tortuous Modoc country, located in extreme southern Oregon and northern California. As terrain went, it would be tough to find a more inhospitable area in which to wage war, unless of course one was on the defensive, in which case it gave you a marked advantage. So harsh and unforgiving was this terrain that one man described it as "hell with the fires gone out."[25]

The Modocs and Klamaths had once been a single tribal entity, although by the mid–19th century their relationship had become adversarial. One source says the name Modoc means "southern people" in the Klamath language. At some point, well before the advent of the white man, the Modocs split off and moved south to the region around Lost River, Klamath, Tule, and Clear Lakes. The Modocs were no strangers to the early white arrivals in Oregon and California. Although there were clashes between the two cultures, notably involving emigrant wagon trains, it was not until the 1870s that differences with whites blossomed into an actual war.

The Modocs' earliest contact with whites appears to have been in the 1830s when French-Canadian trappers took some Modocs to the Columbia River Basin and introduced them to other tribes as well as a lively trade that existed between these people. Although the Modocs were not trappers as such and did not have furs to barter, they did discover that slaves were a very tradable commodity and could be used to acquire horses, along with other goods. The Modocs apparently took advantage of this and it led eventually to their reputation as slave traders. They raided Pit River or Shasta villages for children and young women, which were then taken north to trade. By all accounts, they were ruthless in their sudden attacks, slaughtering those who were of no use to them.

John Charles Fremont may have been the first American—or at least the first of any note—to visit the Modoc country in 1843. While nothing of particular importance seems to have occurred on this visit, three years later, on his second visit to the area, Fremont was ordered to leave California (then Mexican territory) by military commander, General Jose Castro and was attacked by Klamath Indians near Tule Lake. Although Modocs were not involved in this incident, Fremont's presence made all the Indians in the area aware of the Americans.

An interesting aspect of the Modoc relationship with Americans was the giving of white nicknames to various Modoc leaders by miners around Yreka. This was likely due to the Modocs' willingness to adopt white customs, such as wearing their hair short and dressing like cowboys. In any case, Kintpuash (or Kientpoos), who was soon to become the most notorious of the Modocs, was dubbed Captain Jack. His brother was called Black Jim (owing to his unusually dark skin). Others were Humpy Joe, a hunchback; Scarfaced Charley with a large scar on his left cheek; Schonchin John, Hooker Jim, and Curly Headed Doctor, reputed to be the worst of the lot.

With the opening of the Applegate Cut-off in 1846, travelers could depart from the Oregon Trail at The Dalles on the Columbia River and head south to California. During the first two years of the trail's existence the Modocs offered little opposition to southbound wagon trains. By the early 1850s, however, that picture had changed considerably. Surprise attacks and ambushes by the Modocs became increasingly frequent. Immigrants were killed and apparently more than a few were mutilated, though exact or even approximate numbers are unknown. A favorite spot for an attack was Tule Lake, where in 1852 some sixty-five white immigrants were killed. The spot, appropriately enough, came to be known as Bloody Point.

White revenge was swift. At a peace council convened in 1852, Ben Wright, reputed to be the most notorious Indian hater in that part of the world, arranged for the meat served to the Modoc invitees to be well laced with strychnine. The Modocs were not so easily duped, however, and grew suspicious when their white hosts did not eat. When the poisoned meat plan failed, Wright and his henchmen turned to their back-up plan, pulling out concealed weapons and opening fire. Of the forty-six Modocs present, only five survived. Wright was celebrated as a hero.

When Ulysses S. Grant was elected to the presidency in 1868 it ushered in a new era of Indian-white relations and a genuine reason for optimism. A strong core of humanitarians persuaded the president that the Indian problem demanded a peaceful approach. Grant thought so, too, and initiated his Peace Policy. Grant's administration is not remembered for its sterling accomplishments, rather it is known for scandal and failures, of which the Peace Policy was one.

A big part of the so-called Indian problem was bickering within the Federal government as to who should be responsible for overseeing Indian affairs: the Indian Bureau or the War Department, and responsibility seemed to vacillate with each change of administration. When he took office in 1868, many in the Army figured Grant the soldier, would be their friend; much to their chagrin that proved not to be the case.

The Peace Policy seemed to get off to a good start, at least in the Northwest, where Alfred Benjamin Meacham was appointed Superintendent for Indian Affairs in Oregon. An influential figure in Indian-white relations, Secretary of the Interior, Carl Schurz, regarded Meacham as the foremost spokesman for Indian rights in the country.

Thought by some to lack forcefulness, Meacham was nevertheless well intentioned and otherwise quite able, but he also inherited a very troubled and vexing situation. Four years earlier, in 1864, the U.S. Government had managed to sign a treaty with the Klamaths and Modocs who agreed to live on a reservation set aside for them in Oregon. The section particularly set aside for the Modocs was known as Yainax. The Modocs and Klamaths, like the whites in the area, often felt the sting of raids by Paulina and his band of Northern Paiutes. Acceptance of this treaty was an act of self-preservation, for in doing so, the Klamaths and Modocs placed themselves under the protection of the U.S. Army.

Not surprisingly, the arrangement did not work out. Unable to co-exist peacefully with their traditional enemies, the Modocs left the reservation in 1865. Four years later, new superintendent Meacham was able to persuade them to return and have another go at it, but after three months the Modocs once again abandoned the reservation. In 1870, Captain Jack returned to the Lost River area with a band that included some seventy warriors and their families. Whites who had in the meantime settled in that area were not at all happy with the development.

Agent Meacham believed the Modocs should be sent back to the Klamath reservation using force if necessary. However, Lieutenant Colonel George Crook, temporarily in command of the Department of Columbia, refused Meacham's request. When Crook was reassigned to Arizona Territory in July 1871, his successor, General Edward R.S. Canby likewise refused, because Congress had not yet ratified the old 1864 treaty.

In 1872, Meacham was replaced by Thomas Odeneal, who shared his predecessor's belief that the Modocs should be returned to Yainax using force if necessary. In July 1872, the Indian Bureau finally authorized the removal of the Modocs. Accordingly, from Canby's headquarters, orders went out to Lieutenant Colonel Frank Wheaton, 21st Infantry, commanding the Lakes District (near present Lakeview, Oregon) and Major John Green (known to his men as Uncle Johnny), 1st Cavalry at Fort Klamath to be prepared to provide the necessary muscle should it be requested by Odeneal.

Notwithstanding his position that the Modocs belonged on the reservation, Odeneal, for some reason, seemed not inclined to act promptly, perhaps clinging to the hope that the Modocs would agree to return to the reservation without being forced to do so. Through the summer the situation remained static, and finally in September, General Canby sent Major Green on a reconnaissance through the Modoc country to get a better feel for a situation of which he had little understanding. Word of the mission slipped through to Captain Jack, however, who imagined that Green was coming to arrest him.

Green reached Lost River on the 14th, established camp and sent an interpreter to reassure Jack that he had nothing to fear. Jack then sent a messenger back to the major, asking whether Green wished to see him. Green said no via a third message, adding that if Jack had anything to say he was welcome to come in and talk, but Jack declined, with the explanation that his mother was dying. The exchange suggested that things were quiet enough and Green continued his reconnaissance. Settlers he encountered said the Modocs were occasionally troublesome but there had been no major problems.

Meantime, Odeneal continued to waffle. He intended to arrest Jack, or so he vowed, but seemed unable to issue an order to that effect. Finally, in late November, he sent a message to Jack asking him to attend a meeting in Linkville (Klamath Falls) on the 28th. Odeneal's messenger, Ivan Applegate, whom Jack disliked, was a poor choice for the job. Not surprisingly, Jack ignored the invitation. As this was unfolding, Odeneal advised Colonel Wheaton that if the Modocs did not go to Yainax peacefully, the Army would be needed. If Odeneal imagined a prompt response would be forthcoming it was surely an unrealistic expectation because it would likely be mid-December before troops could actually be on hand in any event.

As for the Modocs, there was no real clear consensus as to a course of action. Indeed, when Ivan Applegate reported to Odeneal he told of a heated discussion among the Modocs. Some of the young men favored war; to begin right now by killing Applegate and a companion who had accompanied him. Cooler heads managed to prevail, however. When he learned of this, Odeneal promptly sent a messenger to Fort Klamath requesting help from Major Green, who in turn dispatched Captain James Jackson and Troop B, 1st Cavalry to the scene.

On a cold and wet 28th day of November 1872, a date one historian targets as the beginning of the Modoc War, Jackson left Fort Klamath with thirty-eight men, and orders to arrest Jack, Black Jim, and Scarfaced Charley—without a fight if possible. Ivan Applegate served as guide. Rendezvousing briefly at Linkville, Jackson and Odeneal agreed that there would be no firing—unless necessary—and Jack should be escorted peacefully to Yainax.

Reaching the Modoc camp near Lost River, which contained seventeen families, Jackson deployed his command, sending Lieutenant Frazier Augustus Boutelle and ten men to move on the other Modoc camps, while Jackson assumed responsibility for Jack's band. Jackson had originally planned to slip into the camp before daylight, surprise the Modocs and demand the surrender of their weapons. Unfortunately for the Army, as with most of the plans and schemes made during this unusual war, this one did not quite pan out the way Jackson envisioned.

Even as this was developing, Oliver Applegate (of that ubiquitous family) who was in charge of one Modoc band actually in residence at Yainax had gotten permission from Odeneal to go to the Modoc camps and round up his charges, who he had recently learned had left the reservation to visit their friends and were then camped just across Lost River. Learning that the Army was about to enter the picture, Applegate wanted to bring his people back to Yainax before there was any trouble, although Odeneal assured him this was unlikely.

That night, apparently because he was feeling ill, Jackson scrapped his original plan and decided to keep Lieutenant Boutelle with him. Later, during a meeting with the Applegate brothers, Jackson directed Oliver to proceed to the area and await the arrival of the troops. Jackson further instructed him to be alert. Should firing break out, Applegate was to enlist as many settlers as he could locate and assist the troops. Meanwhile, several civilians who seemed to have followed the troops, perhaps curious to see what was going to develop, met up with Oliver Applegate at the cabin of a local man and there settled down to await the arrival of Jackson's soldiers.

Meanwhile, Scarfaced Charley, out early after a night of gambling, accidentally discharged his rifle. The sound seems not to have disturbed the Modocs, but Applegate and his companions wondered if trouble had begun. Charley then noticed men advancing toward the Modoc camps. However, as the soldiers approached, the Indians were quickly alerted and the camps were filled with confusion. Jackson had lost the element of surprise. However, now that they were inside the Modoc camp, Jackson would try and make the best of a difficult situation. Oliver Applegate's brother, Ivan, acted as translator during a heated discussion that reportedly lasted nearly an hour.

From their vantage point, Oliver and his companions watched the discussion taking place between Jackson and the Modocs and concluded that everything was under control. Accordingly, they decided to enter Hooker Jim's camp, containing some seventeen inhabitants and collect the Yainax Modocs. It quickly became clear, however, that Jim's band was armed and ready, but Oliver was able to defuse the situation with a show of friendship, saying he had come to take them back to Yainax and they should lay down their weapons and after a moment, some complied with Oliver's request, save for Jim himself who tried to flee across the river to Jack's camp but was caught and brought back.

This little episode stands as a microcosm of the entire Modoc War. Perhaps nowhere else during the Indian wars of the West do we find as much confusion, misunderstanding and ineptness (on the part of the U.S. Army and Federal officials) as in the Modoc War. In the minutes that followed Jackson's confrontation with Jack and his band, and the sub-episode with Hooker Jim, tension increased and led to the first real fight of the war.

Jackson ordered Lieutenant Boutelle to collect the Modoc weapons and that's when things began to fall apart. As he attempted to disarm Scarfaced Charley, the latter fired, slightly wounding Boutelle who returned the fire. The situation quickly deteriorated into a confusing little firefight that lasted but a few minutes. The cavalry horses stampeded and both sides retreated. Given the nature of the terrain, Jackson was not at all anxious to pursue the Modocs beyond their camp, but the soldiers later returned to the camp site and destroyed whatever they could.

It did not seem like much as fights went, but eight troopers lost their lives and a number of others were wounded. Jackson, who sought to put a better face on the incident, later claimed to have killed sixteen Modocs, whereas only one was actually killed and another wounded. In the aftermath of the fight, the Modocs withdrew toward their so-called Stronghold, a huge area, pocked with lava rocks, caves, and caverns—en route, they murdered thirteen settlers—some accounts say eighteen—and in any case it spurred Uncle Johnny Green to immediate action, followed soon by Wheaton who reached the field on the 21st and took command.

Following Jackson's debacle, Wheaton ordered reinforcements into the area, swelling troop strength to 225 men. Two companies of Oregon volunteers and another from California added yet another 100 men. Wheaton, who arrived on the scene and assumed personal command on December 21, figured he was facing 150 warriors, at least double the Modocs actual strength.

Canby, meanwhile, was trying to get a handle on the situation and not having much luck. The governor of Oregon advised him that there were not enough troops in the area to deal with the crisis, and ordered up a volunteer unit. Canby was a trifle miffed at the governor's high handedness and ordered troops to move from Fort Vancouver to Fort Klamath.

In addition to the Modocs regarded as hostile, the Stronghold was also occupied by Shacknasty Jim's Hot Creek Modoc band, who were making an effort to remain neutral and had intended to remove to Yainax. However, upon learning that settlers in the area were angry and out for blood because of the murders committed by the Modocs when they withdrew to the Stronghold, the Hot Creek band also opted for the safety of the Stronghold.

What to do? Lieutenant Colonel Frank Wheaton found himself with a sticky wicket, but he was nothing if not determined. He had little choice but to advance on the Stronghold, which he proceeded to do. Through the night of January 16 and into the early hours of the 17th, his troops moved into position, with Major Green on one flank and Captain Reuben Bernard on the right flank. A tough and extraordinarily able Civil War veteran, Bernard was now making his mark on the Western frontier. Indeed, when his forty-year career ended he would have participated in 103 battles.

Maneuvering in the Stronghold was a tough proposition under the best of conditions, but on this occasion fog made it even worse. Skirmishers advanced slowly, preceded by shell bursts from the 12-pounder mountain howitzer. However, owing to the poor visibility and a fear of friendly casualties, the bombardment was soon lifted. As the troops advanced the Modocs maintained a heavy and accurate fire. Neither the soldiers or the Modocs could see much of anything, but the Indians knew this land as well as the back of their hand and it gave them a leg up on the soldiers. Wheaton's plan was to attack on both flanks, while also covering the Stronghold on the south to prevent the Modocs from slipping away. However, between the fog, the rough ground and steadily mounting casualties, the advance ground to a halt. By late afternoon the fog had lifted, improving visibility, but any hope of resuming the advance now was a pipe dream. Green and Bernard attempted to rendezvous along the shore of Tule Lake, but Modoc rifle fire kept the soldiers pinned down behind rocks, of which there were many. As twilight and then darkness closed in on this cold January day, the Army had suffered seven dead regulars and two volunteers. Additionally, thus far, nineteen regulars and nine volunteers had been wounded. There were no Modoc casualties. And so in this war as in most wars, things did not seem to develop quite as one expected.

Not content to simply defend themselves a war party of Modocs slipped out of the Stronghold on the 22nd and attacked an Army supply train at Scorpion Point, burning the wagons filled with grain, and capturing the horse herd. Learning of the attack, Captain Bernard promptly dispatched a relief column that drove off the Modocs and recovered the horse herd, but the incident illustrated the aggressiveness of the Modocs.

Meanwhile, back at department headquarters, General Canby continued his frustrating effort to put together a clear picture of what was happening. Bits of information in the form of letters and an official report or two gradually filtered in, but it was a murky picture that confronted him. He was not at all pleased with Wheaton and Green. He had specifically directed that if the use of force *was* necessary sufficient troops should be employed to get the job done, but it did not appear that either Wheaton or Green had taken his directive seriously. All in all, the whole business had been rather botched, but it wasn't just the Army. Odeneal's waffling had also been a factor.

On the 23rd Canby changed pitchers, naming Colonel Alvin Cullem Gillem, 1st Cavalry to replace Wheaton. A Tennessean and an 1851 graduate of West Point, Gillem was a close friend of former president, Andrew Johnson. He had seen action against the Seminoles in Florida and fought for the Union in the Civil War. It was Gillem's command that killed the famous Confederate raider, John Hunt Morgan. Gillem seems not to have been a popular officer and his rise in rank, it has been suggested, was due less to his soldierly qualities than to Andrew Johnson's influence.

Gillem reached northern California at the end of January in the middle of a blizzard. En route he had plenty of time to reflect on the situation just handed him and how he would deal with matters. The Modocs were not Gillem's only problem. He had inherited a command with low morale. The soldiers, having been stung by the fierceness of the Modoc resistance, were feeling disgruntled and down. The fact that Gillem was not well liked did nothing to raise their spirits, either. To round it off, the colonel was also in poor health, so it appears he was not a good choice to replace Wheaton. Nevertheless, Gillem seems to have formed a reasonably clear picture of the situation confronting him and so reported to Canby. He decided on a strategy of attrition. He would wear the Modocs down, constantly tightening the noose, but also giving those who wished to surrender an opportunity to do so.

Even as the blizzard was raging, Jack sent one of the Modoc women to Gillem's camp with word that he, Jack, was tired of fighting and wanted to parley. He wanted John Fairchild, a local rancher who Jack trusted, to meet him in the Stronghold. By early February, the storm had abated enough for Gillem to reach his field headquarters. Learning Jack's terms, Gillem agreed and stipulated that as soon as weather permitted, Fairchild and a second rancher, one Pressly Dorris, would go out to the Stronghold.

Meantime, the army was cooling its heels, awaiting word as to the next move. As for the Modocs, nearly a month had passed since their repulse of Wheaton's effort. Despite this there was divisiveness among the bands. As in all cultures there was an ongoing struggle for power; control. Those who thought they understood the dynamics of Modoc "politics" believed there were three and possibly four factions vying for control, but be that as it may, it was really Jack and Curly Headed Doctor who determined the course of events, and at the moment, Jack was the *de facto* leader. At this stage, Jack apparently wished to end the war. However, when confronted with the prospect of surrendering his leadership role to the army if they left the Stronghold, he chose to remain.

None of the principals involved in these events had any idea as to what the future held and it is well they did not, for the events of the next few weeks would climax in one of the great tragedies of the Western Indian wars.

As January progressed into February, events plodded along with maddening slowness; resolution of the Modoc problem seemed a light year distant. Alone, Jack left the Stronghold to meet with one of the army officers and several ranchers he knew and trusted. Nothing of particular note seems to have occurred, except that it was an amicable gathering. Jack invited them to come to the Stronghold for a conference, but was advised that negotiations would have to await the arrival of a new peace commission.

Meantime, the former agent, Alfred Meacham, now a member of Oregon's Electoral College, was in Washington to certify Grant's re-election. Discussing the Modoc situation with Secretary of the Interior Columbus Delano, Meacham suggested that peace commissioners might be able to persuade Jack to leave the Stronghold. This sounded good to the Grant administration. The War Department liked it too, as the Army was not especially anxious launch another offensive into the Stronghold. Accordingly, Meacham was appointed to head a three-man commission composed of himself, Jesse Applegate, and Samuel Siletz.

In mid–February, Canby met with Commissioner Applegate and acting Indian Agent, Samuel Case in Linkville to hold preliminary talks while awaiting Meacham's arrival. The local press, meanwhile, had no clear idea as to what was going on, but it was not difficult to discern that something was surely in the works and the uncertainty inspired rumors. Anti-Modoc feelings were running high. A Jacksonville, Oregon, grand jury indicted eight Modocs for murder [*in absentia*].

On February 18, Meacham having now arrived on the scene, the full commission met with Canby at the ranch of John Fairchild. The press was on hand to cover the event and subsequently reported that Applegate and Case favored unconditional surrender and exile to some distant locale yet to be named. Canby and Meacham, on the other hand, believed the Modocs would never agree to such terms and why should they after all? They had whipped the soldiers. Why surrender now? Thus, Canby and Meacham reasoned that a negotiated settlement offered the best chance of resolution.

Accordingly, in an effort to get talks started, the peace commission sent out feelers to Jack. During the next few weeks there was an exchange of messages between the two sides, while the press played up the hard feelings between Californians and Oregonians over the latter's duplicitous dealings with Indians. And of course there was the issue of those grand jury indictments, and Jack would never surrender with those hanging over his head. The whole business was a mess and prompted Jesse Applegate to resign from the commission.

During February and March rhetoric flowed, but there was little real progress toward any kind of meaningful discussion. The whole situation seemed to grow more confused with each passing day. Canby was hard pressed to know just what to believe. Jack had let it be known that he wanted no more war; one day he was ready to parley, only to change his mind the next. He was stalling; possibly hoping to slip out of the Stronghold and into the mountains when warmer weather arrived. As well, keeping the army off balance with his vacillating strengthened his position. Truth be told, Jack couldn't afford to surrender without losing prestige and quite likely his role as leader of the Modocs and that was unacceptable. Notwithstanding, as long as there was a flicker of hope left, Canby clung to it, but he was beginning to see the Modoc strategy for what it was.

During this preliminary negotiating period, emissaries, some white, some mixed-blood, and some Indian who were deemed acceptable to the Modocs, made several trips into the Stronghold in an effort to establish some ground rules that hopefully would lead to serious progress. And for a moment Canby felt his pulse quicken when, in mid-February, several Modoc leaders visited the army camp and had a good look around, declaring that they were ready to surrender. It wasn't true, of course, but Canby was encouraged enough to advise General Sherman that it was over; that the Modocs were ready to surrender even as others were saying no.

The Modoc presence in the army camp angered the Oregonians who had attached themselves to the camp. They saw little point in negotiating. After all, a grand jury had indicted eight Modocs and as far as they were concerned, these Indians should be hanged and they made no bones about threatening them. When they returned to the Stronghold and reported these threats it produced a good deal of agitation among the Modocs.

And so progress remained only a hope. Jack refused to negotiate outside the lava beds and Canby would not enter the lava beds without an escort, so for the moment it was a standoff. Seeking a compromise, the commission told the Modocs that if they surrendered to military authorities they would be taken to a temporary reservation and held in protective custody until a permanent reservation was established. The powers in Washington approved this plan, stipulating only that said reservation be somewhere in Indian Territory.

The situation seemed to defy resolution. After visiting with the Modocs, emissaries brought back warnings of what would happen if Canby or the others were to enter the lava beds, and Meacham passed the warning on to Interior Secretary Delano; if the peace commission entered the lava beds they would surely be killed, but the secretary thought not, a conclusion he would have cause to deeply regret. Meacham was to continue his efforts to negotiate, while he, Delano, checked with Grant and the War Department.

There was word, too, that the Modocs had been reinforced by another twenty warriors and a renewal of the fighting seemed imminent. For Canby, who had tasted a moment of optimism, the picture had turned grim again. On March 7, an exasperated General Sherman—presumably with President Grant's authorization—finally instructed Canby to more or less take charge of the peace commission. The government, it seemed, had lost confidence in Meacham, but in typical bureaucratic clumsiness, failed to advise him of the change. The Modocs had no monopoly on duplicity.

Progress inched forward. There was more back and forth but little real progress. The Modocs seemed unable to make a decision. One day they were ready to surrender, only to change their mind twenty-four hours later. Jack continued to express a desire to surrender and move to the new reservation, but Canby grew ever more suspicious. Divisiveness continued to split the Modocs. Jack took a middle position, though inclined toward peace. His strongest opponent was the hard liner and shaman, Curly Headed Doctor.

During the next few days, Jack continued to stall and Canby—along with just about everyone else from Washington to the lava beds—was growing increasingly impatient. If at all possible, Canby wanted to avoid another offensive into that hellish lava rock country, but it was beginning to look as though that was the only way get the Modocs out. Accordingly, Canby moved his troops closer to the lava beds, first to show the Modocs he was serious, but secondarily to remove his men from the influence of the traders and prostitutes who had attached themselves to the periphery of the bivouac area to feed on the bored soldiers.

On March 21, Canby, in company with Gillem and a small escort made a personal reconnaissance to observe what they could of Modoc activities. The Modocs watched and grew nervous. Finally, several of them, including Jack, Curly Headed Doctor, and Scarfaced Charley, confronted the officers, inquiring as to their purpose. It was a tense moment. Canby tried to persuade Jack to bring his people out of the Stronghold, but he demurred and that was the extent of progress.

And so another two weeks with more of thesame, which is to say nothing much happened. Neither side, it seemed, was prepared to make a decisive move, though both threatened to do so. But if there was little movement up front, there was activity behind the scenes when Secretary Delano officially appointed Canby head of the peace commission. Delano's action of course only confirmed what had been the *de facto* arrangement in place since Sherman's directive. So, Canby was now armed with all the authority he needed.

By April 1, the situation was showing some progress. On the 2nd, Jack advised Canby that he would meet with the peace commission at a neutral point halfway between the Stronghold and the army camp. On that very day, joining Canby and Meacham at the appointed spot were L.S. Dyar, the Klamath agent, and Eleasar Thomas, a Methodist minister who seem to have been appointed to the commission as a gesture to the humanitarians pressuring President Grant to end the Modoc war peacefully. Also present as interpreters were Frank Riddle and his Modoc wife, Winema, or Toby as she was better known to the whites.

The tenor of the meeting was peaceful enough. Canby sought to assure the Modocs that his intentions were not hostile, but if that were true, the Modocs wondered, why had the soldiers taken up positions as if to attack? He did not intend to attack, said Canby, but the Modocs remained suspicious. Jack repeated his demands: send the soldiers home and provide a reservation on Lost River. He also wanted assurance that those of Hooker Jim's band charged with murder would not be punished, to which Canby could only say that if the Modocs surrendered to him, the army would decide their fate. At this point, weather in the form of heavy rain pretty much stifled progress for the day. Canby suggested a tent be erected for the next meeting to which Jack agreed, after mocking the white men for being afraid of a little weather.

During the following week, a tent was erected and preparations moved ahead for a second meeting. Toby, meanwhile, expressed her distrust of the Modocs to Meacham. She had heard rumors that troubled her. Meacham reported this to Canby who discounted the notion as idle gossip.

On Saturday, April 5, a second meeting took place. Canby was not present this time, but Meacham and four others met with Jack and a party of Modocs. During the ensuing discussion, Jack stated that if they could not have a reservation on Lost River, the Modocs would agree to remain in the Stronghold. Meacham saw this as the opportunity they had been waiting for. If the Modocs would agree to become prisoners of war, he promised to see what he could do about allowing them to remain in the Stronghold. Meacham's hope dimmed quickly, however, when Jack also demanded that if the members of Hooker Jim's band accused of murder were to be hanged, he wanted equal justice for those white men who had committed outrages against the Modocs. This, Meacham knew, would never ever happen, and so after several hours of further talk, the meeting ended.

Meanwhile, Toby, who had been sent into the Stronghold to advise Jack that any of the Modocs who agreed to surrender would be protected from their militant brethren, had learned from a Modoc informant of plans to kill the commissioners. When she asked Bogus Charley if the story had any basis in fact, he threatened to kill her if she repeated the rumor. Frightened, Toby told Canby, who allowed as how it might be true, as did Meacham and Dyar. Colonel Gillem, however, dismissed the idea out of hand, and the Reverend Thomas naively refused to believe that anyone would want to kill him.

Strangely, the next act to play out in this strange situation involved Toby ... again. The Modocs sent word that they wanted to see her. She was terrified, but Canby, Meacham, and the others felt it was important that she go in the interest of furthering negotiations. Canby instructed her to advise the Modocs that should any harm befall her, the army would respond with an immediate attack. And so, filled with trepidation actually fearing for her life, Toby returned to the Stronghold.

Much to everyone's relief, Toby and her husband's most of all, she returned, reporting on the ugly mood inside the Stronghold. The Modocs would not surrender, but agreed to come out of the Stronghold if the soldiers left. This of course was never going to happen. A showdown was inevitable. Until then, however, Canby continued to urge for a reopening of negotiations and sent Toby and her husband back to the Modocs to encourage further negotiations.

It had to be one of the most, if not *the* most protracted standoffs between the U.S. Army and Native Americans. That 50 to 60 Modocs were able to hold off an army force at least ten times their number for three months seems completely inconceivable today, and yet it speaks volumes about the great equalizing factor of the unbelievably difficult terrain of the Lava Beds that so dominated the picture. In a real sense, the terrain strengthened the Modoc position more than additional warriors would have done.

Although neither side perhaps realized it, the situation was rapidly coming to a head. Convinced that the time for action was now, the militant Modoc faction played hard ball with Jack in an effort to prod him into resuming hostilities. Black Jim, Scarfaced Charley and others argued that their only hope was to strike quickly before the soldiers devastated them with their artillery. Jack could clearly see his control slipping away. He agreed to kill Canby at the next meeting while other Modocs dispatched the remaining commissioners.

On Good Friday, April 11, 1873, Major General Edward Richard Sprigg Canby, impressively attired in his full dress uniform, met with Jack in the tent. It was exactly the gathering the Modocs had planned for. Canby was joined by Commissioners Meacham, Dyar, the Reverend Thomas, together with Toby and Frank Riddle, acting as interpreters.

Canby's overture was to pass out cigars, which all present lit up, save for the Reverend Thomas. In the midst of the negotiations, Jack suddenly produced a revolver, pointed it at Canby and pulled the trigger, but the weapon misfired. On the second try he shot Canby dead and seriously wounded Meacham. Somehow the Reverend Thomas, the Riddles, and Dyar managed to escape. It was a scene of horror. Modoc blood was up. Canby was shot again then stabbed by Jack and stripped of his uniform. The unthinkable had happened.

Canby's murder shocked the nation and sounded the death knell for Grant's Peace

Policy. Canby was the only general officer of the regular army to lose his life in the Indian wars and the Army was outraged. General Sherman was mightily displeased with the way the Modoc situation had been handled. From here on, the gloves were coming off. Canby was soon replaced by brevet Major General Jefferson Columbus Davis (no relation to the former Confederate president). Davis had seen considerable field service during the Civil War and had a nasty reputation, having once shot and killed his commanding officer over a reprimand.

Colonel Gillem, however, did not wait for Davis's arrival to take action. Gillem thought Wheaton's strategy had been sound, if perhaps poorly executed. Consequently, he now figured to use that strategy against the Modocs, albeit more effectively. During a seventy-two-hour period, Gillem, employing two columns of troops, carefully but steadily pushed ever deeper into the Stronghold. Major Green got the ball rolling on the west flank with two companies, while on the east or right flank, Major Edwin Cooley Mason with the 21st Infantry, together with Bernard's Troop G, 1st Cavalry, pressed forward. This time there was no fog and both sides fired at each other as opportunities permitted. The Modoc warriors, cleverly wrapped in rawhide to prevent cuts, were able to slither their way through the sharp lava rock formations.

At night, Gillem's artillery—he had both howitzers and mortars—lobbed shells into the area where the Modocs were suspected to be. The war had become a siege. With little water, Jack was forced to take his people ever deeper into the Stronghold. Thus far, the Modocs had three warriors and eight women killed, while Gillem's troops had lost two killed and three wounded. It was fifty against a thousand.

Gillem tried to keep up the pressure on the Modocs, but then on April 16 a shortage of water finally compelled Jack to abandon the Stronghold. It was a victory of sorts for the army, which had been trying to accomplish this all winter, but the problem now was where had the Modocs got to? There was fear that if they escaped the army's loop they would be free to raid throughout the area and catching them would be time consuming and very costly. Gillem ordered outposts established in the Stronghold in the eventuality the Modocs should decide to return. Then, on the 18th, the Modocs made a little feint at Gillem's camp. Some shots were exchanged but nothing more.

Within a day or so of this incident, a mixed-blood scout, Donald McKay leading a party of Warm Springs Indian scouts located the Modocs in rough lava flow country only about four miles from their old Stronghold. Here, the terrain was, if anything, even more difficult and treacherous. It would be tough and probably costly to move through this country with infantry. Gillem decided to see if his mortars could not flush the Modocs out of their new stronghold. The campaign was attracting attention, too. Visitors came from afar, curious to see how a war was conducted, reminding one of the spectators that looked on at Bull Run and the Battle of Nashville during the Civil War. Photographers were present, as well. The whole business must have resembled a latter day movie set.

On April 26, Gillem dispatched a scouting party under the command of Captain Evan Thomas with Batteries A and K, 4th Artillery and Company E, 12th Infantry under Captain Thomas Wright. Altogether there were sixty-four officers and men, plus packers who managed the supply train. McKay with a dozen of his Indian scouts was supposed to rendezvous with the column at Hardin or Sand Butte around noon. Thomas's movements could be monitored at least part way by a detachment on Signal Rock near Gillem's base camp.

Thomas's orders were to proceed carefully and not seek a fight unless the Modocs started something. Whether Thomas took his orders a little too literally is not clear, but in any event he seems to have proceeded with little caution. His advance, for example, was not covered by flank guards, which suggests he believed there was little to fear. Reaching Hardin Butte his command lolled about as though on a social outing. It was an invitation to disaster. The Modocs could scarcely believe their good fortune. The ambush, not surprisingly, was a rousing success. Five officers and twenty enlisted men were killed and another sixteen were wounded.

Gillem had not fared well and he must have realized it. When Davis reached Gillem's headquarters on May 2, he did not officially relieve Gillem, but in taking charge himself it amounted to the same thing. Davis found troop morale badly in need of restoration. Poor leadership had sucked the marrow out of their morale. Davis recognized the need to reequip and restore some of their lost élan. While Davis reorganized, the Modocs—numbering some 160 souls—were experiencing a shortage of water, which they sought to alleviate by moving about from one ice cave to another. Jack retained control of the bands, but continued to face challenges to his leadership.

During their shifting about from one cave to another, the army lost track of them for several days. Then on May 7, McKay's scouts located them in the southeastern section of the Lava Beds, an area they had not previously used. Some on Davis's staff questioned the accuracy of the scouts' report. However, when the Modocs suddenly attacked an army supply wagon around Scorpion Point, it confirmed their presence in the area. According to historian Keith Murray, this supply train carried, among other things, a supply of whiskey which the Modocs consumed and enjoyed a thoroughly jolly time, ransacking the wagons and chasing the horses. Later an army patrol managed to recover some of the horses.[26]

Determined to respond quickly, Davis ordered Captain Henry Hasbrouck with Troops B and G, 1st Cavalry and a battery of the 4th Artillery and five days rations to seek out and engage the Modocs. Hasbrouck had not yet fought the Modocs, but he was an experienced leader and Civil War veteran in whom Davis had confidence.

Hasbrouck set out on Friday, May 9. That night, the cavalry and Indian scouts bivouacked at Sorass or Dry Lake. The artillery, oddly, seems to have established camp about a mile distant. The Modocs watched Hasbrouck's movements carefully, and under cover of darkness that night crept close to the soldier camp. Opportunity had once again knocked on Jack's door. A dog belonging to one of the civilian packers sensed the presence of the Indians and alerted its owner who did his best to warn the guard, but just about that time the Modocs struck. The troops stumbled out of their tents and tried to return the fire of the onrushing Indians. In the melee, someone spotted Jack wearing Canby's uniform. Somehow, though, the soldiers recovered their composure. Resistance to the Modoc attack stiffened and suddenly the Indians found themselves on the defensive. On top of this, Hasbrouck had ordered McKay's scouts to work their way around behind the Modocs, who soon discovered they were being fired on from front and flank, but they finally managed to break through McKay's scouts and escape. While it lasted it had been a fierce fight, which cost the Modocs the life of Ellen's Man, one of those who challenged Jack's leadership. Hasbrouck's command suffered several casualties.

In the wake of their defeat at Dry Lake, the Modocs withdrew from the field. After the cremation of Ellen's Man, there was a heated disagreement between Jack and some of the others, particularly the Hot Creek faction which held Jack responsible for the death of Ellen's Man. The outgrowth of this was that Hooker Jim and about thirteen of his followers and their families decided they'd had enough and left. Jack and his followers, meanwhile, moved over to Big Sand Butte.

At this point, Jack had discovered a hard truth, namely that loyalty belongs to the winners. Until Dry Lake the Modocs had come out on top in each clash with the army, but now that they had tasted defeat, Jack's leadership was under fire. There was murmuring in the ranks; resistance did not seem like such a good idea anymore. Suddenly, those who cried for war had changed their tune. Many of those who had urged Jack to murder Canby had grown tired of fighting; a shift in attitude that must have infuriated Jack. They had pressured him to fight and he had agreed; and he was now wanted for murder. The Modocs had lost a number of horses which put a crimp in their mobility. Besides, water was scarce, and irreplaceable ammunition was running low. In all of these conflicts, time and attrition was always the Indians' arch-enemy and so it was now.

While the Modocs dispersed, Hasbrouck regrouped. Mounted patrols fanned out in search of the Indians and on the 18th one of them found Hooker Jim's band. A fight followed with the Modocs suffering several casualties before they were able to escape. Then, four days later, Jim and his followers surrendered to Gen. Davis and offered their services as scouts. In his report to Davis—which he must have genuinely enjoyed writing—Hasbrouck recommended bringing forward all the available cavalry—his own mounts were played out—and more artillery. Davis agreed and directed Colonel Mason to so organize the available forces and proceed in accordance with Hasbrouck's recommendations.

During the next two weeks, Davis sought to bring about closure to this maddening, frustrating Modoc problem. Aided by Hooker Jim's band—they had offered to serve as scouts for the army, perhaps in the hope of receiving consideration—Jack's band was finally located along Willow Creek. Jim attempted to persuade Jack to give up, but he refused, knowing of course that the gallows awaited him. Most of the other Modocs were ready, however, and on May 28, hungry, weary of war and altogether sorry-looking, thirty-seven warriors and their families surrendered. Jack and his family continued their hold-out for a few more days. Finally, on June 3, Captain David Perry's cavalry ended it. Recognizing the futility of further resistance, Jack surrendered. A handful of Modocs remained at large, but the threat they had once posed to settlers in the area was ended.

And so at long last it was finally over. Washington authorized General Davis to convene a military court to try six of the Modocs with murder and criminal behavior. All six were found guilty; however, Grant commuted the sentence of two to life imprisonment. The remaining four, including Jack, were hanged at Fort Klamath on October 3, 1873. Later that month, some 150 Modoc survivors were transferred to Oklahoma's Indian Territory.

Among the Indian wars of the Trans-Mississippi West, the Modoc War occupies a unique niche for two reasons: first, because the extended and convoluted length of negotiations dragged on far longer than with any other tribe or band of Native Americans. Second it was the only Indian war in which a general officer of the regular army lost his life.

III

New Mexico

Prologue: Poco Tiempo

The Land of Poco Tiempo, as one writer described it, translates into Land of "Pretty Soon," a name implying little haste, and indeed much of its landscape conveys a feeling that time is of little importance here. It is as well a land of marked contrasts, from the high peaks of the Sangre de Cristo and Sandia Ranges in the north, to the sun-splashed Upper Sonoran desert country in the south, to the stunning canyon lands in the northwest. And is there a more romantic spot than Santa Fe? Excluding Alaska and Hawaii this was, along with Arizona, the last major land acquisition of the U.S., completing the layout of the forty-eight contiguous states.

The Territory of New Mexico, as defined by the Mexican Cession and the Gadsden Purchase included the present states of New Mexico and Arizona as well as California, Nevada, Utah, and parts of Colorado and Wyoming. Additionally, the western boundary of Texas, after a good deal of wrangling, was permanently fixed at the 103rd Meridian.

U.S. presence in the area was preceded by more than two hundred years of Spanish-Mexican tradition which in turn was preceded by centuries of Native American culture. Thus, by the time the Treaty of Guadalupe Hidalgo (1848) and the Gadsden Purchase (1853) brought the region under U.S. control, there existed a long-standing cultural base to which was now added an entirely new and different civilization.

Spanish settlements had largely been confined to the Rio Grande Valley. The provincial capital, Santa Fe had been founded in 1610, Albuquerque in 1706. Prior to the arrival of the United States, an estimated 40,000 Native Americans resided in the territory, of which perhaps 50 percent could be considered war-like.

Insofar as the various Native American cultures are concerned, the pattern of settlement was somewhat fluid, but mainly found the Navajos west of the Rio Grande, particularly in the northwest, along with Zunis and Hopis. Utes, specifically the Capote and Moache (Muache) bands, together with Jicarilla Apaches also frequented the area, while Mescalero Apaches were found east of the Rio Grande. In the western reaches, in what would later become the Arizona Territory would be found Apaches whose domain also included the southwestern portion of New Mexico Territory.

For two centuries the Spanish had to deal with Indian problems, most of it brought on by their own exploitation of these indigenous people. In 1680, for example, harsh treatment of native people by the Franciscan priests led to the bloody Pueblo Revolt from which Spain did not recover for decades. The attainment of Mexican independence from Spain in 1821 saw little change in the pattern of relationship that had been in place for generations.

In its position as the new authority of the land, the U.S. found itself facing a two-edged challenge: dealing not only with the usual problems posed by Native Americans, but also developing a rapport with the New Mexican population, which was, no doubt, hopeful that the new rulers would put an end to Indian raids, particularly those of the Navajos. The Indians, for their part, thought little of such distinctions.

Commercial traffic between New Mexico—specifically Santa Fe—had been ongoing for more than two decades prior to the official arrival of the U.S. in 1846. Although these traders were largely welcomed by New Mexicans, there were incidents with Indians along the Santa Fe trail and with Spanish authorities after the caravans reached Santa Fe. Trail troubles were usually, though not entirely, the work of Comanches, those fierce Lords of the Southern Plains, as they have been called, who occasionally penetrated as far west as eastern New Mexico Territory, and about whom more will be said later.

Mostly Indian troubles prior to the arrival of the U.S. revolved around the Navajos, but they by no means had a monopoly on mischief-making for the New Mexicans. Here, though, it might be pointed out that this was not a one-way street. New Mexicans, sometimes in company with one or more bands of traditional Navajo enemies, e.g., Utes and Jicarilla Apaches, frequently raided Navajo villages for livestock, and for women and children to be used as slaves.

As we have seen, the Indian wars of the Northwest and California were essentially localized conflicts, unrelated except in a general sense, while those in New Mexico Territory were very much interrelated, which is to say that the regular U.S. Army units when available were usually spread dangerously thin and the department commander was frequently compelled to deal with more than one eruption at the same time.

Between 1846 and 1865, the U.S. military authorities in New Mexico were compelled to deal with the Navajos in the northwest, Utes and Jicarilla Apaches in the north, Mescalero Apaches in the east, and the Gila Apaches in the southwest. The three decades following General Stephen Watts Kearny's 1846 proclamation, saw a mixture of raids, punitive expeditions large and small, and parleys about peace, especially where the Navajos were concerned. Apaches and Navajos had long held up expansion of the Territory. Spanish land grants had become quite meaningless. Insofar as the United States was concerned, of course, these land grants merely complicated the picture of settlement, but it serves to illustrate the impact of Native American activity.

During the decade of the 1850s, the Navajos were unquestionably the most powerful of the three tribes with which Americans were forced to contend. Not only were the Navajos raiders *par excellence*, but like New Mexicans they were superb farmers and sheep herders and therein lay the crux of the problem. Navajos made it a high art to steal sheep—sometimes sizeable herds—from the New Mexicans. Lest it be thought, however, that this was a one-sided relationship, the New Mexicans gave as good as they got; it was a two-way street. Indeed, it might be argued they were as adept at thievery as the Navajos. And both sides were equally ruthless in taking prisoners for slaves. Historian Robert Utley has pointed out that both the Navajos and Apaches were more elusive foes than the better known Plains tribes. And the Navajo homeland with its rugged terrain and scarce water, added immeasurably to the challenge of subjugating them.

By definition, the Navajo name means "cultivated fields," a perfectly appropriate designation typifying their excellence as agriculturalists; as farmers they were at least as good as they were at raiding. Like virtually every Indian tribal group, Navajos referred to themselves collectively as Diné, "the people." Although boundaries of the Navajo homeland were somewhat fluid, their home territory essentially lay west of the Rio Grande and south of present day Colorado. The heart of their homeland was Canyon de Chelly, in present day northeastern Arizona, to which place they migrated, probably about 1775, under pressure from the Spanish in the south, Comanches in the east, and Utes in the north. Here they found a natural fortress-like homeland that proved difficult in the extreme for predatory enemies to inflict serious damage on them in this place.

Navajo Wars

On August 15, 1846, with war rhetoric flowing, Brigadier General Stephen Watts Kearny seized New Mexico for the U.S. and proclaimed from a Las Vegas rooftop that New Mexico now belonged to the United States, but the general was a bit premature here and betting on the come, for war with Mexico had only begun three months earlier and disposition of the region was still two years in the future. Notwithstanding, Kearny made his ebullient declaration, promising New Mexican citizens protection from raiding bands of indigenous people who stole sheep and kidnapped women and children. Kearny wasted no time appointing various civil officials, including Charles Bent (brother of William Bent, founder of Bent's Fort on the Arkansas River).

THE MISSOURI VOLUNTEERS ARRIVE

Whether Kearny appreciated the vast extent of the region for which he accepted responsibility on behalf of the United States is questionable, but probably not. Nevertheless, Kearny was nothing if not confident and an able soldier besides. He did not linger long here. In September, pursuant to orders, he detached part of his command for duty here and headed west to California with the remainder. Of those units left behind, Colonel Edwin Vose Sumner was stationed near Rio Abajo, while Colonel Alexander Doniphan, with his Missouri Volunteers was divided between Santa Fe, Abiquiu, and Ceboletta.

Doniphan once refused to shoot the Mormon leader, Joseph Smith, and others, despite a court-martial order to do so; later the order of execution was rescinded anyway. As an attorney, Doniphan's main duties ostensibly involved functioning more as a civil administrator rather than a soldier. However, during the first four years of American presence in the Territory, military commanders were much too pre-occupied with Indian troubles to do more than pay lip service to civil administration.

Before departing for California, Kearny directed Doniphan to lead an expedition into Navajo country with the object of addressing past wrongs and establishing a peaceful future relationship with the United States. It was to be the first of many such efforts that were to take place during the next two decades.

Sometimes those efforts seemed to quickly dissipate in the high thin desert air. All too often the Army was compelled to respond to Navajo raiders who had stolen sheep and on occasion murdered the New Mexican herders. Lest it be thought that this was all one-sided, there were plenty of instances where parties of New Mexican raiders swept down on Navajo camps and rode off with prisoners to be sold into slavery. Truth be told, it was no more than a continuation of what had been taking place for two centuries.

In the fall of 1846, Colonel Doniphan in company with Lieutenant Colonel Cosgrove Jackson and Major William Gilpin parleyed with the Utes and arrived at an arrangement of sorts, though apparently nothing was put down on paper. In November, Doniphan talked peace with a large gathering of Navajos—said to number several hundred—at Ojo del Oso (Bear Spring).

As would those military leaders who followed him, Doniphan attempted to get the Navajos to understand that all citizens of the territory were now subject to U.S. laws and would be protected, but they must obey those laws. Be it understood, though, that such laws would *not* extend to Native Americans anymore than to Black slaves. The agreement also stipulated that raids on New Mexican villages and herds must cease; as well, all prisoners taken by the Navajos on these raids must be returned. Interestingly enough, no mention seems to have been made of ending the slave trade. Nevertheless a document was signed by a number of Navajos. Signatures on paper or parchment always seemed to satisfy U.S. treaty-makers, never mind that those signing were not empowered to do so, and moreover they had little understanding of what exactly it was they were signing anyway. Indeed, it seems most unlikely that the Navajos even grasped the significance of the transition from Mexican to U.S. rule. They had, after all, been engaged in raiding the New Mexicans for generations and could hardly have been expected to, overnight, change this habit for some abstract concept.

These were the basic ground rules the U.S. authorities sought to establish with the Navajo nation on numerous occasions during the next two decades. That all of these efforts failed to yield lasting results was due entirely to the failure of U.S. authorities to understand the political structure—if indeed it may be described as such—of any Native American tribe. Later, Governor Charles Bent wrote to Secretary of State James Buchanan expressing his doubts that the treaty would last, which proved a moot point at any rate since the treaty was never ratified.

That autumn, Doniphan and his regiment pulled out of the territory under orders to join U.S. forces fighting in Mexico. Doniphan seems not to have considered reporting the results of his parleys with the Utes and Navajos to local authorities. His failure to coordinate activities established an adversarial relationship between the Army and local government that never quite mended. In any case, Doniphan was replaced by Colonel Sterling Price who shortly arrived in Santa Fe with the 2d Regiment of Missouri Volunteers.

Price's Missourians were a wild, unruly, and scurvy-ridden lot. Barely had they arrived in New Mexico when two of their number dispatched to investigate some missing sheep were found full of Navajo arrows. And there was more to come. Price quickly learned how skilled the Navajos were at raiding. Not only did they prey on the herds of New Mexicans, they took a fancy to Price's livestock as well.

In January 1847, the Taos Pueblo Indians, angry over harsh treatment from both Spanish and Mexican governments retaliated in a massacre that resulted in the deaths of many New Mexicans, including Governor Charles Bent before order was finally restored.

In early September 1847, Major Robert Walker, commanding the Santa Fe Battalion of Price's command, set out for Navajo country, bent on chastising the Navajos for breaking Doniphan's treaty, which seems odd since it had never been ratified to begin with. It was the first American expedition against the Navajos; it would not be the last. The general mood of the battalion was cocky and carefree; they would whip the Navajos in a month. Liquor apparently was in abundance, as one private noted that "Nearly every man left drunk."[1]

Crossing the Rio Grande south of Albuquerque, Walker pushed on west. After establishing a wagon camp at Ojo de la Jara, he sent three separate columns out in search of Navajos. Two of the columns found nothing, but the third did have a minor skirmish with some twenty Navajos, of whom two or three were reportedly killed. Walker did manage to reach as far as Canyon de Chelly and though he reported being observed by Navajos from the canyon's heights, there was no contact. With supplies now running low, Walker had no choice but to end the campaign and return to Santa Fe with a small detachment, while the remainder of the battalion remained at Ojo de la Jara where they subsisted on mule meat while awaiting the arrival of a supply train.

As usually happened, raids slacked off during the fall and winter. Colonel Edwin Newby assumed command of the Military Department Number 9—in 1853 it would become the Military Department of New Mexico. He would be the tenth to occupy this billet during the next fifteen years. One of Newby's first official duties was to receive a delegation of Navajo leaders who presented themselves in Santa Fe and requested a peace council. Newby's response was precisely what Doniphan's had been: raids must cease and stolen livestock and prisoners must be turned over to the proper authorities. And the Navajos, as they always did, promised to comply.

The arrival of spring brought on a resumption of raids by both Navajos and New Mexicans, and, predictably, a military response. Accordingly, in May 1848, Newby, with some 200 Missouri and Illinois volunteers, along with a few New Mexican guides, marched west to the Chuska Valley in what is today extreme northeastern Arizona. A few Navajo herders were captured, while others fired into Newby's camp from the surrounding hills. Reasoning that he was not going to accomplish much here, Newby shifted his camp to the shadow of 9,000-foot Beautiful Mountain, southwest of present Farmington. From here he sent out feelers, inviting Navajo leaders to a parley. Some accepted the invitation and on May 20 a treaty of sorts was agreed to, with both sides pledging to return prisoners taken in past raids.

Newby would have no opportunity to build on what he surely regarded as a significant accomplishment, either. In June 1848 Lieutenant Colonel John Macrae Washington, 3rd Artillery replaced Newby as civil and military governor of New Mexico. A second cousin of George Washington, the fifty-one-year-old John Macrae Washington was a West Point graduate and veteran of thirty years' service, including the recently concluded Mexican War. In five years he would die in a freak accident when he was washed overboard during a fierce storm near the mouth of the Delaware River. In the meantime, during that summer of 1848 Washington and all of Santa Fe witnessed jubilant U.S. troops passing through on their way home, following the end of the Mexican-American War.

The winter of 1848–1849 was unusually severe. The Navajos were mainly quiet during the late fall and early winter, but then in February, with total disregard for the terms of Newby's treaty the previous May, they ran off some 8,000 sheep in Valencia County. A detachment of dragoons was dispatched but to no avail. Elsewhere, Jicarilla Apaches along with some Utes also took to raiding, prompting Washington to request Federal troops as well as authorization to enlist four companies of six-month volunteers. Local communities, ever-ready to take action against Indian raiders agreed. These volunteers would be discharged upon the arrival of regular army troops from Fort Leavenworth. Washington stationed detachments at Jemez, Abiquiu and at other key points where it was expected they could provide the quick respond needed. Washington soon discovered that his outlying detachments not only lacked the strength to respond, but were, in his opinion, not even qualified to go campaigning.

Ute and Jicarilla raids continued through the spring. A California-bound wagon train was attacked near Tucumcari, but was driven off by Captain Randolph Marcy, commanding the train's escort. Marcy, who would later become the father-in-law of Union General

George B. McClellan would make his mark on the West as both soldier and explorer, laid out the Marcy Trail, which would later become the Butterfield Overland Stage route. Elsewhere, the Navajos were active, too, stealing sheep and murdering herders.

But the picture seemed to brighten with the arrival in late July of the regular army troops requested by Washington. Unfortunately, many were suffering from the effects of a cholera epidemic that swept across the Plains that summer. The new arrivals included four companies of the 3rd Infantry, commanded by Lieutenant Colonel Edmund Brooke Alexander. Accompanying the troops was one James S. Calhoun a native Georgian. As the first Indian agent in New Mexico, Calhoun's impact would be noteworthy.

Washington, who had intended to resign the department command when the regulars arrived, reconsidered his decision because of the heightened Indian activity. He had also planned to release his volunteers when the regulars arrived, but thought better of that, too, and began assembling a column to operate against the Navajos. Washington now had at his disposal 500 well equipped and well armed troops, plus some artillery that included a large, cumbersome 6-pound field gun and three 12-pound mountain howitzers, packed on mules. Behind all this rolled a wagon train with rations for thirty days.

On August 16, Washington, his staff and two companies of the 2d Artillery set out from Santa Fe, followed shortly by the main body under Lieutenant Colonel Alexander. Accompanying Washington was the new Indian agent Calhoun, together with interpreters James Collins and James Conklin.

Three days later Washington reached Jemez where he was reinforced by one of his outlying detachments—about fifty men—under Captain Henry Dodge, who had elected to name his volunteer company the Eutaw Rangers. The terrain between Santa Fe and Jemez was rugged, forcing Washington to abandon his wagons and rely on pack mules.

Beyond Jemez at least one man in the column found the campaign a rewarding experience. Lieutenant James Simpson, 3rd Artillery and Macrae's Chief Topographical Engineer was under orders to survey the country where practical. Simpson, one of those observant souls to whom we should be forever grateful, maintained a diary that provided a personal view of the expedition. In his diary, Simpson recorded his delight at being able to make the first archeological surveys of what is today Chaco Canyon National Culture Park.

On August 30 Washington, having now reached the Chuska Valley, was approached by a Navajo delegation wanting to talk. Many were colorfully decorated with war paint and naked except for breechclouts, no doubt prompting some to wonder about their intentions. Seemingly, hundreds surrounded the camp. Washington ordered the artillery unlimbered and set up. He informed the Navajos that he had come to punish them for their murders and robberies, but the Navajo head men replied that this was the work of a criminal element over which they had no control. As a gesture, however, they offered to surrender livestock in numbers equal to what has been reported stolen.

The discussion quickly came to a halt when the Navajos refused to return army horses they were alleged to have stolen. Fighting soon erupted. Macrae's artillery swung into action driving the Navajos back into the hills in small groups. Washington's only casualties were a few mules who stampeded away in fright. However, old Narbona, a peacemaker and one of the great Navajo leaders was killed and scalped. Washington broke camp and pressed on, reaching the western end of Canyon de Chelly on September 6. Here, a pair of Navajos were rounded up and brought in to discuss peace, which Washington reminded them they could have simply by returning stolen property as they had agreed to do when they signed Newby's treaty. Mariano, a prominent headman agreed to comply with Washington's terms; a treaty resulted, the first such agreement between the U.S. and Navajos that will subsequently be ratified by Congress. Thus did the campaign end on a satisfactory note. The column returned to its duty stations, having marched 587 miles in 42 days. Washington was pleased with the turn of events. He had recovered several captives and livestock, killed seven Navajos, suffered no casualties himself, and most important, consummated a treaty.

The Ugliest Man in the Army

Having successfully completed a treaty with the Navajos, Washington, returned with head held high, and he would depart on a more or less positive note. There would, however, be a hiatus until his replacement arrived. Washington's successor was a Scotsman, Colonel John Munroe. An artilleryman reputed to be the ugliest man in the Army, Munroe finally marched out of Fort Leavenworth on August 25 with two companies of the 2d Dragoons, commanded by Colonel Charles May. Accompanying the column was a detachment of new recruits for the 3rd Infantry, under Captain William Gordon. Delayed by weather, it was not until October 22 that Munroe was finally able to assume the duties of military governor, an assignment that was not to his liking. Indeed, to put it in the mildest of terms, Munroe hated New Mexico and he would, accordingly, prove to be the least energetic of all the Territory's military governors.

The autumn of 1849 was a busy one in New Mexico, quite apart from Navajo activity. In October, Ute and Jicarilla raiders attacked a wagon train at Point of Rocks on the Santa Fe Trail, killing the wagon master and kidnapping his wife and daughter. Dragoons, guided by Kit Carson, caught up with them a month later, but the wife was killed before she could be rescued. Congress posted a $1,500 ransom to rescue the daughter but she was never found. Significantly, the incident made headlines in the Eastern papers. A year later another war party struck a train near Wagon Mound north of Santa Fe.

In January 1850, Captain Croghan Ker, stationed at Cebolleta with Company K, 2d Dragoons marched toward the Chuskas through snow and under a leaden sky, hoping to rescue two Zuni women reportedly kidnapped by the Navajos. Ker made contact with the Navajos who proved unresponsive. A minor skirmish followed after which Ker returned to Cebolleta empty handed.

Munroe, meanwhile, was fussing about the available resources to protect his department and he had a good point. With only some 600 men he could hardly be expected to police the great vastness of the territory. On another front, Agent Calhoun was fighting his own battle with the Indian Bureau. He argued that it made more sense to confine the hostile bands within the confines of a single reservation. To his way of thinking that made a great deal more sense than trying to whip an estimated 12,000 warriors from four different tribes.

Sandoval

Enter Sandoval, a controversial Navajo figure. Ambitious, cunning, and a fourteen karat opportunist, Sandoval's band was known as the Diné Ana' aii, a separatist group of Navajos who preferred to live apart from their kinsmen. Sandoval's band sometimes raided and plundered and sometimes operated in conjunction with American military units against other Navajos. One was never quite certain whose side Sandoval was on. But ally or adversary, Sandoval and his followers played an important role during the early days of U.S. rule in the Territory.

In the spring of 1850, Captain Ker, who had earlier set out to secure the release of two Zuni women, mysteriously disappeared with twenty-two dragoons. No one knew where he had gone until he surfaced in Santa Fe some weeks later with a rather preposterous story of having escorted a party of Indian traders to the Gila River. His absence was a court-martial offense, but he chose instead to resign his commission, which satisfied army headquarters. With Ker's resignation, command of the detachment at Cebolleta devolved to Lieutenant John Buford, who, a dozen years later, would initiate the critical first day's action at Gettysburg.

The very significant Compromise of 1850 brought a sense of reorganization to the jumbled political and geographical picture surrounding the territory acquired as a result of the Mexican War. Insofar as the Territory of New Mexico was concerned, the Compromise of 1850 resolved another particularly thorny issue involving the location of its eastern boundary. Texas claimed all the land east of the Rio Grande and that presented a problem. Since Texas had come into the Union as a slave state, recognition of this claim meant that slavery would have to be permitted in part of the territory acquired from Mexico. The Compromise of 1850 resolved the issue when Texas agreed to surrender claim to all lands west of the 103rd Meridian, in exchange for the federal government assuming the burden of debts Texas had incurred from its days as a republic.

Insofar as the Native Americans were concerned none of this meant a very great deal; indeed, it would be surprising if they possessed even a rudimentary understanding of the political fall-out. Colonel Munroe received reinforcements to strengthen his department, and since there were rumors of increased Comanche activity in the east the new troops were a welcome addition. The Navajos were said to be rethinking their policy toward Americans, though this did not extend to other tribes—they continued to raid Zuni villages—or the general New Mexican populace as it pleased them. It was hard for the Navajos to now regard New Mexicans as Americans, too, after all this time. Nevertheless, there was more peace rhetoric in the fall of 1850 between the Navajos, Munroe, and Calhoun.

The New Mexicans, meanwhile, had as much trouble thinking of the Navajos in a neighborly way as vice-versa. In November 1850, for example, Ramon Luna, prefect of Valencia County led some 300 volunteers into Navajo country to punish raiders and recover an estimated 2,000 sheep. The volunteers attacked a Navajo village, destroying much corn and seizing fifty captives including women and children, together with an estimated 5,000 head of sheep, horses, and oxen. Retaliation was swift in coming. On the return march, a small party of volunteers who had left the main column were suddenly attacked near present day Grants and wiped out to a man.

By early 1851, newspapers had grown increasingly critical of the Army's seeming inability to do anything about the Indian problem. Governor James Calhoun—he had been appointed territorial governor early in the year—issued a proclamation on March 18 calling for volunteers to serve against the Indians. There would be no compensation, but the men could keep all booty, including women and children captives. It was a traditional thing dating back to the days of Spanish rule.

The proclamation was evidently well received and attracted, among others, one Manuel Antonio Chaves, a prominent surname dating back to 12th century Spain. Thirty-three-years-old at the time Manuel Chaves had been fighting Indians since he was sixteen. He had lost a brother during Luna's expedition the previous fall, which may well have motivated him to answer Governor Calhoun's call. Chaves had offered to raise a regiment, but wanted the federal government to supply arms and ammunition, a demand that the government rejected and Chaves then withdrew his offer, but he would be heard from again.

As spring 1851 came on apace, Munroe began planning a major expedition into Navajo country, mobilizing a mixed force of 400 dragoons and infantry. His objective was to reach

Canyon de Chelly where he knew the Navajos would be underway with extensive planting. As plans progressed, word of the expedition reached Navajos in the Chuska Valley who began their own preparations to receive Munroe's effort. Elsewhere, other bands of Navajos were still talking peace, but like most of these discussions there emerged little of substance. For one thing, not all bands were represented and there remained confusion over the terms of past agreements.

By June, Munroe felt it necessary to postpone his Navajo expedition due to increased Comanche-Apache activity that was threatening the eastern part of the territory around *Bosque Redondo*. In the northeast, there were occasional reports of Indians stealing a steer or two, but mostly such happenings tended to be more of an annoyance than a serious threat, at least during the spring.

Colonel Edwin Vose Bull Sumner

Munroe had not been a particularly energetic department commander and with the increased Indian activity the War Department saw fit to relieve him. Munroe's replacement was one of the more colorful characters in the frontier army. Colonel Edwin Vose Sumner, fifty-four-years-old (he had served out here earlier it will be recalled), was a veteran soldier dubbed "Bull of the Woods" by the men who served under him during the Mexican War for his especially loud voice in combat. Sumner might have been the frontier army's version of World War II's Admiral William F. "Bull" Halsey. Sumner had cultivated an acerbic personality. If his objective was to get on the wrong side of people he was eminently successful.

Sumner left Fort Leavenworth in July at the head of 500 new recruits (some say 600) and ten officers, including one Major James Carleton, who would have a dramatic impact on Indian white relations—especially the Navajos—during the next decade. Sumner reached New Mexico armed with a directive from Secretary of War Charles Conrad to station his troops at outlying posts rather than in towns. Conrad was convinced that stationing troops in the field would better enable them to chastise Indian raiders. Sumner agreed. Santa Fe was a den of iniquity; it was better for the troops if they were stationed away from those temptations of the flesh.

Sumner took the War Department's directive seriously. Garrison troops were moved from the settlements to the outlying frontier, where, in the Bull's view, they would be better positioned to deal with Indian raiders. Sumner's new cordon of defense ranged from just north of the *Jornada* to Mesilla and Santa Rita del Cobre.

During the march west from Fort Leavenworth the troops were beset by an epidemic of cholera that claimed the lives of thirty-five soldiers by the time they reached New Mexico. Having decided to move departmental headquarters away from Santa Fe, Sumner examined several possible sites and finally settled on a location near Mora where work was begun on a new post to be called Fort Union on July 26. At the same time Sumner was also thinking of a Navajo campaign and on August 17 marched out of Santo Domingo Pueblo with four companies of dragoons and two companies of the 3rd Infantry and one of the 2d Artillery, in all, some 350 men and fifty wagons.

Fort Defiance

By the end of August Sumner was at Pescado Springs, where Navajos ran off some of the expedition's mules. Initially the Bull was irate but was mollified somewhat when the mules were recovered the next day. At a place called *Cañoncito Bonito*—about seven miles north of present Window Rock—Sumner found a first rate spot for another military post. The grazing was excellent and indeed, the Navajos had long regarded it as a favorite gathering place. Detaching his wagons and a part of the infantry to begin construction of the new post that would be called Fort Defiance (the soldiers named it Hell's Gate), Sumner took the rest of his command and a mule pack train and struck out for the western entrance to Canyon de Chelly. Barely was he underway, however, when a lone Navajo approached. Selecting him as an emissary Sumner sent a message requesting that two headmen come in for a parley, but the Navajos were wary and when they failed to show, Sumner then gave orders to fire on any Navajos sighted.

Sumner was spoiling for a fight, of that there was no question, but the canny Navajos remained just out of rifle range. Entering Canyon de Chelly, the troops were fired on from the heights. Musket balls, arrows, even rocks rained down on the troops, none of which did any real damage. However, with the arrival of darkness, the Navajos began to appear in larger numbers, compelling Sumner to withdraw to *Cañoncito Bonito*.

Thus, did Sumner's first campaign end on a rather humble note. True, he had suffered no casualties, unless one counts some 300 horses and mules that perished from exhaustion and hunger. Indeed, the loss of so many animals worked a real hardship on Sumner's dragoons; without horses they were nothing more than dismounted infantry. In the light of this, Sumner began considering the possibility of replacing his dragoons with regular infantry. Not everyone took to the idea. Governor Calhoun was greatly disturbed by the thought of having no mounted troops in the department. In fact, he was of the opinion that the needs of the territory called for at least two more mounted regiments. A citizens group requested permission to form a volunteer mounted unit. Sumner agreed and even offered to provide weapons, but there were a couple of caveats: the volunteers could only take the field in support of regular army units and weapons must be returned on demand.

Meanwhile, Fort Defiance was slowly taking shape, but supplies were running low. Muddy river crossings and a snowstorm slowed a supply train to a near halt. In desperation, Major Electus Backus moved most of his garrison eight miles south to a hay-cutting camp, instructing the small detachment that remained behind to burn the buildings when they could hold out no longer.

But then, learning that the supply train was actually coming on, Backus elected to return to the post. However, someone—either Navajo or white—fired the hay camp, and with little forage left for his horses, Backus was faced with the very real possibility that it might be necessary to abandon Fort Defiance anyway, despite the arrival on December 6 of the long awaited supply train, after thirty-four days en route.

During the course of this year 1851, Navajo peace overtures were rejected on four different occasions. Governor Calhoun and Colonel Munroe stipulated that there would be no more talks until the Navajos complied with the terms of the old 1849 agreement, and since the Navajos had thus far failed to show any sign of willingness to accept those terms, the situation appeared to be stuck on hold. However, hope, as always, found a way to sprout anew and it surfaced once again when Governor Calhoun and Colonel Sumner agreed to meet with the Navajos on Christmas Day. Calhoun and Sumner may have been spurred to this action by Major Backus's unauthorized treaty with Zunis and Hopis on October 26.

In any case, on the appointed day Sumner and Calhoun met with an estimated 2,500 Navajos who agreed to remain at peace and further agreed to surrender all New Mexican captives. Much to Sumner's chagrin Calhoun distributed some $3,000 worth of presents.

But the Navajos were on a short leash and Sumner warned them that if they failed to remain at peace, soldiers from Fort Defiance would destroy their crops.

The year 1852 seemed fraught with changes in the Territory. In May, Governor Calhoun, feeling the effects of ill-health, returned home but died near Independence, Missouri, en route. To replace him, President Millard Fillmore appointed William Carr Lane of St. Louis. Then in August, the very able Major Backus left Fort Defiance on an extended leave and in due course would be replaced by Major Henry Kendrick, who had served out here in '49 under Colonel Washington. Kendrick soon concluded that the Navajo policies established by Backus deserved to be continued.

Kendrick soon proved his level-headedness. In October, Sumner arrived at Fort Defiance on an inspection tour. As it happened, a local New Mexican farmer was wounded by a troublesome Navajo. Sumner wanted punishment, but Kendrick calmed him down, arguing that the farmer was not seriously wounded and besides this lone Navajo did not represent the overall tribe, so a serious rift was averted. However, rumors began to swirl about that the local citizenry had it in mind to launch their own punitive expedition against the Navajo. Here was real trouble brewing. Word reached Governor Lane who promptly dispatched Agent Spruce Baird to try and ferret out the origin of the rumor—Sandoval was suspected—and if possible, snuff it out. Baird's mission unearthed nothing, but in any event it mattered not as the rumors turned out to be nothing more than words in the wind. More importantly the Navajos remained relatively quiet.

Winter tended to be a stable period. Conditions were not generally conducive to making mischief, though now and again Indian raiding parties would take the field, as was the case with the Utes and Jicarilla Apaches who were relatively quiet. Anxious to convert them to farmers, Governor Lane had them moved east of the Rio Grande, with agencies at Abiquiu and Taos. Lane was willing to feed them while they made the transition to farming, but was ruled down by the Commissioner of Indian Affairs who said that would be illegal.

With the arrival of spring—May 3 to be exact—five Indians, said to have been Navajos, attacked a sheep camp near Abiquiu and reportedly killed Ramón Martin and one or more sons. However, a second report suggested that the attackers may have been Pueblos, since 300 sheep were left in the pens and Navajos would never have left sheep behind. Governor Lane was determined to find the guilty parties, but the evidence was scanty and confusing. Whether they were Navajos or Pueblos remained a murky point, though increasingly the finger of guilt pointed toward the Navajos, prompting the governor to issue an ultimatum: surrender the guilty parties or the army will take action. Sumner—uncharacteristically it might be noted—challenged him, arguing that it wasn't fair to hold all Navajos responsible for the acts of a few, but Lane was insistent and Sumner finally acquiesced and advised Kendrick to prepare for a movement against the Navajos. Kendrick in turn suggested they employ the rascally Sandoval to meet with the Navajo leaders and warn them that unless they complied with Lane's demands, war would result.

Henry Dodge

Meanwhile, an event of some importance occurred on May 26 when Henry Lafayette Dodge was appointed Indian agent. Forty-three-years-old, grey-eyed and dark haired, Dodge was already an old hand in the territory. Born in Sainte Genevieve, Missouri, as a young man he worked in the lead mines around Dodgeville, Wisconsin, and may have served as a volunteer in the Black Hawk War of 1832. It seems likely that Henry L. Dodge (he reportedly never used his middle name) came west as a member of General Kearny's command and stayed on as a trader. Some thought he knew the Navajos better than any other white man save for Kit Carson. The Navajos called Dodge *Bi 'ee lichii* or Red Shirt, owing to his propensity to wear red shirts.

In yet another political shake-up, on June 26, Lane was replaced as governor by David Meriwether—he would not reach Santa Fe until August 7—and Bull Sumner was temporarily replaced by Lieutenant Colonel Dixon Stansbury Miles. Maryland born, the fifty-eight-year-old Miles had served at Fort Gibson, Indian Territory, and in the Seminole and Mexican-American Wars. Former Governor Lane once described him as a "walking sponge martinet."[2] Miles had enjoyed some success against the Mescalero Apaches in the eastern part of the territory, but he had no knowledge of the Navajos. Eight years later he would be killed by an accidental shell blast at Harpers Ferry, Virginia, at the outbreak of the Civil War. Although lacking former Governor Lane's enthusiasm for chastising the Indians, Miles was nevertheless prepared to take action against the Navajos.

Arriving in Santa Fe from Fort Fillmore—five miles south of Mesilla—Miles sent Henry Dodge west to Fort Defiance with orders for Kendrick. Miles envisioned a two-column approach. Captain Richard "Dick" Ewell, later a prominent Confederate general, was to march to Fort Defiance with fifty dragoons. At Defiance, Major Kendrick was to reinforce the column as he saw fit and assume tactical command of same. From Fort Defiance, Kendrick would march to the vicinity of Shiprock where he was to rendezvous with a second column of forty dragoons under Lieutenant Robert Ransom. The objective, Miles stressed to his field commanders, was to make the Indians understand that they will be punished if they fail to surrender the guilty parties and return stolen livestock.

Miles's campaign got underway from Abiquiu on July 12 when Lieutenant Ransom led Co. I, 1st Dragoons into the field, marching up the north bank of the Chama River to the headwaters of the Rio Puerco, then south to Largo Canyon. During the next three days they met up with only one Navajo but who confirmed that others were in the area. Two days farther on brought contact with a few more Indians near Shiprock. These Navajos claimed the people were frightened of the soldiers' presence and had crossed the San Juan River.

On July 15, following a fifteen-mile march, Ransom made camp among a grove of cottonwoods. Shortly, a large number of Navajos appeared on the surrounding hills. Several headmen, including Archuleta and the legendary Cayetano came in for a parley. The Navajos pointed out that they wanted only peace; that the guilty parties had been surrendered and the stolen sheep had been returned. Ransom was suspicious. Cayetano, then perhaps seventy-eight-years-old had not signed the treaty of 1849 and had been involved in several clashes with American troops.

Although wary of the Navajos' seemingly good intentions, the next morning, Ransom continued his downstream advance for some fifteen miles, until he came across signs of a large herd of sheep. As well, Navajos also begin to appear in large numbers and despite their outward friendliness, Ransom was a trifle nervous and grew more so when Archuleta caused a disturbance, prompting Ransom to secure him as a prisoner. The action resulted in an estimated 400 Navajos moving into the army camp, demanding Archuleta's release. Ransom was in a tight spot here, but he was shrewd enough to bargain wisely. Supplies were running low, so in exchange for half a dozen nice fat sheep, he agreed to release his prisoner. So for the moment anyway, both parties were satisfied. The Navajos soon disappeared and Ransom's troopers lolled about under a blistering sun, fishing at the confluence of the Chaco and San Juan Rivers and awaiting Kendrick's arrival

Even as Ransom was bargaining with the Navajos, Brigadier General John Garland was appointed to command the Department of New Mexico, relieving Colonel Miles. A veteran of the Blackhawk and Second Seminole Wars, Garland was to prove an able department commander. Kendrick, meanwhile, was en route having marched out of Fort Defiance on the 19th with Ewell's Company G, 1st Dragoons, plus an additional twenty-five men from the 3rd Infantry and 2d Artillery. Accompanying was the mercurial Sandoval with a large party armed with lances, bows, firearms, and painted for war.

After four days on the trail, Kendrick reached Ransom's camp on the 23rd, with a change of plan. Ransom was to return to his permanent station at Abiquiu, while he, Kendrick, would continue the campaign alone. Moving west along the south bank of the San Juan River, Kendrick entered and traversed the entire length of Canyon de Chelly. Agent Henry Dodge, accompanying, noted that the Navajos had done extensive cultivating. Some Navajos were encountered who treated the soldiers with great courtesy and deference. It had been a largely uneventful and peaceful campaign, but also one barren of results.

On August 7, David Meriwether reached Santa Fe and prepared to assume his new duties as territorial governor. About the same time General Garland also arrived on the scene to take up his station as military commander of the department.

Governor David Meriwether

Former Governor Lane's strategy for keeping Indian raids to a minimum emphasized providing the Indians with food and encouraging them to focus on farming. Better to spend federal dollars this way, said Lane, but the power in Washington didn't buy his argument. Initially, new Governor David Meriwether liked his predecessor's idea, but as the weeks passed he changed his mind, saying that the policy would cost $50,000–100,000 annually and that was simply unacceptable. Instead, the new governor turned to a more cost efficient program. Meriwether's approach was to persuade the tribes to surrender—extinguishment being the operative word of the day—title to lands that were closest to white settlements. The Indians would then be moved to an area where they would have little or no white contact. In exchange for giving up their land, they would be offered annuities, from which, of course, would be deducted payment for property stolen in raids. Not surprisingly, the Commissioner of Indian Affairs thought this was a capital approach.

On August 31 more than one hundred Navajos, including Zarcillos Largos and Barboncito arrived in Santa Fe accompanied by Agent Henry Dodge, having traveled 250 miles to meet the new governor. En route they stopped in Albuquerque where they were warmly welcomed by General Garland. The Navajos remained in Santa Fe for three days, which proved long enough for Governor Meriwether to be duly impressed with their conduct and appearance.

Through the course of several meetings, Meriwether advised the Navajos that he expected them to live up to the terms of Colonel Washington's 1849 Treaty. In an effort to sweeten the pot, Meriwether said that any Navajos currently being held in captivity would be released so long as specific names were provided. The quid pro quo was that the Navajos would be expected to release their captives; it was all a familiar refrain. The governor then presented medals to six headmen and presents were distributed to the others, after which the Navajos returned to their own country.

In the fall of 1853, Henry Dodge, with Kindrick's blessing, moved his agency from Santa Fe to Fort Defiance. It was probably a good time to make the change, too, as things were relatively quiet and remained that way through most of the winter, although large herds of New Mexican sheep were being grazed in Navajo country. Kendrick and Dodge feared that the proximity of such a target would be too great a temptation for the Navajos to resist; their concern was not unreasonable.

Kit Carson Reports

On January 9, 1854, Kit Carson reported for duty at the Taos Agency as the new agent for the Utes. Shortly thereafter Carson brought in Tierra Blanca or White Earth. One had to look beyond the Ute leader's face to appreciate the inner man, who had but one eye that glared out of a face scarred by smallpox. Governor Meriwether described him as "one of the most forbidding looking beings I ever saw in my life."[3]

February saw a resumption of raids along the Santa Fe Trail by Utes and Jicarilla Apaches. Lieutenant Colonel Philip St. George Cooke, a veteran, full-bearded officer whose daughter would one day marry the dashing Confederate cavalry leader, J.E.B Stuart, was in command at Fort Union near Watrous. Cooke immediately sent a detachment of the 2d Dragoons under Lieutenant David Bell on a chastisement expedition. An Iowan, three years out of West Point, Bell pushed hard and caught up with the Jicarilla raiders on the Canadian River some fifty miles southeast of Fort Union. The two sides parleyed at first, but things soon turned sour followed by a fierce little fight that resulted in the death of war chief Lobo Blanco or White Wolf, one of the top Jicarilla war leaders, along with some twenty warriors. Bell, a crack shot reportedly wounded Lobo Blanco several times, but the Apache refused to succumb until one of Bell's troopers finished him off with a blow to the head with a rock. Soldier casualties totaled five. Interestingly enough, Bell had chanced upon the same raiding party responsible for the 1849 attack on the White wagon train.

March continued to see flare-ups with the Utes and Jicarillas. On the 30th of the month, twenty-nine-year-old Lieutenant John Wynn Davidson with Company I of the 1st Dragoons was ambushed in the Embudo Mountains south of Taos by a war party of Jicarillas under Chacón. The action was furious before Davidson was finally able to extricate his command and withdraw to Taos. Casualties were high: twenty-two killed and thirty-six wounded. It was surely one of the costliest small unit actions in the Western Indian wars.

Learning of Davidson's fight, General Garland promptly ordered Philip St. George Cooke to pursue Chacón's party with his entire force. Cooke wasted no time in taking the field with 200 men. En route from Fort Union, he beefed-up his command by adding thirty-two Pueblo Indian guides and Mexican spies, all under one James Quinn, a thirty-seven-year-old Marylander who had studied law and emigrated to New Mexico back in those first heady days of '46. General James Carleton would later claim that Quinn's scouts were absolutely the best. As a topper, Cooke also hired Kit Carson to guide the column.

Marching through spring snow showers, Cooke's column moved on in pursuit. A dozen years hence, Cooke would be censured for his command leadership at the time of the tragic Fetterman disaster out of Fort Phil Kearny, Dakota Territory, but at this juncture of his career, the colonel was energetic and enterprising and he wanted Chacón. The scouts had no difficulty following the Indian trail ... and for good reason. The wily Chacón made sure he left a visible track. At the Rio Caliente on April 8 Chacón laid an ambush that was, fortunately for Cooke, detected in time by the Pueblo scouts. Still, a brisk fight soon erupted. Cooke sent one detachment under Captain George Sykes and including Lieutenant Sam Sturgis to charge the Indians directly, while a second unit went after Chacón's pony herd. The strategy worked for soon the Jicarillas broke and fled, leaving behind most of their equipage and horses. The Indians reportedly lost five killed and six wounded. Cooke pursued the survivors through the following week before turning back to Abiquiu.

Through April and May, Garland had detachments in the field constantly, pressing the Utes and Jicarillas, but without any significant clashes of arms. June yielded results, however. Major James Carleton at the head of 100 men of the 1st Dragoons, plus Quinn, Carson, and the Pueblo scouts, attacked a Jicarilla camp near 9,600-foot Fisher's (or Fischer's) peak near present Trinidad, Colorado, said to have been named for Captain Waldmar Fischer and sometimes referred to as Raton Peak. Carleton destroyed the camp essentially ending the Jicarilla War, although a few malcontents would continue to be heard from.

On June 29, 1854, Congress ratified the Gadsden Purchase, signed back on December 30, 1853. The territory acquired as a result of this purchase added an additional 30,000 square miles to U.S. sovereignty. Responsibility for maintaining order in this new region devolved to the U.S. Army, who lacked the manpower and resources to take care of the original New Mexico Territory, let alone the addition of the territory from the Gadsden Purchase.

In the west, meanwhile, Major Kendrick was uneasy over Navajo raids on New Mexican sheep flocks, although thus far there had been no major outbreaks. Indeed, the Navajo frontier remained mostly quiet through the summer of 1854. But the potential for trouble was always present and some bubbled to the surface on October 7 when an Army private on a work detail out of Fort Defiance was killed by a well-placed arrow, possibly in retaliation for raping a Navajo woman. Kendrick favored an immediate military response and urged General Garland to move into Navajo country with a strong force. Garland was sympathetic and agreed in principal with Kendrick's recommendation, but most of his resources were concentrated in the northern sector of the department where pesky Jicarillas continued to prove troublesome, notwithstanding Carleton's June victory over the tribe.

Frustrated, no doubt, Kendrick did what he could, which in this case meant issuing a stern warning to the Navajos of the dire consequences that would follow should they fail to turn over the murderer Kendrick was running a bluff here, knowing full well he was in no position to take any real action. What is troubling is the seeming lack of effort to investigate the incident; to try and determine whether the soldier was actually guilty of raping the woman. Here would have been a splendid opportunity to demonstrate to the Navajos that the white man's law was a two-way street.

Nothing happened of course, and a short time later Kendrick, accompanied by Agent Dodge repeated his warning to the Navajos. Perhaps the force of Kendrick's two warnings was convincing, because the Navajos felt compelled enough to turn over one of their number who had been wounded in the leg. Whether or not this was actually the guilty party seems not to have been established. Indeed, one source claims he was not even a Navajo but a New Mexican captive. Guilty or not, Kendrick hanged him at Fort Defiance on November 5. According to one source, the man hung until he was "dead, dead, dead."[4]

Although the New Mexican frontier was punctuated by periods of relative quiet throughout the decade of the 1850s this by no means indicated that Indian troubles were fading away; quite the contrary. Utes and Jicarillas continued to harass fringe settlements and wagon trains. Kit Carson did his best to explain to Washington bureaucrats that with wild game growing ever scarcer, and feeling pressure from the expanding white settlements, the Indians felt compelled to strike out in the name of survival. There were two choices, said Carson: feed and clothe them or exterminate them. Hard choices but they made sense considering the circumstances. Notwithstanding, the government said it couldn't afford the first and no one wanted to think of the second, at least publicly.

General Garland's military department may have been the most difficult to manage in the entire Trans-Mississippi West. Other departments dealt with one or two tribes in a given area. When one spoke of Indian troubles in the Department of Dakota, for instance, the reference was usually made to the Lakota and Cheyenne; in Arizona it was the Apaches, but in the vast sweep of New Mexico Territory, General Garland, his predecessors and successors, had to contend with Navajos in the west, Utes and Jicarilla Apaches in the north, Mescalero Apaches (and occasionally Comanches) in the east, and the Gila Apaches in the southwest.

JORNADA DEL MUERTO

With things relatively quiet on the Navajo frontier and with his detachments pressuring the Utes and Jicarillas, Garland turned his attention to the Mescaleros who stole 2,500 sheep from a ranch on the Pecos River. They were known to swoop down on travelers plying the *Jornada del Muerto* (Journey of the Dead Man), a dreaded hundred-mile stretch of waterless desert basin east of the Rio Grande between Las Cruces and Socorro. Christened by the early Spanish, a journey across this stretch could take a week or longer. During the Pueblo Revolt of 1680, Spanish settlers fled southward to escape the wrath of the Indians. It was said that of the 2,000 who left Socorro, only 1,200 survived the trek to El Paso del Norte. The barren, sun-scoured stretch remains as waterless and inhospitable today as it did three centuries ago.

Detachments had twice been sent from Fort Conrad near Socorro but accomplished nothing. Now Garland decided on a two-pronged effort. One mixed column of infantry and dragoons under Captain Henry Stanton marched from Fort Fillmore near Mesilla, while a second under the balding and cantankerous Captain Richard "Dick" Ewell left Los Lunas south of Albuquerque and rendezvoused with Stanton's command in the Capitan Mountains near present Ruidoso on January 13. Actually, this effort to punish the Mescaleros transcended departmental lines, as two columns of troops from the Department of Texas were also in the field. One, under Major James Longstreet marched from Fort Bliss and a second under Major John Simonson left from Fort Davis. Both Dick Ewell and James Longstreet were future Civil War luminaries.[5]

Neither Longstreet nor Simonson enjoyed any success, but Ewell and Stanton, however, marched up the Peñasco Valley—in the vicinity of present Artesia—harassed by Indians the entire way. On the afternoon of January 14, 1855, while on a scouting mission, Stanton with a dozen men was ambushed by Mescaleros. Stanton himself was killed before the detachment was able to withdraw. Not only that, but the ambush bought the Indians time for their families to escape. Discouraged by this turn of events, Dick Ewell elected to return to the Rio Grande.

A week later, Lieutenant Sam Sturgis, leading a command of eighteen dragoons and six civilian volunteers, caught up with a Mescalero raiding party southeast of Santa Fe on a bitterly cold 19th day of January. These particular Mescaleros had attacked a ranch near Santa Fe, raped the women (the report does not say how many), killed two herders, and made off with seventy-five horses. How many Indians were in the raiding party is unknown, but Sturgis attacked and in the ensuing fight reportedly killed three and wounded four others. Among those killed was the militant Santa Anna—no relation to the victor of the Alamo. Four dragoons were wounded and the stolen livestock recovered.

By spring, the Mescaleros were wearying of the steady pressure by the Army, specifically Dick Ewell, who tried to be as relentless as resources and circumstances permitted. The Mescaleros were ready to talk peace, but Garland decided to keep the pressure on. To that end he directed Lieutenant Colonel Dixon Stansbury Miles to form a strong column composed of 300 men from the 3rd Infantry and lead it on one final campaign.

On April 2, Miles located the Mescalero camp in the rugged Sacramento Mountains near present Alamogordo. Before he could attack, however, the Indians approached, wanting to talk peace. Miles was sorely tempted to launch one last strike but finally relented and promised to present their request to General Garland, and there things stood for the moment.Garland wished for an excuse to take further military action. These Indians had a habit of raiding and looting and then when you took after them they were ready to talk peace, but how could he justify taking action, particularly since Governor Meriwether had recently been advised by the Indian Office that he had been vested with the authority to discuss terms, not only with the Mescaleros, but with the Mimbreño Apaches, Utes, and Navajos as well.

Armed with this new authority, the governor's first step was to sign a treaty with the Mescaleros at Fort Thorn, some thirty miles north of Las Cruces. For Meriwether, this was just the beginning. On July 17, he and Garland held a council with the Navajos at Laguna Negra, about a dozen miles north of Fort Defiance. As with previous meetings, the terms of this agreement stipulated the two primary conditions: surrender of those guilty of crimes, and restoration of stolen property. This meeting was particularly significant in that most of the major Navajo leaders were present. Meriwether proposed to set aside some 7,000 square miles as a Navajo reservation; a huge chunk of land equal in size to the states of Massachusetts, Connecticut, and Rhode Island, but when one considers that this amounted to less than a third of their original territory the proposed reservation seems much less impressive. This council was also significant in that it marked the emergence of Manuelito as a leader of growing importance. Twice Manuelito voiced his objection to the governor's proposal, but he was overruled as twenty-seven Navajo leaders signed the treaty.

On the face of it this would seem to stand as a watershed in Navajo-white relations, but truth be told neither side apparently regarded the agreement as binding, perhaps because earlier treaties had fallen aprt, so why should this be any different? And there was one more thing: neither side had as yet developed a clear understanding of the other. The two cultures were worlds apart. Indians—Navajo or otherwise—never understood the white man's concept of land ownership and the political structure of his society. As for these Navajos that Meriwether and Garland were attempting to come to terms with, it was a virtual impossibility, given the present circumstances. The Navajo tribe, for example, was structured in such a way as to allow raiders to roam and rob freely, and it was these bands that caused the headaches for U.S. authorities, to say nothing of the New Mexican population in general. These raiders operated beyond the pale of tribal leaders. Thus, in demanding that tribal leaders surrender these raiders was asking for something that was beyond their power to give. Few government officials or military leaders ever quite grasped that fact.

Notwithstanding the foregoing, Governor Meriwether felt pretty good about his treaty, mainly because all of the leaders who signed, were, to his understanding, authorized to speak for—sign—this agreement, thereby giving his treaty force that others lacked. Perhaps he would have been a bit less enthusiastic had he known what the future held for his treaty, one of six, that he would broker, of which none would ever be ratified by Congress.

But some things it seemed would never change. With the arrival of spring 1856 Navajo raiders struck a sheep camp west of the Puerco River, killed the herders and reportedly made off with several thousand sheep. This was followed by a second raid on a camp at Peralta, where they added several thousand more sheep to their own herds. Meriwether and Garland, not surprisingly, were furious. Meriwether demanded that the Navajo raiders be turned over for punishment in accordance with the recently concluded terms agreed on at Laguna Negra, but the Navajos stubbornly continued to refuse. Garland wanted to launch an immediate punitive strike and was only prevented from doing so by a lack of troops. Why on earth the governor imagined that the Navajos would now agree to do what they had always refused to do in the past is puzzling to say the least. In any case, Meriwether continued to press the Navajos who eventually extended an apology that was accepted, not too graciously, we might imagine, by the governor and his military commander. Garland's inability to retaliate swiftly may well have served to convince the Navajos that the United States was unable to back up its tall words.

Meanwhile, Henry Dodge, who had been in Santa Fe on business when the latest round of raids took place, rushed back to Fort Defiance where he and Major Kendrick rounded up all the Navajo headmen they could find and met again at Laguna Negra on May 31. Right away, though, things got complicated. Ten days before the scheduled meeting, Navajo raiders made off with some 400 sheep between Cochiti and Santo Domingo, killing three herders in the process. When word reached Garland, he was set to take the gloves off and advised Governor Meriwether that he was thinking of a July-August campaign and wished the governor to raise three companies of volunteers.

When Dodge and Kendrick reached the council site on the 31st, they found far fewer Navajos than were present at their last gathering. And those who did show up appeared despondent. On the brighter side, they did bring along several hundred sheep and a few horses, hoping this gesture would keep the soldiers from attacking their villages. As well, the Navajos tried a little sleight of hand, trying to pass off a trio of Mexican captives as the murderers Meriwether and Garland sought. But the ruse was soon discovered.

Dodge and Kendrick laid it on the line. Abide by the terms they had agreed to or there would be war. Simple as that. But there was a complication, naturally, because some of the raiders were apparently members of prominent families and so it was a touchy situation. Nevertheless, the Navajos insisted they wanted peace. The hang-up of course was that the Navajo leaders were unable to control these raiders, let alone turn them over to U.S. authorities. And then a new factor was introduced into the equation when Dodge discovered that some of the Navajos were being armed with good weapons by Mormons who urged them to drive the *Bilagáana* from their land, claiming that the Americans would soon want all the land. Although there is no hard evidence as to Mormon complicity, there was a belief that a few individuals may have been guilty of the allegation, as opposed to all Mormons in general.

The talks were getting nowhere, especially when Manuelito stepped forward and haughtily declared that Navajos had been killing New Mexicans for a long time and there was nothing the Americans could do about it. And that's the way things ended. Manuelito was right; there was nothing Kendrick could about it. Wisely the major chose not to press further for the surrender of the guilty parties. Disappointed exhausted, and probably a bit disillusioned, Kendrick and Dodge returned to Fort Defiance.

Kendrick, who likely knew the Navajos about as well as any American army officer, recognized that compliance with Meriwether's demands was simply never going to happen. The way Kendrick saw it, war was certain to result, so preparation was the operative word here. In expressing his views to General Garland, Kendrick pointed out that small expeditions accomplished nothing. He recommended six columns of mounted troops, 150 men each to be sent into the Navajo country. "Better to have a large and short war than a small and long one," said he.[6]

Garland agreed with the major's assessment, but he was also practical enough to appreciate that the Navajos could put some 2,000 warriors in the field if they choose to do so and he could not afford to strip his department in order to mount the kind of expedition Kendrick recommended. That said, he directed Kendrick to recover as many sheep as possible, while continuing negotiations to secure the surrender of the prisoners. The idea of course was to stall until such time as Garland was able to assemble a strong enough force to convince the Navajos to give in. By fall, however, it was clear that Garland's plan for a big campaign was a pipe dream. Short of troops to begin with, he now lost the 1st Dragoons, some to Arizona, but most to California. Eventually, these were to be replaced by a regiment of mounted riflemen, but no one knew when that might be.

Farther west, meanwhile, the addition of those lands acquired through the Gadsden Purchase compelled Garland to divert some of his attention to that quarter. South of Navajo country was the realm of the Gila Apaches. The agent for the Gila Apaches was thirty-seven-year-old Michael Steck, a graduate of Jefferson Medical School in Philadelphia. Steck had served as a contract surgeon with the Army in New Mexico from 1849 to 1851. His work with the Indians of New Mexico prompted no less an authority than Henry Schoolcraft and the Commissioner of Indian Affairs to recommend he be appointed agent. A dedicated and thoroughly professional man, Steck was accordingly appointed agent for the Mimbres and Mescaleros in May 1854. His predecessor, Edward H. Wingfield, somewhat of an idealist where Indians were concerned, had departed under a cloud. Few men were truly qualified to assume the mantle of responsibility that came with the office of Indian agent. Wingfield had not met the criteria; Michael Steck would.

Chandler-Eaton Expedition

Although white presence in the country of the Gila Apaches had not yet become a *casus belli* for the Gilas, some of these bands, notably the Mogollons (Muggy-owns) did occasionally raid the New Mexican settlements along the Rio Grande, prompting Garland to take action. In March 1856, two columns of dragoons and infantry took the field. One column of 100 men under Lieutenant Colonel David Chandler, marched from Fort Craig, south of Socorro. Chandler's column penetrated the rugged Mogollons from the north, while Lieutenant Colonel John Eaton approached the area from Fort Thorn, near Hatch. Rendezvousing on the Upper Gila River, they struck an Apache camp, killing some of the inhabitants and recovering several hundred stolen sheep.

On his return march, Chandler located and attacked a second camp, which, unfortunately, proved to be a friendly Mimbrés rancheria that had expressed a desire to participate in Agent Steck's agricultural program. It was a mistake of the first order. A number of women and children were killed before Chandler was able to call off the attack. Amazingly, the Apaches accepted the colonel's apologies but the damage was done. Chandler was mightily chagrined, but the miscue had happened on his watch and repercussions were felt in Washington. Thus, did the campaign close on an ignominious note.

The Chandler/Eaton expedition was at once both a tactical success and a political embarrassment. Notwithstanding, it did little to discourage mischief on the part of the Mogollons who persisted in raiding ranches along the Rio Grande through the summer and fall of 1856, stealing thousands of sheep.

Thus it was that the Gila Apaches promptly became suspects when Agent Henry Dodge disappeared while on a hunting trip near Haashk'aan Sila Mesa and was surprised, apparently by a party of Apaches. Agent Steck enlisted the services of the powerful Mimbréno leader, Mangas Coloradas to act as an intermediary to retrieve Dodge from the Mogollons, who Steck was certain were holding Dodge for ransom (some said it was Coyoteros another name for the Western Apaches). As it turned out, however, Steck was disabused of that notion after a month's search revealed nothing, and Mangas could only offer his opinion that Dodge had been slain. Not until February 1857 did a detachment out of Fort Defiance stumble across the missing agent's remains. No one could truthfully say who was responsible for Dodge's murder, but the finger of guilt had pointed toward the Mogollons for so long that guilt was confirmed by the passage of time.

Henry Dodge's loss was keenly felt. It was thought by some that if Dodge had lived nine years of war with the Navajos would have been avoided. His scalped remains were brought back to Fort Defiance where he was laid to rest with full military honors. Whether Dodge's murder might have been a backlash from Colonel Chandler's unfortunate raid the previous spring is problematical, but the nagging question is inescapable.

Colonel Benjamin L.E. Bonneville

Regardless of who perpetrated Dodge's murder, Colonel Benjamin L.E. Bonneville, filling in as department commander for General Garland who had departed the territory on leave back in October, believed them to be Mogollons and wasted little time preparing to strike back. Sixty years old in 1856, Bonneville had become something of a minor legend in the Army. Born in France and a West Point graduate, Bonneville had led a caravan west out of Fort Osage in the spring of 1832, on what was purported to be a private fur trade adventure, for which he had been granted a two-year leave of absence. That was the face of it and it was true as far as it went, but the colonel was also under orders to report on the country and its inhabitants, and to assess the British presence in the Oregon country. The story got complicated, however, when Bonneville overstayed his leave by a year and was subsequently dropped from the rolls of the Army. He persevered, however, made a case for himself, and was eventually restored to duty. Now, as colonel of the 3rd Infantry he was seen by his subordinates as something of a bald, rotund, comic figure, an image he would shortly put to rest.

With the arrival of spring 1857, Bonneville's units took the field. Dubbed the Gila Expedition, the participating troop units staged at Albuquerque and Fort Fillmore near Mesilla. One column, led by one-armed Colonel William Wing Loring marched southwest out of Albuquerque with three companies of his own Mounted Rifles and two companies of the 3rd Infantry, about 300 men in total. A detachment of Pueblo scouts under Captain Manuel Chavez completed Loring's column. A seasoned veteran, Loring, called "Old Blizzards," had seen action against the Seminoles in Florida and had lost an arm at Chapultepec. In just a few years, he would serve as a major general in the Confederate Army, and following the Civil War would serve under the Khedive of Egypt.

While Loring headed southwest, Colonel Dixon Miles with three companies from the 1st Dragoons, plus two companies from Loring's regiment of Mounted Rifles, together with a battalion of the 3rd Infantry and one of the 8th Infantry, moved west from Fort Fillmore with Bonneville accompanying. Bonneville was the architect of the campaign, but as General Garland had resumed command of the department by this time, Bonneville would have a first-hand opportunity to see how his strategy unfolded.

By early May, Bonneville and Miles had established a supply depot along the Upper Gila River, while Loring worked his way through the Mogollon Mountains, a rugged country of deep canyons. Meanwhile, some of the officers grumbled that neither Bonneville nor Loring, particularly the former, had any idea what they were doing.

But the picture was about to change. Loring, perhaps a bit intimidated by the rugged nature of the terrain confronting him, and especially given their lack of success to date, seemed hesitant, but Manuel Chavez urged him to press ahead; give the Apaches no respite, said Chavez; it was the only way to get the job done, and Loring, wisely accepted his head scout's advice. Chavez, reportedly descended from a de Vargas Conquistador, was smaller in size than even Kit Carson, no physical giant himself. But Chavez was said to be a tough scrapper and a man who knew how to fight Indians.

Accordingly, with Chavez and his scouts ranging out ahead, following whatever sign the Apaches left, Old Blizzards drove his column on a grueling march, which paid dividends when, on May 25, the scouts located an Apache camp in one of the many canyons in these mountains. In the pre-dawn hours, Loring advanced to the canyon rim. Again, following the advice of Chavez, who counseled against dividing the column, as some of Loring's officers urged him to do, Loring launched a straight ahead attack on the Apache camp, leaving only a detachment on the rim to provide cover if needed. Like Ranald Mackenzie's attack on the Comanche village at the bottom of Palo Duro Canyon two decades later, Loring's attack caught these Apaches completely by surprise. Most of the inhabitants scattered, but eight were killed including the notorious Mimbres chief, Cuchillo Negro (Black Knife), who unfortunately had recently expressed an interest in adopting Agent Steck's agricultural program. Additionally, Loring also captured some 1,500 sheep, plus all of the Apache supplies.

Meanwhile, even as Colonel Loring was winding up his attack, the column of Colonel Miles, some 600 strong, struck a Coyotero Apache camp along the Gila River, not far from Mt. Graham, near present Safford, Arizona. As historian Robert M. Utley describes it, the "fight was short and sharp," a quite complete victory. Some forty warriors were reportedly killed and forty women and children were taken captive. Army losses amounted to two officers and seven enlisted men wounded. The completeness of the victory also managed to restore Bonneville's reputation among his subordinates. In the aftermath, Agent Steck was able to show that these were the Indians who had murdered Henry Dodge. How exactly he was to determine this was not made clear, but in any event, if true, a small irony, perhaps, but for once the Mogollons were absolved of guilt.[7]

While Bonneville was enjoying some measure of success against the Apaches, spotty Navajo raids persisted. The blame of course, fell on Governor Meriwether, who urged Congress to set limits on tribal movements. They should be confined to the reservations he established in his treaties of 1855, which he also pointed out had yet to be ratified. As a postscript, Meriwether reminded Congress that there was much land that will not be available for settlement until the Indians are relocated.

Major Kendrick, who on occasion seemed to evince some sympathy for the Navajos did not regard these raids and thievery as a big problem. He thought the New Mexicans ought to be required to graze their flocks farther from Navajo country, so as not to invite raids. Notwithstanding, Kendrick also saw fit to advise his superiors that the Navajos could field 3,000 warriors (a thousand more than General Garland had estimated) and believed themselves capable of whipping the American soldiers. In view of the fact that the Americans seemed incapable of backing up their threats, he suggested a select group of Navajo headmen be taken east where they could be exposed to a demonstration of U.S. might.

But Kendrick's service out here was drawing to a close. About the time Colonel Loring was preparing to attack the Apache camp of Cuchillo Negro, Kendrick accepted a teaching assignment at West Point. He had been in command at Fort Defiance from the outset, since September 1852. Kendrick's departure, along with Henry Dodge's murder put a real crimp in Navajo-American relations. Kendrick and Dodge had worked tirelessly to avoid conflict with the Navajos. What was going to happen now remained to be seen.

Kendrick's replacement was Major William Gordon, a Virginian who had served on Kendrick's staff at Fort Defiance and was familiar with the situation. Times were changing in New Mexico. Kendrick wasn't the only one to depart. Governor Meriwether decided he'd had enough and resigned, returning to his native Kentucky. Meriwether's replacement was one Abraham Rencher, a lawyer from North Carolina and a loyal Democrat and who had served for a time as minister to Portugal. To complete the changes, James L. Collins was appointed Superintendent of Indian Affairs for the Territory. Previously, this position had been under the governor, but now became an independent office.

A severe drought in Navajo country during the spring of 1857 worked a real hardship on both the Navajos as well as the garrison at Fort Defiance. Back in November Kendrick and Dodge had hammered out an agreement with a Navajo headman named El Gordo (the Fat one) to use a large tract of land near the fort as a hay field. As this unusually dry spring rendered other Navajo lands unsuitable for grazing the Navajos moved their herds to the area reserved by Kendrick and Dodge. The Navajos claimed the pact was invalid because El Gordo lacked the authority to enter into such an agreement. Had there been no drought, the hay field would likely never have become an issue, but history sometimes turns on such caprices of nature and this was one of those occasions. Kendrick's replacement, Major William Gordon, disagreed and promptly dispatched Lieutenant J. Howard Carlisle with thirty men and a pair of field pieces to see that the Navajos departed, using force if necessary. That was well and good except that when Carlisle reached the area he was confronted by several hundred mounted Navajos, well armed and ready for trouble. The lieutenant informed the Navajos that they must leave, but when they stood their ground, Carlisle wisely withdrew to the fort where he unexpectedly found himself in command of the post, as Major Gordon, who had a drinking problem, declared himself indisposed.

When word of Carlisle's experience with the Navajos reached department headquarters, General Garland, sensing big trouble in the offing, ordered Colonel Loring out to assume command at Fort Defiance. Lieutenant Henry Clitz with G Company, 3rd Infantry was also dispatched to reinforce the post. Quite likely, Garland's decision was also influence by Gordon's problem with the bottle. Other duties prevented Loring from immediate compliance, but Lieutenant Clitz arrived at Defiance on July 19, by which time Major Gordon had recovered sufficiently from his indisposition to resume command, though it would not be for long.

On August 27, Loring finally arrived to assume command. The strength of the garrison now increased to 300 men and that apparently gave the Navajos pause, for they soon returned some stolen livestock, and insofar as Loring could tell, seemed peacefully disposed. When he reported same to headquarters, General Garland advised him that he could withdraw his command as soon as the Navajos surrender the hay field. Manuelito, Gordo, and Largos assured Loring that the Army's property would be respected.

Loring was convinced and pulled his command out of Fort Defiance in mid-September, leaving Lieutenant Clitz temporarily in command, as Major Gordon was currently under arrest and awaiting court-martial. Gordon's own command—Company H, 3rd Infantry—had been transferred out of the post as well and was subsequently replaced by Captain John Hatch, Company I, Mounted Rifles.

The fall of 1857 saw yet another change as the post of agent to the Navajos that had been vacant since the death of Henry Dodge was filled by one William Harley a Mississippian. The drought, meanwhile, continued to work a real hardship on both the Navajos and the Army which was forced to send some of its livestock to Albuquerque for forage.

In October, new Superintendent of Indian Affairs James Collins toured Navajo country and saw firsthand the effects of the drought. He found the Navajos to be peacefully disposed and was impressed. To what extent Navajo behavior was influenced by the drought is difficult to say, but in any case, Collins liked Kendrick's old idea of sending a delegation to Washington. However, when he broached the idea to the Navajos he found them only mildly interested. Had Collins lingered in the area a little longer he would have been present when a delegation of Coyotero Apaches, at Agent Steck's suggestion, approached Lieutenant Clitz, appealing for the release of their people who had been taken captive during Loring's campaign and were currently being held as slaves by Sandoval's band. Clitz could do nothing more than kick the idea upstairs to Garland, who in turn passed it on to Collins who was then in Washington. Interestingly enough, at about the same time Sandoval was in Albuquerque ostensibly talking to Colonel Bonneville about the release of members of his band who had been seized by Utes, while Sandoval and the remainder of his band was off fighting Apaches. Sandoval wasn't the only one. The Navajos, generally, complained about Ute raids, claiming that the Utes were killing Navajos with ammunition obtained at the Ute agency in Abiquiu, ostensibly to be used in hunting.

Fortunately for Henry Clitz, he was relieved of the responsibility of dealing with situations like that presented to him by the Coyoteros when he was relieved of command at Fort Defiance on November 26 by Major William Brooks, a handsome, by-the-book soldier who brought along with him a Black slave named Jim who was soon to have an effect on Navajo-white relations at Fort Defiance.

With the arrival of 1858, Superintendent of Indian Affairs, Sam Yost, acting on behalf of James Collins who was still in Washington on official business, persuaded General Garland to try and broker a peace agreement between the Navajos and Utes. Yost, a veteran newspaperman was accustomed to working with Collins and indeed was still editor of the Collins owned *Santa Fe Weekly Gazette*. Kit Carson agreed to cooperate with the peace effort, but was doubtful that anything would come of it. The tribes had been enemies for too long and that kind of enmity doesn't end with a simple conference. Notwithstanding, U.S. officials persisted in believing they could bring about a peaceful resolution to the ongoing conflict between these tribes. What they failed to realize and what Carson understood all too well was that these raids were a deeply embedded part of each tribe's culture and ending it was not quite the same thing as the U.S. negotiating a peace settlement with a foreign power. U.S. officials never really grasped the fact that ending an on-going "war" between two tribes, whether Navajo and Utes or others, meant a dramatic change in the culture of each tribe.

Warfare provided opportunities for personal achievement; the increase of wealth, both personal and tribal, through captured horses, weapons, and anything else of value. Captives taken in raids strengthened the tribal labor pool and replaced warriors lost in raids, or non-combatants taken captive during raids by other tribes. Thus, ending a war that had been ongoing for generations meant a complete change in the tribal way of life.

In April 1858 there occurred yet another terrible and totally unnecessary incident that might have led to far more tragic consequences, when a local militia group, dubbed the Mesilla Guard, attacked a Mescalero Apache camp practically in the back yard of Steck's agency. Before it was over, seven Apaches—men, women, and children—had been killed and several others wounded. An army detachment under Lieutenant William Woods Averell responded quickly, but not in time to prevent the massacre. Even so they managed to capture the attackers who were in the process of withdrawing, taking with them several Apache children. The attackers were imprisoned and later sent to Socorro for trial, where they were subsequently acquitted. The territorial governor later congratulated the group.

During April and May 1858, even as General Garland and Acting Superintendent Yost were attempting to broker a peace agreement between Navajos and Utes, the situation at Fort Defiance was deteriorating over the continuing misunderstanding about use of the hayfield. The Army believed it had negotiated an exclusive use agreement. The Navajos, on the other hand, largely led by Manuelito, continued to argue that the agreement was invalid. Major Brooks dismissed their claim out of hand. Each meeting between Manuelito and the major grew more heated; neither side would back down. During one session, the Navajos handed over a cane and medal presented to Manuelito three years earlier. Manuelito now claimed these were no longer respected icons of authority and attempted to return them, but Brooks haughtily refused to accept them. Both men were hard-liners. Interestingly, Colonel Loring acknowledged that the Navajos did have a point; that Manuelito was partly right. It was a no-win situation, out of which would eventually emerge eight years of war.

At any rate, Major Brooks, apparently feeling the need to back up his words, sent Captain George McLane and eighty-one men to drive off any Navajo stock he found grazing on the hayfield. The thirty-four-year-old McLane was the son of a former senator and congressman from Delaware, who had been Secretary of the Treasury in Andrew Jackson's cabinet. McLane was full of charm, dash, and energy, and had been cited for bravery during the Mexican War.

When McLane arrived at the hayfield, the Navajos opened fire and were subsequently driven off in what turned out to be a fairly brisk little fight until McLane himself was wounded. McLane destroyed what livestock he found, but just to be sure the Navajos did not return with another herd, he remained on the scene for three hours before returning to Fort Defiance, incidentally, bringing along the cane and medal which the fleeing Navajos had apparently left behind.

The furor over the hayfield did not prevent Navajo headman, Zarcillos Largos from doing what he could to broker a peace agreement with the Americans; it was symptomatic of the confused relationship that existed between the Navajos and the Americans. In any event, Major Brooks saw here an opportunity and presented the medal and cane to Largos, declaring him to now be headman of all the Navajos. Brooks had no illusion that this gesture to Largos would result in any meaningful development but the gesture couldn't hurt. As it was he remained very much concerned over the possibility of an uprising—indeed, thought war to be inevitable.

The Black Jim War

Garland shared his subordinate's concern and ordered Lieutenant William Woods Averell with Company F, Mounted Rifles to march from Fort Craig to Fort Defiance immediately. Averell reached the fort around the middle of July 1858, a particularly tense time as it turned out, owing the killing of Major Brooks's slave, Black Jim, who took an arrow in the back and died four days later. The motive behind Jim's murder is unclear. In any event, Brooks immediately huddled with Largos who proved less cooperative, we might imagine, than the major expected, given his earlier treatment of the Navajo headmen. There were bones of contention. Largos pointed out that Manuelito still had not been reimbursed for the loss of his livestock, but Brooks, playing hardball, declared that no payment would be made until the killer of Black Jim was brought forward, else there will be war. Once more, tall words filled the air. One historian has suggested that the murder of Black Jim was the incident that triggered the war; the *casus belli*. Evidence as to the killer's identity seemed to point to Cayetano, who, unfortunately, was related to Manuelito and that of course complicated the politics of the situation.

On July 31, Collins advised the United States Commissioner of Indian Affairs, Charles E. Mix, that war seemed likely and that he supported General Garland and Major Brooks. Collins was evidently pleased with Yost's contribution and appointed him agent to the Navajos, Hopis, and Zunis and sent him out to Fort Defiance with a dual mission: he was to cooperate with the Army, but he was also instructed to confer with Navajo leaders and seek a peaceful solution. In issuing these instructions to Yost, Collins appears to have believed that peace might still be had, even though the wheels of war were already turning.

When Yost reached Albuquerque, he found a major campaign forming. It would be the largest of its kind to ever march against the Navajos. Command of the expedition had been given once again to Lieutenant Colonel Dixon Miles, who, it will be recalled, had commanded a column in Bonneville's Apache campaign, but who appeared to have little enthusiasm for this particular assignment and thus seems an odd choice to command the expedition.

The campaign got underway with Captain George McLane starting out ahead of the main body with the supply wagons and accompanied by Agent Yost. The young captain pushed the supply train and twelve-man escort hard, ripping off fifty miles in one day. En route, he was joined by Blas Lucero's fifty-man contingent of New Mexican scouts and guides. McLane was under the impression that Major Brooks's ultimatum to the Navajos had been ignored and that a state of war existed, or so he claimed.

Approaching Ojo del Oso, a traditional Navajo camping spot, McLane decided to attack the encampment he had discovered here. Leaving half of his escort with the wagons, hidden among a grove of trees, he took the remainder of his escort—six men—plus Lucero's scouts and struck the unsuspecting Navajo camp. It quickly turned into another of those swift little scraps, lasting perhaps a quarter of an hour. The Navajos quickly scattered, but not without returning the fire of their attackers. Several Navajos were killed and some taken prisoner. McLane was hit in the chest and carried off to Fort Defiance where he eventually recovered.

Miles learned of McLane's attack on the Navajo camp on August 31, en route to Fort Defiance, and was not at all happy about it, feeling that McLane had exceeded his orders. Miles arrived at the fort two days later, probably still brooding a bit over McLane's unauthorized attack. Nonetheless, he wasted no time setting up a meeting with key Navajo leaders. Whether angry or fearful because of McLane's attack is hard to say, but few of the leaders presented themselves, which gave Miles further reason to be piqued. Only the ever unprincipled Sandoval and a few others saw fit to comply with Miles's request for a parley. Nevertheless, to these, Miles made it clear that if the murderer of Black Jim was not given up, he would destroy all Navajos and their property. To reinforce his threat, Miles added he would be joined by Utes, Jicarillas, and Coyoteros who will plunder and steal Navajo women and children. The Navajos were given five days to consider the offer.

Then on September 7, it appeared that the murderer might have been found when Sandoval produced a dead body believed to be that of the wanted man. However, an examination by the post surgeon at Fort Defiance concluded that this corpus did not match the physical description of the Navajo who killed Black Jim.

In keeping with his word, at 8 a.m. on September 9, Miles commenced his campaign of chastisement, as he termed it. Blas Lucero's scouts took the point, followed by two companies of the Mounted Rifles and two of infantry. These were followed by the pack train with rations enough for twelve days. In total, Miles had some 350 men under his command. Notwithstanding his hard line rhetoric, Miles advised Garland that he was not at all sanguine about finding the Navajos. He lacked adequate maps and Lucero's scouts seemed unfamiliar with the country ahead. Given this one wonders why he launched the campaign at all.

By mid-September, Miles had reached Canyon de Chelly and proceeded to navigate it from east to west. In doing so, he became the first American to traverse the canyon. Future generations would be mightily impressed with Canyon de Chelly, but to Miles it was merely a "remarkable hole in the earth." To Bonneville, Miles wrote that "No command should again enter it" [the canyon]. Throughout the march, Navajo snipers nipped at the column's flanks. The sniping produced a handful of casualties, but otherwise there was no contact to speak of and after seven days Miles had had enough and started back to Fort Defiance, despite the fact that he had rations enough for another five days. The devastation he had promised to wreak on the Navajo countryside appeared to have gone by the boards.[8]

Miles had mostly abandoned his idea of giving the Navajos a sound spanking. Canyon de Chelly was perhaps a bit intimidating and in any case he was glad to return to Fort Defiance. But Miles was not through yet. On the 19th, he sent a mixed column of mounted men and infantry under Major Brooks to try and locate the Navajos and hit them in a surprise attack. However, word of the movement leaked out and Brooks found nothing.

Five days later a second force of approximately the same size, this time under Captain John Hatch set out to strike the camp of Zarcillos Largos believed to be camped some nine miles to the north, though it actually turned out to be more like fifty. Hatch found the camp and attacked. The Navajos put up a stout resistance before withdrawing into the surrounding brush and thickets. Deciding he'd done as much damage as could reasonably be expected, Hatch did not pursue. Six Navajos were killed in the scrap and much camp equipage was destroyed. Following a grueling twelve-hour march, Hatch was back at Fort Defiance.

Towards the end of September, Miles decided to return to the field himself and see if the Navajos might be found in Chusca Valley. This time he took he took four companies of mounted rifles and two of infantry, plus Lucero and his scouts, altogether a slightly larger force than on his earlier foray. Near Chusca Peak he encountered large Navajo sheep herds but only a few herders. While Miles remained with the infantry, he sent the Mounted Rifles out on what proved to be a three-day search for the Navajos. On October 1, quite by accident, Captain Andrew Lindsay with a dozen men stumbled on Cayetano's band in a remote canyon. Outnumbered by a considerable margin, Lindsay took up a position among some trees and sent for help. Captain McLane responded in haste, driving the Navajos from the canyon. The troops burned the village while the Indians continued to fire on them from the canyon's heights. The affair cost McLane and Lindsay two men killed and another wounded. The Navajos reportedly suffered several casualties, but the exact number is unknown.

While Miles was out trying to take the Navajo's measure, raiding parties attacked a freighter's camp and livestock herds near Fort Defiance. This was followed on October 17 by a big raid on the post's livestock herd at *Cañoncito Bonito*. The raiding party was estimated to consist of at least 300 warriors. A detachment of 25 soldiers guarding the herd would have stood no chance of repelling the attack, but fortunately some 160 Zuni warriors who fortunately were camped nearby provided enough muscle to drive off the Navajo raiders. The guard detachment suffered two killed and four wounded. Zuni and Navajo losses are unknown, but the fact that the Navajos were able to penetrate this close to Fort Defiance emboldened them.

These raids triggered yet another campaign. Miles was named field commander with a force of some 400 men. That the military was taking these raids seriously, Miles would be joined this time by a second column under Major Electus Backus, who, it will be recalled, had been the first commander at Fort Defiance. Backus was directed to march from San Ysidro (near Jemez) with three companies of infantry and one of the Mounted Rifles. His command was augmented by a contingent of New Mexican scouts under Captain José Valdez out of Mora. Finally, some 100 Moache (Muaches) Utes led by war chiefs Sobeta and Kaneatchi (Kaniache), gave Backus a command equal in size to that of Miles. When the two forces came together, Miles—in overall command—would have a force of 800.

On October 18, Miles thought to strike the Navajos before Backus arrived. The Zuni scouts, however, refused to participate unless allowed to operate independently. Miles didn't like it, but it was the price he had to pay if he was to have their help. Notwithstanding, the Zunis were a first class nuisance. Miles feared the smoke from their campfires would alert the Navajos. Whether it did is problematical, but the Zunis did claim to have located and destroyed Manuelito's camp, capturing 100 horses and burning hogans. This was all well and good, but there was no evidence to show that they had inflicted any real damage on the Navajos. This, apparently, was an all-Indian show, as the soldiers seem not to have been involved. So the outing, at any rate, had been of questionable value.

On November 2 Miles and Backus rendezvoused some five miles from Bennett's Peak near present Newcomb, New Mexico (south of Farmington). While awaiting the arrival of their supply train, Miles prepared his report. He, Miles, with Number One column would march north while Backus searched for Cayetano's camp, thought to be near Beautiful Mountain. Accordingly, on November 4, the two columns sortied. Miles marched north toward Washington Pass with some 335 men and Lucero's scouts. Backus, meanwhile, reached Cave Creek on the first day. From this point, Backus agreed to let Captain Valdez take his Ute scouts on a reconnaissance mission. The effort produced one very brief, insignificant skirmish that killed two or three Navajos. By November 5, Backus had reached the vicinity of Beautiful Mountain, where he divided his command and searched the area for any Navajos, but without success, although his Ute scouts did find and burn two Navajo Rancherias.

On November 8, Kaneatchi took his Utes and pulled out, informing Backus that he had no use for the U.S. Army's way of making war. But Backus was determined if nothing else and divided his command into three columns and launched another search. Miles, meanwhile, having reached Lukachukai Creek, the agreed upon meeting point, elected not to wait for Backus and proceeded to strike out and scout the country north of Canyon de Chelly. En route, Miles came upon a large sheep herd even as Navajos harassed his point and flanks. Ironically, now that he had found his objective, his horses were too played out to offer pursuit; some even had to be shot. But it seemed perhaps something good might come out of this after all. Along their route of march Miles came upon a cross covered with a white cloth stained yellow, which, an interpreter informed him that it represented Mexican, Navajo, and American and stood as a sign of peace. What to make of this was hard to say. During the course of any of these expeditions, one was likely to find some Navajos who claimed to want peace and it was difficult to know how seriously to take such claims, but this one appeared to hold real promise.

As the column drew nearer the canyon country north of Canyon de Chelly, they were approached by the much respected Navajo leader Barboncito. Then about thirty-eight, Barboncito was in his natural prime and one of the most influential of Navajos. An eloquent speaker and long a peace advocate, Barboncito had signed the 1846 treaty with Colonel

Doniphan, which of course, along with many others, the Senate had never seen fit to ratify. Miles proposed a peace council to convene in seven days despite the fact that he had no authority to negotiate anything, and in any case nothing seems to have come of the idea.

On November 11, Miles commenced his return march to Fort Defiance, which he reached on the 13th, followed six days later by Backus who had covered some 350 miles. Overall, the campaign had been a fizzle. Whatever chastisement had been worked on the Navajos had come at the hands of the Ute auxiliaries. Perhaps encouraged by his meeting with Barboncito, Miles thought he saw a way to end the Navajo war, or then again, perhaps he was simply weary of campaigning. In any event, he now proceeded, entirely on his own volition, to enter into a peace agreement with Zarcillos Largos and several other Navajo headmen. The problem here was that nothing had changed and Miles had no more authority to talk peace with Largos than he had with Barboncito, and neither Bonneville nor Superintendent Collins had any notion of what he was up to. Early season storms delayed mail delivery and by the time they learned what was afoot it was too late. Both were, understandably furious, and Collins was angry as well at Agent Yost who supported Miles. Notwithstanding, the commitment had been made and both Bonneville and Collins felt they had no choice but to journey out to Fort Defiance in support of Miles.

It was a cold, hard journey for Collins and Bonneville, which probably did not help their mood. Nevertheless, Collins drew up a set of terms embodying the usual demands: free captives and pay for all stolen property. Earlier, Miles had suggested to Bonneville that they ought to drop their demand for Black Jim's killer, but at the time Bonneville had rejected that idea. Now, however, that demand was waived. Significantly, though, from here on the entire Navajo nation would be held responsible for the acts of any individual member of the tribe; a perfectly ridiculous provision. As for Miles, he escaped a reprimand for seizing the initiative and believed he had indeed brought the Navajo war to a close.

In January 1859, Samuel Yost was replaced as agent to the Navajos by Robert Cowart. Superintendent Collins had been less than happy with Yost's role in the recently concluded treaty talks, so his dismissal came as no particular surprise. It was another time of change. In February the irrepressible Sandoval died from injuries received when he was kicked by a horse. Sandoval had been one of only three leaders to be accepted by the *Diné Anni aii* in the last sixty years. It would remain to be seen how his demise would affect the relationship between Americans and this renegade band of Navajos.

Meanwhile, restless young Navajo warriors, impatient and dissatisfied with the new treaty arrangements resumed raiding, striking Zuni, Hopis, and Abiquiu itself. A few of Sandoval's old band may have participated, but it was not always easy to identify these raiders. Bonneville was not especially troubled by such raids, but Collins saw war as inevitable, suggesting he had little faith in the recently concluded peace arrangements.

In June 1859, Fort Defiance received yet another commander in the person of Major John Simonson. A veteran officer with nearly half a century of service behind him, Simonson promptly made a point of saying that he had little interest in killing Indians. En route from Abiquiu with two companies of mounted riflemen, Simonson encountered large numbers of Navajos, all of whom seemed friendly enough and tended to reinforce his point of view.

Reaching Fort Defiance, though, Simonson found new orders. He was to divide his command in half and make a thorough reconnaissance of Navajo country, reporting on herds of horses, sheep, grazing lands, and of course the Navajos themselves. New Mexicans regarded this as a strange tactic, one that ignored the problem. Henry Connelly, for instance, whose supply trains regularly traveled between Albuquerque and Fort Defiance were constantly raided, causing Connelly to scream for a war of extermination and he protested vigorously to Superintendent Collins, but Bonneville was not inclined to take any sort of action until he saw Simonson's report.

On July 18, one of Simonson's probes under Captain John Walker, with companies E and K of the Mounted Rifles, plus C and G, 3rd Infantry, advanced toward Canyon de Chelly. Along the way, Walker drafted several Navajos to act as guides, and perhaps to insure the safety of his column.

As it does most people, the Canyon impressed Walker and others of his command. Lieutenant John van D. Dubois wrote:

> The descent was truly terrific. We were four hours getting down the 800 feet depth.... Mules fell distances of from twenty to forty feet. Two were killed & several only saved by their loads which prevented them from striking the rocks in their fall. Looking up it seems as if there was no escape.... Men and animals on the top as seen from below like mites against the sky. Next to Niagara it is the greatest wonder of nature I have ever seen.[9]

Despite the uneasiness of the Navajos—and we might imagine the soldiers as well—there were no clashes. On August 3, Walker returned to Fort Defiance. In his report to department headquarters Walker said that from what he had been able to observe, the Navajos appeared genuinely interested in peace, but in his opinion, this was due to the strong garrison at Fort Defiance, which now numbered nearly a thousand. He added that claims against the Navajos for depredations they allegedly committed were greatly exaggerated, and that indeed it should be taken into consideration that Navajos have suffered losses at the hands of citizen raiders and Pueblos.

Six days after Walker's return, Simonson's second column under Major Oliver Shepherd arrived at Fort Defiance, having penetrated as far as the Little Colorado River. Although Walker had found the Navajos rather peaceably inclined and Shepherd experienced no sign of hostility, Bonneville apparently remained unconvinced that the Navajos were not preparing for war, and ordered additional reconnaissance. Accordingly, on September 5, two more columns, each composed of four infantry companies, one under Walker and the second under Shepherd took the field once again. Shepherd's assignment was to examine the lower Chusca Valley, while Walker marched north as far as today's Monument Valley, which he would later describe as desolate. Neither column experienced any trouble.

Yet, even as Walker and Shepherd were taking the field, a raiding party of some fifty, probably Navajo, though some thought Apaches, drove off a large herd of cattle west of Albuquerque. Captain Henry Schroeder with a mixed force of cavalry and infantry sortied from Fort Defiance in pursuit of the raiders, but failed to locate them. A few weeks later, another trader en route to Albuquerque to discuss monies owed him from annuities due the Navajos, was attacked and robbed, possibly by Pueblo Indians, though again the identity of the raiders was not clear. It was incidents such as this that kept life at Fort Defiance on the edge. One had the feeling that the pot was going to boil over any day.

In the face of this, Major Simonson and a new Navajo agent, Silas Kendrick (no relation to the Army officer) agreed to meet with the Navajos to discuss the issue of indemnity payments. Here was a real sticking point, not just with the Navajos but with all tribes. Traders would provide credit to Indians, expecting to be paid when the government finally got around to making annuity payments. Often, the Indians simply did not understand what was happening, or at least realize the extent of their indebtedness, and it was not uncommon for traders to pad the bill. In any case, when the annuities were finally paid, the Indians found themselves with much less than they expected, and not surprisingly, this left a bitter taste. The white man could always expect to be justly compensated, but restitution or compensation for Indian losses seemed not to be a part of the equation. Thus, when Simonson and Kendrick met with some 2,000 Navajos on September 25, there was a lot of angry rhetoric. How did the white man propose to compensate the Navajos for six of their tribe recently murdered by Pueblos and New Mexican?

Simonson was a fair man and advised headquarters that those who murdered the six Navajos should be pursued and prosecuted to the fullest extent of the law. To this recommendation he added an overall criticism of government policy. Innocent Navajos, said he, ought not to be pressed for repayment claims. But then, Simonson was about to retire and doubtless felt more inclined to speak his mind than he would otherwise. Indeed, on October 10, the major left Fort Defiance and was replaced, temporarily, by Major Shepherd, who in turn was replaced by Major Charles Frederick Ruff. Simonson's opinion of course carried little weight and would not be acted upon.

On October 22, Bonneville, satisfied with the recent reconnaissance reports, decided it was time for the Navajos to be chastised. Accordingly, orders went out to Major Ruff to send his entire command into the Chusca Valley, where the more militant Navajos were thought to be located. Ruff thought the idea was not a good one and so advised Bonneville, pointing out that this might have an adverse effect on the other Navajos, but Bonneville had made up his mind that the effort would provide a necessary object lesson—that four or five Navajos should be killed as punishment for past depredations. Field command of the expedition was assigned to Major Shepherd.

Thus it was that on November 1, Major Shepherd marched north from Fort Defiance with some 280 men, aiming to strike the Navajos wherever he found them in the Chusca Valley. Had Major Ruff delayed the start of the expedition, Bonneville's order might possibly have been rescinded, as he was replaced on November 2 by Colonel Thomas T. Faunteleroy, a Virginian and veteran of twenty-three years service. As it was, however, on November 4, Shepherd's advance guard under Lieutenant John Hildt moved into Chusca Valley where they attacked a small party of mounted Navajos, killing one and wounding another.

With his main body, Shepherd searched the great sweep of lonely valley for traces of Cayetano's or Armijo's band and pursued a Navajo trail beyond Chusca, but soon discovered that his quarry had split into two groups. Concluding that they were too far ahead and on a course that would take them into country too rugged to justify continued pursuit, Shepherd elected to turn back toward Chusca. On November 5, one of his detachments came upon a herd of several hundred sheep, of which they proceeded to take possession, killing three Navajos and wounding a few others, including a woman. On November 12, Major Shepherd returned to Fort Defiance believing his campaign had been successful, although in retrospect, anyway, it is difficult to understand why. And what exactly the soldiers did with the sheep seems not to have been recorded, but presumably the animals were either turned loose or driven back to Fort Defiance.

There is probably no better illustration of what served to keep New Mexico Territory in a state of turmoil than a December 1859 incident when a war party of Muache and Capote Utes—about 100 strong—together with some Jicarilla Apaches and New Mexicans set out on what amounted to a slave raid against the Navajos. Reportedly the Ute agent, Kit Carson, and perhaps others as well, knew what was afoot but did nothing to interfere with it. And it was a successful undertaking, too. When the raiders returned, they brought with them a large number of goats, sheep, and horses, along with twenty Navajo girls taken as slaves. At about the same time all this was occurring, Major Shepherd had a Navajo man publicly flogged on the Fort Defiance parade ground. What exactly the Navajo had done to deserve such punishment is not clear, but in any event, the incident along with the Ute/Jicarilla slave raid, fueled Navajo determination to make war.

As a result of these two incidents and continuing poor relations with the Navajo, raids along the Rio Grande settlements increased noticeably. Shepherd boys were taken into captivity and a reported 20,000 sheep were run off. Barbancito, ever the champion of non-war, struggled to preserve the fragile peace, if indeed it could even be referred to as such.

Thus, the year 1860 got underway with perhaps more than the usual anxiety in the air. Governor Abraham Rencher approved the formation of two companies of volunteers to deal with the heightened Indian activity. Muskets were issued but Colonel Fauntleroy refused to issue ammunition. It was the old bone between civil government and the federal military. The colonel disapproved of civilian volunteers, while the governor argued that the citizenry preferred to fight Indians in its own way, so there would be no territorial authorized volunteers in the field and for the moment anyway, that's where matters stood.But the Navajos were not idle. On January 17, as part of an overall strategy to force the closure of Fort Defiance, they attacked a wood train ten miles from the fort. Three of the four soldiers guarding the train were killed, but the fourth managed to escape. Later, the raiders swooped down on the post's beef herd at *Ciénega Amarilla*. Thirty-five soldiers were on guard duty here and twice repulsed determined attacks by the Navajos. Pinned down, however, the soldiers managed to get word back to the fort by tying a message around a dog's neck. The faithful canine reached the fort around noon, and, unbelievably, at about the same time a lone Navajo arrived to speak with Agent Kendrick. Major Shepherd, having lost his mounted units, nevertheless immediately assembled seventy-five infantry and set forth on his relief mission. En route, a scout reported that other Navajos were attacking a lumber detail three miles away. Dividing his command, Shepherd took fifty men to relieve the lumber detail, while the remainder under Lieutenant Alexander Shipley proceeded to *Ciénega Amarilla*. By the time each detachment had reached its destination, however, the raiders had already departed. These raids prompted Shepherd to advise Agent Kendrick, on January 20, that a state of war existed between the Navajos and the U.S., in view of which the agent was prohibited from having any contact with his charges. On February 25, Kendrick left Fort Defiance, but not before the Navajos struck yet again.

Navajo activity continued. Early in February 500 Navajos launched a daylight attack on Fort Defiance beef herd, but the forty-four-man guard was prepared, having observed Navajo activity in the area the day before. After a sharp, two-hour fight the raiders withdrew when a mountain howitzer arrived from the fort. An estimated ten Navajos died in the fight and one soldier was wounded.

Governor Rencher, meanwhile, continued to promote the idea of sending volunteers into Navajo country, but Colonel Fauntleroy remained adamant in his refusal to support the idea and, indeed, threatened to withdraw regular troops from the frontier if the governor followed through with his intent. So, notwithstanding citizen support for Rencher's plan, there would be no cooperation from federal authorities. Fauntleroy's refusal to support the use of volunteers in Navajo country apparently did not extend to the Rio Grande Valley where a mixed force of regulars out of Fort Craig near Socorro, and volunteers under Manuel Chavez pursued Navajo raiders and recovered some 17,000 sheep near Cañon del Muerto.

When word of the standoff between Fauntleroy and Rencher reached Washington, Secretary of War John Floyd, supported his department commander, officially declaring that volunteers were not to be used in Indian Territory. However, to mollify angry citizens, the secretary added that more troops would be made available for use against the Navajos.

At dawn on April 30, an estimated 1,000 Navajos—twice the number of the garrison—attacked Fort Defiance. While some of the warriors attempted to threaten the fort from the mesa above the post, a second group advanced from the southwest. Neither effort resulted in any success for the Navajos, particularly for those on the mesa who were mostly armed with obsolete muskets and bows and arrows. However, from the other side of Canyon Bonito the Navajo enjoyed some success, managing to penetrate the fort's perimeter. There was some stiff, hand-to-hand fighting before the soldiers finally forced the Navajos to withdraw. Major Shepherd was later commended for his conduct of the fight. As a consequence of the attack, Secretary Floyd ordered a Navajo campaign to get underway as soon as possible.

Despite the prohibition against it, independent parties of volunteers continued to operate in Navajo country A week after the attack on Fort Defiance, for example, a force of 100 New Mexicans, in company with some *Diné Anaí aii* rode into the fort, reporting that they had killed six Navajos and taken a woman captive. Then in July, 125 volunteers under Jesús Gallegos appeared at the fort, claiming to have killed one Navajo.

Much of July 1860 was comparatively quiet for a change; there was even an exchange of captives between Navajos and New Mexicans out at Fort Defiance. But in Santa Fe, angry citizens were calling for military action against the Navajos, urging Governor Rencher to form a regiment of mounted volunteers. Accordingly, a call went out for a thousand men who would agree to serve without pay and provide their own subsistence. However, before anything came of it, and true to Secretary Floyd's promise, five companies of the 7th U.S. Infantry arrived on August 17 from service against the Mormons in Utah, and Colonel Fauntleroy wasted little time in announcing a full scale Navajo campaign.

Lieutenant Colonel Edward R.S. Canby and Major Henry Hopkins Sibley

The arrival of the 7th Infantry gave Fauntleroy forty companies of infantry in his department and with this as a base, plans proceeded for a fall campaign to be led by the recently arrived Lieutenant Colonel Edward R.S. Canby—the same who would be murdered in the far-off lava beds a decade later. While Canby's force was assembling at Fort Defiance, Captain Henry Selden arrived with four companies of the 5th Infantry relieving Major Shepherd and the 3rd Infantry.

As part of Colonel Fauntleroy's operational design, Major Henry Hopkins Sibley traveled from Albuquerque to *Ojo del Oso* (Bear Springs near present Gallup) where a new post was then under construction. The post was to have been named Fort Fauntleroy then was changed to Fort Lyon in 1861. This site was then abandoned and another was selected fifty miles away. The new post erected on this site was named Fort Wingate.

Sibley, an interesting figure would later command the ill-fated Confederate invasion of New Mexico where he demonstrated a remarkable ineptness for field command. Two years hence, that effort, ironically, would be thwarted by Sibley's current superior, Colonel Canby. Now, however, from *Ojo del Oso*, Sibley marched to Laguna Negra with a mixed force of mounted troops and infantry, hoping to locate some Navajos. All he found, however, was a lone headman who expressed a desire to speak with Sibley. However, in the confusion that followed, probably resulting from miscommunication, the man, perhaps frightened, attempted to run away and was shot.

On September 20, angry citizens, meanwhile, acting entirely on their own volition, formed a regiment of mounted rifles with Manuel Chavez—appointed lieutenant colonel—

in command. However, once it is learned that the volunteers will be required to furnish their own horses, only five companies—about half of a regiment—were actually formed. The five companies, numbering about 470 officers and men were mustered at San Ysidro. Governor Rencher advised citizens that in forming this volunteer unit they were in violation not only of territorial law but federal law as well and he reported on the state of affairs in New Mexico to Secretary of War Joseph Holt who had replaced John Floyd.

Out at Fort Defiance, meanwhile, the Navajo expedition was steadily assembling. On September 28, Sibley arrived, followed on October 4 by Captain Lafayette McLaws—another soon-to-be Confederate general officer—from Fort Craig with two companies of mounted rifles and two of infantry. A week later, Sibley, at the head of 270 men, marched out of Fort Defiance to a point near present Ganado, Arizona. Canby would follow with a column about the same strength. Sibley's orders were to attack any Navajos he came across, then rendezvous with Canby at the entrance to Canyon de Chelly. In concert, they would then wheel around the Canyon's north side where, theoretically at least, they would be in a position to catch the Navajos who were expected to be fleeing in the direction of Kayenta. A smaller, third column under Captain McLaws, meanwhile, would patrol the western sector of the Chuscas.

On the 18th, Canby and Sibley rendezvoused as planned. Up to this point, neither column had accomplished much of note. And things were not bright on the campaign trail, either. Water was a problem as was forage for the horses. Supplies were running low, prompting Canby to send a messenger to McLaws to establish a supply depot at Ojo del Oso. But the picture brightened some on the 23rd when a stretch of good grass was found. Canby took advantage of the moment to give his animals a chance to rest and graze, and Canby an opportunity to revise his operational plan. Sibley was given all of the mounted units—two companies of the 2d Dragoons and two of the Mounted Rifles, plus Blas Lucero's scouts. Sibley's orders were to march southwest, climb Black Mesa, then turn north. Canby, meanwhile, would march toward Marsh Pass, toward which it was believed the Navajos were heading. The idea was to catch the Indians between Canby and Sibley.

As he was approaching Black Mesa on the 24th, Sibley came upon a large Navajo horse herd belonging, as it turned out, to Delgadito's band. Holding the dragoons in reserve, Sibley sent Captain Thomas Claiborne and the Mounted Rifles to round up the horse herd, killing any Navajos they found. And find them they did. A fight followed in which 5 Navajos were killed and 3 women and 2 children taken captive. Lucero's scouts had a field day, capturing some 200 horses and 2,000 sheep. Although he had seemingly had the best of the fight, Sibley now found himself confronted by something of a dilemma. Reluctant to leave the captured livestock and uncertain as to exactly where he would find the main body of Navajos, he revised Canby's orders and instead marched along the north flank of Black Mesa, finally meeting up with Canby on the 26th.

The final days of the month proved an exercise in frustration trying to locate the Navajos. Delgadito did present himself for a parley, but Canby said, in effect, what every field commander had been saying to the Navajos since 1846, namely no peace until the Navajos agreed to abide by the original terms. But Canby had no real leverage, not at the moment anyway. His horses were played out, and finally on November 1, discussions having ended, the expedition began its return march, reaching Laguna Negra on the 8th.

The campaign had lasted six weeks, during which an estimated 28 Navajos, including women and children, were killed. Five women and children were taken captive. The Ute scouts, acting independently, as they most always did, reportedly killed 6 Navajos and took as captives 19 women and children, along with 500 horses and 5,000 sheep. Thus, did

Canby's campaign come to an end. From the white man's point of view it could hardly be viewed as a notable success. Although the Navajos were far from vanquished, in their tribal history this would be remembered as *Nahondzod*, The Fearing Time, a period that would culminate in the epic Long Walk: to the *Bosque Redondo* four years hence.

Canby's campaign was noteworthy in one respect, however. In October, Major Albert Myer, just assigned to Canby's command, developed a new method of signaling that proved especially effective in New Mexico's clear air. The system employed large signal flags that were reportedly able to communicate over distances as great as twenty miles. The system was said to be the birth of the U.S. Army's Signal Corps.

Meanwhile, the Manuel Chavez battalion of volunteers, which had been formed despite the ruling against doing so, spent September and October 1860 in the field where they had the advantage of moving in the wake of Canby's columns and so experienced only brief and minor skirmishes with Navajos. Sheep and livestock were captured, however, and women and children taken as slaves. Although the battalion suffered no combat casualties to speak of, there were significant losses of horses and mules due mainly to excessive work and little forage.

The volunteers returned in late October amidst rumors of a forthcoming winter campaign that soon faded before the disapproval of the Secretary of War. And so, for all intents and purposes, their campaigning finished, the battalion was mustered out on December 3. Canby, however, wasn't quite finished just yet. On November 18 McLaws marched out of Fort Defiance with 180 men and scouts, under orders to make for the Little Colorado River where Canby believed Navajos would be found. McLaws did not fare much better than had Canby, although one of his detachments did have a brief skirmish, following which some Navajos approached, wanting to talk peace but were turned away as McLaws lacked authority to discuss any kind of terms. On December 9, the expedition arrived at Fort Fauntleroy.

Even as these fall campaigns were underway, the territorial legislature, over Governor Rencher's veto, enacted legislation to protect slaves as property, *including Indians taken captive in raids and kept as slaves* [italics added]. The expansion of slavery into the Western territories was the polarizing issue of the day, but had not as yet become law (nor would it be). Thus, this piece of legislation is of particular interest, and indeed, the territorial legislature of New Mexico refused to end peonage and slavery until 1867 when compelled by law to do so.

With the election of Abraham Lincoln to the presidency in November, the United States stood on the threshold of a defining moment in its history. With the year 1861 destined to be forever fateful, Colonel Canby, sensing that perhaps the Navajos were now inclined to surrender, extended an invitation for them to come into Fort Defiance and discuss terms.The gesture was accepted, but where it would lead was yet to be determined.

Edward Canby may not have been a hawk, but he was nevertheless taking no chances. For the moment, war was put on hold, but in the likely event these peace talks fell through, as so often seemed the case, he wanted to establish a supply depot west of Fort Defiance. As well, he requested two more companies of infantry to examine the area around the San Francisco Mountains (near present Flagstaff) where he had reason to suspect the Navajos would be found. Colonel Fauntleroy concurred and agreed to reinforce Canby with three companies of the 7th Infantry, if in fact active campaigning against the Navajos should resume.

The winter of 1860–1861 proved unseasonably cold, with the thermometer frequently registering well below zero. The weather, however, did not deter infantry patrols from ranging out across the countryside west of Fort Defiance. Nor did it prevent all the Navajos from coming in. On February 5, some 2,000, many on the brink of starvation, arrived at Fort Fauntleroy. The talks had to be postponed for two weeks, however, in order for Manuelito and other headmen to forge their way through heavy snows.

Three days later, on February 18, the Navajos signed a treaty, in effect, agreeing to submit, unconditionally, to U.S. authority. The agreement was notable, too, in that for the first time the Navajos also agreed to bring in their own raiders. If they were unsuccessful in this it was further agreed that soldiers would be sent in pursuit of the raiders. The Navajos also agreed to relocate to country west of Fort Fauntleroy—an important stipulation in that it meant surrendering sacred land. Any Navajo found living east of Fort Fauntleroy would be shot. And if any Navajo committed a crime it would be regarded as a crime against the U.S. The treaty was signed by fifty headmen, more than had ever before put their mark on a treaty. Owing to the tough terms, however, the treaty did not bode well for peaceful and harmonious relations with the Navajos. One reason for this was that as news of the treaty and its details began to circulate, bands of New Mexicans resumed their slave raids. The Army made a feeble effort to respond, but it scarcely made a difference.

Meanwhile, in the East, storm clouds were growing ever darker. On February 24, Colonel Fauntleroy ordered Colonel Canby to strip Fort Defiance of its garrison, sending those infantry companies to stations in the Rio Grande Valley, ostensibly to counter hostile Mescalero Apache activities. Further, all supplies then at Fort Defiance were to be sent to Fort Fauntleroy; and Fort Defiance was to be closed.

During the spring and summer of 1861, with the Civil War finally underway, virtually all regular army troops were gradually withdrawn from the Territory and sent east. Colonel Fauntleroy elected to cast his allegiance with the Confederacy and was replaced by Colonel William Wing Loring, but he, too, soon chose the Confederacy. On June 11, Colonel Canby was appointed department commander.

To fill the gap left by the departure of most regular army troops, two regiments of volunteers were formed. Named to command one regiment was Colonel Ceran St. Vrain, a figure of some notable importance in the New Mexico story. A former trapper, trader and shrewd businessman, St. Vrain had been a partner in the well known firm of Bent/St. Vrain Company, founders and operators of Bent's Old Fort. Lieutenant Colonel Kit Carson was appointed second in command, giving the unit two prestigious figures at its head. The second regiment was given to Colonel Miguel Pino, a much respected citizen in his own right.

Manuel Chavez, Navajo Fighter

Elsewhere in the Territory, on August 8, Manuel Chavez took command of Fort Lyon—the name having been changed from Fort Fauntleroy—with some 200 volunteers and 7 officers, thereby allowing three companies of the 5th Infantry to transfer east. A fortnight after Chavez's arrival, Ramón Lana—now the Navajo agent—called for a council of headmen to discuss a new treaty, since Congress, in typical fashion, had failed to ratify Canby's February 18 agreement. And the Navajos responded. Some 2,000 gathered in what seemed a genial enough environment. Canby had issued orders that any hungry Navajos were to be fed. The Indians, for their part, then released four captive New Mexican boys. In this seeming atmosphere of good will, a treaty discussion followed, during which the Navajos expressed a desire to cooperate fully. Then with talks apparently satisfactorily concluded Agent Luna took his leave.

In the aftermath of these more or less official talks everyone seemed to be enjoying a rollicking good time. A race between the horse belonging to the post surgeon and one of the Navajo mounts attracted some sizeable wagers. What happened next is not entirely clear. One story claimed that the young Navajo rider was knocked from his horse by the rider of the doctor's horse. Another source, however, claims that the bridle on the Navajo's horse broke and the rider was unable to control his animal, allowing the doctor's horse to win the race. The Navajos claimed that under the circumstances all bets ought to be off, an argument the soldiers promptly dismissed. Confusion set in and a fight quickly developed, probably encouraged by the loose discipline among the Chavez volunteers. Chavez later claimed that the Navajos had planned to attack the fort. At any rate, during the melee that followed a guard was threatened. Mountain howitzers wheeled out from the fort quickly went into action, scattering the Navajos, killing an estimated dozen and wounding several others. For his role in the affair, or more precisely his failure to prevent the incident from getting out of hand, Colonel Chavez was reprimanded and was to have undergone a court of inquiry. However, the exigencies of the Civil War, during which Chavez rendered valuable service during the Confederate invasion of New Mexico kept that from happening.

At the outset of the Civil War there were visionaries in the South who coveted the recently acquired territory from Mexico for its mineral wealth; gold and silver were needed to fill the Confederacy's coffers. As well, control of one or more ports on the Pacific Coast would enhance the South's chances immeasurably. Accordingly, the concept of a campaign to acquire the Southwest had the backing of no less a personage than Jefferson Davis himself. But if the Confederacy saw the value inherent in this territory, neither was the North blind to the threat posed by a Confederate invasion.

Canby's appointment to command the Department of New Mexico (which included the District of Arizona) was a wise move on the part of the Federal War Department. Canby was an able commander. Indeed, it is doubtful that under existing conditions, the Union could have found a better man to command the southwest than Edward Richard Sprigg Canby.

Canby saw the necessity of strengthening the southern sector of his department against a Confederate invasion. He saw Fort Fillmore, near Mesilla as a key point in his defense system and accordingly, in July, ordered the garrisons at Forts Breckenridge and Buchanan to reinforce the already strong garrison at Fillmore. Somewhat later, Canby learned, much to his chagrin, that Major Lynde, acting entirely on his own volition, left Fort Fillmore and marched his command northeast toward Fort Stanton, near present Ruidoso, leaving Fillmore up for grabs. That wasn't the worst of it, however. En route to Stanton Lynde surrendered his thirsty command to Colonel Baylor in exchange for water. And thus were almost 200 men removed from Canby's operational command for a little water.

Canby had his hands full and the future looked bleak indeed. Union control in southern New Mexico had all but evaporated. Secessionists dominated Mesilla, the key city in southern New Mexico. After paroling Major Lynde's command, Baylor proclaimed himself governor of Arizona Territory and prepared to take control of that area, encouraged, no doubt, by strong showing of support for the Confederacy around Tucson. The Confederate presence in the Southwest was, however, destined to be short lived.

Although the Trans-Mississippi West was not the scene of great and furious battles, the Civil War nevertheless left its mark all across the vastness of this great region. Primarily the impact was felt with Indian troubles, but overall westward expansion was delayed for four long, bloody years. With virtually all regular army troops withdrawn from the Territory, it was up to the volunteers to deal with the Indian problem. The Indians for their part soon came to understand that the soldiers had gone away to fight other white men, leaving a void that provided a golden opportunity.

In addition to being forced to rely on volunteer units to deal with ongoing Indian raids, New Mexico also had to deal with a Confederate invasion. Early in 1862, Canby was compelled to marshal his forces to oppose an invasion up the Rio Grande Valley, led by his old comrade Henry Hopkins Sibley, now wearing a brigadier's star in the Confederate Army. The Confederates managed to squeak out a victory at Valverde in February. But were subsequently defeated at Apache Cañon, and had their wagon train destroyed at Glorieta Pass near Santa Fe in March, by the soon to be infamous, Colonel John Chivington. Chivington's victory forced the Confederates to withdraw. Canby then won another victory at Peralta in April, as the Confederates continued their retreat back down the Valley of the Rio Grande, ending Sibley's dream of conquering the New Mexico. He had come close, but Union determination and Sibley's own fondness for the bottle proved too much to overcome.

THE ARRIVAL OF COLONEL JAMES HENRY CARLETON

The summer of 1862 saw the welcome arrival of the California Volunteers under the command of Colonel James Henry Carleton, who replaced Canby as department commander when the latter was transferred east. It was, in a sense, a homecoming of sorts for Carleton, who it will be recalled, had commanded Fort Union back in 1852 and who, along with the able Kit Carson as guide, conducted a highly successful campaign against the Ute and Jicarilla Apaches the following year. An officer of wide-ranging experience Carleton was known to his troops as "General Jimmy." The avuncular sobriquet did not linger, however, once the rank and file discovered the ruthless side of his nature. An able if arrogant commander, Carleton's handsome features were framed by full side-burns and dark piercing eyes. Carleton would, arguably, prove to be the Army's most effective Indian fighter in New Mexico. Let it be noted, though, that to those Native Americans who opposed him, Carleton especially was a lesser man.

In 1863, Carleton, rearranging his military department, created the District of Arizona, which included the territory south of the *Jornada del Muerto* and west as far as the Colorado River. This essentially, was along the 32d Parallel; the southern third of today's New Mexico and Arizona. At about the same time, Carleton appointed Kit Carson Colonel of the 1st New Mexico Volunteers based in Santa Fe. Together Carleton and Carson would prove to be a formidable duo, probably the most effective military team during the Territory's formative years.

During the first two years of the Civil War—1861–1863—the Mescalero Apaches found it irresistibly convenient to resume their raiding ways. The closure of Fort Stanton and the transfer of the garrison east, left the Mescaleros largely free to raid uninhibited. As with most Indians, they had not taken well to the U.S. Government's efforts to turn them into farmers and raids on nearby ranches was a way to survive without tilling the soil.

This, accordingly, was the first major problem to confront Carleton as the new department commander and he wasted no time swinging into action. Three columns took the field. Carson with five companies of the 1st New Mexico was directed to reopen Fort Stanton and from that base pressure the Mescaleros. Two other columns under Captain Thomas Roberts and William McLeave, respectively, completed Carleton's operational plan. Carleton's directive to his field commanders was plain and simple: all Indian men were to be killed where found. Women and children were to be taken prisoner but not killed. There would be no peace talks. If the Indians were serious about peace their leaders should come to Santa Fe to talk with Carleton.

Faced with unrelenting pressure, the Mescaleros soon gave in and asked Carleton for peace. Again, Carleton's terms were simple: relocate to the *Bosque Redondo*, near the recently built Fort Sumner—where Billy the Kid would later be killed. Those who refused would be hunted down and killed. Carleton had the leverage and most Mescaleros agreed they had little choice, although a few did slip across the border into Mexico. Three months was all that it had taken to put some 240 Mescaleros on the *Bosque*. Carleton credited Kit Carson with ending the Mescalero problem.

Next on Carleton's list were the Navajos. Perhaps more than any of his predecessors, Carleton recognized that the conflict between Navajos and New Mexicans had been ongoing for generations and would not be easy to change. Notwithstanding, he also recognized that if there was to be peace in New Mexico it would take draconian measures.

On February 24, 1863, President Lincoln signed legislation creating the Territory of Arizona. Initially, the new legislation would have little impact on Indian/white relations in New Mexico, though eventually it would redistribute the military responsibility for responding to Indian troubles.

In that spring of 1863—the third of the Civil War—even as General Robert E. Lee's Army of Northern Virginia was defeating the Union Army of the Potomac at Chancellorsville, General Carleton placed a proposal before the Navajos; it was the same ultimatum he had given the Mescaleros: relocate to the *Bosque Redondo*. They were given a two-month deadline to decide—until July 20. Refusal meant they would be treated as hostiles. But of course the Navajos were not going to surrender that easily, it was going to take a campaign; they would have to be rooted out.

And so during that summer of 1863, while the eyes of the nation were focused on places like Gettysburg and Vicksburg, nearly 2,000 miles to the west, Kit Carson's 1st New Mexico Volunteers moved into Navajo country. While half of the regiment built a supply depot at old Fort Defiance, the remainder, some 400 strong, aided by more volunteers under Lieutenant Colonel J. Francisco Chavez operating out of Fort Wingate, relentlessly burned fields of Navajo crops and rounded up livestock. And, as if this was not enough, Zunis, Pueblos, Utes, and Hopis took advantage of the splendid opportunity to strike at their old enemy, killing Barboncito and a dozen of his followers in a December raid.

Kit Carson's Expedition to Canyon de Chelly

With the approach of winter, Carleton, recognizing the Indians' vulnerability at this time of year, pressed Carson to take his volunteers into the Navajo stronghold of Canyon de Chelly. James Carleton was shameless when it came to goading and prodding his field commanders to try harder, to push out farther. As he saw it, the only way to bring about closure in this business was to press the Indians until they couldn't take any more.

Accordingly, on January 6, with heavy snow blanketing the ground, Carson marched out of Fort Canby (a new operational post created in June, approximately thirty miles southwest of Fort Defiance) with 400 men of his 1st New Mexico Volunteers. On the 12th, Carson with the main body of his battalion, working their way through drifted snow, reached the west entrance of the forbidding Canyon de Chelly. Meantime, Captain Albert Pfeiffer, a veteran Indian fighter who had seen his family slaughtered by Apaches the past summer and harbored a deep seated resentment of all Indians, reached the east entrance.

Carson's battalion skirmished briefly with the Navajos and Pfeiffer's column was harassed from the canyon rim from where the Navajos rained down rocks and some arrows, but otherwise the opposition was negligible. Rendezvousing at the west portal, Carson then sent two companies back through the canyon to destroy crops and orchards. It was not an overwhelming victory on fields of battle—the campaign resulted in only twenty-three Navajos killed—that brought the Navajos to their knees; it was this scorched earth policy; this Sherman-like march through the heart of their homeland that destroyed the source of their livelihood that finally compelled them to capitulate. Although military columns had been here in the past, the destructive swath cut by Carson's command served as the strongest possible object lesson to the Navajos in a way that no other expedition had done. For the first time, the Navajos realized that if they were not safe in Canyon de Chelly there was no place they could feel safe from the soldiers.

The Long Walk of the Navajo

Carson's campaign effectively ended the Navajo War. During the next three months some 8,000 Navajos surrendered and commenced their infamous "Long Walk" 400 miles across New Mexico to the *Bosque Redondo*, yet another Trail of Tears. For four long years the Navajo would endure existence at the *Bosque* before finally being allowed to return to their homeland in 1868. It is interesting to note, though, that during their enforced exile, the Navajos did not miss an opportunity to torment their old enemies the Mescaleros and in turn were harassed by westward probing Comanches. Tradition it seems never dies.

Late in 1867, reverting to his permanent rank of Lieutenant Colonel Carleton joined the 4th Cavalry and was replaced as department commander by Colonel and Brevet Major General George Getty, 37th Infantry. Carleton had left his mark on the Territory. The Navajo problem had been resolved and progress, if it could be so called, had been made in bringing about order in the Rio Grande Valley.

Although the Navajo War had indeed ended with the conclusion of Carson's campaign, but such is not to say there were no further troubles. In June 1868, a party of Navajos killed and mutilated four white men near Twelve-Mile Creek, even as preparations to return them to their homeland were underway. However, Navajo leaders, most anxious not to jeopardize their return, agreed to cooperate in finding the guilty parties. Whether the killers were ever actually found and turned over is not known. In any event, the incident seems not to have interfered with returning the Navajos to their homeland.

But if the Navajo threat was largely a thing of the past, bands of Apaches, primarily Mescaleros, continued to raid. On March 11, 1868, Mescaleros raided around the settlement of Tularosa, killing 24 men and 2 women. The raiders also made off with some 2,000 sheep. A detachment of the 3rd Cavalry from Fort Stanton pursued the raiders but lost them in the rugged Guadalupe Mountains.

Through the spring and summer of 1869 roving bands of Apaches struck ranches, wagon trains and outlying settlements. Detachments operating out of both Fort Stanton and Fort Selden were continuously in the field in pursuit of these raiders, though seldom with any real success.

The soldiers did enjoy some success that fall of 1869. On November 18, Mescaleros made off with 150 head of stock from a ranch on the Rio Hondo. On this occasion, they were pursued by thirty-one-year-old Lieutenant Howard Bass Cushing, a gutsy, hard-driving young officer leading F Company, 3rd Cavalry out of Fort Stanton. Wisconsin born, Cushing was one of four brothers who served with distinction in the Union Army during the Civil

War; only two of whom survived that conflict. After serving in the artillery during the war, Cushing transferred to the cavalry where he spent the next six years pursuing Indian raiders in the Southwest. He died in an Apache ambush in Arizona in 1871.

The struggle for peace in New Mexico Territory had been a long, tough struggle, indeed longer than any other region in the Trans-Mississippi West.

IV

The Central Plains

Prologue: Pike's Peak or Bust

For the purposes of this book, the Central Plains are defined as, roughly, the region bounded by the Platte River on the north and the Arkansas River on the south, and including all or parts of the present states of Colorado, Kansas, Nebraska, and Wyoming. The indigenous tribes that called this region home were principally the Lakota, Southern Cheyenne, Arapaho and Pawnee. Occasionally, the mountain-dwelling Utes would also venture out onto the Plains in search of buffalo.

In addition to the steady influx of white immigrants, there were two significant events responsible for bringing about warfare between Indians and whites on the Central Plains: the railroad and the telegraph.

In the years since General Stephen Watts Kearney proclaimed New Mexico to be part of the United States, wagon trains large and small forged across the central corridor of the Great Plains, carving the ruts of Manifest Destiny along the California-Oregon Trail. Overland traffic was light when Marcus and Narcissa Whitman made their way to the new Oregon country, but with the discovery of gold, first in California, then Colorado, immigrant traffic exploded, and as it did, its effect on the natural resources of the country through which these trails passed was significant and felt in a serious way by the region's indigenous peoples.

The country was shrinking, although those who labored across the plains and mountains would no doubt contest the point, but indeed the U.S. of A. was in fact getting smaller in the sense that travel and communication were faster than anyone might have dared imagine just a few decades before. Railway systems were already well underway east of the Mississippi River prior to the Civil War and talk of a trans-continental railroad was reaching the feverish stage. However, before the steel rails could be laid, a route had to first be determined: which course offered the most direct approach with the lowest grades. And finding these routes was the job of railroad survey crews. Mostly, these survey crews did not particularly trouble the Indians, although on occasion they proved a tempting target to young hot-blooded warriors.

Unrelated to railroads, save in a spiritual sense, the telegraph—the Talking Wire as the Indians called it—would be the other half of the continent-shrinking equation. James K. Polk's election in 1846 was the first presidential election to be announced by telegraph. By the mid-1850s parts of California were connected by wire and by 1863 messages could be flashed from the Atlantic Seaboard to Pacific shores and points in between.

As the decade of 1850s opened, the U.S. Army found itself with an increasingly tough assignment and it would get no easier in the years to come. Travel across the great central plains corridor peaked in 1852 as some 70,000 emigrants headed toward Oregon, California, or Utah. Protecting these travelers from raiding Indians with but a skeleton force was a nearly impossible task, particularly when it is realized that the rank and file of this frontier army was underpaid and served under mostly abominable conditions. The 1850s also saw the arrival of monthly mail coaches along the overland trail and the army found itself responsible for protecting these as well. Not only that but these soldiers were also expected to act as common laborers—they built the posts in which they were garrisoned—surveyed routes of travel, and acted as escort for railroad survey crews and exploring expeditions.

Beginning with the last half of the 1840s, notably with the Whitman massacre and continuing into the '50s, Army units had seen action against various Indian bands in the Pacific Northwest, California, Nevada, and New Mexico, but to the east of the Rocky Mtns. conditions were quieter, with only isolated occurrences of trouble. West-bound emigrant wagon trains were generally not bothered, except for sporadic Indian raiders who found emigrant livestock too tempting to resist.

The year 1854 might well be seen as a watershed year on the Central Plains. It marked a defining point in Indian-white relations on the Great Plains and set the stage for the turmoil that was to follow. Notable events often come about as a result of little things and in this case it was arrogance and stupidity that set the stage for conflict and death.

The 1851 Horse Creek Treaty

The Horse Creek Treaty of 1851 was the first significant agreement between the U.S. and a number of the prominent bands of Plains Indians—Lakota, Cheyenne, Arapaho, and others, including Blackfeet, Assiniboins, Mandans, and others; nearly 10,000 in all. The Indians responded warmly to entreaties by Indian Agent Thomas "Broken Hand" Fitzpatrick, who was largely responsible for bringing about this important gathering.[1]

Fitzpatrick was one of the West's more colorful and interesting characters, and he may have been the best Indian agent ever to wear that title. Called one of the three best mountain men of the fur trade era, Fitzpatrick was born in County Cavan, Ireland in 1799 and arrived in this country as a youth of seventeen. Six years later he went up the Missouri River with entrepreneur William Ashley and participated in the great fight with the Arickara. During the next decade he trapped throughout the Rocky Mountains and in the Southwest. In a chancy 1832 fight with the Gros Ventres [pronounced Grow Vont] his hair turned white, after which he was sometimes called "White Hair." But it was the Nez Perce Indians who provided his best known sobriquet, "Broken Hand" owing to a firearms accident that resulted in the loss of two fingers on his left hand. Fitzpatrick was engaged in the fur business either as a trapper or entrepreneur or both until the 1840s when he began guiding wagon trains to Oregon and served as a guide for Pathfinder John C. Fremont's second expedition. In 1846 he was appointed agent for tribes inhabiting the Upper Platte and Arkansas River drainage systems. He died of pneumonia while in Washington on treaty business in 1854.

FORT LARAMIE

Perhaps no military post in the Trans-Mississippi West is as celebrated in history as Fort Laramie. In 1854, however, it had not yet achieved the status it would later enjoy. Orig-

"Old Bedlam," bachelor officers' quarters at Fort Laramie, fallen into disrepair many years after it served an important role during the Indian wars.

inally, a trading post founded in 1834 by William Sublette and Robert Campbell it was purchased by the United States Army in 1849 and renamed Fort Laramie. The post's final name was taken from that of Jacques LaRamee a Canadian trapper killed by Indians in 1822. Now, as droves of Indians began to arrive at Fort Laramie for Fitzpatrick's conference, the site was moved downstream to Horse Creek, because the grazing around the fort had already been drastically depleted by passing emigrant wagon trains, as well as by Indians steadily arriving for the council.

On September 17, 1851, U.S. Government commissioners and representatives of the various Indian bands signed the Horse Creek Treaty. Each tribe was to receive $50,000 in annual supplies for a period of fifty years. Each tribe was also assigned a specific territory, with the Lakota Sioux, now the most powerful of the Plains Tribes, being given all of what was then western Dakota Territory, Nebraska, and northeastern Wyoming. Other tribes were assigned territory in accordance with their power and importance. Notwithstanding the favorable response of the tribes to this parley, the situation rather teetered on the brink of collapse when the huge wagon train bearing the annuities failed to arrive on time. Fortunately, however, the train finally put in an appearance, much to the relief of the government officials and the soldiers in attendance. Annuities, including sabers, and officers' uniforms were presented to the various chiefs, in accordance with their perceived stature.

By white standards the treaty seemed fair and generous, but like all such agreements it was fatally flawed. And perhaps the most fatal defect of all was that of arbitrarily assigning individual headmen as overall chiefs of their respective tribes. Here was yet another instance of U.S. insistence on having one spokesman for each tribe, a concept totally out of sync with reality. Conquering Bear the principal Brule leader was named chief of all the Lakota, despite fact that he was authorized to speak only for the Brules; some of the other Lakota bands over which he now ostensibly wielded authority were not even present. This failure to understand the political structure of Indian tribes would continue to have tragic consequences in the years ahead. It will be recalled that this same flaw had been repeated in the Pacific Northwest and New Mexico, and it would continue to plague U.S.–Indian relations during much of the last half of the 19th century.

1853 Overture

The summer of 1853 was a portent of things to come. A band of Miniconjou Lakotas came down from the Black Hills to the Platte River, in the general vicinity of Fort Laramie, to join their Brulé and Oglala cousins on the annual summer gathering. Three years earlier the U.S. Army had constructed a skiff ferry for crossing the North Platte River, which was fairly wide and at certain times of the year, notably during spring run-off, quite deep. The visiting Miniconjous camped near this ferry.[2]

Only occasionally did the Miniconjous venture this far south, but they soon found the passing immigrant wagon trains to be a source of some amusement. With a little pressure and harassment these trains could often be coerced into providing tobacco, whiskey, or whatever else captured the fancy of the Miniconjous. Although it seems unlikely that these particular Indians sought serious trouble, the threat seemed real enough to the immigrants. The Miniconjous also took a liking to the Army's ferry and on one occasion commandeered it until forced off by a veteran Army sergeant. Angry, one of the warriors fired a shot at the ferry and though the bullet hit nothing but water the Army did not take the incident lightly and post commander, Lieutenant Richard Garnett (a future Confederate general who would lose his life in Pickett's Charge at Gettysburg) sent 2d Lieutenant Hugh Brady Fleming and twenty-two men to arrest the guilty party. Reaching the Miniconjou camp as evening drew near, Fleming, unable to find the guilty warrior, ordered the entire band to surrender. The villagers of course refused. A skirmish followed in which five warriors were felled, but the guilty warrior remained at large. Fleming withdrew taking two women prisoners back to Fort Laramie.

Later, the Miniconjou chief, Little Brave, with a contingent of warriors, rode to Fort Laramie to parley with Lieutenant Garnett. In the discussion that followed the Lakotas swore they were guilty of no wrongdoing. Indeed, they said, the white man was in violation of the treaty and demanded that the Army abandon Fort Laramie. Garnett, however, refused to be intimidated and insisted that the Lakotas had been in the wrong. Nevertheless, to show his good faith he released the two women prisoners. One wonders whether Garnett sensed that major trouble had been averted because the Lakotas could easily have overwhelmed the tiny garrison at the fort had they chosen to do so. It was a warning.

Meantime, annuity goods to be given to the Indians by virtue of the Horse Creek Treaty finally arrived in August and were stored at the Gratiot House, a few miles downstream from the fort. The trading house of one James Bordeaux stood about three miles from Gratiot House. The Lakotas anxiously awaiting their annuities had been arriving in the area since July. The Oglalas camped near Gratiot House, while Conquering Bear's Brulés set up camp near Bordeaux's trading post.

Grattan Massacre

On August 18, a Mormon immigrant came into Fort Laramie to report that an Indian had stolen one of his cows. Lieutenant John Lawrence Grattan, an 1853 West Point graduate urged his post commander, now Lieutenant Fleming, of all people, to assign him the job of arresting a suspected Minniconjou warrior believed hiding in the Brule village. Grattan had arrived at Fort Laramie with no permanent assignment and was awaiting a regimental appointment. Like many other young officers on the frontier Grattan had little regard for the fighting ability of Indians, claiming that with a howitzer and a few regulars he could whip all the Indians.

Conquering Bear, seeing trouble in the offing, urged Lieutenant Fleming not to take action until Agent Fitzpatrick arrived with the year's annuities, but Fleming, who seems not to have learned anything from his own experience a year earlier, caved in to Grattan's insistence.

With twenty-nine men and an inebriated French interpreter named, Lucian Auguste, Grattan marched into the Brule camp, where he unlimbered the howitzer, trained it on the camp and demanded that Conquering Bear surrender the guilty party. For nearly an hour the words flew. Reportedly, the guilty Indian stood in front of his tepee, vowing that he was ready to die. Out of patience, Grattan finally opened fire, mortally wounding Conquering Bear. Grattan next ordered his howitzer to fire into the village, but fortunately it was aimed too high and did nothing more than tear up a tepee. Probably disconcerted at first by the blasts from the artillery pieces, the Indians quickly recovered and seized the initiative. The soldiers withdrew, apparently in an orderly fashion before being overwhelmed. All save one were followed and killed, including Grattan. Later, when the remains of those killed had been found, Grattan's body had been pierced by twenty-four arrows. The badly wounded lone survivor would eventually be helped back to the fort where he later died of his wounds, as did Conquering Bear who had been wounded three times.

Not until the following day did word of the fight reach Fleming when Trader James Bordeaux sent an employee to the fort. In the aftermath of the fight news of the incident got the attention of the nation … and Congress. There was a cry for revenge, despite the fact that Grattan had blundered and Fleming had exercised questionable judgment at best. The Indian Bureau, too, had contributed to the disaster. As historian Douglas McChristian has pointed out, locating the Upper Platte Agency near Fort Laramie was an invitation to the Indians to congregate around the Overland Trail area, where the Indian Bureau specifically did not want them to be. It would appear too, that the War Department gave little thought to the possibility of having to deal with Indian troubles around Fort Laramie, as it had stationed only one company of infantry under a junior officer (Fleming) at the post.[3]

The Grattan incident might well have brought on a major war but it didn't. Although most of the Lakotas feared repercussions and moved north to see what would happen, there were some whose blood was up and who wanted to attack Fort Laramie, particularly since annuities due the Indians by virtue of the Horse Creek Treaty were, as always, slow to arrive and restlessness among the younger warriors began to mount, especially when the annuities were not promptly distributed. Fortunately for the whites, there were cooler heads among the Indians who successfully argued against that striking back. However, angry Lakotas did raid the Gratiot House where the annuities were stored; attacked the stage station, stole livestock and generally vented their spleen on anything white in the area. The Cheyennes and Arapahos who were not involved with the Grattan incident remained in the vicinity of Fort Laramie.

The remainder of 1853 and the first half of 1854 were relatively quiet, but beneath the surface trouble lurked aplenty. News of the Grattan Fight—massacre as it quickly and erroneously came to be called—flashed across the telegraph wires and, capturing the attention of the nation and of Congress. Revenge was in the wind. The Indian Bureau, which seldom trusted the Army's judgment anyway (and vice-versa), placed the blame on Grattan's shoulders, but recognized that Fleming's judgment deserved to be questioned. True, Grattan asked for trouble and got it, but in sending a hot-headed, inexperienced young second lieutenant on an assignment that called for a wiser and cooler head was exceedingly poor judgment on Fleming's part. Be that as it may, one might argue that conditions made it convenient for trouble to erupt. As one historian has pointed out, locating the Upper Platte Agency farther from Fort Laramie would have served to keep the tribes away from the Overland Trail and hence reduce the likelihood of contact with immigrant wagon trains.

In any case, as a consequence of the Grattan disaster and Indian troubles elsewhere in the West, a bill to increase the size of the Army gained momentum. Secretary of War Jefferson Davis declared, ridiculously, that the Grattan business was part of a plan to attack and loot trade stores designed to service emigrant traffic along the Overland Trail. The Sioux must be chastised for Grattan's death, said Davis. To not do so would be to let them think they had done nothing wrong.

When Indian raids on livestock continued through the fall and winter of 1854–1855 they served to reinforce fears of further Indian troubles. On November 13, a Brule Lakota raiding party, seeking revenge for the death of Conquering Bear, attacked a stage bound for Salt Lake, killing three and wounding another, and stealing a strongbox with $10M in gold. The incident demanded some sort of response and accordingly, two companies of infantry under Major William Hoffman came up from Fort Riley to reinforce Fort Laramie, now suddenly thought to be vulnerable. By virtue of his senior rank, Hoffman assumed command of Fort Laramie from Lieutenant Fleming. Faced with continued depredations along the Overland Trail, Secretary Davis decided that the situation needed a firmer hand. The Lakota must be chastised for the Grattan disaster. To do nothing would send the message that the United States did not consider the Lakotas guilty of any wrong-doing. Accordingly, in October 1854, Davis and General of the Army Winfield Scott selected William S. Harney—recently promoted to brigadier general—to lead a punitive expedition against the Sioux.

"By God I'm for battle—no peace"[4]

For the U.S. Army (not so for the Lakota, however), the choice of Harney to command the first punitive expedition against the Plains tribes was a good one. Fifty-four years old in 1854, Harney was a grizzled veteran, having served in the artillery, infantry and dragoons. Indeed, called the "Prince of Dragoons" by one biographer, Harney had seen service in the Blackhawk War, the Seminole and Mexican Wars. Tall and powerfully built, the sometimes cantankerous and fully bearded Harney reminded one of an Old Testament prophet. During the Seminole War he once managed to escape from a surprise Indian attack by fleeing through the forest in his underwear. The following year he disobeyed orders by having his men dress as Indians in an attack on a Seminole Village. In June 1846 he was promoted to colonel and became the Army's senior cavalry officer. On leave in Paris, he was ordered home to lead the expedition against Sioux. On August 24, 1855, at head of 600 dragoons,

Officers of the frontier army at Fort Sanders, Wyoming, in July of 1868. Included are P.H. Sheridan (fourth from left), U.S. Grant (center, hands on fence), William T. Sherman (center, facing left), and W.S. Harney (third from right with white beard).

Harney pulled out of Fort Kearny, Nebraska, with the pronouncement "By God I'm for battle—no peace."

Meantime, the Indian Bureau was making changes of its own. Following Fitzpatrick's demise, John Whitfield was appointed agent at Upper Platte, but then even as Harney was about to set forth, a further change occurred in August 1854. The Upper Platte Agency was seen as too unwieldy and was broken up into two parts. Thomas Twiss was assigned to head the new Upper Platte Agency replacing Fitzpatrick, while Whitfield was given the responsibility of the tribes living along the Arkansas River. Something of an intellectual, Twiss brought an interesting background to his new posting. A West Point graduate, he had also been a railroad engineer and professor of philosophy. In October, he recommended to the Commissioner of Indian Affairs that a new agency be established for Cheyennes and Arapahos at Fort St. Vrain on the South Platte River. This would remove them from the influence of Sioux, who should have their own an agency around Fort Laramie. Such an arrangement, however, would be contradictory to Harney's views.

Blue Water Expedition

The situation with Indian raids along the Platte River Road was not unlike that with the Navajos in that while the Brule headman, Little Thunder, seemed friendly enough toward whites, the young warriors who were causing the mischief lived in his village and ferreting them out without creating a major incident was nigh impossible. Agent Twiss urged Little Thunder to relocate his camp south of the Platte River, away from the main corridor of immigrant travel in order to at least be perceived as non-hostile. Little Thunder, however, failed to heed the agent's advice and so when Harney's scouts located the village on Blue Water Creek, a tributary of the Platte (near present Lewellen, Nebraska) on September 2 the stage was set.

Harney judged this village to be hostile, based on the report of some passing freighters who had experienced a fracas with these Brules who were of Little Thunder's band and said to have played a part in the Grattan disaster. Based on the number of lodges in the camp, Harney expected to be confronted by as many as 120 warriors and made his plans accordingly. Colonel Philip St. George Cooke would take four companies of mounted troops and block the only line of retreat open to the Sioux, while Harney advanced against them with the infantry. More men were positioned along the high ground above the canyon floor. Caught between Cooke's horsemen and the advancing infantry, the Brules had no option but to try and flee while soldiers positioned along the heights fired down on them. Seldom does an opponent behave exactly as one hopes, but in this instance the Indians did precisely that, falling back toward Cooke's waiting horsemen. It was a crushing defeat: Eighty-six Brulés died and some seventy women and children were captured. Harney's losses, meanwhile, amounted to four killed. Soldiers ransacking the village found uniforms stripped from Grattan's men along with things taken from the Salt Lake stage raid.

In the aftermath of the battle, Harney established a temporary post near Ash Hollow he named Fort Grattan, leaving a small detachment of the 6th Infantry under Captain Henry Wharton to man the post, after which Harney began the 140-mile march to Fort Laramie, arriving on September 15. Harney's victory on the Blue Water brought an end to the first encounter of the first Sioux War. Ash Hollow was a defining moment in the Indian wars on the Central Plains because it cowed the Lakota into submission for many months. Ash Hollow ended victoriously for the U.S. Army, but there would be others in the years ahead with results far less positive For his part, Philip St. George Cooke would go on to see considerable service in the Trans-Mississippi West before his career drew to a close.

When Harney, the avenging angel, returned to Fort Laramie he found a huge Sioux camp containing an estimated 4,000 souls, encamped about thirty-five miles above the fort. Flushed with victory, a triumphant Harney addressed the leaders. They must, he warned them, cease their raiding, or else. By his orders, all trade with these Sioux was to be limited to the vicinity of military posts, where the Army could monitor activities. To Secretary Davis, Harney emphasized the growing strategic importance of Fort Laramie. As well, he pointed out the potential out danger of having so many Indians so close to immigrant corridor. In keeping with its new found position of strategic importance, Harney directed that Fort Laramie be reinforced with five companies of infantry, a company of artillery—presently serving mounted as cavalry—and two-plus companies of dragoons. This done, Harney then took rest of his command on a grand march through Lakota country to Fort Pierre, Dakota Territory (present day Pierre, South Dakota) intending to make an unmistakable impression of the Sioux.

In October 1854, Agent Twiss recommended to the Commissioner of Indian Affairs that a new agency be established for the Cheyenne and Arapaho at Fort St. Vrain on the South Platte River. This would remove them from the influence of Sioux, who should have their own agency around Fort Laramie, notwithstanding Harney's views to the contrary. On paper this was perhaps a sensible solution. The problem was that the Lakotas were much more numerous ... and scattered. Altogether there were seven principal bands or council fires (Oglala, Brulé, Miniconjou, San Arc, Blackfoot—no relation to the Montana Blackfeet—Hunkpapa, and Two Kettles) that ranged between the Canadian border and

Platte River, and consolidating them all in and around one agency was a logistical impossibility. Clearly, Agent Twiss lacked a clear grasp of the situation.

On October 17 Brulé chief, Thunder Bear informed Twiss he wanted peace and to prove it would bring in those guilty of the attack on the mail coach. It was a day for surprises. Thunder Bear's declaration was followed by the surrender of Spotted Tail, Long Chin and Red Leaf. The trio was advised that they would be imprisoned at Fort Leavenworth. Amazingly, the three leaders agreed, but asked for time to prepare. To this Major Hoffman agreed, informing them that they were due back on the 27th. The major was informed that there were two others involved—boys, one of whom had since joined a Missouri River band. The second boy was ill with tuberculosis and was too ill to travel. Hoffman stupidly insisted there be no exceptions and eventually all four were brought in and imprisoned.

Having punished the Lakota, who now seemed fairly tractable, Secretary Davis directed Harney to negotiate a new treaty. Accordingly, Harney sent word for a big parley to be held at Fort Pierre on March 1. The Indian Bureau and Twiss, especially, were furious at what they considered Harney's high handed behavior, but the fault actually lay with Davis who had completely ignored the chain of command. When Davis issued his directive he intruded on the authority of the Indian Bureau. Conflict between the War Department and the Indian Bureau would wax and wane during the remainder of the 19th century.

Politicking creates messy situations. Both Twiss and Harney used whatever influence each possessed to undermine the other. Twiss advised the Oglalas and Brules not to attend Harney's planned council at Fort Pierre. Harney of course was furious. In this he was at least given moral support by Secretary Davis. Davis, unfortunately for Harney, had no authority to issue orders to the Indian Bureau. However, Harney did order Twiss to move his office to Fort Laramie, where he was only to have contact with the Cheyenne and Arapaho; contact with the Lakota was reserved exclusively for Harney. As Davis had done with Harney, so too did the Commissioner of Indian Affairs, George Manypenny agree with Twiss that Harney had exceeded his authority. And given the adversarial feeling between the War Department and the Indian Bureau it was unlikely any reasonable compromise could be achieved. Harney was a little high-handed for sure, but Twiss was not lily-white either. He had been lining his pockets by using annuity goods in trade for buffalo robes.

Meanwhile, in March 1856, notwithstanding the Indian Bureau, Lakotas minus Oglalas and Brulés arrived at Fort Pierre, where they signed a second treaty with Harney. The terms were all too familiar. The Indians agreed to return stolen property, surrender guilty warriors, and further agreed not to molest travelers along the immigrant roads. Harney also stipulated that each band was to have a certain number of chiefs who would be recognized as such by U.S. authorities. The new treaty also called for the Indians to form their own police force to watch over each band. Then in late April, the Oglalas and Brules finally reached Fort Pierre and agreed to Harney's terms. On May 20, the Brulés and Oglalas turned over captured livestock, along with those individuals guilty of committing depredations, but Harney was feeling generous these days and chose to release the surrendered warriors with their promise not to commit future wrongs. Harney's position at this time was a strong one. His victory at Blue Water was long-lasting insofar as the Lakotas were concerned. In their collective memories, Blue Water left an indelible mark.

The fruits of Harney's victory at Blue Water notwithstanding, during the spring and summer of 1856, Inter-tribal trouble was brewing south of the Platte River, in the domain of the Cheyenne and Arapaho. Despite the terms of the Horse Creek Treaty, the Cheyennes were unable to resist raiding their old enemies the Pawnees, who were also arch-enemies of the Lakota.

A tribe that inhabited the Central Great Plains around the Loup and Platte Rivers in present Nebraska, The Pawnees were composed of four separate, self-governing bands. They both clashed with and traded with French, and Spanish, as the occasion demanded. Fierce enemies of the Lakota, Cheyenne, and Arapaho, they generally cooperated with the U.S. and at times served as scouts for U.S. Army. The famous Pawnee battalion led by Frank and Luther North played an important role in the later Army expeditions against the Lakota.

It wasn't just the inter-tribal nature of these raids, which caused trouble for travelers along the Overland Trail, to say nothing of the military survey crews then in the process of locating new routes of travel across the central Great Plains. Harney sent the Cheyennes and Arapahos a stern warning to cease and desist. However, growing sectional differences in Kansas, Missouri, and Nebraska over the coming Civil War—especially Kansas—prevented him from taking any real action.

Farther north, in April 1856, disagreement over the ownership of a horse created trouble when the officer in command at Upper Platte Bridge Station (present Casper, Wyoming), Captain Henry Heth (pronounced Heath) attempted to arrest some Cheyennes. Heth would later make something of a name for himself by initiating the opening action at Gettysburg when his division of General A.P. Hill's Corps clashed with John Buford's Federal horsemen.

In the scuffle that followed, one Cheyenne was killed and another taken prisoner. The remainder of the Cheyenne party fled toward the Black Hills, killing a trapper en route. This incident was followed in June by the more or less accidental killing of an immigrant near Fort Kearny by a party of Cheyennes who were actually searching for Pawnees. Then in August another party of Cheyennes attacked the Salt Lake mail coach and wounded the driver. This brought action in the form of Captain George Stewart with a company of the 1st Cavalry who found and attacked a Cheyenne village on the Platte, killing ten. The Cheyennes of course retaliated and all along the great immigrant road where a dozen travelers felt their wrath.

Cheyenne leaders, knowing full well what Harney had done to the Sioux, traveled to the Upper Platte Agency to discuss matters with Twiss. Impatient soldiers and hot blooded young warriors were to blame, claimed the Cheyennes, who promised to remove their people from the vicinity of the Overland Trail if the Army would leave them alone. The War Department had other plans, however. The new Western Deptartment. Commander, General Frazer Persifor Smith took the position that the Cheyennes must be punished and promptly set in motion plans for a major campaign to be launched in the spring of 1857.

Persifor Smith was a twenty-year veteran and one who had distinguished himself during the Mexican-American War. Considering the fact that Smith was in poor health and had but a year to live, he seems to have been an odd choice for the job.

Bull Sumner Takes the Field

On April 4, 1857, following his less than successful term in New Mexico Territory—an assignment he detested—Edwin Vose "Bull" Sumner, now colonel of the new 1st Cavalry, created March 3, 1855, sortied from Fort Leavenworth on May 20, at the head of two companies of his own1st Cavalry and two companies of the 2d Dragoons, moved up the Plate Valley, while Major John Sedgwick led four companies of the 1st Cavalry along the Arkansas River corridor. A third force under the command of Lieutenant Colonel Joseph Eggleston Johnston was also in the field, under orders to survey the southern boundary of Kansas.

Not actually a part of Sumner's command, Johnston, nevertheless, was to cooperate with Sumner should the need for such assistance arise. The plan changed quickly however when issues with the Mormons out in Utah resulted in the need to establish a military presence in that area. Originally, Harney had been the choice to command the Utah Expedition, as it came to be known, but Secretary Davis decided that his skills were better served in troubled Kansas, so the assignment went instead to Colonel Albert Sidney Johnston (no relation to Joseph Eggleston). All three of these men would go on to fame in the soon-to-come Civil War. Albert Sidney Johnston would later lose his life at the Battle of Shiloh; Joseph Eggleston Johnston would also become a major Confederate Army officer. Sedgwick, a veteran officer, who would rise to Major General in the Army of Potomac and be known as Uncle John to his men, and would die at Spottsylvania Courthouse, Virginia. Sumner, too, would become a corps commander in the Union Army.

But for now, Sedgwick marched from Fort Leavenworth west to Bent's Fort, then north to Fort Pueblo, then to Fort St. Vrain. Sumner, meanwhile, marched northwest to Fort Kearny and then to Fort Laramie before turning south to rendezvous with Sedgwick along South Platte River at what Sumner named Camp Buchanan (near Julesburg) in honor of the president.

By July neither column had met up with any Indians. Reaching Fort Laramie Sumner learned that his dragoons had been ordered to join Johnston's expedition to Utah. However, In return for giving up his dragoons, Sumner was given three companies of the 6th Infantry.

General Edwin Vose Sumner.

In any case, from Fort Laramie, Sumner swung south to his rendezvous with Sedgwick near present Greeley, Colorado in July. Here, the expedition remained in camp resting and fitting out for the upcoming expedition. On the morning of the 13th the Sumner column moved out toward the Republican River Valley.

On the morning of the 29th, Pawnee scouts informed Sumner that an Indian camp had been located in the Solomon River Valley—just west of present Hill City, Kansas. Leaving the infantry to protect the howitzers, he advanced along Rock Creek, a small stream in the Solomon Valley. The Indians had learned of Sumner's approach and prepared to fight. At first light, the Cheyennes moved out from their village to a small lake. Here, their Medicine Men, Ice and Dark, advised the warriors that once they had washed their hands in this water, they would be invincible to the soldier bullets, a misguided belief that would be witnessed time and again, notably at Adobe Walls and Wounded Knee, South Dakota Cheyenne scouts fell back as Sumner approached. The day had progressed into afternoon. Rounding a sharp bend in the Solomon, Sumner discovered a large body of Indians advancing toward him. By the Bull's estimate there were some 300. History has not recorded Sumner's reaction at finding a large body of Indians forming to meet him, but he must have been pleased; this was almost too good to be true. Ordering the pack train to the rear, Sumner formed his command into line, right by fours: six companies, four deep. The order to trot was given. The Cheyennes waited patiently, likely a bit awed at the sight of so many soldiers—Veho, as the Cheyennes called them. Here was perhaps the only spectacle of its kind seen in the Western Indian wars: colorfully decorated warriors; horses painted for war, while on the soldier side could be seen fluttering guidons and uniform brass glittering in the sun. Two parties of Cheyennes moved to strike Sumner's flanks. Detaching two companies to deal with this threat, Sumner continued his advance.

Out in advance of the troops, Sumner's Delaware Indian scout, Fall Leaf, fired the first shot, then wheeled his pony around and rejoined the troops. As the distance between the soldiers and the Cheyennes closed, Sumner ordered a full gallop, followed almost instantly by the command "Draw sabers." Suddenly confronted by some 300 flashing steel sabers, the Indians halted their own advance. Then, unloosing a shower of arrows, they scattered down the Valley of the Solomon.

Sheathing their sabers, Sumner now directed his troopers to pursue the fleeing Cheyennes as targets of opportunity. Crossing the Solomon, the Indians, knowing the lay of the land, were able to avoid the pockets of quicksand, but many of the troops were not so fortunate and became bogged down. The pursuit became a running fight for some seven miles before Sumner finally called a halt, as the Indians had largely disappeared. Two soldiers were killed and nine wounded. Sumner reported nine Indians killed. One of Sumner's wounded was Cooke's son-in-law, the soon to be celebrated Confederate cavalry leader, Jeb Stuart. The Bull was pleased to have led this saber-wielding charge, but some were sharply critical, particularly his long-time rival, Harney. Sumner's critics argued that firearms would have killed more Indians.

In the immediate aftermath of what was probably the one true-to-life cavalry charge against the Indians, as so often depicted on the silver screen, Sumner ordered the construction of a small field fortification, which he named Fort Floyd, in honor of Secretary of War John Floyd, who had replaced Davis. Sumner detached a company of infantry to garrison the little fort and guard the wounded, while he with the main body followed the Indian trail. At the site of the Cheyenne village the troops burned anything and everything left behind that might be of value to the Indians. Sumner pressed his pursuit until September 2 without further contact.

The Cheyennes, meanwhile, having fled before the Long Knives, regretted feeling so intimidated by all of those flashing sabers, but the moment offered scant time for regret. Concerned for their families, they sought out the great village along the Saline River, from where they moved again, this time to the Smoky Hill River—known to them as the Bunch of Trees River—in Central Kansas. To immigrants traveling west across Kansas, hills near present Abilene usually appeared in a haze, thus the name Smoky Hill. Here, they would be safe. The village was large and the location remote. But of course this could only be a temporary haven for the larger the village was the faster the natural resources surrounding it expired. Soon the village split off into smaller bands, some going farther south to seek refuge among the Comanches and Kiowas, while others moved into northwest Kansas along the Republican River and its tributaries.

Meanwhile, Sumner's wagon train under the command of the very able and indefatigable

Percival Lowe, formerly of the 1st Dragoons and now a civilian wagon master, trekked to Fort Laramie where Lowe filled his wagons with additional supplies, then moved on to Ash Hollow to await Sumner's arrival. Lest it be imagined that Lowe's job was a cushy rear echelon assignment, be it noted that he bore responsibility for 109 wagons, drawn by some 500 mules. Provisioning a military campaign in the field during the Western Indian wars was a task of the first order and not for the faint of heart.

Back in June, Robert Miller, agent for the Upper Arkansas tribes, left Westport, Missouri, with a wagon train bearing annuities for the Cheyennes, Arapahos, Comanches, Kiowas, and Plains Apaches. On July 12 even as Bull Sumner was firing up his campaign, Miller was distributing annuities near the ruins of old Fort Atkinson near present Dodge City.

All, save the Cheyennes were the recipients of the federal largesse, and all but the Kiowas were relatively friendly. But then these Kiowas tended to be a moody, superstitious lot anyway. Miller subsequently learned that these same Kiowas had recently attacked a ranch near Mora, New Mexico. Miller must have wondered about the Cheyennes, but of course had no way of knowing about the big fight on Solomon's Fork.

Following distribution to the bands present on the 13th, Miller moved on to Bent's New Fort, built in 1853 and located some thirty-seven miles east of the original fort. Here, Miller expected to distribute annuities to the Cheyennes and Arapahos. However, not ten miles beyond Fort Atkinson, he encountered a large ... and very hungry Arapaho village. These Arapahos had been awaiting Miller's arrival at Bent's Fort for several days, but when the agent failed to put in an appearance, they moved out onto the Plains in the hope of finding game. Miller at once distributed goods to them, then continued on to Bent's Fort, which place he reached on the 19th. The Cheyennes of course were not present, so Miller hoped that William Bent would agree to store the Cheyenne annuities until he (Miller) was able to make contact with Sumner. Old Bill Bent hadn't lived and traded with the Cheyennes for as long as he had without learning a thing or two, and he quickly saw Miller's idea as a stacked deck and refused, arguing that the Cheyennes, when they did show up, would not be in a waiting frame of mind and would attack the fort if they knew the annuities were stored there. Bent had a counter-proposal, however. He offered to lease the fort to the U.S., and if Miller still wished to do so, the annuities could then be stored on what would be federal property. Miller agreed. Bent, meantime, took his personal property and headed east on the 21st. The day before, Miller had finally been able to persuade a French trapper to try and locate Colonel Sumner. After what must have been a chancy dodge trying to avoid parties of hostile Indians, the rider returned on the 27th having been unable to locate Sumner. And with the rider's return, Agent Miller saw his chance of survival drop a notch.

Here it should be noted that not all of the Cheyennes were engaged with Sumner. Stragglers began to drift in to the fort, reporting a great fight. True to Bent's word, they were not in a particularly friendly mood, proclaiming that they planned to join the Kiowas and make war against the white man. Spouting anger, they threatened to return and take the annuities along with Miller's scalp.

What, Miller must have wondered, had happened to Sumner? Truth be told, on August 8, Sumner's tired horsemen finally bivouacked a few miles from old Fort Atkinson. The summer's campaigning had pretty well convinced Sumner that travelers along the Santa Fe Trail needed protection. The Cheyennes seemed combative enough, and there were always the Comanches and Kiowas. Trouble was Sumner's command was not exactly fit for more campaigning. Some of his men were sick owing to a poor diet, and his horses were played out as well. As a consequence, Sumner elected to rest his command for a few days and a messenger was sent on to Fort Leavenworth for fresh supplies. With little in the way of shelter and given the enervating heat of the dog days of August here on the plains of Kansas one has trouble imagining any of Sumner's troopers finding much rest. Nevertheless, for forty-eight hours Sumner's command did in fact rest before moving down river to a new site just east of present Dodge City, Kansas.

From a passing mail coach, Sumner was able to learn that Agent Miller was then at Bent's Fort and was fearful the Cheyennes would raid the fort for the annuities they knew were stored there. Sumner had to act. Selecting the strongest horses he set out for Bent's Fort with six companies, sending the rest back to Walnut Creek (near Great Bend), which was closer to Fort Leavenworth and a source of supplies, though not by much.

On August 13, en route to Bent's Fort, Sumner found Indian sign. Scouts advised him that this was the village of Cheyennes he had tangled with at Solomon's Fork. He also came upon a Mexican wagon train, from which he was able to purchase coffee and flour. It seemed to be a day of discovery for on the opposite side of the Arkansas River was a Comanche village. One could not always divine the mood of the Comanches; mostly that mood was hostile, but in this instance they seemed perfectly content to just remain on their side of the river. On August 18, Sumner reached Bent's Fort, where he directed Miller to turn over all of the annuities to the quartermaster, except for any ammunition which was to be destroyed.

Meanwhile, what of Major Sedgwick? It will be recalled that his column departed Fort Leavenworth back on May 21 and proceeded on a southwesterly course. Nearing old Fort Atkinson the column narrowly avoided disaster when it was threatened by a buffalo stampede. Though a veteran soldier, Sedgwick had little experience as a plainsman. Uncertain as to what to do in this particular situation, he turned to Captain Samuel D. Sturgis who had experienced this phenomenon before and knew exactly what to do. After corralling the wagons and horses, Sturgis positioned the companies of the command so as to break up the stampede by firing into the point and splitting the herd.

The column passed the now crumbling ruins of Bent's Old Fort and on June 18 reached Bent's New Fort, where Sedgwick turned north past the future site of Denver City. Amidst the deepening spring, the lay of the land began to change subtly from that of the Great Plains to the foothills of the Rockies. Along the column's western flank rose great ermine capped peaks. By early July Sedgwick had reached Fort St. Vrain on the South Platte River near present Platteville where he bivouacked to await his rendezvous with Sumner. It had been an uneventful, trouble-free march for the veteran major, though it had been hell on the mules. On July 4, the projected rendezvous date, a single boom from one of Sumner's howitzers was answered by a blast from one of Sedgwick's field pieces. The rendezvous had been carried out.

By September 2, Sumner was back at the Walnut Creek bivouac where a department headquarters messenger brought official word to end the expedition. Four companies of cavalry and six of infantry were assigned to Major Sedgwick who was ordered to march to Fort Laramie where they were to become part of the Mormon Expedition. Sumner himself, with two cavalry companies was to report to Harney at Fort Leavenworth immediately.

There was an epilogue to Sumner's Cheyenne Expedition. It will be recalled that the detachment left behind at Fort Floyd—two officers and sixty-eight men of Company C, 6th Infantry—commanded by Captain Rennselaer Foote and included a dozen wounded from the fight at Solomon's Fork. Sumner had directed Foote that if the main body had not returned by August 20, he was to march his command to the Lower California Crossing of the Oregon Trail and rendezvous with Percival Lowe's wagon train. So through a fortnight of depressing, enervating heat, and with little game to supplement their meager diet, Foote's men waited in vain for Sumner's return. It was a desolate, God-forbidden spot: beastly hot, wolves howled at night, and from time-to-time could be seen an Indian or two. Then, on August 6, Pawnee scouts brought word that Foote was to march to Fort Kearny rather than the Lower Crossing. Perplexed, Foote was uncertain what to do. Sumner's orders had been explicit: remain here until the 20th. But these Pawnees had skirmished with a party of Cheyennes, and that caused Foote to feel somewhat vulnerable. Then, too, supplies were running low, so orders or no, Foote elected to begin his march to Fort Kearny on August 8. The 12th found them about fifty miles from Fort Kearny, but it might as well have been 400. The Pawnees deserted them, and in heavy fog on the morning of the 14th, Foote lost his bearings. They tried to rely on a Cheyenne prisoner for directions, but he spoke no English and no one in the company spoke Spanish or Cheyenne. Blindly, they followed their prisoner east through heavy, drenching downpours and somehow miraculously managed to reach Fort Kearny on the 21st.

To Colorado

The late summer of 1862 was a watershed event that brought home to Westerners all the fear and horror of what a full scale Indian uprising would be like. In August and September of that year, even as the Armies of the Potomac and Northern Virginia were saturating the ground with blood around a place called Antietam, Maryland, the Santee Sioux under their leader, Little Crow, were massacring hundreds of whites in southwestern Minnesota.

The Minnesota Uprising sounded an alarm knell throughout the Plains. The central corridor of the West was growing, not in a huge way at first, but the signs were there. Kansas became a state in 1861 and Colorado was given territorial status; helped along by the discovery of gold, which quickly brought on a rising tide of prospectors and opportunists and soon, where there had been nothing, Denver City seemed to blossom overnight. The slogan "Pike's Peak or Bust" had the same magnetic effect as had Sutter's Mill a decade earlier. For Argonaut and immigrant alike, the threat of Indian trouble was never far from the forefront of their mind. Fears grew with the report of each new incident, many of which were wildly exaggerated. Here a strike on the Salt Lake mail route, there a hit on a passing emigrant wagon train; just enough to keep the pot simmering, if not quite boiling. In Washington, the Commissioner of Indian Affairs was not at all sanguine about Indian-white relations in Colorado, reporting that "they are not as favorable as desired."[5]

If the great migration to the Colorado gold fields and the steady immigrant traffic along the Great Overland Trail disturbed some Indians, it seemed not to provoke an especially militant response from the Cheyennes. For even as Harney had intimidated the Lakota at Blue Water, so, too, did Sumner's victory at Solomon's Fork affect the Cheyennes (save for the Dog Soldiers, of whom more later), who had lost much equipage and food stores in that fight.

Although the Central Plains remained relatively quiet between 1858 and 1863 there was justification for uneasiness on the part of the general public and one could empathize with the Commissioner of Indian Affairs for his pessimism. There was, for example, the killing of a Cheyenne by a soldier at Fort Larned, Kansas, and there were Indian attacks on targets of opportunity throughout the region—from Fort Leavenworth to Denver, and including the Salt Lake City mail stage. Taken individually, each of these incidents probably represented no real cause for alarm, but collectively they suggested far more serious trouble ahead. Several tribes were involved in this mischief-making: Lakotas, some Utes, Kiowas, Plains Apaches, and now and again Comanches. Whites responded with a zeal born of hatred for Native Americans that was now several generations deep.

As said, during this period of restless peace, the Cheyennes did not prove especially troublesome. In point of fact, some Cheyenne chiefs, notably Black Kettle and White Antelope, along with Little Raven of the Arapahos were known peacemakers. These men recognized the futility of fighting the white man and had signed the Treaty of Fort Wise (near present day Las Animas and later to be renamed Fort Lyon) in 1861. The territory assigned to them through the Horse Creek Treaty was now coveted by the advancing white frontier, so when Indian land was needed the obvious solution was simply to remove them to a new reservation. In this case, the Treaty of Fort Wise placed the Cheyennes on a reservation along the Upper Arkansas River.

Governor John Evans

Perhaps no Colorado official feared an Indian uprising more than John Evans, the second territorial governor (William Gilpin had been the first). Evans dreamed of statehood and imagined himself as the new state's first senator, but standing in the way of all this was the Indian problem. The territory had to be brought under control; settlers had to come, communities built and a sense of peace and prosperity established. To this end the governor envisioned concentrating all the Cheyennes and Arapahos on their reservation on the Upper Arkansas. With the tribes thus localized the vast lands over which they traditionally roamed would be available for settlement. In September 1863 Evans called for a big parley with the tribes, intended to enforce the terms of the Fort Wise Treaty, but to no one's surprise—except possibly Evans—no one showed. The Indians saw the treaty for the sham that it was: simply another way to grab their land.

Evans saw the failure of his grand council to convene as a sign that a major Indian war was in the offing, and it was of course, but not because of this alone. Nevertheless, Evans was clearly obsessed—and that is probably not too strong a word—with this fear of a general Indian war. He concluded that the solution might be military force. If the Indians refused to cooperate peacefully, perhaps they could be forced to move. The governor couldn't say it in so many words but a trumped-up war was what seemed to be forming in his mind. Notwithstanding his dire prediction of a major Indian war, he was forced to acknowledge that all of the current mischief was the work of small war parties, and did not reflect a general tribal attitude. Notwithstanding, he felt certain that war was just over the horizon and this of course was fueled by events in Minnesota. Indeed, in the wake of the Minnesota uprising some Lakotas had tried to induce the Northern Cheyennes and the Cheyenne Dog Soldiers to join in a war on the whites, but both the Northern and Southern Cheyenne bands, as well as the Arapahos refused to do so.

The more he pondered the Indian problem, which festered in his mind like a sore that refused to heal, the more the governor grew obsessed with the defense of his territory. Due to the exigencies of the Civil War, however, finding enough troops to adequately guard the territory was simply impossible. Territorial militia—as opposed to federally authorized and supported volunteers—was one option on the table, but few men were willing to commit to two years of service, as mandated by the territorial constitution; besides there were no funds. During the fall of 1863, Evans journeyed to Washington to express his fears to Secretary of War Edwin M. Stanton. Indian troubles in the territory necessitated keeping all of the Colorado volunteers within the territory. And his volunteers needed better weapons. Stanton listened but was too completely consumed with the war in the east to give more than a nodding appreciation to the governor's pleas..

Between the summer of 1863 and the spring of 1864, Evans did now and again meet with Indian leaders, but nothing of any real substance ever emerged from these talks, and besides there was never any concerted effort to reach a truly fair and equitable arrangement with the tribes which of course was really quite impossible anyway. Evans was like Sisyphus pushing a boulder up the hill only to have it roll back down. Given the needs of an advancing civilization, there was no way that Evans or anyone else could create a solution that was fair and equitable to both sides. It is easy to be critical of Evans for his disingenuousness in dealing with the Indians, but truth be told his attitude toward Indians was no different than that of the average Colorado citizen. The Indians occupied land that the whites wanted; it was just as simple as that. It had been that way for more than two centuries and it was never going to change. The only real difference between Evans and the average citizen was that Evans was in a seat of power and able to take the kind of action that was not an option to the man on the street.

Colonel John Milton Chivington

Evans was not without powerful allies, the most prominent of whom was his military commander, Colonel John Milton Chivington. Chivington did not share the governor's paranoia about the immanence of a major Indian uprising, but he did see the Indians as a problem … vermin, really, who needed to be exterminated if Colorado Territory was to grow and flourish; there could be no middle ground in Chivington's eyes. There was nothing disingenuous about John M. Chivington. He was perfectly up front about a solution to the Indian problem: extermination.

John Chivington is central to the story of Indian-white relations on the Plains, indeed, in the entire West. Nothing in Colorado or on the Plains would ever be the same after Chivington's handprint was firmly imbedded on the ground at a place called Sand Creek. Few individuals can be said to have had the kind of forceful impact that Chivington did. A physically large man—he stood six feet, four inches and weighed 260 pounds, his sheer bulk made it tough for anyone to oppose him. An Ohioan by birth and a former Methodist minister Chivington had come to Colorado which he viewed as fertile ground for opportunity and power. Although he had forsaken the ministry, he had not abandoned a brutal zeal for his version of Christianity. Chivington saw himself as something of an avenging angel and was just the sort of *hombre duro* to fill Evans's need for a ruthless military commander. He had arrived in Colorado in 1860, carrying the torch for abolition.

With the outbreak of the Civil War Chivington offered his services to then territorial governor William Gilpin and was promptly appointed major in the 1st Colorado Volunteers. With his forceful personality and natural aptitude for command he rose quickly to regimental command. During the Confederate invasion of New Mexico in 1862, Chivington led his regiment to key victories at Glorietta and Apache Pass, thus thwarting the Confederate invasion. When the 1st Colorado returned home, covered with glory, Chivington was promoted colonel and acquired the *non de plume* of the "Fighting Parson."

Chivington was not alone in his desire to kill Indians; some of his officers were at least as racially motivated. Major Jacob Downing, for example, loathed Indians and was eager to follow Chivington's dictum to kill Indians wherever they found them. As a powerful and forceful personality, Downing was probably second only to Chivington.

In the army chain of command—after January 1, 1864—Chivington was responsible to General Samuel Ryan Curtis, commanding the Department of Kansas and Indian Territory, which included Chivington's Military District of Colorado. For the most part, however, Chivington operated more or less independently. Yet despite his success in New Mexico Curtis was not all that enthralled with Chivington's management of Indian affairs. The colonel knew he was skating on thin ice with Curtis and made an effort to avoid further exacerbating their rather tenuous relationship.

Confederate activity had compelled Curtis to siphon off some of the Colorado Volunteers for duty in Missouri and Kansas and this in turn fed into Chivington's big fear that he would lack sufficient troop strength to take hard action against the Indians. And be it noted that John Milton Chivington was not without political ambition either. A resounding victory or victories over the Indians would almost surely mean stars on his epaulets, to say nothing of his political goals. It is instructive to note that the Colorado territorial press largely supported Chivington's perspective *vis à vis* an Indian war.

During the winter of 1863–1864, things were relatively quiet along both the Arkansas and the Platte Rivers and their tributaries. The Cheyennes and Arapahos were divided into northern and southern bands, with the former located along or near the Platte, while the southern bands tended to gather along the Arkansas and Republican River watersheds. The northern bands seem to have enjoyed more successful fall hunts and were thus better prepared to withstand the rigors of winter. In particular, Cheyennes and Arapahos around Fort Lyon in southeastern Colorado and in western Kansas had suffered through a bad drought and hunting was poor. They had tried to turn themselves in to the army, but were advised their reservation was not yet ready, although one wonders what in the world had to be done to make ready a reservation? It was these Cheyennes and Arapahos who were to figure prominently in the Sand Creek story.

With the arrival of spring the Indians, as they always did in the warm weather months, became more active. There were raids on traditional enemies: Cheyennes and Arapahos raiding Pawnee villages, Utes attacking Cheyennes and so forth. Although the tribes of the Central Plains did not consider themselves at war with the white man, at least not in the sense that an official sate of war existed, a growing number of Coloradans went about their day-to-day endeavors feeling that a war was imminent. And, when one considered the upswing in raids along the South Platte River and across Kansas a case for war could surely be made.

It is important to make a distinction here between what are called incidents as opposed to a major uprising, as occurred in Minnesota. Indian mischief such as a livestock or stagecoach raid, an attack on a surveying party, or even a sudden strike on some lonely homestead did not indicate a tribe was at war with the whites. In a sense, Coloradans recognized this distinction, but if one operated a small homestead out on the Plains, fear of Indian trouble was always in the forefront of one's mind. Mostly, it was the Cheyennes who were judged guilty of so-called mischief, and Chivington, with the blessings of Governor Evans, sent detachments of volunteers into the field with orders to kill all Indians and burn any villages they found.

On April 7, 1864, Indian raiders stole 175 cattle from government contractor Irwin-Jackman, east of Denver. Apparently the fact that the raiders had stolen from federal contractors captured General Curtis's attention and orders promptly went out to General Robert Byington Mitchell, commanding the Nebraska District, to pursue the raiders, ignoring district lines if necessary. Mitchell, who had received his brigadier's star, in April of '62, was a veteran who had seen some hard fighting in the Mexican and Civil Wars, notably at Wilson's Creek and Chickamauga, being severely wounded in the former. A man of unquestioned physical bravery, he could also be something of a tyrant as commander. At Chickamauga, by way of example, he arrested some 300 of his own men and threatened to shoot them for mutiny. The order was later rescinded. In 1864, he was reassigned to the District of Nebraska.

Although Curtis suspected the raiders would be found in Mitchell's sphere of command, the same set of orders went out to Chivington, who advised Curtis that the raiders were Cheyennes and that he had ordered a 54-man detachment of the 1st Colorado, under Lieutenant George Eayre to go in pursuit. The civilian contractors who had tracked the thieves for several miles also believed them to be Cheyennes. Chivington also advised his counterpart up at Fort Laramie, Colonel William O. Collins "to look out for them [the Indians] and kill them. They are raiding in every direction." In any event, it was a fruitless hunt. Eayre and his command took the field from Camp Weld (near Denver) and scoured the country to the east, but found nothing.[6]

The spring was peppered with reports of Indian raids that threatened to further exacerbate tensions. In early April, for example, a band of Dog Soldiers en route to join some Lakotas in a raid against the Crows, happened to chance upon four stray mules that they promptly appropriated. Later, a rancher, W.D. Ripley by name, out searching for his animals came upon the Dog Soldiers and demanded the mules be returned. The Cheyennes in turn demanded a reward. Angry and believing he ought not to have to pay for his own property, the rancher stalked off in high dudgeon and later filed a report at Camp Sanborn on the Cache La Poudre near present Fort Lupton.

A 40-man patrol under Lieutenant Clark Dunn left Camp Sanborn with rancher Ripley in tow. Dunn's patrol caught up with the Dog Soldiers near Fremont's Orchard east of Denver. Dunn tried to parley for the return of Ripley's mules, but his powers of persuasion left something to be desired and the Dog Soldiers rejected his overtures. Frustrated, Dunn then tried to confiscate the Indians' weapons. Bad idea. A fight ensued in which two soldiers were killed and two others were wounded. Three Cheyennes were reportedly wounded, but managed to escape—presumably with Ripley's mules. The incident prompted the Dog Soldiers to rethink their plans and instead of continuing north to join the Lakotas, they retired toward the Smoky Hill country to avoid further contact with the soldiers.

The theft of Ripley's mules, the Irwin-Jackman incident, and a Cheyenne attack on Moore and Kelly's stage station near Julesburg, where a horse herd valued at $800 was run off were typical of the Indian raids that typified the spring and summer of 1864. Reports from one incident or another usually exaggerated the number of Indians involved. Dunn's experience did serve to reinforce the general feeling that the Indians were in a threatening mood. One rancher near Fort Lyon, however, was of the opinion that the Cheyennes did not want war, and since he was married to the daughter of the Cheyenne chief, Lone Bear—known to the whites as One-Eye—his opinion was probably a little better informed than most. And this—not wanting war with the whites—was probably true enough, perhaps even of most bands, though certainly it did not reflect the attitude of the Dog Soldiers, for instance. A splinter group of Southern Cheyennes who had once been cast off from the main band and had since been reconciled with the tribe, probably as much because their strong anti-white stance now found favor with many headmen of the tribe. Although reports of these raids were usually exaggerated—sometimes wildly so—the almost constant presence of military detachments in the field—often chasing nothing more than a rumor—managed to create an illusion of grave trouble.

That firebrand Indian hater, Major Jacob Downing reported that "Everything indicates the commencement of an Indian war." With a 60-man patrol, Downing located a Cheyenne village just north of the South Platte River. Here can be found a striking illustration of the racial bias shared by Chivngton, Downing, and others. A captured Cheyenne was tied to a stake and set on fire, until he agreed to serve as a guide. With no other option available to him the Indian agreed and guided the column to the village.

Although Downing struck while the village was asleep, the Cheyennes reacted quickly enough to respond and establish a defensive position. Eventually Downing called off his attack, claiming he had killed twenty-six Cheyennes, which was almost certainly an exaggeration. Downing later informed Chivington that he had dealt the Cheyennes a harsh blow. Here it might be noted that this was not the first time an Indian village was taken by surprise, nor would it be the last. The myth that an Indian village could not be surprised because Indians were so well attuned to nature is just that: a myth.[7]

As spring deepened the only incident of note had been the attack on Kelly and Moore's stage station yet on May 28, Evans wrote to Curtis painting a gloomy picture: "we are at war with a powerful combination of Indian tribes [said Evans] who are pledged to sustain each other and to drive the white people from their country."[8]

Just how seriously Curtis took Evan's dire view of the situation is not known, but Curtis was growing edgy about the Indian problem. For one thing there had been a flare-up of Kiowa raids and perhaps Evans's words caused him some unease as well. In any event, he came to believe that the corridor between Fort Lyon and Fort Larned, Kansas, was vulnerable to raids. Accordingly, on June 7, he ordered Chivington to take up station near Fort Lyon so as to be in a position to address any troubles that might crop up in that area.

When he learned that Chivington was at Fort Lyon, William Bent paid the colonel a visit, hoping to convince Chivington that Black Kettle was sincere in his desire for peace, but Chivington was not at all receptive. Meanwhile, in Denver, Evans was approached by the Cheyenne chief Spotted Horse who appealed to the governor to bear in mind that not all Indians were hostile. If Chivington dismissed Bent's entreaties out of hand, Evans was only slightly more open minded in his skepticism of Spotted Horse's pleas.

The Hungate Massacre

The flash point of what finally did become the Indian war so long feared by Governor Evans was the murder of the Hungate family. On June 11, 1864, Indian raiders struck the ranch of Isaac Van Wormer, southeast of Denver, killing the foreman, Nathan Hungate, his wife and two daughters. Later, their mutilated bodies were brought to Denver and displayed in a wagon. The incident served to instill both fear and rage among Coloradans. It was one thing to make off with a herd of horses or a brace of mules, but the beastly murder of a man and his family was quite another matter. At the time it was thought the raiders were Cheyennes, though it was later learned the attack had been perpetrated by Arapahos. In the immediate aftermath Governor Evans wired Curtis stressing the need to have all of the Colorado volunteers available to respond to these Indian attacks. Curtis, who clearly did not share the governor's fear, wired Evans saying "Little howitzers surrounded by irregular troops will overpower Indians."[9]

Evans also set about organizing a militia force and wired the Commissioner of Indian Affairs in Washington for permission to raise a regiment of 100-day volunteers, but the commissioner was not quite ready to press the panic button. True enough it was that the Hungate Massacre struck fear into the hearts of Coloradans and there were wild, frenzied reports of growing Indian activity, prompting Evans to order a curfew in Denver. However, despite how the situation appeared on the face of it, as historian Gary Roberts makes abundantly clear, "Evans's tales of horror did not stand up under close scrutiny."[10]

Evans was stuck between a rock and a hard place. As a result of the Hungate Massacre the general public was nervous and wanted reprisals. Evans wanted statehood, and he aimed to be the first U.S. Senator from Colorado. He was also on the Union Pacific Board of Directors and wanted the trans-continental railroad to come through Denver, but none of this was gong to happen until the Indian problem was resolved.

In the wake of the Hungate Massacre, armed bands of whites set out to hunt Indians—any Indians, it didn't really matter—and killing whoever they happened to find. And of course the Indians struck back. Ranches and stage stations felt their fury all along the Platte, Smoky Hill, and the Arkansas, as well as the Solomon and Saline Rivers in Kansas. Mostly the raiders were Cheyennes with some Arapahos. The South Platte corridor was, then as now, a favorite route into Denver, following a course generally parallel to today's Interstate Highway 76. The Smoky Hill Trail ran across central Kansas, in some places paralleling Interstate Highway 70.

On June 27, 1864, Evans issued a proclamation, inviting all friendly Indians to separate themselves from hostile bands and set up camp near military posts where they were assured of army protection and not regarded as hostile. Despite his horror at the Hungate Massacre and his long standing fear of a general Indian uprising, Evans did not intend his June 27 proclamation to be a trap, but in effect this is the way it worked out.

Notwithstanding the demands of the Civil War on his military department, Curtis, finally feeling the need to respond to the Indian problem, assembled a 400-man column at Fort Riley and from there, marched to Fort Larned—southwest of Great Bend, Kansas—where he rendezvoused with Chivington and four companies of the 1st Colorado. Following this, Curtis split his command into three probing columns that wound up finding no Indians. The presence of so many of the soldiers had prompted the Indians to simply fade away. So, with not much of anything to do, by August 8, Curtis was back at Fort Leavenworth. Actually, all the Indians had done was simply make sure they avoided contact with the soldiers. Thus, for the moment anyway, immigrant traffic was again flowing west unimpeded. So it might be argued that the campaign had enjoyed a measure of success after all.

As a consequence of recurring Indian raids between Forts Lyon and Larned, Curtis concluded that better control of the area could be managed by changing the command structure. Accordingly, on August 9, 1864, he created the District of Upper Arkansas, the command of which he assigned to General James Gilpatrick Blunt, whose new sphere of responsibility would include Kansas and southeastern Colorado.

A former seaman from Maine and a medical school graduate, Blunt had come west and gotten involved in Kansas politics. An ardent abolitionist, he had been once been an associate of John Brown. He was appointed lieutenant-colonel in the Kansas Volunteers in 1861, and received his brigadier's star the following year. Blunt had acquitted himself well as a field commander against Confederate forces in Missouri and Arkansas. His first assignment as commander of the District of Upper Arkansas was to organize a 600-man column to take the offensive. Curtis's strategy was to strike the hostiles—as they were then judged—during the autumn months, giving them no time to prepare for winter. There would be no talk of surrender.

The 3rd Colorado Volunteers

On August 11, Governor Evans received the necessary authority to raise a regiment of 100-day volunteers. Finally, it must have seemed to Evans, someone was listening to his cries for help. Twelve days later, on August 23 the governor issued a proclamation for volunteers to form the 3rd Colorado Volunteer Regiment. And almost immediately there developed a rivalry for command of the regiment. Chivington was impressed by Lieutenant George L. Shoup, and based on Chivington's recommendation, Evans named him [Shoup] the regimental commander on September 21.

Meanwhile, on the 15th, General Mitchell arrived at Fort Kearny and was also quick to see that an organizational change was needed. Accordingly, he created two new sub-districts. Responsibility for protecting travel along the Platte Road as far as Julesburg was assigned to Colonel Samuel Summers, an aging Iowan who was soon replaced by Colonel Robert Livingston, 1st Nebraska Cavalry. Responsibility for protecting the route from Julesburg to Fort Laramie fell to the elderly but dignified Colonel William O. Collins. Unlike many frontier commanders, Collins made a genuine effort to familiarize himself with the Indian problem.

Barely had Mitchell settled into his billet than word arrived that a Cheyenne war party had struck along the Little Blue River in Kansas, killing fifteen settlers and taking others captive. The news brought Curtis charging out from Fort Leavenworth to Fort Kearny, where he quickly organized a punitive expedition: 600 men of the 1st Nebraska, 7th Iowa, 16th Kansas Cavalry, plus a few Nebraska militia and some Pawnee scouts. With two general officers, Curtis and Blunt, plus a pair of regimental colonels, there was no shortage of brass on this expedition.

On September 7 the column reached the Solomon River, where Curtis divided his command. With one half under his personal command, Curtis turned east, reaching Fort Leavenworth on the 17th. Meanwhile, Mitchell, with the remainder of the expedition, searched the Upper Solomon and Republican Rivers and reached the Platte on the 16th having had no more success than Curtis. And so the story of yet another empty-handed expedition was recorded in the record books.

Meanwhile, General Blunt, at the head of a 400-man column reached the Cimarron Crossing of the Santa Fe Trail which put him in the land of Kiowas and Comanches. Here he learned of the Cheyenne raids along the Little Blue and turned north in response. On September 25, from Pawnee Fork of the Arkansas River, Blunt's scouts located a substantial force of Cheyennes and Arapahos camped along Walnut Creek. When some gunfire erupted, Blunt sent Major Scott Anthony with two companies of the 1st Colorado to investigate. En route, Anthony came under attack and soon found himself surrounded. Fortunately, a messenger was able to get through to Blunt, who arrived in time to put the Indians to flight. Blunt's troops pursued the Indians for two days before exhausted horses compelled Blunt to call off the pursuit and return to Fort Riley.

In September (some sources say July), word of Governor Evans's proclamation finally reached Black Kettle. The Cheyenne leader took the governor's proclamation seriously and sent word to Major Edward Wynkoop at Fort Lyon, proposing to end all hostilities and to return captive white prisoners. Unsure what exactly to make of this, but willing to give Black Kettle the benefit of the doubt, Wynkoop assembled a column of 125 men from the 1st Colorado, and marched to the Smoky Hill River to participate in what he gambled was going to be a peace conference. And he found the Cheyennes and Arapahos mostly sincere. Indeed four white captives were turned over to Wynkoop then and there. Still, there was tenseness in the air. Some of the Cheyenne leaders, notably Bull Bear, fired angry rhetoric at Wynkoop, arguing that it was foolish to surrender all captives without gaining something in return. But Bull Bear and his cohorts were in the minority and at length the Cheyennes finally consented to turn over all captives. The conference further produced an agreement for Black Kettle and seven others to travel to Denver and formalize a peace agreement with Governor Evans.

When the Indian delegation arrived in Denver, Evans was discomfited; this was a completely unexpected development. He had already, in fact, rescinded his June proclamation, primarily because eastern Colorado had, in his opinion, lived with the perceived threat of an Indian uprising all summer. Whether this was a realistic view of conditions seems now to have been a mot point. But it was true that supplies from the east had been delayed or cut off entirely and Evans was feeling the pressure. He urged citizens to seize any property belonging to hostile Indians, killing them in the process if necessary. Here again, the term "hostile" strictly speaking referred to those Indians who committed depredations, but in actual practice it came to mean literally any Indian. Thus, by fall 1864 it seems clear that Evans had abandoned his peace policy and was gearing up for war.

At the Camp Weld council on September 28, Evans washed his hands of the whole business, advising Black Kettle and the others that peace could still be theirs, providing they distanced themselves from known hostile bands, but, and here was the kicker: they would have to arrange details with the military, which of course meant Chivington. The chiefs agreed and departed, believing they had a peace agreement. But whoa not so fast. The chiefs may have believed a peace agreement was in place, but both Evans and Chivington were quick to let it be known that the Indians were misguided in their belief.

Sand Creek

The story of the Sand Creek tragedy is convoluted and yet at the same time painfully simple. It was arguably *the* defining event in the history of Indian-white relations on the Great Plains; nothing would ever again be quite the same. Although there were clashes aplenty before Sand Creek it would not be unreasonable to suggest that the Indian wars of the West, at least, on the Great Plains, began with Sand Creek and concluded with Wounded Knee.[11]

As much as anything else, Sand Creek is a story of political intrigue on the part of a territorial governor who sought statehood and a senate seat. And it is a story of disputes among the military over command jurisdiction, and the role of volunteers versus regular army troops which was an on-going dispute that had been around for as long there had been a Western frontier. It will be remembered that the squabbling over regulars versus volunteers/militia had played a key role in the Pacific Northwest, in California and Nevada, and in New Mexico as well. But all of the above were contributory factors to the overarching reason that fueled every Indian-white conflict in the West—or East, for that matter: land, either what was on it or under it, or both.

On September 30, 1864, Chivington met with Ben Holladay, owner of the Overland Stage Line. Chivington, in his huge, blustering, intimidating manner, rather demanded that Holladay shift his route farther south for better protection. But tough Ben Holladay was not easily intimidated and refused in no uncertain terms. What Chivington did not seem to appreciate at this point was that Holladay had a bevy of powerful and influential friends and business associates, leverage of which he was quick to take full advantage.

Accordingly, this promptly brought about a swift response from General Henry Halleck, Army Chief of Staff [although alike in name, the position was not the equivalent of the same position today]; there would be no change in stage line's route. Further, Halleck sent a directive to General Patrick Connor in Salt Lake, ordering him to provide protection for the Overland Stage Line. In doing so Connor was to ignore departmental boundaries. The directive did not go so far as to compel district commanders, such as as Chivington, to cooperate with Connor's efforts, however. It was a typical sort of military order that made little sense. As might be expected, Chivington was not at all pleased by Connor's unexpected new role. Chivington, who had his own political agenda, sensed that there was a magnificent opportunity here for a great victory over the Indians and he wanted that glory for himself; there was no way he was going to share the fruits of that victory with Patrick Connor.

Understanding that his orders did not give him the authority to compel any district commander to cooperate, Connor, in a surprise visit to Denver, asked for Chivington's cooperation, but was turned down. Chivington advised Curtis of the situation and as a sort of courtesy—and not much more—he did strengthen outposts along the South Platte Road. Chivington may have been annoyed by Connor's presence, but Governor Evans was encouraged by Connor's idea for a winter campaign against the Indians.

In October, General Curtis, facing the reality of his situation, advised frontier settlements in his jurisdiction that they would have to defend themselves. General Blunt, for example, had been called east to assist Curtis in repelling Confederate General Sterling Price's invasion of Missouri, which meant the district was temporarily without a senior grade officer in command. To look after affairs in his district in his absence, Blunt left Major Benjamin Henning in command resulting in a peculiar command situation. Even though Chivington was senior to Henning, he was answerable to him as Blunt's deputy.

Chivington needed a big score. He had been a hero at Glorietta Pass, but that was two years ago. He had lost his first bid for Congress and that did not sit well with him. Complicating the picture was the fact that his popularity in Colorado had fallen big time. With Denver under martial law following the Hungate murders Chivington's arrogant behavior had made him more than a few enemies, some of whom had once supported him. Nor was he appreciated by General Curtis. In dealing with the Indian question, for example, he had seen fit to ignore the fact that he was answerable to Blunt and in the latter's absence, to Major Henning. Yet another consideration was that Chivington's volunteer commission was due to expire soon, though with Curtis and Blunt busy in Missouri, there was little likelihood any action would be taken until the Confederate invasion had been turned back, so he almost certainly had little to fear on that score.

But Chivington had one concern that weighed on him more than a worry about his volunteer commission. The 3rd Colorado Volunteer Cavalry—the "Hundred Dazers," as they were called, had been created by enlisting many who were nothing more than deadbeats, anxious to kill Indians, and there was grumbling among the rank and file over the fact that they had enlisted to kill Indians but so far most of them had never seen an Indian. Organized in August, their time would soon be up but as yet they had fought no Indians, earning them a second sobriquet "The Bloodless Third."

On October 10, 1864, the Bloodless Third finally drew first blood near Valley Station on the South Platte River, about 100 miles east of Denver. In a brief clash, ten Cheyennes—six men, three women, and a boy—of Big Wolf's band were killed. It could scarcely be called a fight worthy of praise, but the Thirdsters were proud of themselves. Historian Gary Roberts has pointed out that the men of the 3rd Colorado were not really veteran Indian fighters as such, but they had all seen or known of friends who had suffered at the hands of the Indian raiders, and perhaps more importantly they carried in their hearts generations of racial bias toward Indians.[12]

Meanwhile, the Cheyennes and Arapahos were operating under the assumption that they had a deal, but the waters were getting murkier. When Wynkoop agreed to let Black Kettle and the others surrender to him at Fort Lyon, thereby placing themselves under his protection, he did so without the authorization of Major Henning to whom he was responsible as district commander. Here one begins to tangle with the complicated army chain of command. Both Wynkoop and his successor Major Scott Anthony, were officers in the 1st Colorado, Chivington's regiment and answerable to him. However, when acting in the capacity of post commander at Fort Lyon they were directly responsible to Major Henning. Naturally, the loyalty of each man rested with the regimental commander, so it is not difficult to imagine how this arrangement managed to complicate an already tenuous situation.

When Wynkoop left his meeting with the Cheyennes back in September, he believed he had reached an accord of peace with the Indians. However, when the Indians failed to show up at Fort Lyon Wynkoop wrote to Curtis for clarification of orders *vis a vis* his peace arrangement with the Cheyennes (by-passing Henning it might be pointed out), but there had been no response from Curtis, who was probably a little busy dealing with the Confederate invasion of Missouri.

Meanwhile, after duly pondering the offers of Evans and Wynkoop, the Cheyennes under Black Kettle and White Antelope, finally decided to join the Arapahos and give themselves over to the army at Fort Lyon. The small band of Arapahos had already preceded them. Wynkoop was undoubtedly relieved to be able to accept the Indians' surrender and accordingly issued rations and blankets to them. The act, though admirable in and of itself, exacerbated the command structure because Wynkoop acted without proper authorization, and indeed, also clearly exceeded departmental orders. Curtis, in fact, had specifically said he wanted the Indians chastised before there was any talk of peace, and that included parceling out rations to Indians. "I want no peace until the Indians suffer more," Curtis informed Chivington the end of September.[13]

When the Cheyenne-Arapaho contingent arrived at Fort Lyon, Wynkoop issued rations to them for the remainder of his tenure as commander at Fort Lyon. The Indians' delay in reporting to Fort Lyon was due to the Bloodless Third's attack at Valley Station which had created some doubt in their minds as to the sincerity of the white man's offer. As a result the body divided into three groups. Some 500 under Black Kettle and White Antelope elected to go into Fort Lyon, which place they reached the end of October. The Dog Soldiers headed toward the Solomon River, while a third band, uncertain and confused, elected to watch and wait along the Smoky Hill River and see what happened.

What Black Kettle, White Antelope and their followers did not realize, and there was certainly no reason they should have been expected to, is that they were still technically considered hostile because department headquarters had not approved Wynkoop's arrangement. Thus, to Chivington, there was every reason to attack. Notwithstanding, as historian Robert Utley has wisely pointed out, history has not been critical of the Indians for their failure to grasp this subtle distinction.

By November 1864, Chivington was formulating plans for a big strike on the Cheyennes, whom he believed to be camped along the Republican River. Accordingly, orders went out for a concentration of his command at a place called Bijou Basin some seventy miles south of Denver. There was now little doubt left as to Chivington's intentions. His strategy was aided and abetted by both Wynkoop and Anthony who saw fit to keep their regimental commander apprised of what was happening, as opposed to informing Curtis. The picture changed, however, when Major Anthony arrived to take command, pursuant to orders issued by Curtis on October 17. Anthony immediately ordered the Indians to camp along Sand Creek where they would be free to hunt buffalo as he was not in a position to continue to feed them. Anthony was adhering to the directive issued by Curtis and reaffirmed by Henning. The Indians of course were puzzled and failed to understand why Wynkoop had issued provisions to them but Anthony could not. Nevertheless, the Indians went into camp along Sand Creek, secure in the understanding that they were under the army's protection.

Thirty-four years old, Scott Anthony hailed from New York State and was a cousin of Susan B. Anthony the well known suffragette leader. Anthony had been active in mining in the Leadville, Colorado area before accepting a commission in the 1st Colorado Volunteers. He had acquitted himself well at Apache Canyon and Pigeon's Ranch near Santa Fe during the Confederate invasion of New Mexico. Although not a rabid Indian-hater like some of his brother officers, Anthony was nevertheless somewhat more militant than Wynkoop. Scott Anthony was to play a key role in the Sand Creek story.

From reports supplied by both Wynkoop and Anthony, Chivington had learned of the Cheyenne-Arapaho encampment on Sand Creek; this was the intelligence he had been waiting for. Accordingly, on November 24, 1864, in bitter cold and snow two feet deep, Chivington began his march from Bijou Basin to Fort Lyon; his destination known to only a few. Two days later, on the 26th, Anthony, unaware of Chivington's approach, sent John Smith down to Sand Creek to ascertain the number of Indians in the encampment. Smith had friends in the village. He was married to a Cheyenne woman and had a mixed-blood son, Jack, who accompanied him, along with David Louderback, a private from G Company, 1st Colorado, and one Watson Clark, a teamster in the employ of Dexter Colley, the son of Agent Sam Colley. Exactly what role, if any, these other men were intended to play is not clear.

At noon on November 28 Chivington reached Fort Lyon. Though unexpected he was nevertheless welcomed by Major Anthony. As noted, Chivington's movements had been cloaked in secrecy. He had stationed guards along the route of his march and upon reaching Fort Lyon had posted additional guards around the post with orders to shoot anyone attempting to leave. Chivington's plan called for the utmost secrecy. The last thing he wanted was for the Indians to learn that a large body of soldiers was in the area.

When Major Anthony learned of Chivington's plan he reportedly informed his commander that in his opinion the Indians should be punished. Moreover, he would have taken on the task himself if he had possessed the resources. What Anthony seems not to have made clear at this point, however, was that he meant he lacked the resources to attack, *not just those Indians at Sand Creek*, but the bands still at large along the Smoky Hill and Republican Rivers. As will be seen, Scott Anthony was something of a paradox in the Sand Creek saga.

If Anthony welcomed Chivington and was receptive to his plan, such was not the case with all of the officers at Fort Lyon. Some regarded it as downright wrong, since the Indians were at peace. Lieutenant Joseph Cramer argued that such an attack would be nothing short of murder, and Captain Silas Soule was so angry that fellow officers had to keep him away from Chivington. Soule went to Anthony and argued strongly against an attack, whereupon Anthony advised Soule not to accompany the troops if he was opposed. To all those who questioned or stood against his plan, Chivington responded that it was just and proper to kill any Indians who would kill women and children and that any man in sympathy with the Indians should be damned.

At 8 p.m. on November 28, in the frigid blackness of the autumn night, Chivington departed from Fort Lyon leading ten companies of the 3rd Colorado, commanded by Colonel George Shoup, plus three companies of the 1st Colorado. Four mountain howitzers accompanied the expedition. The old mountain man, Jim Beckwourth and young Robert

Bent, son of William Bent served as guides. In all, the expedition totaled some 700 men. Although Chivington could not directly order Major Anthony to be part of the expedition, the major, who later was critical of the attack nevertheless did not refuse to accompany Chivington.

At dawn on November 29, following a bone-numbing cold, forty-mile march, the troops reached the vicinity of the village spread out along Sand Creek. Chivington and Colonel Shoup, out in front of the main body reached a rise of land overlooking Sand Creek. A line of bluffs caused the creek to make a great bend that stretched for nearly a mile, east and west, before looping back to the south.

The Cheyennes of Black Kettle, White Antelope and One Eye was encamped in a grove of trees in a bend of Sand Creek, called Ponoeohe or Little Dried River by the Cheyennes. The river was appropriately named; barely a trickle of water moving along its course in this late season of the Freezing Moon. The Arapahos of Sand Hill and Left Hand were camped nearby. It was a somber late autumn morning. Here and there snow still covered the ground. There were no sentries. After all, this was a peaceful camp under army protection.

The key question here is whether or not this was a hostile encampment. In a sense, it was really a moot point for who could really say which Indians were hostile (as whites understood that term) and guilty of depredations. Evidence suggests that the village contained perhaps 100 warriors. If that estimate is correct, and further assuming all of them might be considered hostile, we must conclude that the bulk of the encampment—70 to 80 percent would have to have been non-hostile. Unquestionably there were some in the village who had been guilty of participating in raids, but in any case Chivington's judgment that the entire village was hostile and as such constituted a legitimate target was a smoke screen to justify his attack.

With his objective spread out before him, Chivington deployed his command along a ridge above the unsuspecting encampment. A few of the inhabitants were up and about at this early hour, some hunting, some checking on the horse herd. The troops seemed to have made no particular effort to be quiet, and presently the noise and clatter of the howitzers being moved into position, together with the thudding of the hooves of the cavalry horses soon alerted the Indians to the presence of the soldiers. Curious, certainly, and perhaps with some apprehension, the Indians watched the soldiers moving about, wondering what was happening. Black Kettle was no less puzzled than the others by these goings-on. Tying both a white flag and an old American flag to a pole he stood it upright next to his lodge as a sign that his people were at peace. But confusion and anxiety were spreading. Still, Black Kettle exhorted his people to remain calm, reminding them that they were safe; the soldiers would not attack, but his words must have seemed weak in the face of what was happening.

If there was any doubt as to what was happening it was erased when Lieutenant Luther Wilson led three companies of the 1st Colorado across the creek, northwest toward the horse herd, while another company moved to capture the smaller herd on the southwest fringe of the village. While these units advanced on their objectives, troops along the ridge began firing into the village. The Cheyenne, White Antelope ran toward the soldiers, exhorting them not to fire. By reputation White Antelope was one of the bravest and on this day showed why, standing in the center of the village, arms folded, believing that stance would signify his peaceful intentions. He died there along with his peaceful intentions.

As the attack continued to unfold, Major Anthony now led his battalion—three companies of the 1st Colorado—across the creek, their line of advance taking them between the Cheyennes and Arapahos. Once across Sand Creek, however, Anthony, inexplicably, took no action, electing to wait on Chivington's initiative. At this point, the mountain howitzers, positioned along the ridge, begin to open up lobbing shells into the village, scattering and terrifying the Indians who fled upstream.

As the Indians fled upstream some of the soldiers followed, but there was no organized pursuit. Indeed, at this juncture, there was a complete tactical breakdown. Officers lost control of their units as troops tore through the village. Some of the chiefs tried desperately to stop the attack, but it was a fruitless effort and resulted in the deaths of three Cheyenne chiefs: Standing-in-Water, War Bonnet, and Old Yellow Wolf all were killed.

As the Indians withdrew upstream, some warriors attempted to delay the soldiers, so as to give non-combatants a chance to escape. However, besides the soldiers coming on in pursuit, there were others on both sides of the creek firing at the fleeing Indians. Along the creek banks a series of high bluffs afforded an opportunity for some warriors to scoop out defensive pits from where they were able to fire effectively at the soldiers. A few non-combatants tried to seek shelter here as well. Most of the casualties inflicted on the soldiers came from the warriors in these pits.

The mixed-blood, George Bent, another of William Bent's sons, was among the villagers who attempted to mount a defense against the attack. Later, he recalled the events of that morning:

> Hardly had we reached this shelter under the high bank when a company of cavalry rode up on the opposite bank and opened fire on us. We ran up the creek with the cavalry following us, one company on each bank, keeping right after us and firing all the time. Many of the people had preceded us up the creek, and the dry bed of the stream was now a terrible sight: men, women, and children lying thickly scattered on the sand, some dead and the rest too badly wounded to move.[14]

The soldiers killed wantonly on this day; "slaughtered" would probably be more appropriate. There was little mercy shown and no distinction between age and sex. "Remember our murdered women and children," Chivington admonished his troops. Major Anthony later told of troopers spotting a small boy walking naked and tried twice to shoot the child, but missed him each time. Then another soldier came along and said, "Let me try. I can kill the son-of-a-bitch" and did. Not all carried Chivington's blood lust, however. Captain Silas Soule (pronounced Soul), whose Company D, 1st Colorado, moved along the south bank of Sand Creek, was appalled at what he saw and refused to order his men to open fire. He would later testify against Chivington at an inquiry.[15]

Back in August Chivington had reportedly ordered his troops "to kill and scalp all, little and big ... nits make lice." The order became a catchphrase and was certainly put into practice this day. It is well to note that by 1864, the expression had been in use for some years. It has sometimes been erroneously attributed to General Philip Sheridan of Civil War fame, who later commanded the huge Military Division of the Missouri, but in fact originated in 1810 with one, John Sevier, Governor of Tennessee and noted Indian fighter. It will be recalled that the expression had been used during the Rogue Wars of the Pacific Northwest.[16]

That unspeakable atrocities were committed by Chivington's command seems indisputable. Mostly these seem to have been the work of the Bloodless Third. Some have argued that atrocities were committed by both sides and truth be told there were a few soldiers whose bodies were mutilated, but these were mostly the few troopers who wandered over the field later that day in search of grisly souvenirs, only to themselves become an object of Indian wrath. In any case, given the circumstances it seems hard to believe that the Indians had an opportunity to commit many atrocities.

We will never know the exact number of Indians in the encampment, but the consensus among historians seems to be 400–600, of which approximately 100 were estimated to men of warrior age, leaving 300–500 as women, children and old people. Immediately following the attack, Chivington wired Curtis that he had attacked a village of 130 lodges, containing 900–1,000 warriors, plus 400–500 other Indians. The claim was absurd and would have meant 7 Indians per lodge, an extraordinarily crowded village. Chivington undoubtedly wanted to impress Curtis with a stunning victory.

Notwithstanding the suddenness and intensity of Chivington's attack, a surprising number of Indians somehow managed to escape; both small and large groups slipped away in the darkness. Some hid wherever they could find good cover, hoping to reach their brethren along the Smoky Hill, but however they managed, it was a long and painful night. George Bent remembered it as the "worst night I ever went through. There we were on that bleak, frozen plain, without any shelter whatever and not a stick of wood to build a fire with. Most of us were wounded and half naked; even those who had time to dress when the attack came, had lost their buffalo robes and blankets during the fight."[17]

On the morning of November 30, Chivington ordered the village burned, along with any equipage which surviving Indians might find useful. The fight—if such it may be called—was over, but atrocities continued. One officer blew out the brains of a still-alive baby, while another cut off the fingers of a dead warrior for rings, and as noted, a few soldiers wandered over the battlefield in search of trophies. A few who strayed too far were summarily killed and mutilated by a few warriors who kept watch over their now torched village.

On December 1, Chivington formed his command and marched south toward the Arkansas River where it was believed Little Raven's Arapahos were camped. En route they met Major Anthony and a supply train from Fort Lyon. Two days earlier, Anthony had escorted a few prisoners back to Fort Lyon and returned with the wagon train. That night Anthony penned a report to Henning at Headquarters, District of the Upper Arkansas, calling Sand Creek "the most bloody and hard fought *Indian Battle* that has ever occurred on these plains."[18]

On December 7, after six days of futile searching, Chivington elected to turn back. There had been no further sign of Indians, his horses were played out, and the men of the 3rd Colorado were due to be mustered out soon. Leaving Colonel Shoup in command, Chivington returned to Denver alone. Anthony was dumbfounded. Why not continue on to the Smoky Hill and finish the job? This was what he had assumed was Chivington's intent all along.

Once the news of Sand Creek reached Denver, the mood was euphoric! The Central City *Miner's Register* said, "The good work is begun, and we hope no respite will be given to the savage till at least four thousand of them have been killed." And from the *Rocky Mountain News*, "Our people may rest easy in the belief that outrages by small bands are at an end, on routes where soldiers are stationed." And among the returning soldiers themselves, Lieutenant Colonel Leavitt Bowen declared that "The Third Regiment cannot any longer be called in Denver the bloodless Third."[19]

On December 20 Chivington, perhaps sensing what the future held requested to be relieved of command. Curtis honored the request. He had never approved of Chivington to begin with and so the change was undoubtedly welcomed.

But Chivington was not about to bow out quietly. Two days later, on December 22, he led the 3rd Colorado on a proud march through Denver with a live eagle tied to a pole. The regiment, preceded by the 1st Colorado band was hailed as conquering heroes. That night there was plenty of celebrating in the old town. The streets were filled with strangers, described by one on-looker as "chiefly Indian killers." Judge Stephen Harding, a political enemy of both Chivington and Governor Evans, called the spectacle a "horrible sight, with the plunder with which they [the soldiers] were loaded and the bloody scalps which hung from their saddle horns. Most of these were the scalps of women and papooses." Harding was not the only one who was horrified. Indeed, back when the 3rd Colorado had returned to Fort Lyon following Sand Creek on December 10, some of the garrison's officers were appalled at the sight of these trophies and thought Chivington ought to be prosecuted.[20]

Sand Creek was not the first nor would it be the last instance of white barbarity in U.S. history; such examples, unfortunately are all too plentiful, and not only where Native Americans are involved. In the aftermath of the 1831 Nat Turner uprising angry Blacks murdered fifty-seven whites, including forty-six women and children. Avenging whites responded by massacring an estimated one hundred Blacks, many of whom were beheaded and their heads then displayed atop pikes.

In the press, Sand Creek was being favorably compared to Harney's victory on the Blue Water and Patrick Connor's at Bear River; the Colorado volunteers were the heroes of the day and applauded from one end of the Territory to the other—or at least Denver—for their stunning victory. Many believed that now the tribes would sue for peace.

Yet even as kudos were flying around, ugly stories were beginning to surface. There were rumors of a tainted victory. Some members of the 1st Colorado were sharply critical of what they had witnessed at Sand Creek. Based on these allegations, Judge Harding—never passing up a chance to be critical of Chivington—said "the truth will doubtless show that the attack on the defenseless savages was one of the most monstrous in history."[21]

In a letter to Commissioner Samuel P. Dole, Samuel Colley, agent for the Upper Arkansas District was also critical of the attack. Likewise, Agent Jesse Leavenworth, agent for the Comanches and Kiowas at Fort Larned, penned an angry letter to Dole saying that the whites had now lost the influence and support of nearly all the so-called peace chiefs. In his report to the Secretary of the Interior, Commissioner of Indian Affairs, N.G. Taylor offered another somewhat exaggerated official report, describing the event as "the horrible Sand Creek Massacre of friendly Cheyennes and Arapahoes. Exasperated and maddened by this cold-blooded butchery of their women and children," he went on to say, "disarmed warriors and old men, the remnant of these Indians sought the aid and protection of the Comanches and Kiowas, and obtained both." So over and above the horror of the event itself, it was becoming increasingly apparent that Sand Creek had not ended the Indian problem, but in fact had exacerbated it big time.[22]

As 1864 drew to a close, accounts of Sand Creek were beginning to reach the Eastern media. Chivington had both critics and supporters, though most of the latter were either Coloradans or at least Westerners. Sand Creek was becoming a highly charged political issue. Easterners, mainly, tended to be horror-stricken over the reports that reached them. In Denver, the air was filled with fiery rhetoric; charges and counter-charges; speculation was rampant. Congress was now being urged to investigate. On the whole, though, Coloradans continued to stand by Chivington, notwithstanding the allegations of horror that were emerging. As historian Gary Roberts so aptly points out, "The alternative was so monstrous that Coloradans could not accept it without destroying their image of themselves as defenders of home and hearth." Thus, Chivington continued to bask in the glory of a great triumph, and curiously did not seem concerned enough to even prepare a rebuttal or defense.[23]

As word of the horror of Sand Creek began to filter through official channels, General

Henry Halleck directed General Curtis to look into the matter, and, given the circumstances, Halleck could scarcely have done less. Curtis, who certainly had learned of the attack, was skeptical as to the accuracy of the allegations, but he acknowledged that if true it meant that Chivington had deliberately violated his (Curtis's) standing order not to kill women and children.

By February, however, with the allegations mounting, Halleck further directed Colonel Thomas Moonlight, now commanding up at Fort Laramie, to convene a formal inquiry into Sand Creek, with the focus to be mainly on the conduct of Chivington and the 3rd Colorado Regiment. Lieutenant Colonel Samuel Tappan of the 1st Colorado who had not been at Sand Creek, and was a well known opponent of Chivington, was named president of the inquiry board. Given that he was an avowed enemy of Chivington makes it seem odd that he would be selected as president. However, despite his personal feelings toward Chivington, he was the only senior officer of the regiment who had not been at Sand Creek and therefore ostensibly able to render an objective judgment on contentious issues.

The Tappan Commission Investigates

On February 15, 1865, the Tappan Commission got underway with its proceedings. The furor stirred up by Sand Creek had mightily embarrassed Governor Evans, who journeyed to Washington to assure President Lincoln that the attack had not been of his doing; that disloyal federal officials were responsible—he did not provide names—and should be dismissed. The president seemed sympathetic, for whatever that was worth to Evans. However, the Joint Congressional Committee on the Conduct of the Civil War was viewing Evans with a jaundiced eye. Chivington was not the only one with enemies it seemed.

On March 20, the Tappan Commission reconvened at Fort Lyon to hear further testimony. The general public was largely ignorant insofar as the full facts of the case were concerned. No official reports had been published, and what information did manage to reach the local populace was fragmentary and unclear, which only served to strengthen the public's support of Chivington and, for the most part, the local press as well. But here and there could be found cracks in the body of favorable opinion that had supported Chivington. For example, the *Blackhawk Mining Journal* which had originally supported the attack now reversed itself and said that Chivington had killed peaceful rather than hostile Indians, and that this was the real reason for the court of inquiry. By and large, though, the Western press continued to support Chivington.

On April 20 the Tappan Commission completed hearings at Fort Lyon and returned to Denver. The evidence against Chivington had been slowly building, prompting the colonel to finally begin preparations for his own defense. Three days later, however, on April 23, the case against Chivington suffered a severe blow when Captain Silas Soule was murdered under rather mysterious circumstances. While visiting friends with his bride, the sound of gunfire nearby apparently drew him to investigate where he was shot and killed by a member of the 2d Colorado Cavalry.

Soule, it will be recalled, had been adamantly opposed to the attack and had ordered his troops not to open fire. Soule's testimony, together with that of Lieutenant Joseph Cramer stood as the core of the evidence against Chivington. Although at this point the majority of Coloradans still supported Chivington, Soule's views continued to be highly respected. Indeed, his murder changed the attitude of many Coloradans who were now convinced that it was somehow tied to Sand Creek and his anti–Chivington stance. Suspicion even lurked in some quarters that Chivington had arranged for the murder, Edward Wynkoop among them, and Soule himself confided to friends that he expected to be murdered. In retrospect, given Chivington's record it seems not too far-fetched to imagine him behind such a scheme, but on the other hand no evidence was ever forthcoming to support such a claim. Soule's killer, Charles Squier fled to New Mexico, but was later apprehended.

Soule had been much beloved by the men of the 1st Colorado. He reportedly was a warm, outgoing personality with a wonderful sense of humor. Once, while on leave he reportedly walked from La Junta, Colorado, to Lawrence, Kansas, and back, to see his mother. An ardent abolitionist Soule had helped his father develop an Underground Railroad station in Kansas. In company with two others, he also developed a plan for rescuing John Brown from Harpers Ferry, but the plan was cancelled when Brown refused to be rescued.

On May 30, 1865, Chivington concluded his own defense such as it was. Fourteen witnesses appeared on his behalf, but only junior officers and enlisted men. No senior officers testified, which meant that there was nothing to substantiate or deny the major decisions made immediately prior to and during the battle. Chivington's defense stressed the hostile nature of the village, based on the many white scalps found among the lodges. He also argued that the so-called sand pits were actually rifle pits prepared in advance. The implication was that this was a hostile village that *expected* to be attacked. Chivington took the opportunity to lash out at his critics, saying that if "you desire to become the servile dogs of a brutal savage [criticism] will suit you, though I thought differently and acted accordingly." Perhaps as much as anything else, this statement sums up the case of John Milton Chivington, man and soldier. In assessing the guilt or innocence of the Nazi Adolph Eichmann, the question was asked whether a criminal is "anyone who decides what races will and will not inhabit the earth and decides to eliminate 'undesirables.'" The question might well be directed toward Chivington and others of his ilk.[24]

After reviewing the testimony of the Tappan Commission the Judge Advocate General Joseph Holt, called Sand Creek a "cowardly and coldblooded slaughter" that covered "its perpetrators with indelible infamy" and recommended that Sand Creek be officially condemned. Despite Holt's recommendation, however, the War Department failed to issue an official statement to this effect. Had it been within his province to do so, Holt likely would have preferred charges against Chivington but since the colonel had cannily resigned his commission he was no longer subject to military authority.[25]

Yet even as the Tappan Commission was hearing testimony, the Congressional Committee on the Conduct of the War was also looking into the Sand Creek business and taking testimony from Governor Evans, Major Anthony, and others. Pressed for an explanation as to his role, Evans was not convincing and the committee severely castigated him for his prevarication and shuffling, and recommended he be removed from office. Chivington did not personally testify, but did provide a written deposition outlining his own role. In conclusion, the Committee denounced the attack as infamous; that Chivington "deliberately planned and executed a foul and dastardly massacre which would have disgraced the veriest [sic] savages among those who were the victims of his cruelty." Once the Congressional report was made public, the *Rocky Mountain News* called it a disgrace for having based its conclusions on the testimony of a few scoundrels.[26]

In the aftermath of the investigations, Evans, Anthony, and others who had come under fire sought to justify their own actions. Evans claimed, and rightly so, that he had no foreknowledge of Chivington's plans, yet that scarcely excused his disingenuous dealings with the Indians. Further, Evans staunchly held to his belief that the village at Sand Creek was hostile. Scott Anthony, for his part, argued that the attack had been a military blunder, *not because of the atrocities committed, but rather because Chivington failed to carry out a major campaign against the Indians.* In a letter to Colonel Thomas Moonlight, Anthony wrote that by itself Sand Creek did nothing more than infuriate the Indians. The letter, later published in the *Rocky Mountain News* brought criticism down on Anthony's head. The Colorado press saw this as a betrayal by Anthony who had once seemed to be on Chivington's side, but as historian Gary Roberts suggests, perhaps better than anyone else, Scott Anthony understood the realities of Sand Creek. To Anthony, Sand Creek was a blunder because it simply failed to get the job done. Shortly, he, too, resigned his commission.[27]

No other event better exemplifies the "terribleness" of the Western Indian wars than Sand Creek. There were of course other tragic events in the West: the Massacre on the Marias and the Bear Creek Massacre among others, to say nothing of the genocide of California Indians, but none ever quite resonated with the public consciousness like Sand Creek. One might argue that the Battle of the Little Bighorn is better known and perhaps it is, but the circumstances of the two events are poles apart.

The Indian-white conflicts, both East and West are filled with a long litany of massacres and atrocities. Insofar as Sand Creek is concerned, the average Colorado citizen never really possessed all of the facts; never knew the full story. What developed was a war of words between the Eastern press and the humanitarian crowd versus the Western press and Westerners themselves who were convinced that the only way to deal with Indians was to treat them as they treated whites. Fight fire with fire. Them or us. *The New York Tribune*, for example, wrote that it [Sand Creek] "proves to have been a most brutal and unprovoked slaughter of men, women and children, who were living in a quiet manner in a state of entire peace with the whites." By contrast, the *Montana Press* in far-off Virginia City, Montana, proclaimed that after Sand Creek Chivington would be received like David after smiting Goliath.[28]

It has been suggested that Sand Creek did not really provoke an all-out Indian war that in fact, war between Indians and whites had existed on the Plains long before Sand Creek. But what we confront here is a question of semantics: what exactly defines a war? If raids and depredations by a handful of warriors does in fact constitute war, then one may legitimately argue that war between Indians and whites was indeed on-going prior to Sand Creek. But if we define war as a concerted effort by a tribe (or nation) to right what it believed were wrongs inflicted on it—and the operative word here is *concerted*—then we can hardly argue that a state of war existed between Indians and whites on the Central Plains at the time of Sand Creek. What followed Sand Creek could—and is—properly defined as a state of war, but prior to November 29, 1864, the argument that a state of war existed because of the behavior of a minority of Indians loses force.

There can be no denying that Sand Creek provoked a strong response from the Indians. Indeed, here it can legitimately be said that the Indians vowed to take a *concerted* action against the whites. All out war became the order of the day. In the weeks that followed, there was a wave of raids and attacks that very arguably would never have happened, or certainly happened with less intensity had it not been for Sand Creek. Sand Creek was a watershed event. Insofar as Indian/white relations were concerned nothing would ever again be quite the same on the Great Plains. Perhaps what was to come in the three and a half decades to follow would have happened anyway, but if there was a slender thread of hope that somehow a less violent solution to the so-called Indian problem might yet be found, it was dashed to the frozen, tawny turf at Sand Creek.

The War of 1865

Back in November 1864, on the day after Sand Creek, as a matter of fact, General Grant, having grown dissatisfied with Curtis's management style, created a new military department to be called the Department of Missouri which now included the Departments of Northwest—Minnesota and Dakota—plus Missouri and Kansas. The commander of this new department was Major General John Pope, who had fallen into some disfavor after the Battle of Second Manassas in 1862. As a consequence of that messy situation, Pope had been sent up to St. Paul to take over the Department of the Northwest. Considering what was happening elsewhere in the country, it was a backwater assignment, but far from an easy one. That late summer of 1862 had seen a bloody Indian uprising that ravaged southwestern Minnesota but Pope took charge and got things under control and was now being handed a broader sphere of responsibility. Forty-seven years old, Pope had a tendency to be loud and sometimes boastful, but withal he was a solid professional soldier who saw extermination as the solution to the Indian problem.

The change became official on January 30, 1865. The Department of Kansas was abolished and that region was added to the Department of Missouri, commanded by General Grenville M. Dodge, who was soon to play a pivotal role in the creation of the transcontinental railroad. Dodge's new command was further expanded to include Utah and a portion of Dakota Territory. General Samuel Curtis, who had commanded the Department of Kansas, was sent up to St. Paul to take over the Department of the Northwest from Pope, a position Curtis would hold until his death in July 1866. Creating a military infrastructure to deal with the Western Indian troubles was no simple matter, as is evident from the administrative shuffling that took place in 1865–1866. Resources were lacking, and it was hoped that rearranging command responsibilities might serve as an answer.[29]

In the wake of Sand Creek, the Colorado press was largely confident that the Indian problem had been resolved, but all too soon in fact there was an escalation of trouble on the Central Plains, and beyond for that matter. Scott Anthony and others had been quite correct to predict that there would be a strong Indian response to Sand Creek. At military posts across the area, from Forts Laramie and Lyon, word began to trickle in that the Indians were preparing to retaliate. Mixed bloods George Bent and Edmund (Edmond) Guerrier, who moved freely among the Cheyenne bands learned that things were going to happen. Bent and Guerrier shared a similar heritage. Guerrier's mother was a full blood Cheyenne; his father, William was a Fort Laramie trader, and like George Bent, the twenty-four-year-old Guerrier had been educated in St. Louis.

And indeed, the Indians were serious about a strong response. Sand Creek had sent a loud and clear message. The Indians heard and responded. Cheyenne runners were sent forth to the Lakotas and Arapahos inviting them to smoke the war pipe. By early January 1865, a great village was forming along Cherry Creek, a tributary of the Republican River in northwest Kansas [not to be confused with the better known Cherry Creek in Denver]. As the village grew, there was an estimated 400 lodges of Cheyennes, 100 of Arapahos, and as many as a thousand Lakota lodges—Oglalas, Miniconjou, Brules, and Sans Arc. Some sources say 800–900 Lakota lodges, but in any case, the overall village contained between 1,000 and 1,500 warriors. Even allowing but one warrior per lodge, a total of 1,500 warriors would seem conservative. The plan was to terrorize the busy South Platte Trail corridor between Julesburg and Denver. Participating chiefs made a formal declaration of war. "We have now raised the battle-axe until death," vowed the Cheyenne chief, Leg-in-the-Water.[30]

The site that would be the first to feel the wrath of the Indians was Julesburg in extreme northeast Colorado. Established about 1850 on the right bank of the South Platte River opposite Lodgepole Creek by the firm of Russell, Majors, and Waddell, Julesburg was later acquired by Ben Holladay and soon became a key station on his Overland Stage Route. From Julesburg, stagecoaches and mail carriers rode east to Atchison, Kansas, and west to Salt Lake City. Julesburg also became an important supply hub for east and west bound travelers and freighters from Denver—180 miles to the west. Near Julesburg the South Platte Trail connected with the Oregon-California Trail. The name Julesburg took its name from the station's founder and first manager, Jules Beni (or Bene) who seems to have been a dour individual and not above dipping his hand into the company till, but word seems to have gotten out. Consequently, when Division Manager, John "Jack" Slade arrived at the station ready to fire Beni a quarrel ensued during which Slade—known as Bad Jack—shot and killed Beni, reportedly cutting off one of his ears for a watch fob. The story is one of those anecdotes of the Old West, which has some basis in fact but contains more color than fact.

In any case, eventually a small settlement grew up around Julesburg, including a telegraph station, blacksmith shop, a large warehouse filled with supplies, a saloon, and boarding house where travelers could rest en route to their destination. The east side of the station featured a sod wall from which a defense could be mounted if necessary. Just a few miles to the east stretched a deep gulch that would play a prominent role in the coming festivities.

A mile to the west was Fort (or Camp) Rankin, situated on the south side of the South Platte River. It was a one-company post established in 1864 near the site of old Camp Buchanan occupied by Major John Sedgwick's column of Sumner's expedition. The post would later be renamed Fort Sedgwick. The deep gulch mentioned earlier ran northeast and entered the South Platte just below Fort Rankin.

In January 1865, Fort Rankin was garrisoned by Company F, 7th Iowa Volunteer Cavalry, commanded by Captain Nicholas O'Brien. A former enlisted man and veteran of Civil War artillery service, O'Brien had been commissioned a lieutenant the previous spring and then promoted to captain. O'Brien's two sub-alterns were forty-five-year-old First Lieutenant John Brewer and twenty-three-year-old Second Lieutenant Eugene Ware, who would one day chronicle a history of the war that was about to come his way. O'Brien's company reached Julesburg on September 4 and purchased the ranch of one Samuel Bancroft, on which the soldiers of Company F would construct their new post.[31]

Attack on Julesburg

Early in January advance elements of a large Indian war party, estimated to number a thousand or more, and including the Bent brothers, George and Charley, made camp in the hills south of Julesburg, followed by the main body a day later. The camp was made with care so as not to alert the garrison at Fort Rankin. Guards made certain that no anxious young warriors would slip out in search of an early coup. Fort Rankin and Julesburg both were the targets. The strategy was to try and lure soldiers out of the fort using a decoy party while the main body of warriors remained hidden in the sand hills, in the deep gulch described above. The decoy party was to consist of five Cheyennes and two Lakotas. It was a favorite Indian tactic was to send a small party to entice the soldiers to come on in pursuit. Then at the right moment the soldiers would find themselves trapped by an overwhelming force.

On the 6th, the decoy party sallied forth and fired on the post guards at Fort Rankin near Julesburg. The ruse worked well, at first, anyway, promptly bringing out Captain

O'Brien and thirty-seven soldiers in pursuit. However, as so often happened in these situations, impatient young warriors sprang the trap prematurely. Yet even at that it was a close encounter of any kind. Suddenly confronted by a howling mass of painted Indians, O'Brien ordered the bugler to blow retreat, but he became a target in doing so and lost his life in the frantic scramble that followed. Pinned beneath his horse who had stumbled the bugler became easy prey for the Cheyennes.

O'Brien and his troopers were something like 300 yards from Fort Rankin when they were confronted by the main body of Indians. In a fighting withdrawal that spoke well for their tenacity of spirit, O'Brien's command managed to reach the fort just behind the west bound stage. Inside the fort, O'Brien, ever the artilleryman, unlimbered a Parrott Gun—a rifled, muzzle-loading cannon invented appropriately enough by one, R.P. Parrott.

Opening up on the Indians, O'Brien scored a direct hit, killing several warriors, which gave the Indians pause about further attempts on the fort. Instead, they turned to looting the Julesburg general store and well stocked warehouse, capturing large stores of bacon, sugar, and flour, but that wasn't all. The haul included a strongbox containing paymaster funds. Stacks of green bills were tossed away by warriors who did not realize the value of the greenbacks. The Bent brothers and their comrades had a marvelous time partaking of freshly prepared food. George Bent confiscated a brand new U.S. Army major's uniform. All totaled, there was so much loot it took the Indians three days to haul everything back to the Cherry Creek village.

Meanwhile, a pair of mountain howitzers from the fort continued to discourage the Indians from any further attempts on the post. When the Indians finally departed on the 8th, O'Brien sent a detachment out to recover the bodies of those who had been killed; all had been horribly mutilated. Uncertain as to whether or not any Indians remained in the area, O'Brien sent out scouts and got a wire off to General Mitchell advising him of recent events. Mitchell, in turn, reported to Curtis (who had not yet moved to the northwest) and suggested that more adequately garrisoned posts were needed if the Indians were to be controlled. It was not an unreasonable suggestion, except that it was well beyond the limit of current resources.

On January 10 O'Brien was ordered to join General Mitchell at Cottonwood Springs, east of Julesburg on the Oregon-California Trail. O'Brien was to march with his entire command, leaving Fort Rankin to the protection of dismounted men, walking invalids, and any available citizens. Meanwhile, the Indian coalition cut a dreadful swath of destruction up and down the South Platte Valley. No stage or telegraph message reached Denver for a month. The telegraph line to Salt Lake City was also destroyed. Colonel Robert Livingston observed that this "was no trifling Indian war."[32]

On January 14 the *New York Times* reported that the overland mail to California had been suspended until the Indian problem was resolved, a goal that General Mitchell set out to achieve on the 15th with a strong column of 650 men from the 7th Iowa and 1st Nebraska, plus two companies of Nebraska militia. For artillery support, Mitchell had four 12-pounder mountain howitzers and two 3-inch Parrott guns. Supplies were carried in a train of 100 mule-drawn wagons. Mitchell's second was Colonel Robert Livingston, while Captain Nicholas O'Brien managed the artillery. For ten days this column searched the headwaters of the Republican River and its tributaries, but found nary an Indian. What they did find was bitter cold and more than a few troopers, Mitchell included, suffered frozen fingers and toes. A number of wagons eventually had to be abandoned before Mitchell returned to Cottonwood Creek on January 26.

The Indian war whoop as depicted by artist Charles Schreyvoel.

Mud Springs and Rush Creek

On February 4, a large war party numbering perhaps as many as 500, attacked the telegraph station at Mud Springs, an important watering stop on the Overland Trail a few miles northwest of Julesburg, midway between Forts Laramie and Mitchell. The station was guarded by 14 men, 9 soldiers and 5 civilians. From a defender's perspective, the station was a nightmare, surrounded by bluffs and low knobs of hills. Despite their disadvantage, the defenders resisted stoutly. Meanwhile, upriver at Fort Laramie, Colonel William O. Collins, commanding that post, learned of the attack by telegraph. Apparently in their initial attack at least, the Indians had failed to cut the "singing wire." Reacting promptly, Collins ordered a relief column to march immediately from Fort Mitchell, downriver. The relief column, 36 men of the 11th Ohio under Lieutenant William Ellsworth, reached Mud Springs early on the 5th. Ascending one of the bluffs behind the station, the troops pecked away at the Indians, until finally they were compelled to seek the quasi security of the telegraph station, where their arrival undoubtedly lifted the flagging spirits of the defenders, who now numbered 50.

The evening of the attack—it was a Saturday—Colonel Collins left Fort Laramie at the head of 120 men from the 7th Iowa and 11th Ohio with a second relief column for Mud Springs. By noon on the 5th Collins was at Fort Mitchell. After a few hours' rest, an advance detachment, led by Collins himself, pushed on to Mud Springs, followed soon thereafter by the main body. Early on the 6th, Collins and the twenty-five men comprising his advance detachment finally reached Mud Springs, but it had been a hard bone cold, two-day ride with some of the troopers suffering frostbite.

Collins's first act upon arriving was to form a corral out of four wagons, from behind which the defenders, some armed with seven-shot Spencer repeating carbines, were able to keep the Indians at bay. Warriors, though, fired arrows into the compound, killing and wounding a number of horses and mules. By the morning of the 7th, the soldiers had managed to force the Indians back. Quite likely this had more to do with the Indians preparing to move their huge village. As well, Indian patience with a prolonged siege was limited. That night Collins sent a detachment out to repair the telegraph line.

On the morning of the 8th, the siege of Mud Springs having been lifted, scouts reported finding a trail and Collins set out to locate the Indians with 185 troopers. He seems not to have been discouraged by the fact that he would be outnumbered, probably two or three to one. Notwithstanding, Collins divided his command into four squadrons and an artillery section. Squadron one, under Captain William Fouts with his company of the 7th Iowa, remained behind at Mud Springs to guard the station.

As they marched down the Platte they were watched the entire time by the Indian war party which positioned itself between the soldiers and the big village, now on the move to a new location. Near Rock Springs, they found the freshly abandoned camp, which included debris from the Julesburg raid: empty food cans, flour sacks, and more.

Approaching the frozen Platte River, the soldiers spotted a huge war party riding out to confront them. Collins estimated 2,000 Lakotas and Cheyennes, which is almost certainly an exaggeration, but that the Indians were present in overpowering numbers is certain. From a not too distant vantage point, George Bent remembered that "the Indians were hurrying, looking like a swarm of little black ants, crawling across the river on the ice."[33]

The mountain howitzers fired a couple of shots at the advancing phalanx and that gave the Indians temporary pause. Once again, Collins ordered his wagons corralled. This was to prove a wise decision. After circling the wagons, the soldiers dug rifle pits, throwing up sand to form a wall. Collins later reported that the men were cool and "had confidence in their officers."[34]

Barely were their preparations made when the Indians attacked with vigor. Collins claimed that the fire of the soldiers was deadly and it likely was to a point. Not at all discouraged by the ire of the defenders, the resourceful Indians found a ravine that enabled them to sneak up close to the breastworks. Here was a serious threat which Collins met by sending a detachment of sixteen Iowans under Lieutenant Robert Patton to clear them out. A lieutenant unafraid was Robert Patton who led his detachment straight at the Indians and in a fierce fight drove them out. Indian casualties, as usual, were reported to be heavy. Patton suffered two killed. That night the Indians withdrew across the river, but they were not quite finished.

If Collins and his troopers entertained thoughts of a leisurely breakfast they were soon disabused of that notion when an estimated 400 warriors appeared on the bluffs with an obvious intent of yet another attack. A few shots were exchanged and a salvo from the trusty howitzers sent the Indians scrambling. Later, Collins sent out a reconnaissance party to ascertain whether the Indians were still in the area, but they had moved on. The party did, however, find the mutilated body of one of their comrades who had been killed the previous day. According to witnesses his body was filled with nearly 100 arrows.

On February 11, Collins commenced his return march to Fort Laramie. In his official report, he listed his casualties as 3 killed and 16 wounded, plus another seven disabled from frostbite. He estimated Indian losses at 100–150. Interestingly enough, George Bent declared that in all the action from Julesburg to Collins's final fight at Rush Creek, there were *no* Indians killed and only 2 wounded: a stunning declaration in light of Collins's estimate. As we have noted elsewhere, reports and estimates of Indian casualties were almost always exaggerated, along with the number of Indians engaged; it looked better on one's official report to say that heavy casualties were inflicted on an Indian force much larger than our own. Still, it seems hard to believe that not a single Indian lost his life in all that fighting. Like Major Scott Anthony writing about Sand Creek being the greatest Indian battle ever fought, Colonel Collins's son Caspar, wrote to his mother describing Rush Creek as "the largest Indian battle ever fought at the greatest of odds, of any ever fought in this country."[35]

The Connor Expedition

The attacks on Julesburg and up and down the South Platte Valley, along with the fights at Mud Springs and Rush Creek, prompted Secretary of War Edwin Stanton to assign the protection of the Overland Stage route and railroad survey crews to General Patrick Connor, who, it will be recalled, had come to Denver back in November of '64, hoping for cooperation from Chivington and failed to find it. Chivington of course rode on to infamy at Sand Creek, while Connor thought of other ways to put a bell on the cat. In February 1865, Connor submitted his plan for protection of the Overland Route. General Halleck approved the plan, and on March 28 Dodge and Connor put their heads together and created a District of the Plains to include Utah, Colorado, Nebraska, and Wyoming. Connor would be in command, with headquarters in Denver. Connor's first step was to send five companies of the 11th Kansas (the regiment had arrived at Fort Kearny in March) under Lieutenant Colonel Preston Plumb out to Fort Halleck, from which post their sole job was to protect and keep open the stage line to Salt Lake.

Connor wasted no time dividing his new district into four sub-districts: Colonel Guy V. Henry was assigned the south sub-district consisting of the territory of Colorado (except for Julesburg). The Territory of Nebraska—the east subdistrict—was under Colonel Robert Livingston who had his headquarters at Fort Kearny. The northern sub-district included most of Dakota Territory (except for Fort Halleck, west of Fort Laramie) and Julesburg. The fourth sub-district, Utah, was commanded by Lieutenant Colonel Milo George.

While Connor completed his organizational plans, Pope and Dodge laid plans for a major campaign against the Lakotas, Cheyennes, and Arapahos. The idea was to locate and attack the Indians before their ponies grew strong from the new grass. This was to be a mighty effort against the Plains tribes. As the War Department saw it, the vast sweep of land between the Arkansas and Platte Rivers needed to be protected. Immigrant traffic was growing and there were railroad survey crews to protect as well. But the need for protection wasn't limited to the Arkansas and Platte region. North of the Platte—nearly to the Canadian line—restlessness and raids by the northern bands of Lakotas, Cheyennes, and Arapahos presented additional cause for concern, particularly with the discovery of gold in southwestern Montana (then part of Idaho Territory).

The plan envisioned by Pope and Dodge called for General James Ford to take the field against the Southern Plains tribes, while Connor, in cooperation with General Alfred Sully aimed for the Powder River Country, revered hunting grounds for the northern tribes, supported since Sand Creek by bands from the Arkansas and Platte River drainage systems. The plan looked impressive on paper because at its birth in February 1865, Pope's Military Division of the Missouri contained more than 52,000 men available for duty. In addition there were two regiments of Confederate prisoners who had volunteered to fight Indians rather than languish in some Yankee prison camp. Such men were dubbed Galvanized Yankees. Besides these, there was a brand new Colorado militia—120 strong—whose job was to guard the South Platte Trail between Julesburg and Denver. Additionally, a company of Pawnee Indian scouts under Captain Frank North reached Fort Kearny in late February. Finally, the 11th Kansas Volunteers, who had arrived at Fort Kearny in March, might be viewed as a liability more than an asset. They were an unhappy lot, these Kansans, as their enlistment was nearly up and they were thinking of home not fighting Indians. In any event, with numbers such as these at their disposal, it was no wonder that Pope and Dodge oozed optimism over their new campaign plan.

Even as Pope and Dodge talked over their plans, conditions along the Platte seemed to be stabilizing. The Overland Stage was on the move again but just barely. With news that the Civil War had ended with Lee's surrender to Grant at Appomattox Courthouse on April 9 the picture began to change. Although there was much celebrating, the end of the war was to have a profound effect on the carefully crafted plans of Pope and Dodge. Meanwhile, throughout the summer of 1865, pressure mounted for Governor Evans to resign and finally on August 1, he did so, being replaced by Alexander Cummings.

West of Fort Laramie was a series of small outposts designed to protect the overland telegraph line. These posts were seldom garrisoned by more than fifteen or twenty men and often fewer than that. The Indians had come to understand the importance of the telegraph and sought to interdict it wherever possible. Accordingly, these little outposts became important targets of opportunity. Thus, if conditions through February and March of 1865 were relatively quiet in the eastern sector of Connor's district, it was not so west of Fort Laramie, where there were a number of skirmishes between the 11th Ohio and Oglala and Brule Lakotas.

On March 28, a detachment of the 11th Ohio collected more than 1,400 Lakotas and a few Arapahos north of Fort Laramie. It should be noted quickly that these were not hostile Indians. They were, in fact, quite peaceably disposed and were en route to Fort Laramie to join up with Oglalas and Brules who had made a more or less permanent home around Fort Laramie. Some of these Indians inter-married with white traders, evidently regarding this form of existence as being more sensible and secure than trying to war against the white man. Their chosen style of life earned them the dubious sobriquet of the "Laramie Loafers." In one of the earliest instances of employing former hostiles the army arranged for some of these warriors to serve as gatherers of information, providing them with arms and old uniforms in return.

Colonel Thomas Moonlight

On April 9, the very same day that saw General Robert E. Lee surrender the Army of Northern Virginia to General Ulysses S. Grant, four companies of the 11th Ohio were replaced by the 11th Kansas Volunteers, commanded by thirty-two-year-old Colonel Thomas Moonlight, who, it will be recalled, had presided over the military inquiry into Sand Creek. Now he had been named to command the recently formed Northern subdistrict of the Plains, with headquarters at Fort Laramie.

Thomas Moonlight, a heavily bearded man of Scottish descent, had a service record dating back to the Seminole Wars. During the Civil War he had been commissioned lieutenant colonel of the 11th Kansas and was later promoted to the colonelcy of the regiment. Like many of his contemporaries, Moonlight had political ambitions. He was also said to have had a fondness for the bottle.

As always the onset of spring led to an increase in raids. However, in this spring of 1865 what tended to overshadow these raids was the hanging of a Cheyenne named Big Crow who had been charged as a murderer and spy, although the latter charge seemed specious without evidence to back it up. In any case, General Connor ordered him hanged and accordingly, on April 22, Moonlight and Lieutenant Colonel William Baumer dutifully carried out Connor's orders ... while under the influence it was said.

On May 3, Moonlight took the field aiming to strike a band of Cheyennes, estimated at 300 in number, who were reportedly raiding west of Fort Laramie. It was a strong force that followed Moonlight, at least in terms of numbers. Altogether he had 500 men from the 11th Kansas and 11th Ohio (those not yet mustered out) and 7th Iowa. The nearly legendary mountain man, Jim Bridger, served as guide, along with a party of Indian scouts.

While Moonlight was searching for the Cheyennes, Connor relocated his headquarters to Julesburg on the 21st. Forty-eight hours later Moonlight estimated that his quarry could be found in the Wind River Valley, however, a reconnaissance by Bridger and other scouts revealed no sign of Indians in that area. Moonlight's official report summed up the often fruitless effort of pursuing Indian raiders. Finding no Indians, Moonlight concluded that his Cheyennes had gone north into the Powder River country, and pursuit into that region would require a major effort, exactly what Pope, Dodge, and Connor were contemplating, and beyond the scope of Moonlight's authority.

The success enjoyed by the Lakotas, Cheyennes, and Arapahos in upsetting travel along the Overland Trail between Platte Bridge Station and Fort Laramie emboldened other bands to try their hand at making trouble for the white man. On May 18, a raiding party struck a detachment of Galvanized Yankees en route from Fort Leavenworth to Fort Kearny, Nebraska. The men were fresh out of the hospital and unarmed. Two were killed and six wounded. Two days later, Pawnees attacked a stagecoach, but were repulsed by the steady fire from two of the passengers. Ordinarily, Pawnees proved friendly toward whites, not particularly because they liked the white man, but rather because they saw whites as allies against their hated and traditional enemies, the Lakotas and Cheyennes. This strike on the stagecoach was likely an impromptu act motivated by a target of opportunity to tempting to resist.

On May 26, Moonlight, who seems to have been in a hanging mood this spring, hanged two Oglala Lakota chiefs, Two Face and Blackfoot, as punishment for depredations, including the maltreatment of two white women, one of whom, Lucinda Eubank had been taken captive by a Cheyenne raiding party in Kansas back in August of '64. The camps of the two Lakota chiefs contained sufficient booty and evidence to convince Moonlight of their guilt.

In June 1865 Secretary of War Stanton decided to move the so-called "friendlies" around Fort Laramie east to Fort Kearny where they would be less likely to cause trouble and less likely to have contact with the hostile bands. The transfer was to be supervised by Captain William D. Fouts with 135 men from the 7th Iowa. Strangely, however, when preparing to depart from Fort Laramie Fouts had directed that his rear guard not be issued ammunition. En route to Fort Kearny a disagreement broke out among the Indians. One faction wanted to break away rather than live closer to their old enemies the Pawnees. The disagreement turned into a fracas. Soldiers attempted to bring the situation under control, but the Indians had their dander up. Suddenly there was an exchange of gunfire. Fouts himself was killed and the Indians fled, managing to get across the North Platte before the soldiers caught up with them.

When Colonel Moonlight learned of the Fouts disaster on June 14, he immediately assembled a mixed force of 234 cavalrymen from various California, Ohio, and Kansas regiments and set out in pursuit of the Indians. Moonlight pushed so hard in pursuit that half of his men were compelled to turn back because of exhausted horses. Then, on the 17th, 200 Lakotas surprised Moonlight and ran off nearly all of his horses. The men later managed to recover a few animals, but most of the command, including its colonel, was forced to return to Fort Laramie on foot. Shortly afterward a disgusted Connor wasted no time relieving Moonlight of his command. Although embarrassing in the extreme, the incident seems not to have affected Moonlight's future political career. In later years, President Grover Cleveland appointed him governor of Wyoming and following that he served as Minister to Bolivia.

Colonel Nelson Cole, Lieutenant Colonel Samuel Walker and Colonel James H. Kidd

In anticipation of the spring offensive, Connor moved his headquarters back to Fort Laramie. But plans were going awry. Spring floods and a shortage of horses caused significant delays as did the rapidly decreasing size of the federal army. General James Ford's southern column had to be temporarily grounded when the enlistments of its volunteer troops expired. Indeed, Ford himself was mustered out and replaced by thirty-nine-year-old General John Benjamin Sanford. A former lawyer and politician, Sanford had served throughout the Civil War. A cautious officer, he would take no unnecessary risks. Although peace feelers were in the wind, Sanborn was ordered to send small columns up the Republican and Smoky Hill Rivers; a sort of reconnaissance in force.

The end of the Civil War brought about another change to command jurisdiction in the West. No less than General William Tecumseh Sherman was now in charge. His new command, The Military Division of the Mississippi encompassed everything between the Mississippi River and the Rocky Mountains. Sherman's new command replaced the old Military Division of the Missouri, which now became simply the Department of Missouri, embracing the states of Wisconsin, Minnesota, Iowa, Kansas, and Nebraska, plus Dakota and Montana Territories.

Meanwhile, west of Fort Laramie, Cheyenne and Arapaho war parties, ranging in size from 50 to 300, continued to strike overland wagon trains, killing some immigrant travelers and wounding others, but the wagons continued to roll.

As plans for Connor's spring campaign stuttered and stammered, the U.S. Congress still wrestling with the growing ignominy of Sand Creek ordered an inquiry into the condition of the Western Indians and their treatment by the civil and military authorities. Chairmanship of the two-pronged committee was vested in Senator James R. Doolittle of Wisconsin. Two members would look into matters on the Northern Plains, while three, including Doolittle himself, would investigate affairs in Kansas, Indian Territory, Colorado, Utah, and New Mexico. Oddly, at its conclusion, the Doolittle Committee issued no official report of its own, but a general report issued by the joint committee in January 1867, stated that "in a large majority of cases Indian wars are to be traced to the aggressions of lawless white men."[36]

Notwithstanding the logistical problems and delays spawned by the weather, Connor's campaign, which came to be called the Powder River Expedition, gradually began to take shape, but it would be well along in the summer season before these three cumbersome and uncoordinated columns actually took the field. The expedition was to consist of three segments: the eastern wing under Colonel Nelson Cole consisted of two Missouri cavalry regiments, plus a section of three-inch rifled guns and assorted supply wagons—some 1,400 men in all. A native New Yorker, the thirty-three-year-old Cole had been a businessman in St. Louis prior to the Civil War.[37]

From its staging point at Omaha, Nebraska, Cole's column was to head west along the Platte and Loup Rivers then swing north along the eastern apron of the Black Hills. The departure date was set for July 1. In his orders to Cole, Connor warned his subordinate to anticipate finding large numbers of "hostiles" around Bear Peak (or Butte). In theory, anyway, Cole was expected to thrash any Indians he found, as his orders specifically called for him not to enter into any peace discussions, and to kill every male Indian over twelve years of age. Exactly how Cole was to tell who was twelve or over was not made clear, but it was irrelevant in any regard because when Pope learned of the order, he promptly rescinded it. After completing this phase of the campaign, Cole was then to proceed around the northern rim of the Black Hills where he could expect to find the supply depot that Connor planned to build.

General Patrick Connor. Except for the attack on Black Bear's village, his Powder River campaign was largely a bust.

Number two column was commanded by Lieutenant Colonel Samuel Walker, who had six companies of the 16th Kansas Volunteers, together with some from the 15th Kansas Volunteers, a total force of around 600 men. A forty-three-year-old Pennsylvanian, Walker had migrated to Kansas where he ultimately joined the volunteers. These were troubled times in Kansas and Missouri and many men, such as Walker, with strong political feelings were drawn to volunteer military units. Walker had been appointed lieutenant colonel of the 16th Kansas the previous October. His column had actually taken the field in midwinter, marching from Fort Leavenworth to Fort Laramie, in order to be available for the spring/summer campaign.

Cole got started on July 1 as planned, but Walker's Number 2 column ran into snags. He had anticipated a July 20 departure date, but a mutiny in the ranks threw everything into turmoil. Some of the 16th Kansas figured their tour of duty would soon be up and refused to march off to fight Indians. When he learned what was afoot, Connor was irate and sent two companies of his California Volunteers to make the Kansans an offer they couldn't refuse, said offer taking the form of a brace of mountain howitzers loaded with canister, and after due reflection, the Kansans decided that maybe they could manage one more campaign. In any case, after all of this ruckus, Walker did not actually get boots and hooves on the ground until August 5; it was the last of the three columns to take the field. Confusingly, an independent column headed by one James Sawyer was to rendezvous with Walker in the field. As events were to demonstrate Sawyer's column would complicate life for Walker.

The third column was headed up by Colonel James H. Kidd, commanding the 6th Michigan Cavalry. Kidd had served with distinction in the late Civil War. He and his regiment had been a part of the famed Custer brigade that dueled Jeb Stuart at Gettysburg during that fiercely fought battle two years earlier. In June 1865 Kidd received orders to join Connor's Powder River Expedition then forming at Fort Laramie. Kidd and his Michiganders were clearly an unhappy lot; their term of service, too, was nearly up and they were anxious to head home. A summer of campaigning on the Plains against Indians had not been on their agenda. Nevertheless, the regiment reached Fort Laramie on July 25 with only half the men under arms.

General Connor, meanwhile, reached Fort Laramie at the end of June and began preparations to take the field with Kidd's Number 3 (the main column). Cole's command was already in motion of course and now it remained for the other two forces to get underway. The month of July was largely spent gathering supplies and finalizing organizational plans. The Fort Laramie garrison as well as the troops designated for the upcoming campaign did take time out to celebrate the 4th of July. Connor's departure was delayed because supply wagons were in short supply, forcing him to purchase more from civilian sources, thereby incurring Pope's wrath for going outside normal channels, but after expressing his displeasure, Pope relented; he had little choice if he wanted to see the campaign get underway. Connor's operational plan called for a convergence of Cole's and Walker's two columns on the Powder River in present southeastern Montana.

Finally, on July 30, with wagons stuffed full of supplies and grain for the cavalry horses, the western column, under Colonel Kidd's command (with Connor accompanying), marched out of Fort Laramie. One of the logistical problems that mounted troops always had to deal with was sustenance for the horses. Cavalry horses were, by and large, bigger than the wiry Indian ponies. Unlike the smaller Indian ponies who were able to subsist on native grasses, cavalry mounts were accustomed to being fed grain, which had to be hauled in wagons, thereby adding to the Army's logistical burden.

The westernmost column would proceed north, skirting the eastern apron of the Big Horn Mountains. Once all three columns were in the field, The Powder River Expedition would have three prongs aimed at the heart of the Powder River region: Cole's to the east, along the east side of the Black Hills, Walker's along the west side of the Black Hills and the Connor—Kidd column the farthest west. In addition to four companies of the 6th Michigan, Connor's western column included three companies of the 11th Ohio, and one each of the 2d California and 7th Iowa, plus a detachment of 2d Missouri Light Artillery. A bevy of Indian scouts fleshed out the strength of the column with 75 Pawnees under Captain Frank North and 70 Winnebago and Omaha scouts under Captain Henry Palmer. In all, the western column numbered about 475 men. Kidd and his Michiganders would not be expected to participate in any of the anticipated clashes with the Indians. Rather, Kidd's job was to build and garrison a fort on the Powder River that would serve as a base for future operations.

THE PLATTE BRIDGE FIGHT

Indian raids along the Overland Trail continued, pretty much unabated. General Connor reported that the southern sector of the Overland Route between Virginia Dale (north of Fort Collins) and Fort Laramie was largely controlled by Indians and that mail was moving through that sector only with a strong escort. In Denver, *The Rocky Mountain News* reported that Indians were running wild from Minnesota to California. This, of course, was more than a slight exaggeration, but truth be told, raiding parties were plenty active along the Overland Trail. Platte Bridge (present Casper), and Sweetwater Stations some fifty miles west of Fort Laramie seemed perfect targets for the raiders. By early July, it had become necessary to increase the garrison at Platte Bridge to a hundred men. In fairness, the Lakotas and Cheyennes did not confine their raids to the Overland Trail stations. On occasion they took time out to strike their traditional enemies the Shoshones. During one such raid they killed Snowbird, son of the prominent Shoshone chief, Washakie. They also ran off several hundred horses, which the Shoshones were later able to recover.

Even as Connor's western prong was preparing to take the field, Lakotas and Cheyennes struck the Platte Bridge Station. At a mid-month council, the Indian leaders decided that with the Platte Bridge destroyed, whites would be unable to cross the North Platte River and thereby penetrate the Indians' prime hunting territory. As a strategy this appears not to have taken into account the fact that the bridge could easily be rebuilt and any delay would be very temporary.

The station at Platte Bridge consisted of a stockaded enclosure garrisoned by some 120 men of the 11th Kansas, 11th Ohio, and the 3rd U.S. Infantry, all under the command of Major Martin Anderson. The garrison also included a detachment of men awaiting assignment to a permanent duty station. Of particular interest here was that numbered among the garrison was Lieutenant Caspar Collins, son of Colonel William O. Collins. Twenty-one years old on the morning of this 26th day of July 1865, and much liked, Lieutenant Collins was given command of a twenty-five-man detachment and ordered by Major Anderson to provide an escort for a wagon train approaching from the west. Indians in large numbers were plainly visible from the stockade and, indeed, a ten-man detachment en route to Fort Laramie had passed the east-bound wagon train, under the command of Sergeant Amos Custard, and advised Anderson that it was liable to be attacked, which prompted the major to organize an escort.

When none of the Kansas officers volunteered—they were due to be discharged shortly—Collins said he would go if the size of the relief column was increased. Anderson apparently did not believe a larger force was necessary and turned down the request, but Collins volunteered anyway. Reportedly, the young officer did not expect to return from his mission, for he rode out attired in a brand new, recently purchased dress uniform. Whether or not Collins actually expected to be killed is problematical, but certainly none of the garrison imagined there were perhaps as many as 3,000 Lakotas and Cheyennes secreted in the hills just beyond the station, watching young Collins and his men ride forth. A direct attack on the stockade held no appeal for the Indians. Instead, they planned to employ the time-honored decoy approach.

The hour was 7:30 a.m. as Collins and his men passed through the gate. The young lieutenant, a cigar clenched jauntily between his teeth, handed his cap to Private James Williamson as a remembrance. A half mile beyond the bridge spanning the North Platte, Collins saw two Indians cutting the telegraph wires and ordered an attack, but it was too late to seize the initiative. Even as Collins prepared to attack, the Indians moved in, with one group aiming to secure the bridge and cut off any retreat, while the main body of warriors struck the soldiers from all sides. After firing a volley with their carbines, the troopers turned to their side-arms. Collins ordered a retreat to the bridge, but with warriors swarming all over his position it was nearly hopeless. Being surrounded by so many Indians may have actually worked in Collins's favor. Fearful of hitting their own comrades, the Indians attacked with spears and tomahawks rather than firearms. Collins was wounded in the hip, yet stopped to aid one his fallen men and in so doing took an arrow in the head.

In an effort to open a line of retreat for Collins, Major Anderson sent a howitzer toward the bridge, supported by a detachment of infantry. Surprisingly, most of Collins's men were able to reach the bridge and cross into the safety of the stockade. Only Collins and four of his men lost their lives; all were badly mutilated, and Collins, reportedly, was filled with more than twenty arrows.

This little action, along with that of the earlier Grattan Massacre, would become one of the more notable fights in the Indian wars of the Plains. Neither was particularly costly in terms of Army lives lost—only Collins and four of his troopers were killed—but both fights signaled what the Army was going to have to contend with in the years ahead. When strength of numbers and the right circumstances prevailed, as they did with Collins and Grattan, the end result could and did indeed prove all too costly, as was the Fetterman disaster a year later, and the Little Bighorn a decade later. The Platte Bridge battle was a big score for the Indians, although they were said to have lost 60 killed and 130 wounded.

Meanwhile, even as Collins and three of his troopers lay dead a half mile from Platte Bridge Station, Sergeant Amos Custard, in charge of the east-bound wagon train, heard firing up ahead and sent four of his men to ascertain what was happening. The four soon found themselves confronting hundreds of howling Indians. Somehow, though, three of the men managed to cross the bridge and reach the stockade. A savvy veteran, Amos Custard did not waste a lot of time pondering his situation. With the remainder of his escort—twenty men—Custard formed a defensive position with his two wagons. From here, Custard and his men, armed with .50 caliber carbines, gave a good account of themselves but in the end were overwhelmed and killed to a man. When their bodies were recovered later all had been horribly mutilated. When word of the attack on Platte Bridge Station reached Fort Laramie, Connor dispatched Colonel Kidd and nine companies of the 6th Michigan to march immediately to the station's relief. Two days out, however, Kidd learned that the Indians had moved north after the fight. So, retracing his steps, Kidd returned to Fort Laramie to prepare for the departure of Connor's column two days hence.

On August 5, five days after Connor's departure, Walker's column finally got underway, marching north out of Fort Laramie with forty days supplies packed on mules and aiming for the western flank of the Black Hills. At long last, all three wings of the Powder River Expedition were finally in the field.

By mid-August the Connor column had reached the Powder River east of present day Kaycee, Wyoming, where the river more or less joined with the Bozeman Trail (or Road), a recently created overland route to the gold fields of southwestern Montana that branched off from the Overland Trail near present Casper. Although the Bozeman had not yet become the route of notoriety it would become in the next year, some overland traffic was flowing along its lonely often rugged course and Connor elected to build his supply depot at this point.

While Kidd and his Michiganders went to work constructing the new post, Winnebago scouts ranging out in search of hostile Indian sign, found same in the form of a large Lakota war party and a scrap ensued. The Winnebago chief, Little Priest suddenly found himself cut off and surrounded until his tribesmen swooped into the rescue. Tight moment though it was, Little Priest nevertheless managed to take two scalps. Other than this, however, clashes with hostile Indians were few and minor, but for the men of the expedition, there was the constant awareness of being in "Indian country." On the afternoon of the 16th, Indians appeared on a bluff near the construction site, prompting Connor to send North and his Pawnee scouts after them. After a long, arduous pursuit, covering some sixty miles, North and his scouts caught up with the Cheyennes, killed all—or so they said—and returned to the new fort.

These encounters were something less than what Connor had in mind, however. They were minor affairs and the purpose of the expedition after all was to punish the heart and soul of these bands, not simply a few raiders. Accordingly, since the main body of warriors seemed to be elsewhere, Connor elected to examine the Tongue River watershed to the west, leaving Kidd and his troopers to their labors on the fort. Connor was prepared, indeed hopeful of finding the hostiles, but his movements also took into account the planned rendezvous with Cole and Walker.

Then it seemed as though the God of Good Fortune chose suddenly to smile on Connor. On August 28 his scouts reported a large Arapaho village near the present site of Ranchester, Wyoming. Acting swiftly, Connor assembled 215 cavalrymen from the 7th Iowa, 2d California, and 11th Ohio, together with a pair of 6-pounder howitzers, plus 90 Pawnee and Omaha scouts and marched upriver toward the village, some 36 miles distant.

Connor Attacks Black Bear's Village

In the early hours of August 29, Black Bear's Arapaho village, numbering between 200 and 300, was preparing to move when Connor attacked. The warriors recovered from their initial shock quickly and fought back, giving the non-combatants together with a few warriors a chance to flee to the south. Connor led a pursuit some ten miles before discovering that only 14 men were behind him. Noting this, the Indians seized the moment and drove Connor back toward the village, where the Pawnees were having a field day, capturing an estimated 500–600 Indian horses. Meantime, the troops went about destroying the village. While the troops were so engaged, the Arapahos decided to counter-attack and might have been more successful had it not been for Captain Nicholas O'Brien's howitzers which kept the Indians at bay, until at length they withdrew. O'Brien, it will be recalled, had conducted a sterling defense of Fort Sedgwick back in '65. "The fight was something terrific," one of the officers said. The howitzers fired so furiously that one overheated and was temporarily put out of action. In the immediate aftermath of the fight, Indian casualties numbered 63 killed, including Black Bear's son. Seven soldiers were wounded. Some 250 lodges were burned, along with much jerked buffalo meat and equipage, though not before the troops replenished their own stock of supplies.[38]

The Odyssey of Cole and Sawyer

The month of September found Connor searching up and down the Tongue, Rosebud, and Powder Rivers in a vain search for Cole and Walker. The weather had turned nasty, too. Rain and some snow made for miserable conditions, and Connor was concerned that his two field commanders would be running short of supplies.

There was no way Connor would likely have known about it in advance, but his Powder River Expedition was going to have company. As previously noted, the discovery of gold in southwestern Montana had created a demand for a faster overland route to the "diggings," hence the birth of the Bozeman Trail. But a group of business-minded folks from Sioux City, Iowa, on the Missouri River, pressed for yet another overland route from their city, up the Niobrara River to the Black Hills, eventually to connect with the Bozeman Trail. The advantage of such a route would mean prosperity for Sioux City which would become a major supply point for travelers who followed the Niobrara Route. Command of this expedition was entrusted to one James Alexander Sawyer. Forty years old, Sawyer, a former Tennessean and successful Sioux City merchant, was a veteran of the Mexican War and a former officer in the Iowa militia. His expedition consisted of 15 wagons and 53 men, plus two companies of the 5th U.S. Volunteers, altogether about 140 men with their own wagon train, which General Pope, undoubtedly with some pressure from the War Department, agreed to furnish as an escort. Additionally, there were some emigrant travelers and private freight wagons.

Sawyer marched from the mouth of the Niobrara on June 13 and for the first month travel was smooth and uncomplicated. The picture changed on August 13, however, when he was attacked by a mixed party of Lakotas and Cheyennes, 600 strong, near Pumpkin Buttes, Wyoming, a large land mass between the Black Hills and the Powder River. The Cheyennes were led by Dull Knife, the Oglala Lakotas by their powerful leader, Red Cloud. The attack was a monument to persistence. For four days the Indians hammered at the Sawyer train. Worn down by the continual attacks, though they managed to repulse each Indian effort, Sawyer and the commander of his military escort Captain George Williford, argued over whether it made more sense to head for Fort Laramie, or continue on to the rendezvous with Colonel Walker, about whom nothing was known at the moment.

At noon on the 15th, the Indians signaled for a parley. George Bent, looking very striking in the major's uniform he had picked up at Julesburg, acted as interpreter for Sawyer and Williford. Sawyer thought perhaps a bargain might be struck and offered to purchase safe passage for his wagons, but Bent said the only price was the hanging of John Chivington. Both parties knew this was out of the question, but it undoubtedly gave Bent much satisfaction to demand the execution of the Sand Creek demon. Still, Sawyer did present the Indians with some food and tobacco, hoping perhaps that this gesture might buy them enough good will to get through. However, barely had the gifts been given when fighting broke out. Two men were killed before Williford's artillery finally drove the Indians off. Perhaps because they were tired of fighting for the moment, the Indians allowed the wagon train to proceed without further disturbance.

As a result of the parley Sawyer and Williford heard of the death of Caspar Collins in the Platte Bridge fight, but more importantly, learned about Connor's new fort on the Powder River. At this juncture, Williford informed Sawyer that his escort service was at an end. In the meantime, however, scouts had located Fort Connor, some thirteen miles to the south and by August 25 the entire Sawyer train, plus Williford and his troopers, were camped near the new post.

Even as Sawyer and Williford were enjoying the security—if such it may be called—of Fort Connor (soon to be renamed Fort Reno) General Connor was searching for the Indian village, which as previously noted, he found along the Tongue River on the 29th. Meantime, one of the couriers Sawyer had sent out to locate Connor returned with a message from the general, directing Williford to remain at Fort Connor. Colonel Kidd was to replace Williford's escort with a detachment of the 6th Michigan whose assignment was to take Sawyer as far as the Big Horn River, by which point it was assumed they would have passed beyond the pale of harm.

On August 29, Sawyer resumed his northward march. In addition to his escort, there were 57 wagons and several hundred cattle. Three days later, the caravan, slogging its way through heavy rain, passed Lake DeSmet, even as Connor was attacking the Arapaho village on Tongue River. The lake itself, just beyond present day Buffalo, Wyoming, was named for the Jesuit, Father Pierre Jean DeSmet, a tireless worker among the tribes and an important figure in the history of the West. Interestingly enough, just four days earlier, Connor's command had also passed this way. There were buffalo in the vicinity which invited a sport for some of the men, Connor included. Not insignificantly, animals provided meat for the column's larder.

Thus far, Indians had not really molested the train, though the wagon masters made it a point to form their wagons in a corral each night. The picture changed on September 1 when a war party attacked the rear guard and managed to make off with some loose livestock. And it got worse. Vengeful Arapahos, angry after Connor's attack, now swarmed around the Sawyer train. The defenders put up a stout fight with a curtain of fire that prevented the attackers from penetrating the corral. The Indians, estimated to number about 600 made a grand display of their horsemanship, riding around the corral, firing from underneath the necks of their mounts.

This initial attack was followed by a lull, during which the Indians seemed happy to exchange riding and shooting for a barbecue using the captured livestock. Sawyer concluded from this that it was safe to un-corral the wagons and resume the march, but the idea proved a bit premature. The wagon masters were compelled to reform their corral when the Indians resumed the attack pouring a heavy volume of fire at the position without, however, inflicting many casualties due to poor ammunition. A very similar scenario would be played out two years later in the better known Wagon Box Fight. Not generally appreciated in so many of these fights is a shortage of ammunition for Indian weapons. It was one thing for an Indian to acquire a repeating rifle, for example, but in order to use the weapon he needed ammunition which was not always available in substantial quantities. Historian John D. McDermott also points out that in reloading their ammunition, the Indians often used insufficient powder, which in turn reduced the striking power of the bullets.

Intermittent fighting continued, but the Indians evidently had no interest in another direct attack on the corral. Although the defenders had held their own and repelled every Indian effort, it had become clear to Sawyer that his position could not be maintained without reinforcements and offered a reward to any who would undertake to carry a message to General Connor. That night, three volunteers, ignoring the odds, slipped away under cover of the chilly September darkness in search of Connor. As luck would have it, a committee of Arapaho leaders approached the next afternoon under a flag of truce. Connor had burned their village, they reported, and taken many horses. They proposed to send three of their own along with the three volunteers Sawyer had already dispatched. The *quid pro quo* here was that the Arapahos were bargaining for the return of at least some of their horses. The Indians further agreed to leave a dozen of their own behind as hostages. The proposal seemed straight forward enough and Sawyer agreed.

On September 5, quite by accident, a few reinforcements arrived in the form of another detachment of the 6th Michigan also in search of Connor, for whom they carried mail. From them Sawyer learned that his three messengers had gotten through to Fort Connor, but as to the general's whereabouts, no one seemed to know. So here, the Sawyer train and escort remained for a week, hoping perhaps Connor would put in an appearance, but if that was indeed Sawyer's hope, it was a forlorn one and he now found himself between the proverbial rock and a hard place. On the 12th, with his escort under orders to proceed no farther than the Big Horn River, some of the men refused to continue. There was disenchantment in the ranks, too. Some were of the opinion a change of pitchers was in order and faced with that unpleasant fact, Sawyer elected to return to Fort Connor.

Barely had the train commenced its journey, however, than it met Captain Albert Brown leading a company of the 2d California Cavalry, plus a company of Omaha and Winnebago scouts. Here at long last were the reinforcements Sawyer had requested. Brown would have arrived earlier but heavy rains had delayed his movements.. In any event, his arrival brightened the picture. Optimism was restored and the Sawyer train was soon in motion north once again. By September 19, the train was at the banks of the Big Horn, where Brown and his escort bade them farewell and turned back south. With Indian troubles were behind it, on October 5, the Sawyer wagon train finally rolled into Bozeman, Montana.

Having escorted Sawyer as far as the Big Horn River, Brown turned about and rejoined Connor, which was something more than either Cole or Walker had managed to accomplish. In retrospect, the Powder River Expedition seemed to have an almost comic opera quality about it, although to the participants it surely seemed anything but funny. Here were three Army columns—four if Sawyer is included—at times struggling through a tortuous landscape, while suffering through dramatic changes in weather that ranged from intense heat to freezing temperatures, together with snow and drenching downpours, all the while searching for one or both of the other two columns.

Nelson Cole, meanwhile, had proceeded west from Omaha as directed and then north along the eastern slope of the Black Hills without finding any trace of Indians. His orders had been to kill every male Indian over the age of twelve, but as he rounded the northern point of the Hills in mid-August, he had found nothing resembling the gathering of hostile Indians he had been led to believe would be found in the area. Disturbingly, neither had he heard from Colonel Walker with whom he was to rendezvous. At this juncture, Cole's command had marched nearly 600 miles and his horses were showing signs of fatigue. Moreover, some of his men were afflicted with scurvy. Then finally, on August 18, some 40 miles north of present day Devil's Tower, Wyoming, Cole and Walker finally found each other.

Walker's command was a little better off than Cole's, mainly because it had covered less ground and hauled its supplies on mules, rather than wagons. Walker had started out with forty days supplies on August 5, but his provisions, too, were beginning to run low.

In assigning Cole and Walker command of their respective columns General Connor seems to have expected independent operations to be conducted by each commander, without anticipating the need for one officer to assume overall command in the event of joint operations, even though the two columns were expected to junction at some point, which of course was the situation after August 18. For the next two weeks, Cole and Walker proceeded northwestward into Montana toward the Powder River. The two columns marched independently, though close enough to support each other should trouble arise.

On August 29, Cole dispatched scouts to look for Connor and on the following day the combined forces reached the Powder River at a point approximately fifty miles south of the Yellowstone River. Although Indians monitored their movements they seemed uninterested in bothering the troops, but that was about to change.

On September 1 Cole's scouts returned having found no sign of the general after a wide ranging search. Seeing smoke to the north and thinking this might be Connor, Cole and Walker headed down the Powder River, but progress was soon delayed and then halted completely by weather which turned ugly with wicked storms and winter-like temperatures. Discouraged by conditions and with supplies dwindling daily, Cole, cut rations in half and, apparently with Walker's concurrence, elected to turn about and head towards Fort Laramie.

Before they were able to get underway, however, Cole learned that a raiding party estimated to be some 500 strong attacked the horse herd about a mile from the main camp. These attackers were Hunkpapa Lakotas. The Hunkpapas were Sitting Bull's band, though Sitting Bull himself had not yet attained the status he would enjoy a decade hence. Interestingly, these Hunkpapas had not joined the Cheyennes and southern branches of the Lakotas in raiding along the Overland Trail farther south, but they had been pressured by

General Sully's troops since the Minnesota Uprising and now perhaps felt threatened by Cole and Walker.

Reacting quickly, Cole sent a detachment to drive off the raiders, who nevertheless managed to capture twenty horses. The soldiers pursued and recovered the horses, killing several Lakotas in the process. The situation turned about unexpectedly, however, when the troops found themselves confronted by a larger war party, numbering near fifty and putting the pursuers back on the defensive. The fight that followed was fierce enough. Four soldiers were killed and three others were wounded. One man was able to get back to the main camp and report and that brought Cole out with the main body. The reinforcements compelled the Indians to withdraw, but Cole's weakened horses were too exhausted to pursue.

On September 3, the two columns commenced their journey to Fort Laramie with Walker's command taking the point. The combined commands had lost more than 200 horses due to exhaustion and starvation, and with no horses to pull them a number of wagons had to be destroyed. On the 4th, Indians harassed the rear of Cole's column until driven off by the soldiers. The next morning, the tempo increased as the Indians attacked with larger numbers. Aided by artillery support, the Spencer-armed soldiers repelled several attacks.

Their travails were far from over, however. On September 8, along the Little Powder River, Cole's column—Walker was some miles ahead—quite unexpectedly came upon the huge village of Lakotas, Cheyennes, and Arapahos that had attacked Platte Bridge Station. The village, according to historian John D. McDermott, could have contained as many as 3,000-4,000 warriors; if so, it may even have exceeded the size of the village Custer found on the Little Bighorn, eleven years hence. Cole immediately ordered his wagons formed into a corral. What followed was a fight of the stiffest sort, with both sides trading counterattacks, but again it was Cole's artillery that made the difference, along with the seven-shot Spencer carbines of the troops. After three hours of combat, the Cheyennes withdrew and headed for the Black Hills to hunt buffalo, leaving the Lakotas and Arapahos to carry on the fight. Meanwhile, Walker's column, some fifteen miles ahead, had also been surrounded, but, oddly, not attacked. Hearing the sounds of battle from Cole's column, Walker left a detachment to guard his nearly empty supply wagons and marched to the sound of the guns, only to find that the Indians had pulled out by the time he arrived. On the night of September 9, a howling Norther struck with freezing temperatures, and rain mixed with snow. More than 400 horses, already weakened, perished in the frigid conditions.[39]

On the 10th, Cole and Walker resumed their southward march, with Indians continuing to nip at the rear guard. Meanwhile, on September 11, General Connor finally learned something of the whereabouts of Cole and Walker when Frank North's Pawnee scouts came across hundreds of dead cavalry horses, many of which had been shot to put them out of their misery. Four days later, North and his scouts located Cole and Walker, and sent word of their finding back to Connor, who promptly sent supplies on ahead to his two wandering and starving columns.

The combined columns of Cole and Walker reached Fort Connor on September 19-20, where they rested, bathed, and received welcome rations, before heading on to Fort Laramie, which they reached early in October, preceded by Connor who arrived on the 29th to find that headquarters had cut new orders officially ending the Powder River Expedition, terminating the District of the Plains and restoring Connor to his old billet command of the District of Utah. Connor was furious. He saw no reason to end the campaign and, indeed, was ready to take the field again. Connor of course thought the campaign had been a grand success, but in truth the Powder River Expedition had accomplished little. True, Connor had destroyed an Arapaho village and Cole and Walker had managed to repel several attacks, but if the purpose of the expedition had been to chastise the Indians it had fallen far short of the mark. One historian has suggested that the expedition was important because it marked the beginning of the post Civil War Indian conflicts on the Plains; it was also the last major campaign in which Civil War volunteers would see action.

Following the Treaty of the Little Arkansas, Edward Wynkoop, who, it will be recalled, was relieved of command after Sand Creek, was appointed Special Indian Agent for the Cheyennes. Viewed as fair and honest in his dealings with Indians, Wynkoop was respected by the Indians, even as he respected them. If he was not unique in this respect Wynkoop was at least unusual. On April 4, 1866, Wynkoop met with a group of Dog Soldiers near Fort Larned. The gathering included several prominent Dog Soldier leaders. When the parley ended the Indian leaders promised to abide by the terms of the Little Arkansas treaty. However, they were also given to understand that it was permissible to remain in their home territory between the Arkansas and the Platte. It was almost inevitable that there would be some kind of misunderstanding during any one of these sessions and this one proved no exception. In agreeing to abide by the terms of the Little Arkansas treaty—which in essence meant withdrawing all opposition to the principal corridors of travel along the Arkansas, Platte and Smoky Hill Trails—the Indians imagined they were in full compliance with the specifications of the treaty, quite naturally, and since nothing seems to have been said about being prohibited from living in their traditional territory they believed it was acceptable to do so. Had the terms been stated precisely they would have understood that this was simply unacceptable.

Through the summer of 1866 scattered incidents suggested that serious trouble was not far off the grid and underscored the futility of the early April meeting with Wynkoop. The ever militant Dog Soldiers refused to abandon the Smoky Hill country, and prompted Wynkoop to call another meeting with Cheyenne leaders at Fort Ellsworth. Once more the Indian leaders proclaimed their support for the treaty, but complained that the U.S. Army had failed to return two Indian children captured at Sand Creek. The Dog Soldiers and Sutaio bands of Cheyennes had only agreed to certain parts of the treaty, while Wynkoop, it appears, wanted to believe that the Indians had understood and agreed to the treaty in all its ramifications and signed accordingly. Meanwhile, though the summer and early fall had been remarkably free of violence, the Cheyennes had warned garrisons at the military posts and employees at stagecoach stations to leave the country; if the whites could be persuaded to leave without violence so much the better.

Hancock Takes the Field

In August, General Winfield Scott Hancock replaced John Pope as commander of the Missouri Department. A celebrated figure, renowned for his magnificent defense of the Union center at Gettysburg on the third day of that bloody battle, Hancock was tall, handsome, physically imposing and looked every inch the beau ideal of a professional soldier. He was one of those generals who emerged from the Civil War seemingly assured of a place in the pantheon of American heroes, only to find his star tarnished on the Great Plains of the West. Like others of his ilk, Hancock had difficulty making the adjustment from waging a conventional war to fighting Indians.

In December 1866 the U.S. Army's worst disaster in the Trans-Mississippi West up to that time occurred when Captain William J. Fetterman and the eighty men of his command were surprised and wiped out to a man near Fort Phil Kearny in what was then Dakota Territory. As a consequence of the Fetterman Massacre—by which name it soon came to be known and would continue to be so called until well into the 20th century—the Army was shaken to its core. "We must act with vindictive earnestness against the Sioux," said General Sherman to General Grant (now general of the Army). Indeed, there was—still is—nothing quite like a disaster to change one's perspective, for it will be recalled that Sherman spoke with a much less strident voice only a year earlier. Anti-Indian sentiment in the West was a force to be reckoned with and when Sherman spoke in such terms he talked the kind of talk that appealed to contractors, operators of trans-Mississippi stage lines, railroaders, and a good many citizens.[40]

From the late 1860s into the '70s there was a continuous battle between the Indian Bureau and the War Department over which federal agency should be responsible for the welfare (and discipline if necessary) of the Indian tribes. The Indian Bureau favored a peace policy and in this was supported by a powerful lobby of like-minded citizens, most of whom lived east of the Mississippi River. Not surprisingly, the approach represented by the War Department favored a military solution. One particular sticking point revolved around whether it should be legal for traders to sell firearms to Indians. The pro side of the argument was that the tribes needed these weapons for hunting; for their livelihood. No one, at least in the Indian Bureau, seemed to recall that Indians had managed to get along quite nicely without firearms for generations The Army of course strenuously objected, arguing that so long as the Indians were armed they represented a threat. During the last half of the 19th century this would remain a contentious issue.

On January 25, 1867, the official report of Senator James R. Doolittle's investigating committee was published. The report claimed that the Indian troubles were caused by the white man's greed and aggression. Supported by the Doolittle report and pressured by peace elements, President Andrew Johnson agreed that a peaceable approach was the best way to deal with the Indian difficulties. Accordingly, a formal commission was established to examine the cause/s of the Fetterman Disaster; to get a finger on the pulse of the Plains tribes; to better understand their mood.

General Winfield Scott Hancock. His much touted campaign against the Cheyennes accomplished little more than to stir up trouble.

Meanwhile, though, Sherman moved ahead with plans for retaliation. His plan took the form of two major expeditions; one under General Hancock. The second would move north into the Powder River region, covering much the same ground as Patrick Connor had covered back in '65. "No peace should be shown these Indians," said Sherman.[41]

South of the Arkansas River, Hancock was ordered to make a demonstration against the Cheyennes and Arapahos, who reportedly were ready to make war. Should Hancock find this to be true he was to oblige them. As it worked out, however, the Powder River expedition had to be postponed because the peace commission—which included General Alfred Sully—was already en route to parley with the Lakotas. Thanks to dime novels and lurid pulp stories, Easterners formed an image of the Indian warrior of the West who was probably best personified by the Plains tribes. With feathered war bonnets dancing in the wind; faces and ponies painted for war, these superb horsemen of the Great Plains quickly became a romanticized western version of Cooper's woodland Indians.

These were the warriors to test Hancock's mettle; they would be his nemesis, but he would never really understand them. And in truth he would confront a paradox in that the older, respected leaders were not at all anxious to go to war with the U.S., and were willing to relinquish rights to *some* of their territory in order to avoid war. Had it been left strictly up to these men there likely would have been much less bloodshed on the Great Plains and elsewhere in the West for that matter. But the young warriors and the militant hot heads saw it differently. This faction resented the steady encroachment of the white man and expressed their displeasure through their raids. To Hancock and his superiors the dilemma was how to tell the good guys from the bad guys.

In March, Hancock advised Indian Agents Edward Wynkoop and Jesse Leavenworth that he would be marching into Indian country with a powerful column of troops. It was his intention, he told the agents, to parley with the chiefs and leading men; to let them know that they must not interfere with the routes of travel. If they, the Indians, wanted war, however, he was ready to oblige. "No insolence will be tolerated."[42]

As winter gradually faded Hancock began planning his spring campaign. By the end of March, lead elements of his expedition—the Expedition For the Plains, as it was officially named—departed from Fort Riley, traveling via the old Military Road that ran between Forts Riley, Leavenworth, and Harker, thence on to Fort Larned which would serve as the expedition's staging point. En route they were joined by one, Henry M. Stanley, a reporter for the *Missouri Democrat* out of St. Louis. Stanley was to go on to fame as the man who would find Dr. Livingston in darkest Africa. A bond quickly developed between Stanley and General Hancock.

By early April, Hancock had organized a formidable force consisting of eight troops of the 7th Cavalry and seven companies of the 37th Infantry and a battery of the 4th Artillery; 1,400 men in all. Additionally, there was a large wagon train carrying supplies and equipment, together with a train of pontoon bridges for crossing rivers. Brand new to the West, Hancock had little understanding of the terrain, particularly that there would be little call for bridging the small watercourses found on the Great Plains. And as usual for an expedition such as this there was a coterie of Delaware Indian scouts, plus three white scouts, one of whom was James Butler "Wild Bill" Hickok.

The 7th Cavalry was a relatively new regiment, having been organized less than a year earlier. As with all mounted regiments, the 7th consisted of twelve troops, but with some troops assigned to various duties throughout the Department of Missouri, only eight troops were available for this expedition. Destined to become one of the Army's storied units, the 7th was commanded by Colonel and Brevet Major General Andrew Jackson Smith a crusty thirty-year veteran. Smith had a dual role. In addition to commanding the 7th Cavalry, he also commanded the District of Upper Arkansas. As a consequence, de facto command of the 7th Cavalry devolved to Lieutenant Colonel George Armstrong Custer, who was about to begin his education with the Plains Indians. As commander of the Upper Arkansas District, Smith also served as Hancock's deputy, and earlier than that as a young captain had seen action during Oregon's Rogue Wars.

Above: Journalist Henry Stanley recorded his impressions of Hancock's campaign. He would later make history by meeting Dr. David Livingstone in darkest Africa, as shown in this illustration (Stanley is shown left of the flag, while Livingstone is to the right). ***Below:*** General Andrew Jackson Smith. He was named first commanding officer of the 7th U.S. Cavalry, with Custer as his second in command.

On March 31, the expedition passed through Salina and on April 1 reached Fort Harker. Originally named Fort Ellsworth it had once been a stage stop and trading post. The post was garrisoned by two troops of the 7th Cavalry which gladly joined the main body of their regiment, grateful for the opportunity to take the field and leave the monotony of garrison duty behind them.

Travel across the high plains was likely a monotonous trek for Hancock: few trees and many small streams to cross, perhaps prompting the general to wonder why he had bothered to haul pontoon bridges. Little evidence of white presence was found; occasionally a small ranch, stage station, or trading post. The presence of graded railroad beds, however, indicated that railroad survey crews were working the area.

On April 3, the Hancock column left Fort

Harker and pushed southwest along the Military Road toward Forts Larned and Zarah. At Walnut Creek their route intersected briefly with the old Santa Fe Trail, which ran from Franklin, Missouri, southwest across Kansas to Santa Fe, New Mexico. Not far from Zarah stood Allison and Boothe's Fort, or trading post, where, it will be recalled, Bull Sumner's column had bivouacked back in '57. By the time of Hancock's visit the combination trading post/stage station was operated by one Charles Roth, whose ethics, if not an outright violation of the law, drew Hancock's ire because of a report from the commanding officer at Fort Dodge (present Dodge City) stating that Roth had been violating specific military orders by selling whiskey to the Indians.

For a brief time in 1865–1866, Fort Zarah was the seat of the Cheyenne-Arapaho Agency, but when Edward Wynkoop was appointed agent, he moved the agency back to Fort Larned in the fall of 1866. The Indian Bureau seemed to be in a moving mood at this time, for even as Wynkoop was moving back to Fort Larned, Jesse Leavenworth, agent for the Kiowas and Comanches, removed his agency from Larned to Zarah.

In the order of march, the infantry, wagons, and artillery formed double columns with the cavalry out on the flanks. At Fort Larned, Hancock hoped to have his meeting with some of the so-called "hostile" leaders. To Sherman, Hancock wrote that he trusted the Indians would give them "proper cause for chastisement." Although the road itself was in tolerably good condition, spring rains and snow had filled many of the arroyos and streams, some with as much as a foot of water. Otherwise, a sharp biting wind seemed to affect everyone but Custer who appeared impervious to inclement weather, hot or cold, wet or dry. In typical spring fashion, however, mild weather returned on the 4th.[43]

On April 6, the weather changed again. Skies remained clear but the column was buffeted by powerful winds and dust storms. Along the way they encountered a party of buffalo-hunting Plains Apaches, but the meeting was peaceful enough. However, of more import to Hancock was the arrival of a group of Cheyennes from a nearby village. The spokesperson, dressed in the uniform of a lieutenant 3rd Cavalry, was taken to Hancock carrying a message from Agent Wynkoop, requesting that Hancock meet with a gathering of Cheyenne-Arapaho and Plains Apache chiefs at Fort Larned on the 10th.

En route to Fort Larned, the expedition passed historic Pawnee Rock, a huge sandstone outcropping that rose some sixty feet above the surrounding terrain. The rock gained its name when at some earlier time a party of Pawnees, on a horse-stealing foray were chased and attacked by Cheyennes or perhaps Comanches. The Pawnees took up a defensive position on top of the rock, which provided great protection until food and water ran out. Recognizing the inevitability of their end, they chanted their death song, then descended and after what was probably a furious fight were slain to the man.

On April 7, Hancock reached Fort Larned, one of the oldest posts on the Santa Fe Trail. Built in 1859, the post was responsible for protecting the mail station and guarding a stretch of the Santa Fe Trail. Indeed, it was once called "Camp Alert" because of the frequent Indian attacks in the area. The expedition camped a mile east of the fort.

The freakish spring winter that had assaulted the column on the 6th continued, with strong winds, snow and plunging temperatures. In Hancock's mind the weather should have no effect on his planned meeting with Cheyenne and Kiowa leaders on the 10th. Moreover, he expected the Indians to agree to the terms he planned to propose, which meant they were to move at least 100 miles south of the Smoky Hill Road. If this worked out—and Hancock saw no reason why it shouldn't—his expedition would move to either Fort Harker or Fort Hays, remaining in that vicinity until May, at which time the expedition would officially end. Should the Indians refuse his terms he would take immediate action.

Fort Larned, Kansas.

As the historian of the expedition, William Chalfant, points out, Hancock was not actually authorized to make any treaty with the Indians, so it is incorrect to think that he planned to do so. He could of course inform the Indians as to what was expected of them. He intended to meet with the chiefs, lecture them sternly, and demand that they relocate south of the Smoky Hill corridor.[44]

On April 9, even as Lee and Grant were discussing surrender terms at Appomattox Courthouse, the spring storm began to ebb. Nevertheless, the storm caused the meeting slated for the following day to be postponed, much to Hancock's irritation. To Hancock's mind, this was nothing more than "an excuse" to avoid meeting with him.[45]

On the 11th, Wynkoop advised Hancock that the Cheyennes were on the way but had stopped to hunt buffalo, which Hancock regarded as another stalling tactic. Here, the hero of Gettysburg demonstrated yet again his ignorance of Plains Indian culture, which depended almost exclusively on the bison for so very much, and after a long winter when game was often scarce, a herd of bison near their village would have been cause for great excitement. Nevertheless, setting his irritation aside, Hancock elected to grant them another day.

Finally, late on the afternoon of April 12, a group of Cheyenne Dog Soldiers, including their principal leaders, Tall Bull, Bull Bear, and White Horse, in company with a few others from smaller bands, in all perhaps a dozen, came in to parley with Hancock. After furnishing them with rations, as a gesture of good faith, Hancock had a large fire built in front of the headquarters tent and arranged for seating around the fire, informing the chiefs that the council would be held that night, yet another *faux pas* on Hancock's part. Had he bothered to discuss this with any of his guides he would have learned that Indians only held council during the daylight hours. As it was, the parley would get off on the wrong foot right away.

Hancock and his officers presented themselves in full dress uniforms. After introductions all around, Hancock addressed the Indians, reminding them that he had previously advised their agents—Wynkoop and Leavenworth—of his intention to meet with the tribes. Hancock went on to say that he had more soldiers than all of the tribes put together, and that he intended to visit the village the next day. Soldiers would remain among them to insure peace; those who walked the path of peace would be treated like brothers, but those who chose the path of war would be punished severely. Hancock then persisted in perpetuating the misguided notion that each tribe must have one all powerful leader who can be held responsible for all wrong-doings. As we have seen, the idea of one central leader to speak for all was a completely foreign concept to the Indians, even as the antithesis of it was equally foreign to whites, and why, after all these years, white leaders should have failed to grasp that is a vexing question. Said Hancock, those who violate the trust of peace— on either side—would be punished. Whether the Indians understood this, or more importantly, believed it, is doubtful.

Theodore Davis, an artist for *Harper's Weekly* who observed the meeting, thought Hancock's presentation was simple and straight forward: hostiles would be punished, others would not. Custer's view was that Hancock said he was not there to make war but rather promote peace, but given his earlier statements to Sherman and others, it is hard to accept Hancock as a promoter of peace. His demeanor was more like that of a stern parent rebuking his wayward children, but it went beyond that; his words were arrogant and provocative. Indeed, Dr. Isaac Coates, expedition surgeon, who commented on the proceedings more like a doctor of philosophy, opined that it must have been galling for the Indians "to be talked to as if they were children."[46]

In any case, the sacred pipe was lit and passed around, beginning with the tall, dignified Tall Bull, leader of the Dog Soldiers. An impressive fellow, Dr. Coates, thought he looked like Shakespeare's Cassius, while General Smith compared him to Andrew Jackson, a comparison Tall Bull would surely have resented had he known anything of Jackson.

Tall Bull then addressed Hancock, saying that whites could travel on any road they chose, although the Indians did not want a railroad across their land. Indians had no wish to harm the whites, said Tall Bull. Tall Bull, was in fact speaking with the authority of an all powerful leader, albeit one who had little control over young warriors, whose raiding antics belied his statement that the Indians had no wish to harm the whites. To this, Tall Bull offered an observation that wild game particularly buffalo, were growing scarce and that as a result Indian would eventually find it necessary to come to the soldier forts for food.

Hancock had expected to parley not just with the Cheyennes, but also with the Kiowas, Comanches, Arapahos, and Lakotas and he was thoroughly ticked that these tribes failed to put in an appearance. Tall Bull said he knew nothing of these other bands. Hancock operated under the assumption that Tall Bull and the others were authorized to speak for all the Cheyennes. He seems not to have been aware that there were other Dog Soldier chiefs to be dealt with, to say nothing of other bands of Cheyennes who were not in the village he proposed to visit.

Hancock made a grand show of telling the Indians that he was honoring the Treaty of the Little Arkansas because he was returning the boy captured at Sand Creek and that the Cheyennes should do likewise. Ironically, the lad's story is an interesting one. He was not actually a Cheyenne (though Hancock was unaware of this) but an Arapaho who wound up in the Wilson-Graham Circus, hence his white name Wilson Graham. Two Cheyenne girls had also been taken captive at Sand Creek. One wound up with a family in Denver. The other became a member of the circus along with the boy and later disappeared. Eventually, federal officials recovered the boy from the circus and returned him to Sherman, who passed him on to Hancock, who instructed the commanding officer at Fort Larned to return the boy to his people.

The council ended about 10 p.m. with Hancock reiterating his intention to visit the village the following day. This, the Indians found more disturbing than the general's words about war and one all powerful Indian leader. To the Cheyennes, the thought of Hancock visiting their village was a frightening prospect, for it conjured up memories of Sand Creek. These Cheyenne leaders had, after all, come forth to meet Hancock purposely to keep him away from the village. It was Hancock's intent to expose the Indians to the might of the U.S. Army; if they could be made to see the power they were up against, the Indians would be much less inclined to make war. Thus, it was imperative that the expedition visit the village, for only by doing so could Hancock make his point.

On the morning of April 13, Hancock, disgruntled but still determined, left Fort Larned for the Indian village he expected to find on the north branch of Pawnee Fork. The day began with wind, overcast, and a little rain. Wynkoop attempted to reason with Hancock that the approach of a large military force was certain to frighten the Indians with whom the memory of Sand Creek still resonated powerfully. Hancock's explanation was that because the principal chiefs had not been at the council it was necessary to march on the village, which of course was nonsense because the village had been on his agenda from the outset.

Hancock undertook this campaign with a glaring lack of understanding about the culture and political structure of the Plains Indian tribes with which he was dealing. In this he was of course not the first military commander to be handicapped by his own ignorance, nor would he be the last. Still another misconception was his fixation on the idea that Roman Nose, a warrior of the Ohméséheso band of Southern Cheyennes, was the principal Cheyenne chief. Although renowned for his prowess in war, Roman Nose was not a chief and his presence at the Fort Larned council would have been inappropriate; an understanding of this rather basic fact might well have made a noticeable difference in Hancock's efforts to deal with the Cheyennes.

On April 14, the expedition marched out of Fort Larned, deeper into the southern reaches of the Smoky Hill country. As the landscape subtly changed, scattered stands of timber became increasingly evident. South of the Smoky Hill Trail was the historic Santa Fe Trail. From a distance, Indians watched as the column marched steadily onward.

Crossing Pawnee Fork they were approached by the Lakota war chief, Pawnee Killer and several others. The chief informed Hancock that he was camped up ahead near the Dog Soldiers and the Sutaio, another band of Southern Cheyennes. Pawnee Killer assured Hancock that his village would remain there until Hancock had held his council. Later, another band of Dog Soldier chiefs paid a visit as well. In all probability the Indian strategy here was to delay Hancock's approach, giving the non-combatants time to flee, as the general was soon to discover.

By late afternoon, Hancock ordered camp to be made. It had been a laborious day, especially for the wagon train. That evening several Indian leaders, including Pawnee Killer, came in to talk and elected to spend the night. Later, Hancock wrote to Sherman, reporting that he planned to talk to the Indians and advance to the village the next day. Early the next day, Pawnee Killer departed, but promised to return with other chiefs and they would hold a council at 9 a.m.

Although Hancock was focused on his objective, the Indians, he was not blind to the beauty of his surroundings. It was a land where earth and sky came together on the far horizon. It was spring. The grasses were fresh and prairie wild flowers were coming to life; immense herds of bison once literally blackened these plains. Modern travelers only glimpse the land from the highway and imagine what it must have been like to see the great buffalo herds. Our perspective is distorted by fences, power lines, and occasional buildings, but Hancock's view was fresh and clean. He told Sherman he was not surprised that the Indians did not want to give up this land.

When the chiefs failed to arrive at the appointed hour, Hancock felt his ire rising again. He could not understand why it should take so long, but the village was farther away than the general realized. Then at 9:30 the Dog Soldier leader, Bull Bear rode in to report that the others were coming, which improved Hancock's frame of mind. However, by late morning with still no sign of the Indians, Hancock broke camp and began his march to the village. Barely had they started, though, when a contingent of Indians was seen approaching, and it was a good size party, too, composed of Cheyennes and Oglala Lakotas, estimated at 300–400 and including the renowned warrior, Roman Nose.

To Hancock this surely did not look like a group of chiefs come to talk things over; this was a formidable looking bunch, to which he responded by forming a line of battle. Custer ordered sabers drawn, 500 of them flashing in the April sun. Here was another moment of high drama: two bodies of armed warriors, drawn up in line of battle, facing each other. Theodore Davis thought the Indians presented a "bold and spectacular sight."[47]

Well aware of Roman Nose's reputation, Agent Wynkoop urged him to keep the Cheyennes quiet and above all not to flee. Under a flag of truce, Roman Nose, Bull Bear, White Horse, and several other leading men approached Hancock, who was accompanied by General Smith, Custer, and several others from the general's staff. While introductions were made, Roman Nose fixed his gaze intently on Hancock.

Edmund Guerrier again served as interpreter. With the curtness that typified his demeanor thus far, Hancock bluntly asked whether there were any Indians who wanted to fight because if so he was ready. To this, Roman Nose replied that they were not looking for war; that if war was their objective they would not have "come so close to your big guns." We cannot say whether this response took a bit of the bluster off of Hancock's words, but we might imagine that it did. Hancock then explained that as commander of the District of the Upper Arkansas, General Smith would remain in the area after the expedition left.[48]

Theodore Davis tells us that Roman Nose was the most impressive Indian present and Dr. Coates thought he was one of the finest physical specimens of his race. According to Coates, Roman Nose was resplendent in the full uniform of a major general, and in addition to a bow and arrows, he was armed with a Spencer carbine and four Navy Colt revolvers. However, as historian William Chalfant points out this has to be an exaggeration as both Davis and Dr. Coates were several hundred yards away and could hardly have noticed that kind of detail. In all likelihood Guerrier or one of Hancock's officers provided them with a description with which they then took certain liberties. It seems safe to say, though, that Roman Nose was splendidly dressed and well armed.

It continued to stick in Hancock's craw that Roman Nose had failed to present himself at the Fort Larned council and he now asked the great warrior directly why that was so. It seems surprising that someone such as Guerrier had not pointed this out to Hancock, but if they did the general apparently rejected the explanation as unacceptable. Roman Nose undoubtedly wondered why Hancock would have expected him to be present and responded by saying, oddly, that he had heard conflicting accounts of the general's intentions.

As he had done earlier, Hancock reminded the Indians that he still intended to march to their village; camp nearby and convene a council. The Indians apparently had no vocal reaction to this, but did exhibit great nervousness that even Hancock noticed.

When the words were finished, the expedition prepared to resume the march to the village, preceded by the Indian retinue. Wynkoop continued his effort to try and make Hancock understand that the presence of his command was going to frighten the Indians who were likely to flee, but Hancock remained unmoved and reaffirmed his intention to camp near the village.

By late afternoon, the expedition, under watchful Indian eyes, had reached what Hancock described as "a charming spot" about a mile from the Indian village. Theodore Davis rode into the village with a small detachment, probably out of nothing more than curiosity. But if they expected to see a live, functioning village they were quickly disabused of that notion, for all the women and children had fled just as Agent Wynkoop had predicted.[49]

Not surprisingly, the news angered Hancock and he demanded an explanation. Roman Nose replied that while he and his warriors did not fear the soldiers, the women and children did. Be that as it may, Hancock ordered the women and children returned at once. Angered at the general's arrogance, Roman Nose told Bull Bear he was going to kill Hancock. At this point, Hancock accompanied by a small party set off for the village, perhaps to see for himself. Roman Nose, meanwhile, reaffirmed his intention to kill Hancock, causing the others to be frightened because they feared the consequences.

Sometimes the course of history teeters on a single moment, as it did in this instance. An incident of major proportions was narrowly averted when Bull Bear, fearful that Roman Nose was about to carry out his threat, grabbed the bridle of Roman Nose's horse and led his warrior friend away, thus defusing what could have been a deadly moment. In retrospect, it seems likely that Roman Nose had every intention of killing Hancock. According to Guerrier, Roman Nose told Bull Bear that Hancock wanted a fight and he would give him one. Hancock, meanwhile, was apparently unaware that his life hung in the balance of a moment. Had it not been for Bull Bear's timely maneuver Hancock would likely have joined General E.R.S. Canby as the only two general officers of the regular army to lose their lives during the Indian wars.

Although by now, Hancock, probably through the persistence of Wynkoop and Guerrier, and perhaps others, seems finally to have understood that the presence of his expedition might unnerve the Cheyennes with their memories of Sand Creek, but he saw no reason for the Lakotas to harbor the same fear, and in any case, this did not to his mind excuse the absence, which he viewed as a sign that they planned mischief, and he insisted that the women and children return to the village immediately, as though they were hiding just around the next bend of Pawnee Fork.

That afternoon of April 14, Hancock sent Edmund Guerrier to the village with orders to report back with information about Indian movements: had the women and children returned? what if anything was happening? Guerrier returned that night with word that in fact nothing had happened; the women and children were still absent. Hancock was chagrined and embarrassed. His strategy to cow the Indians had fallen apart, and Winfield Scott Hancock was not a man who liked to see his plans go sideways. But there was more to it than that. As William Chalfant, the historian of the expedition points out, this development had to hurt Hancock's political ambitions, which included a vision of the White House.

But the Union hero of Gettysburg did not waste time wallowing in his frustration. Custer and his 7th Cavalry were immediately dispatched to surround the village, estimated to contain some 300 lodges, of which a little more than half were Cheyenne, the remainder Oglala Lakota. True to Guerrier's report Custer found the village abandoned, save for an old Lakota couple, and a ten-year-old mixed blood girl who reportedly had been raped. In their haste to flee from the soldiers, the Indians had left behind much equipage.

By midnight Custer had completed his assessment of the village situation, and by sunrise on the 15th, guided by Guerrier, Wild Bill Hickok, and a coterie of Delaware Indian scouts, the 7th Cavalry set out to locate the Indians. For the next three days Custer and his troopers, following the trail picked up by the Delaware scouts, pursued their quarry, watched all the way by the Indians. Like the dog trying to catch the hare, the Indians managed to stay just ahead of the soldiers. Finally, on April 19, Custer reached Fort Hays, his command exhausted and his horses badly in need of forage.

Even as Custer was in futile pursuit, Indians attacked and burned Lookout Stage Station, ten miles west of Fort Hays. When Custer arrived he learned that another raiding party was active, to the east of Fort Hays. Wild Bill Hickok was directed to carry a message to the commanding officer at Fort Harker, fifty miles distant, requesting forage and supplies for the 7th Cavalry. Hickok, armed with a brace of revolvers and a carbine, successfully ran the gauntlet and delivered the message to Fort Harker. This incident later served as the basis for a C.B. De Mille movie, *The Plainsman*, starring Gary Cooper as Hickok and Jean Arthur as Calamity Jane.

After sending Hickok on his mission, Custer wrote a report to Smith and Hancock, updating them on his lack of success in catching the Indians. On the same day that Custer reached Fort Hays, Hancock made what was arguably the biggest blunder of his campaign. Having thought it over for three days, he concluded that the village must be destroyed; it must be eliminated as a base of operation for the Indians. Further, destruction of the equipage and food supplies left behind would work a real hardship on the Indians. Destruction of the village would have far reaching effects on Indian-white relations on the Central Plains.

On the morning of April 19, three companies of the 37th Infantry tore down the teepees and created a huge pile of skins and teepee poles, along with the equipage left behind and put it to the torch. Several lodges were preserved as housing for Indian scouts. Hancock apparently had hopes of recruiting some Cheyennes and Lakotas to serve as scouts.

The day before, Hancock had written to Sherman, setting out his views on the Indian situation. He was terribly frustrated that his relationship with the Cheyennes and Lakotas had gone sour, but he also remained convinced that the Cheyennes, at least, had demonstrated their treachery by running away. Hancock was also angry that neither Wynkoop nor Leavenworth had taken action to insist that the Indians be forced to make restitution for their raids.

Meantime, Indian raids along the Smoky Hill route continued, which lent some substance to Hancock's argument about Indian treachery. On the 20th, Hancock returned to Fort Dodge and ordered Custer to pursue the Indians, promising forage and supplies would be forthcoming.

If Hancock felt frustrated by his lack of success with the Cheyennes and Oglala Lakotas, it by no means discouraged him from holding further council meetings. On April 23 he parleyed with a trio of Kiowa chiefs, and on the 28th with Little Raven of the Arapahos. Then, on the 29th it was back to Fort Larned for a meeting with the famous Kiowa leader Satanta, a man noted for his oratorical ability and diplomatic skills. Hancock was so impressed with Satanta that he presented the chief with the full uniform of a major general. Hancock was not alone in his admiration of Satanta. Correspondent David Stanley was also singularly impressed.

By April 25, supplies for Custer's regiment had arrived at Fort Hays, but only a minimal amount; much more would be needed in order for the 7th Cavalry to take the field again. Fresh fruit and vegetables were desperately needed. There was no room at Fort Hays to quarter the regiment so camp was made at Big Creek, about a mile west of the fort, where the troopers were forced to endure heavy spring rains with little or no protection. Fortunately, Custer's horses were able to graze around the fort and recover their strength somewhat.

Custer was to spend a month and a half here at the Big Creek campsite. The enforced idleness may have been harder on the regiment than being in the field. The desertion rate was high and Custer himself was in a bad frame of mind, annoyed by almost anything; everything seemed to get under his hide. He missed Libbie and wrote to her frequently, saying how beautiful their camp was and he longed to have her close. She agreed to visit him, and he longed to have her close. In May, she and a friend, Anna, from Monroe, Michigan (her home town) traveled in an army wagon to Fort Hays, escorted by a detachment provided by General Smith.

With the arrival of spring and new grass, the Indian ponies just like Custer's horses, fattened and grew stronger. The difference was that the wiry Indian ponies subsisted on native grasses for much of the year, while the bigger cavalry horses needed grass (forage) supplemented by grain periodically. The rich buffalo hunting grounds between the Platte River and the Smoky Hill provided ample opportunity for the Indians to fill their larder with fresh meat, hides, and more, to replace what Hancock had destroyed in the village on Pawnee Fork, while raids along the Smoky Hill corridor also seemed to replace some of the weapons and equipage that had been lost. The 7th Cavalry also took advantage of the buffalo herds. Early in May, Custer organized two hunting parties. The hunt raised the spirits of the command, providing a welcome relief from the daily monotony, and provided fresh meat as well. Custer himself did not manage to bring down a buffalo, but did accidentally shoot his horse while dismounting.

Despite the supply shortages, the 7th Cavalry was not overlooked. While here at Big Creek, Custer received orders to protect the Smoky Hill stage route between Fort Harker and Denver. The distance between the two points is about 360 miles, give or take, and exactly how Custer with a worn down regiment was expected to accomplish this was not specified. One of the companies of his regiment, I, commanded by Captain Myles Keogh was stationed at Fort Wallace, west of Big Creek. Keogh would later die with Custer at the Little Bighorn, and his famous horse Comanche would become legendary as the only survivor of that battle. This campaign had convinced Custer that the Indians in the area were hostile, and he warned Keogh to be alert; that Indians loved to employ the decoy strategy to surprise a command.

Mostly the raids during this spring of 1867 were the work of the Dog Soldiers, but other bands were active as well and Hancock was anxious to chastise these mischief makers. Accordingly, early in May, through General Smith, Custer was ordered to march north with six companies of his regiment to Fort McPherson, Nebraska (near present North Platte) where additional supplies would be waiting for him. Hancock was apparently convinced that a movement into the Republican River country provided the best opportunity to hit the Indians hard. Raiders along the Smoky Hill Trail would have to be dealt with by the garrisons stationed at the posts along that route. From Fort McPherson, Custer was to proceed to Fort Sedgwick and then Fort Morgan. If he found no Indians, Custer was to turn south to Fort Wallace and await further orders.

Although Hancock had been anxious for Custer to get underway as soon as possible, the 7th Cavalry did not take the field for nearly a month. True, there were problems of supply that delayed departure, but the primary reason was that Custer simply hated to leave his wife behind. Finally, on June 1 six companies of the 7th Cavalry began their northward march. The remaining two companies were left behind on detached duty After relocating Libbie and Anna to a more secure location, Custer with a few scouts rode north to catch up with the main body.

For the 7th Cavalry the march to Fort McPherson was largely uneventful, except that on June 8, Major Wyckliff Cooper, the regiment's second major, committed suicide. Cooper had served with distinction during the Civil War, but had finally lost his battle with the bottle.

On June 9, the regiment arrived at Fort McPherson. The rails of the Union Pacific had reached this point the previous fall, so there was a stockpile of supplies awaiting Custer. The next two days were spent resupplying the regiment while Custer reported his arrival to General Sherman, who was then at Fort Sedgwick only 86 miles to the southwest. Sherman planned to be at Fort McPherson in a few days and ordered Custer to await his arrival.

On June 12, Custer shifted his campsite ten miles west of Fort McPherson where Pawnee Killer and several other Oglalas and some Cheyennes rode in for a parley. Custer immediately wired Sherman who responded promptly, but the Indians had already cleared out, promising, however, to return for more talks. For the officers responsible for dealing with the Indian problem, this sort of thing was maddening; it was like playing tag. Sherman had directed Custer to make certain that Pawnee Killer checked in at Fort McPherson, but the Indians had gone by the time Sherman's wire arrived.

With regard to the Indian situation, Custer was as frustrated as Sherman, but over and above that he was testy because he missed Libbie. The regiment remained in camp here through the 13th. Custer wrote to his wife expressing his hope for an early reunion. Then on June 14, Pawnee Killer and a Cheyenne chief, Turkey Leg in company with four warriors returned as promised. Custer fed them, as was customary at these gatherings, after which they talked. The Indians declared their wish for peace. What, they wanted to know, were Custer's intentions? It was a small conference and we shall never know exactly what was said because no interpreter was present. Custer imagined that the Indians were simply curious, which may well have been true. No pledges were made on either side and the Indians were soon on their way.

Custer moved camp closer to Fort McPherson on the 15th and was joined by Sherman the following day. While Sherman and Custer discussed future movements, the regiment's horses were shod and looked after by the farriers at the fort. Sherman said that there were reports of a large Indian village on the Upper Republican River. If these reports proved true Custer was to take his regiment and move on in pursuit.

Since assuming the reins of his new command (The Military Division of the Mississippi), Sherman had been nearly deluged with cries for help with the Indian problem and he had come west on a fact-finding tour to judge the status of affairs himself. No one pestered him more than Colorado Territorial Governor Alexander Hunt, who wailed about Indian raids along the Smoky Hill Trail; virtually every station had come under attack several times. The raids had caused supplies into Denver to slow to a trickle. The governor begged Sherman for permission to organize 300 volunteers, to which Sherman agreed, providing it could be done right away. Sherman stressed, too, that there was no guaranty that the Territory would be reimbursed by the federal government. This warning dampened Hunt's enthusiasm noticeably, but his anxiety over Indian raids remained high. Sherman did his best to calm the fears of a general Indian uprising. These raids, he argued were being carried out by young hot bloods. It may have eased Governor Hunt's mind to know that Custer's regiment would soon be scouring the Upper Republican in an effort to locate the troublemakers.

From Sherman went orders to both Hancock (then en route to Denver from Fort Hays) and Custer. To both officers he reiterated his belief that all Indians between the Arkansas and Platte were either hostile or supportive of the hostiles. At the moment the hostiles seemed to be roaming and raiding at will and he warned Hancock to take every precaution.

Custer's orders called for him to scout both forks of the Republican River and then march to Fort Sedgwick where he would find further orders awaiting him. Presumably, any solid contact with Indians would necessitate a departure from Sherman's orders.

Before departing on his new assignment, Custer again wrote to Libbie of his wish that she might join him. He of course had no way of knowing that rumors of impending Cheyenne raids had prompted General Smith to transfer the ladies first to Fort Harker then to Fort Riley.

On June 18 the 7th Cavalry commenced its march to the forks of the Republican. No one of course can ever know what is on anyone's mind at any given moment, but it does appear that Custer was preoccupied with thoughts of his wife and whether that preoccupation affected his judgment as a field commander may only be imagined. Notwithstanding, on the 22nd he sent two companies to Fort Wallace as escort for a wagon train which was intended to pick up supplies *and return with Libbie and Anna* [author's italics]. This, opines historian William Chalfant, was the underlying reason for sending the wagon train to Fort Wallace in the first place. The following day, Major Joel Elliott was sent with a detachment to Fort Sedgwick. Elliott carried with him dispatches for General Christopher C. Augur who had been appointed commander of the Department of the Platte in Omaha back in January. Forts McPherson and Sedgwick would have been in the Platte jurisdiction. As such Custer would have been obligated to inform Augur while operating in his sphere of authority.

While Custer searched vainly along the Republican and its tributaries, the Cheyennes, Oglalas, and Arapahos were raising all kinds of trouble along the Smoky Hill Trail. From Fort Harker, General Smith wired Sherman (now back in St. Louis), pleading for Custer's return. Sherman, who seemed genuinely surprised to learn that Custer was still in the Republican River country, sent an order to Custer through Augur to return to Fort Wallace post haste. Why Sherman should have been surprised is puzzling since the orders under which Custer was now operating were fairly recent. In any case, Custer was to march to Fort Wallace and report to Hancock who was then returning from Denver.

At dawn on June 24, the "peace-seeking" Pawnee Killer's Oglalas struck the 7th Cavalry bivouac, but thanks to a prompt response by the troopers the raiders were driven off and thwarted in their effort to capture the cavalry horses. The Indians remained in the area, watching the soldier camp from a distance. Custer desired to meet with the raiders and sent his interpreter to arrange for a parley and, ultimately, persuade the Indians to check in at Fort McPherson. Whether Custer knew this was Pawnee Killer's band is not clear, but in any event the Indians failed to be enticed by the prospect of another meeting with Custer.

Unsuccessful in persuading the Indians to return to Fort McPherson, Custer now ordered a pursuit, but the elusive raiders proved too slippery and the chase was soon abandoned. A bit later, however, a small party of Indians appeared on a nearby hill, prompting Custer to send Captain Louis Hamilton (grandson of Alexander Hamilton) and Company A to investigate. In typical Plains Indian style, the decoy party led Hamilton's detail on and on. When the Indians divided Hamilton followed suit, pursuing one group, while Capt. Tom Custer went after the others. Dr. Coates, who had been with Hamilton, somehow got separated and soon found himself the quarry, but managed to make it back to the main camp just in time. The incident had turned into something more serious than Custer expected and he quickly formed up the remainder of his command and set off in relief, only to meet Hamilton and Tom Custer returning. The Indians, it seemed, had broken off their attack and withdrawn.

Given the Indian activity in the area, Custer was growing concerned for the safety of

Major Elliott's small party, and even more so for the wagon train he expected would be bringing Libbie. Custer was concerned enough for his wife's safety that he had instructed Lieutenant William Winer Cooke, who was in charge of the train, to shoot Libbie if it appeared she might be taken captive. His frustration finally reached a point where on the 25th he sent Captain Edward Meyers and a squadron (two companies) to escort the train from Fort Wallace.

The wagon train, meanwhile, left Fort Wallace the same day and was attacked by Cheyennes on the 26th. Journalist Davis estimated several hundred Indians, but the Cheyennes had not that many warriors to begin with, so a more reasonable estimate would probably be 100–150. In any event, they would have outnumbered the escort, which, nevertheless, stood fast. Discouraged from further head-on attacks by the accurate fire of the cavalry carbines, the Indians then circled the train, which had continued to move forward. Now and then an individual warrior would demonstrate his courage and prowess, but the wagon train pressed ahead. When Captain Meyers' squadron arrived on the scene, the Indians, recognizing the futility of their effort, broke off the attack and disappeared.

On June 28, both the wagon train and Major Elliott were safely back at the forks of the Republican, each with its own adventure to relate. Elliott and his small party had managed to avoid all Indian contact, and the wagon train had survived its ordeal with no loss of life. Custer probably greeted the wagon train with very mixed feelings. On the one hand he was relieved that Libbie had not been a passenger, but on the other hand he must certainly have been disappointed not to have her with him at last. Lieutenant Cooke would only have been able to tell him that Libbie and Anna had been moved to a safer location, but he probably did not know that by now she was at Fort Riley.

When Custer headed north to Fort McPherson on June 1, he left behind two companies of his regiment to provide protection for Forts Hays and Harker, as well as the railroad construction crews who were working in the area. Farther west, Captain Myles Keogh's Company I had been trying, mostly in vain, to secure that area from repeated raids by Cheyennes and Oglala Lakotas.

The survey crews were then plotting the future course of the U.P.E.D. (Union Pacific, Eastern Division), which would eventually cross Kansas and Colorado, New Mexico, and Arizona to the Pacific, with a branch line connecting Denver. The new railroad would roughly parallel the Butterfield Overland Dispatch Route along the Smoky Hill corridor.

Indian raids along the Smoky Hill Route took place nearly every day during the month of June. Much, though not all of the mayhem was the work of the Dog Soldiers, which included the Bent brothers, George and Charley, particularly the latter.

It will be recalled that William Bent, the founder of Bent' Fort, had three mixed blood sons: Robert, George, and Charley. George and Charley had both been at Sand Creek (along with their sister, Mary), Julesburg, and the Platte Bridge battle, and Robert had been forced by Chivington to guide his command to Sand Creek. George, though he had great respect for his mother's people, and indeed lived and fought with them, tended to be more favorably disposed toward whites than Charley, whose white-hating attitude was perhaps unequaled. Charley reportedly had once vowed to kill his own father.

On June 26, even as Custer awaited the arrival of Major Elliott and the wagon train, Captain Albert Barnitz, with Company G of the 7th Cavalry, responded to a raid on an incoming stagecoach. It was rumored that the great Roman Nose was among the attackers, mounted on a white steed. Although the number of Indians present was estimated to be as high as 300, a more likely figure would be half that many. In any case, a stiff fight followed that cost the lives of 6 troopers, about 12 percent of the number engaged. Several of the dead troopers were horribly mutilated. Interestingly, the fight managed to draw national attention. Some newspapers reported it as a bigger fight than the Fetterman battle. So the month of June 1867 had been a tough month for the 7th Cavalry, but nine years later it would prove a tougher month still.

For George Custer himself, it was a time of intense frustration. He wanted desperately to be with his wife, but the likelihood of that now seemed remote. He hoped for orders that would take him back to one of the posts along the Smoky Hill and thus, closer to Libbie. In the absence of new orders from Sherman—he apparently had not received the orders sent to him through General Augur—Custer could only follow his last set of orders, namely to continue to scout the forks of the Republican River.

Although Custer's orders called for him to thoroughly examine the Upper Republican River watercourses, Custer was obviously distracted, and while he did pay lip service to those orders he seems to have been far more interested in reaching Riverside Station on the South Platte, west of Fort Sedgwick, where it was to be hoped, he would find fresh orders from Sherman, sending him back to the Smoky Hill and Libbie.

And new orders, directing Custer to return to Fort Wallace and report to Hancock, had indeed been cut, just twenty-four hours after Major Elliott left Fort Sedgwick on his return journey. However, since Custer's exact whereabouts were unknown and the new orders could not be communicated to him by wire, they were entrusted to Lieutenant Lyman Kidder, 2d Cavalry, who was ordered to take a detachment, and find Custer, who was presumed to be in the Republican River Valley somewhere, and present him with the new orders. The Kidder story, rather well known to students of the Indian wars, is a one-act tragedy of the Central Great Plains.

The Kidder Tragedy

Twenty-five-year-old Lyman Kidder was a native Vermonter. His father had served as lieutenant governor of Vermont until moving his family to Minnesota when Lyman was seventeen. During the Civil War young Kidder joined the Minnesota Volunteers and participated in actions against guerrillas in Tennessee, and later again the Santee Sioux during the bloody Minnesota uprising in 1862. Liking military life he applied for an appointment to the regular army and was commissioned second lieutenant in the 2d Cavalry in the fall of 1867. The following June he was posted to Fort Sedgwick from which place he set out on his mission to find Custer.

Kidder rode out of Fort Sedgwick on June 29 with a ten-man detachment and an Oglala guide named Red Beard who had lived among the whites for many years and was presumed trustworthy. Custer, meanwhile, reached Riverside Station on July 5 after a grueling and exhausting march, which worked a real hardship on both his troopers and their horses, and for no sound military reason. When he reached Riverside, Custer learned of his new orders and that Lieutenant Kidder had left six days earlier to deliver those orders.

For Custer, the news was disconcerting. Although undoubtedly pleased to learn that new orders had been issued that would allow a reunion with Libbie, he was, at the same time, worried about Kidder's safety. With these thoughts in the forefront of his mind, and with scarcely a chance to rest his tired command, Custer began his march to Fort Wallace (near present Sharon, Kansas) on July 7, not knowing that a dozen or more of his troopers planned to desert from that night's camp. Somehow, though, word leaked out and Custer sent a detachment to pursue the men, with orders to shoot the deserters. Subsequently, six were captured, including three who were wounded attempting to defend themselves. Seven, mounted on good horses, however, managed to escape.

Pushing steadily south toward Fort Wallace, generally following the route taken by the wagon train Custer had sent back earlier, there was speculation as to the fate of Lieutenant Kidder. Said speculation ended on the 12th when Custer's scouts discovered Kidder and his men in what was known as Beaver Creek Valley. All were dead and badly mutilated: scalped and their bodies bristling with arrows. A sketch of the grisly scene by artist Theodore Davis later appeared in *Harper's Weekly* and once more brought the horror of Indian warfare to the nation's attention. The attackers were believed to have been Cheyenne.

On the 13th Custer established camp one-half mile from Fort Wallace. Not at all surprisingly, the horses were in shabby condition, needing grain and a prolonged rest before being again fit for field service. The troopers, too, were worn out. In point of fact, Custer had driven his command to the point of exhaustion unnecessarily.

Impatient and possessing a well of nervous energy, Custer immediately rode into the fort looking for Hancock and hoping, perhaps expecting, to find letters from Libbie; he found neither. Hancock who had arrived from Denver on the 3rd, had already moved on to Fort Harker (near Ellsworth, Kansas) which place he reached the day before Custer arrived at Wallace. Sherman was already at Harker, so he and Hancock had ample time to discuss the Indian problem, which showed no sign of abating, a hard truth that could not have pleased Sherman. And Indians were not the only problem. An outbreak of cholera began to manifest itself near the end of June.

Before leaving Fort Harker, Hancock promised that the 7th Cavalry would be resupplied and ordered Custer, through General Smith, to resume operations in the region between the Arkansas and the Platte, using Fort Wallace as a base of supplies. Hancock almost certainly would have had no idea as to the condition of Custer's regiment else he would not have expected the 7th to take the field again so quickly. On the 16th, General Smith sent Hancock's orders to Custer via a wagon train that was then en route from Fort Harker to Fort Wallace.

Custer Is Court-Martialed

Also on July 16, Custer, with a seventy-six-man escort, rode out of Fort Wallace on yet another punishing ride. His destination was Fort Harker, his purpose, ostensibly, to see about new orders. In reality he was bound to find his wife, be she at Fort Harker, Riley or elsewhere. Forty-eight hours later they met the Fort Wallace-bound wagon train. Custer accepted his new orders from Lieutenant Charles Cox then pressed on to Fort Harker. Presumably Custer read those orders and based on that presumption one wonders why he did not about-face and return to Fort Wallace and prepare to operate in accordance with his new orders? The answer of course is simply that seeing his spouse trumped his orders.

In any event, Custer reached Fort Harker in the early hours of the 19th; awoke General Smith and gave him a cursory report of his activities before informing the general that he was going on to Fort Riley to see his wife. It appears that General Smith did not at first fully grasp what Custer was up to. Only later, after Custer had already departed on the early morning train—the first passenger train had reached Fort Harker on July 1—did Smith come to understand that Custer, with a large escort, had made what amounted to a forced march to Fort Hays before continuing on to Harker in an army ambulance. This was unacceptable and Smith immediately sent a wire to Custer ordering him to rejoin his command immediately. Custer replied, requesting permission to wait until the 22nd, but Smith ordered him to return by the first train. On the night of the 21st, Custer finally arrived ... with Libbie and all of their baggage. Subsequently, Smith, who seems to have been fond of both Custer and his wife, informed Hancock that Custer had been delayed a day, probably because it took extra time for Libbie to pack. Nevertheless, Custer was in hot water and Smith immediately placed him under arrest. However, with cholera spreading, the general elected to send both Custer and Libbie back to Fort Riley where Custer was confined to quarters, pending further action.

When presented with the facts, Hancock approved court-martial charges for being absent from his command without authorization; also for conduct prejudicial to good order and military discipline. Appended to this was a further charge of pursuing and shooting deserters from his regiment. All charges were approved by General of the Army Grant, who ordered a court-martial. The trial was conducted at Fort Leavenworth on Sept. 17. Custer pled not guilty and put up a spirited defense. On October 11, he was found guilty on all counts and sentenced to be suspended from rank, command, and pay for a year.

In retrospect, one cannot help but wonder how Custer could have imagined that his actions in going AWOL—for that is precisely what he was—could possibly be justified? One would have to look far to find a more flagrant and egregious example of conduct unbecoming an officer, indeed, any soldier. His attitude and behavior throughout the campaign portrayed a commander who was astonishingly indifferent to both the letter and spirit of his orders. From the moment he marched north to Fort McPherson; his focus was almost entirely on his wife and not on his mission; little attention was paid to orders or Indians. This was not the dashing hell-for-leather cavalryman of the Civil War, and certainly he did not here exhibit the image of the famous Indian fighter he had come to be thought of by the time of his demise nine years later. Perhaps the explanation lies in the fact that in 1867 he had only been married three years; he was still a newly-wed and quite possibly his sexual appetite was much stronger than it was in 1876, by which time he had been married a dozen years, and the pressing urge for sexual companionship had ebbed a bit.

George Armstrong Custer (seated), with Elizabeth "Libbie" Custer and Tom Custer (standing).

In any case, the verdict was upheld by the adjutant general. Custer was angry and bitter, convinced that his court-martial was a smoke screen to cover up the failure of Hancock's expedition. He could take at least a small measure of comfort knowing that Sheridan agreed about that. But what Custer seemed unwilling to recognize was that his travails were his own undoing; this was not about Hancock. Custer vented his spleen in a series of articles written for *Turf, Field, and Farm*, which seemed to be more of a vehicle for salvaging his bruised reputation than in providing an accurate historical recounting of what had taken place during Hancock's ill-fated expedition.

Custer had not won many friends during the recent campaign. Indeed, his treatment of the officers and men under him gave rise to anger and bitterness that would shadow him to the Little Bighorn. He was a complex individual, arrogant and selfish to a fault, and a man not likely to win the admiration and loyalty of most men, though he did a cabal of followers.

It seems odd that even as Custer marched north to Fort McPherson in early June, presumably searching for a large body of Indians, Cheyenne and Oglala war parties in some strength continued to raid along the Smoky Hill route. By 1867, the Dog Soldiers had become closely allied with the Oglala Lakotas and Northern Cheyennes. Raids intensified as the summer progressed. No matter, railroad construction crews continued with their labors. Despite the Indians' most persistent efforts, the Iron Horse was making its way across the Plains.

On July 22, Cheyenne raiders, including Roman Nose and the infamous Charley Bent attacked Monument Station east of Fort Wallace, and the next day yet a second raiding party struck a train of eighty wagons led by Captain Francisco Baca who had a ninety-man escort. Among the passengers was one Jean Baptiste Lamy soon to be the first archbishop of Santa Fe.

The raids persisted through the summer and into the fall of 1867, prompting Kansas governor Samuel Crawford to write Secretary of War Edwin M. Stanton, asking for authorization to raise volunteers. The governors of Colorado and Montana also chimed in, as did railroad president John Perry. Such authorization of course assumed federal financial support. Stanton referred the matter to Sherman, who, as we have seen, was diametrically opposed to the use of federally funded volunteers; they were rowdy and undisciplined and Sherman undoubtedly felt besieged. He held off on this as long as he could but this summer the pressure was too great to resist and on July 1, he authorized the creation of six to eight companies of mounted volunteers. Apparently, however, only enough men to fill the ranks of four companies could be found. In any case, the 18th Kansas Volunteer Cavalry, 385 officers and men, was mustered in on July 15th. The regiment would acquit itself well during its four-month term of service.

Hancock's expedition had been a fizzle. Before the year was out he was named to command the Department of Louisiana and Texas. This assignment would be followed later by command of the Department of Dakota. His arrogant, blustering ways, instead of cowing the Indians, had instead stirred up more trouble. In particular, his order to burn the big village on Pawnee Fork had aroused anger and indignation among the Indians, not unlike that of Sand Creek, which made any peace discussion all the more difficult. In fact, his campaign, culminating in the destruction of that village, led to two years of fighting. It was called Hancock's War and rightly so.

On the positive side, it might be said, Hancock's War resulted in the creation of a peace commission that would enter into treaties with the Cheyennes, Arapahos, Kiowas, and Comanches. There followed then the Treaty of Medicine Lodge consummated in October 1867. The Medicine Lodge Treaty, along with the Horse Creek Treaty, and the 1868 Fort

Laramie Treaty were arguably the three most important treaties between the United States Government and the Western Indian Tribes. In August 1869, President Grant signed the executive order creating the reservation in Indian Territory and the Great Sioux Reservation in Dakota and Montana.

Philip H. Sheridan

Hancock's replacement as commander of the Missouri Department was the redoubtable Philip H. Sheridan, who seemed to always be in a combative mood; it was his nature as his black hair. Sheridan's behavior as military commander in Texas did not sit well in Washington. Little Phil's harsh application of the president's reconstruction policy rubbed President Andrew Johnson the wrong way and led to his (Sheridan's) replacement by Hancock who was expected to be more politic in his dealings with Southerners. In short, Hancock was a political animal, Sheridan was not.

Although Sheridan's appointment dated from September 12, 1867, he did not actually take office until March 2 the following year. (A.J. Smith served as department commander between Hancock and Sheridan). In the pantheon of the Union's Civil War heroes, Sheridan ranked behind only Grant and Sherman. A feisty, combative, black-eyed little Irishman, Little Phil, as he was known, was determined to bring order to the Plains, which meant enforcing the terms of the Medicine Lodge Treaty, albeit with limited resources, which translated into manpower. Sheridan had some 4,000 men in his entire military department, which embraced the present states of Missouri and Kansas, plus the Indian and Colorado Territories. It wasn't that there were so many more Indians, but rather so few soldiers to watch over thousands of square miles.

If nothing else, Philip H. Sheridan was a hard-headed realist who understood perfectly that he had to be tough and resourceful if he was to succeed where Hancock had failed. Sheridan approached his job by creating an intelligence system, using veteran frontiersmen to keep him apprised of Indian movements. If he was to get after these raiders he had first to have some idea where to find them.

General Philip Sheridan. As commander of the vast Military Division of the Missouri he oversaw most of the military activity between the Great Plains and the Rockies.

As Indian raids continued, units from the 7th and 10th Cavalry Regiments (the 10th was one of the Buffalo Soldiers, a Black regiment that was so named because the hair of the Black troopers reminded Indians of buffalo fur), pursued the raiders frequently and mostly without success. Sheridan was itching to launch a major campaign against the Indian villages, but he lacked the manpower. Not only that but Sheridan was forced to curb the starting date for a major offensive until the Peace Commission met in late 1868. But events worked in Little Phil's favor; it was his good fortune that the commission convened without

Senator John Brooks Henderson, thereby giving the Army a majority (the commission was composed of both military and civilians). Even so, it was a delicate line he had to walk. Because of Sand Creek and in view of how Hancock had conducted his expedition, it was imperative not to attack "peaceful" Indians. Sheridan's solution was to order all peaceful Indians to return to their reservations as stipulated in the Medicine Lodge Treaty.

And Sheridan had another thought: create an independent, sort of flying column that would have more flexibility than a regular army unit. His idea was to form a company of frontiersmen and send them after the Indian raiders. Thirty-year-old Major George Alexander "Sandy" Forsyth, then serving as an aide on Sheridan's staff, was appointed to the command of this new scout company. Forsyth had served under Sheridan during the Civil War and acquitted himself well. Sandy was excited about the idea and jumped at the chance to command a company of frontiersmen.

Sandy Forsyth (perhaps so named to distinguish him from James Forsyth, also an aide on Sheridan's staff, but no relation) wasted no time assembling his company: fifty men, most all of whom were veteran frontiersmen. A few were young and inexperienced in the ways of Indian fighting, but anxious for the adventure, and in need of money. Pay was fifty dollars a month (seventy-five if you furnished your own horse). They were armed with the 7-shot Spencer repeating carbine, plus a Colt revolver. Forsyth's second was Lieutenant Frederick H. Beecher, nephew of the famed abolitionist, Henry Ward Beecher. Young Beecher had suffered a severe knee wound at Gettysburg that continued to bother him, and perhaps was responsible for him developing a fondness for the bottle.

On August 29, Sheridan ordered Forsyth to take the field with his command and scout the country north of Fort Wallace. For nearly a week the scouts searched and found nothing, but then on September 5, word reached Forsyth by courier that a war party had attacked the terminus of the railroad, by that time some thirteen miles west of Fort Wallace. Forsyth immediately went off in pursuit, eventually picking up a large trail that led into the Republican River Valley—where Custer had investigated the summer before. The trail grew larger and it soon became evident that they were following a major body of Indians. The veterans in Forsyth's command predicted a big fight ahead.

Forsyth seemed undaunted by the prospect of a big fight. Indeed it was in young Forsyth's mind. He wanted to give the Indians a sound thrashing and in this he was driven by much the same sort of emotional fire as were the young Indian hot bloods. Notwithstanding, on September 16, one of the men, perhaps chief scout Abner Sharp Grover, managed to persuade him that it would be unwise to press on and risk running into a trap. Forsyth took the advice to heart and that evening the command made camp along the Arickaree Fork of the Republican River, which was mainly a dry stream bed in this late season of the year.

Forsyth had managed to locate what Custer had sought a year earlier. Although he didn't know it then, only a dozen miles away were three large camps of Dog Soldiers, Arapahos, and Lakotas. Had Forsyth been privileged to see into these camps he would have known that among those present was Roman Nose and Pawnee Killer, who had taken advantage of Custer's naiveté the year before, and the Dog Soldiers, including the Bent brothers, George and Charley.

The Battle of Beecher Island

The Indians were by no means ignorant of Forsyth's presence and on the morning of the 17th they seized the initiative, attacking from the east and stampeding some of the horses. Caught by surprise, the scouts scrambled to a small sandy spit of an island in the middle of the mostly dry stream bed. The island itself, about seventy-five yards long by thirty yards wide was covered with long grass, willow and plum trees.

After the initial attack, Forsyth ordered a defensive perimeter with the men digging shallow rifle pits; anything to provide some protection from the Indian attackers who were swarming around the little island, held at bay only by the determined scouts and their 7-shot Spencers. There were casualties among the scouts early on. Surgeon J.H. Mooers was killed in the first attack and Forsyth himself suffered a leg wound; he would later suffer two more wounds. With the blessed arrival of night, a few of the scouts who had been unable to reach the island did so under cover of darkness. Forsyth's situation was perilous in the extreme.

With the arrival of day two, other assaults followed, but were repelled each time by the withering fire of the Spencers. Up to this point Roman Nose had not been involved in the fighting, but as other warriors urged him to join in he finally agreed. Unfortunately, for Roman Nose, just before leaving the village to join the fight, he had inadvertently eaten some bread with an iron spoon. His medicine in battle required him to avoid eating anything touched by iron. Urged to go through the purification ceremony, he declined, probably believing there was not enough time. In their third and final charge Roman Nose fell mortally wounded. From this point on, the fight devolved into one of sniping and attrition.

Forsyth's scouts had suffered a number of casualties. Rations were running low and help was needed, but Fort Wallace was a hundred miles away. Fortunately, the men were able to find water by easily digging down through the sandy soil. The Indians too had taken casualties; the loss of so renowned a warrior as Roman Nose would hurt, but Forsyth's situation was perilous. With each passing day suffering among the wounded increased and the survivors were compelled to survive on the rancid flesh of any dead horses within reach. There was talk of pulling out, but Forsyth refused to countenance any notion of abandoning the wounded.

On the night of the 18th Forsyth sent two volunteers for help. With no horses available, the

The death of Roman Nose at the Battle of Beecher Island (drawing by Colonel Forsyth).

men were forced to travel on foot. The following night, uncertain whether the first pair had gotten through, Forsyth sent out two more. On the morning of September 20, a company of the 10th Cavalry under Captain Louis Carpenter, Forsyth's old comrade from Civil War days, arrived in relief, guided by the first pair of scouts who had indeed managed to reach Fort Wallace.

Sheridan's concept of using a company of frontiersmen was not a bad idea; there were plenty of precedents: Roger's Rangers in the French and Indian War being one. In this instance, however, it nearly resulted in a disaster. Once it was ascertained that they were following a huge Indian trail, prudence would seem to have dictated that it would have been wise to back off, for obviously the Indian force they were following was much too large for one company of frontiersmen, no matter how experienced. A courier could have been sent back to Fort Wallace, while Forsyth shadowed the Indians. Whether a large enough force could have been assembled in time to strike the village before it dissolved is problematical, but in any case this was clearly no job for a company of fifty men. The Battle of Beecher Island (sometimes erroneously called Beecher's Island) would be remembered as one of the great fights of the Western Indian wars.[50]

Sheridan, naturally, was much relieved that Forsyth had not met with disaster, but at the same time he felt frustrated over what seemed to be an effective way of dealing with the Indian problem. He had counted on Forsyth's company to harass the Indians and instead Forsyth had come within a whisker of being wiped out. However, Little Phil was nothing if not determined. Even as Forsyth was taking the field Sheridan sent Lieutenant Colonel and Brevet Brigadier General Alfred Sully with eight companies of the 7th Cavalry (minus Custer) and one of the 3rd Infantry, along with a single piece of artillery out of Fort Dodge aiming to strike the Cheyennes and Arapahos south of the Arkansas River. It was Sheridan's hope that this would cause the Dog Soldiers to move south away from the Republican River country. It was a dismal failure and did nothing to draw the Dog Soldiers south. In November, Custer, finally restored to active duty, would score a signal victory for Sheridan and the Army at the Battle of the Washita..

Sheridan also arranged for the bulk of the 5th Cavalry (seven companies) under Major and Brevet Major General Eugene Asa Carr to report for duty at Fort Harker. The 5th, temporarily under the command of Colonel William B. Royall, took the field on September 29. Carr, who had been on detached duty in Washington, joined his new command then en route to the Republican River country.

The Battle of Summit Springs

Indian raids continued. Especially hard hit this autumn were the Saline and Solomon River Valleys. On October 5, Royall had a fight with the Dog Soldiers that cost him the lives of two troopers and the loss of several horses. Three days later, on the 17th, a party of Dog Soldiers attacked Captain Louis Carpenter's squadron of the 10th Cavalry at Beaver Creek. These were the same Buffalo Soldiers who had rescued Forsyth's beleaguered command. Carpenter was escorting Carr to his new billet as commanding officer of the 5th Cavalry. One of the attackers was a medicine man named Bullet Proof (originally Wolf) who claimed he had special medicine that could make those who wore skins treated with his medicine safe from bullets, hence his new name. When the Dog Soldiers charged, the Buffalo Soldiers drove them back. Several of the attackers who wore the protective shirts were among those cut down and later scalped by the Buffalo Soldiers.

On October 25, Carr, having by now joined his regiment, caught up with the Dog

Soldiers and had a running fight that lasted several days but settled nothing. The Dog Soldiers moved on and Carr returned to Fort Wallace, later to be transferred to Fort Lyon, Colorado.

Winter, as usual, saw a diminution of Indian raids, but as Spring came on, activity increased, especially with the Dog Soldiers. By May, Carr's 5th Cavalry changed post again, this time to Fort McPherson, from which station it was felt Carr could operate more effectively against the Dog Soldiers, who continued to hold forth in the Republican River Valley. The hope was that Carr could round them up for eventual relocation to Indian Territory. It was a forlorn hope if ever there was one. Nevertheless, in May, Carr with Buffalo Bill Cody as guide struck the Dog Soldier camp, which contained perhaps 500 warriors. Two dozen Cheyennes were killed, while Carr lost 4 killed and 3 wounded. But again the fight proved inconclusive, as the Indians were able to escape by dividing into small bands. Later, coming together again, they soon resumed their raiding ways.

In June, General Christopher Augur, commanding the Department of the Platte, ordered Carr to clear the Indians out of the Republican River country. This time, Carr's cavalry was augmented by the Pawnee Indian Battalion, 150 strong, under Major Frank North. Buffalo Bill continued on as Carr's chief of scouts.

By July, Tall Bull's Dog Soldiers were camped at a place called Summit Springs near present Sterling, Colorado. About 3 p.m. on July 11, following a forced march through the night of the 10th, Carr surprised the Dog Soldier camp. In a rare mounted charge that destroyed the camp and killed more than fifty Indians, including Tall Bull himself. Soldiers recovered a wounded white woman who had been held captive forty-two days. The Pawnee scouts captured hundreds of horses and mules. As with the village on Pawnee Fork there were also supplies of food and many weapons. Here was the victory the Army had been seeking for two years. Carr's victory broke the back of the Dog Soldier resistance forever. Summit Springs largely brought to an end, Indian troubles on the Central Plains corridor. From this point on, Indian resistance would largely be confined to the Southern and Northern Plains.

V

The Southern Plains

Prologue: Llano Estacado

> *In a short time I found myself surrounded by at least 1,000 Indian warriors, mounted on first class horses.* —Christopher "Kit" Carson at the first battle of Adobe Walls, November 25, 1864[1]

As herein defined, the Southern Plains essentially covers the present states of Oklahoma (then Indian Territory) and West Texas. Generally, the area is bordered on the north by the Arkansas River and the state of Texas west of Dallas–Fort Worth.

South of the Arkansas River, the land stretches away through Indian Territory (Oklahoma), down through the Texas Panhandle and on across the vast loneliness of the *Llano Estacado*, or Staked Plains. A vast mesa, extending from the Canadian River on the north to Midland Texas on the south, the area reaches into New Mexico nearly to Fort Sumner and Tucumcari. If ever a region seemed ideally suited to provide a secure hiding place for Indians seeking to avoid detection by pursuing soldiers, the Staked Plains was it. With immense, deep canyons cut into the Cap Rock, a party of Indians could seemingly vanish into the bowels of one of these canyons, as though some spirit God had sprinkled them with the dust of invisibility.

The precise origin of the name remains obscure. Early Hispanic hunters and travelers used the name *El Llano Estacado* and Coronado seems to have used the name *Llano* or Plain. The addition of *Estacado* suggests a stockade, perhaps from the natural bluffs and escarpments in the region. The sheer sweep of the *Llano* seemed to early explorers as though they had set sail across a great uncharted sea. As one traveler described it, "Leaving behind the rims that form the canyon we began to travel over plains so immense that the eye could not see their end. There was nothing but grass and a few small pools of rain water, with very little water, and some dry holes [buffalo wallows], on these plains." But however it was defined this was the homeland of those Lords of the Southern Plains, the Comanches, the ever superstitious Kiowas, and the southern bands of Cheyennes.[2]

Thought to have been a branch of the Shoshone tribe at one time, the Comanches migrated from the Northern and Central Great Plains onto the Southern Plains probably beginning in the very early 17th century. During the next hundred years they evolved into what might arguably be called the most powerful Native American tribe in the Trans-Mississippi West, and by the mid–19th century they had created an empire that was unequaled. By the late 18th century, the Comanches were said to have numbered 40,000, but disease, smallpox especially, made drastic inroads into the tribal population base and by the 1870s, that number had been reduced by perhaps fifty per-cent . Nevertheless, the Comanches were the dominant power on the Southern Plains from the Indian Territory to New Mexico, and from the Arkansas River to the Staked Plains

Perhaps the earliest of the Western tribes to obtain horses, the Comanches became the finest of equestrians; equaled by few and surpassed by none. Like other Plains tribes theirs was a buffalo-hunting society, and they became exceedingly adept at trading, not only with other tribes, but with the *Comancheros* from New Mexico, who developed a system of trade with the Comanches from whom evolved their name. It was one of the more unusual economic enterprises in Western history. In exchange for whiskey, firearms and horses, the Comanches traded captives and plunder from their raids. From their Ute allies, the Comanches also learned how to penetrate the Spanish—Mexican—New Mexican market, where they traded buffalo robes and Navajo slaves for horses and blankets among other items.

Masters of the bow and arrow and the lance and tomahawk as well, they were fierce fighters and showed no mercy to young or old. Rape, mutilation, and torture were commonplace. They spared no one but often took captives. So fierce was the enmity between Comanches and Texans that Mirabeau Lamar, who succeeded Sam Houston as president of the Lone Star Republic called for "total extinction," or "total expulsion," echoed by other state officials in the years ahead; California comes to mind.[3]

The overall Comanche tribe were composed of eight subdivisions which generally defined their way of life: Yamparikas or Yap Eaters, Kotsotekas or Buffalo Hunters, and Jupes or People of the Timber, Nakoni, and Kwahadi were generally thought of as the Northern Comanches, with a population estimated to be perhaps as many as 15,000. The Penateka who operated around the Brazos River and were known as the Southern Comanches, numbered a thousand or fewer. These major groups were further divided into smaller bands much like other tribes. Principal Comanche allies were the Kiowas, Southern Cheyennes and Arapahos and occasionally others when circumstances suited Comanche needs.

In barely a generation after acquiring the horse, Comanches became feared raiders, who usually struck suddenly and with devastating effect. Yet it was not their military prowess alone that made them the dominant power on the Southern Plains. Rather, it was a combination of their enterprising economic drive and their far reaching expansionism—a surprising form of Native American colonialism. During the 18th century as they solidified their hold on the Southern Plains they defeated both the Spanish and the Apaches. As historian Pekka Hämäläinen puts it so succinctly and precisely, theirs was most definitely an empire.

As for Comanche allies, by the middle of the 19th century, the Cheyenne and Arapaho tribes numbered about 4,000 for the former and perhaps 2,500 for the latter. A small branch of Cheyennes, maybe a thousand strong along with a few Arapahos seemed to prefer the territory north of the Platte and so became more commonly associated with the Lakota bands. The separation seems to have been amicable enough, but in any case the Cheyenne and Arapaho tribes have come to be defined as the Northern and Southern Cheyennes and Arapahos.

The Kiowas and the closely related Kiowa-Apaches, arrived on the Southern Plains around 1800. Pushed south out of Black Hills region by Lakotas, the Kiowas settled in the northern reaches of *Comancheria*. A smaller tribe than the Comanches, the Kiowas and Kiowa-Apaches together numbered 1,500–2,000. The Kiowas and Comanches became allies early in the 19th century.

A number of smaller, less influential tribes also inhabited Texas and the periphery of

Comancheria. Among these were the Tonkawas, Lipan Apaches, Hasinais, and Taovayas, who had once been allies of the Comanches during their wars with the Spanish Crown. However, when Mexico achieved its independence the basis for the alliance gradually faded and eventually they became enemies of the Comanches. Inter-tribal relationships, such as this usually survived as long as a military or economic need for such an alliance existed.

Conflict on the Southern Plains

Indian trouble on the Southern Plains was hardly a recent development. Conflict dated back to the early Spanish colonial period and never faltered with the arrival of Americans which, for all hard purposes, began with the establishment of the Santa Fe Trail in 1821. There had been traffic along the Trail before that time, but it was erratic and many of those who made the trek often wound up being imprisoned by the Spanish. However, when Mexico acquired its independence traffic began to flow freely, and the Santa Fe Trail quickly became a thriving road of commerce and continued as such until the advent of the railroad in the 1870s.

There was a brief hiatus of travel on the Trail during the early 1840s due to internal problems in New Mexico, but even more so because of angry Texans who launched several expeditions into New Mexico nourished by the belief that the western boundary of Texas was fixed at the Rio Grande. The argument was based on an interpretation of the Louisiana Purchase and would have expanded the western boundary of Texas well into eastern New Mexico. It was a heated issue that was not resolved until Texas joined the Union in 1845 and agreed to accept its western boundary as presently defined, in exchange for the U.S. absorbing the republic's indebtedness.

Indian troubles on the Santa Fe Trail began around 1828 when Comanches struck a home-bound caravan, killing one man and making off with the train's livestock. Although not every caravan was attacked and many made it to Santa Fe and back with no Indian trouble, veteran travelers knew that if they no longer had to fear Spanish reprisals they were well advised to recognize the potential threat from Comanches and Kiowas.

It might be said that nowhere on the western frontier was settlement more furiously resisted than in Texas, which grappled with the Indian problem from the time the first Anglo settlers arrived in the early 1820s. However, inhabitants of Texas had actually been dealing with the Indian problem even earlier. In 1836, following Houston's victory at San Jacinto, Texas, achieved its independence from Mexico and for the next nine years it carried on as the Lone Star Republic's war against the Comanches.

THE TEXAS RANGERS

New immigrants arriving in Texas found indigenous people along the coast. Farther inland they were confronted by Tonkawas, Wacos, and other tribes. But by far it was the Comanches and Kiowas who posed the strongest threat to expansion. Before joining the Union in 1845, Texans, as they referred to themselves, had to rely on their own resources for protection. This eventually gave birth to citizen-soldier type groups—militia, if you prefer—formed to provide protection against Indian raiders, bandits, and Mexicans. Out of such a need was born the legendary Texas Rangers. As we have seen elsewhere this was an approach to the Indian problem that was employed throughout the West. These volunteer groups, however they are defined, differed from one another in name only.

Texas took the position that a good defense was to strike the Indians first. In 1839, Colonel John Moore launched a highly successful attack on a Comanche village near the San Saba River, but the wily Indians managed to make off with the Ranger horses, thereby taking the edge off the victory.

In March 1840, a band of Comanches arrived in San Antonio to talk peace. They had with them a white woman named Matilda Lockhart who had been captured a year before and had been horribly treated. As a result, the Texans were really in no mood to talk peace. When the Indians prepared to leave they were attacked by soldiers hidden around the compound. Thirty-five Comanches were killed, including women and children; twenty-seven others were taken prisoner. Seven whites were killed and eight others wounded. The incident came to known as the Council House Fight.

Once Texas joined the Union, protection of her frontier became the U.S, Army's responsibility. And Texas was not all. The Mexican-American War cessions added a vast new theater of operations; indeed more than a million square miles. And as was evident elsewhere in the West during this ante-bellum period namely Oregon, California, Nevada, and New Mexico, the United States Army was simply ill-prepared to meet the challenge of meeting this greatly enlarged responsibility.

As the U.S. expanded west in the years preceding the Civil War the Army had a mission to safeguard three major corridors of travel and commerce: The Oregon/California Trail on the north the Smoky Hill corridor across the Central Plains, and the Santa Fe Trail on the south. As happened throughout our history, after a war, the military is greatly reduced in size, and so it was following the Mexican-American War. Now the U.S. Army was compelled to administer this vast new territory with a force of 10,000 men.

In 1853, Indian Agent Thomas Broken Hand Fitzpatrick brokered a treaty with several Comanche and Kiowa bands at Fort Atkinson in southwest Kansas. Essentially, the terms of the agreement called for the tribes to allow the Army to build roads and forts, and permit travel across their territory. Fitzpatrick's Treaty of Fort Atkinson also called for Comanches to cease their Mexican raids and return all Mexican captives, which of course the Indians flatly refused to do. Despite their rejection of this caveat, the Comanches did sign the treaty though probably just to obtain the firearms and other gifts promised by treaty.

General Stephen Watts Kearny's Army of the West, which followed the Santa Fe Trail into New Mexico and took possession of that territory for the Union stood as the first major U.S. military force to pass over the Trail and more or less reopened it to brisk commercial traffic, but traffic that nonetheless found itself under frequent attack by Indian raiders.

During the 1840s and 1850s, especially, the War Department's philosophy to control the various Indian tribes who interfered with westward expansion was to construct military posts at what were perceived as key locations from which control could be exercised over the tribes. Sometimes these posts were crudely built, often consisting of nothing more than a few mud huts. Many lasted but a short time while others such as Fort Ripley on the Upper Mississippi and Forts Leavenworth and Riley are still in existence, albeit serving a different need.

When Texas entered the Union, it did so retaining ownership of unoccupied lands, which in effect meant that the Indian Trade and Intercourse Act of 1834 did not apply here. The Act was a crucial piece of legislation affecting the nation's early Indian policies. Its provisions were many, but one of the salient points allowed the Federal government to create Indian Territory out of public lands ... everywhere except in Texas.

The Texas frontier was an issue unto itself: 1,000 miles east to west and nearly half that from north to south. By mid-point of the 19th century the Army was able to assign fewer than 1,500 soldiers to the task of defending the new state of Texas. During its time as an independent republic—1836–1845—Texans had defended themselves with Ranger companies and militia. They welcomed the U.S. Army, but the Ranger concept was by now firmly embedded in the Texas consciousness, and they wanted the Rangers retained but at Federal expense. The Rangers stayed but at state expense.

After the treaty of Guadalupe Hidalgo in 1848, the War Department addressed its new responsibility by creating a new and separate military division, at first called the 8th Military Department and later the Department of Texas. To foil Indian raiders crossing into Mexico, a string of forts were erected on the International Boundary, along the Rio Grande in extreme south Texas. Secondarily, these posts were intended to deal with the Indian problem. Farther inland and defining the advance of the settlers' frontier were other forts created along key river systems: Trinity, Brazos and Colorado Rivers.

As the frontier advanced, these posts were intended to prevent the Indians from preying on the settlements, a task that turned out to be nearly impossible because most of the posts were garrisoned by infantry and there was little that foot soldiers could do to stop Indian raiders on horseback. Technically, each post was supposed to have a contingent of cavalry, but in practice they seldom did.

The concept of a string of army posts as a means of controlling these horseback Indians may have looked good on paper, but in practice the policy left much to be desired. For one thing, garrisons were seldom strong enough to take offensive action, and for another the rapid advance of the frontier meant that frontier settlements were soon beyond the protection of these posts, however minimal that protection may have been. By the early 1850s new settlements were springing up beyond the pale of forts, which in turn called for the creation of still more posts to keep up with the advancing settlements.

Captain Randolph B. Marcy

When the California gold rush began in 1849, Captain Randolph B. Marcy who had been active in guiding emigrant wagon trains to California pioneered a new route that ran southwest from Fort Smith, Arkansas, to the Rio Grande near El Paso. The route became a favorite and was known as "Marcy's return route," with a series of forts eventually established at various points. In addition to being a favored overland route to southern California, the forts created along the route were intended to discourage Indian raiders, mainly Comanches and Kiowas.

Massachusetts born in 1812, Randolph Barnes Marcy was an 1832 graduate of West Point. Commissioned a second lieutenant in the 5th Infantry upon graduation, he would prove a figure of some importance in the development of the West. Posted to Texas at the time of the Mexican-American War he served with distinction in that conflict. By 1849 he had escorted some 2,000 emigrant from Fort Smith to Santa Fe and on to California. He would go on to lead four major expeditions in the great West. Later, he traced the course of the Red River to its source; created the first accurate maps of the southwest, and was instrumental in the creation of a series of forts from eastern Indian Territory to Texas, including Fort Sill.

During the winter of 1857–1858, Marcy led a dramatic mid-winter march from Fort Bridger, Wyoming, to New Mexico for relief supplies. His daughter married George Brinton McClellan, the well known Civil War general. During the Civil War Marcy served as McClellan's Chief of Staff. A literate man, he was the author of *Prairie Traveler* a handbook for the emigrant traveler, along with several other volumes. Those who remember the television series, *Centennial*, based on James A. Michner's novel, may recall that actor Chad Everett's character, Major Maxwell Mercy was based on the real life Randolph Marcy.

By 1852, Major General Persifor Smith, newly assigned to the Department of Texas had enlarged on the system of defense established by his predecessor, General George Brooke. Smith's job was a tough one, calling for him to protect Texas, prevent Indian incursions into Mexico, while seizing the initiative against the raiding Indians, and of course cut expenses while doing all of this. Notwithstanding the enormity of his task, Smith oversaw a system of defense with an inner and outer line. When Indians struck, infantry would alert what cavalry was available and the latter would respond accordingly. In theory it looked good, in practice it faired poorly, reason being the territory was too vast and the soldiers far too few in number.

General Randolph B. Marcy.

Some help for Army forces in Texas arrived at the end of 1855 in the form of the brand new 2d Cavalry Regiment: 750 officers and men. No expense was spared; this was to be a first class unit. The regimental commander was Colonel Albert Sidney Johnston, who shortly took over command of the Texas Department from General Smith. Being a Texan himself, Johnston was especially welcomed. The 2d Cavalry was without question the premier regiment in the Army; its officer cadre was a who's-who of future Civil War luminaries: second in command was Lieutenant Colonel Robert E. Lee; others included George H. Thomas, William J. Hardee, Edmund Kirby Smith, and John Bell Hood. Seven of these officers would go on to serve as general officers of the Confederacy, including Johnston who would shortly take over command of the Texas department from General Smith. That the balance of the regiment's officer cadre should have Southern sympathies is not surprising, considering that the reigning Secretary of War was Jefferson Davis. That said, however, the regiment was not entirely pro–South as a dozen of its officers would serve the Union.

Faced with the geographical vastness of the territory for which he was responsible Johnston divided his regiment into squadrons—two companies each—and stationed them around the edge of the state's defense system. It was not a bad plan, had there been enough troops to make it effective, but in truth there simply were not. With another half a dozen regiments like the 2d it might have been a different story. As it was for the next four years—until the onset of the Civil War—the 2d Cavalry units were almost constantly in the field chasing Indian raiders; during this period there were forty clashes, mostly minor scrapes—save for those who were wounded or lost their lives—but nothing that had any lasting effect on the Indian problem.

In 1858, Albert Sidney Johnston was given command of an army being sent out to Utah to cope with an uprising in Mormon land. Johnston was succeeded by General David

Twiggs. Meanwhile, the governor of Texas was given a green light to raise another body of 100 rangers. The idea was to seize the initiative and strike the Indians. If the strategy proved successful it jut might go a long way toward discouraging further raids. General Twiggs seemed willing to cooperate, but the plan fell apart when the 2d was tagged to join Johnston in Utah. At the last minute that order was changed, but by then Rangers were already in the field.

THE COMANCHE: LORDS OF THE SOUTHERN PLAINS

In May 1858, a company of Rangers under Captain John "Rip" Ford surprised a Comanche village along the Canadian River in northwest Indian Territory near the Texas line. Called the Battle of Antelope Hills, the Rangers reportedly killed more than seventy Comanches and put 300 to flight. It marked the first time the Comanches had been hit hard by Texans. Although there had been Comanche losses in other fights this one was especially costly. Yet, if the Ranger victory at Antelope Hills was expected to cow the Comanches into submission it did not. If anything it roused their ire. In July, raiders struck a train on the Santa Fe Trail before returning to their agency to accept annual presents from agent, Robert Miller.

Indians prided themselves on their independence in battle. The warriors of the Plains were not subject to discipline like the white soldiers; they pretty much did as they pleased. But that could be a detriment too. An example of this can be seen in summer of 1858 when a party of young Comanche warriors, wanting to replace horses lost to Rip Ford's Rangers, raided the camps of peaceful Choctaws and others around Fort Arbuckle on the Washita River in Indian Territory. One Southern Comanche chief named Buffalo Hump who had been the bane of Texans promised to repay the whites for Antelope Hills, but first he had to journey to the peaceful villages on the Washita to replace the horses his young warriors had stolen. One thing Buffalo Hump realized was that he needed to avoid antagonizing neutral Indians who might otherwise ally themselves with the whites.

It should be noted that inter-tribal warfare had been on-going long before the white man arrived in North America. Through warfare, strong tribes became stronger. Warriors gained renown through their exploits. Both tribes and individual warriors benefitted greatly from the acquisition of horses captured in raids on other tribes. Captives, mainly women and young boys were also much sought after as a means of strengthening the tribal population from losses to disease and war. But war with the white man was not quite the same. Warfare with other tribes was a way of life, whereas war with the white man was a war for survival.

Meanwhile, General Twiggs had been contemplating an offensive, and accordingly, on September 15, 1858, four companies of the 2d Cavalry under brevet Major Earl Van Dorn (another future Civil War luminary) marched out of Fort Belknap. In addition to the cavalry, Van Dorn also had a company of the 1st Infantry and a detachment of Indian scouts. The Wichita Expedition, as it was dubbed, reached the Wichita Mountains eight days later and established a base camp on the north fork of the Red River called Camp Radziminski, after a former 2d Cavalry officer. When scouts reported a Comanche camp near Rush Springs, Van Dorn figured to attack. He of course was unaware that this was Buffalo Hump's camp and that the wily Comanche leader was having his powwow with the Army and the Wichitas who happened to be camped nearby.

At dawn on the morning of October 1 Van Dorn struck. While one company and the Indian scouts went after the horse herd, Van Dorn with his other three companies smashed into the village. The surprise was complete. Although the Comanches reacted quickly they suffered many casualties. The fight raged for an hour over broken ground that at times was obscured by fog. The Comanches lost about 56 killed; a number of others were wounded but managed to escape. Troops later destroyed more than 100 lodges, along with ammunition and food supplies. Perhaps even more important, the Indians lost some 300 horses. Van Dorn himself was badly wounded in the fight. Three soldiers were killed and another ten wounded. As historian Robert Utley points out, the battle underscored the almost total lack of communication between the War Department and the Indian Bureau. Treaty terms were being discussed even as plans were being carried out to attack the very Comanche village that was talking treaty terms.

General of the Army Winfield Scott further complicated the command structure by sending two companies of the 1st Cavalry to Fort Arbuckle under another future Civil War general, William H. Emory, who would have to obey orders from General Twiggs as well as from his own department headquarters, the Department of the West. Ordinarily there would be no problem unless one order happened to contradict another, which of course happened from time to time.

In addition to Camp Radziminski, other key military outposts during these years were Fort Cobb, established in 1859 on the Washita River near present Anadarko, Oklahoma, and Fort Arbuckle, also on the Washita, established in 1851, near present day Byars.

Twiggs sent a recovered Van Dorn out scouring the various river drainage systems for Comanches through the winter of 1858–1859, but it proved a futile effort. The Comanches had been twice burned and were skittish. Speculation had some going north; others to Mexico, while a few bands continued to harass the Texas settlements.

In the late spring of 1859, Twiggs sent Van Dorn on yet a second mission, this time with six companies of the 2d—nearly 500 men—along with nearly 60 friendly Indian scouts. Van Dorn suspected that the Comanches could be found somewhere in the vicinity of the Arkansas and his suspicions proved well founded. On May 13, Van Dorn forced a young Comanche boy, captured by his scouts, to lead him to the village of who else but Buffalo Hump, camped near the now abandoned Fort Atkinson on Crooked Creek. Attacked, the Comanches took up a defensive position in a deep ravine. This was a job for foot soldiers and a brutal affair. When finally it was over forty-nine Comanches had been killed and five wounded; thirty-two were taken prisoner. Not a warrior escaped. But the soldiers had paid for their victory. Two of Van Dorn's officers were badly wounded, two enlisted men killed and another nine wounded. Four Indian scouts died as well. The Comanches gave a good account of themselves. They "fought without giving or asking quarter until there was no one left to bend a bow," Major Van Dorn later wrote.[4]

Mostly, the Army's role against Comanches and their allies was adversarial, but there were exceptions and one was in 1859 when Van Dorn and four companies of his regiment were called south to San Antonio to protect reservation Indians from angry, vengeful whites. Five years earlier, in 1854, Texas had agreed to let the federal government create a reservation system on public land—recall that Texas retained its unoccupied land when annexed to the Union. Indian Agent, Robert Neighbors, then created a 50,000-acre reservation on the Brazos River for Southern Comanches, and a number of other smaller tribes.

Here, the Indians seem to have taken to the idea of farming, which of course is what the white man wanted them to do all along. At least they made a sincere effort, but after generations of living as a nomadic, buffalo hunting culture, making the transition to tilling the soil was no simple and easy matter. At first, whites responded to this effort enthusiastically, but then into the picture came one John Robert Baylor a disgruntled former employee of the Indian Bureau who began a war of words against the Indians, charging that these reservation bands, not the wild bands of the north were responsible for raids and thievery.

JOHN ROBERT BAYLOR

A thirty-seven-year-old native of Kentucky, Baylor arrived in Texas in 1840 and went on to gain wide experience in fighting Comanches. After serving as a teacher at the Indian agency out of Fort Gibson in the Indian Territory, he returned to Texas and served briefly as agent at the Brazos Reservation. His harsh treatment of Indians, however, led to his dismissal by Superintendent Robert Neighbors. Baylor seems to have had a deep-seated bias against Indians from the start and his dismissal by Neighbors undoubtedly played a key role in accusing the reservation Indians of crimes of which probably only a very few were guilty. At the outset of the Civil War Baylor was appointed lieutenant colonel of the 2d Texas Mounted Rifles. Marching his command into Arizona, he promptly proclaimed himself governor there. He let it be known that in his opinion the Confederate Congress had decreed that all hostile Indians should be exterminated. John Chivington was not the only one, it seems, with a solution to the Indian problem. Baylor's career as a biased and controversial figure in Western history lasted until his death in 1894.

Baylor planted the seed of suspicion about the Brazos Reservation Comanches and their allied bands and by 1859 he had managed to convince a good many whites that the Indians were guilty. In May 1859, he led 300 men who called themselves rangers, most of whom were probably guilty of more deviltry than the Indians they sought. Some had been active raiders in Kansas and Missouri and had now come to Texas. Baylor—elected captain—and his rangers took the field determined to kill any Indians found off the reservation.

On May 23 Baylor prepared to attack the reservation, on which could be found some of the same "friendlies" who had not long ago scouted for Van Dorn. The officer in command of the troops at the Agency, Captain Joseph Bennett Plummer, with two companies of the 1st Infantry ordered Baylor to back off, but he would not be cowed and defiantly told Plummer he would fight the federal troops too. What tipped the scales was when a large party of the reservation Indians showed up to reinforce Plummer. Seeing this, Baylor pulled in his horns and retreated. After an eight-mile chase Baylor took up a position on an old homestead where the reservation Indians held him under siege until dark.

Meantime, Major George Thomas, now the senior officer of the 2d Cavalry since Johnston had departed for Utah and Robert E. Lee was away on extended leave, ordered four companies of the 2d down from Radziminski to the Brazos Reservation to maintain order and protect the Indians. Baylor's vigilantes—and that is exactly what they were—continued to attack any Indians they found off the reservation, but did not again attempt to challenge the regular troops. In July, authorization came through to remove the Indians to a new location and in August, with an escort of the 2d Cavalry, the Indians trekked to their new home on the Washita River in Indian Territory. That night, Superintendent Neighbors wrote to his wife that the Indians had been moved "out of the heathen land of Texas and [that he, Neighbors was] now out of the land of the Philistines." It was a troublesome time, and not just in Texas. On October 16, 1859, John Brown raided Harpers Ferry on his mission of evangelical fervor. He would die at the end of a rope on December 2.[5]

The relocation of the Brazos Reservation bands, together with the continuing pressure applied by the regular army units and by ranger companies and groups such as Baylor's pushed the Comanche and Kiowa bands farther north. William Bent of Bent's Old and New Fort—and who now served as Agent for the Arkansas River bands thought new military posts were now needed in the area because the Indians, who were now operating farther north, posed a threat to the Santa Fe Trail, as indeed they did.

As a consequence, the War Department decided on an ambitious campaign for the summer of 1860. The most ambitious of its kind yet on the Plains, the campaign did not set a pattern for success and it could be said that the similar undertakings that followed were seldom any more successful.

Major John Sedgwick took four companies of the 1st Cavalry and two of the 2d Dragoons, 500 men, plus a contingent of Delaware Indian scouts, on a march from Fort Riley down the Arkansas to Antelope Hills where Van Dorn had scored his stunning victory. Aside from one trivial skirmish with Kiowas that involved the soon-to-be-famous Confederate cavalryman, Jeb Stuart, there was no action. Two Indians were reportedly killed and a number of non-combatants were captured.

Meanwhile, a second column of six companies, 400 men of the 1st Cavalry under Captain Samuel Sturgis headed north out of Fort Cobb. In July they found a large Kiowa party on Solomon's Fork and fought with the warriors who played rear guard while the villagers escaped. Sturgis claimed twenty-nine casualties, but worn out horses prevented him from following up his victory, if such it could be called. A third column left Fort Union, New Mexico, and marched east, searching the Canadian River and its tributaries without finding anything save a deserted Comanche village. The last effort was by Major Thomas who, with a column from the 2d Cavalry fought with a band of Comanches along the Concho and Colorado Rivers, killing one Indian. Thomas himself was wounded. It could be said that all the columns were successful in wearing out their horses, but insofar as accomplishing anything of strategic or tactical importance, the result was nil.

The onset of the Civil War and the departure of regular army troops from Texas, left a void in the state's frontier defense system, as indeed it did elsewhere in the West. In Texas a new ranger regiment was authorized to replace those whose enlistments had expired. Interestingly, the Confederacy refused to reimburse the Texas for Ranger expenses. Getting the Federal government—or in this case the Confederate government—to pay for frontier defense was a hard sell in Washington and it seems, in Richmond as well.

The Texas solution was to create a frontier regiment that would be supported by state funds. Success with this approach was mixed during the first two years of the Civil War. Despite exhaustive patrols there were only occasional clashes with Comanche/Kiowa raiders and these were hardly effective deterrents. Raids continued and war parties had little trouble eluding ranger patrols. By 1863, The Confederacy, feeling that Texas was vulnerable to Union incursions from the north, created a Confederate military district, and assigned Confederate forces to the state's defense. Where exactly Confederate authority ended and ranger responsibility began was a touchy point.

In December 1863, a powerful Comanche war party, estimated to be some 300 strong struck settlements northwest of Fort Worth in deadly style. How, some wondered, could so large a war party fail to have been noticed? How indeed? Then the following October an even larger war party—perhaps as many as 600, struck ranches, and farms along the Brazos, slaughtering any whites they found.

There was an understandable thirst for revenge among the Texans and when ranger scouts discovered a large Indian trail in December 1864, a punitive strike force was hastily assembled. Unfortunately, these particular raiders were neither Comanche or Kiowas but rather Kickapoos, who were guilty of their share of thievery, but were aiming to leave Texas and relocate to Mexico. These Kickapoos had had nothing to do with any of the raids of the preceding year, but an Indian was an Indian insofar as Texans were concerned.

On January 8 a mixed force of some 300 militia and rangers struck a large encampment of Kickapoos on Dove Creek, a tributary of the Conchos River. The rangers struck from one direction, the "flop-eared" militia as they called by the rangers from the other. The militia suffered nearly twenty casualties right off and panicked in the face of Indian fire from the timber and brush-choked ravines. By contrast, the rangers fought back for five hours before falling back at dark. The rangers had thus far acquitted themselves well, but with darkness closing in, they suddenly found themselves caught in a deadly crossfire and they, too, panicked, even abandoning the Indian horses they had captured at the outset of the attack. Ranger/militia losses numbered twenty-six killed and a like number wounded. Rangers claimed one hundred Kickapoos killed. Perhaps more than anything else, the attack on the unprovoked attack Kickapoos angered them and justifiably so. They had posed a minimal threat in the past; occasionally stealing some livestock, but they had never posed the same threat as the Comanche/Kiowas. As historian Robert Utley has said, "Dove Creek displayed a leadership so poor that it bungled a battle that should not have been fought, cost unnecessarily heavy casualties, and planted in Mexican lairs an enemy unlikely to forgive or forget."[6]

In the late fall of 1864, General James Carleton prepared to launch another campaign against the Comanche/Kiowa coalition. Colonel Kit Carson would be the field commander. Between his own 1st New Mexico and the 1st California, he was able to assemble about 350 horsemen, plus 75 Ute warriors, and a pair of 12-pounder mountain howitzers at Fort Bascom, near present Tucumcari, New Mexico. Carson's objective would be the Comanche/Kiowa bands that had been harassing the Santa Fe Trail caravans. But as much as he was after the hostile Indians, Carson was also after the *Comancheros* who in a very real sense, made it possible for the Indians to continue operations by furnishing them with weapons and ammunition in exchange for loot collected by the Indians on their raids. Interestingly, Carson's expedition took the field at almost the same time as did Colonel John Chivington. There was no connection of course, but it remains an interesting coincidence. Carson's line of march followed the Canadian River into the Panhandle of Texas. Intelligence reported that a huge village, said to contain perhaps 3,000 Indians—Comanches, Kiowas and Kiowa/Apaches was encamped on the Canadian some 200 miles northeast of Fort Bascom.

The Indian encampment was spread out for several miles along the river. Near the ruins of an old adobe trading post, built by William Bent, founder of Bent's Old (and new) Fort, was a camp of 150 lodges of Kiowas under Chief Little Mountain. Included in the village was the thirty-four-year-old Satanta, feared warrior and skilled orator, whose name will be recalled from Hancock's campaign.

At dawn on November 25—just 4 days prior to Sand Creek—Carson's command surprised Little Mountain's village. Once more we see how time and again the army had no difficulty surprising an Indian village, contrary to the popular myth that Indians, being so attuned to nature could not be taken by surprise. Despite being caught unawares, the Indians recovered their composure and fought back, allowing the non-combatants to escape downriver, with Carson's troops in hot pursuit. The fleeing Indians alerted the larger Comanche encampment. Soon, Carson found himself embroiled in a fight of the first magnitude with perhaps a thousand warriors.

The Indians pressed forward and it was only the mountain howitzers that prevented them from overwhelming the soldiers. Now it was Carson's turn to fall back to the site of Little Mountain's camp. Fierce fighting continued, while the soldiers and their Ute allies took what they could from the village before putting it to the torch. There was much evidence in the camp of plunder from raids on the Santa Fe Trail. Carson returned to Fort Bascom on December 10. He had inflicted some serious losses on the Indians, but had been fortunate to return with losses of only two killed and ten wounded. Indian casualties were estimated at sixty.

With the end of the Civil War some regular army units returned to the West, but even though the regular Army had been somewhat increased there were still not nearly enough soldiers to protect the frontier; not only that but many regiments or parts thereof were assigned to the South to maintain order during Reconstruction. Additionally, the Army was compelled to divert troops for other duties such as coastal defense.

Indian activity did not slack off with the return of regular army units. What did make a difference, though, was that now the army did not have to concern itself with a multitasking mission. For the most part, army leaders were free to focus on the Indian problem. When fiery Philip Sheridan—Little Phil, owing to his diminutive stature—replaced Hancock the army had a tandem of Sherman and Sheridan, who both saw the solution to the Indian problem in the same light. The concept of complete war was a means of destroying one's opponent was nowhere during these years better demonstrated than by Sherman on his March to the Sea, and Sheridan in the Shenandoah Valley of Virginia. The "Indians require to be soundly whipped," said Sherman, and to Sheridan went the job carrying out that philosophy.[7]

Expectations were high for the Treaty of Medicine Lodge. Here at last was the agreement that would end Indian trouble on the Plains. For ten rather pleasant autumn days beginning on October 19, 1867, they came together to talk of peace along a creek called Medicine Lodge—known to the Indians as Medicine River because of healing properties in the water. It was a bucolic setting, back-dropped by the buttes and tablelands of southeastern Kansas. Today, one can visit the small community of Medicine Lodge, population about 2,500, without having any sense of what happened there that long ago autumn of 1867. One can visit a small marker in City Park, but the actual site is several miles away on private property. It was surely the most important event to have happened in the area.

They gathered here at this place to discuss an end to hostilities between the whites and those Indian tribes for whom this area had been a homeland for generations. It was an immense gathering, headed by seven U.S. Commissioners, nine journalists, including the soon-to-be celebrated Henry M. Stanley, and their military escort. Unexpectedly, the commissioners found themselves joined by a group from Kansas that included Governor Samuel Crawford, that perennial voice crying in the wilderness for authority to raise volunteer troops. Obviously, the U.S. was solidly represented for the solemn and momentous events that were expected to unfold here. And yet, as sizeable as it was, the official party was as nothing compared to the Indian gathering which numbered nearly 5,000.

During the ten days of talks, treaties were signed with the Kiowas and Comanches (except for the Kwahadas (or Quahadi), strongest and most militant of all the Comanche bands), Plains Apaches, Cheyennes, and Arapahos. The tribes were assigned two reservations in western Indian Territory. The U.S. agreed to furnish everything necessary for Indians to become farmers, including food, housing, and farm equipment. The Indians, however, found this proposal unappealing; they were not interested in farming, but wanted to continue their life as nomadic hunters. Here was a stalemate, but the commissioners, anxious to conclude a working agreement, finally agreed to allow the Indians to continue to hunt buffalo, south of the Arkansas River, *but only for so long as there were buffalo to hunt* and that was the operative phrase: *for only so long as there were buffalo to hunt*. The commissioners were willing to bend this far, knowing that the life span of the buffalo was going to be brief. Whether the Indians fully understood this caveat is questionable. What seems more likely is that they could not (or would not) see the demise of the buffalo, and therefore having permission to hunt south of the Arkansas was like a license to continue to live in the traditional way forever.

When it was consummated the Treaty of Medicine Lodge was expected to provide a solution to the Indian problem, but like others designed to achieve the same end, it failed. If General Carr's destruction of the Dog Soldier camp at Summit Springs more or less brought an end to serious hostilities on the Central Plains, resolution of that conflict on the Southern Plains was not yet within reach.

During the years 1865–1867, Indian raids on the Southern Plains continued. Texas Rangers, various militia units and—after 1865—regular Army troops, clashed frequently with raiders; sometimes these actions were mostly small, but sometimes involving larger numbers. Farms, ranches, outlying settlements, anything could be a target. In July 1867, a school in Hamilton County, Texas, for instance, was attacked by raiders. In October 1869, six companies of the 9th Cavalry—Buffalo Soldiers—plus two of the 4th Cavalry, together with a detachment of the 24th Infantry, and some Tonkawa scouts (called Tonks) sortied from Forts Bascom and Concho to look for Indians along the Brazos and Colorado River systems. On the 29th Captain John Bacon, in overall command, was attacked in camp on the Brazos by several hundred Comanche and Kiowa warriors. A fierce fight followed; some of it hand-to-hand. The Indians were finally forced to fall back. Bacon took up pursuit the next day, found the Indian camp and largely destroyed it, but the Indians managed to escape. Bacon's casualties amounted to eight wounded, while the Indian losses were estimated to be forty killed and several captured.

The year 1868 saw the return to active duty of Lieutenant Colonel George Custer, suspended from active duty for a year, it will be recalled, but pressure from Sherman and Sheridan shortened his sentence. Both commanders were determined to bring about an end to the Indian troubles and Custer was needed.

Actually, Sheridan had two areas of concern: north of the Arkansas and Platte Rivers, Indian opposition consisted of Cheyennes, Arapahos and Lakotas. South of the Arkansas he had to deal with the Comanche/Kiowa problem. For Sheridan the question that loomed was to decide which was the more serious and immediate threat. While his far-flung units clashed with Cheyennes, Arapahos, and Lakotas, Sheridan sought to hold the Comanches and Kiowas at bay by enticing them to remove to the newly created reservation in Indian Territory. In September Sheridan and General William B. Hazen parleyed with the Comanches and Kiowas at Fort Larned and encouraged the Indians to move to Fort Cobb, where the new agency was located. The move would be escorted by the Army once the Indians had concluded a buffalo hunt which would provide them with meat to sustain them through the winter.

Thirty-eight-year-old William Babcock Hazen was a Vermonter and a career officer; an 1855 graduate of West Point. He had a solid Civil War record and later served across much of the Western frontier. Although his name does not resonate like that of Custer, Sheridan, Miles, and others of the Western Indian wars period, he was an active field officer in the West during the last half of the 19th century. At times his record was controversial. Hazen had a habit of occasionally crossing swords (so to speak) with those who could harm his career. For example, like Custer, he was a key witness against Secretary of War William Belknap in the scandal that helped undermine the Grant administration. Later, as head of the Army Signal Corps Hazen was involved in a controversy over an Arctic Expedition.

The Comanche/Kiowa alliance agreed to Sheridan's proposal but did so with suspicion. While his units were busy dealing with the Cheyennes and Arapahos Sheridan was unable to provide the promised army escort, so the Comanches and Kiowas started off on their own hook. That would probably have been all right except that the Indians decided to engage in a little raiding en route, which prompted Sheridan to regard them as hostiles, and one imagines he needed little persuasion to change his mind.

Winter was coming on and Sheridan had long since decided that winter campaigning had much to recommend it. The biggest asset of the Plains Indians was their mobility and winter greatly reduced their mobility. Sheridan figured to take advantage of this right away. Accordingly, from New Mexico, General George Getty (who had replaced Carleton as commander of the Department of New Mexico) was ordered to strike east from Fort Bascom down the Canadian River with six troops of the 3rd Cavalry two companies of the 37th Infantry and 4 mountain howitzers, in all nearly 600 men. Getty's field commander was the twenty-nine-year-old, book-loving Major Andrew Wallace Evans, Once described by a fellow officer as "one of the queerest men I ever met in the army," Evans had served honorably in the Civil War. Newspaper correspondent John Finerty described him as a melancholy officer, fond of literature, and a man who apparently never smiled, perhaps from the pain of an old war wound. Nevertheless, before his career ended, Evans would see wide service on both the Southern and Northern Plains.[8]

The second column was headed up by Major Eugene Carr, 5th Cavalry, whose force consisted of seven troops of Carr's own regiment, plus four troops of the 10th Cavalry and one of the 7th Cavalry; in all, some 650 men. Carr pulled out of Fort Lyon, Colorado on December 2 (Evans left Bascom on Nov. 18) guided by Buffalo Bill Cody, not yet the household name he would one day become. The object of these two columns was to stir up, the Indians who would then be the target of the third and most powerful of the three columns in the field, commanded by Brigadier General Alfred Sully, who had enjoyed considerable success up north against the Lakota following the Minnesota Uprising. The son of a noted watercolor artist, Sully was something of an actor, having once acted in the same play ("Our American Cousin") which President Abraham Lincoln was watching at the time of his assassination.

Sully's column would consist of eleven troops of Custer's 7th Cavalry, plus five infantry companies, and Governor Samuel Crawford's 19th Kansas Volunteer Cavalry. Sheridan himself would accompany Column 3, perhaps not wanting to take a

General Eugene A. Carr. As commander of the 5th Cavalry, he ended the power of the Dog Soldiers at the Battle of Summit Springs.

chance on another lackluster performance by Sully, who appeared to have left his aggressiveness back at Fort Dodge the past September.

Some 100 miles south of Fort Dodge, Sully and Custer established a base camp at the confluence of the North Canadian River and Wolf Creek. Appropriately enough they named it Camp Supply. In Sheridan's mind, there was little doubt that there would be plenty of campaigning in this area in the future, so Camp Supply was expected to see a good deal of service and it did. The idea was for the infantry to garrison and protect the base, while the cavalry took the field against the Indians. Sheridan himself, accompanied by two companies of the 19th Kansas Volunteers arrived on Nov. 21 even as an early season snowstorm ripped through the area. Crawford and the remainder of his 19th Kansas were still to come. Sheridan was excited because a fresh Indian trail headed north had been discovered and it was assumed these particular Indians were bent on attacking settlements in Kansas.

The Battle of the Washita

Sully and Custer did not see eye-to-eye. Sully wanted to take command of the expedition using his Civil War brevet rank of major general as the basis for doing so. Custer, however, countered with his own brevet rank of major general. To further complicate matters, whenever Crawford and the rest of his volunteers showed up, Crawford outranked them both. In any case, Sheridan, having little confidence in Sully anyway, sent him back to Fort Harker to command his District of the Upper Arkansas, and gave Custer the field command, which was probably what Sheridan had in mind all along.

It is worth noting here that even at this early stage in its history the 7th Cavalry had become a regiment of cliques: those who favored Custer and those who didn't, and this campaign would result in a deepening of that divide. On the morning of November 23, under a depressing overcast, the 7th Cavalry marched out of Camp Supply. Twelve inches of heavy, wet snow had already fallen and more was coming down. The troopers were sent on their way to the lilting melody of "The Girl I Left Behind," played by the regimental band. The snow worked in the Indians' favor, hiding their trail and scouts temporarily lost their way. Custer took over using his own instincts and a small compass. On the following day, the snow stopped and the sun appeared causing some snow-blindness. Warmer weather melted some of the eighteen inches of snow that had fallen and softened the ice in the creeks and streams. It was not pleasant weather in which to be campaigning, which of course, was exactly why Sheridan judged it the perfect time to go hunting Indians. But perseverance rewards its own kind. The night of the 26th, the regiment located the Indian village in the valley of the Washita River. Custer's plan, such as it was, called for the village to be surrounded and at dawn attacked from all sides, but strangely, no effort was made to scout the Indian position. The night was bitterly cold, and long. Troopers wrapped in their coats and blankets were forced to sleep on the hard-crusted snow.

At daylight on the 27th, the 7th Cavalry—800 strong—charged to the sound of the bugle, and the regimental band—believe it or not—managed to get off a few bars of Custer's favorite, "Garryowen," before their instruments froze.

Irony of ironies, this was the village of Black Kettle, the ever-seeking peace chief of the Cheyennes. It was Black Kettle it will be recalled, who had been attacked at Sand Creek. Just days before Black Kettle had met with General Hazen at Fort Cobb to discuss peace. Black Kettle admitted to Hazen that while he genuinely sought peace, he had no control over the young warriors who continued their raids up into Kansas. But it mattered little in the long run as Sheridan had lumped them into one package: they were all hostiles and would be dealt with accordingly, hence here was Custer storming into the village of Black Kettle on a cold and snowy November morning; the same month and almost the exact day as Sand Creek, but four years later. Sand Creek had happened on the 29th.

Just as the Cheyennes had reacted to Chivington's attack four years earlier, these Cheyennes bolted from their tipis, searching for cover, some fighting back wherever they found a position. It took but minutes for the troopers to clear out the village, but it was tougher to dislodge the Indian defenders who had taken up positions in ravines, and behind trees and boulders. Here and there small groups of Cheyennes managed to escape down the valley. Major Joel Elliott and fifteen men pursued one group, only to find themselves suddenly cut off and there wiped out to the last man. As he galloped off at the head of his little band, Elliott is reported to have shouted "Here goes for a brevet or a coffin." He got the latter.[9]

Had Custer bothered to do a little reconnaissance, he would have learned that there were other villages of Cheyennes, Arapahos, Comanches, and Kiowas farther down the valley, and when word of the attack reached them, via those escaping Black Kettle's village, war parties from these villages began forming up and counter-attacking; it was a band of these warriors that wiped out Elliott's command.

At the outset, Custer was flushed with what appeared to be a total victory. While his troopers burned tipis and destroyed what supplies they could find, including food, buffalo robes; anything that might be of use to the inhabitants, hordes of warriors from the other encampments down the valley began to arrive on the scene and Custer suddenly found himself on the defensive. The situation immediately puts one in mind of the Little Bighorn, but the two situations, while seemingly similar on the face of it were actually quite different and although Custer suddenly found himself in a tight spot, it does not appear that these Indian reinforcements threatened to overwhelm him as they did nine years later. Indeed, and undaunted, Custer formed-up the regiment and prepared to attack down valley, but re-thought that strategy as the day waned and evening approached. Instead, Custer judged that it would be prudent to withdraw and return to Camp Supply, which place he reached on December 2. Custer had done serious damage to the Indians and Sheridan was pleased. The winter campaign had paid off handsomely.

Victory or not, the attack brought a renewed onslaught from critics. Those who had been critical of Chivington renewed their verbal assault on Custer and the War Department for massacring women and children. Meanwhile hard feelings were brewing within the 7th Cavalry. Initially, Custer had detached Captain Edward Myers to ascertain what had become of Elliott, but Myers reported back that he had been unable to find out anything, and Custer made no further effort to try and locate the missing major. In Custer's behalf, Indian resistance was building due to the arrival of more warriors from the villages down valley and Custer would have been risking the entire regiment by undertaking a more thorough search. Nevertheless, there were those in the regiment who never forgave him for his failure to search for Elliott, and leading this group was Captain Frederick Benteen, whose behavior at the Little Bighorn, would forever brand him, in the minds of many, as the officer who left Custer to his fate. The growing feeling of disharmony within the regiment was certainly reinforced here at the Washita. Besides Elliott, Custer had lost Captain Louis Hamilton and nineteen enlisted men. In addition, three officers—including Custer's brother, Lieutenant Tom Custer, were wounded, along with a dozen enlisted men. Custer reported in excess of 100 Cheyennes killed, including Black Kettle, but that number is almost certainly inflated. Many years later, George Bent claimed eleven Cheyennes were killed.

There were a number of Cheyennes who were taken captive, including a twenty-year-

Cheyenne prisoners after the Battle of the Washita, 1868 (sketch by Theodore R. Davis).

old woman named Monahsetah or Meotzi. Monahsetah was apparently an extremely attractive young woman. It seems clear from the testimony of Captain Benteen (avowed enemy of Custer), and scout Ben Clark that Monahsetah did sleep with Custer, a not uncommon practice among military men on the Western frontier. And Custer had developed something of a reputation as a womanizer, but as historian Robert Utley points out, it is impossible to know where gossip about such matters ends and truth begins. In any event, Monahsetah remained with Custer for some time and provided valuable service as a negotiator. Later she was said to have given birth to a blond child that could only have been Custer's, some claimed. Such stories, however, ignore the fact that Monahsetah was seven months pregnant at the time of her capture.

The Battle of the Washita, or the Washita Massacre, as some prefer to characterize it, was one of the most important clashes between Indians and whites in the Trans-Mississippi West for several reasons. First it established the effectiveness of winter campaigning and struck a devastating blow to the Southern Cheyennes. Whether the attack deserves to be called a "massacre" or a "battle" is still debated. One might argue that if the side being attacked is capable of providing a *strong or determined* resistance, as opposed to a mere token resistance, the affair might justifiably be called a battle. Massacre, on he other hand, implies an indiscriminate killing of non-combatants, or the wanton and continued slaughter of an opponent after that opponent has surrendered, or reached a point of being unable to offer further resistance, then we might regard it as a massacre. Insofar as the Washita is concerned, "battle" would seem the more appropriate designation. While there are certain similarities between Sand Creek and the Washita, the former would truly seem to justify the appellation of massacre.

Although there were atrocities committed by the soldiers, Custer appears to have made a genuine effort to prevent such actions. His orders were to attack the village, kill or hang all able bodied warriors, and take women and children captive. The problem is that in the heat of fighting complete control is not possible. To a large extent, a fight takes on a life of its own; it is never a choreographed production.

If the issue of whether the Washita should be called a battle or a massacre seems to present an irreconcilable semantic problem, perhaps the more important issue to address is was the Army justified in attacking the village of Black Kettle? Those who generally supported the Indian position advanced the argument that Black Kettle's village lay within the boundaries of land guaranteed the Indians by the Treaty of Medicine Lodge. Sheridan countered by pointing out that the Indian village was far beyond the land set aside by Medicine Lodge.

The real problem, here as elsewhere in the West, was the failure—refusal—on the part of the military and the civilian populace to make a distinction between peaceful Indians and hostiles. How could one tell? They did not have an "H" branded on their foreheads, and it was easy enough to mingle with non-hostiles when it suited one. There really was no way of telling hostiles apart from non-hostiles, and the military never really attempted to make that distinction; such would have been an exercise in futility in any event. In Black Kettle's village at the Washita were any number of warriors who had been involved in raiding along the Saline and Solomon Rivers in eastern Kansas the past summer and fall. Now they were wintering along the Washita, part of Black Kettle's "peaceful" village. Black Kettle himself admitted he could not control the young warriors, and it was based on this realization that Sheridan and Sherman believed the only way to end these raids was to attack villages such as Black Kettle's, and in Sheridan's opinion, the most effective way of accomplishing this was by a winter campaign.

Although Washita was regarded as a glorious success, Sheridan wasn't finished with winter campaigning just yet. While Custer was attacking Black Kettle's village, the rest of the 19th Kansas Volunteers finally arrived. Several days were needed to refit the unit which had lost horses in the blizzard that gripped the region. But on December 7, Sheridan followed up Custer's attack by sending a second column, including both the 7th Cavalry and the 19th Kansas—1,500 men in all—down the Washita Valley in bitterly cold temperatures, following the trail of the Indians who had moved on after Custer's attack. En route they found the badly mutilated bodies of Major Elliott and his men.

Following the Washita attack, the Indians moved south; a mixture of Cheyennes, Arapahos, Kiowas and Comanches, banding together for mutual protection, uncertain as to what might happen next, but eventually there was a diaspora of sorts, as some concluded that it made more sense to avail themselves of the Army's protection—which meant rations—remember it was winter after all—as opposed to fighting. So they began to trickle into Fort Cobb, there to receive Hazen's assurance of protection ... and rations.

Meanwhile, on December 17 the Indians were tracked heading toward Fort Cobb. When Sheridan and Custer reached Cobb they found Kiowas under Satanta and Lone Wolf carrying documents signed by General Hazen confirming that they were non hostile. Sheridan was livid. Here were hostile warriors (and no doubt their non-combatants) who had been at Washita for sure but now enjoyed the Army's protection. They had, it seems, managed to persuade Hazen of their peaceful intentions.

Here was a dilemma for Little Phil. What to do? His solution was to arrest Satanta and Lone Wolf and issue an ultimatum: if the villages failed to report to Fort Cobb in forty-eight hours they would be hanged. Most, though not all of the Comanches and Kiowas complied leaving Sheridan with no choice but to free the chiefs. Some of the bands, notably the Cheyennes and Arapahos; but also some Comanches and Kiowas chose instead to take their chances beyond the pale of Sheridan's sword.

All the while, Majors Carr and Andrew Evans were still in the field looking for Indians. Evans discovered a Comanche village—with Kiowas nearby—along North Fork of the Red River, at a place called Soldier Creek, appropriately enough. Unleashing his artillery on the village, Evans soon had the Indians in flight. However, the Comanches meantime reinforced by some of the Kiowas, struck back. While the troopers burned the village the two sides exchanged fire for the better part of two days, at the end of which the Indians pulled out, some returning to Forts Cobb or Bascom, while others toughed the winter out on the Staked Plains. Sheridan trumpeted the fight on Soldier Creek as the death knell of the Indian resistance, but it was hardly that. Much tough campaigning and fighting lay ahead.

Although some of the bands remained free, thousands of Indians, fearing a repeat of the Washita, gradually arrived at Fort Cobb creating a problem of congestion, which was exacerbated by the presence of Sheridan's own troops. Conditions were dreadful. There were not enough rations to feed all, and heavy rain made life miserable ... for everybody. As a consequence, in January 1869, Sheridan ordered Colonel Benjamin Grierson, commanding the 10th Cavalry, to continue with construction of a new post thirty miles to the south. Grierson had earlier selected this site on which to build a small cavalry post. Now it was to be enlarged and named Fort Sill in honor of General Joshua Sill, killed at the Battle of Stone's River in the Civil War.

A fine soldier, Benjamin Grierson is frequently overlooked in the ranking of the Army's Indian-fighting officers. A Civil War veteran of more than a little distinction, he led the famous "Grierson's Raid," south from LaGrange, Tennessee, through Mississippi to Baton Rouge as a diversionary effort in support of Grant's Vicksburg Campaign. An Illinois music teacher before the war, Grierson disliked horses yet wound up becoming a splendid cavalry leader. After the war he was appointed to command the 10th Black Cavalry Regiment. Grierson was of the few officers who judged his troopers on their ability not on the color of their skin.

For the moment, the relocation of the Comanche/Kiowa tribes at Fort Sill gave Sheridan the opportunity to direct his attention to the Cheyennes and Arapahos, who were understandably gun-shy as a result of the Washita and had yet to come in to the new agency. The Washita Campaign revealed the possibility of white captives still held by those bands. Through the efforts of Black Kettle's sister a parley with Cheyennes and Arapahos was set up. The leaders appealed to Sheridan; their people were suffering; they needed food and shelter. They wanted the Indian prisoners taken at Washita to be returned. However,

Colonel Benjamin Grierson. One of the few white officers who commanded and respected the Black soldiers in his regiment.

Sheridan said not until *all* the bands came in. To this ultimatum he added that white captives must also be delivered.

But Sheridan figured to press the thing. At the end of January 1869, Custer took forty sharpshooters and guided by the Cheyenne, Little Robe and the Arapaho, Yellow Bear, they located and persuaded an Arapaho band to come into Fort Sill. This was a start but a significant number of Cheyennes—perhaps as many as 1,500—were headed for the Staked Plains. As a consequence of the Cheyennes' refusal to come into Fort Sill—and who could blame them—Custer marched out in early March with eleven companies of the 7th Cavalry and ten of the 19th Kansas Volunteers, guided by some white scouts and Osage Indians. Meanwhile, with the election of Grant to the presidency, Sherman moved up to become general of the army and Sheridan replaced him as commander of the Military Division of the Missouri, leaving the frontier for his new office in Chicago.

Custer, still in the field, marched southwest along the Wichita Mountains. The men and horses suffered so much that Custer was compelled to send some 400 animals back to a supply depot on the Washita River, not far from where the 7th had attacked Black Kettle's village. His command, it would seem, was scarcely in any condition to continue operations, but Custer persisted. On the 11th, scouts reported a large trail headed northeast and Custer followed. There was scarcely enough forage for his horses, and the men were reduced to eating mule meat, but on March 15 they approached the large Cheyenne camp of Medicine Arrows along Sweetwater Creek. This village, Custer learned, contained two captive white women. Now Custer found himself with something of a dilemma: much as he would liked to have attacked, if he did so, the women would probably be killed. The village he gradually learned contained some 250 lodges, many of them Dog Soldiers, which meant a sizeable body of warriors. Directing his men to take up positions around the camp, Custer parleyed with the Cheyennes. Afterward, the leader reportedly knocked ashes from the ceremonial pipe both had smoked, on Custer's boots. This was the Cheyenne version of breaking a mirror, in that it was intended to bring Custer bad luck, and somehow this became part of the Custer mythology that ostensibly helped bring about his demise at Little Bighorn.

Custer was determined to obtain the release of these women, but it was an unsettled situation to say the least. While many of the villagers began to pull out of the encampment, some of Custer's officers urged him to attack, but Custer held off, and when four Indians—three of whom were Dog Soldiers—were sent to parley further, the three Dog Soldiers were grabbed by the cavalrymen. Suddenly Custer had a trump card. If the women weren't released, he would hang the Dog Soldiers. That did it. Promptly the two women: twenty-four-year-old Anna Belle Brewster Morgan and eighteen-year-old Sarah Catherine White were released. They were in pitiable condition, garbed in rags and buckskin. Anna Morgan's brother, Daniel Brewster who had been allowed to accompany Custer from Fort Sill was there to greet his sister. One can only imagine the emotions felt by both.

Custer did not attack the village, which was probably a good thing, given the condition of his command. Actually, it would be difficult to say who was worse off the Indians or the soldiers. Custer did keep the hostages in custody, however, and began his return march to Fort Sill, after first making the Cheyennes promise to come in to Camp Supply, presumably in return for not hanging the Dog Soldiers or attacking the village. Custer reached Camp Supply on March 28. In retrospect, one wonders whether Custer actually expected the Cheyennes to come into Fort Supply on their own volition. In any case, ten days later, the exhausted troopers marched into Fort Hays, where the Kansas men would shortly be discharged.

It is tempting to suggest that the Battle of the Washita and the campaigns that followed broke the power of the Southern Plains tribes, or at least the Cheyennes. Sheridan seemed to think so, or at least that's what he wanted the Press to believe. In reality, however, such was far from the truth. For the moment the Comanches and Kiowas were drawing rations at the new Fort Sill agency, but that did not mean they no longer posed a threat. And the Cheyennes were still at large. Despite Custer's strong words, they had failed to show up at Camp Supply. Prisoners taken at Washita were turned loose in June, but the militant Dog Soldiers refused to be cowed and returned to the Republican River country, where Carr's 5th Cavalry would break their power at Summit Springs come July.

The decade of the 1870s was to prove the high water mark for Indian resistance on the Great Plains, north to south. The decade got underway with President-elect Ulysses S. Grant's inauguration on March 4, 1870. Insofar as Indian-white relations were concerned, Grant's administration began with a Peace Policy. Although well intentioned, the policy proved a dismal failure as subsequent events demonstrated. Grant's idea was to use the power of the churches to pacify the Indians, and transform them into Christians, who would take up the plow and become good citizens. It was one of those ideas that sounded so good when you talked about it, but was quite another matter to implement it, and, most importantly, no one seemed to see fit to ask the Indians what they thought of the idea.

Enter the Quakers

Down in Indian Territory, the Society of Friends, better known as Quakers, took charge of Indian affairs. As historian Robert Utley points out, those Indians who would be "guided" by the Quakers—the Kiowas and Comanches—were probably the most warlike in the West. Whether the Quakers actually understood this is not clear, but in any event, they asked Grant to appoint some of their members and Grant complied.

The agent for the Comanches and Kiowas was one Lawrie Tatum, a man of upstanding character and a tireless worker on behalf of those for whom he was responsible. Born in New Jersey, Tatum moved to Ohio as a boy and later taught school in Iowa. At the Fort Sill Agency, Tatum was not only agent, but just about everything else, including judge and sheriff. Many years later he would author a book entitled *Our Red Brothers and the Peace Policy of President Ulysses S. Grant*. Meanwhile, the Cheyenne-Arapaho Agency, formerly located at Camp Supply was moved to a site about 100 miles north of Fort Sill on the Canadian River. Here, the agent was one Brinton Darlington, to be followed three years later by John Miles.

In order to appreciate the problem faced by both the civilian and military authorities in attempting to bring about closure to the Indian problem on the Great Plains (or most anywhere in the West for that matter), one needs to constantly bear in mind the failure of the reservation system to achieve the desired results. It is hard to find anything at all positive about the reservation concept; it was a system that failed both the whites and the Indians.

The Indians were expected to reside on their designated reservations, and it was understood (by the whites of course) that the Indians would be under the control of the agent. It was further understood that the Indians would be allowed to hunt outside the reservations, but only so long as there was game—particularly the buffalo—to hunt. The treaties also stipulated that the tribes would offer no opposition to travelers, surveying crews, and settlers, though again a full realization of what this would mean to their way of life, seemed beyond the grasp of most Indians. While some of the Indian bands did indeed find hanging around the agency (or military post) an easier way of life, most of them much preferred to live the old nomadic lifestyle and come into the agencies to receive their promised annuities and rations; it was the best of both worlds. During the spring and summer they could live as they always had, knowing that they could come into the agencies for the winter. One might accuse the Indians of taking advantage of the situation, but in truth they were only taking advantage of an opportunity provided by the treaty.

Meanwhile, Comanches and Kiowas plus some Cheyennes and Arapahos continued to raid across the Texas frontier and down into Mexico. In one sense, Grant's Peace Policy worked to their definite advantage. Troops could pursue these raiders right up to the very border of the reservation, but not across that line, and of course they were prohibited from crossing the border into Mexico.

Some, Sherman among them, thought reports of the raids were blown out of proportion. There was also a question as to whether most of the raids were caused by the Kwahadis, regarded as perhaps the most militant of all the Comanches, and who lived deep in the Staked Plains. It seemed a question of whether the raiders were from the reservation, or the Staked Plains.

Agent Lawrie Tatum who ran the show at the Ft. Sill Agency was a solid supporter of Grant's Peace Policy, but he expected the Indians to abide by the rules. And Colonel Grierson who commanded at Fort Sill proved an able supporter of Tatum. Although Grierson treated the Indians—and his Black troopers—with respect, he enforced the rules.

A new element was added to the equation on Feb. 25, 1871, when thirty-one-year-old Colonel Ranald Slidell Mackenzie assumed command of the 4th U.S. Cavalry at Fort Richardson, Texas. An officer who had served with much distinction in the Civil War, Mackenzie would prove an outstanding cavalry commander and Indian fighter. Hard-driving, at times ruthless, and a martinet, he was one of Sheridan's favorites, along with George Custer. U.S. Grant once called Mackenzie the most promising soldier in the Army. Some would argue that he was the Army's most effective Indian fighter. Under Mackenzie's command, the 4th Cavalry arguably became the army's premier cavalry regiment.

Although Sherman believed that reports of Indian depredations on the Texas frontier were exaggerated, he agreed to strengthen the state's defenses. General Christopher Augur was named to command the Dept. of Texas, but the boundaries of Sheridan's Division of the Missouri were also expanded to give him authority as far as Fort Sill.

The Warren Wagon Train Raid

In the spring of 1871—May to be exact—Sherman decided to have a personal look at the Texas defense system and make a personal assessment of the Indian problem. On the 18th, Sherman along with Inspector-General Randolph Marcy and a small escort reached Fort Richardson, near present Jacksboro, having had an uneventful journey. Unbeknownst to Sherman and Marcy, however, they had been uncomfortably close to a large Kiowa war party, which refrained from attacking the Sherman/Marcy party only because a more tempting target in the form of a large wagon train was passing through.

The train of ten wagons belonging to the freighting company of Warren and DuBose had organized under the supervision of Henry L. Warren at Weatherford, west of Fort Worth and was bound for Jacksboro, some forty miles north. On May 17 as the mule train plodded northward a severe thunderstorm struck. Rain lashed the train and lightning flashed everywhere. The teamsters attempted to corral the wagons, but it was hard to control the frightened mules. In the midst of this chaos the Kiowas of Satanta, several hundred strong attacked. Though well armed, the teamsters had little chance. The train was destroyed and all the teamsters save one were killed. The sole survivor somehow managed to make his way to Fort Richardson. The episode came to be known as the Salt Creek or Warren Wagon Train raid.

Not until that night when they were at Fort Richardson did Sherman learn how close they had come to annihilation, when the badly wounded, lone survivor from the raid reached the fort and related his story. Ten wagons burned, forty mules stolen and eight of the dozen wagon masters killed. The report finally convinced Sherman, who wasted no time ordering Mackenzie to go in pursuit.

The peace policy, it seemed, wasn't quite playing out the way its proponents had expected. When an angry Sherman reached Fort Sill, likely still fuming over the wagon train raid he himself had been fortunate to escape, he found Agent Tatum beginning to have some doubts. What rocked Tatum's belief in the peace policy was when Kiowas, headed by Satanta, appeared for rations and demanded—not requested—arms and ammunition. Old Satanta had the cheek to boast about their part in the Salt Creek wagon train raid. When he heard this, he sent a message to Colonel Grierson, requesting that Satanta be placed under arrest.

This led to a subsequent and tense stand-off when Grierson and Sherman faced Satanta, Kicking Bird, Satank and a couple of other Kiowa leaders. Once more, Satanta repeated his prideful boast and Sherman ordered the lot of them placed under arrest, to later be tried in the Texas courts. The angry Indians immediately threatened Sherman and Grierson with their weapons, but Sherman had been prepared for just such an eventuality, and at a given signal the Indians found themselves facing the carbines of Grierson's Black troopers who had been secreted inside the colonel's quarter, causing the Indians to think twice. Most stood down then although one later let fly an arrow at Sherman that missed. The Indi-

General William T. Sherman. When Grant was elected president, Sherman was appointed General of the Army.

The Kiowa chief Satanta who was known for his oratorical prowess.

ans were subsequently placed in the guardhouse to await their fate. Later, Satank was killed in a scuffle with his guard. The others were tried by a jury in Jacksboro and found guilty. However, Texas Governor Edmund Davis commuted the death sentence. If hanged, the Indian leaders might have served as martyrs, so they were sentenced to life in the state penitentiary at Huntsville.

If federal authorities imagined that the hard hand of Sherman would cause the Indians to think carefully before continuing their raids, they were badly mistaken. True, some of the Kiowas and Comanches did decide to forsake the war path, but others were galvanized into their own brand of retribution. From their isolated and nearly inaccessible strongholds in the Staked Plains, they struck the west Texas frontier with a savage fury, on occasion even threatening Fort Sill itself. Kiowas under Lone Wolf and Kwahadi Comanches under Quanah Parker were the devils of the Llano as far as the U.S. Army was concerned.

Of all the noted Indian warriors who opposed the U.S. military in the vast reaches of the Trans-Mississippi West: Sitting Bull, Crazy Horse, Cochise, Geronimo, and a number of others, perhaps none presents quite as interesting and compelling a picture as does Quanah Parker.

Quanah Parker

Born 1845 (some sources say '48), Quanah Parker was the son of a white woman, Cynthia Ann Parker and the Kawhadi Comanche chief Peta Nocona. Nine-year-old Cynthia Ann had been captured in a raid on Parker's Fort, Texas, in 1836. Unlike most white females who were captured by Indians, Cynthia Ann seems to have had a different experience. Although the known facts surrounding her life as a Comanche are murky, she does appear to have taken a liking to the Comanche way of life. She later married her captor, Peta Nocona and bore him two sons and a daughter. Among the Comanches Cynthia Ann was known as Nautdah. The stories surrounding her life—of which there are many—tell us that she rejected opportunities to return to her own people. And yet sightings of her in the aftermath of her capture are rare so we really don't know how many such opportunities actually existed. We do know that when she was captured

The extraordinary Comanche chief, Quanah Parker. As the son of a captive white woman and a Comanche chief, he rose to become one of the most respected and feared Indian war leaders. After the fighting was over he willingly embraced the white man's way of life.

in a retaliatory raid by a mixed force of Texas Rangers and U.S. Cavalry, at the Battle of Pease River in December 1860, twenty-four years later, she looked every inch a Comanche and did not easily revert to the white way of life.

Cynthia's and Peta Nocona's two sons were named Quanah and Peanuts—whom she reportedly named out of a fondness for peanuts. Their younger sister was known as Prairie Flower—Tohtseeah. Of Cynthia's three children it was the one called Quanah who was to become a legend in his own time. As a boy he was physically large and strong, like his father, growing into a physically imposing and handsome man. The given name seems to mean Eagle, although other translations range from "odor" to "stinking" leaving us with a completely unclear picture as to the name's true meaning. Neither is it clear exactly when—or why—Cynthia Ann's surname was added to Quanah's.

Regardless of exactly how he came by his name, or its precise meaning, as a war chief Quanah Parker was equaled by few and exceeded by none. When compelled by circumstances to finally surrender, he came into Fort Sill of his own accord in 1875. Once Quanah abandoned the war trail he became as strong a proponent of peace as he once had been for war. Although he embraced a peace policy Quanah never abandoned his Indian culture. Until his surrender at Fort Sill he was the Army's major nemesis on the southern plains.

From the time of his arrival at Fort Richardson in early 1871, Mackenzie and his 4th Cavalry were almost continuously in the field pursuing Indian raiders. What was particularly galling for the young colonel—as it was for every soldier from Sherman on down—was to find that a band of raiders had crossed into the sanctuary of Fort Sill where they could effectively thumb their noses at the soldiers who were prohibited from following.

So, frustrated though far from deterred, Mackenzie was determined to strike the Indians in their strongholds on the *Llano Estacado*. His reasoning was that attacking the Indians here would reduce the threat of their raids on the west Texas settlements. On one occasion he led his regiment across the vastness of this unknown region as far west as Fort Sumner, New Mexico, where just a decade later an outlaw named Billy the Kid would meet his fate.

Mackenzie's expeditions into this region along with another led by Lieutenant Colonel William R. Shafter, later to command the U.S. expeditionary force sent to Cuba, revealed the depth of the Comanche's extraordinary trading relationship with the *Comancheros*. As a dependable supplier of firearms, ammunition and captives for the Comanches, the Army would need to destroy this relationship before it could seriously hope to bring about an end the Indian threat.

Mackenzie's efforts paid off. On September 20, 1872, he led eight troops—450 men—of the 4th Cavalry north from Fort Concho along the eastern apron of the *Llano Estacado*. To provide security for his advanced supply base, he also had three companies of infantry while another two companies of infantry guarded the wagon train.

It was a miserable expedition as cold, drenching rains soaked the troopers. On the night of September 26, an estimated 250 Comanches struck the camp near Tule Canyon, aiming to drive off Mackenzie's horses, but he recalled what had happened in 1872 when he had lost horses to the Comanches at McClellan Creek. This time Mackenzie was prepared. His horses were well tied down and ringed with pickets. The position was solid. The Indians were driven off, and both sides sniped away at each other through the night. At daylight, Mackenzie attacked and sent the raiders reeling.

Meanwhile, behind the scenes, Quaker forces pressed the government to release from prison at Huntsville (and others at Fort Concho) the Kiowa chiefs Satanta and Big Tree in the misguided belief that by so doing the Kiowas would be moved to abandon their raids against the Texas settlements. The military knew better of course and opposed the idea, but they were swimming upstream. Sherman, Sheridan and others were irate. The assassination of General Canby during the Modoc War in April 1873 had fired public opinion, but the Quakers prevailed in their argument and in the fall of 1873, the Texas governor released the prisoners, and as the army feared, their incarceration did little toward persuading the Indians to abandon the war trail.

Ordinarily, the Indians went into semi-hibernation with the arrival of winter and raids tended to fall off, but the winter of 1873–1874 proved an exception to the rule. Although Kiowa raiding activity did ease up, other bands were more active than usual. And politics continued to exert an influence. When Agent Lawrie Tatum called on Grierson for support after the Jacksboro affair, he did so using the authority of his office. However, Governor Davis's release of Satanta and Big Tree, in effect, overrode Tatum's authority and so, disillusioned with the system, Tatum resigned in April of 1873. His replacement, James Haworth apparently saw no point in a military presence around the agency. It was a sign of the times.

Not only had the peacemakers largely failed to bring about order on the Southern Plains (or elsewhere in the West) but as the decade of the 1870s deepened, troubles intensified. In large part this was due to the efforts of the hide hunters. Buffalo hides were in great demand around the country, and accordingly, buffalo hides became a prime target for hide hunters operating out of Forts Dodge, Hays and elsewhere on the Plains.

In 1868, one year after the Medicine Lodge Treaty, an Englishman traveling cross Kansas on the railroad described how the train was forced to stop frequently because the Plains were blackened with herds of buffalo. Yet only a few years later one could make the same journey and count but a handful of the shaggy animals.

In 1870, two New England brothers, John and Josiah Mooar recognized the commercial potential of selling buffalo hides. Buffalo were being slaughtered for meat, but the hides were going to waste. Eventually, it was discovered that hides, especially those from cows and young bulls, made wonderful robes to cover sleigh riders. Hides also made warm overcoats, caps and gloves, along with leggings and boots for soldiers. And the hides from older animals could be made into machinery belts. Hides could bring up to $3.50 each and when multiplied by thousands of robes the profit was substantial. In 1873, some 750,000 hides were shipped east from Dodge City, and it was estimated that between1872–1874 more than 4 million buffalo were killed. Slaughtering buffalo became a genuine art. A hunting crew consisted of the hunter plus skinners and a driver. A good hunter could kill upwards of 100 buffalo a day. The favored weapon was the famous Sharps "Big Fifty" .50 caliber buffalo rifle, which packed an enormous punch and was accurate for up to three-quarters of a mile.

The Red River (Buffalo) War

Although it was the destruction of the buffalo herds that led to what was known as the Red River or Buffalo War of 1874, there were secondary reasons as well. Gun runners and bands of white men who raided Indian horse herds exacerbated a tense situation. As might be expected, the Indians responded to this intrusion with attacks wherever they happened to find a likely target. The particularly superstitious Kiowas targeted surveying parties, fearing white men who moved through the region, planting stakes in the ground. Although it is not nearly as well known as the Great Sioux War of 1876 the Red River War was arguably a war of greater fierceness. No fewer than seven major battles were fought as opposed to five during the Great Sioux War.[10]

By 1874, the vast buffalo herds that roamed north of the Arkansas River had been drastically reduced by the hide and meat hunters, who now began to prey on the herds as far south as the Canadian River in the Texas Panhandle, which was Indian country. Ostensibly off limits by virtue of the Medicine Lodge Treaty, the U.S. Army was responsible for seeing that those terms were enforced. However, senior military commanders, including Sherman and Sheridan recognized that once the buffalo were destroyed so was the Indians' commissary. Hence, the Army winked and made no effort to prevent the hunters from crossing the Arkansas River—the so-called dead line—and attacking the great southern herd that still populated this region. It was quite like the situation in the Black Hills of Dakota where—the very same year, 1874, gold was discovered and whites were prohibited from entering. The difference was that here on the Southern Plains, the Army did nothing to stop the invasion of the hide hunters. In a lame sort of gesture, the government moved the southern boundary from the Arkansas River to the Cimarron. As a consequence, the hide hunters enjoyed a banner year in 1873 and planned on an even bigger one in 1874.

It is helpful to have an understanding of exactly where the reservations were located. There were two: both in extreme southwestern Indian Territory—today's Oklahoma. The Cheyenne-Arapaho Reservation—which had been located right on the Kansas line in 1867—had been moved south so that its northern border was now touched by both the Cimarron River and the North Fork of the Canadian River, while its western flank was anchored by the eastern boundary of the Texas Panhandle. The agency headquarters was at Darlington. Immediately south of the Cheyenne-Arapaho Reservation was the Kiowa-Comanche Reservation. The Kiowa-Comanche agency was located at Anadarko, southwest of present day

A buffalo herd on the Southern Plains.

Oklahoma City and north of Lawton. Although it was technically illegal to enter Texas by passing through the reservations, it was not considered a violation of the treaty's terms to enter Texas by by-passing the reservations—through No Man's land, as it was called. Here was yet another of those subtleties that eluded the Indians' grasp of reality. Insofar as the Indians were concerned, all the buffalo south of the Arkansas was on their land.

The treaty terms of Medicine Lodge made it illegal to hunt buffalo in territory reserved for Indians, but Indian agents lacked the power to prohibit hunters from doing so. Prior to 1874 when the Kansas herds were decimated, only a few hardy souls had dared hunt south of the line, and sometimes these failed to return, but in any case, agents lacked any real authority to halt the incursions. Nor was there any federal authority to halt horse thievery. It is pointless to pass any law that is unenforceable, or which the government refuses to enforce. Notwithstanding the terms of the Medicine Lodge Treaty, Indian Commissioner Columbus Delano took the position that it was a proper course for a civilized nation to grow and survive at the expense of a "barbarous" people.[11]

It would be misleading to suggest that the southern tribes had been entirely peaceful since Medicine Lodge and yet there was some truth to the notion. The four major tribes: Cheyenne, Arapaho, Kiowa, and Comanche had been relatively quiet since the treaty—relatively being the operative word here. Indeed, several Kiowa and Comanche leaders had even been taken to Washington to view first hand the power of the white man and returned suitably impressed. Although the hard-liners remained, many were ready to walk the white man's road. Was there an opportunity here that just might have led to a better solution than war? Perhaps, but if so, said opportunity was let to pass. Further, it seems not to have occurred to white authorities—civil and military alike—that while the destruction of the buffalo herds would end the Indian way of life, it would also bring about retaliation. The Indians, after all, were not going to sit idly by and watch their livelihood go down the tube without fighting back. But even with the loss of the buffalo, war might have been prevented had the government made a genuine effort to see that annuities—especially food—had been delivered in a timely manner. Instead, time after time, annuities were delayed or cut short. Colonel Nelson Miles, one of the key field commanders during the Red River War later observed that a major cause of the war was the government's broken promises.

Against this backdrop in the nascent spring of 1874 a band of hide hunters, some fifty in all with thirty wagons, set forth from Dodge City bound for the forbidden territory. Among the group was twenty-four-year-old Billy Dixon reported to be one of the finest marksmen on the Plains. Dixon's young companion was William Barclay "Bat" Masterson, who would go one to make a name for himself as a lawman. When he learned about the adventure, a mixed-blood army scout named Amos Chapman observed that there were a great many Comanches and Kiowas down there, whereupon one of the hunters replied that they could "shoot their way through all the Indian nations of the Southwest" if necessary. Part of the entourage was a man named A.C. Myers who ran a thriving business out of Dodge, buying hides and selling supplies to the hunters. The Kansas market had nearly dried up and Charley, as he was known, saw plenty of potential in this enterprise and so signed on.

Adobe Walls

A week out of Dodge found them some 150 miles deep into the Panhandle of Texas. En route they had passed a couple of other camps of hunters, but none so large as their own. Along the north bank of the Canadian River, they found a site that suited them amidst the ruins of an old adobe trading post built three decades earlier by William Bent and

Ceran St. Vrain, who had planned to open up what was expected to be a brisk trade with the Kiowas and Comanches. It was not a bad idea, but the Indians for some reason proved uninterested. The sturdily constructed buildings were called "soddies" and were constructed of logs placed end-to-end, with sod to fill in the gaps. The hunters called their camp Adobe Walls, appropriately enough. It was here, back in '64 that Kit Carson had had such a stiff fight with Kiowas and Comanches and had managed to escape only by the hair of his field pieces. The coming battle would go Carson's fight even one better.

Meanwhile, if the Southern tribes deplored the slaughter of buffalo north of the Arkansas they were understandably furious to discover that hunters had begun to encroach on their territory. The Indians could ill-afford to allow the hunters to do to the southern herd what they had done to the northern herd. As tension among the Indians rose there appeared on the scene a prophet named Isatai of the Kwahada Comanches. Isatai was an emotional adolescent whose name freely translated means "Wolf-Shit." Like others before and after him, notably, Wovoka during the 1890 Ghost Dance, Isatai proclaimed that he had great powers. He was immune to bullets and could restore the dead to life. He also claimed to have the power to vomit up cartridges for Indian weapons. Isatai preached war against the hide hunters threatening to destroy their major food source; his words were well received. As noted, had the government been at all attentive to the needs of the Indians, war might well have been averted. Through the winter of 1873–1874 and on into the spring, Indian agents pleaded in vain for more supplies. The buffalo of course remained the principal staple of the Indians' diet, and when hide hunters began to threaten the southern herd the Indians responded in the only way they could.

As spring came on, Isatai, his medicine growing stronger, sent out word for all Comanches to attend a great Sun Dance where his inflammatory war rhetoric reached a responsive audience. Early in the morning of June 27, 1874, a mixed force of Comanches and Kiowas, led by Isatai and Quanah Parker, struck the buffalo hunter's camp at Adobe Walls. What followed was one of the fiercest fights of the Western Indian wars. Within the Adobe Walls perimeter were twenty-eight men and one woman. Encouraged by Isatai's proclamation of invincibility the Indians struck hard, but were stunned to find that Isatai's word failed to provide the promised protection. The hide hunters' big buffalo rifles quickly proved deadly. Surprised by the accurate and deadly fire from the hunters, the Indians withdrew. Although some of the hide hunters, fearing a general uprising, did return to Dodge, their fears quickly subsided and it was soon business as usual.

Adobe Walls, along with other incidents of Indian resistance, moved General of the Army William T. Sherman to take swift action. The intensity of Indian raids could no longer be ignored. From the secretary of the interior to the secretary of war to General Sherman went the welcome order to take off the gloves. From Sherman to his *numero uno* lieutenant on the western frontier, General Philip H. Sheridan, was transmitted the operational plan to move against the Indians with multiple columns: press the Indians from all corners. And from Sheridan's headquarters went orders to the next level of command: General Christopher Augur, commanding Texas and a portion of Indian Territory, and to Gen John Pope in charge of the Missouri Department which included Kansas, New Mexico, part of Colorado and that part of Indian Territory not under Augur's immediate command.

COLONEL NELSON APPLETON MILES

By late July 1874 a major multi-pronged campaign against the Southern Plains tribes was taking shape. To Colonel Nelson Appleton Miles, commanding the 5th U.S. Infantry went orders from General Pope to assemble a strike force consisting of eight troops of the 6th Cavalry and four from his own 5th Infantry. Miles's command was to stage at Fort Dodge then strike south into Indian Territory. A second column out of General Pope's department was commanded by Major William Redwood Price who led a second column of some 200 men of the 8th U.S. Cavalry east from New Mexico Territory.

Nelson Miles may have been the vainest man ever to wear the uniform of the U.S. Army, but if not, he was surely a close second. Miles was no "West Pointer." He had been nothing more than a clerk at the time of the Civil War, but he was given a commission in a Massachusetts infantry regiment and soon found himself leading troops into battle. Here he found his true calling. Miles participated in nearly all the major battles of the Army of the Potomac and by war's end had been brevetted a major general of volunteers. In the postwar army he found himself as colonel of the 5th Infantry, but his quest for promotion and advancement never subsided. It didn't hurt Miles's career either that his wife was the niece of General Sherman and the daughter of Sherman's brother, John, though both men might have from time to time wished that Miles was not related to them, so hard did he push for advancement. But all of that aside, Miles was a tough campaigner. From here he would go north to finish off the troublesome Lakotas, Cheyennes, and Nez Perce, before turning his attention to the Apaches. To some, Nelson Miles was the best of all the Army's Indian fighters.

Colonel Nelson Appleton Miles. Vain and ambitious, he was one of the Army's most effective Indian campaigners. Later he would rise to become General of the Army.

But Sheridan's plan was not limited to the resources of Pope's department. General Augur planned to put an additional three columns in the field. Augur's first step was to shift Mackenzie's 4th Cavalry from Fort Clark and the Mexican border north to Fort Concho. A supply base was to be established for Mackenzie on the Brazos River. From here he would operate against the Comanches and their allies on the Staked Plains. A second column from Augur's department was headed up by forty-year-old-year-old Lieutenant Colonel George Pearson Buell with five companies of the 11th Infantry. Indiana born, Buell had served with honor during the Civil War and he proved himself an able field commander here in the west. As department commander, Mackenzie had Buell placed under arrest for failing to call formally on his commanding officer (Mackenzie) upon arriving at his station, but the incident seems not to have impacted Buell's career. Yet a third column under forty-nine-year-old Lieutenant Colonel John Wynn "Blackjack" Davidson, marched out of Fort Sill with his 10th Cavalry. A crusty Virginian who had graduated from West Point in 1845, he had seen his share of hard duty in the years since. Davidson was one of those rare Virginians who chose the Union over the Confederacy during the Civil War, despite being offered a general's star in the Confederate Army. A decade earlier, Davidson had marched from Fort Tejon, California, through the Owens Valley. Davidson was the polar opposite of the kindly Grierson, whom he replaced as commanding officer at Fort Sill and as commander of the 10th Cavalry.

Sheridan's strategy may have looked good on paper, but there was a flaw. Five columns would be operating independently with no overall commander. Miles, who was under Pope's umbrella, had little respect for his department commander anyway, and thought he (Miles) ought to have been the man in charge. Miles had little good to say about the other expedition commanders either, but he feared Mackenzie. Both men were young and aggressive. Miles had influence, but knew that Mackenzie was well liked by both Sheridan and Grant. What Miles feared was that Mackenzie would win the race for the next brigadier's billet. It had, after all, been Mackenzie whom Sherman summoned to pursue the Warren Wagon Train raiders. Politics indeed.

Meanwhile the situation at Fort Sill and the agency at Anadarko was growing tense; once again it was a matter of distinguishing between "friendly" and "hostile." Those Indians who wished to be treated as friendly were directed to enroll at their respective agencies. At Darlington there was little difficulty with the Arapahos, but the Cheyennes were proving troublesome. To complicate matters further, there was tension between the Comanche/Kiowa agent James M. Haworth and Davidson over the handling of the Indians. In due course, the Indians who had reported in were finally enrolled. Later, however, some Comanches and Kiowas decided they wanted to be added, but by that time it was too late. Haworth saw trouble in this and requested help from Davidson, who dispatched four troops of the 10th Cavalry. When the Indians were ordered to lay down their arms and submit, however, fighting broke out, resulting in the soldiers and Indians exchanging fire over a two-day period. The most important thing to emerge from this standoff was that, insofar as the Army was concerned, it served to clearly define hostile elements from friendlies.

As summer 1874 wound down the U.S. Army found itself confronted with a tough situation. Although many Indians had returned to the agencies, many "hostiles" remained in the field: in all, nearly 4,000 Comanches, Cheyennes and Kiowas, men women and children. Of this number, perhaps a third—1,000 to 1,500—were warriors. As far as anyone knew these bands were to be found deep in the Texas Panhandle, south of present day Amarillo, along such various watercourses as the Washita and Red Rivers, many of which were dry in this summer of great drought.

On August 11 Miles' column—some 750 strong—marched out of Fort Dodge and by the 30th had pushed deep into the Panhandle crossing the Prairie Dog Town Fork of the Red River. Along the edge of what was called the Cap Rock, the escarpment that signals the edge of the Staked Plains, they were suddenly attacked by a war party of 200 Cheyennes. Miles coolly put his infantrymen in the center while a mounted detachment protected each flank. Responding to the attack, Captain Adna R. Chaffee, who would later command the American relief expedition to China during the Boxer Rebellion, told his troop that he would make any man who lost his life a corporal. There was nothing brief about this fight. For five hours, under a merciless sun, and over a distance of a dozen miles, it was soldier against Indian. Comanche and Kiowa reinforcements had strengthened the Indian force to about 600, making it nearly as large as that of Miles. Supported by mountain howitzers and Gatling guns, the soldiers pushed the Indians out onto the Staked Plains. A lack of supplies finally forced Miles to contain his advance, but not before putting to the torch any supplies and equipage left behind by the Indians.

On the Great Plains—Southern, Northern or Central—the weather is seldom tepid or timid. When it's hot it blisters; when it's cold it is the bone-numbing variety, and during turbulent weather the wind can howl with a demoniac fury. Campaigning here was tough at any time of year, but this late summer of 1874 was one to remember. The heat was stifling—well in excess of 100 degrees—106 at Fort Sill, and a drought lay everywhere on the land; there was no rain for forty-six days. And as if this was not enough, a plague of locusts stripped the land of whatever vegetation the drought had not killed. To slack their thirst Miles's men were forced to cut the veins in their arms and moisten their lips with their own blood.

During this late summer of 1874, Nelson Miles and his men had suffered greatly from the drought and heat—the Indians no less, but that picture changed abruptly on the 7th day of September when autumn storms raged through the region. Suddenly there was water in abundance; it filled watercourses and turned the prairie to mud. At this juncture, Miles had done about all he could. Between the weather and a steadily worsening supply situation, he had no choice but to halt operations for the moment. He had two options: he could march back to Camp Supply—about 100 miles southwest of Fort Dodge—which in effect would mean abandoning the field to the Comanches, and also to Mackenzie, Davidson and Buell, both of whom he knew were in the field leaving these officers to perhaps win the glory that might have been his own.

Confronted with this dilemma, Miles elected to send his supply train back to Camp Supply to re-provision. To provide protection for the train he sent Captain Wyllys Lyman and a company of infantry, thereby setting the stage for a small drama. Miles was gambling that the train would return before his men were forced to kill their horses or starve. Obviously, if his cavalry had no horses his campaign would be largely useless, since infantry alone had no hope of catching the Indians.

On September 6, word reached Miles that a large force of Cheyennes had somehow managed to get between his command and Camp Supply. The original idea behind the strategy of Miles's operation had been to sweep the area clear of so-called hostiles, so this was not good news. Indeed, Miles's strategy had been to move south with his command marching in echelon, so to speak, so as to prevent any Indians from sneaking around his flanks, but somehow they managed to do so all the same. So now, Miles had good reason to be concerned about the fate of his supply train; a large party of Cheyennes roaming at will behind him posed a real threat to his line of supply. As a consequence, Miles detached his chief of scouts and probably his most trusted subordinate, Lieutenant Frank Dwight Baldwin and three former buffalo hunters turned army scouts to carry dispatches to Camp Supply and also check on the wagon train.

Miles, meanwhile, had earlier sent couriers to Camp Supply with instructions for a supply train to meet up with and re-provision Lyman's wagon train en route. The rendezvous was to have taken place on the 5th, but on that date, Lyman found no supply train waiting for him. Sending a six-man detachment on ahead to ascertain what had happened, he proceeded on toward Camp Supply. Meantime, Baldwin and his companions managed to reach Lyman's supply train late on September 9, following a harrowing three-day ordeal of dealing with horrid weather and eluding Indians. From here, Baldwin pushed on to Camp Supply, while Lyman's train lumbered along. When they found the scalped body of a teamster who had gone hunting, it was obvious that Indians were in the area, despite Miles's plan to clear the area and drive them before his column, rather like a roundup. Precautions were clearly in order. Putting half of his infantry escort on each side of the wagon train and positioning his few cavalrymen in front, Lyman continued on to Camp Supply, loaded his wagons and started back.

Lyman, probably fearing that Indians would strike the train before he rejoined Miles, had his fears confirmed on the 9th when a large Comanche/Kiowa war party attacked. The fight began as a long range affair, but grew closer as the day progressed. Lyman's men, well disciplined, maintained their positions until sunset at which time the Indians withdrew. For the next twenty-four hours, the two sides fought on and off until the Indians finally tired of the fight. Having been unsuccessful in penetrating Lyman's defenses they judged that there was no point in continuing the fight. Lyman reported to the commanding officer at Camp Supply that he had suffered one killed and two wounded.

The Indians had not fared well. In the aftermath of the Lyman Wagon Train fight, they found themselves continually pressed by the various army columns in the field, as well as by the same harsh weather that beset the army columns. Even as Miles, Mackenzie and the others suffered through the fierce thunderstorms, lightning, and drenching rain that followed in the aftermath of the brutal heat wave, so too did the Indians suffer. Drenched and just as cold as the soldiers, the Indians who fled from the pursuing army columns, called this the Wrinkled Hand Chase.

When Miles assembled his expedition he brought together most of the available troops in the Kansas garrisons. This would have presented no problem had Miles been successful in driving the Cheyennes out of the area. Unfortunately, a war party of about twenty-five led by a tough warrior named Medicine Water avoided the net and managed to spread a web of terror across southwestern Kansas. Medicine Water's wife was a large woman named Mochi or Buffalo Calf Woman. Because she was a full participant in all the raids, Mochi was known as a Warrior Woman. According to historian James Haley, neither could be considered particularly bright, but both were adept at raiding. How Medicine Water's party managed to elude Miles's scouts is not clear, but it was a small and probably fast-moving party that was apparently savvy enough to avoid being spotted.

In any case, during June and July 1874, two surveying teams platting the Kansas Territory, were attacked by Medicine Water's band in Meade County, close to the Indian Territory line. Both surveying parties were devastated and one was wiped out. Medicine Water's trail from this point on is rather sketchy, but he seems to have traveled north and west, perhaps reaching as far as southeastern Colorado and northeastern New Mexico. Medicine Water is next heard from on September 11 when his party came across the lone immigrant train of one John German, a former Georgia farmer who had left that state four years earlier in April 1870, after spending time in a Union prisoner of war camp during the Civil War. After his release, German envisioned a better life awaiting his family in Colorado. There were seven in the family, six of whom were girls. Reaching Kansas they paused for two and a half years to set up a homestead, but German had his heart set on Colorado, and despite his family's great reluctance to move yet again, John German pulled up stakes and started west once more on August 15, 1874, following the Smoky Hill Road.

On the morning of the 11th, Medicine Water's party struck the German camp. John and his wife, Lydia, were killed in the initial assault, as was Stephen and the eldest daughter, Rebecca who was raped. Seventeen-year-old Catherine German saw her father shot and her mother tomahawked in the head. An Indian woman, perhaps Mochi then buried a tomahawk in the lifeless John's skull. The remaining five German sisters, Catherine, with an arrow in her thigh, recalled a big Indian pulling the arrow out and then thrusting her on a horse. Catherine, along with her sisters, Joanna, fifteen, Sophia, thirteen, Julia, seven and Adelaide, five, were taken captive. It was a morning of horrors that put one in mind of the Whitman family in far-off Oregon nearly three decades earlier. Eventually, the four German sisters would be rescued, but the suffering and humiliation they endured during their weeks of captivity may only be imagined. The two older girls, especially, were beaten, raped frequently, and forced to perform the most menial of tasks.

Meanwhile, even as Miles struggled with his supply problem, his competitor, Ranald Mackenzie marched his crack 4th Cavalry out of Fort Clark north to Fort Concho on September 17, arriving three days later. This campaign was the third in four years for the 4th regiment. For this campaign, Mackenzie had at his disposal eight companies of the 4th, plus four of the 10th Infantry and one of the 11th. A contingent of Tonkawa, Lipan Apaches, and Seminole—Negro scouts rounded out the expedition; in all some 600 men. Unlike Miles, Mackenzie paid closer attention to his supply line. The expedition passed in review for Mackenzie and his boss, General Augur, after which Mackenzie and Augur rode on to Fort Griffin so Mackenzie could make certain that supplies would follow. Augur then issued his final instructions. Mackenzie was to follow the Indians wherever they went. Meanwhile, the expedition had taken the field, marching northwest to establish a base camp 150 miles west of Fort Griffin.

Rejoining the expedition, Mackenzie did not tarry long at his base camp but pushed on north, skirting the edge of the Cap Rock, which he reached on the 22nd. A severe storm, not unlike the one that had pummeled Miles now struck Mackenzie's column, forcing a halt. When the storm passed on the 25th, Mackenzie resumed his march toward Tule Canyon with the cavalry, leaving the five Infantry companies to protect the wagon train. Mackenzie divided the eight companies of his regiment into two four-company battalions, one under Captain Napoleon Bonaparte McLauglin (McLaughlin) the other under Captain Eugene Beauharnais Beaumont; both Civil War veterans.

The Battle of Palo Duro Canyon

At Tule Canyon, Mackenzie's far ranging scouts reported crossing the trail of a large pony herd. Mackenzie sent Beaumont and his battalion in pursuit, while he (Mackenzie) waited in Tule Canyon with the rest of the command. Beaumont's horsemen pursued the Indians for five miles under a full moon—a Comanche moon it was called in these parts—but was unable to overtake the Indians. Mackenzie meanwhile had selected a new campsite five miles down-canyon, where the expedition rested and awaited a further move on the part of the Indians. The wait also gave time for Captain Henry Lawton to bring up the wagon train. Indian sign was present everywhere and Mackenzie guessed the Indians might strike, but if so he would be ready. Security was tight, especially around the horses. The men slept with weapons handy. About midnight, just as Mackenzie had sensed, some 250 Indians attacked, but the well prepared defenses repelled the attackers, who only managed to wound three horses. After two hours of exchanging fire, the Indians withdrew. At midnight, Lawton's supply train lumbered into camp, having been unaware of the stiff fight just ended. Throughout the rest of the night, the Indians maintained a sniping fire on the troops until Mackenzie dispatched a detachment of scouts to drive them off. At dawn they appeared in mounted force across a mesa. It was an impressive sight, but when challenged, the Indians refused to accept the challenge and withdrew, to seemingly simply disappear from the face of the earth.

There was an explanation, of course, for presently scouts reported locating the main Indian encampment deep in one of the many canyons cut into the Cap Rock. This was Palo Duro Canyon—literally, canyon of hard wood. Canyons such as this—and there were many—provided wonderful hiding places for the Indians. Besides, the Kiowa prophet Maman-ti said they would be safe in Palo Duro Canyon. The story is told that a former *Comanchero*, José Tafoya, impressed by Mackenzie as a scout, finally revealed the location to Mackenzie but only after the colonel made him an offer he couldn't refuse, namely his life. Tafoya had developed a successful business relationship with the Comanches as a cattle trader and was understandably reluctant to see that brought to a close, but when threatened with hanging the old reprobate leaned in favor of immediacy. Tafoya well knew what the Comanches would do to him if they learned he had divulged the location of their hideaway, but he was faced with death here and now. The story may or may not have a basis in fact. Mackenzie never reported the incident officially and said only that the canyon was discovered by his scouts. It is interesting to note here that Mackenzie's father, Alexander Slidell Mackenzie, earned a reputation for himself when, as captain of the U.S. Naval ship, *Somers*, he hanged a young midshipman named John Spencer, who happened to be the son of the Secretary of the Navy. The young man, it seems had been inciting mutiny and Captain Mackenzie took it on his own authority to hang the three mutineers. As might be expected, the incident raised a considerable furor. Mackenzie was subsequently cleared in a court-martial and went on to serve during the Mexican-American War. Whether the harsh type of discipline imposed by his father played any part in shaping young Ranald Mackenzie is not known, but throughout his army career, Ranald frequently employed harsh tactics. He was a martinet of the first rank.

However the discovery of Palo Duro Canyon came about, it was now Mackenzie's turn to seize the initiative and he prepared to do just that. It appeared the Indian trail led southwest, but Mackenzie now knew they would be found in Palo Duro. He also knew that the Indians would be watching to see whether he followed the trail they had set for him. So, the colonel who could be just as canny as the quarry he was chasing waited until past midnight on September 27 then marched his command north toward Palo Duro Canyon.

Early morning of the 28th, just about the time that the pre dawn light allows some visibility, Mackenzie and his scouts reached the edge of the giant canyon—located south of present Amarillo. If Mackenzie was a gloating man there was no better time to gloat than this very moment. For down in the abyss of this magnificent canyon, 1,000 feet deep and 120 miles long, could be barely discerned the dim shapes of tipis. A collection of Indian villages, Cheyenne, Comanche, and Kiowa, stretched for two miles along the Prairie Dog Town Fork of the Red River. The soldiers would not realize the extent of the encampments until they reached the floor of the canyon and opened the fight. Clearly Mackenzie had outsmarted the Indians. The Seminole-Negro scouts were aghast at what they took to be the huge number of sheep and goats, though so great was the distance it was impossible to distinguish goats or sheep from horses; this was what Mackenzie had prayed for.

To Lieutenant William Thompson, his chief of scouts, Mackenzie said "Mr. Thompson, take your men down and open the fight." The question now was how to get down into the canyon? Day light was building and Mackenzie feared he would lose the element of surprise. Then a narrow, winding path that barely deserved being called a trail was discovered. The Tonkawas and Seminole-Negro scouts led the way followed by A and E Companies of Beaumont's battalion, the men leading their horses, ever so carefully down this goat track trail in the still dim light of the emerging day.[12]

Halfway down, a lone warrior spotted the soldiers. Unbelievably, however, instead of sounding a general alarm he seems to have dashed into his lodge to apply war paint. The soldiers were totally vulnerable as they descended the rocky face of the canyon wall. Had this lone warrior sounded the clarion call, the Indians might well have turned Mackenzie's surprise attack into a grand disaster. As it was the advance elements reached the canyon floor, formed a skirmish line and promptly charged through the first village, guns blazing.

Meanwhile, leaving Captain McLaughlin's battalion on the rim as a reserve, Mackenzie joined Beaumont's other two companies, H and L and followed the advance elements down the narrow and dangerous trail to the valley floor. Wasting no time Mackenzie and Beaumont drove the two companies on down the valley, through one village after another. Bedlam reigned on the valley floor: soldiers, some on foot some on horseback, firing, Indians yelling, fleeing. Some Indians tried to fight back, taking up positions along the canyon walls.

Like all military commanders who conducted campaigns against the Plains tribes, Mackenzie knew that nothing would destroy their ability to carry out hostile activities more than the loss of their horses; without mobility they were lost. Accordingly, Beaumont at the head of his own Company H charged down the canyon some two miles and returned driving more than 1,400 Indian horses before them.

Although there was some resistance on the part of the Indians, it was not a tough fight as such affairs went; only three Indians were killed. Mackenzie lost a dozen horses and mules and one man wounded. By mid-afternoon, the villagers had largely fled and Mackenzie, reinforced now by three of McLaughlin's four companies, began a systematic destruction of the village and its contents. The Indian scouts had a field day, looting.

Mackenzie's victory at Palo Duro Canyon was one of the most important in the Western Indian wars. Although the battle did not end Indian resistance on the Southern Plains, the loss of so many horses and so much equipage proved a serious setback for the tribes. Although the loss of warriors was slight and the various bands remained intact—indeed, Quannah Parker's band of Kwahadi Comanches were among those not present, being camped far to the south—the loss of so many horses and much needed supplies robbed the tribes of mobility and the ability to survive. Following the destruction of the villages, Mackenzie, who chose not to follow the fleeing Indians, marched his command, along with the captured horse herd, to the rim of the canyon, then twenty miles to their supply camp at Tule Canyon. Of the 1,424 horses captured, Mackenzie had 350 of the choicest animals cut out for the scouts and his regiment. The rest, more than a thousand horses, were systematically slaughtered by firing squads in what must have been a thoroughly depressing assignment. Eventually, the carcasses of these animals would be picked clean by the buzzards and their bones—a huge bleached pile—would be a gruesome landmark in Tule Canyon for years to come. Later, there would be reports of a ghost herd thundering through the canyon.

Even as the 4th Cavalry was working its way down the treacherous path to the bottom of Palo Duro Canyon, Colonel Davidson was searching the headwaters of the Red River, looking unsuccessfully for Mackenzie. Davidson had formed his expedition and issued marching orders on September 4. His force consisted of seven troops of the 9th Cavalry, two troops of the 10th Cavalry, and four companies of the 11th Infantry, plus a section of mountain howitzers and forty-four Tonkawa Indian scouts; in all some 600 men, took the field on the 10th, marching west out of Fort Sill.

None of the five field commanders had any idea where the other four columns were or how they had fared. Not even the department commanders had heard anything. It was one of the hazards of having multiple columns of troops in the field simultaneously; it was almost impossible for them to communicate with each other. By mid-October Mackenzie had reported in and word of his victory went out over the wires to Sheridan and beyond.

The other columns had not been idle. On October 11 and 12 Colonel Buell, with five troops of the 9th Cavalry and one from the 10th, plus two companies of infantry, headed northwest out of Fort Griffin, Texas, following a warm trail. After burning two deserted villages on the Salt Fork of the Red River he continued on toward the Canadian River, at which point the Indians he had been following, dispersed and Buell, his horses fatigued and in need of supplies, turned back. At the same time, Major Price's troops, operating out of New Mexico, had also been searching the region for hostiles, though without any particular success.

Nelson Miles, who had been the first column in the field and the first to strike the Indians, and who likely had his nose out of joint upon hearing of Mackenzie's victory, had at last gotten re-supplied and had taken the field again in late October. Intelligence reported that Indians had taken refuge in the western reaches of the Staked Plains. Miles hoped to get behind the Indians and drive them east to be caught by the other columns. The operational strategy worked, to a degree. On November 8, Lieutenant Frank Baldwin's detachment attacked Grey Beard's Cheyenne camp—more than 100 lodges on McClellan Creek. Baldwin, as able a field leader as one could hope to find, stormed into the village, surprising the occupants and pursuing them for a dozen miles. Baldwin's victory had an added bonus, for here they found two of the four German girls, Adelaide and Julia. The rescue of the two girls built hope that the two older sisters, Catherine and Sophia, might yet be found as well. Baldwin's victory would have been complete had Major Price attacked Grey Beard's band as it fled eastward, but Price failed to take advantage of the opportunity. Displeased by Price's failure to nab Grey Beard, Miles relieved him of command, replacing him with Captain Charles Hartwell, who responded to the promotion by attacking a small body of Cheyennes, possibly from Grey Beard's band, and chased them into Palo Duro Canyon where they managed to elude the troops.

As fall deepened west Texas was struck by a series of "Blue Texas Northers," a weather condition, that, while not unique, seems so to those who experience its fierceness. The norther season runs from November to March and is characterized by precipitous drops in temperature, fierce winds, and drenching rain or snow storms. The term "blue norther" seems to have originated because in the vastness of the region the sky often appears a dark threatening blue while the storm shrieks through the area. Other parts of the Great Plains also experience such fierce storms, but only those that strike Texas are named after the state.

During November 1874, the Staked Plains were hit time and again by these northers. Rain, snow, sleet, and biting cold made campaigning a true nightmare. As miserable as conditions were, though, Miles's troops still found cause to sing "Marching Through Georgia," as they slogged along. Miles himself suffered frostbite on one ear and despite a buffalo robe and six blankets found it difficult to sleep. Horses died and men suffered greatly, and it was no less hard on the Indians. Under such conditions, weather proved the more challenging adversary for soldiers and Indians alike. The Indians, though, would survive somehow; they were in their natural element. For the Army, further campaigning under such conditions was pointless and field operations were terminated. Horses were worn out and the regiments were badly in need of rest and refitting. Accordingly, field commanders returned the troops to their duty stations. Aside from Mackenzie's victory at Palo Duro Canyon and Baldwin's strike on Grey Beard's village, the five-pronged campaign could hardly be thought of as successful in the tactical sense, but overall it did achieve the desired end by forcing the Indians to seek the security of the agencies. The Army won the Red River War not so much because they whipped the Indians in battle but through an aggressive policy of pursuit that resulted in victory through attrition.

If the weather had been tough on the troops in the field, it had made life equally difficult for the Indians, who gradually began to drift into the agencies. By early March 1875 more than 800 Cheyennes came into Darlington and surrendered their weapons. Stone Calf who had acquired the two remaining German sisters, Catherine and Sophia, surrendered them as well. And other bands followed. The outstanding Comanche bands proved the most recalcitrant. In April 200 turned themselves in, and in June Quanah Parker and his band finally surrendered, essentially ending serious resistance on the Southern Plains.

Although the so-called hostile bands had now joined the less militant groups, it did not mean they also surrendered their disaffection and unrest. The Indians were tired and hungry, worn out from constant pursuit by the army. As detested as was the reservation life, their backs were to the wall. The federal government was now faced with the decision of what to do with the troublesome leaders, especially ones like Satanta, who it will be recalled had been released from the Texas State Prison earlier in the hope that in so doing he and his followers might be persuaded to walk the path of peace. That didn't happen of course and this time there would be no second chance. The Kiowa chief was returned to the Huntsville, Texas, prison, where, three years later, he took his own life by jumping from an upstairs window.

Elsewhere at the agencies, there was an effort underway to compile a list of hard-core offenders. At Darlington, a Cheyenne named Black Horse was being manacled when some of his own people chided him for not trying to escape. Unable to stand the taunt, he tried to escape and was quickly shot down, but the gunfire threatened others who had been watching. Probably a little uncertain and fearful enough as it was, the ruckus caused about 150 Cheyennes to flee to a spot on the North Canadian River where a stash of weapons was awaiting those who attempted to escape. They were promptly pursued by three troops of cavalry, supported by a Gatling gun. The troops poured volley after volley into the Indian positions, but were unable to dislodge them and the fugitives escaped in the darkness. Notwithstanding, it had been a fierce little fight, with nineteen soldiers wounded and half a dozen Indians killed.

Some of these Cheyennes eventually returned to Darlington, having learned of an amnesty offered by General Pope. However, sixty, under a warrior named Little Bull, elected to try and reach their Northern Cheyenne brethren and by late April had reached northwestern Kansas, where at last they were caught on the morning of April 23, 1875, near the town of Atwood, Kansas, not far from the Nebraska line, by Troop H of the 6th Cavalry commanded by twenty-six-year-old Second Lieutenant Austin Henely. Young and boyish looking Austin Henely was an Irish immigrant who had served on the Kansas frontier since his graduation from West Point in 1872. In the ensuing fight on Sappa Creek—called Dark Water Creek by the Cheyennes—twenty-seven Indians were killed, of whom eight were women and children. Two soldiers were killed. From a numerical standpoint, there were more Indians killed in this small fight than in any of the other battles during the Red River War. Interestingly enough it was the last battle of that War and largely ended major Indian-white conflict on the Southern Plains.

The Mexican Border Crisis

Compared to Canada, the Mexican border was a nest of trouble and not just by Indian raiders either, although they were the principal source of trouble. Bandits and cattle rustlers were also active along the border, where the harsh, rugged terrain lent itself to outlaw activity. Since the days of the Texas Revolution it had never been a truly peaceful area.

The decade of the 1870s saw a rise in Indian depredations in extreme southwest Texas. Bands of Indian raiders who established villages in the mountains of northern Mexico periodically swept across the border to raid and plunder in Texas. The region southwest of San

Antonio was particularly hard hit by these raiders who consisted mainly of Kickapoos, but Lipan and Mescalero Apaches were also involved. It was a win-win situation for the Indians who could dash across the border, raid ranches and outlying settlements in Texas then return to the safety of their camps in Mexico knowing that they were safe from U.S. troops who dared not cross the border in pursuit.

By 1865 the Kickapoos, who had been migrating to Texas from Kansas over the years, were present in the state in substantial numbers and may actually have been in the area as early as 1812. Originally the Mexican government had invited them to Texas as mercenaries of sorts to fight the Comanches and Kiowas. Texans, however, saw them in pretty much the same light as they did Comanches and Kiowas, which is to say, as enemies, and attacked their villages whenever the opportunity presented itself. And of course the Kickapoos were quick to strike back. Suffice it to say that neither side was particularly careful about making a distinction between friend and foe.

Public outcry over these raids prompted the U.S. State Department to seek Mexican permission for U.S. troops to cross the border when in hot pursuit. Not surprisingly, the effort was destined to fail because of the complicated political picture. As a consequence, President Grant elected to skirt international protocol.

It might have been called Operation Retaliation, but it wasn't; indeed, it had no official name. In fact, officially, no such operation existed. It was a back-door deal in the truest sense of the word and the man selected to carry it out was Colonel Ranald Slidell Mackenzie, long a favorite of both Grant and Sheridan. In March 1873, Mackenzie began preparing his 4th Cavalry regiment at Fort Clark, near present day Brackettville, where a century later John Wayne would film his version of the Alamo.

Early in April, Secretary of War William Belknap, General Christopher Augur, commanding the Department of Texas, and General Sheridan huddled with Mackenzie in deep secret at San Antonio. No record was committed to paper, for obvious reasons, but as it happened, present also was Mackenzie's adjutant, Lieutenant Robert Carter who gave us his version of the meeting in a later book chronicling his experiences as a frontier officer in a book entitled *On the Border with Mackenzie*. As Carter recalled, Sheridan directed Mackenzie to cross the border and weave a path of destruction through the villages of the Indian raiders. The colonel was told not to worry about repercussions; his actions would be backed by the president and himself (Sheridan). It is interesting to note that General of the Army Sherman was not taken into confidence here; quite possibly because he would have opposed such a plan and in fact did so when a similar situation arose several years later, involving Nelson Miles and Sitting Bull along the Canadian border.

As Mackenzie prepared for his covert mission, his scouts slipped across the border to locate the enemy and in mid–May reported finding three villages of Kickapoos, Lipans and Mescaleros—perhaps 150 lodges in all—near Remolino, some forty miles west of Piedras Negras, southwest of San Antonio. This was the report Mackenzie was waiting for, but even better, the scouts reported that most of the warriors were away on a raid. Here were conditions made to order. Wasting no time, Mackenzie struck south with 6 companies of the 4th Cavalry—some 400 men—plus a mule pack train and two dozen Seminole Indian scouts.

On the morning of the 18th Mackenzie struck the village. Surprise was complete. What Indians were able, fought back, but there was little opportunity for a successful defense. The nearby camps of Lipans and Mescaleros, hearing the sounds of battle, had managed to escape. When it was over, nineteen Indians were dead and another forty were taken captive. Mackenzie's losses were one killed and two wounded. After torching the village,

Mackenzie returned to U.S. soil. The Mexican government complained about the violation of its border of course, but it was a timid protest and quickly faded.

The swift attack captured public fancy particularly in Texas, but the attack could scarcely be seen as even a tactical victory, since Mackenzie's troopers faced almost no opposition. And the actual raiding power of the Indians had not been affected. Still, the raid did serve its purpose in that it temporarily resolved the border problem with Indian raiders at least it did with the Kickapoos who seemed to take the attack more seriously. The mere fact that U.S. soldiers had crossed the border and attacked villages that were presumed safe was enough to prompt the Kickapoos to negotiate for permission to return to the U.S. and by 1874 most of them had abandoned Mexico for residence in Indian Territory. The Lipan and Mescalero Apaches, on the other hand, persisted in being a source of periodic trouble for several years.

Between the years 1875 and 1881, Brigadier General Edward Ord commanding the Military Department of Texas had to deal with a persistent problem of Indian raiders, a responsibility he met head on and which endeared him to Texans who had suffered at the hands of raiders. Fifty-seven years old in 1875 and bearing the long and rather unusual name of Edward Otho Cresap, Ord was a West Point graduate and veteran of the Seminole, and Civil Wars. Sherman, who had been his West Point roommate, once characterized him as an officer who would swim an ice-cold stream even if there was a bridge available. An engineer by training, Ord would one day design Fort Sam Houston, Texas.

There was nothing timid about Ord's approach to dealing with the Indian problem, and his field commander during these years was poured from the same mould. Thirty-eight-year-old Lieutenant Colonel William Rufus Shafter was another Civil War veteran with a Medal of Honor to his credit. In 1866, Shafter had been promoted to lieutenant colonel and given command of the Black 24th Infantry, which he tirelessly led across west Texas on a series of tough campaigns against Indian raiders, which included crossing the Mexican border on occasion and earned him the sobriquet of "Pecos Bill." Two decades later, now a ponderous 300 pounds and afflicted with gout, Pecos Bill Shafter, carrying the twin stars of a major general, would lead the American Expeditionary Force into Cuba. Shafter also carries the distinction of being the officer who initiated court-martial proceedings against Lieutenant Henry Flipper, the first Black graduate of West Point.

On July 30, 1876, a twenty-man detachment of the 24th, under the command of thirty-five-year-old Lieutenant John Lapham Bullis, supported by twenty Seminole scouts surprised a Lipan village near Zaragosa, destroying two dozen lodges. Bullis, who would prove to be Shafter's hammer in these campaigns, would in later years, be honored by citizens of West Texas for his service in ending the Indian menace.

But the border situation was steadily becoming a thorny political issue. Mackenzie's unofficial raid had strained relations, even though it resulted in no reaction. Tension was growing and businessmen were anxious for a restoration of normal relations. Meanwhile, however, the Indian problem simply refused to go away. Violation of the border by U.S. troops in pursuit of Indian raiders continued although crossings were infrequent. The picture changed on June 1, 1877, however, when President Rutherford B. Hayes officially authorized a penetration of the border when in "hot pursuit" of raiders; this being the operative phrase. Up to this point border crossing violations by military commanders had been under the table and on the sly, but the Hayes pronouncement made it official and public, and that raised the ire of Mexican officials. President Porfirio Diaz could hardly ignore such a slap at the inviolability of his nation and promptly authorized his military commander in the north to repel any U.S. troops who had crossed the border, but despite the rhetoric, neither side really wanted a full blown conflict and managed to avoid a head-on meeting.

The Diaz revolution, begun in 1876, had come to power a year later. President Diaz, sensitive to the strong anti–American feeling in his country, used that to good advantage in his dealings with the U.S. There was plenty of quid pro quo here, too, as President Hayes refused to recognize the Diaz regime. Thus, the famous order of June 1 exacerbated tension between the two countries. Some in Congress suspected that President Hayes was looking for an excuse to go to war with Mexico, resulting in the formation of congressional committees to look into the tortured border situation. General Ord and Colonel Shafter both testified. Shafter especially argued that there ought to be no limitations placed on their pursuit of Indian raiders, and that if Mexico objected we should declare war. It was a volatile situation and one not helped any by the attitudes of General Ord and Colonel Shafter.

Both Sherman and Sheridan were increasingly coming to believe that Ord should be replaced. The situation needed a less aggressive commander who appreciated the politics involved. To relieve Ord, however, would raise the ire of Texans; especially the Democrats who represented a powerful influence in Washington, but that might have to be risked.

Meanwhile, there were fears aplenty that the winter of 1877–1878 would witness costly raids by the Indians and the elected representatives from Texas clamored for more border protection. The situation called for Sheridan to walk a fine line. On the one hand he was to avoid doing anything that might exacerbate matters, while on the other he was encouraged to take whatever steps he deemed prudent to provide protection, which led him to send Mackenzie's 4th Cavalry back to Texas from Crook's Department of the Platte in December 1877.

At this juncture, General Ord decided that a good old fashioned demonstration might serve to impress Mexican authorities and Indians as well with the power of the U.S. Actually it was to be a comparative flexing of muscles, with both countries demonstrating its military might. On June 12, 1878, a grand parade was held just across the Rio Grande. Eight troops of Mackenzie's cavalry, three battalions of Shafter's infantry, and three batteries of artillery paraded their might. The Mexican force lined up to challenge this show of force was quickly intimidated.

Although the demonstration was highly satisfying from the U.S. perspective, especially Texans, it did not win the United States any Mexican friends and tensions along the border remained strained for the next two years. At long last, in 1880, President Hayes opted to recognize the Diaz government and two years later, a border treaty was signed.

Sherman, meanwhile, was on the verge of replacing Ord, but in a stunning development President Hayes took it upon himself to direct that Ord be retired from active duty, thereby making room for Nelson Miles to receive his long coveted brigadier's star. Sherman was furious. Ord had been his West Point roommate and he had great respect for the man as a soldier. A congressional delegation, consisting mainly of Texans who appreciated Ord's service saw to it that he was retired as a full major general.

VI

Iowa, Minnesota and the Northern Plains

Prologue: Little Crow to Sitting Bull

Unlike the Southern and Central Plains, settlement on the Northern Plains—herein defined as the region lying between the Platte River and the Canadian line—was somewhat slower to develop and as a consequence, Indian troubles had been minimal, comparatively speaking. However, as a result of the bloody 1862 uprising in Minnesota and the discovery of gold in southwestern Montana (then part of Idaho Territory) that picture began to change rather quickly, particularly as the Northern Pacific Railroad commenced to spread west in earnest.

During the years immediately following the passage of Lewis and Clark, the only U.S. penetration of the Upper Missouri River region was by fur companies who sought to make a fortune trapping—mainly beaver—and trading with the tribes of the region, of which the Blackfeet, Lakota and Arikara (commonly called Rees) were the dominant powers. Relations with these tribes were unpredictable and tense, and clashes did occur. In the spring of 1823 an attack on a Missouri River trading post resulted in the death of a prominent Ree chief, thereby exacerbating tensions between these Indians and Americans.

But there was more to it than that. Although the Treaty of Ghent (1815) ending the War of 1812 had finally compelled the British to abandon their outposts in the what was then known as the Northwest Territory, the British managed to retain a presence in the Upper Mississippi River Valley, the Missouri River basin and the Columbia River region. To what extent the British may have been involved in stirring up trouble between American fur companies and the Indians is somewhat muddy and controversial, but certainly there were those who saw the British as instigators.

Conflict on the Northern Plains: War with the Arickaras

> *I deplore the death of those of my brave Countrymen who fell victim to the scalping knife of the A'rickaras.*—Benjamin O'Fallon, June 19, 1823[1]

For the most part, clashes between trappers and tribes of the region did not involve the U.S. Army. However, an exception to that occurred in 1823 when a party of Rees attacked a trapping brigade in the employ of one, William Henry Ashley. Given the fledgling U.S. government's concern about protecting its interests in this region, military intervention was deemed warranted.

As a consequence, in the spring of 1823 Col Henry Leavenworth, commanding the 6th Infantry at Fort Atkinson, Nebraska (Council Bluffs), moved up the Missouri River with a 200-man force and two pieces of artillery in relief of the Ashley party. Meanwhile, the Blackfeet, scourge of the mountain men, had also attacked a party of trappers along the Yellowstone River and killed seven. This turn of events resulted in another 100 reinforcements sent to Leavenworth, who, in the meantime, was joined by 50 trappers, led by one Joshua Pilcher of the Missouri Fur Company. Augmenting this force was a party of 750 Sioux—hereditary enemies of the Arikara. Perhaps harkening back to General Anthony Wayne's "Legion of the U.S." Leavenworth decided to call his expedition the "Missouri Legion."

The Arikaras were grouped in two pallisaded or walled villages. As the expedition approached, the Sioux, ranging out ahead attacked and forced the Rees to retired behind their palisade. Arriving with his troops, Leavenworth surrounded both villages. After lobbing a few shells into the villages, Leavenworth prepared an all-out assault but then changed his mind, notwithstanding the pleas of his officers and especially the Sioux, who hungered for an attack. Leavenworth, however, stood by his decision, hoping that the Rees might be persuaded to talk peace without a fight. Disgusted, the Sioux pulled out. But Leavenworth's patience paid off and on August 11, the Rees signed a peace treaty, but did so knowing that the American traders wanted more in the way of satisfaction than simply a signature on a piece of paper. That night the Arikaras burned their villages and fled west out of harm's immediate way. Casualties on both sides were negligible, with Ashley's company having suffered the loss of fifteen. Leavenworth reported no casualties and soon took his command back down the river to St. Louis. The whole affair was called a war, though it scarcely deserves to be tabbed as such.

Spirit Lake, Iowa, 1857

He was called Inkpaduta of the Wahpekute band of Santee Sioux. The name is variously translated as Scarlet Point, Red Cap or Red End, depending on the source. Along with a few other hard-liners, Inkpaduta refused to sign the 1851 Treaty of *Traverse de Sioux*, notwithstanding its acceptance by the large majority of Santees.[2]

Born about 1805—date of his birth varies from 1800 to 1815 near the Canon River in southern Minnesota, Inkpaduta survived smallpox as a child, but his pocked-marked face bore permanent ravages of the disease.

As a consequence of the murder of the chief of the Wahpekutes by a rival named Wamdesapa, who also happened to be Inkpaduta's father, Inkpaduta and a group of followers—supporters of Wamdesapa—were banished from the tribe and regarded as renegades. Having been thus ostracized, they did not see the necessity or importance of signing of the *Traverse de Sioux* treaty. As outcasts, they roamed through eastern Dakota and parts of western Minnesota and Iowa.

At some point in his life, Inkpaduta became an avowed hater of whites, possibly because his brother, along with his entire family were slain by a white whiskey seller and horse thief, though one historian has suggested that a more likely explanation is simply that he inherited a rather sociopathic bent from his father who was well noted for his temper and violent ways. But however he came by it, Inkpaduta seems to have had it in for the whites, although historian/biographer Paul Beck suggests that historians have created an image of Inkpaduta that is not entirely true; that is he was not the evil incarnate figure that some have made him out to be.

The winter of 1856–1857 was particularly severe. All the Indians suffered even those receiving annuities. For Inkpaduta and his followers conditions were even tougher because having refused to sign the treaty they received no annuities. Game was scarce and these Indians took to begging among the settlements in order to survive. On one occasion they dined on a dog that had bitten one of the Santees. Confronted by a posse the Indians were forced to surrender their weapons which left them with no way to survive. What happened next was predictable. Angry and hungry, on March 8 and 9 the Indians attacked a small settlement on the Okoboji Lakes—west of present Estherville—killed thirty-four people and took three women prisoners. Moving north, they killed a settler near Spirit Lake and took his wife prisoner. Continuing their northward movement, they struck again at Springfield, west of New Ulm in Jackson County, Minnesota. Here they attacked a trading post, operated by Charles, William, and George Wood. Charles and William were killed in the attack, along with some forty settlers.

When he learned of the events around the Okoboji Lakes, Indian Agent Charles Flandrau, who would later play a pivotal role in the Minnesota uprising, requested military assistance from Fort Ridgely in the Minnesota River Valley. The request sent Captain Bernard Bee marching out of Fort Ridgely with a relief column which unfortunately did not reach Springfield until after the Indians had departed. As one historian has pointed out, though, this was probably a good thing as Inkpaduta and his followers would probably have killed the captives. As for Captain Bee, he would later join the Confederate Army and as a brigadier general, his brigade was one of two to receive the initial Union attack at Bull Run in July 1861.

Flandrau and the Commissioner of Indian Affairs in Washington were the ones most responsible for resolving the crisis which understandably had settlers in the region on edge. Indeed, there were rumors that a major uprising was unfolding. Confronted with the fact that the Indians still held captives, Flandrau and the commissioner were forced to back off from taking any punitive action that might endanger the lives of the hostages. They finally managed to persuade some of the friendly Indians to see if Inkpaduta and his band might be amenable to negotiating for the release of the hostages.

When this led to no resolution, in May 1858, the territorial legislature voted a $10,000 reward for the return of the captives. Interestingly enough, the legislature did not actually have the money. Nevertheless, no sooner was the announcement promulgated—five days, actually—some Wahpetons came in to one of the missions with a captive. In return they asked for and were apparently paid $500. This surely seemed like a solution to Flandrau, who promptly sent out another party of Wahpetons to bring back the remaining captives. They returned with one of the captives and reported that the other two had been killed.

With the captive issue unfortunately only partially resolved, Flandrau was now ready to take punitive action. Dame Fortune then appeared to grant him a boon when it was reported that Inkpaduta's son and his wife were at the Yellow Medicine Agency. Backed by a detachment of soldiers from Fort Ridgely, Flandrau went immediately to the agency where Inkpaduta's son was killed, evidently while being apprehended; his wife was taken prisoner. But then Flandrau suddenly found himself surrounded by angry Indians, forcing him to release the woman. Flandrau himself and his escort, apparently, were allowed to remain at the agency as prisoners until finally relieved by a battery of artillery from Fort Ridgely.

During that summer of 1858 there was tension at the agency. The Indians were restless and many were angry. Incidents such as the one where a Sisseton stabbed a soldier reflected an underlying current of hostility that burst into flame four summers later. Meantime, Charles Flandrau left his post to participate in the political affairs of the new state, Minnesota having entered the Union that year. Flandrau's replacement, one William Cullen urged the Santees to assume responsibility for the apprehension and punishment of Inkpaduta and his followers. The Indians refused unless backed by soldiers, which the new Indian Commissioner, James Denver, was reluctant to do. Finally, Little Crow, now the nominal head man of the Santees, volunteered to try and tack down Inkpaduta. With a hundred followers, Little Crow set out on his mission. On August 4 he returned, reporting that they had killed three of the Wahpekutes, but Inkpaduta and several followers had managed to escape into Dakota Territory.

The Spirit Lake Massacre, as it came to be called, laid the groundwork for the bloody uprising in Minnesota that followed four years later. Although there were plenty of signs pointing to the troubles of 1862, but like most such events they become visible only retrospectively. Inkpaduta remained an implacable foe of the whites until his death. He would fight General Sully at Whitestone Hill in 1863 and, so far as is known, was in the big Indian village that Custer found on the Little Bighorn. Like Sitting Bull, Inkpaduta refused to surrender and fled to Canada, where he died in 1879, although the year of his death like that of his birth is uncertain.

Bloodbath in the Heartland: Minnesota, Summer 1862

[Bishop Whipple] talked to me about the rascality of this Indian business until I felt it down to my boots.—President Abraham Lincoln, December 17, 1862.[3]

During the late summer of 1862, even as events in the east were building toward a terrible confrontation in Maryland, at a place called Antietam by the Union and Sharpsburg by the Confederates, an event of equal horror was unfolding in southwestern Minnesota.

Sunday, August 17, 1862

Four young Indian men: Brown Wing, Breaking Up, Killing Ghost, and Runs-Against-Something When Crawling, frustrated after an unsuccessful hunt, approach the farm of one Robinson Jones in Acton Township. Anger was building in these four young men, as it was in many Santees in the Minnesota River Valley that troubled summer of the Civil War's second year. The hunt had been unsuccessful, but they were also smarting over ill treatment at the hands of whites. The annuities guaranteed their people by treaty were delinquent ... again. Approaching the farm they discovered a cache of eggs. One of the four thought to take the eggs, but was warned by the others that these belonged to the farmer. Angered, the one who had found the eggs smashed them on the ground and accused his companions of being afraid of the white man. Emboldened by this the four approached farmer Jones and demanded liquor. Jones refused. A stand-off ensued, following which Jones decided to take the two friends who were then staying with him to join Mrs. Jones who was then visiting her son (by an earlier marriage), Howard Baker on his nearby farm. The four Indians decided to follow. Obviously not particularly fearful, Jones left behind his two children, ages fifteen and eighteen months.

Arriving at the Baker farm, the Indians proposed a shooting match, to which Jones and Baker consented. Whether this was a ploy on the part of the Indians is not clear, but in any event, once the shooting started, the four Indians suddenly turned on the whites, killing everyone, then stole horses and departed for their village. The incident triggered what soon came to be known as the Minnesota Massacre, an orgy of killing seldom equaled in U.S. history.

By the middle of the 19th century, the greater Siouan family was composed of three major divisions: the Teton Lakotas dwelled generally west of the Missouri River. The Yanktons and Yanktonais, who together were known as the Nakotas, lived generally in that portion of what is today central North Dakota. To the east of the Nakotas in the western and southwestern parts of Minnesota were the Dakotas, sometimes called the Santees. The Dakotas were further sub-divided into four tribes: Mdewakantons, Sisseton, Wahpeton, and Wahpekute.

During the 17th and 18th centuries, all Sioux—a French corruption of the word *Nadouessioux*, meaning snake or snakes, or enemy—had been primarily woodland Indians, until pressure from the larger and stronger Ojibways (Chippewa) forced them to seek a new homeland farther west. The Nakotas settled in central Dakota, while the Teton Lakota branch continued on to the Missouri River Country. Only the Dakotas remained in their traditional woodland environment.

In 1849, Congress created Minnesota Territory and nine years later, in 1858, granted full statehood to the region whose fertile land was attracting an increasing number of settlers. This was followed three years later in 1861, by the creation of Dakota Territory.

The Santees

With the steady influx of settlers into the Minnesota River Valley the federal government found it necessary to make arrangements with the native tribes of the region to accommodate the growing number of settlers.. The first such agreement took place in 1837 when the Mdewakanton band of the Santees agreed to sell five million acres of land on the east side of the Mississippi and remove to the west bank. Twenty years later, in 1851 the Santees (Dakotas) entered into two treaties with the United States at Mendota and *Traverse des Sioux*. By virtue of these agreements, the Santees ceded their land in southwestern Minnesota, plus a small tract of land in the southeastern part of the state. In return, the Indians were to receive something in excess of three million dollars in cash and annuities, which were to be paid annually for a period of fifty years. Additionally, the bands were to be relocated to a pair of twenty-mile-wide reservations situated along both sides of the Minnesota River between the community of New Ulm on the south and Big Stone Lake, approximately 140 miles to the north and bordering the present state of South Dakota.

The two reservations were arbitrarily divided by the Yellow Medicine River near present Granite Falls. The Upper Sioux Agency which was tasked with serving the northern reservation was located near the confluence of the Yellow Medicine and the Minnesota Rivers. The Upper Agency was home to the Sisseton and Wahpeton bands, in all, about 4,000 souls some of whom ignored the reservation boundary and lived in Dakota Territory. Near Redwood (present day Redwood Falls) was the Lower or Redwood Agency, which served 2,000–3,000 of the Mdewakanton and Wahpekute bands of Santees. With the arrival of statehood in 1858, a second treaty further reduced the size of the two reservations by taking more land along the north side of the Minnesota River.

A third ethnic group composed of mixed bloods, was to play a pivotal role in the uprising of 1862. Numbering perhaps 700, these people were mainly the offspring of Indian women and French traders. Some represented a second or third generation. It would have been hard to differentiate between whites and many of the mixed bloods who conducted their lives in much the same way that whites did farming and attending church regularly. These mixed-bloods stood as a shining example of what the U.S. Government wanted to see happen with all Indians: they had become acculturated, and in return for walking the white man's road, they were given preferential treatment by the Indian agents.

Between the signing of the Treaties of *Traverse des Sioux* and Mendota, the living conditions of the Santees had not improved any, indeed they had actually deteriorated, especially after the loss of the additional land in 1858. Some Indians had turned to farming, but were scorned by their kinsmen who refused to abandon the old ways and referred with derision to those who farmed as "farmer Indians" or Cut-Hairs because they had cut their hair short like the white men. Those who embraced the old ways were known as blanket Indians.

For these Santees reservation life was not working anymore than it did for other tribes. Whether things might have been different had the government done a better job of living up to its treaty promises is a moot point, but its failure to do so certainly exacerbated a worsening situation. The food shortage, brought on by the steadily declining wild game population could have been alleviated had the annuities guaranteed by the treaties, arrived in timely fashion, but they did not, and as a consequence, resentment among the Indians grew, particularly when alternate means of survival were reduced because of severe winter weather. And, as if that was not enough, when the annuities did arrive, the cash payment portion was first divided up and paid to the traders who had been selling merchandise to the Indians on credit, with the understanding that they would be reimbursed *first* when the annuities arrived. Whether the Indians fully understood this is doubtful. So, in any case, when the money did arrive, the Indians usually found themselves receiving far less than they expected.

By 1862 the Civil War had imposed on the federal government an almost crushing financial burden. Confronted by this obligation, the government was undecided as to whether it ought to honor the responsibility of paying the Indians their annuities in gold or paper, and so payment was delayed while officials argued about which to send. Second, the Homestead Act resulted in an increased number of new settlers in the area that proved more than a little disturbing to the Indians. On top of this, the wild game population was shrinking, and 1861–1862 was one of the coldest winters on record. Food was scarce and although traders' warehouses were full of food Agent Thomas Galbraith refused to distribute any to the Indians without payment, and the cash portion of the annuities was late. The Indians pleaded for food, but were turned down. Several thousand congregated around the Upper Agency, begging for food, and when their pleas were ignored they broke into the warehouse and helped themselves to flour. It was a tense moment. A call for help went out to Fort Ridgely, bringing on a detachment of soldiers commanded by Lieutenant Timothy Sheehan who arrived with a detachment of soldiers and two pieces of artillery. When Sheehan informed the Indians that he would open fire if they did not disperse, they finally backed down. For the moment, serious trouble was averted, but here was a sign that rebellion was at close at hand.

This then was the situation that existed when the four young Santees struck down the five white people on that otherwise peaceful Sunday afternoon in mid–August 1862.

When the four Indians returned to their village and reported what they had done, it created a mighty stir among villagers. Some feared retribution, but others saw it as the time to make war on the whites. The action at the Baker farm stirred up buried resentment among many of the Santees, but there was no real consensus as to what action, if any, ought to be taken. After conferring among themselves, village leaders decided to seek the counsel of Little Crow, most prominent and respected of the Santee leaders.

Little Crow

Little Crow or Taoyateduta, was a powerful and influential figure, who merits more attention than he has been given. Intelligent and shrewd, Little Crow became a leader of the first rank. Among indigenous people leaders, , he was, arguably, the most astute politician of them all. As his biographer, Gary Clayton Anderson, put it so succinctly, Little Crow "was a politician who happened to be an Indian."[4]

Born about 1810 in the Mdewakanton village of Kaposia, near the confluence of the St. Croix River with the Mississippi, southeast of present Minneapolis, Little Crow's early years were spent in the generally traditional way. He learned about woodland lore, hunting and war. He seems to have been possessed of great stamina and was known to be a fearless hunter. When he was about nine years old, white presence in the area of his home increased, due to the creation of Fort Snelling. By the time Little Crow reached his twenties his father Big Thunder, assumed the chieftainship of the Mdewakantons and no doubt provided Little Crow with a closer opportunity to learn how to deal with the steadily increasing number of whites who were moving into the area.

In addition to providing annuities to the tribes, the federal government also sought to bring an end to inter-tribal warfare. Big Thunder, however, seemed ill-inclined to honor these efforts, for in 1841, he led a war party north up the St. Croix River to attack a village of Ojibways, traditional enemies of the Santees. Two of Big Thunder's sons were killed in the raid. The attack brought retaliation from the Ojibways who killed a dozen Santees. As a consequence, the federal government hosted a peace parley at Fort Snelling in1843. This resulted in Big Thunder and the other principal chiefs agreeing to surrender the young men who broke the peace; whether the leaders agreed to surrender themselves is not clear.

Then, in 1845 Big Thunder died as a result of an accidental gunshot wound. Big Thunder had originally favored his youngest son, one of Little Crow's half brothers, to replace him as chief, a choice that caused trouble. Little Crow was apparently not thought of by Big Thunder as a good candidate because he had been living west of the Mississippi and had been too far removed from the political scene to be qualified.

Unwilling to accept the choice of his half brother as chief Little Crow challenged the choice. But Big Thunder seems not to have been the only one who doubted Little Crow's leadership qualities. Others among the Mdewakantons felt the same way. Moreover, Little Crow had earlier been rebuked for breaking the traditional hunting protocol by moving ahead of the main hunting party to gain a personal advantage. Little Crow had also come under fire for gambling and the use of liquor, and trading with the distant Teton Lakotas for buffalo robes. He was also reputed to have been a skillful card player. But if these were flaws, for which his tribesmen criticized him, they also recognized other qualities: physically strong, energetic and smart. And if he had been something of a rebel, he had also made friends among the whites and studied their ways. Indeed, it might be said that he was fascinated by white culture.

Things came to a head when Little Crow arrived at his home village of Kaposia soon after Big Thunder's death. Confronted by his two half-brothers who demanded that he leave, Little Crow challenged them to shoot which they did severely wounding Little Crow in the forearm. Taken to Fort Snelling, the surgeon recommended amputation, but Little Crow refused and returned to his village to recover, which he did eventually, though his arm remained crippled for the rest of his life. His two half brothers were later killed by some of Little Crows supporters. Thus, with challengers eliminated, Little Crow was now able to ascend to the position of chief.

Little Crow proved equal to the task of leading his people, too, displaying the qualities of leadership that many doubted he possessed. What seems to have set Little Crow apart from other noted Indian leaders was his curiosity about the white man's lifestyle and his efforts to adapt to that lifestyle, without at the same time forsaking the old tribal ways. Whether this was motivated by a genuine desire to truly become white in spirit, or whether it was fueled by political ambition is not entirely clear, but one is inclined to suspect the latter. In any case, by 1860, Little Crow had become the unquestioned leading figure of the Santees and was well regarded among the white community where he was considered a friend of many. He was a regular attendee at church, and moved among the white community as though he was one of them.

When confronted with the report of what had transpired at the Baker farm, Little Crow initially voiced his opposition to any further action, convinced that an all out war against the whites could only result in disaster for the Indians. Little Crow well knew that the whites had the men and resources to eventually devastate his people. At the same time, however, he had a powerful ego and took great pride in his skills as a warrior. Although opposed to war it seemed that the initiative had been seized; the first step taken. Many of his people were unhappy with the treatment they had been receiving from the whites and sought recourse. Faced with this surprising chain of events, Little Crow may well have wondered if perhaps the hour had at last come to strike back. The Indians were aware that many white soldiers had gone off to the east to fight in a great war, which meant there weren't as many of them in the area as there might otherwise have been. Exactly how big a factor this played in Little Crow's consideration is unknown, but in any case, he finally agreed to lead his people in a war against the white man, somewhat reluctantly we suspect, but only somewhat.

The Uprising Begins

War it would be. Early on August 18, 200–300 warriors came together at the Lower Agency even as some 80 agency employees went about their daily routines, completely unaware of the storm that suddenly descended on them. In the initial assault some 20 workers were killed and another 50 were taken captive. Their blood up, the Santees swept thru the agency looting and burning. One of those killed was a trader named Andrew Myrick, who had refused to extend credit to the Indians. Asked how the Indians would live if he refused them credit, Myrick reportedly said "let them eat grass." We can't say that Myrick actually uttered those words, but whether he did or didn't is a moot point; in all probability he said something along those lines. However, the exact wording is less important than the intended meaning. The Indians did not forget and when his body was found his mouth was stuffed with grass.[5]

About noon Captain John Marsh, commanding the 5th Minnesota Volunteers at nearby Fort Ridgely was alerted to the trouble at the Lower Agency by one of the survivors who had managed to elude capture. Others followed with more reports. Still Marsh was not convinced that the trouble was serious. Clearly, something had happened, however, but what kind of response was needed? Notwithstanding his doubts, Marsh assembled a column of 46 men and started out for the Lower Agency, leaving young Lieutenant Thomas Gere and twenty-seven men to hold the fort. At the same time, Marsh sent a dispatch to

Lieutenant Timothy Sheehan, commanding Company C, to return to Ridgely post haste. Recall that Sheehan, who had left Fort Ridgely the day before to march to Fort Ripley on the Upper Mississippi River, had actually stifled a potential outbreak at the Lower Agency just the month before and was sensitive to the mood of the Indians.

Ironically, on this same day, $70,000 in gold and silver specie arrived; the annuity payment for the Indians. It was of course late and one wonders whether if it had arrived earlier the trouble that erupted on August 17 might have been avoided? As it was, the money was now returned to Washington.

En route to the agency, Marsh reached Redwood Ferry, unaware that the Santees had overpowered the ferryman and taken control of the ferry, then hidden themselves in the bushes along the river. When Marsh approached, the Indians suddenly opened fire. Unable to retreat, Marsh led his men through the underbrush to the river, with Indians firing on the stunned soldiers. With no other option open to them, Marsh led his men into the water, where the captain himself soon drowned. Whether he was struck by a bullet, suffered a cramp or just panicked is not clear. In any event it fell to nineteen-year-old Sergeant John Bishop to extricate the fifteen survivors and try to make it back to Fort Ridgely. More than half of Marsh's original command had been killed.

Elsewhere, the Upper Agency had thus far been relatively quiet. There had been a few scattered reports of the trouble at the Lower Agency but nothing to really upset anyone here. Like Captain Marsh, most whites at the Upper Agency thought the stories they were hearing were exaggerated. As for the Indians at the agency, some had begun to think of joining the uprising, while others counseled against such a move.

For many of the full bloods and mixed bloods alike it was not an hour of easy choices. Most if not all bore a deep resentment of ill-treatment by the whites, and of course made no distinction between traders, government officials, and the average white settler, who in turn made no distinction among Indians. Notwithstanding, many full and mixed bloods, while anxious for pay back, also recognized the futility of turning on the white man, while others were angry and felt the time was ripe to strike back. Two notable exceptions at the Upper Agency were John Other Day, a Wahpeton Santee who had become a Christian and married a white woman and Joseph LaFramboise, a French mixed-blood. Both men reading the signs correctly, warned whites of the great danger that was unfolding and led many to take shelter in a large brick warehouse. That night, rampaging Santees torched a nearby trading post, but for some reason seemed not interested in bothering with the agency. Those whites who had taken refuge in the brick warehouse were temporarily safe. In the morning, Other Day led his group of sixty-two on a three-day march to the safety of Cedar City, some sixty miles distant. Angry Santees burned Other Day's farm for helping the whites. For his courage, Other Day would later be awarded $2,500 by the U.S. Government.

Word had also reached two missions located near the Upper Agency about the troubles. About thirty whites from the immediate neighborhood banded together and managed to make their way down to Fort Ridgely, while somehow managing to avoid roaming Santee war parties.

First Attack on New Ulm

As the summer of 1862 wound down, the settlers in the Minnesota River Valley quite unexpectedly found themselves living in the midst of a terrifying turn of events that just twenty-four hours earlier would have seemed completely unbelievable. Between New Ulm on the south and the Upper Agency, a sixty-mile swath, immigrant farmers—many of them

Refugees from the bloody Minnesota Sioux uprising.

German—were terrorized by angry Santees. Many were slain outright, with little distinction being made between gender and age. Some were taken captive and brutalized. Farms were burned. What perhaps was most terrifying was that many settlers suddenly found themselves attacked by Indians they had known personally and with whom they had been friendly. Some settlers tried to flee only to be caught, killed and mutilated. One woman who had been raking hay was found with a pitchfork sticking in her body, while nearby a man had been butchered by a scythe.

Back at Fort Ridgely, the garrison that had been stationed there to monitor and control the Indians, was now reduced to twenty-nine with the disaster that had befallen Captain Marsh, and seven of those were in the post hospital. The trouble didn't stop there, either. With Marsh's death, command of the post devolved to nineteen-year-old Lieutenant Thomas Gere, who was hardly in any condition to command, having come down with a case of mumps. No matter, Gere had to deal with nearly 300 panic-driven settlers who swarmed into the fort in a steady stream, looking for protection from the army. Although he must have been feeling lousy, young Gere wrote that night to Governor Alexander Ramsey and to the commanding officer at Fort Snelling, pleading for help. The letters were carried by a lone rider, Private William Sturgis, who made an amazing ride of 125 miles in 18 hrs. Gere didn't stop there, however. He also sent off an urgent plea, also carried by Sturgis, to Lieutenant Sheehan, urging him to return as quickly as possible.

Whether help would arrive in time was a good question. Gere ordered the women and children placed inside the large stone barracks and meanwhile established a defensive cordon around the perimeter of the post. Wagons, barrels—anything that could be used as protection made up the defensive line.

At this point, the Santees made their first major error in judgment. Little Crow, Big Eagle, and Mankato recognized the vulnerability of Fort Ridgely. Had they attacked they almost certainly would have had no difficulty overrunning the garrison and in that eventuality it surely would have had a significant impact on the outcome of the uprising. But as it was, the majority of Santees were enjoying the thrill of rampaging and looting. Downriver, a mere fifteen miles, New Ulm loomed as an irresistible prize, and so the moment passed. Little Crow and the others were unable to persuade their followers to strike Fort Ridgely now.

Then again, an immediate attack would have proven more difficult than it appeared at first to Little Crow and the other leaders. Even as the Indians began to move down river toward New Ulm, Lieutenant Sheehan and his company arrived at the fort, much, we might imagine, to Lieutenant Gere's great relief. As the senior officer, Sheehan assumed command of the post. Not only that, but hard on the heels of Sheehan came some fifty Renville Rangers who had been organized for Civil War service, but had not yet departed for the east. Private Sturgis had encountered them en route to delivering his messages. Advised of what was happening in the Minnesota River Valley, the Rangers elected to help out and rode to Fort Ridgely, where they arrived on the evening of August 19. Between the Rangers and Sheehan's men, there were now about 180 defenders at the fort, plus some 300 settlers.

Meanwhile, the seven-year-old community of New Ulm was the largest in the area with a population of 1,000. Word of the uprising had reached the residents of the town through a party of volunteers bound for the Union Army who themselves had been attacked. Survivors rushed back to New Ulm to warn the residents. Shortly thereafter groups of settlers arrived, bringing terror-filled stories with them. The residents wasted no time doing what they could to prepare for the defense of their town. Barricades were put up and noncombatants were put inside the strongest buildings. At the same time, word was sent out by riders to nearby communities asking for help. By noon on August 19, 100 volunteers from the town of St. Peter, twenty-five miles to the east, made ready to march to New Ulm and similar groups prepared as well. Joining the relief party from St. Peter was Judge Charles Flandrau, who it will be recalled had organized the pursuit of Inkpaduta after Spirit Lake. A former Indian agent to the Sioux and well known political figure, whose father had once been a law partner with Aaron Burr, Flandrau had been appointed a justice of the state supreme court when Minnesota joined the Union four years earlier.

Back in New Ulm, citizens prepared for the expected attack, which came about three p.m. when Indians began firing into the town from high points to the east. Defenders fired back with the few weapons they possessed. Every firearm in town had been confiscated for defense, but even at that there were only a few available. Some defenders armed themselves with nothing more than farm tools. Probably the most important weapon the townspeople possessed was the Indians' lack of organization. There was no real coordinated effort. Each individual Indian pretty much did what he felt like. Had the Indians marshaled their forces and responded to white incursions in an organized way, the Santees would surely have overrun New Ulm. As it was the defenders also had the weather on their side. A powerful thunderstorm with rain and lightning put an end to the fighting. Casualties were light—a dozen—and for the moment, the town was safe. That night, Judge Flandrau arrived with reinforcements from St. Peter and took command of the situation.

Elsewhere, as the uprising spread, the settlers of the Minnesota River Valley were confronted by a wave of terror such as hadn't been seen since the bloody days in the Ohio River Valley of the 18th century. It took some time and the loss of many lives, however, before authorities began to take the uprising seriously. At Fort Snelling, Governor Alexander Ramsey took the first step in dealing with the uprising when he appointed Henry Hastings Sibley colonel of volunteers and authorized him to respond with military force. Sibley was the perfect choice, too. A well respected legislator and former governor of Minnesota he had been a trader among the Sioux for some thirty years. If there was a flaw in Ramsey's choice it would have been that Sibley possessed no military experience.

To deal with the uprising, Sibley had four companies of the 6th Minnesota—some 400 men—who were then forming up at Fort Snelling for Civil War service. Sibley wasted no time in assembling these troops and marching to St. Peter. Here, word reached him that the situation was worsening. Confronted by this news and taking into consideration the inexperience of his troops, Sibley decided to pause here until reinforcements and supplies arrived. During the next several days additional companies of the 6th Minnesota arrived, along with more rangers and individual volunteers. On August 26, his force now swelled to some 1,400, including 400 mounted troops, Sibley resumed his march to Fort Ridgely.

Even as Sibley headed for Fort Ridgely, Little Crow had finally managed to marshal his forces for an attack on the fort. On Wednesday, August 20, some 400 Santees, including many who had been involved in the earlier attack on New Ulm, were now finally ready to follow Little Crow in an attack on Fort Ridgely.

Unlike some military posts of the 19th century, Fort Ridgely was not enclosed by a stockade. Rather it was a collection of buildings grouped a quadrangle or, if you prefer an assembly area or parade ground. The post was located on a tableland about 150 feet above the valley floor. Refugees were placed inside the barracks, a stout building made of native granite that serves as today's visitor center. It was thus, not a post not well suited for defense. And to make matters worse, attackers could advance up through ravines to the east and southwest without being seen until they were practically at the edge of the fort. Not surprisingly, this was the approach selected by Little Crow. Shrewdly, the Santee leader had a small war party create a diversionary movement from the west while the main body of warriors crept up through the ravines to the east, then struck the ne corner of the fort.

Attack on Fort Ridgely

Fort Ridgely had served as an artillery post in the 1850s, and still on duty at the fort from those by-gone days, was one Sergeant John Jones, an old-time artilleryman, and his presence at the fort would now prove invaluable. Jones had made it his mission to see that the garrison knew how to work the guns. Now, as the Indians attacked, Jones took charge of the fort's five field pieces: a six-pounder, three twelve-pounders, and one twenty-four-pounder. Working like the veteran that he was, Jones and his cannoneers fired their pieces with desperation and kept the Indians at bay. After several efforts, the Santees finally withdrew. That night rain began falling, further discouraging another attack from the Indians. But Sheehan and his garrison were certain another effort would come the following day and in expectation of this, they strengthened their defense.

Meanwhile, the uprising was spreading. Forty miles south of the Lower Agency was Lake Shetek, the center of an area that had attracted a number of settlers, among whom was the John and Lavinia Eastlick family. On Wednesday, August 20, the Lake Shetek community was swept up in the terror of the uprising, when some 200 Santees moved through the area, killing whites wherever they found them. Along with a number of other settlers, the Eastlick family took refuge in the large log cabin of a settler named Smith. This seemed like a good place to fight off the Sioux, but some of the men apparently felt they ought to try and escape the area, and guided by a Santee named Old Pawn, who was perceived as friendly, they set out for Fort Ridgely. Unfortunately, Old Pawn turned out to be something less than trustworthy and the fleeing settlers were soon set upon by rampaging Sioux. Fifteen whites were slaughtered in a marshy area that came to be known as "Slaughter Slough"; among them John Eastlick, along with three of his children. Lavinia Eastlick was seriously wounded and feared she was dying. Fearful for the life of her fifteen-month-old baby, Johnny she turned him over to eleven-year-old Merton who had managed to survive. There were many acts of individual courage demonstrated during these terror-filled days, but none more heroic than that of young Merton Eastlick. Somehow, with very little food and water, this eleven-year-old boy managed to trudge fifty miles to Mankato much of the time carrying his fifteen-month-old brother on his back. En route, astonishingly enough, they met their mother, Lavinia, who had also somehow managed to survive and struggle along despite her wounds. Together, the remains of this family reached the safety of Mankato.

Frustrated over the failure of his first attempt to take Fort Ridgely, Little Crow now prepared for a second effort. On Friday, August 22, some 800 Santees struck. When fire arrows failed to ignite the roofs of the fort's wooden buildings, Little Crow and Mankato launched an attack from the southwest quarter, and managed to penetrate as far as the stables before Jones's artillery turned them back once more, this time aided by Mrs. Eliza Müller, wife of the post surgeon. Along with other women, she also helped with the wounded and making ammunition in the blacksmith shop. As said, there were a number of heroes during these August days. Unquestionably, Sergeant Jones and his artillery made the difference between repelling the attack and being overrun. Big Eagle, one of the Santee leaders, later said that if it had not been for the artillery, they would have taken the fort.

Second Attack on New Ulm

Like Fort Ridgely, New Ulm was attacked a second time. In the meantime, however, Judge Flandrau had directed a determined effort to strengthen the town's defenses. Also additional reinforcements had arrived from Mankato and elsewhere, bringing the total number of defenders to 300. Before launching their second attack on August 23, the Sioux decided to employ a bit of trickery. They started a rumor to the effect that it was the Winnebagoes—traditional enemies of the Sioux—were really responsible for all the trouble. Exactly how they set such a rumor in motion is not clear, but it must have been effective as it compelled some 100 of Flandrau's defenders to return to their homes around Blue Earth, south of Mankato, near the Iowa border to deal with the supposed Winnebago threat.

On Saturday, August 23, the Sioux resorted to more trickery by creating a diversion in the direction of Fort Ridgely. The ploy worked, too, drawing off another hundred or so of Flandrau's defenders. Having accomplished the task of weakening New Ulm's defenses, some 650 Santees under Big Eagle, Mankato, and Wabasha, attacked the town. As the defenders fell back abandoning buildings, the Indians took up positions in these buildings and set others afire. Smoke from the burning structures hovered over the besieged town. The fighting was furious, with the Indians gradually enveloping New Ulm around both flanks in a giant pincer movement. It was a critical moment. The Santees were on the verge of overpowering the town when suddenly Judge Flandrau, supported by covering fire, led a counter-attack that drove the attackers back. Regaining occupancy of some of the buildings, defenders and attackers continued to exchange fire until dark. Thus far, the defenders had suffered ninety-four casualties, of which a third were deaths. Sunday, August 24 saw a resumption of sporadic firing. Flandrau and other community leaders decided it would be best to evacuate the town and so it was that the entire community supported by an armed escort marched twenty-five miles downriver to Mankato.

Meantime, Colonel Sibley finally reached Fort Ridgely on Aug. 28, with about 940 new recruits of the 6th Minnesota, commanded by Colonel William Crooks. Additionally, Sibley had nearly 400 mounted volunteers under Colonel Samuel McPhail; half of these were members of a local unit called the Cullen Frontier Guards, formed by Major William Cullen. At no other time during the course of the uprising would Sibley have as many mounted troops at his disposal. Unfortunately, soon after Sibley reached Ridgely most of the cavalrymen left to return to their homes to harvest crops. As a consequence, Sibley was left with only a small contingent of cavalry. And that was not all. More important than anything else, Sibley's troops were untrained and poorly armed and Sibley undoubtedly realized that this would limit his effectiveness. There was simply no substitute for trained soldiers, but trained, experienced troops were needed in the East. Clearly, Sibley's volunteers were not ready to fight much of anybody. So here at Ridgely the men were given some rudimentary training while Sibley asked Governor Ramsey for experienced soldiers and better weapons.

By August 31, intelligence from scouts and local leaders suggested that the Indians no longer posed a threat, at least to the area around Fort Ridgely. Based on this intelligence Sibley was able to assemble a force of cavalry and infantry from the 6th Minnesota under Captain Hiram Grant, with mounted troops from the Cullen Guards under Captain Joseph Anderson. This force, augmented by wagons and a civilian detachment moved upriver to bury the dead. Each man carried two days' rations and forty rounds of ammunition. An additional 3,000 rounds of ammunition was carried in the wagons. Importantly, the men had recently been armed with the 1862 Springfield muzzle-loading rifle. Overall command of the expedition was assigned to Major Joseph Renshaw Brown, whose appointment as Indian agent had only recently ended. Although some felt that Grant should have been named the overall commander, Brown technically outranked him, owing to his former position as Indian agent, which appointment traditionally carried the rank of major.

Fifty-seven years old at the time of the Minnesota uprising, Brown was a man of wide experience, having served as a legislator, Indian agent and trader. He was also an inventor, having designed a steam engine which he visualized being used on the plains. A lack of capital seems to have prevented the machine from attaining any level of success. A tall, muscular man, Brown had extraordinary self-confidence and prided himself on his knowledge of Indians.

Slowly Brown's column moved upriver, burying the dead wherever they found them. Corporal Joseph Coursolle, a mixed-blood of French and Indian descent left a vivid account of the gruesome task:

> The things we saw that day were too terrible to describe. [he wrote] Scattered along the road and at burned cabins we found the bodies of settlers, mostly men and boys. Fifty we buried before reaching the ferry. There the most gruesome sight of all awaited us. On the road lay the bodies of thirty-three young men [soldiers of Marsh's command] most of them in two files where they fell when the Sioux fired from almost point-blank range—killed in their tracks without firing a shot.[6]

On the night of August 31, the command bivouacked on the valley floor, near the head of Beaver Creek. Above them rose high bluffs, which some saw as a dominating position for Indians to fire down on the troops. Brown thought they should camp on the bluffs, but Grant seemed to feel they were perfectly safe here, which suggests that even though Brown was officially the commander, Grant still influenced the decision and would continue to do so. Whether there were still Indians in the area was a troubling question. Brown suspected some were still around, but opined that most had pulled out because of the soldiers now in the area. Brown further judged that that most of the Sioux had moved west into Dakota, taking captives with them. He was right in that the Sioux had vacated the area, but only temporarily. Even as Brown's horsemen were scouting the area and examining the now abandoned site of Little Crow's village, the Sioux, under Gray Bird were then moving back down the Minnesota River.

The Battle of Birch Coulee

Nothing happened that night and on the morning of September 1, the burial column continued north along the river, finding a few more bodies and several refugees. Now and then it was thought Indians were seen, but it always proved a false alarm. Still, the men remained jittery. That night the column bivouacked on open ground adjacent to Birch Coulee, a gouge in the earth some sixty feet deep. The sides of the coulee were covered with bushes and stands of Birch and Oak trees. Grant had been ordered by Sibley to avoid camping in a locale favorable to attack by the enemy, and Birch Coulee would seem to have been exactly the sort of spot to avoid. Grant, however, saw it differently; the open plain afforded an unobstructed view of the surrounding area. Ostensibly the column's commander, Brown, for some reason seems not to have been involved in the decision to camp here.

Grant was not exactly oblivious to the possibility of a surprise attack and ordered his wagons corralled, with the open end facing the coulee. Inside the enclosure, the men slept in Sibley tents. Picket posts were set up along the perimeter of the encampment. Meanwhile, the cavalry had ranged out ahead, but found nothing and returned to the camp. Nevertheless, some were nervous about the campsite and sensed the presence of Indians. Corporal Joseph Coursolle was one who did.

Coursolle's instincts were good. During the night, Gray Bird's war party slipped across the river and surrounded the encampment. With first light, a sentry thought he observed movement and opened fire, which was promptly returned by the Indians. The opening salvos proved costly to the soldiers who suffered thirty casualties in the exchange, but the alert sentry may well have saved the command from being overrun.

The sound of the battle drifted downriver some sixteen miles to Ridgely where Sibley immediately organized a relief column of the 6th Minnesota, plus some rangers and artillery, all under the command of Colonel Samuel McPhail. However, as McPhail marched upriver he suddenly found himself facing a large war party; larger he imagined than was actually the case. As it turned out, McPhail had been bluffed by Mankato and a party of perhaps fifty braves. Deciding caution was the smart move, McPhail dispatched Lieutenant Sheehan on a rather perilous sixteen-mile ride back to Ridgely for reinforcements. Sibley immediately assembled his entire remaining force—seven companies of the 6th Minnesota and marched out of Fort Ridgely in relief. Joining up with McPhail's command, Sibley's force reached Brown's besieged command on the morning of September 3. Artillery fire soon caused the Indians to withdraw, lifting the siege. After attending to burial of the dead, Sibley turned about and returned to Fort Ridgely. Birch Coulee had been a costly affair for the soldiers, with thirteen killed and forty-seven wounded. More important, Sibley had yet to really take control of the situation.

Elsewhere in the region, Captain Richard Stout with fifty men of the 10th Minnesota and two dozen civilians moved into Meeker County to provide protection to settlers. It will be recalled that the uprising had started in this county at the Jones and Baker farms just a few days earlier and settlers were still plenty nervous ... and for good reason. About 100 warriors led by Little Crow himself were preparing to threaten Meeker County. The Santee leader saw the area as ripe for attacking and looting. However, once again, Little Crow found his authority challenged. Walker-Among-Sacred-Stones took the bulk of the war party to a point near the Jones farm, while Little Crow with the remainder, about thirty-five warriors, camped southeast of the Jones place. On September 1, some militia skirmished with Santees (who may or may not have been part of Little Crow's party), near the community of Litchfield.

Meanwhile, Stout had learned of the militia action near Litchfield and mobilized his command for action, which was not long in coming. On the morning of September 3, Stout's command had a brisk encounter with Little Crow's warriors. The two sides were well matched in terms of numbers, with Stout perhaps having a slight edge, but the picture changed when the larger Santee group under Walker-Among-Sacred-Stones arrived on the scene. Then it became a hot affair, with Stout's men having to use bayonets to cut their way out and reach the safety of Hutchinson, twenty miles away. On the morning of September 4, Little Crow (who was apparently once again in overall command) divided his force into two wings, with one attacking Forest City, while the other struck Hutchinson. Both settlements, however, were ready, having built stockades from which they were able to repel repeated attacks. Thwarted, Little Crow could only destroy whatever he could find outside the stockades.

By September 3, the uprising had been terrorizing southwestern Minnesota for more than two weeks. There had been attacks on Fort Ridgely and New Ulm twice and a battle fought at Birch Coulee. For all intents and purposes, the Indians appeared to be in full control of the situation and to the nearly 300 whites and mixed-bloods that had been taken captive by the rampaging Santees, it must have seemed more than a little hopeless. Those who had been herded along by angry Indians had witnessed horrible scenes of killing and mutilation that would be forever etched in their memory. Twenty-five-year-old Nancy Faribault Huggan with her husband and eight-year-old daughter had joined up with the mixed-blood family of Louis Brisbois when they were caught by the Sioux.

> The Indians at once disarmed my husband. They seemed a little surprised to see the Brisbois family, and declared they would kill them, as they had not agreed to spare their lives. Poor Mrs. Brisbois ran to me and asked me to save her, and she and her husband got behind me. My husband asked the Indians what all this meant—what they were doing anyhow. They replied "We have killed all the white people at the agency; all the Indians are on the warpath; we are going to kill all the white people in Minnesota."[7]

The Indians told Nancy Huggan they would not kill her or her family and put them in a nearby house. About this time, more settlers came along in wagons and the Huggan family could only watch in horror as most were killed. Nancy Huggan and her family then became members of a growing body of refugees. When they reached the agency they saw dead and mutilated bodies everywhere. Later they were taken to Little Crow's camp.

When Little Crow learned that his old friend, Henry Sibley was marching against him with a column of soldiers, he moved the hostages to the Upper Agency where he was unsuccessful in persuading the Sissetons and Wahpetons to join him. The settlers and military authorities did not realize it yet, but the uprising had actually stalled, owing to Little Crow's failure to persuade these Upper Agency bands to join in the uprising. Indeed, some of the Upper Agency Indians argued for the release of the captives, but Little Crow and his followers were adamant. If the uprising failed and the Indians were killed, the captives would die along with them.

General John Pope Is Appointed Department Commander

The uprising had struck like a thunderclap and spread like wildfire. Largely occupied with the tumultuous events of the Civil War, neither state officials nor the federal government had been immediately prepared to respond to such an unexpected trauma and one with which they were ill-prepared to deal. Nevertheless, as stories and reports of events in the Minnesota River Valley continued to flow into St. Paul it became ever clearer that a disaster of the first order was unfolding. Governor Ramsey soon concluded that the situation required more muscle than Sibley had. His next step was to create a full fledged state militia. Charles Flandrau was appointed colonel and named to take charge of the state's southern defenses. Flandrau immediately organized the construction of a series of defensive structures that reached to the Iowa line. The Indian scare was not limited to Minnesota. In the wake of the Spirit Lake Massacre in 1857, the state of Iowa had formed a Northern Border Brigade charged with guarding that state's northern reaches.

And at long last the federal government was beginning to take action as well. On September 6, President Lincoln named General John Pope to command a newly created Military Department of the Northwest that included the states of Minnesota, Iowa, Wisconsin, Nebraska, and Dakota Territory.

The biggest hurdle facing Pope was a shortage of men and horses. As the Civil War progressed, cavalry commanders everywhere screamed for horses and Pope screamed as loudly as any. Although cavalry played an important role in the Civil War, that conflict was essentially decided by the foot soldiers, but on the frontier there was little chance of defeating Indians without mounted troops. There were mounted militia units around the state, but they were needed for local protection and were thus off limits to Pope, who fumed over their unavailability.

The Minnesota uprising by the Santees, triggered fear from another quarter. Suddenly rumors were afloat that the Chippewas (Ojibways), whose territory was traditionally in the valleys of the St. Croix and Upper Mississippi Rivers, were planning to join their traditional enemies in driving out the white man. The rumor was basically unfounded, but Indian agent Major Lucius Walker bought into it. When a troublesome chief of the Chippewas named Hole-in-the-Day seemed to Walker to be preparing to start something, Walker requested help from Fort Ripley, which had but little to offer, since Lieutenant Timothy Sheehan was busy down at Fort Ridgely. Thus, only twenty men could be dispatched to Crow Wing Agency. Along the way the detachment met a fearful Agent Walker fleeing south. So distraught was Walker over the perceived trouble, that he later committed suicide.

While this minor drama was unfolding, Commissioner of Indian Affairs, William Dole had actually been en route to work out a treaty with some of the Chippewas when he learned of the trouble from Walker. After reporting to Governor Ramsey at St. Paul, Dole, supported by two companies of infantry, headed for Crow Wing Agency to see about settling

Fort Abercrombie

Meanwhile, north along the Minnesota River, some 165 miles from the Lower Agency, sat Fort Abercrombie, on the west bank of the Red River, just inside the present North Dakota line. Established in 1858 its mission, like those of Ridgely and Ripley was to act as a control point for the Sioux in the area. At the time of the uprising in 1862, it was commanded by thirty-one-year-old Captain John Vander Horck, formerly a grocer in St. Paul. Bearded and distinguished looking, Vander Horck might easily have passed for a Prussian nobleman, though he completely lacked military training or experience. He had, under his command, some eighty men of Company D, 5th Minnesota.

Even as the uprising was unfolding downriver, a wagon train of goods and supplies plus a herd of cattle reached Fort Abercrombie. When word of events downriver reached Vander Horck he ordered the train brought into the fort and also recalled a detachment of soldiers that had been sent downriver on detached duty.

Vander Horck was edgy and more than a little concerned about how the uprising might affect his command, and he had every right to feel nervous. Most of the ammunition his soldiers had for their muskets was of the wrong caliber. The post was blest with a field piece, which Vander Horck may well have imagined would have to carry the burden of defense if it came down to that. Vander Horck had sent urgent requests to Governor Ramsey for the right ammunition along with reinforcements, but as of late August his requests were unanswered. Fortunately, there had been no Indian activity as yet.

Finally, on August 30 Indians ran off the post's cattle herd, but made no effort against the fort itself, thus beginning a 26-day siege of Abercrombie. On September 3, about 100 Indians attacked the fort, only to be driven off by canister fire from the post's lone field piece, after a two-hour fight. Earlier that day, Vander Horck was accidentally wounded by one of his own men while checking the fort's defenses. Fortunately, the Santees chose not to launch a second attack that day; had they done so, it seems likely they would have overrun the fort.

On September 6 the Santees attacked again, this time about 200 strong, but once more they were repulsed by artillery fire. Vander Horck had no way of knowing whether his requests to Governor Ramsey had been received, but indeed they had. Even as the first attack against Abercrombie was taking place, a sixty-man relief column marched out of St. Paul, to be joined en route by additional units that finally totaled 450 by the time they reached the fort, ending the siege of Fort Abercrombie.

Birch Coulee had convinced Sibley that he needed strong reinforcements of men, equipment and horses—he had hardly any cavalry—and he bombarded Governor Ramsey with pleas for reinforcements, particularly mounted troops. While he pondered, seemingly weak, but hardly weary, Sibley also began to consider the possibility that perhaps Little Crow might be amenable to the idea of surrender. He was visited by this thought because some of the Santee leaders who had been opposed to war suggested this might be the case, but whether it was or wasn't Little Crow had let it be known that he was adamantly opposed to releasing any of the captives and as far as Sibley was concerned there could be no discussions until the captives were released.

By mid–September Sibley had at long last gotten the reinforcements he had been begging for. Some 300 veterans of the 3rd Minnesota who'd been captured at the Battle of Murfreesboro, Tennessee, had been paroled and sent home to fight Indians. These, together with others from the 6th, 7th, and 9th, Minnesota plus local militia and artillery now gave Sibley more than 1,600 men.

The Battle of Wood Lake and the End of the Uprising

At long last on September 19, two weeks after Birch Coulee and a month after that eventful Sunday at the Baker farm, Sibley marched up the Minnesota River Valley reaching a small body of water on the 22nd. Sibley was mistakenly informed that this was Wood Lake but in reality was Lone Tree (now sometimes referred to as Battle Lake) and which no longer exists

Sibley's intelligence at this juncture assured him that the Indians he sought were located much farther to the north, so the colonel saw no particular reason to post a strong guard. Unbeknownst to him, however, Little Crow—well aware of Sibley's movements—had crept stealthily down from the north with more than a thousand warriors, intending to ambush the soldiers.

As at Birch Coulee it was judged that the Indians were not in the immediate vicinity, a judgment that came perilously close to being fatal and might well have been except for one of those chance events that dropped in the midst of history's lap to tilt the balance in favor of, in this case, Henry Hastings Sibley.

On the morning of the 23rd, a party of the 3rd Minnesota decided, entirely on their own volition, to make a journey to the Upper Agency for a supply of potatoes. En route, the soldiers stumbled upon Little Crow's waiting warriors, who fired on them, wounding some, but more importantly, sounding the alarm. No surprise this morning for Little Crow. Hearing the sound of guns, the rest of the 3rd Minnesota—quite without orders—promptly stood to arms and marched toward the sound of fighting. The 3rd was a tough outfit and much inclined to act on its own. Upon the approach of the regiment, the Indians began to fall back, but fluid-like, gradually commenced to envelop Sibley's flanks.

Quickly alerted to this danger, Sibley immediately directed the 7th Minnesota to address the new threat, supported by fire from the 6-pounder howitzer. The right flank was quickly secured, but on the left flank, it took the 7th, reinforced by a company from the 6th Minnesota, to turn back the Indians. The battle continued for two hours, by which time the Santees, unable to achieve the success Little Crow had hoped for, broke off the fighting. They had suffered a number of casualties, including the death of Mankato.

The mixed-blood John Other Day who had returned to Fort Ridgely to offer his services as guide was the one who mistook Lone Tree Lake for Wood Lake. For some reason, Sibley failed to pursue the Indians after the fight, claiming that he lacked the cavalry for a pursuit, which was true as far as it went.

Although Wood Lake had been a solid victory for Sibley, the hostile Indians were still at large, and the hostages had yet to be rescued. Nevertheless, the fight at Wood Lake marked the end of the uprising, at least insofar as military action was concerned. A growing number of dissident voices among the Santees, especially from among the Upper Agency, called for an end to the troubles and a restoration of the old ways; they also called out for the release of the captives. The "friendlies" as they came to be known actually provided the whites with an additional ally. During the Battle of Wood Lake, some of these friendlies took it upon themselves to transfer the captives to their own village. The Wahpeton chief, Red Iron, vowed to attack Little Crow's warriors if they attempted to recover the hostages.

The Release of the Hostages

When Sibley learned of this, and feeling comfortable in knowing that the hostages were now out of immediate danger, resumed his march north, reaching the village of the friendlies on 25th. Seventeen-year-old Samuel Brown, a mixed-blood, recalled the moment of Sibley's arrival. "I shall never forget it while I live." [said Brown] "We could hardly realize our deliverance had come."[8]

These friendlies wasted little time in turning the hostages over to Sibley. In all, there were 150 mixed-bloods, and 91 white captives; an additional 28 were released during the next few days for a total of 269 of which 107 were whites and 162 mixed-bloods. This site marking the place where the hostages were returned was appropriately enough named Camp Release. Some of the hostages were taken to Fort Ridgely for questioning. Children whose parents had been killed in the uprising were distributed among various settlers to be cared for. Some of the women captives were detained at Sibley's camp for a time to help identify Santees who would subsequently be charged with war crimes. Nancy McClure Huggan remembered that there were seven wagons of white and mixed-blood women.

For Little Crow, the failed uprising had been both a personal and tribal humiliation. "I am ashamed to call myself a Dakota," he said. "Seven hundred of our best warriors were whipped yesterday [at Wood Lake] by the whites. Now we had better all run away and scatter out over the plans like buffalo and wolves." Little Crow had gambled that his prestige would unite the Lower and Upper Sioux, but he misread the signs. Without the support of the Upper Sioux bands the uprising was doomed to failure and fail it did, though not before inflicting a swath of horror on the heartland of America that had not been seen since the bloody days of the Old Northwest Frontier, along the Ohio River.[9]

Sibley meanwhile remained at Camp Release for nearly a month, attending to the dispersement of captives and collecting Indians who had been involved in the uprising. By the end of October he reported having in captivity (and irons), about 500 Santees, some of whom had drifted in of their own volition, while others had been rounded up by army patrols. Gradually, the number of residents grew too large for the camp site. Between Sibley's 1,600-man force and the Indian captives, the logistical burden became too heavy. To ease matters, some of the Santees were sent out to harvest what crops might still exist in the fields. Meanwhile, Army patrols continued to search the area for more Santees or white captives still at large.

The Hanging of the Condemned Santees

Now that the uprising had finally been put down, Sibley next needed to address the disposition of the perpetrators. To this end, he was directed to establish a military commission to adjudicate the guilt or innocence of the Indians involved. The objective here was to try and separate those guilty of criminal action that is rape, murder, etc., from those who had simply been involved in the uprising. It was all clear enough in some instances but not so in others. If an Indian had raped a woman, for instance and then tomahawked her to death that was clearly a criminal act. On the other hand an Indian who killed a white person during the course of the uprising was doing nothing more than any soldier would do in the course of battle. Charges including murder, rape, and robbery were brought mainly by former women captives. The Rev. Stephen Riggs, a missionary who had worked among the Dakotas for a quarter of a century acted as a sort of secretary for the commission, collecting and organizing the various allegations of criminal offenses.

In January 1862, the War Department had authorized the use of military tribunals for dealing with crimes such as those with which the Santees were charged. But there were voices that cried out against the use of such tribunals, claiming that in so doing the War Department had exceeded its authority. Such crimes, it was argued, should be dealt with in a civil court. It is interesting and instructive to note that these same issues would surface 150 years later in dealing with terrorists.

Notwithstanding, the commission pressed ahead, taking testimony over a six-week period. In the end, 303 Santees were judged guilty and sentenced to death. General Pope gave the commission's findings his blessing. Although at the outset, it was clear that some Indians were going to hang, no one, including Pope, expected that number to reach 300. Uncomfortable with hanging so many, and yet recognizing that all had been found guilty, left Pope in an uncomfortable and awkward position. Fortunately, he had a way out. The articles of war allowed him to kick the issue upstairs to President Lincoln, which he did.

On November 10, Lincoln responded by asking for the trial records. Before signing a man's death warrant, the president wanted to feel as certain as possible that the individual was guilty as charged. For nearly a month, Lincoln studied the records and finally on December 6, signed death sentences for 39, which was later reduced to 38 due to conflicting evidence. Some, especially among the clergy, had pressured Lincoln to be merciful, pointing out the abominable conditions that served as a prelude to the uprising. Angry Minnesotans, however, wanted their pound of flesh and were not pleased that the president had commuted the death sentences of 265.

On December 26, the 38 condemned Santees were hanged on a public scaffold in Mankato. The grim event was witnessed by some 1,400 soldiers and a huge crowd of civilians. It remains the largest mass execution in U.S. history. But it was not the finale. Two years later the Santee leaders, Shakopee and Medicine Bottle, who had escaped to Canada were lured back across the border, apprehended and hanged on November 11, 1865.

For those Santees not found guilty of criminal wrong-doings, the uprising spelled the end of their days in Minnesota. One is tempted to say their days were numbered anyway; that the uprising merely hastened the inevitable end and perhaps that is so. Eventually about 1,658 Santees were taken to Fort Snelling. As they passed through New Ulm on the way, angry whites attacked them and had to be forced back by the bayonets of soldiers. The Santees were housed (imprisoned) at Fort Snelling until 1866 when they were transferred to reservations in eastern Dakota Territory. In the spring of 1863, 326 other Santees who had been held in custody at Mankato were transferred to Camp McClellan at Davenport, Iowa. The entire Santee population paid the price for the uprising. They received no annuities for the next three years.

Settlers of western Minnesota, still angry over what they had lost and endured during the uprising, wanted all Indians removed from their state and that included the Winnebagos, who had not been part of the uprising at all. Accordingly, by 1863, the Winnebagoes found themselves on a reservation in eastern Dakota, uncomfortably close to their traditional enemies the Sioux. During the next two decades, small groups of Dakotas managed to drift back across the line into Minnesota, but they were few in number.

The Death of Little Crow

As for Little Crow, within a year his band of followers had dwindled from about 200 to a handful. In the summer of 1863, he and 15–20 Santees made their way back into Minnesota. Some of the party was involved in the killing of a white family near Howard Lake. Little Crow was said to have participated, but the evidence is sketchy. Following the attack, the band dispersed, with some heading for Canada. Little Crow and his son, Wowinape, however, chose to remain in the area, where Little Crow was subsequently shot and killed, after an exchange of fire, by a farmer, Nathan Lamson and his son Chauncey, who had been out picking berries when they spotted Little Crow and his son. Lamson had no idea as to the Indian's identity, but assumed he was one of the fugitive Santees. Meanwhile, Wowinape had managed to escape into Dakota where he was later captured by Sibley's command in August 1863. Wowinape's description of the shooting helped in identifying his father's body. Little Crow's remains were taken to the town of Hutchinson where it was dismembered and scalped. A year later, Lamson would be awarded a $500 bounty for killing the leader of the uprising. Tragically, some of Little Crow's remains were nabbed by souvenir hunters. Finally, in 1896, what remained of the chief's corpus was given to the Minnesota Historical Society where it remained until 1971 when they were finally returned to his descendants.

The total number of settlers who lost their lives in the Minnesota uprising varies widely. Some sources say around 400, but the Minnesota Historical Society claims 644. The Society also claims 113 soldiers were killed. As always, Indian casualties were nearly impossible to determine, but taking everything into consideration, a figure of perhaps 200 seems reasonable, including those who were hanged at Mankato.

On October 9, 1862, General Pope informed General Henry Halleck in Washington that "The Sioux War may be considered at an end," and Governor Ramsey sent a similar message to President Lincoln. In the larger sense, then, the uprising was over, though that did not mean the Minnesota frontier no longer need fear Indian raids. In the months that followed the Battle of Wood Lake and the recovery of the captives, there were sporadic raids that kept fears stoked.[10]

The recurrence of these raids prompted settlers to pressure state officials to take action, resulting in the formation of mounted volunteer units that were enlisted to patrol Minnesota's western frontier. In addition to their pay of $2 per day, they would also receive a bonus of $25 for the scalp of every hostile Sioux they brought in. In fact, any non-volunteer who brought in a Sioux scalp would receive $75. Of course it had to be proved that the scalp belonged to a hostile Sioux, although exactly how it could be proved that this particular scalp belonged to a "hostile" Sioux was not explained.

As commander of the Department of the Northwest, Pope, and Sibley, as commander of the Department of Minnesota were irate to have their authority ignored. It was yet another illustration of the sparks that so often flew when local volunteers attempted to take military action, horning in, so to speak, on the Army's sphere of authority.

Although Pope and Governor Ramsey had stated publicly that the war was over, there were fears the Minnesota frontier would be stripped of troops to be used in the east, but Pope and the governor hastened to quell those fears by assuring citizens that the state would not be left unprotected. If the generals and politicians considered the uprising over, such was not the case with the rank and file of the citizenry and the press.

The Dakota Campaigns of Sibley and Sully, Summer 1863–1864

In 1863 Dakota Territory—the present states of North and South Dakota, along with parts of Wyoming and Montana—was a vast region about which little was known except that it was the habitat of large numbers of Plains Indians: Lakota, Cheyenne, Arapaho, Arickara (Rees), Mandans, and others, and now as a result of the Minnesota uprising a substantial number of Santees—perhaps close to 5,000—were judged as new additions to the population of the region. These bands had fled west because they did not trust Sibley's assurances that there was safety in surrender.

Although Pope regarded the Minnesota uprising as over, he also saw the presence of so many Sioux roaming free in Dakota Territory, as a potential threat, and the continuing sporadic raids, across the line into Minnesota certainly seemed to reinforce the idea that such a threat was in fact real enough. As a consequence, he determined, early in 1863, to take the initiative by sending two strong military columns into Dakota Territory. As such, these would mark the start of a series of campaigns against the Teton Lakota or western Sioux. From Minnesota, the scene would now shift west into Dakota and Montana.[11]

Pope's two field commanders would be General Henry Sibley—he had been promoted to brigadier—and forty-two-year-old Brigadier General Alfred Sully. An 1841 graduate of West Point, Sully, the son of an artist, had served in the Seminole and Mexican-American Wars. He had also seen action against the Rogue Indians in Oregon and commanded the 1st Minnesota during the Civil War's Peninsular Campaign. Although he seems to have acquitted himself well up to this point, his later career on the Central Plains left something to be desired.

Sibley's column was composed mainly of infantry. In June 1863, he assembled 3,300 men at the newly established Camp Pope near present Redwood Falls. The 6th, 7th, and 10th Minnesota Regiments, the Minnesota Mounted Rangers, and the 3rd Battery of Light Artillery commanded by Captain John Jones formed the core of Sibley's command. Additionally, one hundred men from the 9th Minnesota also joined the column as did a detachment of Indian and mixed-blood scouts. True to his word, Sibley left behind the 8th Minnesota to protect the frontier settlements and lines of supply.

Pope's plan called for Sibley to march northwest to the Devil's Lake region in present North Dakota, where it would rendezvous with General Sully's column, composed mainly of cavalry that would be coming up the Missouri River from Fort Randall (near the present Nebraska South Dakota line). It was hoped that the Indians would be caught between the two columns and whipped.

THE BATTLE OF BIG MOUND

Sibley moved out on June 16; a ponderous column, five miles long with more than 200 wagons. Under a scorching sun and fighting dust, the column plodded its way across a land that had been touched by drought and stripped clean by a plague of locusts. Water quickly became scarce with the troops forced to dig wells to find good water. By July 4th the column had reached the Sheyenne (as opposed to Cheyenne) River where it was necessary to halt and await additional supplies en route from Fort Abercrombie.

Resupplied, the column resumed its march across what was known as the *Coteau des Missouri*, a 200-mile-long plateau which early French explorers called New France, and which Sibley described as uninhabitable. On July 17, the expedition reached a point southeast of Devil's Lake and established a base camp which Sibley decided to call Camp Atchison. There had been no contact with Indians up to this point, but here it was learned that several hundred lodges of Sioux had recently left the Devil's Lake area, bound for the Missouri River.

Assembling a strike force of 2,300 men, Sibley set out from Camp Atchison on July 20.

A week later his scouts reported a large camp ahead. Sibley's presence in the area had not gone unnoticed, while Lakotas watched from the surrounding hills. Establishing a new camp, Sibley watched while a sizeable party of Indians approached. He had entertained hopes that the Indians might be willing to talk of surrendering. His feeling was based on the understanding that Standing Buffalo and several other chiefs who favored peace were numbered among this band and might be responsive to peace feelers. With this in mind, Sibley dispatched a scout, Joseph LaFramboise with an invitation for Standing Buffalo to meet with him. Meanwhile, taking no chances, Sibley prepared to fight. Circling his wagons, he placed the 6th Minnesota on the northern perimeter, the 7th and 10th Regiments on the east side, and his mounted detachment along the south side. All the while Sibley was making his preparations, the Indians continued to observe, most of them from the highest point called Big Mound (in present Kidder County, North Dakota).

The composition of the Indian band was a volatile mix of militants and quasi friendlies. Sibley's scouts parleyed with a small group who invited Sibley to come forth for a talk; however the scouts also learned that some of the young warriors were spoiling for a fight. Sibley agreed to parley but only in his own camp. From here, relations deteriorated and threats were exchanged. When Surgeon Dr. Josiah Weiser joined the scouts who had been parleying, he apparently believed he saw some friendly faces he had known in the days before the uprising. In this he may have been right. However, one warrior, an earlier follower of Inkpaduta suddenly shot the doctor through the heart. Further shots were exchanged and the battle was on; the first major confrontation between Army troops and the Lakota Nation in Dakota Territory.

Overhead, black skies, thunder and lightning added drama to the scene. Sibley sent a company of mounted rangers out to recover Dr. Weiser's body while the remainder of the command deployed for action. Positioning one company of the 7th Minnesota on the left and two others on the right flank, and three dismounted companies of the rangers in the center, Sibley advanced, accompanying the artillery. Drawing within range of the Big Mound, the artillery commenced lobbing shells on the Indian position, killing several. Following this, the infantry and dismounted cavalry advanced and soon had Big Mound secured. As the Indians withdrew, Sibley directed one company of rangers to pursue the Indians, who fought a rear guard action to allow their village time to move out of harm's way. From what he could see, Sibley judged the Indians to number 1,000–1,500. The battle cost Sibley one man killed by lightning, oddly enough, and wounded several others. Indian casualties were believed to be around eighty killed and wounded.

The Battle of Dead Buffalo Lake

The mounted rangers, led by thirty-seven-year-old Colonel Samuel McPhail (a founding father of Redwood Falls, Minnesota), meanwhile, pursued the Indians to near Dead Buffalo Lake, managing to kill a few more during the chase. Fortunately for the Indians, the rangers received orders to return to Sibley's main body, though there seems some reason to suspect that the orders were misunderstood, since it seems clear that Sibley's intentions were to pursue the Indians. Had McPhail done the campaign might well have ended right there. In any case, the day's fighting had exhausted both sides, so the campaign paused for the moment.

On July 26, Sibley resumed his advance. That there was a sizeable number of Indians out there to be chastised was clear, but what was not so clear was exactly how many? One could never be certain of numbers in these Western Indian campaigns. Villages were fluid critters. A camp of fifty lodges today might be twice that number a week hence, or conversely it could also be smaller. In this case, what Sibley probably did not know was that the less militant groups had split off and headed north, attracting other splinter groups who were not at all anxious to fight the soldiers. Within a year this group, numbering perhaps as many as 3,000 would seek refuge in Canada, at Fort Gary (present Winnipeg).

Among the militant factions that remained, however, was the one that included Inkpaduta. Exactly how much influence the old warrior wielded is unclear, but more than likely his reputation as the perpetrator of the Spirit Lake Massacre together with his overall defiance of the white man would have made his medicine strong. Again, what Sibley most likely did not know was that the Wahpekutes and Yanktonais had been joined by several hundred Teton Lakotas that included an upcoming warrior named Sitting Bull. The addition of the Tetons, said to have numbered nearly 700 meant that Sibley now had to confront something like 1,600 warriors; all militant.

Continuing his southward march, Sibley's command found the remains of the Indian village from two days earlier and torched what was left. About noon on the 26th Indians began appearing around Sibley's advance unit, the 6th Minnesota. A pair of companies of that regiment formed a skirmish line and, along with a battery of 6-pounders, drove the Indians off. Inkpaduta, who seems to have been the guiding force here, tried a strike on the left flank of the 6th Minnesota, but was repulsed by mounted rangers. This was followed by a second attack that was similarly driven back. As the afternoon waned it appeared that the Indians were finished for the day and had moved off. The soldiers, accordingly, prepared to bivouac around Dead Buffalo Lake about thirty miles east of the Missouri River, only to have the Indians launch one more attack, which turned out to be the fiercest of the day. In the mêlée, dust was thick, making it difficult for Indians to see soldiers and vice-versa. Finally, the Indians, having lost Grey Eagle, a renowned warrior were discouraged and withdrew, having lost fifteen others besides. Sibley lost two men. With the approach of darkness Sibley ordered earthworks created to protect against a possible night attack, but the Indians had had enough for the time being.

Sibley had hoped to rendezvous with Sully by this time but he had heard nothing of the other column. Although he had been successful in two encounters thus far, he remained disappointed that some of the Indians had already crossed the Missouri and he was determined to prevent more from escaping into that region beyond the Missouri River.

On the 27th, Sibley reached a small, fresh water lake with stony shores, hence the name, Stony Lake. On the morning of the 28th, he resumed his advance and was soon confronted by a sizeable force of Indians who threatened his flanks. The Indians had evidently intended to try and strike the soldiers while the expedition was in the process of preparing to get underway but were late in doing so. Sibley estimated a force of 2,000–2,500 warriors and a total Indian encampment of 10,000. Sibley's estimate was inflated, but even so, it was a sizeable body of warriors.

And they came to fight. Painted and marked for battle they threatened to envelop the brigade, but Sibley directed Colonel James Baker to deploy two companies of the 10th Minnesota as skirmishers to provide a holding action while the wagon train moved up. For the men of the 10th it seemed as though they were going to be overwhelmed. In the meantime, though, the other two regiments were forming on the flanks of the brigade and long range fire from the artillery was having an effect that discouraged the Indians from making strong frontal effort.

With the wagon train finally closed up, Sibley was now able to seize the initiative. With the 6th and 7th Minnesota Regiments and McPhail's cavalry operating on both flanks, and the 10th in the center position, Sibley ordered a general advance. Both sides exchanged heavy fire to which was added the spherical case shot (shrapnel) from the artillery of Captain Jones. Finally, discouraged by this, the Indians withdrew, shouting jeers and taunts from nearby hills, but the battle was effectively over. A determined pursuit would probably have yielded good results to what had been three encounters favorable to Sibley. However, the cavalry horses were played out and Sibley elected to rest his brigade.

After a brief rest, Sibley resumed the advance, hoping to strike yet another blow at the Indians before they crossed the Missouri River. On the night of the 28th, the brigade bivouacked along the Apple River, ten miles south of Bismarck and a dozen miles east of the Missouri. Early on the 29th, McPhail's cavalry, escorting a pair of six-pounder howitzers pressed on ahead of the main body hoping to catch the Indians, most of whom had already begun crossing the previous night in bull boats; an ingenious river craft, constructed of buffalo hides stretched across a frame made of willow branches.

Still, enough Sioux remained behind to make things interesting. As the cavalry approached, the Indians responded from wooded thickets along the river, but these were quickly encouraged to depart by artillery shells lobbed into their positions. It was a lively time as Sibley's main body moved into the picture and added the fire of their muskets to that of the artillery. From hills across the river, the Indians taunted the soldiers; some were spoiling for a fight, but others shouted that they did not want to fight the soldiers. Firing continued through the remainder of the afternoon, but by dark it was clear that the Indians had made good their escape, although minus much equipage had been left behind. Scattered pockets of Indians remained on the east side of the river from where they continued to harass the troops.

On the 30th, Sibley detached 700 infantry, some and cavalry to search for missing soldiers. Now and again their work was interrupted by sniper fire from Indians across the river. For the next two days Sibley remained in camp, resting his tired brigade and hoping to finally hear something from Sully, but at length, in the absence of any word from the other column, Sibley elected to return to Minnesota. His brigade had marched nearly 600 miles and fought three battles, plus a number of skirmishes. Supplies were running low. His campaign had been a success and there was little more he could do at this point. Including Dr. Weiser, Sibley lost 6 killed. Estimates of Indian losses ranged from 120–150. One Sioux source claimed 13 had been killed while another said 58. On August 1, Sibley commenced his return march to Minnesota. As he did so, the Sioux followed and attempted to recover anything of value the troops had not destroyed.

About the same time, a large raft, carrying twenty-seven miners (including several mixed bloods) with a large cache of gold dust from the Montana diggings, approached the area. From ambush, the Sioux attacked. The miners put up a vigorous fight, but seventeen were killed, and when the others ran out of ammunition they, too, were killed. The Indians vented their anger on this group, but it proved a costly victory. One Indian source claimed ninety warriors had been killed, while another said thirty-five killed and forty-five wounded.

Sibley considered his campaign an unqualified success, and if it is assessed from the standpoint of securing the Minnesota frontier, then the answer would be yes. If however, it is judged on the basis of what was accomplished in terms of resolving the Indian threat in Dakota, then the answer would have to at least be debatable, although one might well argue that if Sully had been able to cooperate as planned a more decisive outcome might have evolved.

The Battle of Whitestone Hill

And what of Sully? The Missouri River column, unlike that of Sibley's, was composed mainly of two mounted regiments: the 6th Iowa, commanded by Colonel David Wilson, and eight companies of the 2d Nebraska under Colonel Robert Furnas. These two regiments were further augmented by two companies of Dakota Cavalry and another from the 7th Iowa. Artillery support was provided by a battery of eight mountain howitzers. Sully's column totaled about 1,200 men, compared to 3,000 for Sibley. Unlike Sibley's troops, Sully's command had yet to be blooded.

On June 20, four days after Sibley took the field, Sully left Sioux City. The march, roughly paralleling that of the Missouri River, was slow and plodding. At this stage of the campaign Sully was unencumbered by wagons as his supplies were carried aboard steamboats, but the downside of that was that the progress of the column depended on the progress of the boats, which were moving upstream and agonizingly slow in this low water period.

As a consequence of low water, heat and generally lousy travel conditions, Sully got no farther than Fort Pierre (in present South Dakota) by July 25, which had been Pope's projected rendezvous date with Sibley, and by which time Sibley was engaging the Sioux at Big Mound. Here, Sully languished, waiting vainly until August 7 for the steamboats to arrive with supplies. Pope, meanwhile, fussed over Sully's slowness, though in fact Sully was a prisoner of conditions. From his advance base at Fort Pierre, Sully was finally able to resume the march and, fortunately, on the 16th was able to re-provision his troops from a steamer that had finally made it to a point near the mouth of the Little Cheyenne River.

A week later, this time with supplies hauled in some seventy-five wagons, Sully was able to cut lose from his dependence on the river and resume his advance overland. By the end of the month, he learned, from an old Indian that Sibley had fought the Sioux and was now returning to Minnesota. The old man also reported on the massacre of the miners. Sully's scouts more or less confirmed the old man's story. According to the scouts, the Indians were faced with two choices: return to the east side of the Missouri where they could hope to find good hunting in territory familiar to them, or move still farther west. With Sibley no longer in the area, option one seemed the most attractive of the two choices.

With Sibley no longer in the picture, and now with an understanding that the Indians had re-crossed the Missouri, Sully elected to push on in pursuit. So, Pope's grand plan to catch the Indians in a great pincer movement had failed to materialize. Notwithstanding, Sibley had not fared badly and now Sully would take his chances. A favorite spot for the Indians this time of year was along the James River and Sully accordingly moved in that direction.

As the column moved toward the James River it was trailed by Sioux who sought an opportunity to make off with some of the column's livestock, but Sully, a veteran Indian campaigner, was familiar with those tactics and had the column protected by guards on all sides, making thievery nearly impossible. Early on September 3, with Indian sign growing stronger, Sully dispatched a 300-man battalion of the 6th Iowa under Major Albert House to push ahead and pinpoint the location of the Indians. Sully's instructions to House were to keep about five miles ahead of the main body. House's scouts included a mixed blood named Frank LaFramboise and a party of friendlies.

Late on the afternoon of the 3rd, LaFramboise came upon what he believed to be a small village. Leaving the other scouts to watch the Indians, LaFramboise returned to the column, some two miles back, and reported his finding to House. Ordering his troopers to load their weapons, House started the battalion forward, first at a trot, then a gallop, scouts out ahead, keeping a low profile by advancing through the little valleys which were plentiful in the area.

The Indian encampment was situated around a small lake, the shores of which were strewn with white rocks. The lake itself was dominated by small hills, and the intervening ground was cut by ravines. The slopes of the most prominent hill in the area were also dotted with white rocks, giving rise to the name Whitestone Hill, located north of present day Ellendale, North Dakota. As they moved closer to the Indian campsite the scouts soon discovered that it was much larger than they had originally thought. Revising their earlier estimate, they now figured the encampment contained 300–600 lodges, with perhaps 1,500 warriors. The Sioux would later claim there were only 1,000 warriors, but either way Major House's battalion was substantially outnumbered.

Now aware that he was up against a sizeable body of Indians, House sent LaFramboise and two men from Company C to advise Sully, who was then some ten miles in the rear with the main body. Barely had LaFramboise spurred his mount back toward the main body then he and his companions ran into a party of Sioux—perhaps 200 strong—the same ones who had been shadowing the brigade. Belligerent and threatening, they told LaFramboise that they had beaten Sibley and were ready to kill these soldiers. This was not a time for diplomacy and suddenly LaFramboise and his companions spurred their mounts forward and raced back toward the main brigade. The Indians did not attempt to follow perhaps they enjoyed seeing the scared white men riding off. In any case, about 4 p.m. LaFramboise reported to Sully who promptly prepared to ride to Major House's aid.

As House slowly advanced, he presently found himself confronted by a delegation from the Indian camp. Drawing closer to the scene, House formed his battalion in line of battle. Uncertain as to the strength of the Indians, the first step was to try and get a clearer picture of what he was up against. Consequently, he sent two companies out to the left to assess the situation and then later two more to the right. Meanwhile, several Indian leaders approached the battalion to parley under a flag of truce. The leaders, who were undoubtedly buying time to allow their non-combatants to move out of harm's way, offered to surrender some of their chiefs as temporary hostages, but House insisted that the entire camp would have to surrender. This "the Indians refused to do, [wrote Major House] and having sent away their squaws and papooses, together with their stock of provisions, they placed themselves in battle array."[12]

The situation was ripe for action. If the Indians chose to start something House would more than have his hands full, although it appeared that the Indians were more concerned with seeing to the security of their non-combatants. Notwithstanding, there was no shortage of militants in the Indian ranks, including the seemingly ever-present Inkpaduta.

Inkpaduta's role here as well as in the later campaigns later, seems to have been questionable. Some sources credit him with playing a major figure in all the Indian-white clashes from Spirit Lake to the Little Bighorn. That he was among the most militant of Indians there is little doubt, but what role he actually played and whether he was actively involved in every action seems questionable. In any case he does appear to have been present at Whitestone Hill.

Even as the Indian leaders were trying to parley with House, others began to creep around the flanks of the battalion. Fortunately for House, Sully arrived with the main body around 5 p.m. With the approach of the main body the Indian village began to disperse, causing Sully to conclude that the Indians were preparing to flee, and that, above all else was what Sully did not want to happen. Throughout these Western Indian campaigns, army field commanders consistently made an effort in formulating a plan of attack to prevent a village from dispersing. If a village was able to scatter, the opportunity to strike a damaging or even decisive blow was lost. As will be seen later, this concern undoubtedly figured into Custer's operational plan at Little Bighorn.

Wasting no time, Sully immediately directed the 2d Nebraska under Colonel Furnas to reinforce House. Meanwhile Colonel David Wilson, commanding the 6th Iowa was sent out to the left flank with the 1st battalion of his regiment dismounted, while Sully took personal charge of the center with the two remaining companies of House's battalion, supported by a company of the 7th Iowa and the brigade's battery of howitzers.

Although Sully thought the Indians were preparing to vacate the area, the situation was not all that clear to House. Were the Indians preparing to attack or flee? But then, welcome news reached House as he prepared to advance. The 2d Nebraska arrived to assume responsibility for the right flank. So, with the 6th Iowa on the left and the Nebraskans on the right they charged the Indians, who, meanwhile, had taken up positions in a ravine, which seemed a poor choice for a defensive position, but no matter, they seemed determined to fight it out. Reaching the head of the ravine, the soldiers reformed and poured a heavy fire in on the Indians, who returned the fire themselves, giving about as good as they got. By this time, Major House had swung his entire battalion around to the left to get behind the Indians, and, from dismounted positions, began to apply pressure on the Indians from that quarter.

Although Sully appeared at the outset to have a plan of battle, his control of developments on the field seemed to evaporate, as Furnas, Wilson and House, each seemed to be controlling the action in his own sector as it unfolded. The day was waning, though, and darkness was beginning to settle in. Furnas feared that the Indians might escape through one of the ravines, or possibly attack the battalion's left flank, and indeed they did try but were driven off by the Nebraskans, reportedly with heavy losses.

Meanwhile, on House's front, regimental commander, Colonel Wilson, had arrived on the scene and ordered the battalion to remount. In his zeal to launch a mounted charge, perhaps encouraged by the approaching darkness, Wilson neglected to order weapons loaded, but some of the men, probably directed by company commanders, or perhaps Major House, issued orders to load weapons on their own volition. In any case, as the battalion came onto line, it moved to a trot, and finally full charge. Firing was heavy. Well out in front of the battalion, Wilson's horse was killed, though not before carrying its rider back to the main line. Apparently, with the Indians in the middle between House and Furnas, some of the Nebraskans' bullets carried into the ranks of the Iowans, inflicting a fair amount of damage, according to one observer, but House's battalion also inflicted a number of casualties on the Indians. The horses of Wilson's troopers, evidently unaccustomed to such noise became impossible to manage, causing the charge to unravel.

House's initial contact with the Indians had been about three p.m. and Sully reached the field around five. Twilight in North Dakota on September 3 set in around 6:30, with sunset following a little after eight. As the light faded, confusion became a key factor. Fighting was brisk all across a widespread brigade front, but heaviest on the flanks where House and Furnas had engaged the Indians.

Sully meanwhile advanced the center portion of his line toward the Indians. As he moved forward, a small party of Indians under Chief Little Soldier, approached the general, professing friendship for the Americans, while assuring Sully he and his followers were not hostile. Sully took the chief's word with some suspicion and had the Indians placed under guard. Resuming his advance Sully next came upon a cluster of tepees belonging to a party under Chief Big Head. Here, there was no question about the Indians' allegiance. Big Head and a number of his warriors were dressed for battle, but Sully quickly surrounded the small encampment taking prisoner some thirty warriors and ninety women and children.

Noise and confusion were rampant in the gathering darkness. Major House ordered his battalion to dismount and fall back, forming a square with the horses behind the soldiers. Colonel Furnas also retracted his line in order to maintain better control of his men.

One might argue that had Sully waited until dawn to send House's battalion on its mission of reconnaissance, thereby allowing the battle to unfold during full daylight his victory would have been far more complete, but as it was most of the Indians were able to avoid capture and escape through one of the many ravines that scarred the area. On the other hand, had the attack been delayed the Indians might well have slipped away before Sully had a chance to bring them to battle.

Under strong guard, the brigade bivouacked on the field. The following morning, September 4, Sully brought his wagon train forward and dispatched details to gather up any Indian fugitives still in the area, but only a few were found, including some children who had been separated from their families and left behind. During the next two days, the brigade rounded up 32 warriors and 124 women and children. An examination of the battlefield also revealed that the soldiers had inflicted heavy casualties, judging from the bloody evidence and the bodies left behind. Estimates of Indian casualties ranged from 100–150 killed and 300 wounded. Brigade losses were put at 20 killed and 38 wounded.

Many dead horses were found along with much plunder, some from the Minnesota uprising, including weapons, ammunition, and bags of gold dust, probably taken from the miners killed in the attack on the Mackinaw boat. Sully's troops spent two days burning some 300 lodges and an estimated 400,000 to 500,000 pounds of dried buffalo meat—the winter's supply.

The Battle of Whitestone Hill, though perhaps not as widely known as other engagements stands as one of the more important major clashes between the Army and the Northern Plains tribes. Tactically, the battle belonged to Sully; strategically it was another matter. In Pope's eyes Sully got an "A" plus because Whitestone Hill made him (Pope) look good to his superiors and blessings along with criticisms flow downhill. On the other hand, the Sully-Sibley Campaigns had failed to resolve the Indian problem in Dakota. The resident Indian Agent and the Dakota Territorial Governor, Newton Edmund, were of the opinion that the campaign did not achieve lasting results. It could, however, be pointed out that the Minnesota frontier was largely secure and the eastern part of Dakota was now available for settlement. Then, too, the Indian equipage and meat destroyed by Sully certainly worked a hardship on the Indians, but not one from which they were unable to recover. Indeed, they not only recovered but remained a force with which to be reckoned for another two decades. Sully felt that if he had had enough supplies to prosecute the campaign for another month he could have insured the end of the Sioux problem, which in retrospect seems unrealistic. The power of the Teton Lakota had hardly been tested as yet and Sully's brigade, even given more supplies, would hardly have been in a position to do that.

As it was, given his present situation, Sully commenced his homeward march on September 6 and reached Fort Pierre by mid-month. The threat of further Indian trouble on the Dakota frontier was evidenced by the fact that Sully detached part of his brigade to construct a new post north of Fort Pierre, eventually to be named Fort Sully; it would serve as his supply base during the forthcoming 1864 campaign. The rest of the brigade meanwhile, moved into winter quarters at Fort Randall.

Between the Sully and Sibley campaigns Minnesota citizens could feel relatively secure from further uprisings of the sort that had brought terror to the Minnesota River Valley. The dynamics of the region had changed. Many of the Santees had fled to Canada and those Lakota bands, notably the Yanktons and Yanktonais who had previously dwelled in eastern Dakota Territory, were now largely beyond the Missouri River, leaving the settlement of eastern Dakota to proceed with little trouble from the Indians. And the fertile Dakota prairie definitely beckoned to settlers, who found additional incentive in the new Homestead Act which had become effective on January 1, 1863. And then there was gold! Discovered in southwestern Montana in 1862, it was as much or more of a magnet, even than the promise of land, so much so that political pressure had resulted in an attempt to create an overland route to the Montana gold fields from St. Paul.

Between the lure of land and gold, there was plenty of rhetoric calling for a second Dakota campaign from speculators, settlers, indeed, almost anyone who stood somehow to profit from another campaign. And perhaps no one profited more from military operations than contractors and traders who supplied the troops.

It is sometimes imagined or implied that the federal government or the War Department, or both together, were responsible for creating the Western Indian wars, when in fact, it should be noted and well remembered that it was the public clamor for land and access to the gold fields, together with pressure from commercial interests that compelled the government to take military action. "All the people in this territory and western Iowa, great and small, [noted one observer] are doing their best to get another expedition sent up the river (object to make money), and iff [sic] lying can affect anything they will gain their point." Thus it was that between the end of Sully's 1863 campaign and the arrival of spring 1864, General Pope and his superiors in Washington finally came to see the need for a second campaign.[13]

It was true that scattered Indian raids did perhaps provide some additional justification for a renewal of military action. Sibley had already been thinking along such lines. His overall strategy embraced the reinforcement of Forts Ripley, Abercrombie, and Ridgely. Beyond that, he envisioned launching a strong column from Ridgely to sweep through the Devil's Lake region, putting the finishing touches on his own campaign of the previous summer. Pope liked the idea but thought it fell short and authorized another two-brigade campaign. Once again the field commanders would be Sibley and Sully, with the latter acting as overall commander of the Northwestern Indian Expedition, as it would be called.

The Minnesota Brigade

The Minnesota brigade would march to the Missouri River, with the objective of punishing the Sioux still in the Devil's Lake area and making sure that eastern Dakota was free of any remaining Indian threat. A second objective was to build a new fort at Devil's Lake and a second one on the James River. The presence of these two posts, together with Fort Sully, built the year before, were intended to provide protection for travelers heading up the Missouri, for the Montana gold fields. Colonel Minor Thomas would command the 2d or Minnesota brigade. Sibley, at his own request, would remain behind. This 2d brigade would consist of the 8th Minnesota, which included a company of Confederate deserters who had been drafted into federal service and would see action against the Indians. Galvanized Yankees, as they were known, these former Confederates preferred fighting Indians to life in a Union POW camp.

In addition to the 8th Minnesota, Thomas's brigade included six companies of the 2d Minnesota Cavalry, and two sections of artillery from the 3rd Minnesota Battery, led by that outstanding hero of Fort Ridgely, Captain John Jones. A group of 45 scouts along with mule teams and wagons rounded out the column. Altogether, the brigade mustered about 1,500 men.

The 1st Brigade, which Sully would personally accompany, was made up of the 6th Iowa, about 900 troopers in eleven companies, commanded by Lieutenant Colonel Samuel McLean Pollock. Additionally, Major Alfred Brackett's Minnesota Battalion of cavalry, some 360 men, three companies of the 7th Iowa Cavalry, about 240 men, commanded by Colonel John Pattee, and two companies of Dakota Cavalry, about 160 men under Captain Nelson Minor. Captain Christian Stufft [spelling correct] was in charge of some eighty scouts. Finally, Captain Nathaniel Pope commanded four mountain howitzers. In terms of overall numbers the 1st Brigade was about the same size as the 2d, perhaps slightly larger.

In 1864, Dakota Territory was a vast land and, apart from Indians and a few trappers and traders, was mostly uninhabited. Pope envisioned a campaign of no more than three months, and advised his field commanders that they could expect to deal with as many as 6,000 hostile Sioux, many of whom were believed to be well armed and supplied by Canadian mixed-bloods, known as Red River traders.

Two things differentiated the 1863 columns from those of 1864: first there was better balance in that both brigades had strong contingents of cavalry, second, and perhaps most important, with the exception of the 8th Minnesota, which had served as Sibley's Minnesota frontier defense force, the officer and men were veterans with a year of Indian campaigning under their belts.

Colonel Thomas's Minnesota Brigade left Fort Ridgely on June 5, whereas the 1st Brigade did not commence its departure from Sioux City until the 14th and by the 28th was at the Little Cheyenne River in Potter County, not far from a place named Gettysburg, a name that undoubtedly resonated among the men. But this particular spot resonated with the men for another reason, too. Here Captain John Felner, a topographical engineer, and two troopers, riding out ahead of the expedition to gather geological specimens, was killed in a surprise ambush, along with one of his men. The third member of the trio, though wounded, managed to escape and reach the main camp. Angry, Sully immediately ordered a twelve-man patrol of the Dakota Cavalry—called Coyotes—led by scout Frank LaFramboise, to go after the ambushers. The Coyotes had a fearsome reputation as Indian killers. After a furious chase and fight, they found the three Sioux and promptly dispatched them. When Sully learned of their success he ordered them to return and cut off the heads of the Indians and mount them on poles to serve as a warning to other Sioux. It appears, however, that, rather than being cowed the Sioux were instead infuriated.

Unlike the '63 Campaign, this one was also better organized and coordinated. On June 29, Sully bivouacked near Swan Lake in present day Walworth County. Here, they fired off rockets to let the Minnesota Brigade know where they were. On the following day the two columns rendezvoused and Sully and Thomas laid plans for the continuation of the campaign.

Once again, Sully's artery of supply was the Missouri River, and as in 1863, it proved an impediment. Water level was low—by mid-summer the spring run-offs had ended. On July 7, Sully established a second Missouri River fort, south of present day Bismarck. The new post would be called Fort Rice and would serve as Sully's supply post. Four companies of the 30th Wisconsin Infantry, under Captain Daniel Dill came up the Missouri to provide the new post's garrison.

Thus far, no Indians had been located and informants, such as Father Pierre-Jean De Smet, a Belgian Jesuit priest who had been doing extensive missionary work among the

Indians for many years visited the camp and advised Sully that most of the Indians had crossed to the west side of the Missouri. Lately, the 61-year-old Belgian Jesuit had been unsuccessfully trying to broker a peace agreement with the Indians, while acting as an emissary for the Indian Bureau. On July 9, De Smet paused on his way downriver from Fort Berthold to provide Sully with the latest tribal information.

According to De Smet, the Indians were concentrating in the Little Missouri River Badlands in present day western North Dakota. Among other news, De Smet reported an increasing number of Teton Lakotas. The Indians were upset, too, to learn that more soldiers were moving into the region, and anger lingered over the beheading of the three Indians.

Sully spent the next week transferring supplies across the river and working on the construction of Fort Rice. On the 19th he was ready at last to march toward the Badlands, but it was a ponderous column that finally headed west. In addition to his own wagons, he had also been charged with the protection of 123 emigrant wagons containing some 200 Idaho miners plus their women and children. The miners and their families, of course, had a wagon train that was close behind and also required protection. Settlement of the western territories was not to be denied. Opportunity lay to the west, but the journey to that land of fresh opportunity would be contested and so political pressure brought on by elected representatives compelled the government, through its War Department to provide protection for that journey. The problem was that such demands tended to hamstring the army. Conducting an Indian campaign was tough enough without having to provide escort service at the same time. Sully was not a happy camper, but he had little choice here; the emigrants would have to come along.

The Battle of Killdeer Mountain

On July 19, notwithstanding his unwanted baggage, Sully commenced his march northwest toward the Badlands with 2,200 men from both brigades. Eleven companies of Pollock's 6th Iowa; three of Pattee's 7th Iowa, two companies of Dakota Cavalry, four companies of Brackett's Battalion, and four mountain howitzers. From the Minnesota Brigade, came ten companies of the 8th Minnesota, six companies of the 2d Minnesota Cavalry, and the four howitzers under Captain Jones.

Their route took them through high prairie country, with high buttes that rose to a peak. Travel was difficult beneath a blistering sun; the temperature reportedly reached 110 degrees. Indian sign was plentiful and Sully was certain he was following the same Indians he had fought at Whitestone Hill. And indeed, he was right. Well aware of his presence, the Sioux consortium was preparing to confront the soldiers and planned to do so from a huge land mass on the Little Missouri River; and they had chosen well. It was about as good a defensive position as one could hope to find. The Indians called it Tahchakuty Mountain—"the place they killed the deer." To whites who knew the area, it was simply Killdeer Mountain. How much information Sully possessed about the composition of the Indian force we don't know, but in any case, he would be up against elements of three bands of Sioux: Lakotas led by Sitting Bull and Gall, plus Yanktonais, and Dakotas, reportedly led by old Inkpaduta.[14]

On a clear and very hot July 28, 1864, Sully's brigade approached Killdeer Mountain, having been marching six hours since dawn. It was a dry and barren land over which their boots tramped, having been baked and seared by two months of summer sun. Again, it was scout LaFramboise who reported a huge Indian camp up ahead.

There would be no surprise by the soldiers. The Indians could see them coming and prepared for battle. Sully judged some 6,000 Sioux awaited the troops, but in fact, there were probably only 1,500, still a sizeable force nonetheless. It will be recalled that Pope had estimated 6,000 and Sully may simply have repeated his superior's estimate. The lay of the land favored the Indians. The hills approaching Killdeer Mountain were covered with deep, wooded ravines. This would not be a job for the cavalry.

Dismounting his troops, Sully formed them into a square with the horses and artillery in the center, and advanced. Indians sniped continuously, probing at his outer line, but the square held firm and the Indians gradually fell back into the cover of the ravines. Sully's artillery pounded the ravines and the Indian camp, farther up. Additionally there was a good deal of vocal haranguing, with both sides slinging taunts at each other.

One soldier of the 6th Iowa recalled the battle:

> Our battle of the 28th began about 2 o'clock and lasted until dark. When we were dismounted and formed in line of battle, the Indian town appeared to be about 2 miles distant, but when the ground was measured it was found to be nearly ten. We had to fight them all the way. At first they were very couragious [sic], getting up on top of hills and buttes, daring us to come on, etc. Our two batteries were soon in position and began throwing shell [s]. At first the reds appeared to be astonished. And after three or four rounds of shell plainly showed sig[n]s of fear, began to complain that we were not fighting fair. Said if we would leave the wagons that shot twice at home they would come out and fight us. In our briad[e] is one company of scouts composed partly of half breeds and friendly Indians. They fought like tigers, and while fighting with their carbines, acted as interpreters between soldiers and Indians, and when the Indians began, they abused them terribly in their way of blackguard. In the morning we started in pursuit of the retreating foe, found the country very rough. The general, after going a few miles, gave up in disgust, saying it was the dam[n]dest country he ever saw.[15]

As daylight waned, the Indians, possibly led by Inkpaduta, made a serious demonstration against Sully's right flank, probably to allow their village time to flee. Sully responded by ordering thirty-five-year-old Major Albert Gallatin Brackett to mount his battalion and charge the Indians with sabers drawn. Already an officer of distinction for his service during the Mexican War, Brackett would go on to have a long and distinguished military career in the Civil War and in the West against various Indian tribes.

An officer of great courage, Brackett, who two years later would author *A History of the U.S. Cavalry*, responded to Sully's directive with enthusiasm. With sabers drawn, the Minnesotans charged the attacking warriors, while Brackett shouted taunts at the Sioux. The fight that followed was the fiercest of the day. The troopers wielded their sabers, while the warriors slashed back with tomahawks. But eventually, the Indians gave way and fell back into the timber choked ravines of Killdeer Mountain, from where they loosed volleys of arrows, forcing Brackett to dismount his men and fight on foot. Then presently, Captain Jones and his field pieces were brought into action, scattering the Sioux.

Indian losses on Brackett's part of the field amounted to twenty-seven killed. Brackett's casualties were one killed and eight wounded, the lone fatality being a man named George Northrup who had earned something of a reputation as a frontiersman and Indian fighter. Northrup had also served with distinction in the Civil War when he carried out a successful covert mission against the Confederacy. In 1864 he was assigned to Sully's expedition as a member of Brackett's Minnesota Battalion. His experience on the frontier had earned him the sobriquet of Kit Carson of the Northwest.

On the other side of the field, Sully attempted to flank the Indian right. This action, supported by the artillery of Captain Nathaniel Pope, and coupled with Brackett's strong effort, compelled the Indians to fall back here as well and disperse. In the fading daylight,

Sully halted his advance, but ordered the artillery to continue to pour fire on and over the high points of Killdeer Mountain. By day's end, the Indians had fled from the battlefield and Sully chose to go into bivouac so men and horses could be rested and fed.

On the morning of the 29th Sully delegated the task of destroying what remained of the Indian encampment to a detachment of the 2d Minnesota, while he swung around Killdeer Mountain with the remainder of the brigade and went on in pursuit of the Indians, whose trail led toward the Badlands. The pursuit proved brief, however. After considering what lay ahead, Sully declined to take his brigade into such forbidding terrain that would prove more of an enemy than the Indians.

Returning to camp, Sully had to assign a second detachment to help in the destruction of the Indian camp, which had proved more extensive than at first realized. Stores of buffalo meat, robes, and blankets, plus tools and weapons needed to be destroyed, if the Indian capacity for waging war was effectively shut down. Two papooses were discovered by the Winnebago scouts who bashed their skulls in with tomahawks, explaining that "Nits make lice."

Killdeer Mountain ended the first phase of the 1864 campaign. Sully returned to his base camp on Heart River where he was welcomed by the emigrants and the guard detachment he had left behind. Once again, he had scored a tactical victory. The Indians had been driven still farther west and much of their equipage had been destroyed. But such success notwithstanding, the Indians remained a serious threat to any western expansion in the region. Sully estimated the Indian dead at 150, but the Indians later refined that number to 31. The actual figure probably lies somewhere in between the two estimates. Sully's loss was 5 killed and 10 wounded.

Sully now addressed the other two objectives of his campaign: escorting the emigrant wagons as far as the Yellowstone River and constructing a post at some point along that river. As plans presently stood, Sully was scheduled to rendezvous with steamboats on the Yellowstone in early August, but this posed something of a dilemma because it would mean taking his wagons through the Badlands. The more reliable but longer route, however, would put him at the Yellowstone too late to meet the steamers.

The dilemma was resolved when one of the Indian scouts claimed that he thought it possible to take the wagons west via the shorter route. Sully accepted the recommendation and after a two-day rest, resumed his westward movement.

Although the march proved uneventful, it was also interesting and illuminating to a man with the natural bent of an explorer such as Sully, who thought the region looked like good coal country—which of course it is. On August 5, the column reached the Badlands and Sully was impressed. "It was [he wrote] grand, dismal and majestic." But impressed though he was, the sight of this rugged, broken country prompted him to wonder about getting through it before reaching his rendezvous point but once more the Indian scout assured the general that the expedition could pass through successfully.[16]

On the morning of August 6, the brigade began the job of moving through the Badlands. It was hard and hot work preparing the way for the army wagons as well as those of the emigrants. Other than one small raid on a few soldiers who had strayed beyond the main lines, though, the brigade's main opposition was the terrain and the searing heat. Then on the 7th an estimated 1,000 warriors appeared on a high bluff across the river from the brigade's camp. From here they harangued the troops with jeers and taunts, boasting that there were 10,000 warriors ready to fight the soldiers. Sully ordered his field pieces to open fire, and as usual the effects of the artillery shots caused the Sioux to disperse at least temporarily. That night Indian warriors, supported by a pack of wolves, managed to maintain a heightened state of alertness, particularly among the emigrants who fired into the threatening darkness almost endlessly.

Early on the 9th Sully resumed the advance. Being somewhat incapacitated by rheumatism he turned tactical command of the column over to Colonel Thomas. Progress was slow on this another scorching day, with the expedition being forced to cross and re-cross the Little Missouri River several times. Approaching a steep defile, they were confronted by a large body of warriors, which Sully estimated to number 1,000. Jones's artillery drove the Indians from their positions and kept them out of rifle and musket range of the column, which allowed it to proceed albeit very slowly.

In the waning afternoon daylight, as the brigade made preparations to establish camp, the Sioux launched another strike. A bevy of several hundred warriors swept in to attack. Had it not been for the soldiers, the emigrants were close to panicking, but as it was the troops reacted quickly and soon drove off the attackers.

Indians continued to deploy against the brigade as it moved forward, but with strong dismounted units protecting the wagons and artillery, Sully was free to counter Indian aggressions with his mounted units. Sully's three-day campaign in the Badlands, while often intense was also at times a war of words, at least on the part of the Indians who seemed always ready to challenge the soldiers, but not Jones's artillery, however. Sully judged 100 Indians had been killed in the 3 days, while others of his staff thought many more than that. In all likelihood, though, the actual number killed was probably far fewer than even Sully's estimate. Army casualties were 9 killed and 100 wounded. Interestingly, the Blackfoot Indian scout who had encouraged Sully to follow his route was among the seriously wounded.

On August 12 the brigade rendezvoused with two steamers, near the site of present day Sidney, Montana. A third steamer had run aground and sank, and its loss caused Sully to abandon plans for building an outpost at this point. It is difficult to say whether the men of the brigade were hungrier or thirstier, but in any event, their rations were replenished and the river provided water. The steamboats brought news from back east as well. The fall of Atlanta to Sherman's army would have been encouraging to all save the Galvanized Yankees. There also seems to have been an erroneous report declaring that Richmond had fallen.

Sully renewed his pursuit of the Indians though not for long. A plague of grasshoppers had devastated the surrounding countryside. Whether Sully was aware of it or not, the Indians had dispersed into smaller bands, which in itself would have necessitated abandoning the chase. On August 14, with the assistance of the steamers, Sully shifted his expedition to the west side of the river and reached Fort Union three days later. From here, the emigrant miners left the expedition doubtless much to Sully's relief. The miners and their wagons had been a real burden on this campaign, and to add insult, to the experience, they managed to help themselves to army property upon leaving. Exactly how this might have come about is not clear, but some forty of Sully's troopers, excited about the prospect of finding gold, also elected to desert and join the miners. An effort was made to catch them, but to no avail. After resting his command at Fort Union, Sully finally reached Fort Rice on September 8.

No sooner had Sully reached Fort Rice than he learned Captain Fisk's Montana and Idaho Expedition had come through two weeks earlier, bearing 200 miners bound for the gold fields. And what really annoyed Sully was that the commandant at Fort Rice saw fit to provide these people with an escort. It would be Fisk's wagon train that fought the last action of the 1864 campaign when it was attacked on September 2, 160 miles west of Fort Rice.

By early October most of Sully's brigade was back in Minnesota. The campaign just concluded had been an ambitious one. The brigade had been in the field four months, marched 1,600 miles and fought two major actions. Although the Indians had been soundly chastised one could hardly say they no longer remained a threat. Pope, with a fair amount of naiveté, believed the campaign had established a foundation for peace talks and while it was true that there was a peace faction among the Lakotas, there were remained plenty of hard-liners who would be heard from in the years ahead.

If nothing else, the Sully/Sibley campaigns of 1863 and1864, together with Patrick Connor's expedition of 1865 surely alerted the Northern Plains tribes to the escalating threat posed by the white man.

The Teton Lakota: Lords of the Northern Plains

South of the Platte River white traffic across the Central Plains corridor had begun in the 1850s. In Texas and on the Southern Plains, as we have seen, whites began moving in even earlier but until the discovery of gold in Montana in 1862, those tribes north of the Platte River had not suffered from the effects of white intrusion nearly as much.

The dominant Indian power between the Platte River and the Canadian border was the Teton Lakota, westernmost of the three Sioux divisions. The Teton Lakota were further sub-divided into the seven council fires: Hunkpapa (Camps at the End of the Camp Circle), Oglala (Scatters their Own), Miniconjou (Planters by the Water), Sans Arc (Without Bows), Brulé (Burned Thighs), Sihasapa (Blackfoot, though no relation to the Blackfeet of Montana), and Oóh Núnjpa (Two Kettle). Of these, those best known to history are the Hunkpapa—Sitting Bull's band, and the Oglalas of Crazy Horse and Red Cloud. The former was the northernmost branch of the seven council fires, their habitat being generally north of the Yellowstone River and west of the Missouri. The Oglala territory tended to be along the Platte River drainage system, ranging north into Nebraska, the Black Hills and the Powder River country of northeastern Wyoming. The territory of the remaining five bands was generally throughout the region of the Oglalas and occasionally farther north. The Lakotas were frequently allied with the smaller bands of Northern Cheyennes and Arapahos.

The southern bands had already had plenty of contact with both the military and the emigrant wagon trains following the Great Platte River Road, and north into the Powder River Country during Patrick Connor's 1865 Campaign, but it was the creation of the Bozeman Trail (Road) that really opened the door to white incursion into the treasured Powder River Region.

The Powder River drainage system, encompassing some 24,000 square miles in northeastern Wyoming, is bordered on the north by the Yellowstone River, on the south by the North Platte River, and flanked, roughly, by the Big Horn Mountains on the west and the Black Hills on the east. It is a diverse landscape, ranging from high desert on the south to the beautiful timbered foothills of the Big Horns. It is also an area rich in coal deposits (it currently supplies about 40 percent of the nation's coal), and hunting resources. The Powder River country was, accordingly, prized by the Indians. It was also to be one of the most contested regions in the West.

By virtue of the Horse Creek Treaty of 1851 the region had been assigned to the Crow tribe, numerically smaller than the Lakotas and their traditional enemies as well. As the Lakota had migrated west from their original woodland home in the 18th century, they came to covet the resource rich Powder River Country, which in turn meant that the Crows must be driven out, and so it was that the Lakotas (and their Cheyenne and Arapaho allies) came to be the dominant power in the land of the Powder River. It is interesting to take note of the fact the white man was not the only one capable of wresting land he found desirable from a tenant who lacked the resources to successfully resist. The Lakota took the land from the Crow and now the whites would take it from the Lakota; it was the natural progression of things.

Gold and Fire: Red Cloud's War, 1866–1868

Red Cloud was an imposing figure. At six feet, he stood taller than the average Indian of his day; that alone being enough to set him apart. With his strong, powerful features, his profile could easily have been the one that adorns our nickel (it was actually a composite of three different Indians), but it was his commanding demeanor and charisma that made others know they were in the presence of a powerful personality.

As the decade of the 1860s began, Red Cloud (Makhpiya-Luta) was arguably the most dominant Lakota (Sioux) leader of his generation. At age forty he was a *nonpareil* warrior who had achieved status through the sheer force of his personality and accomplishments in war. Although not a hereditary leader, Red Cloud quickly demonstrated his skills as a warrior, and that attracted followers who recognized the power of his medicine. He came up the hard way, collecting his first scalp at age sixteen. He was whipcord tough and as ruthless as he needed to be.

By 1860, Red Cloud had evolved from warrior into a forceful and persuasive leader. No longer needing to prove himself in battle, he had ascended to the eminence of elder statesman; in in that capacity he was rivaled by none save perhaps Spotted Tail. Red Cloud was one of only five Indian leaders who had the dubious distinction of having a war named in his honor: King Philip, Pontiac, Little Turtle, and Blackhawk being the others. During its two-year run, Red Cloud's War left its mark from one end of the Bozeman Trail to the other. It was a war that began with gold and ended with fire.[17]

And so it began. The discovery of the yellow metal in southwestern Montana (then part of Idaho Territory) in 1862 quickly attracted prospectors, plus the usual complement of those who sought their own riches by catering to the needs and wants of those who worked the soil for the color they hoped to find. But southwestern Montana was not the easiest of places to reach. Some worked their way east from Washington and Oregon, along what came to be known as the Mullin Road, but most came from the east. The Missouri River offered one route: upriver to Fort Benton, then overland to Alder Gulch, Bannack, and Virginia City. The problem here was that river travel was expensive and was only available during those months when the river was free of ice. Other travelers, bound for the gold camps, could journey across the Oregon-California Trail, as far as Fort Hall, Idaho (today's Pocatello), then turn north to Montana. This route worked well enough but it was longer and circuitous. What was needed was a more direct overland route. Enter one John Bozeman.

THE BOZEMAN TRAIL

A Georgian by birth, Bozeman had not fared well when it came to finding much color in the "diggings," but he did see the need for a more direct route to Montana. In fairness to history, it needs to be pointed out that John Bozeman was not the first to perceive this need, but it would be his name that labeled the trail he and a partner first blazed in 1862.

The Bozeman Trail aka the Bozeman Road or Montana Road, split off from the Oregon-California Trail near present day Casper, Wyoming, and snaked its way north, roughly paralleling today's Interstate Highways 25 and 90, passing along the eastern flank of Wyoming's majestic Big Horn Mountains. Not far north of present Sheridan, the route curved to the west as it moved into and across Montana, until, finally, it came to rest among the tents and shacks of Virginia City, Alder Gulch, and Bannack. It was along this route, not far from the city that would also one day bear his name that John Bozeman perished at the hands of Indians in 1867.

Actually, the old mountain-man-turned-guide, Jim Bridger, pioneered a similar route, but the canny old guide, knowing how troublesome the Lakota could be, laid its course west of the Big Horns. The Bridger Trail, accordingly, was safer, insofar as Indian harassment was concerned, but it also offered even less forage and water than Bozeman's route. And so it was that the Bozeman Trail came to be the overland route of choice for most Montana-bound travelers.

The Bozeman Trail—it was more a general direction rather than one precise trail—wound through what was known as the Powder River country, so named because much of this area is drained by the Powder River. The River itself rises in central Wyoming's Natrona County, west of Casper, and flows mainly north (and some east) through Wyoming and on into Montana until it junctions with the Yellowstone a few miles west of Terry.

In places the Powder barely seems to qualify for river status, particularly after the spring run-off has ended and the brassy heat of summer has sucked the winter moisture back into the atmosphere from whence it came, no doubt giving rise to one well known description labeling the river as being "too thin to plow and too thick to drink." Supposedly the river acquired its name because of its perpetually dark coloration.

The Powder River Basin is a land of some considerable contrast: rugged, barren, and arid between the North Platte River and the Big Horn Mountains, north to the Montana line before it reverts to its earlier described barrenness along the final leg of its journey to the Yellowstone River. During the course of an 1851 journey from Fort Union to Fort Laramie, the well known Jesuit missionary, Father Pierre Jean De Smet, recorded his rather bleak impression of the Powder River country.

"On the 27th of August we reached Powder River, ... Our wagoners will not soon forget the difficulty of conducting their teams through this last route, for it was a very miserable, elevated, sterile plain, covered with wormwood and intersected with countless ravines, and they vowed they would never be caught driving a wagon there again."[18]

The Lakotas had been steadily forced out of the upper Midwest (today's Wisconsin and Minnesota) beginning about 1700 by the stronger Ojibways (Chippewas) and Crees, who had the decided advantage of possessing firearms provided by French traders. By 1800, the Lakotas had reached the Black Hills and Powder River country, where in turn they forced the Crows and Cheyennes still farther west in an illustration of the domino theory. By this time and possibly earlier, the various Indian tribal groups of the region had all acquired horses and become proficient in the use thereof, establishing themselves as the buffalo hunting, horseback Indians of popular imagery.

The Lakotas regarded the Powder River country as the heart of their territory, "theirs" meaning the land belongs to he who is strong enough to control it. By virtue of the 1851 Horse Creek Treaty, this region had been awarded to the Lakota's traditional enemies the Crows, an assignment of secondary importance, however, even though the Crows had occupied the region far longer than the Lakotas. What mattered was that the Lakota had the muscle. Nevertheless, the dilemma poses an interesting, question for writers and historians attempting to place the events of 1866–1868 in their proper historical perspective.

Is it fair to take the position that the Lakota, in failing to recognize the terms of that treaty, were thereby in violation of that agreement when they attempted to defend territory not legally their own through the terms of the 1851 Horse Creek Treaty? Were the Lakota bound to accept the conventions of the white man's treaty, even assuming they fully understood what exactly it meant? In attempting to address this question, one quickly finds that in the broader sense of history the very same question lies at the root of many if not most misunderstandings and conflicts between Native Americans and Euro-Americans. It is a legitimate question, right enough, and it is well to bear the ramifications in mind in reflecting on Red Cloud's War.

At any rate, in the years 1863 and 1864, traffic along the Bozeman Trail increased though not without the sting of Indian resentment. By 1865, however, there was plenty of Indian trouble to be found up and down the Great Plains. The massacre of the Cheyenne chief, Black Kettle's village at Sand Creek, Colorado in November 1864, prompted the government to close the trail and prohibit emigrant traffic while the army cleaned out the region. The effort, a four-column campaign, under the leadership of tough-minded General Patrick E. Connor achieved little, except for a hard-won victory over Chief Black Bear's Arapahos on Tongue River, north of present Dayton, Wyoming.

Accordingly, as the nascent spring of 1866 deepened, United States treaty commissioners at Fort Laramie faced the fact that they had failed in their efforts to persuade the Powder River Lakota to grant safe passage to emigrant wagon trains headed north along the Bozeman Trail to Montana. Unwilling to grant travelers access to the Powder River region, and disgusted, finally, with the proceedings, Red Cloud stalked off in high dudgeon, promising war should the soldiers invade the land of the Lakota! With the powerful and influential Red Cloud out of the picture, there was little the commissioners could now hope to achieve, yet they sought to pick up the pieces and put together some sort of agreement, meaningless though it would be.

Then, into the midst of this rather discouraging situation, came a large army column, bound, indeed, for the Powder River region. The Indians watched and were further disturbed. Later, Red Cloud was reported to have said that the white man came to steal the land while others talked of peace. Perfect rhetoric for the moment, but unfortunately, since Red Cloud had departed Fort Laramie before the arrival of the army column, he could hardly have made the statement. But whoever uttered the statement (perhaps a waggish journalist) it surely captured the mood of the angry Lakotas.

The column included three battalions of the 18th U.S. Infantry, a blend of veterans and raw recruits; some cavalry, a regimental band, and a long wagon train carrying wives, assorted supplies and a pair of saw mills. Before leaving Fort Kearney, General William T. Sherman urged the several wives who would accompany the expedition to record their experiences and observations in a diary. One at least, Margaret Irvin McDowell Carrington, the colonel's wife, did exactly that and her journal subsequently became the basis for *Absaraka: Home of the Crows*. Much of what we now know of life at Fort Phil Kearny is revealed through the pages of *Absaraka*.

At the forefront of this retinue rode a bearded, scholarly-looking officer by the name of Henry Beebe Carrington. In appearance he emanated an aura of culture and refinement. An 1845 graduate of Yale Law School, he had later taken up practice in Ohio. As a reward for political service, he was appointed colonel of the 18th Infantry during the Civil War.

But while his regiment was being bloodied on various Civil War battlefields, Carrington remained on the home front, serving as assistant to the governor of Indiana. After the war, Carrington finally joined his regiment at Fort Kearney, Nebraska, from which place he received orders to lead his battalions west to Fort Laramie, then up the Bozeman Trail. Carrington's mission was to insure the safety and protection of emigrant travelers by establishing three outposts along the Bozeman Trail. As his eyes and ears, Carrington could rely on the legendary mountain man Jim "Old Gabe" Bridger.

In the brassy heat of that early summer, the Carrington column wound its way north into the Powder River country. Aside from utility poles and fences, the area is little changed today from what the Carrington people would have seen. The modern traveler, gazing east while speeding north along Interstate 25, would see essentially the same landscape.

On the 28th of June, eleven days after departing Fort Laramie, Carrington and company reached the site of Fort Reno (east of present Kaycee, Wyoming), a crude post established the year before by General Connor and named for him. However, since military posts were to be named in honor of fallen heroes, this one was renamed Fort Reno after General Jesse Lee Reno killed in the Battle of South Mountain (during the Civil War). Discovering that the post contained more supplies than expected and was, after all, an extant post, Carrington elected to retain Fort Reno, which would become the first of the three outposts he had been ordered to create along the Bozeman Trail. After relieving the disgruntled Civil War volunteer garrison still stationed there a year after Appomattox, Carrington detached two companies of the 18th Infantry to serve as the post's new garrison and resumed his march north.

At Fort Reno, Carrington had his first taste of what the future held, when Indians ran off some of the sutler's livestock. The colonel sent a detachment of cavalry in pursuit, but the troopers returned later, much wearied by the chase and with only a single Indian pony in tow.

Fort Phil Kearny: The Hated Post on the Piney

By mid-July, Carrington had reached the forks of Piney Creek. Here, in the shadow of the strikingly beautiful Big Horn Mountains, about twenty miles south of present Sheridan, Colonel Carrington elected to build the second and flagship post of his new command. The post would be named Fort Phil Kearny, in honor of General Philip Kearny, killed at the Battle of Chantilly, Virginia, during the Civil War. Soon after arriving, Carrington sent two additional companies of infantry, under Captain Nathaniel Kinney to construct a third outpost, to be named Fort C.F. Smith, after General Charles Ferguson Smith of Civil and Mexican War fame. C.F. Smith would be located some ninety miles northwest of Fort Kearny, near the Big Horn River.

Shortly after getting underway with the construction of his fort, Carrington learned that a trader, one Pierre Gasseau, more commonly known as "French Pete," and five companions had been killed, just north of the work site. French Pete, who dispensed firewater and perhaps weapons as well, apparently got into a disagreement with some of his Indian customers, who promptly did in Pete and his companions. Carrington later sent a work party to retrieve the bodies and bury them in the new post cemetery, which was to grow and flourish in the coming months if nothing else at Fort Phil Kearny did.

Throughout that summer of 1866, work on Carrington's fort progressed. Much like the British colonel in "Bridge on the River Kwai," Carrington became obsessed with the construction of this post. If his life had a singleness of purpose, this seemed to be it. Wood parties ranged out into the virgin pine forests, to the northwest, cutting and hauling timber for the fort. And by the time autumn gold began to tinge the foothills of the Big Horns, an impressive and massive 600 by 800-foot stockade stood as testimony to Henry B. Carrington's sense of purpose. On a departmental inspection trip late that summer, Colonel William B. Hazen pronounced it a splendid structure, albeit excessive in size, considering the garrison, which had been reduced to about 300 men, after detaching units to serve at Forts Reno and C.F. Smith.

And, meanwhile, what of the Indians, who looked on with anger at this intrusion: the "hated post on the Piney," as they called it. True to his word, Red Cloud's warriors did not sit idly by while Carrington's soldiers labored mightily to erect this stockaded white man's symbol of authority. Almost daily, raiding parties swept down from the surrounding hills to run off livestock, strike the slow-moving wood train, hauling freshly cut timber to the fort, or fall on some unsuspecting solitary hunter foolish enough to venture beyond the pale of the fort's protection. Case in point being one Ridgway Glover, a photographer/writer, whose naked and mutilated body was found a mile and a half from the fort at dawn one September morning. Carrington was learning just how deadly serious these Indians were when they predicted war if the soldiers came into the Powder River country.

As well, virtually any wagon train plodding up the Bozeman was a ripe target for attack. The larger trains were generally able to drive off the attackers, but if nothing else, the Indians were usually successful in running off a few head of livestock. On July 21, 1866, a mixed train of military personnel and civilians, under the command of Lieutenant George Templeton, came under attack on the Crazy Woman Fork of the Powder River, roughly halfway between Forts Reno and Phil Kearny. Reacting promptly, the resourceful twenty five-year-old Templeton directed the train to high ground and corralled the wagons, from where, in the best Hollywood tradition, the defenders kept the circling attackers at bay. Later, forty-eight-year-old Methodist clergyman David White led a charge to drive Indian snipers from a nearby gulch, then, with a companion, rode back to Fort Reno for help. As it turned out, though, the defenders were relieved by a column of cavalry under Captain David Starr Jordan, en route to Fort Reno from Fort Phil Kearny.

There is some irony to be noted in the fact that part of Carrington's mission was to provide protection for emigrant wagon trains traveling along the Bozeman Trail. However, owing to the surprising vigor of Indian attacks, the government was forced to close the trail to all immigrant traffic after 1866. However, in that first full year following the Civil War, some 2,000 immigrants traveled the Bozeman Trail to Montana. Thereafter, however, the Bozeman would see only military traffic for the next two years. But that was not all there was to it. Three hundred miles to the south, the Union Pacific's "Iron Horse" was pushing steadily west and the government was mighty keen on keeping the Indians from interfering with construction of those steel rails. So, in a sense, the Bozeman Trail dangled as something of a carrot keeping the Indians occupied while railroad construction proceeded.

In the beginning, anyway, Carrington's orders did not allow him the latitude to take offensive action, even if he had had the resources to do so, which he didn't. As noted, he was there to protect emigrant traffic, not prosecute an Indian war. Although the federal government recognized the need to provide protection for travelers along the Bozeman, it was not of a mind to undertake punitive operations at this time, nor had it really expected to have to do so.

Following the end of the Civil War, a drastically reduced peacetime army had to find the resources to fulfill its mission of reconstruction in the South, be prepared to respond to French Emperor Maximilian's aggressive posturing in Mexico, while also dealing with the Western Indian problem. It was clear to many that eventually, the Indians would have to be subjugated by military force, but for now, the idea was simply to see that travelers along the Bozeman Trail were accorded such protection as army was able to provide.

Thus, the army's role along the Bozeman was intended to be strictly defensive, and Henry B. Carrington, not being of an aggressive temperament to begin with, was probably not a bad choice, given the restrictive nature of his assignment. Fortunately, Carrington did not see fit to interpret his orders in any other light, a position that a number of the officers in his command found intolerable. Most of these men, having seen plenty of combat in the Civil War, were incensed over the boldness of the Indians and more particularly, over Carrington's refusal to retaliate in like kind. As the weeks passed at Fort Phil Kearny, what had begun as a disagreement with their commander's Indian philosophy soon blossomed into outright resentment.

THE FETTERMAN DISASTER

That fall, there arrived at Fort Phil Kearny, two figures who were to play a key role in the soon-to-unfold December tragedy. In October came Lieutenant George W. Grummond and his pregnant bride, Frances Courtney Grummond, a lovely young woman out of Franklin, Tennessee, whose life was to be forever changed by the events of the next few weeks. A month later, Captain and Brevet Lieutenant Colonel William Judd Fetterman arrived at the fort and promptly made clear his views on the Indian problem.

In the meantime, a directive had come through from department headquarters in Omaha authorizing Carrington to take some offensive action. The Indians, it was imagined would be hunkered down in the warmth of their lodges and hence more vulnerable than would otherwise be the case. Whether or not the directive set Carrington's pulse to racing is not clear. He did not exactly have a plethora of resources at his disposal. A goodly portion of his command was new and they had little combat experience, including their commander. Moreover, training was sorely lacking; most of the garrison's time and energy was expended on building the fort. Neither were these troops well-armed, being mostly equipped with the old Civil War Springfield muzzle loader. In the sometimes inscrutable ways of the military, the regimental band had marched up the Bozeman armed with seven-shot Spencer breech-loading carbines, which Carrington had the good sense to promptly transfer to his cavalrymen. Thus, when all was said and done, the garrison at Fort Phil Kearny, seemed to have its hands full trying to take care of itself and provide some reasonable degree of protection for north-bound travelers.

In all likelihood, Carrington probably did not entertain anything like a bold strike on the Indian villages, though a cabal of his officers led by the newly arrived Captain Fetterman and Lieutenant Grummond, had been urging punitive action right along. But the issue became a moot point when bold Fetterman, battle wizened veteran that he was, requested permission to set a trap for the Indians. Carrington agreed. It wasn't exactly what the Omaha directive called for, but it was close enough for the colonel. As it turned out, the Indians refused to be enticed by the lure of tethered livestock and so the ploy fizzled. Notwithstanding, Fetterman thought little of the Indians' fighting prowess and bragged that with a company of regulars he could whip a thousand Indians. Fetterman's boast, it should be noted, reflected a general feeling among many officers in the frontier army that regular army troops were more than a match for savage Indians.

On the morning of December 6, lookouts reported that the wood train was again under attack. Fetterman, with thirty men, was sent to relieve the wood train, while Carrington himself, with Lieutenant Grummond and twenty-five mounted infantry would swing around and strike the raiders from behind. On paper the plan looked pretty good, but unfortunately, Fetterman's green troopers rather panicked when confronted by the Indians. Fetterman's second-in-command, Lieutenant Horatio Bingham was cut off and killed. Instead of cornering the raiders between them, Carrington and Fetterman each had their hands full and were fortunate to escape with no further losses.

After this incident, Carrington was probably a bit cowed. He had witnessed first-hand how quickly a relief effort could fall apart. Thereafter, he would be careful to avoid such situations. A fortnight later, when the wood train was struck again, Captain and Brevet Major James Powell, also a veteran combat officer, but one less impetuous than his comrade Fetterman, relieved the wood train but refused to pursue the raiders. But all of this set the stage for the defining moment of Red Cloud's war.

December 21 was a pleasant enough morning to begin with, Margaret Carrington recorded in her journal, but it was soon to be a day that would harbor the grimmest of memories. Once again, lookouts signaled that the wood train was under attack. Carrington ordered Major Powell to form a column and relieve the wood train, but Fetterman, perhaps still smarting from the little debacle on the 6th, claimed the right to command by virtue of his brevet rank of lieutenant colonel. Carrington acquiesced. Fetterman was ordered to relieve the wood train, but under no circumstances was he to pursue the raiders beyond Lodge Trail Ridge, a large land mass just east of Fort Phil Kearny.

In short order, Fetterman had his column assembled: a mixed force of cavalry and infantry, the former under Lieutenant Grummond, the latter to be commanded by Fetterman himself, along with Captain Fred Brown, another veteran of the old 18th Infantry who was about to leave Fort Phil Kearny for a new assignment, but longed to take himself an Indian scalp before departing. Interestingly enough, Fetterman's party numbered eighty-one, including himself; just about the size of a regular army company, with which he had claimed he could whip all the Sioux.

Exactly what happened next is clouded in some controversy. Carrington claimed to have issued a clear directive to Fetterman when he assigned him to lead the relief party, then repeated his order as the column was leaving the fort, but there is some evidence to suggest that this was perhaps an afterthought on Carrington's part. In any event, Fetterman did pursue the Indians beyond Lodge Trail Ridge, only to disappear into a shroud of mystery and speculation, like George Custer a decade later.

Beyond Lodge Trail Ridge the Indians lay in wait. A favorite tactic of the Indians was to conceal the main body of warriors, while a decoy party craftily drew the pursuers into a trap from which there was little chance of escape. The ploy failed about as often as it succeeded, however, usually because a few impulsive young braves were unable to restrain themselves. But here on this late December day with snow on the ground and under thickening skies, the ruse worked to perfection, orchestrated perhaps by a rising young Oglala warrior named Tasunka-Witko—Crazy Horse to the whites. Whether Crazy Horse was actually there is not clear, though it seems likely he would have been present on such an occasion.

Teasingly, the decoy party drew the blue coats onward, Lieutenant Grummond and the cavalry thundering on in pursuit, followed some distance back by Fetterman, Brown and the infantry. Near the end of a long sloping ridge that roughly parallels the old U.S. Highway 87, the trap was sprung. Caught between warriors concealed along both flanks of the snowy ridge, Grummond, too late, tried to pull back, but he had crossed his Rubicon. Retreat was no longer an option.

An exaggerated artist's depiction of the Fetterman disaster.

Fetterman and Brown were coming on, but in a heartbeat, they too were caught up in the jaws of the ambush. The foot soldiers tried to fall back, but were quickly overwhelmed as desperately they struggled to reload their Civil War vintage muzzle loaders, with cold-numbed fingers. Two civilians, Isaac Fisher and James Wheatley who had elected to accompany the relief column, were anxious to test their new sixteen-shot Henry repeaters against the Indians. And a good account of themselves they gave, their bodies found behind a copse of boulders, surrounded by spent shell casings. The final stand took place near the present large rock obelisk. Here, Fetterman met his end at the hands of American Horse, who brained Fetterman with his stone war club, knocking him from his horse, then finished off the brash captain by slitting his throat. In the end, none of the eighty-one survived to tell the story of this December day. It was the worst disaster the United States Army had suffered in the Trans-Mississippi West up to that time and would so stand until eclipsed by the debacle on the Little Big Horn a decade later. For the Indians, it was an electric success; the victory of the "Hundred in the Hands," they called it.[19]

THE AMAZING RIDE OF PORTUGEE PHILLIPS

Back at Fort Phil Kearny, a nervous Carrington dispatched Captain Tenedor Ten Eyck with a second column of troops to see what had happened to Fetterman. Ten Eyck reached a high point overlooking the ridge of destruction. He was too far for the naked eye to discern details, but it was clear that what his gaze beheld was a tragedy of the first magnitude. Returning to the fort, he reported his findings to Carrington. The bodies of Fetterman's command would have to be retrieved. And so, preparing a column of all the troops the post could spare, together with wagons, Carrington sallied forth on his grim mission.

Once the hasty burials were effected, Carrington turned his thoughts to the defense of the fort, now seen as quite vulnerable to the Indians, who were sure to follow up their destruction of Fetterman's command with an attack on the fort itself. With reinforcements needed, one of the civilian employees working under the post quartermaster, thirty-four-year-old John "Portugee" Phillips volunteered to carry a message to the nearest telegraph at Horseshoe Creek, 190 miles to the south. With a weather system moving in, Phillips and a companion, Daniel Dixon set out on their mission. At Fort Reno, the pair picked up a third companion, and here, Phillips was also asked by the post commander, Lieutenant Colonel Henry Wessells, to carry a message to Col. Innis Palmer, commanding at Fort Laramie. On Christmas Day, the Phillips party reached Horseshoe Creek, where a report was wired to department headquarters in Omaha.

Meanwhile, Phillips then continued on to Fort Laramie, some forty-six miles further, and apparently alone, through bitter cold weather, arriving at that post at 11 p.m., in the midst of a gala holiday ball. In the wake of the Fetterman disaster, department commander, General Philip St. George Cooke, ordered Lieutenant Colonel Wessells to assume command of Fort Phil Kearny and the recently created Mountain District. On January 18, Wessells arrived at Fort Kearny with two companies of the 2nd Cavalry and four more of the 18th Infantry, bringing the garrison's total strength to approximately 650. Unfortunately, the new commander brought nothing in the way of supplies, which were more in need at that point than additional mouths to feed. Although the Fort Kearny community was mightily worried about an attack on the post, there was, as it turned out, little to fear on that score, since the weather encouraged the Indians to remain in their villages.

And what of Carrington? Back in July, a reorganization of army units had been authorized by Congress. The second and third battalions in each existing regiment would be designated new regiments. Thus the first battalion of the 18th would remain as such, while the second battalion became the new 27th Infantry and the third battalion became the 36th Infantry. The plan called for headquarters and the first battalion of the 18th to be shifted from Fort Kearny to Fort Caspar. Ironically, the new directive arrived on the very day Fetterman's command was destroyed. The second battalion, now the 27th Infantry would remain behind at Fort Phil Kearny. Carrington, however, asked to remain with his old regiment, the 18th. His request was approved though actual orders had not been cut. But then came the news of Fetterman. Back in Omaha, General Cooke, stunned, like everyone else, at the news, nevertheless issued the directive sending Carrington to Fort Caspar and replacing him with Lieutenant Colonel Wessells. Although the transfer had been all but made official prior to the Fetterman tragedy, it appeared to all parties that Carrington had been relieved of command as a result of the disaster. An 1867 inquiry would subsequently clear him of responsibility for the Fetterman debacle, but the man in charge always wears the mantle of responsibility and like Lord Chelmsford in the wake of Isandlwana, Henry B. Carrington never again held a field command.

Following the arrival of Colonel Wessells, Carrington and his family (wife and sons), together with a few other wives and children, in company with a saddened and very pregnant Francis Courtney Grummond departed Fort Kearny, escorted by a twenty-man cavalry detachment, bound for Fort Caspar, plodding through the snow and sub-zero temperatures. It was indeed a cold and bitter journey, one filled with haunting memories.

But an interesting postscript: in 1870, Carrington retired from active duty to take a teaching position at Wabash College in Indiana. That same year Margaret died of tuberculosis, two years after the publication of her book, *Absaraka: Home of the Crows*. Meanwhile, in her home town of Franklin, Tennessee, Francis Grummond, reading of Margaret's death, wrote Henry a note of condolence. The note led to further exchanges and eventually the two were married. Later they removed to Hyde Park, Massachusetts, where Francis, like Margaret before her, penned her own account of those days trying days beneath the shadow of the Big Horns, entitled *My Army Life and the Fort Phil Kearny Massacre*.

Although it might appear so, Red Cloud's War was not confined solely to Fort Phil Kearny. True enough, the "Hated Post on the Piney" did seem to receive most of the Indians' attention, but they by no means totally ignored the other two outposts. Of these two, Fort Reno got off easiest, but Fort C.F. Smith had tough times of its own: small parties attacked, travelers killed and mutilated, livestock run off, but fortunately, nothing on a par with the Fetterman debacle. It will be recalled, that in early August, Carrington sent Captain Nathaniel Kinney north to build the third Bozeman Trail outpost. Guided by grizzled old Jim Bridger, Kinney, with two companies of the 18th Infantry (165 men) established the site of the new fort, ninety-one miles north of Fort Kearny, near the Big Horn River. By December, C.F. Smith was largely finished. Then late that month, Crow Indians, mostly white-friendly and on whose reservation the fort had been built, brought disturbing rumors of the Fetterman disaster; it was not reassuring news to the garrison.

The Hayfield and Wagon Box Fights, August 1867

The winter of 1866-1867 passed with no further disasters and no all-out attacks on any of the Bozeman Trail forts, though harassment tactics persisted. However, as spring came on and the new grass fattened winter-thin Indian ponies, activity picked up. Spring also meant a resumption of supply trains lumbering up the Bozeman hauling much needed supplies. Early in July 1867, one such train arrived at Fort Phil Kearny, carrying among other things, a shipment of the new Springfield-Allin breech-loading rifle and 100,000 rounds of ammunition.

The rifle was actually not new in the true sense of the word, but was rather, a revamped version of the old Civil War vintage muzzle-loader that had been converted to the breech-loading system. What this meant was that instead of having to ram powder and ball down the muzzle of the weapon, the soldier now had only to flip up a hinged plate on the top of the rifle and insert a ready-made cartridge. A giant improvement over the old system, the breech-loader was soon to pay rich dividends.

The army that Carrington left behind was growing up, too. By the summer of '67, they had a year of seasoning under their belts and, along with the new breech-loaders came a new commanding officer, Colonel John Eugene Smith, a solid leader with combat experience. During the Carrington regime, the garrison spent most of its time building Fort Phil Kearny; little time was devoted to training. Accordingly, one of the first things Colonel Wessells had done upon his arrival in January, had been to institute a training schedule, which Colonel Smith continued and expanded on. Coincidentally, Smith's second-in-command was Major Benjamin Smith, no relation. Both Smiths had served with distinction in the Civil War. Jonathan carried a brevet major general's rank, while Benjamin had been brevetted brigadier general.

Although Fort Phil Kearny was essentially complete, a few structures were still under construction and of course, firewood was always needed. As a consequence, wood parties continued to harvest timber for the fort's two sawmills from an area known as Piney Island, some five miles north of Fort Kearny. A civilian contractor, hired by the post quartermaster, provided the cutting crews, while the fort's garrison provided protection against Indian raiders, who continued to find the lumbering wood train a most tempting target, as it plied its way from Piney Island to the fort.

In July 1867, it was decided to assign one company to provide protection for the wood cutters each month, rather than to delegate that responsibility on a daily basis. In July, Company A, 27th Infantry drew the duty and was replaced on the last day of the month by Company C, Captain James Powell commanding. Company C numbered about fifty men, not including Powell and his second, Lieutenant John Jenness.

Out at the cutting area, a wide, grassy plain, the woodcutters had arranged a makeshift oval-shaped corral using the wagon tops or beds, as some of the men referred to them. The canvas tops had been removed, along with the chassis or running gear. Overall, the corral measured approximately seventy by thirty feet. The corral served a dual purpose: as a place to put livestock at night to prevent their being run off by Indians and as a defensive enclosure in time of attack. The soldiers and woodcutters slept in tents just outside the corral. The running gear of the wagons (the wheel assembly), meanwhile, was used to haul freshly cut timber back to the fort. Each morning, cutting crews fanned out into South Piney Creek Canyon to harvest more timber, returning to the corral in the evening with the fruits of the day's labors. With half of his command detached as escort for the wagon train and to watch over the woodcutters, Powell was left with some twenty-four men at the corral.

The month of July had been a comparatively quiet time insofar as Indian harassment was concerned. Mostly, the various Lakota and Cheyenne bands had been busy with their annual Sun Dance ritual, an event that stood as the apex of their spiritual year. However, once that was finished they were again able to devote their undivided attention to driving the soldiers from their territory.

As it turned out, though, the Indians were unable to agree on a target. One faction thought their effort ought to be directed against Fort C.F. Smith, while others argued for a strike on Fort Phil Kearny and its always tempting wood train. They settled for the best of both worlds. One contingent, composed mainly of Northern Cheyennes, led by Dull Knife and Two Moons, would attack the hay-cutters working out of C.F. Smith, while the second war party, made up mainly of Lakotas led by Crazy Horse, High Backbone and other prominent war leaders, and most likely including Red Cloud, would go for Fort Phil Kearny.

Up at Fort C.F. Smith, they cut timber, too, but the fort did not require as much wood as at Fort Kearny. Hay was also harvested from a large meadow located two to six miles from the post, depending on the point from which one was measuring. Like their wood-cutting counterparts at Fort Phil Kearny, the hay cutters had also constructed a corral of sorts, theirs being made out of brush and saplings, but it served the same function in both places.

Only twice so far in this year of 1867, had Fort Smith experienced any Indian harassment. The Crows foretold that a major attack by the Sioux and their allies was imminent, but they had been warning of this and one was never quite sure just how much credence to give these predictions. In any event, Lieutenant Colonel Luther Prentice Bradley, recently installed as the new commander at Fort Smith, thought it probably made good sense to provide an escort for the hay cutters. At the end of July, twenty-nine-year-old Lieutenant Sigismund Sternberg, was assigned to command the escort. A German-born Jew, and a veteran of the Prussian army, Sternberg had served the Union in the Civil War, but like most of these officers in the frontier army, he had no experience fighting Indians.

About 11 a.m. on the morning of August 1, Sternberg's command discovered a large Indian war party, judged by the defenders to be 700–800 strong, preparing to attack. Like the garrison at Fort Phil Kearny, the troops at C.F. Smith were also armed with new Springfield-Allin breech-loading rifles. While workers outside the corral rushed frantically toward its security, the Indians launched a decoy party, hoping to lure the defenders out in pursuit, and a few of the twenty-six men inside the corral thought to do exactly that,, but were, fortunately, restrained by a coolheaded Sergeant James Norton, who recalled that Fetterman, too, had chased a decoy party to his everlasting regret.

The decoy ruse failed to click on this day and so a large body of mounted warriors charged the brush and wood corral, only to be met by a withering blast of rifle fire from the new breechloaders. Grabbing a Springfield, Lieutenant Sternberg immediately placed himself in an exposed position and was warned by one of the enlisted men to get down before he got hit. Sternberg berated the private for speaking that way to an officer and then promptly fell dead with a bullet in the head.

Here the Indians met a totally unexpected reception, one that called for a change in strategy. To this end, the attackers decided to enlist the support of a grass fire. And so, the "fire came on in rolling billows, like the waves of an ocean," recalled one defender. But as it approached the corral it swept upward to a height of forty feet before running out of gas, snuffed by a sudden wind change that carried smoke and burning grass back toward the Indians.[20]

The Indians now resorted to a rain of arrows, which streaked through the haze and burning ash-filled air to wound a number of mules inside the corral. Most of the Indians appeared to be armed with bows and arrows, but enough had firearms, so that between arrows and bullets, the defenders were pinned down for some four hours, before a relief column from the fort arrived on the scene to discourage the Indians from further activity.

Meanwhile, down at Fort Phil Kearny, the Indians were preparing to unleash their second strike in as many days. About 7 a.m. on the morning of August 2, one large war party of Lakotas made a feint against the fort, hoping to draw the soldiers out to give battle. Meantime, others attempted to run off livestock grazing out beyond the wagon box corral, while simultaneously swooping down on the wood cutters working up in Little Piney Creek Canyon. Soon, these were joined by the war party demonstrating against the fort and presently the combined Indian war party, numbering perhaps as many as 1,000–1,500, turned their undivided attention to the wagon box corral, where Powell and Jenness had managed to muster twenty-six soldiers and six civilians.

As the anxious defenders watched and waited, the mounted Indians massed on a broad plain to the southwest. Nervously, they fingered their new breech-loaders and prepared for the onslaught. And then it came, a thundering mounted charge swept toward the corral. As with the hay cutters, these wagon box defenders met that charge with a furious blast that turned back the attackers. Regrouping, the Indians launched a second and then a third charge, only to be turned back each time by the steady volume of fire. This was unexpected; not at all like fighting Fetterman's soldiers. Here, there was no pause while the soldiers loaded their rifles; the fire was nearly continuous.

From a drop-off north of the corral, Indian snipers enjoyed some success against the defenders. Indeed, three of Powell's five casualties were incurred as a result of fire from these snipers. At one point, Lieutenant Jenness, like his counterpart Lieutenant Sternberg in the Hayfield Fight, was cautioned to keep low, but the brash young officer brushed aside the warning and soon lay dead with a bullet in his head. Since the mounted charges had been unsuccessful, the Indians now turned to a new tactic. From the north, a massed body of warriors surged toward the corral, only to be repulsed.

Meanwhile, back at Fort Kearny, Colonel Smith, aware of Powell's predicament, dispatched a relief column under Major Smith. Approaching the corral, Smith unlimbered his 12-pounder mountain howitzer and lobbed a shell or two at the attackers, who elected to withdraw. There had been fighting enough for this day and there would be wailing in the camps tonight for warriors who would not be returning. There is no consensus on Indian casualties in the Hayfield and Wagon Box fights. One observer claimed fifty in the former, and Powell thought sixty were killed in the Wagon Box Fight, but the actual number was probably less than that.

But if the Indians had been thwarted at the Hayfield and Wagon Box Fights, neither setback in any way diminished their zeal for harassing movement along the Bozeman Trail. On August 1, just ahead of the attack on the hay-cutters, a government supply train left Fort C.F. Smith, bound for Fort Phil Kearny. Pursued and harassed by the Indians en route to its destination, the train reached Big Goose Creek (present day Sheridan) and continued on. Approaching the site of the wagon box corral, they were greeted by the still smoldering grass, dead cattle, and a white man's scalp hanging from a pole. The following day, the gates of Phil Kearny swung open to receive the new arrivals, who only then learned of what had transpired out on that grassy plain twenty-four hours earlier, when a corral of wagon boxes made history.

Near the end of October, a thirty-eight-year-old lieutenant with the uncommonly long name of Edward Richard Pitman Shurly was ordered to take an escort of forty men to rendezvous with a Wells Fargo train north bound from Fort Phil Kearny to Fort C.F. Smith. Shurly's orders were shepherd the train on into Fort Smith. On November 2, the train came under Indian attack some six miles north of Fort Kearny and the wagon master wisely corralled the wagons. In this state, Shurly found the train and assumed the escort duty. An early season snow storm struck the next day, but let up enough for the train to resume its journey on November 4. Fifteen miles out, Indians struck again, this time at the Goose Creek crossing. And a perfect spot it was. The descent to the crossing was steep and footing insecure due to the snow, thereby causing the train to be widely separated, the wagons having to be guided downhill using ropes.

Shurly's hole card, though, was a mountain howitzer at the rear of the train, along with the last two wagons. The cannoneers promptly loaded their piece and sent a shell screaming toward the attackers. The Indians figured that if they captured the big medicine gun, they could have their way with the wagon train and, accordingly, moved to secure that objective. But Shurly, who was at the rear of the train with seven men, recognized the peril and ordered the howitzer limbered up and driven at full speed down the slope toward the rest of the wagons, which by now had been corralled. Despite an arrow in his foot, Shurly, and his detachment managed to fight their way downhill to safety of the corral. With the arrival of darkness, the attack tapered off and two volunteers set off to Fort Kearny for help. With the arrival of daylight, the Indians renewed their efforts, but fortunately for the defenders, the two volunteers had reached their destination and a relief column soon arrived to break the siege.

By the spring of 1868, renewed efforts were underway to reach a settlement with the Plains tribes. In April, representatives of the United States government gathered with the Lakotas and their Cheyenne and Arapaho allies at Fort Laramie. Most notably, however, Red Cloud and his followers were not among those presence. Notwithstanding, a treaty was agreed to and signed by both the Indians and the representatives of the United States. In essence, the government agreed to abandon its three Bozeman Trail forts. The Powder River country would henceforth be regarded as strictly Indian territory, with whites not allowed. But Red Cloud was not so easily persuaded. When the soldiers left, then he would come down to Fort Laramie and put his mark on the treaty, not before. The proof of the peace commission's promise came to pass in August, and Red Cloud saw the troops march out of the Bozeman Trail forts. And scarcely had the dust from the departing bluecoats settled, than the "Hated Post on the Piney" was ablaze, probably torched by the Indians themselves. At long last, Red Cloud believed and journeyed to Fort Laramie to finally put his mark on the Laramie Treaty.

And so it had begun quietly enough, as wars go, but during the course of its brief two-year life it accounted for hundreds of casualties. No war can be studied and certainly not fully evaluated in terms of what it might or might not have accomplished unless the assessment considers the impact on all parties. Insofar as Red Cloud's War is concerned, it may be said that in addition to inflicting a painful and embarrassing defeat on the U.S. Army, the Indians also achieved a limited strategic victory by compelling the army to abandon its Bozeman Trail forts ... or so they thought. In reality, however, the stoutness of the Indian resistance to the military presence in the Powder River region probably had less to do with the abandonment of the forts than did the inexorable westward movement of the Union Pacific Railroad, which had made the Bozeman largely obsolete anyway. But even without the railroad in the picture, the cost of maintaining a corridor of travel through the Powder River country had become prohibitive and would likely have forced the road's closure in any case. By 1869, the railroad made it possible to reach Montana, traveling by rail as far as Salt Lake, from which point travelers could then turn north and continue their journey overland. This same route had always been open to travelers, but it was a longer course than along either the Bozeman or Bridger Trails. Now the railroad negated that longer distance and offered a far safer route than by traveling up the Bozeman and risking Indian attack, or going along the Bridger route, which, though safer than the Bozeman, offered reduced forage and water.

Red Cloud's War clearly demonstrated the need to resolve what was then called the "Indian problem." Where the treaty negotiations of 1866 had failed so dismally, hopes were higher for the Laramie Treaty of 1868, arguably the most significant such agreement between the United States Government and the Plains tribes. It would not be reasonable to say that without Red Cloud's War there would have been no Laramie Treaty, but the war did underscore the rather immediate need to find something approaching a permanent solution to the Indian problem. If it cannot be argued that Red Cloud won his war, it at least must be said that he did not come away empty handed. The victory of the "hundred in the hands" was certainly noteworthy, even if the Wagon Box and Hayfield Fights proved downright disappointing. But the forts were abandoned and the army was gone and that was what it had all been about in the first place. So as far as Red Cloud was concerned the effort had paid off in that it bought some time, if nothing else.

The 1868 Laramie Treaty

It could be argued that Red Cloud's War was the only conflict of the Western Indian wars in which the Indians emerged triumphant. Notwithstanding, it was a hollow victory because only briefly were the Indians able to savor the fruits of that victory. The three key posts along the Bozeman Trail had been shut down and burned, and that was something to feel good about, if one happened to be a Lakota. (There were actually five posts on the Trail, but Forts Fetterman and Ellis were at the beginning and end and therefore did not manage to disturb the Indians nearly as much as Forts Reno, Phil Kearny, and C.F. Smith).

Abandonment of the three most antagonizing posts, then, along with the closure of the Bozeman Trail itself were cause aplenty for jubilation, even if only short term. The Indians believed they had brought the U.S. to its knees, not realizing it was simply a case of the Bozeman Trail and its forts having become unnecessary. The Iron Horse—Union Pacific—was approaching Cheyenne and would soon reach Salt Lake City, so that emigrant traffic could travel the railroad to Salt Lake, then head north to Montana without having to fight the Sioux on the Bozeman Trail, which, in effect, had now become obsolete. The Trail would, however, continue to serve as an important corridor for military traffic, but its days as a route for the immigrant wagon trains had come to an end.

Unquestionably, the most significant legacy of Red Cloud's War was the Laramie Treaty of 1868. Of the three treaties affecting the Indian tribes of the Great Plains, the 1851 Horse Creek Treaty and the Treaty of Medicine Lodge, the Fort Laramie Treaty of 1868 was arguably the most important.

Consummated during the spring and summer of 1868, the terms of the treaty, while calling for the federal government to close the hated Bozeman Trail, also stipulated that the tribes agreed to settle on a large tract of land that essentially covered all of present day South Dakota west of the Missouri River; to be called the great Sioux Reservation. Here the Indians were expected to reside and here they would receive food, medical treatment and in short whatever was needed to sustain life. Both Red Cloud and Spotted Tail were among the many Lakotas who chose to settle here. Warrior years were behind both men now and this way of life would not have seemed unattractive. But there were others, such as Sitting Bull, Crazy Horse and Gall who refused to change their life style. These recalcatrant's chose instead to live in the old way, roaming free, without government interference. It was these bands *who did not sign the treaty or agree to its terms* that would constitute the core of the so called "hostile" element and would prove the most troublesome to the U.S. Army.

Unquestionably, the Laramie Treaty's most ambiguous and troublesome clause was the one that set aside, as unceded Indian territory, a huge tract extending from the Black Hills on the east to the Big Horn Mountains on the west and from the North Platte River on the south to the Yellowstone River on the north. Here in this vast region, the tribes would be permitted to live and hunt for so long as the buffalo roamed. Of course it was understood—by the whites—that the white man would be allowed to build railroads across this land without interference by the Indians. In retrospect certainly, and probably at the time as well, to anyone who bothered to give the treaty a serious look, it was an invitation to trouble. But there was something to be said for the treaty from the Indians' point of view; it wasn't all bad. Many found that it was nice to be able to accept government handouts during the winter then trot off to join their wild brethren in the unceded territory during the summer months. In a way it was the best of both worlds. For the moment the government was willing to go along with this arrangement, in the misguided belief that eventually the buffalo would be gone and even the wild bands would then be forced to come into the agencies, where they would all be one happy family, learning to farm and become educated while the paternalistic hand of the Great Father provided their umbrella of security. Of course unforeseen circumstances—such as the Black Hills gold rush and the continued advance of the *Northern Pacific Railroad* would cause that timetable to be accelerated, but in 1868 those events were yet to happen.

Massacre on the Marias River, January 23, 1870

Meanwhile, farther to the west of where the Indians sought to stem the white advance along the Bozeman Trail, there were other clashes as well. It will be recalled that upon taking office President Grant, heavily influenced by Quakers and other peace-minded groups, had put into play his own peace policy, and barely had that policy taken effect when it received what might have been a crippling blow. On January 23, 1870, four companies of the 2d Cavalry and some fifty mounted. infantry from the 13th Regiment, under the command of Major Eugene Baker, attacked and virtually wiped out a Piegan [pronounced as pagan] village on the Marias River near present Shelby, Montana. Piegans from the band of Mountain Chief had been raiding and stealing stock since the past fall and outraged citizens were clamoring for action. From General Sheridan in Chicago came orders to chastise the raiders. Major Eugene Mortimer Baker, an officer who had served with distinction in the Civil War and was now in command at Fort Ellis, near Bozeman, was directed to go after Mountain Chief's Piegans. Sheridan's orders, delivered through department commander, Colonel Phillipe Regis de Trobriand, were "Tell Baker to strike them hard." Baker took his instructions at face value. The problem was that there were two camps of Piegans; Mountain Chief's was one and the second was a mostly peaceful band under Heavy Runner. However, Baker's chief scout assured the major he would be able to distinguish between the two camps. So with that in mind, on a bitterly cold 19th day of January, Baker set out from Fort Ellis on his mission.

As it turned out, though, Heavy Runner had gotten word of what was afoot and moved his village. Only at the last minute was Baker informed that the encampment he was preparing to strike was not that of Mountain Chief. However, in Baker's view, one Piegan was as good as another and he authorized the attack to proceed. When the smoke had cleared, more than 170 Piegans had been killed, 40 were wounded and another 140, along with 300 horses were captured. Baker's casualties amounted to 1 killed. Winter weather precluded the pursuit of Mountain Chief's band, and so, after burning the encampment, Baker returned to his station at Fort Shaw. Although it did not receive the press that Sand Creek had, some saw this as a repeat of that tragedy.

The Northern Pacific Railroad

It could perhaps be considered part of the legacy of Sully and Sibley's Dakota campaigns in the sense that those campaigns made it possible to begin work on the construction of the Northern Pacific Railroad. Chartered in 1864, and given a massive land grant by Congress, the object of the Northern Pacific Railroad was to connect the Great Lakes with Puget Sound in the Pacific Northwest. In addition, a rail line across the Dakota prairies and up the Valley of the Yellowstone would open new lands to lumbering, mining and of course farming. Between the years 1864–1870 backers of the new enterprise struggled mightily to find financing. Then, into the breach stepped Jay Cooke, entrepreneur and banker, who brought some much needed financial stability to the operation. By1871, the line had reached the North Dakota border and a year later the Missouri River. The railroad's arrival at the Missouri promptly resulted in the creation of the town of Bismarck. This, in turn, resulted in the creation of a new military post some three miles downstream from the new community. The post, eventually to be named Fort Abraham Lincoln, would become one of the best known forts in the West.

As the Northern Pacific crawled across, first Minnesota, then present day North Dakota, the concern of the Lakotas mounted in direct proportion to the railroad's advance. General Sherman (now General of the Army) was only too willing to support the advance of the railroad with his troops. At first glance, it would seem that any extension of the railroad up the Yellowstone Valley was in violation of the Laramie treaty of 1868. However, a careful reading of the terms of that agreement stipulated that corridors of transportation across "Indian lands" would be allowed.

From President Grant, through Generals Sherman and Sheridan, protecting these railroad enterprises was a top priority. Where the Northern Pacific was concerned, military protection was provided through 1872 by troops from General Winfield Scott Hancock's Department of Dakota and after that time by Brigadier General Alfred Terry, who replaced Hancock. The nationwide panic of 1873—actually initiated by Jay Cooke's house of finance—slowed but did not entirely stop progress on the railroad. During 1871 and 1872, surveying parties worked their way across the vast expanse of Dakota prairie and by 1873 had reached the Yellowstone. Teton Lakota war parties harassed the surveyors at every opportunity, but such action was scarcely enough to even delay progress.

With the arrival of 1873, surveying crews prepared to continue their work up the Valley of the Yellowstone. This section of the route was expected to be the most contested and so it was. Anticipating the need for a strong military presence, a formidable expedition was organized at Fort Rice under the command of Colonel and Brevet Major General David Sloan Stanley. The expedition was a huge thing to behold and included Lieutenant Colonel George Armstrong Custer and ten companies of his 7th Cavalry, along with nineteen companies of infantry and a pair of Rodman field pieces. The 7th Cavalry's regimental band provided a musical backdrop. Even President Grant's family was represented in the person of Colonel Fred Grant, and Custer had his own personal cook, a Black woman named Mary Adams. Some 300 wagons, a large beef herd and a contingent of scouts rounded out the expedition, which numbered 1,500 men. Although Custer had little respect for Stanley, he was no doubt relieved not to have to answer to Hancock as he did in Kansas.

Although providing protection for the surveyors was their number one priority, there remained ample opportunity for Custer to indulge himself hunting elk, antelope, and deer with his beloved hounds, and by all accounts he was mightily successful at supplementing the expedition's kitchen. Custer seems also to have acquired a new interest in paleontology, collecting fossilized specimens to take back with him. Interestingly enough Custer's old West Point classmate, Tom Rosser a former Confederate cavalry leader was now in charge of the Northern Pacific engineering party. As the expedition wound its way across the prairie, Rosser and Custer relived their war experiences. To one looking on from afar it might well have seemed as though the expedition was nothing but a grand lark on the prairie.

Once again, Custer found himself at odds with a superior officer; it seemed to be a trademark of his personality to quarrel, or at least challenge his superior. By all accounts, Stanley had a drinking problem; indeed seems to have been in his cups most of the time. Once, while under the influence, Stanley placed Custer under arrest, over what, is not exactly clear, and compelled him (Custer) to march at the rear of the column for two days. Later, when he sobered up a contrite Stanley revoked the arrest and apologized. But Custer was never timid about following his own instincts, with or without orders, a trait Stanley probably found more than a little irritating. Stanley boasted a distinguished Civil War record. It was Stanley's division, for example, who had borne the brunt of the furious Confederate assault at Franklin, Tennessee, on that pristine last day of November 1864. He was awarded the Medal of Honor for his conduct at Franklin.

Custer Meets the Sioux

Knowing that fresh supplies had come upriver and were awaiting the expedition on the Yellowstone, Custer took two companies of his regiment and set out in search of the supply steamer which he found moored to the south bank of the Yellowstone near present Glendive, Montana. Here the expedition constructed a temporary supply post which they named Stanley's Stockade. Captain Fred Benteen, whose dislike of Custer was soon to propel him to the forefront of Custerphobes, was detailed to stay behind with two companies to guard the stockade while the remainder of the expedition proceeded up the valley.

Thus far the Indians had presented no real opposition to the survey crew, but that was about to change. As was his custom, Custer could always be found with the advance party and so it was this day. Two companies of the 7th constituted the expedition's advance point; some ninety men. At the Yellowstone's confluence with the Tongue River, near present day Miles City the advance paused for lunch. The respite was probably most welcome on a blistering hot August 4.

Suddenly, a party of mounted warriors appeared and tried to stampede the horses, but the troopers were quick to take up their arms and drive the Indians away. Taking his brother Tom—who commanded one of the two companies—and twenty men, Custer pursued the raiders, while the main body of the advance under Captain Myles Moylan, followed behind.

It quickly became clear to Custer that the Indians were using the old decoy trick. When a large party of warriors suddenly appeared along the timbered shores of the river, Custer and his orderly—out in front—found themselves nearly cut off. Tom Custer quickly formed a skirmish line and provided covering fire while Custer and the orderly made a mad dash to safety.

Custer's small advance party soon found itself in a perilous situation. Far outnumbered by the Indians who threatened to swamp them, Custer coolly formed a perimeter around his horses, while at the same time withdrawing to a stand of timber downriver where he was reinforced by Captain Moylan with the rest of the advance party. Fortunately, an old riverbank formed years earlier by the river, provided a strong, natural defensive position. From here the cavalrymen thwarted every Lakota attempt to dislodge them, which included setting fire to the surrounding grass. During the course of the action, the regimental surgeon and three soldiers left the main body to reach Custer's command, but were surprised and ambushed en route; all were killed save one man who managed to escape and reach Custer's position. Late that afternoon, Custer was reinforced by the rest of the regiment, allowing him to pursue the Indians for several miles up the valley. It had been an intense sort of fight that surprisingly resulted in only one soldier being wounded, other than the surgeon and his two companions.

Further pursuit up the valley revealed the site of what had been a large village, one the Arikara scout Bloody Knife—who would later lose his life at the Little Bighorn—judged to have consisted of 400–500 lodges; which in all probability meant a thousand warriors. Custer proposed to strike that village with his entire regiment and Stanley agreed. Accordingly, on the night of August 10, Custer set out on a night march with eight companies of his regiment.

Thirty-six hours later, the soldiers found that the Indians had crossed to the south side of the Yellowstone and taken up positions among the timber on the south shore, about three miles from the mouth of the Big Horn River. Custer attempted to follow, but the river was deep and swift, owing to spring run-offs (one wonders how the Indians managed?). Lieutenant Charles Braden, Company L, 7th Cavalry sets the scene for us:

Next day, August 10, at sunrise, parties were sent up and down the river to look for a crossing. The main force went o a small island. Someone had discovered a narrow ford to the island capable of holding two or three abreast, but between the island and the south bank, the water was deep and the current strong. Efforts were made to swim some of the horses across, their riders carrying a rope made by tying a lot of picket lines together. The efforts failed, for the long line was too heavy to be dragged through the water with its strong current. Lieutenant Weston and several teamsters succeeded in crossing with mules.

Our men and horses had never been drilled in swimming. When the water reached about halfway between their bellies and their backs, the strong current nearly carried them off their feet and the animals refused to go further, but turned around and started for shore. The swimmers were advised to keep on their underclothing, but they did not do so, and long before the day was over, the sun had blistered their bodies, and the next morning they were stiff and sore all over.[21]

From the timbered other side the Indians opened fire on the cavalry, even as their non-combatants looked on from the bluffs. Meanwhile, war parties crossed the river with the intention of striking Custer on each of his flanks. Alert to the danger, however, Custer sent one squadron upriver and a second downriver to counter the threat.

Although Indian resistance was not only spirited; indeed they displayed a more aggressive nature than was ordinarily the case. The '73 fight—as it's often referred to among students of Custeriana, also demonstrated that Indians were well equipped with repeating rifles. But Custer and his troopers acquitted themselves well, and if they did not administer a sound thrashing to the Indians, they nevertheless turned back each Indian effort.

The Northern Pacific survey continued up the Yellowstone Valley for another thirty miles before turning north to the Musselshell River and heading back to the Missouri River, their work for the summer completed. By September, half of the 7th Cavalry was back in quarters at Fort Lincoln, while the other half (minus two companies detached for the northern boundary survey) was sent to Fort Rice. Stanley, meanwhile, returned to Fort Sully.

Looked at it in retrospect, this 1873 expedition and Custer's fight with the Sioux along the Yellowstone carries an eerie similarity to the Little Bighorn, which would be fought just a few miles to the south, three years later. The Washita and this fight on the Yellowstone firmly established the 7th Cavalry as the nation's premier Indian fighting unit.

Custer's 1874 Black Hills Expedition

To western travelers, the Black Hills of Dakota Territory (South Dakota after 1889) loomed as a sort of dark, forested island, hence the name Black Hills. Until the mid–1870s there wasn't much to attract settlers or railroads and as a consequence, few white men did anything more than occasionally pass through. Lakotas and Cheyennes, on the other hand, viewed the Hills not only as sacred, but an area rich in game. And, among other provisions, the Laramie Treaty of 1868 made it clear that the Black Hills was part of what was defined as the Great Sioux Reservation and would remain sacrosanct; whites were prohibited from entering the Hills. At first there wasn't much difficulty enforcing the ban because there was little reason for whites to be there in the first place. But the discovery of gold changed the picture dramatically, as it always did, and it was none other than George Custer and his 7th Cavalry who opened the door.

How the 1874 expedition came about is a fascinating tale of subterfuge and disingenuousness. The vigorous resistance of the Lakota to Custer and the Northern Pacific survey of 1873 was further reflected in the attitude of many Indians at their respective agencies, a brazen sort of attitude that made agents and military authorities wary of what to expect. Although the so-called hostile bands—Hunkpapa in particular—remained the most recalcitrant, even the agency Indians were less submissive than government authorities would have liked them to be.

The Indians' insolent attitude reinforced the notion that, notwithstanding the Laramie Treaty, they remained a troublesome lot and needed close watching. The problem was, though, the closest military post to the Great Sioux Reservation was Fort Laramie, 100 miles south of the Black Hills. To General Sheridan the solution was clear: build a fort in the Black Hills, never mind that to do so would be a direct violation of the Laramie Treaty, but military officials who had been part of the treaty negotiations, disagreed; roads and military posts were exempted. White settlers figured their rights were being violated by banning them from the Hills. At any rate, Sheridan pitched the idea upstairs and, not surprisingly, found a ready audience from both President Grant to and General Sherman. A reconnaissance was needed to select exactly the right site for Sheridan's new fort. At first, Sheridan thought to launch his expedition from Fort Laramie, until it was feared that this might stir up the Indians at Red Cloud and Spotted Tail agencies. As a consequence, Sheridan then turned to Custer and the 7th Cavalry, which may have been in the back of the general's mind all along. Custer had always been his favorite, going back to Civil War days.

Custer didn't need a second invitation, either, and as spring 1874 deepened the 7th Cavalry prepared for another summer afield. The expedition sortied from Fort Lincoln on July 2. It was a huge affair, perhaps the largest of its kind ever to take the field. All twelve companies of the 7th Cavalry were present, along with two companies of infantry which marched alongside more than a hundred supply wagons. Should it be needed there was firepower support in the form of a three-gun battery of Gatling guns and a Rodman field piece. Sixty-one Arikara Indian scouts, three journalists, and a photographer were also part of the entourage, as were two miners and a coterie of scientists. It was hardly a secret that the miners were along to investigate long standing rumors that there was gold in the Black Hills. The scientific party was anxious to report on the flora and fauna of the region. Four reporters would report on the expedition for the *New York World*, *Chicago Inter-Ocean* and *Bismarck Tribune*. Sheridan's staff was represented too, in the person of Major George "Sandy" Forsyth, hero of Beecher Island and Lieutenant Colonel Fred Grant who had been on the Yellowstone adventure the previous year. Custer had taken a liking to the president's son back then, but here in the Black Hills his drinking became something of a problem. Finally, it was an outing for the Custer family no less. In addition to George and Captain Tom Custer, the younger, twenty-five-year-old Boston Custer rode with his brothers, just as he would two years later at the Little Bighorn.

Whether or not the expedition would encounter Indians or at least Indian resistance, was a good question, but most seemed to think they would be challenged, especially considering the Indians' attitude last year along the Yellowstone. In any case if the Indians resisted, the expedition had plenty of firepower. However, for two weeks the only Indians seen were a few small parties who seemed to be observing from a distance.

The last week in July saw the expedition entering the Black Hills from the northwest and soon thereafter came upon five lodges of Lakota. Five lodges scarcely posed a threat but Custer surrounded them with a company of the 7th then entered under a flag of truce. The headman of this group was an aging Sioux named One-Stab. The Indians, One-Stab reported, were on a hunting trip from Red Cloud Agency. Custer and Stab smoked the pipe and Custer then invited the chief to bring his people to the expedition camp where they would be given gifts of sugar and coffee. Angry because Custer would not let them kill the

Sioux, the Arikara scouts nevertheless taunted the Sioux and finally drove them off into the hills, much to Custer's chagrin.

And this would be as close as the expedition came to encountering Indians. The next two weeks were like a big picnic as the expedition made its way through the interior of this enchanting region. Custer and companions climbed to the summits of 6,300-foot Inyan Kara (rock gatherer) a sacred mountain to the Lakotas, and 7,200-foot Harney Peak (named for General William S. Harney), the highest point in the Hills. And of course the region was rich with wildlife. There was plenty of hunting; antelope and deer abounded, and Custer even managed to kill a grizzly. Other members hiked,

Custer and his trophy bear killed in the Black Hills. Although he believed it to have been a grizzly, it may not have been. On the left is his favorite scout, the Arikara Bloody Knife, who would later die at the Little Bighorn.

played baseball and drank in the scenery. But the big news came on July 30, when Horatio Ross, one of the prospectors on the expedition discovered glimmerings of gold in French Creek. *Quod erat demonstrandum.* Ross's findings proved what had long been suspected. Subsequent discoveries only reinforced Ross's findings and the expedition celebrated with champagne. Custer dispatched the scout Lonesome Charley Reynolds on a solitary ride to Fort Laramie to report the news of gold.

Not forgotten amidst the fun and scenery was Sheridan's order to find a suitable site for a military post. On August 7, the expedition camped near historic Bear Butte where the Cheyenne peace prophet, Sweet Medicine reportedly received the Sacred Arrows, and directions for how his people were to conduct their lives. In Custer's view, the site seemed ideal and he so recommended it in his report. Seldom had a military reconnaissance enjoyed such an idyllic time in the field. But all things come to an end. As the expedition prepared to depart the Black Hills, Colonel Sandy Forsyth noted in his journal that they would depart with regret. But depart they did and by the end of August Custer and the 7th Cavalry were back at Fort Lincoln.

News of the discovery of gold in the Black Hills quickly made headlines even though the reports from the Custer expedition were far from conclusive. Indeed, the expedition's official geologist claimed he had not actually seen any gold. But Custer himself had made it a point of proclaiming that the Black Hills was a rich lode and prospectors immediately began flocking to the area in search of riches. If it was the federal government's intention to keep the Black Hills off limits to white settlers and entrepreneurs, the Custer Expedition was a strange way of showing it, but then again perhaps President Grant, and Generals Sherman and Sheridan recognized that the public pressure that followed Custer's announcement was just the excuse that was needed to justify moving into the Hills. But first, something more in the way of proof was needed and it was forthcoming the following year when an official scientific expedition headed by Professor Walter Proctor Jenny, acting under the auspices of the Department of Interior entered the Hills to determine once and for all if gold was present in serious quantities.

And so in July 1875 the Jenny expedition marched into the Black Hills from Fort Laramie escorted, not by Custer, as had been expected, but by Brigadier General George Crook, now commanding the Department of the Platte, which included Fort Laramie. Of Crook, more will be said later, but it will be remembered that we last saw him as a young lieutenant during the Indian troubles in the Pacific Northwest. Historian Robert M. Utley speculates that Sheridan may have chosen Crook over Custer to lead Jenny's escort for political reasons. The Black Hills were a sensitive area and Sheridan may have feared that Custer's presence—a second time—might stir up unneeded controversy, what with the Hills technically being off limits to whites. It was all a sort of charade, however, as a large party of miners accompanied Jenny and, indeed, there were more than a thousand prospectors already in the Hills.

Jenny and his colleagues did indeed confirm the presence of gold in the Black Hills and now the government would be forced to take some sort of official position on a very touchy issue. The Army vowed to turn back trespassers and so it did, but the effort was weak one at best. One of Crook's officers involved in patrolling the Black Hills recalled the futility of trying to keep prospectors out of the area: "The day before Christmas, 1874, an Indian courier rode into our camp near Red Cloud Agency, Nebraska, bringing orders from the department commander for troops to be sent to the Black Hills to remove miners who were supposed to be there in violation of treaty stipulation."[22] A party of prospectors would be turned back, only to reenter the Hills once the army patrol disappeared. No one was deceiving anyone either. The federal government was going to have to reinforce the terms of the Laramie Treaty or ignore it publicly. They came up with a third option. Even as Jenny and company were investigating the mineral potential of the Hills, the Interior Department was exploring the possibility of buying the Black Hills from the Indians. Accordingly, in September a government commission met with several thousand Lakotas on White River for the purpose of discussing a possible sale. Between the Northern Pacific surveys and the two Black Hills expeditions, the Indians were not in a selling mood and moreover, the federal commission appointed to negotiate the matter seems not to have made a very effective presentation. At any rate, some of the more militant Lakotas threatened bodily harm to any Indian who agreed to sell the Black Hills, and so not surprisingly, the conference collapsed. It is worth noting that here were planted the seeds of the litigation over the so-called theft of the Black Hills, which remains unresolved to this day.

In the weeks that followed the abortive attempt to purchase the Black Hills the various Indian bands remained relatively calm, though there was an air of mounting tension in the area, like a darkening sky that presaged a coming storm. In November 1875 at a closed-door meeting, President Grant and Secretary of War William Belknap, along with Generals Sheridan and Crook hammered out a strategy. The rule prohibiting whites from entering the Hills would technically remain in place, but would not be enforced, and perhaps most importantly, the so-called wild bands would now be required to reside on the reservation. No longer would they be permitted to roam at will in the unceded territory. In effect, this meant that the U.S. Government was arbitrarily abrogating the Laramie Treaty and white settlement of the Black Hills could now proceed apace.

With just a bit of hindsight we can quickly recognize that Custer's intrusion into the Black Hills during the summer of 1874 was a prelude to war. One might say that if it hadn't been the Black Hills it would have been something else, which is probably true, but it was the Black Hills nonetheless. Given the prevailing attitudes of the day, war was simply inescapable. There was no way for settlement to proceed without a clash of arms, so why all the duplicity on the part of the federal government? The answer to that is we need always appear to be in the right; there must be just cause.

The strategy decided on by President Grant and his military advisors would be orchestrated with a little sleight of hand; the federal government could not simply declare war on the Indians; proper procedure had to be followed and the way around this was with smoke and mirrors.

The responsibility for managing the Indians belonged to the Indian Bureau, which was under the auspices of the Interior Department, and the War Department could take no action until and unless Interior requested military help. Fortunately for the Army, the newly appointed Secretary of the Interior, Zachariah Chandler former senator out of Michigan, unlike some of his predecessors, was not an Indian rights advocate and supported the administration's new policy to deal with the Indians by force if necessary. There had to be an excuse. And the way they worked it out was to have the Indian Bureau send out a notice to all the so-called hostile bands, generally referred to as the Sitting Bull bands, advising the Indians that they were no longer free to reside in the unceded territory and were now required to be on the Great Sioux Reservation by January 31, 1876. Failure to comply with this directive meant they would be considered hostile and subject to military action.

Although there were a number of wild bands, all were collectively thought of as hostiles with Sitting Bull (Tatanka-Iyotanka) the titular or at least symbolic head. By 1875 Sitting Bull was in his mid–40s. As a young man, he had earned his chops as a warrior and now in middle age he had ascended to a place of prominence, becoming, arguably, the most influential Indian leader in history. He was not a medicine man per se as some have portrayed him, but by mid-life had earned his reputation as a warrior; his political acumen, and spiritual leadership set him apart as a leader of unequaled proportion. He was unquestionably the dominant figure among the Lakota. Few Native American leaders have equaled him in stature; none has surpassed him.

Since the Indian Bureau's announcement was only promulgated early in December it meant the Indians had less than two months to comply. December and January are harsh months on the northern plains and to expect these bands to trek across country to the reservation agencies—even if they were inclined to do so which they were not—was ludicrous, but the strategy was sound enough. If you wanted to justify putting boots on the ground in the unceded territory, this was a good way to go about it, since there was no reasonable way for the bands to pick up and move into the agencies by the end of January. It was simply not going to happen and it didn't. Indeed, not all the wild bands even received the message. Thus, when the deadline came and went ... unmet as expected, the issue was turned over to the military for further action. And so, soon would be heard the steady thump of Walt Whitman's "Drum of War" from military posts across the Northern Great Plains.

It is an easy enough matter, from the vantage point of the 21st century to look back on the Trans-Mississippi West in the middle of the 19th century and decry how the U.S. treated the indigenous tribes of the West. And it is easy enough to point a finger at military leaders who sought nothing more than an excuse to take the field and whip those hostiles into subjection; and there were some in the military who certainly fit that description; but not all. There were military leaders—Custer among them—who sympathized with the Indians' plight, and there were supporters of Indian rights both in and out of government. It is always convenient to accuse the government, and conniving politicians of being primary culprits, responsible for the way indigenous people were treated. Likewise, scheming businessmen and opportunists are scarcely to be ignored for the role they played in the subjugation of the tribes. But let's not forget the average American citizen. From its earliest days the U.S. had been a westering nation. The movement, first across the Appalachians, then the Mississippi was an irresistible tide. Not every American wanted to cross the Great Plains of course, but a great many did, and in any event, the great migratory wave that swept across the Mississippi was nothing more than an extension of what had begun two centuries earlier. The hunger for land and a fresh start was the driving force behind Manifest Destiny, not some vague, moral or spiritual concept. It was land; land; always the land: what was on it or under it: grass, minerals and timber. It was this unstoppable force that drove the government, the railroaders, and the military to clear the western lands for use. For the government not to have responded to *vox populi* would have been unthinkable. Whether our treatment of the Indian tribes was morally defensible is a question for philosophers, but suffice it to say here that given the existing circumstances it is difficult to envision how any other scenario might have worked.

Now that the fat was in the fire, Sheridan proceeded to alert his department commanders. Three powerful columns would take the field. Number one column to be commanded by Custer would strike west from Fort Lincoln. Column number two, under Colonel John Gibbon, would march east from Forts Ellis and Shaw in Montana, through the valley of the Yellowstone. Finally, the third and largest of the three columns, under General George Crook, would strike north from Fort Fetterman, Wyoming (near present Douglas) along the old Bozeman Trail. The idea of course was to catch the Indians between the three converging columns. Exactly where the Indians would be found was not clear, although the most recent intelligence suggested somewhere between the Little Missouri and the Big Horn Rivers.

General George Crook.

It had been Sheridan's intent to reprise the Washita, but between the weather and Custer's propensity for getting himself into a jam, things just didn't come together in time for a winter campaign. As the campaign played out, George Crook's command came the closest to achieving Sheridan's objective. With a force that included five companies of the 2d and five of the 3rd Cavalry, plus two companies of infantry, a train of 80 wagons and a coterie of scouts, Crook's column—dubbed the Big Horn and Yellowstone Expedition—marched out of Fort Fetterman, Wyoming, on the first day of March. With nearly a thousand men in his column, Crook felt supremely confident of whipping any body of Indians he might encounter. It was a fine day, too, with a great vault of blue sky above, but that would soon change. March on the Northern Plains can shift from pleasant and pretty to wind, snow, and bitter cold, in nearly an instant and shortly it would, but George Crook was no fair weather soldier.

Following his tenure in the Pacific Northwest, Crook had served with distinction in the Civil War, rising to the rank of brevet major general of volunteers. A favorite of Sheridan (until later in his career), Crook returned to the west after the Civil War and saw action against the Snake Indians in Idaho. In 1870, he moved on to Arizona where he compiled an outstanding record against the Apaches. His Arizona success prompted Sheridan to move him up to command the Department of the Platte with the rank of brigadier general. Sheridan felt confident that Crook's skills would lead to the same kind of success against the Sioux.

George Crook was the antithesis of George Custer. Where Custer was outgoing and flamboyant Crook was taciturn and introspective. In the field, it was never difficult to spot Custer, but one could easily mistake George Crook for a common soldier. Typically, Crook shunned the formal uniform, preferring to take the field in plain unpretentious clothes. Interestingly enough the Northern Plains tribes came to call Crook Three Stars, evidently because of one star on each shoulder and a third on his hat. Both Crook and Custer were fond of hunting and both enjoyed eminently successful reputations as Indian fighters, at least until 1876. Custer's career would end ignominiously at the Little Bighorn and Crook's reputation would forever be tarnished by his fight on the Rosebud. About the only thing the two men had in common was their given name.

Meanwhile, up in remote western Montana Colonel John Gibbon's Montana Column, as it would soon be known, was not far behind Crook. Gibbon's was the smallest of the three forces to take the field, with six companies of the 7th Infantry and four of the 2d Cavalry and a detachment of scouts, in all about 450 men. On March 17, Gibbon's infantry marched out of Fort Shaw on the Sun River, near Great Falls, bound for Fort Ellis near Bozeman. From Ellis, Gibbon's column would proceed east along the north bank of the Yellowstone. Gibbon's mission was to thwart any attempt by the Indians to cross the Yellowstone and escape from the Dakota Column under Custer which would be marching west from Fort Lincoln.

Like George Crook, John Gibbon was a soldier of wide ranging and distinguished service. A West Point graduate, he served in the Seminole War and saw considerable action during the Civil War, where he commanded the famed Iron Brigade for a time. He was wounded at Mayre's Heights (Fredericksburg) and again at Gettysburg. Gibbon was promoted to major-general of volunteers for his Civil War service. After the war he reverted to the rank of colonel and went on to see considerable service on the western frontier. As a result of his Civil War wounds, Gibbon walked with a limp, prompting Indians to refer to him as "No Hip Bone." It would be No Hip-Bone Gibbon's unenviable task to bury the Custer dead after the debacle on the Greasy Grass.

Although it was never stated as such, the Dakota column featuring Custer and the 7th Cavalry was the principal striking force. Crook's role and Gibbon's role were seen as supportive; they would be beaters who would drive the Indians into Custer. This is not to say that Crook and Gibbon, particularly the former, were not expected to act offensively for indeed they were, but it was imagined by Sheridan at least, that Custer and the 7th Cavalry would be the one that got the job done. Notwithstanding, Sheridan was fully confident that each column was capable of taking care of itself.

Owing to Custer's predilection for shooting himself in the foot, the Dakota column was the last of the three to take the field and by the time it did, spring was well under way. What it all came down to was those ancient human conditions: politics and greed; the hidden enemy in all of mankind's endeavors.

The Great Sioux War

On March 3, three days after leaving Fort Fetterman the spring-like weather that had attended their preparation and departure changed dramatically, as described by newspaperman Robert Strahorn:

> When tattoo sounded the night before, and the troops looked up toward the little sky that Fetterman needs for a cover, it was found that even that little was hid by clouds that hung black and heavy as a pall. A northeastern wind—which brings the worst storms here—whistled a refrain to that tattoo, which did anything but lighten spirits and unburden hearts. Snow came down in great thick flakes and promised faithfully to gather to the depth of a foot before ceasing, and then up came up the declaration of General Crook, which drowned all hopes of camping until the storm was over in this wise: "The worse it gets the better; always hunt Indians in bad weather."[23]

On St. Patrick's Day, the 17th day of March 1876, even as John Gibbon's column was marching out of Fort Shaw, Montana, the spear point of George Crook's expedition, operating under the tactical command of Colonel Joseph J. Reynolds, struck what was thought to be the village of Crazy Horse on the Powder River near the present site of Moorhead, Montana. In reality this was a Cheyenne village with a few lodges belonging to the Oglala leader, He Dog, friend and confidante of Crazy Horse. Just as it had been at the Washita eight years earlier, the weather was atrocious. Through deep snow and bitter cold, the mixed-blood scout, Frank Grouard brought the troops to the outskirts of the village.

Down in Apacheria, it was thought that no white scout knew the Apaches better than Al Sieber and Crook had come to see Frank Grouard as the Northern Plains equivalent of Sieber. And it was faith well founded, for it would be difficult to find another man more knowledgeable about these Sioux than Grouard. The son of a Mormon missionary and a Hawaiian woman, he had once been captured by the Sioux and later adopted by Sitting Bull with whom he lived for several years. And he seems to have been well thought of by Crazy Horse as well. After several years living with the Sioux, however, Grouard decided to abandon his Indian ways and return to the white lifestyle, which he did, eventually becoming a scout for the army. During the wars of the 1870s on the Northern Great Plains, Frank Grouard would play an important part in George Crook's campaigns, of which Reynolds' attack on the Powder River village was the first.

REYNOLDS ATTACKS THE CHEYENNE ON POWDER RIVER, MARCH 17, 1876

On the 16th, Grouard and the other scouts picked up an Indian trail that led toward Powder River. Crook accompanied the expedition in the role of department commander, with Reynolds in tactical command. The avuncular looking, fifty-four-year-old Reynolds was a veteran officer who had acquitted himself well in the Civil War officer, emerging from that conflict a brevet major-general. of volunteers. After the war he was appointed colonel of the 3rd Cavalry. The command structure for the campaign was possibly intended to allow Crook the freedom to observe the practicality of a winter campaign on the Plains, while Reynolds concentrated on the day-to-day business of running the campaign. In any case, on the morning of March 17, Reynolds moved out with six troops of cavalry, while Crook remained behind with four troops and the pack train.

His attack unfolded well. One squadron, mounted, under Captain James "Teddy" Eagan ripped through the village, pistols blazing, followed by a second squadron under

Captain Anson Mills. Meanwhile, Reynolds' third squadron led by Captain Henry Noyes secured the substantial pony herd, numbering some 700 horses. Then everything went downhill.

Although caught by surprise and driven from the warmth of their lodges, Indian warriors quickly recovered their composure and, taking up positions in the bluffs overlooking the village, began to rain fire down on the troops. Notwithstanding the unexpected resistance, Reynolds remained in command of the field, but the situation was beginning to get a bit dicey. While the Indians continued to fire from the bluffs, the soldiers proceeded to destroy the contents of the village. This done, Reynolds prepared to move out and rejoin Crook, driving the captured pony herd ahead of them, but he reckoned without the tenacious Indian resistance. Despite the falling temperature and gathering darkness, the Indians continued to harass the column and eventually recaptured most of the pony herd. When finally he was able to rejoin Crook, Reynolds could only report that the Indians had snatched victory from the jaws of defeat. Seldom had a battle turned around so completely and with such abruptness. Irate, Crook assembled his expedition and began the return march to Fort Fetterman, where charges were brought against Reynolds and Captains Noyes and Moore. Crook was not the only one who felt that Reynolds had really botched the job. Major Thaddeus Stanton wrote:

> We got back to Fetterman March 23, and I arrived home the thirty-first. Altogether we beat the Indians badly, but nothing like we should have done if it had not been for the imbecility of Reynolds, to call it by no worse name. Crook has preferred charges against him for disobedience of orders for leaving dead and wounded on the field, and letting the herd go, etc. So there will soon be a big court martial here.[24]

Subsequently, Reynolds was tried and found guilty and suspended from rank and pay for one year, but the sentence was remitted by President Grant. Disgraced, Reynolds retired the following year. Moore was suspended from rank and pay for six months and Noyes was found not guilty. Although Crook was displeased with all three officers, Moore and Noyes would serve under him again in the coming summer's campaign. The late historian Jesse W. Vaughn who studied the campaign and subsequent court-martial proceedings was convinced that Reynolds was unjustly charged.[25]

And so Sheridan's campaign had gotten off to a rather inauspicious start. Briefly it appeared that Crook would have something positive to report, but what had begun on a triumphal note in the deep snow along Powder River soon dissolved amidst courts-martial proceedings at Fort Fetterman. And then, Custer's Dakota Column had yet to march out of Fort Lincoln, so that only John Gibbon's Montana Column, marching east along the Yellowstone, was the only one of Sheridan's three columns actually in the field.

Meanwhile, as "No-Hip-Bone" Gibbon was marching east along the Yellowstone and George Crook was refitting down at Fort Fetterman, George Custer, back in Washington, had once again managed to run afoul of topside, and this time it was not General Winfield Scott Hancock but President Ulysses S. Grant and that did not bode well for G.A. Custer, who seemed not to realize that when in uniform one was well advised to be careful about making public statements that reflect on the reigning administration.

What happened was that a nasty little scandal involving the licensing of post traderships on military posts had begun to taint the Grant administration. Custer, of course, had more than a little knowledge of how the system was being worked to the advantage of certain individuals, and he spoke freely about what he knew, both first and second hand. And it was a system that easily lent itself to exploitation. The sutler, or post trader, was nearly as old as the army he served, providing soldiers with tobacco, liquor, and delicacies such as canned fruit. In some locations prostitutes were also a part of the sutler's business. The precise meaning of the name is not clear, but may have been of Dutch origin. During the Civil War, sutlers usually operated out of the back of a wagon, but as the army moved west, military posts of any substantial size began to include a post trader located on the premises.

In order to operate on an army post, a trader needed to be licensed by the War Department. The way the system worked was pretty slick. An appointment would be made to a middle man, through a person with enough influence to secure an appointment. The middle man, in turn, would then transfer that license to a third party, who often was an established trader that wanted to renew his license. The third party, in turn, paid a fee to the original appointee, who shared that fee, with the individual of influence. In some cases, apparently, the person of influence was the no less than the Secretary of War himself. In other instances, the president's brother, Orvil was also known to be a peddler of such influence. The practice was not new. Most recently it had swirled around a post tradership scandal at Fort Sill, Indian Territory.

Eventually, the allegations were given a hard look by the powerful House Committee on Expenditures in the War Department, chaired by a Pennsylvania Democrat named Heister Clymer. President Grant had some notion of running for a third term, but the growing scandal did not reflect favorably on his chances for reelection.

Because Custer's views on the practice of selling post trader licenses were well known he was summoned to testify before the Clymer committee. And he spoke freely, apparently without any thought as to how it might impact his career, to say nothing as to how his views might affect the president, his commander-in-chief. And Grant took umbrage. Angry that Custer not only implicated the presidency but cast aspersions on his family as well, the president retaliated by forbidding Custer to command the Dakota column. And thus was the machinery of Sheridan's campaign slowed to a crawl.

Stunned and mortified, Custer tried to see the president but Grant would have nothing to do with him. There was nothing Sheridan could do without directly challenging Grant. But General Alfred Terry, commanding the Department of Dakota and Custer's immediate superior was in something of a bind himself. Terry was no Indian fighter and, like everyone else, assumed that the Dakota column would be commanded by Custer, who would do the Indian fighting. Suddenly, that picture had changed and Terry would either have to do the job himself, or select a subordinate from within his department to command the column, and nobody with the necessary rank and experience was available.

A quiet, cerebral officer who also happened to be a lawyer, Alfred Howe Terry had acquitted himself well in the Civil War, from which conflict he had emerged as the "hero of Fort Fisher" with a promotion to major general of volunteers and brigadier general in the regular army. To the kindly Terry, Custer pleaded for intervention. And Terry agreed to help. He may have done so simply out of compassion for a brother office or perhaps it was a self-serving reason, in that he wanted Custer to command the Dakota column. In any case, drawing on his lawyerly skills, he drafted a wire for Custer to sign. To the president, Custer begged not to have to suffer the ignominy of seeing his regiment march off to war without him at its head. Despite his ill-conceived public statements, Custer's plea must surely have been moving to the old soldier, Grant. And Terry's endorsement—also supported by Sheridan—was couched in language which made it almost impossible for the president to turn down. And so at length Grant compromised. Custer could go in command of his regiment, *providing Terry accompanied in overall command of the column.*

And so, while March and April vanished amidst the swirl surrounding Custer's indiscretion and the new grass fattened the Indian ponies, Terry and Custer made preparations for getting underway at long last. Assembled, the Dakota column was an impressive force, not quite as large as what George Crook was bringing together down at Fort Fetterman, but sizeable nonetheless. For only the second time in its history, all twelve companies of the 7th Cavalry would be together and would constitute the core of the Dakota Column. The cavalry would be supported by two companies of the 17th Infantry and a third from the 6th Infantry. The infantry's responsibility would be to provide protection for 150 wagons. Additionally, there would be three Gatling Guns, operated by a detachment from the 20th Infantry, plus a coterie of some 40 Arikara Indian scouts.

During the month of May Fort Abraham Lincoln was a beehive of activity and through it all ranged the now ebullient Custer in his "dashing suit of Buckskin," as the reporter Mark Kellogg, who would cover the expedition for both the *Bismarck Tribune* and the *New York Herald*, wrote. By mid-month, all was ready and on the 17th the Dakota Column, headed by Custer and the 7th Cavalry, marched out of Fort Lincoln and its date with destiny. Elizabeth Custer and several other wives accompanied the column for a short distance before adieus were said. And so it happened that when finally she had bade farewell to her beloved Autie and watched the column plod on toward a fate no one would have predicted, a mirage created the illusion of the column marching between earth and sky. An omen, perhaps?

As it happened, twelve days after the Dakota Column began its westward march, on May 29, George Crook's Big Horn and Yellowstone Expedition was again striking north out of Fort Fetterman to have another crack at the "hostiles" who had embarrassed Crook two months earlier. Actually, it had been Reynolds who embarrassed Crook, but the debacle on Powder River had only made Crook all the more determined to restore the luster to his reputation. And this time the Big Horn and Yellowstone Expedition had added more muscle to insure a sound thrashing of the Indians.

The Big Horn and Yellowstone Expedition was now composed of ten companies of the 3rd Cavalry and five of the 2d Cavalry, plus five companies of the 4th and 9th Infantry; more than a thousand men, plus 120 wagons and one thousand pack mules, under forty-four-year-old Tom Moore, veteran plainsman and mule-packer extraordinaire, who Crook had brought along from Arizona. Crook's Expedition was a tough and formidable outfit, but its mettle would be severely tested before this campaign was finished.

Of the three Army columns in the field, none would have as much newspaper representation as George Crook's outfit, which is surprising as one would have expected that Custer would have had all the news hounds. There had been newspaper coverage with the Reynolds column back in March, but now the number of reporters had grown to five. It was an energetic group representing two Chicago papers, *The New York Herald*, Denver *Rocky Mountain News*, and the San Francisco *Alta*. Perhaps the most colorful of the lot was John Finerty, representing the *Chicago Times*. Finerty was sometimes called the "Fighting Irish Pencil Pusher," owing to his passionate support of Irish independence. One of his colleagues said, "It is alleged by some that he is seven feet in height, but this is not credited. It is not believed that his altitude is more than six feet two, but his great lack of longitude and circumference gives him the appearance of greater height." Later, Finerty would author an account of his experiences on the expedition in a volume entitled *War-Path and Bivouac or the Conquest of the Sioux*, which would become one of the classic accounts of the Western Indian wars.[26]

Meanwhile, what of the Indians? It was commonly known that many of the Indians who spent the winter months at the agency joined the so-called wild bands during the summer months to hunt and participate in the annual Sun Dance ritual, which meant that any one of Sheridan's three columns in the field might well expect to be confronted by a sizeable body of warriors. Indeed, as the summer season of 1876 approached, there were indications that more agency Indians than usual were heading west to join their wild brethren and enjoy the fruits of the old traditional way of life, but truth to tell, this was not a big concern for the military. What did worry Sheridan and his field commanders was the nightmare of having the Indians disperse in small bands; thereby preventing the army from rounding them up and escorting them back to their agencies. It was axiomatic that in Western Indian campaigning one needed not just to defeat a war party; the object was to capture the entire village, for only in so doing could the Indians be brought into submission.

The Battle of the Rosebud, June 17, 1876

And so up the Bozeman Trail marched the Big Horn and Yellowstone Expedition; Crook and staff first, followed by the infantry, wagons, and cavalry. For a time at least, the weather remained fair. Spring was blooming on the Northern Plains. On June 5, the expedition passed Lake DeSmet and camped near the charred ruins of old Fort Phil Kearny. On the day following, the route took them over Lodge Trail Ridge, crossed by Fetterman's unlucky command a decade earlier. Meanwhile, the fair days of late spring had given way to rain and under the lowering skies. Unbeknownst to the soldiers, they had been accidentally spotted by a roving Cheyenne hunting party who subsequently reported the Army's presence to their village, then on the Rosebud.[27]

On the 8th, Crook elected to give the expedition a day of rest, establishing a bivouac along the Tongue River close to the present day Wyoming-Montana line. Thus far, the expedition had proved grueling but uneventful except for one poor 3rd Cavalry trooper who died as the result of a self-inflicted though accidental gunshot wound. The unfortunate soldier was buried with full honors in a somber, rain-dampened setting. For a soldier to die in battle was one thing but to die an ignominious death from a self-inflicted gunshot wound was quite another matter.

But the 8th brought other developments, too. A party of sixty-five miners bound for the Black Hills attached themselves to the expedition, in effect, adding another nearly full strength company to Crook's command, and their worth would soon be demonstrated. And there was more to come. A pair of couriers rode in from Fort Fetterman carrying a message from Sheridan to the effect that a large contingent of Shoshone and Crow allies would soon be joining the expedition. Not only that, but the 5th Cavalry had also been alerted to support the expedition if needed. And we might imagine that such news gladdened Crook's heart. But then Sheridan also reported that substantial numbers of agency Indians had headed west. No surprise here. That night, unknown Indian voices were heard across the river. One of Crook's scouts responded in Sioux, but there was only silence from the darkness beyond. Crook was annoyed, imagining that these might have been the friendly Crow and Shoshone who were frightened by the sound of a Sioux voice.

On the evening of June 9, hostiles fired on the expedition from atop bluffs across the river, prompting Crook to send three companies of infantry and a battalion of cavalry to respond. Fired up, the troops crossed the river in pursuit, but the Indians, whose intention was nothing more than to harass the soldiers did not wait around to give battle, but fled to their village on the Rosebud, there to give an account of what they had seen.

On the 14th the long awaited Crow and Shoshone allies arrived amid much cheering and that night a massive celebration took place, much to Crook's chagrin; he feared the festivities would alert the Sioux, but to forbid the merriment might risk losing his allies and Crook was nothing if not practical. And he could ill-afford to turn away more than 200 well-armed allies.

A week later found the Big Horn and Yellowstone Expedition at the Rosebud River, so named because of the profusion of wild roses along its banks. Here, on a pleasantly warm summer morning—it was the 17th day of June—the anniversary of the Battle of Bunker Hill—Crook decided the expedition should take a break. It was a bucolic setting; lovely and inviting. The Crow and Shoshone scouts were scouting ahead and the troops relaxed in the lazy morning sun. Crook and his staff enjoyed a game of cards.

The respite on the Rosebud would prove brief, however, for shortly the Indian scouts came ripping into camp with word that "Heap Lakotas" were on the way! And with that report, the expedition uncoiled and prepared for action. It was a most unlikely development—the Indians seizing the fire. Reynolds had proved an embarrassment at Powder River and now Crook had been caught with his pants down, but sturdy soldier that he was, he promptly deployed his battalions, and presently all were engaged with their hands full. How many Indians were present is not clear, but their numbers likely approximated what Crook had, including his Indian allies, which is to say in excess of a thousand. As much as any Indian war party could be said to have an overall leader, Crazy Horse was the guiding spirit of this force.

The terrain—which is little changed today from what it was in 1876—was rough and broken and not well suited to cavalry operations, thus compelling Crook's battalions to fight dismounted. Of all the battles of the Western Indian wars, Rosebud was the most hotly contested. Back and forth the fighting raged through the day, beneath a merciless June sun that poured down fire on the combatants below. The Crow and Shoshone allies who had so annoyed Crook with their celebratory antics just a few nights earlier, proved their worth on this afternoon.

Hard by the left flank, where the Virginia veteran, Colonel William Bedford Royall was in command, the fighting was furious, probably more so than on any other part of the field. At one point, Captain Guy Verner Henry, commanding Company D, 3rd Cavalry was hit in the face, the bullet passing through the cheek beneath the left eye and emerging beneath the right eye. Driven to the ground, Henry laid prostate, blood filling his mouth. Seeing one of the soldier leaders down, the Lakota rushed in to count *coup*, but were driven back by the Crows and Shoshones who rushed to the stricken captain's defense. Helped back into the saddle by some of his troopers, Henry, in a blood-choked whisper that was barely audible, asked the attending surgeon only to be fixed up so that "I can go back." It was seemingly a day for heroics on both sides. A diminutive Crow named Humpy rescued Sergeant Van Moll who had been unhorsed and cut off from his command, and a Cheyenne warrior, Comes-in-Sight was saved from certain death by a comrade who dashed in and, oblivious to fire from the soldiers, picked up the horseless Cheyenne and rode to safety.

It was charge and counter-charge with both sides giving as good as they got. One plus for Crook was his infantry. The foot soldiers were armed with the 1873 Springfield rifle, as opposed to the carbine with which the cavalry troopers were armed. The rifle version had a longer barrel and was accurate over a greater distance than the carbine. In the central part of the battlefield, where Crook had established his command post, the infantry, supported by the Black Hills miners, laid down a devastating rain of fire.

Convinced that the Indian village was not far off, down the dead cañon of the Rosebud,

Crook detached Captain Anson Mills and his battalion of cavalry to move down the cañon and strike the village. Barely had Mills and his troopers started on their mission, however, than the intensity of the fighting increased compelling Crook to send a courier to recall Mills. Mills was stunned to receive the recall order, for like Crook, he believed the village lay just a few miles beyond. Good soldier that he was, however, Mills obeyed the order and returned to the field of battle. Neither Crook nor Mills had any way of knowing that the village they sought had moved to the Little Bighorn, some thirty miles to the north, where Custer would find it a week later.

A small mystery of the Rosebud battle surrounds this so-called dead *cañon*. Virtually all contemporary accounts describe the cañon as a steep, narrow defile, ideally suited to ambush a column of troops, and word reached Mills that the Sioux had indeed prepared just such a reception for Crook's soldiers. In fact, however, the *cañon* does not fit this description at all, and in any case, the Lakota had not prepared any sort of ambush.

With the return of Mills to the battlefield, the fighting began to taper off. The Indians, having made their statement, gradually withdrew. Crook elected to camp on the field for the night. On the one hand, he felt victorious, for he was in possession of the field of action, a yardstick that might have counted for something under the white man's philosophy of waging war, but meant nothing insofar as the Indians were concerned. Despite the fierceness of the six-hour fight, Crook's casualties were light: nine killed and twenty-three wounded. Indian casualties were said to have been thirty-nine killed and sixty-three wounded.

The next day, Crook elected to return to Goose Creek (present Sheridan, Wyoming) and reorganize his command which had been roughly handled. Although he never admitted it publicly the fight on the Rosebud had proved to be a much sterner test of arms than he had anticipated. Although his troops had given a sterling account of themselves, the valor of the Indian allies cannot be overstated. Historians have been critical of Crook's decision to withdraw to Goose Creek, thereby removing one-third of Sheridan's striking force from the field. After all, he had not suffered heavy casualties and had plenty of ammunition remaining. It seems reasonable to propose that Crook had received an unexpected jolt and simply needed to recover his own aplomb. He had not been whipped, but he had been stymied and that was going to take some getting used to. Had Crook regrouped and pushed forward the next day instead of retiring to Goose Creek, he almost certainly would have found the Indian village several days before Custer arrived; what the outcome would have been must remain one of those tantalizing but forever unanswered questions of history.

The Little Bighorn: Custer's Nadir, June 25, 1876

Notwithstanding Crook's setback, Sheridan's campaign still had the green light. On June 9, Terry and Gibbon met aboard the steamer *Far West* to assess the situation. Intel suggested that no Sioux would be found west of the Rosebud, but Terry wanted further assurance and ordered Major Marcus Reno of the 7th to take six companies of the regiment to examine the Powder and Tongue River drainage systems. Subsequently, Reno, uncharacteristically exceeding his orders pressed on to the Rosebud where he discovered the trail of a big village.[28]

On the 21st, four days after the Rosebud fight, General Terry, along with Colonels Gibbon and Custer got together on the steamboat *Far West* at the confluence of the Rosebud and Yellowstone Rivers. They were of course ignorant of what had transpired thirty odd crow flight miles up the Rosebud. Lack of communications was the gremlin that bedeviled multiple military columns in this day and age; nobody ever knew where the other columns were or what had happened. On board the *Far West*, Terry and his two field commanders discussed what strategy to pursue. Where exactly the Indians were to be found was not clear.

Terry was infuriated that Reno's scout had taken him as far west as the Rosebud, fearing it might have alerted the Indians. Angry or not, Reno's reconnaissance was the most recent intel available and would form the basis for the strategy that emerged from the conference on the *Far West*. As worked out during on the Far West, the operational plan called for Custer to follow the Indian trail up the Rosebud. If the trail turned west toward the Little Bighorn as expected, Terry wanted Custer to continue up the Rosebud before turning west. Gibbon, meanwhile, would proceed west along the Yellowstone to its confluence with Big Horn. From here, Gibbon, with Terry accompanying, would follow the Big Horn to its junction with the Little Bighorn. No one was sure exactly where the Indian village might be found, but the general idea was to catch the Indians between the two columns. It was expected that the 7th Cavalry would strike the decisive blow, with Gibbon's Montana Column acting as a back-up, with the primary mission of preventing the escape of the Indians to the north across the Yellowstone. The tenor of the operational plan made it abundantly clear that the Army's main worry was preventing the Indians from eluding the soldiers.

Understanding the fluid nature of Indian tribal movements during that spring and early summer of 1876 provides an illuminated background for General Sheridan's military operations. Insofar as the movement of the various bands was concerned, it is more than a little important to understand that this was not a typical year; indeed it was most atypical. June was the month for the Lakota to celebrate the annual Sun Dance. For those who partook of that ceremony it was a time of spiritual renewal. For others, it was a time for renewing friendships; it was a coming together. Ordinarily, bands and groups would journey to the pre-appointed gathering place for the Sun Dance ritual. At the conclusion of the celebration the gathering would disperse into smaller groups simply because it became difficult for one spot to support a large gathering of people for any length of time, to say nothing of supporting several thousand horses. Reynolds' attack on the Cheyenne village on Powder River had made it abundantly clear that the soldiers were on the hunt and there was safety in numbers. The size of this assemblage has long been debated and ranged upward as high as 20,000 with as many as 3,000–4,000 warriors. Although certainly a huge village, its size has been exaggerated. Indeed, Historian Robert Utley thinks that as late as mid–June the village contained about 3,000 souls of which perhaps 800 were warriors.[29]

By early June the great village was camped along the lower reaches of the Rosebud, not far from that river's confluence with the Yellowstone. Here, probably about the 7th or 8th, during the Hunkpapa Sun Dance ceremony, Sitting Bull had some fifty small pieces of flesh removed from his body, as part of the Sun Dance ritual.

By the time the Dakota Column reached the mouth of the Rosebud, the village had moved farther upstream. A day's march or so up the Rosebud at a place called Deer Medicine Rocks, soon to be passed by the 7th Cavalry, Sitting Bull reportedly had a vision of soldiers falling into camp; soldiers with no ears and grasshopper legs. Whether the vision was a premonition of what was to occur on the Little Bighorn a few days hence will forever remain one of the intriguing stories of Custer's last campaign. On the 15th, the village camped along a small watercourse called Davis Creek from where Crazy Horse and the big party set out to assault Crook on the Rosebud. Meanwhile, it was clearly evident from all the signs discovered by Major Reno on his reconnaissance that this was indeed the gathering that was the object of the present campaign.

On a bright, warm 22nd day of June, the first full day of summer, the 7th Cavalry paraded in review before Terry, Gibbon, and Custer. The regimental band had been left behind at the Powder River base camp, so the musical send-off was provided by the blare of regimental trumpets. About noon, the review completed, the 7th Cavalry headed south up the Rosebud, led by the Arikara scouts along with half a dozen Crow scouts, loaned by Gibbon. The Crows were more familiar with this country than the Rees and their knowledge of the terrain, it was believed, would prove more than a little useful. Numbered among the Indian scouts was Custer's favorite, Bloody Knife. Half Hunkpapa Lakota and half Arikara, Bloody Knife had followed the path of his mother's people and had developed a powerful hatred for Sitting Bull. A contingent of white scouts, led by "Lonesome" Charley Reynolds, one of the savviest scouts on the plains, and thirty-year-old Minton "Mitch" Bouyer, a mixed-blood scout, said to be half-Sioux and half Crow, accompanied the Indian auxiliaries. Bouyer had reportedly been a protégé of the legendary mountain man, Jim Bridger. Custer could hardly have had two more skilled frontiersmen than Charley Reynolds and Mitch Bouyer. Custer had also been offered a battalion of the 2d Cavalry under Major James "Grasshopper Jim" Brisbin from Gibbon's command and a platoon of Gatling Guns, all of which were refused by Custer.

"Now Custer, don't be greedy," Gibbon shouted. "No, I will not," Custer replied, and with a jaunty wave cantered after his regiment. Within seventy-two hours, the 7th's controversial commander, together with some 250 of his troopers would cross the grand divide into eternity.[30]

By June 24, the regiment had traveled some seventy miles since leaving the Yellowstone; it had been a grueling three days. As suspected, the Indian trail, which had grown substantially larger, did indeed continue west from the Rosebud toward the Little Bighorn. Moreover, judging from the sign they had been following, the Crow scouts were quite certain that the Sioux would be found on the lower reaches of the Little Bighorn. Here was a crucial piece of intel that left Custer with a decision: obey the letter of his instructions, or stay on the Indian trail. If he chose the former, he risked losing touch with the Indians who could conceivably slip away, exactly what Terry and Custer hoped to avoid happening. At this juncture Custer made a command decision and chose to redefine his orders from Terry and follow the Indian trail.

Perhaps no single factor in the whole drama surrounding the Battle of the Little Bighorn has been more controversial than the orders Custer received from General Terry before departing on his final march. In fact, Terry's so-called "orders" were really couched as "advice," which granted Custer the autonomy to depart from that "advice" if he found that circumstances justified him doing so. Not being there himself, of course, Terry could only state what course of action he desired Custer to take, while at the same time giving his field commander the freedom to act as he saw fit. The timetable under which Custer (and Gibbon) would operate was fluid as well, since no one could predict exactly when or precisely where either column would be found. However, it was generally expected that Gibbon's command would be at the confluence of the Big Horn and Little Bighorn around the 26th, and if Custer could time his movements accordingly, the campaign could be brought to a successful conclusion.[31]

Based on the trail signs and the reports from his Indian scouts, Custer roughed out an operational plan that had the regiment crossing the low divide separating the Rosebud Valley from that of the Little Bighorn on the night of the 24th. He would rest the men and horses the next day and strike the Indian village at dawn on the 26th. Whether he saw his plan as part of Terry's overall strategy, or whether he was only focused on achieving a glorious victory will of course never be known, but it should be remembered that Terry and Gibbon were expected to be at the Little Bighorn on the 26th.

The morning of the 25th brought word from Lieutenant Charles Varnum, Custer's acting chief of scouts, that the Crows and Rees had spotted smoke from the Indian encampment as well as an immense pony herd in the valley of the Little Bighorn. With a small party Custer rode to the crest of the divide separating the valleys of the Rosebud and Little Bighorn and joined his scouts. Here, from a high point called the Crow's Nest, Custer strained to see what the scouts claimed to see. On a bench across the river from the village grazed the immense pony herd, but Custer, who possessed excellent vision, still could not make it out. "Look for worms crawling on the grass," he was told, but that didn't help. It was a clear day, but the morning was getting on and there was a haze forming over the valley where the big village lay, some fifteen miles distant and obscured from view by the intervening bluffs.[32]

Circumstances cause plans to change rapidly and unexpectedly, and Custer was now forced to rethink his operational plan of twenty-four hours earlier. Even though he himself had been unable to spot the village, there was no reason to question his scouts. Although certainly not infallible he had to assume they had sighted the quarry; the trail the regiment had been following had been growing. Clearly the Indians were in the area. What he didn't know was the exact location of the village and its disposition; nor did he have any solid evidence as to its size. True, Mitch Bouyer and others had warned him that there were a great many Indians in this village, but that warning in and of itself had less influence on Custer's analysis of the situation than the same piece of information has had on some historians of the fight. And there was one more thing that played a crucial role in Custer's decision at this juncture: a report that the regiment had been spotted by several parties of Indians was a grave piece of news. It seemed likely that these Indians would be certain to report their discovery to the village, thereby jeopardizing the regiment's movements. Ironically enough, these particular Indians were apparently returning to their agency and would not reveal the presence of the soldiers, although Custer of course had no way of knowing this.

Custer could hardly develop a plan of attack without knowing exactly where the village was located and the absence of such information left him with two options: he could hold the regiment in a high state of readiness and await more detailed information on the size and disposition of the village, or he could advance and make a final decision as more information became available. He chose the latter, out of fear that the regiment had been discovered which in turn could result in the breakup of the village and the escape of part of the inhabitants.

Up ahead, at a small watercourse known as Reno Creek, Custer made command assignments, dividing the regiment into three battalions: Major Reno was given Companies A, G, and M, plus the Indian scouts. To Captain Frederick Benteen went Companies D, H, and K. Custer himself retained personal command of five companies: C, E, F, I, and L. The single remaining company, B, under Captain Thomas McDougall, had charge of the pack train. Historian Robert Utley has given us a portrait of the jaunty, still flamboyant, thirty-six-year-old Custer on this the last day of his physical existence: dark blue shirt, buckskin trousers and wearing a broad brimmed white felt hat. The famous Custer curls were gone; he was balding and besides had gotten a haircut prior to leaving Fort Lincoln.

The trail toward the Little Bighorn led past an abandoned teepee. In the vast ocean of literature surrounding the Little Bighorn, this "Lone Tepee," as it is known stands as one of the icons of Custeriana; it is impossible to study the battle without coming across reference to the Lone Tepee, which seems to have been a burial lodge containing the remains of a warrior killed in the Rosebud fight with Crook. From a high point near the tepee interpreter Fred Girard (Gerard) told Custer that he could see the Indians running. Based on Gerard's observation, reports from other of his scouts, and his own instincts as a field commander, Custer may have formed his final plan of action at this juncture. Considerable smoke, possibly indicating Indian movement, could be seen rising above the Little Bighorn Valley, still hidden by the surrounding bluffs. Accordingly, given the intelligence he had in his possession at that particular hour, this would seem to have been the moment for another command decision.

In any event, initial assignments were now handed out. Since there remained a strong likelihood that some of the Indians might slip away to the south, Benteen was instructed to take his battalion on a scout to the left to block any escape attempt. Major Reno, meanwhile, with his three companies reinforced by the scouts was to charge down the valley toward the village, while Custer with the remaining five companies swung around to the right, apparently with the intention of striking the village from the other side of the river while Reno kept them engaged. There is much disagreement over the precise wording of Custer's orders to Reno, but the consensus seems to be that Custer stated or at least implied that Reno could expect to be supported by the entire regiment.

From this point on, the character of the rapidly evolving battle becomes murky, and impossible to reconstruct in any definitive way. What is known for certain is that Reno charged down the Little Bighorn Valley with his battalion of about 112 men plus the Indian scouts. At about the same time, a body of warriors moved forward to meet this threat. Reno of course he had no way of knowing the number of Indians suddenly forming up on his front, but it appeared to be sizeable and so confronted by this, he made a command decision to halt the charge, dismount and form a skirmish line. Although he has been roundly criticized for this it should be remembered that as the commander on the spot he was within the sphere of his authority to redefine Custer's orders if circumstances so demanded, and in Reno's mind that seemed to be the case.

As Indian resistance stiffened, Reno, perhaps wondering where the rest of the regiment was, halted his advance and took up a position in the timber adjacent to the river. Command structure seems to have disappeared by this time and Reno soon decided to abandon the position in the timber. In a confused withdrawal that quickly became a rout, the battalion fled the timber, scrambled across the river and made its way to the bluffs above the river, pursued as they went by howling Indians. Up on the bluffs, a much disconcerted Reno formed a defensive perimeter and waited for the attack that seemed likely to come. Most historians who have studied the battle believe that Reno lost his composure after withdrawing into the timber; possibly even earlier, but in any case, his effectiveness as a commander was completely lost thereafter. The Valley Fight, as it came to be known, was costly. Forty men were killed and another dozen wounded. Among the dead were Lonesome Charley Reynolds and Custer's favorite, Bloody Knife. Struck in the head by a Lakota bullet, during the fighting in the timber, Bloody Knife's brains splattered over Reno. If nothing else served to unstring Reno during the fight, this moment would surely have done so.[33]

Benteen, meanwhile, had moved off to the left over rough terrain and after several miles, concluded there was nothing to suggest any body of Indians were moving in that direction, and he opted to turn back. Benteen's assignment had taken him some several miles away from Custer. He had carried out his assignment as ordered, but he may not have appreciated being sent off on a mission of questionable importance. Nevertheless, he was a soldier and followed his orders. In executing his assignment Benteen probably covered some six to seven miles during a nearly three-hour period.

At one point he stopped to water his horses. En route to rejoin the regiment, he was met by Sergeant Daniel Kanipe from Tom Custer's C Company. Kanipe carried instructions for Benteen to hurry the pack train along. Not long after this, he was met by a second courier, Trumpeter John Martin (Giovanni Martini), carrying the famous message from Custer: "Benteen. Come on. Big village. Be Quick, bring Packs. Ps bring packs." The message was signed W. Cooke (Lieutenant William Winer Cooke was Custer's adjutant). Thus it was that young Trumpeter Martin, a recent Italian immigrant was the last white man to see Custer and his men alive.[34]

It is impossible to know exactly how much credence Benteen attached to the "Big Village" message. It does seem reasonable to propose that any responsible officer receiving such a communiqué would have pressed ahead with a great sense of urgency, but not so Benteen. Fred Benteen's hatred of Custer bordered on the pathological and dated back at least as far as the Washita. Benteen never forgave Custer for abandoning Major Joel Elliott in that fight. Others in the regiment were also critical of Custer for leaving Elliott behind, but none as much as Benteen. Whether his hatred of Custer was so strong that it caused him to ignore his soldierly responsibilities will of course never be known, but his hatred of Custer notwithstanding, Benteen was a fine soldier and it seems a real stretch to imagine him sacrificing all of the men with Custer just to satisfy his own blind hatred. Of course, there was no way for Benteen to know that his decision to ignore the directive might result in the destruction of Custer and five companies of the regiment. In all likelihood, Benteen, for whatever reason simply did not view the message with the same sense of urgency that hindsight suggests. It is also possible that Benteen may have been peeved at being sent off on a mission of questionable importance, while the rest of the regiment was going to engage the enemy.

Whatever his motivation Benteen continued along the trail that would reunite him with the regiment. Eventually he reached Reno's beleaguered battalion in its defensive position on the bluff. Reno, obviously distraught at this point, pleaded with Benteen to add his battalion to Reno's now frazzled command. The question where was Custer was on everyone's mind. Some firing had been heard, but there had been no word from Custer. Some conjectured that he was even then attacking the village, or perhaps had attempted an attack, been repulsed, and had moved off to unite with Terry and Gibbon, and some wondered if he had abandoned them as he did Major Elliott? In any case, Benteen elected to throw in with Reno and quickly became the de facto position commander, although Reno was the senior officer present. As said, Frederick Benteen was a first rate soldier and it was his leadership skills and combat experience that would save the day for the combined battalions.

And so what indeed had become of Custer? After sending Trumpeter Martin back to hurry Benteen along, the Custer battalion—actually two battalions, one of three companies and one of two—proceeded north, behind the bluffs that obscured their movement from Reno's men then still in the timber, although some of Reno's command claimed to have caught a momentary glimpse of Custer before he disappeared from view. About the time Martin was sent off on his mission, or perhaps shortly thereafter, twenty-eight-year-old Boston Custer rejoined his brother's command. Young Boston had been employed as a forage master for the expedition. Not that he had any particular experience in this area, but it served as an excuse for him to join his brothers, brother-in-law, James "Jimmi" Calhoun, and nephew Armstrong "Autie" Reed, on this grand adventure. Boston had been with the pack train, but was anxious to be with his brothers when the fighting began. As he hurried to rejoin the Custer battalion he passed Benteen and Martin. It seems unbelievable that Boston would not have informed his brother that Benteen was coming on, and knowing this may well have influenced Custer's course of action from then on.

At this point there occurred another command division. Moving down Medicine Tail Coulee from the bluffs above the river, Custer now sent one, two-company battalion (F and E) under Captain George Yates to effect a crossing into the village at Medicine Tail, while Captain Myles Keogh with the remaining battalion (companies C, I, and L) moved to secure the higher ground to the northeast.

Only through the power of conjecture can we can reconstruct Custer's movements from this point forward. It would appear that his decision to send Yates across the Little Bighorn at Medicine Tail was designed to relieve the pressure on Reno while simultaneously diverting Indian attention, thereby allowing Custer to move north and strike the upper end of the village. If so, the plan rather rapidly deteriorated owing to the rout of Reno's command which freed many warriors to join in the effort to repulse Yates, who was soon forced back from the ford and driven to the higher ground along with Custer's other battalion. It must have become clear to Custer by this time that he was losing the initiative; the battle had now become a defensive fight for survival. Still, half of his regiment was yet to be committed. If Reno and Benteen were asking where was Custer? Custer was surely asking where they were.

It was a sultry Sunday, and the day was steadily deteriorating for the 7th Cavalry. Yet despite this, Custer was not quite ready to surrender the initiative, for the evidence suggests that he continued to press on north, hoping to strike the village from the north end. It is possible that this final movement carried him as far as the present national cemetery. But even if he was successful in penetrating this far north, he was soon driven back, probably to a point approximately where the big monument stands today. By this point, the Custer battalion had pretty much lost its cohesiveness The five companies were now distributed over the back trail along the high ridge and fighting for their lives. Horses were killed to provide a barricade from which to fire at the growing number of warriors who were joining the battle.

As the soldier positions gradually crumbled, some forty gathered on what is now known as Custer Hill, just below the present monument. Here were grouped the Custers, their nephew Autie Reed, several officers and the remnants of surviving companies. The killing blow was delivered by Crazy Horse, leading a phalanx of warriors in a sudden unexpected sweep from the north. And then suddenly it was over and nothing was left but the dust, and the heat, and the stink of battle. At one point a handful of soldiers rushed down the slope toward the river only to be killed in a huge cut in the earth known as Deep Ravine.

Exactly where Custer was killed will never be known. His body was found on last stand hill with a wound in the left breast and another in the temple. Some have speculated that he may have been wounded while attempting to ford the Little Bighorn at Medicine Tail and was helped—perhaps even carried—to Custer Hill where he may have received his second wound. There is little likelihood that he died as did Errol Flynn in the classic *They Died with Their Boots On*. Like most of his men, Custer was stripped, but unlike many of his troopers, his body was not scalped and mutilated, although Cheyenne testimony claims that in the aftermath of the battle, women pierced each ear with an awl, as a gesture to his failure to listen when he smoked with the Cheyennes during the Hancock campaign in 1867.

The precise number of men who died on Custer Hill will forever be debated. After careful study and research, the late John Gray concluded that 210 died with Custer. Indian casualties are even more difficult to determine because most of the bodies were later removed from the battlefield. Estimates range from 30 to 300. Although there were reports of mass suicides among the soldiers, Indian accounts testify to the bravery of the soldiers. Undoubtedly, there were some who elected to take their own life, but it appears that most of the troopers gave a good account of themselves.

Stories of a Custer survivor are legion and while some are intriguing, none have yet been proven true, but the idea that one man, somehow, managed to avoid the swarms of hostile Indians grabs the public consciousness with an unbreakable grip. So far as is known, the only living creature to survive the battle was Captain Myles Keogh's horse Comanche, who was found wounded on the battlefield along with several other horses. The others were too badly wounded to survive, but Comanche was cared for and eventually brought back to Fort Lincoln where he was retired from active service and treated as the 7th Cavalry's symbol of the Little Bighorn. The eighteen-year-old Crow scout, Curly, apparently watched some portion of the fight, though he was not a participant, and how much he actually witnessed is unclear because of early reporters interviewing him managed to scramble his story to the point that it became impossible to tell exactly what he saw.

Meanwhile, some five miles back along the trail that had brought Custer to this place, the combined Reno-Benteen battalions waged a purely defensive fight for the next thirty-six hours. Once Custer had been disposed of it allowed the Indians to concentrate on the hilltop defenders and although there was never any serious effort to overrun the position the Indians maintained a constant pressure on the soldiers through long-range fire. Suffering among the wounded was severe and a shortage of water added to the discomfort. Finally, a party of water carriers braved a descent to the river to fill canteens. On the night of the 26th, the village broke camp, and, cloaked by billowing smoke from a grass fire they had ignited, began moving toward the Big Horn Mountains.

On the morning of the 27th, the beleaguered defenders discerned a column of blue troops. Was it Custer? Terry?, or perhaps even Crook? Shortly it proved to Gibbon's Montana Column. The good news was that the defenders had been relieved. The bad news was that Lieutenant James Bradley, leading Gibbon's scouts, had discovered the bodies of the Custer command, leading one observer to remark that they all looked so white. After an examination of the battlefield and a cursory burial of the bodies of Custer's command, Terry and Gibbon, accompanied by the Reno-Benteen survivors, including the wounded, began a march to the Big Horn River where the steamer *Far West* was tied up. The wounded were placed on board the boat which then began its record-setting, fifty-four-hour journey to Bismarck and Fort Lincoln, arriving late on the night of July 5. That same evening, out across the singing wire went the startling announcement that Custer and his command had been wiped out by Indians.

No one would argue that the Battle of the Little Bighorn is not one of the most written about events in U.S. military history, indeed, out of all proportion to its ostensible importance. On the face of it, the overall battle accomplished nothing other than the deaths of some 300 soldiers of the 7th Cavalry and an indeterminate number of Indians, together with the downfall of one of the nation's most charismatic military figures. And so the fight on the Little Bighorn—Greasy Grass, as the Indians referred to the river—slid almost immediately and effortlessly into legend, to become the stuff of enduring myth. But in fact, the disaster on the Little Bighorn galvanized the American public, the U.S. Congress, and the War Department as never before. Although the battle is often seen as the high water mark of Indian resistance in the West, or at least the Northern Plains, it was surely the death knell for the old free way of life for the buffalo hunting warriors of the Plains. That Pyrrhic triumph on the Greasy Grass awakened a white nation and filled it with a grim resolve to bring about a hard and final end to the Indian problem.

But how had it all happened? How did a horde of savages manage to wipe out nearly half of the renowned 7th Cavalry, and bring down the celebrated Yellow Hair Custer, hero of the Civil War? The answer is in three parts: first, Custer not only encountered more

Indians than expected, but found that for once the warriors were determined to respond with everything they possessed, and here one needs to remember that for once the Indians failed to scatter when the soldiers appeared.

Second, these Indians were better armed than the soldiers expected; many carried sixteen-shot Henry repeating rifles, which gave them a distinct advantage over the single-shot 1873 Springfield carbine carried by the soldiers. Although the Springfield had great range and stopping power the circumstances of the fight negated that advantage; dust and smoke often made it difficult for the soldiers to pick out a target. Then, too, many of the Indians, operating on foot, were able to work closer to the soldiers and using the traditional bow and arrows inflicted many casualties. Third, unwise battalion command assignments probably did as much to doom the Custer battalion as anything else. For example, had Custer given Reno's assignment to, say, Captain Myles Keogh and assigned Captain George Yates to do Benteen's job he would have had two dependable commanders to count on, and that might have made a world of difference. Keogh would surely have been more aggressive than Reno, and Yates would undoubtedly made haste to rejoin Custer upon receipt of the "Bring Packs" message.

On the evening of the 26th, the big Indian village, having exhausted the resources of the immediate area, broke camp and moved out after a rousing celebration. Such a victory had never before been theirs, nor would be again. Beyond the horizon, for those with a vision of the future, could be seen the nadir of their way of life, but for now there was reason for a celebratory mood. A portion of the great camp followed Sitting Bull north across the Yellowstone, on into the region of the Upper Missouri River and eventually across the border into Canada. Others moved east toward the Black Hills. No thought was given to preparing a collective response to further attacks by the soldiers. Unfortunately for the Indians, the absence of any over-arching political structure that might have provided for the common defense did not serve them well. For now, the soldiers had been whipped and it was time to seek out *Pte*, the buffalo. It was the season of the long grass, but provisions had to be got up to carry them through the long, cold winter moons. Whether or not the Indians realized they were fighting Long Hair Custer is debatable.

Meanwhile, Generals Sherman and Sheridan were at the Continental Hotel in Philadelphia celebrating their nation's centennial. Unexpectedly, on Independence Day, as it turned out, there came a news report out of Salt Lake City announcing that Custer and his command had been wiped out. Both generals regarded the report as preposterous until an official dispatch from General Terry confirmed the sad news. Custer and half of the 7th Cavalry had been destroyed ... to a man. It was the worst disaster ever experienced by the U.S. Army on the Western frontier, eclipsing by a considerable margin, the Fetterman Disaster of 1866.

Both stunned and angry, Sheridan nevertheless wasted no time reacting, and neither did Congress, who now quickly approved his long-standing request for funds to build two new posts in the Yellowstone Valley, and also authorized an increase in the size of the Army. As it has throughout U.S. history, it seems Congress fails to appropriate the necessary resources until forced to do so by a disaster.

The "first scalp for Custer"

From various posts throughout his military department, units received orders to take the field. Colonel Wesley Merritt, another of the Civil War's "boy generals" was given command of the 5th Cavalry, replacing Lieutenant Colonel Eugene A. Carr, who had commanded the regiment at Summit Springs seven years ago when the power of the Cheyenne Dog Soldiers had been broken. Of all the young Indian-fighting commanders in the Western frontier army, only Wesley Merritt would remain on active service and rise to high rank, surpassed only by Nelson Miles. During the Spanish-American War, Merritt, now a major general, was given command of the American expeditionary force that was sent to the Philippines.

Some regarded the 5th Cavalry as the finest mounted regiment in the Army, notwithstanding Custer's 7th and Mackenzie's 4th. Merritt picked up his new command at Fort Laramie and prepared to join Crook. Additionally, six companies of the 22d Infantry under Lieutenant Colonel Elwell Otis were assembled from posts as far away as the Great Lakes region. Finally, Colonel Nelson Miles was directed to march from Fort Leavenworth with six companies of his 5th Infantry to reinforce Terry, who went into camp along the Yellowstone near its confluence with the Rosebud.

Crook, meanwhile, bided his time back at Goose Creek, and it wasn't an unpleasant sojourn, either. Much of the time was spent fishing and hunting in the Big Horn Mountains, while awaiting reinforcements. On July 6, Crook determined to send out a scouting party to see if there was any sign of Indians in the area. Lieutenant Frederick Sibley was given the assignment, along with twenty-five men and the *non-pareil* scouts Frank Grouard and Baptiste "Big Bat" Pourier. John Finerty, the "Fighting Irish Pencil Pusher" asked for and got Crook's permission to join the group. Two days later found them approaching the site of the big Indian village on the Little Bighorn. Beyond that, near the Tongue River, they were discovered by a large war party and fled back toward Goose Creek post haste. It proved a narrow escape. Finerty would later write that "Close acquaintance with death is not a pleasing sensation."[35]

On July 15, Colonel Merritt was advised that some 800 Cheyennes under Little Wolf had left Red Cloud Agency in northwestern Nebraska, near Fort Robinson, intending to join the large coalition that had stymied Crook and destroyed Custer. Merritt, whose new command responsibilities included the District of the Black Hills, had been operating between Fort Laramie and Red Cloud Agency. When word of the Cheyenne movement reached him, Merritt moved immediately to intercept the Cheyennes. On the 16th, the 5th Cavalry, guided by the celebrated long-haired scout, Buffalo Bill Cody, caught up with the Cheyennes at War Bonnet or Hat Creek in northwestern Nebraska. The skirmish, if one can even call it that, produced a single casualty: the warrior Yellow Hair, who reportedly was promptly scalped by Cody, who added to his reputation by claiming the "first scalp for Custer."[36]

After disposing of the Cheyenne threat, Merritt and his entire regiment joined Crook on August 3. Now reinforced by Merritt, Crook at long last seemed finally ready to resume the campaign begun nearly two months ago. His striking force, powerful back then, was now almost doubled: 2,000 men, including twenty-five companies of the 2d, 3rd, and 5th Regiments of Cavalry, plus ten companies from the 4th, 9th, and 14th Infantry regiments, and more than 200 Shoshone allies.

A week later, Crook rendezvoused with Terry in the Rosebud Valley. The meeting was not planned and may even have been a trifle embarrassing; instead of finding the Indians they had found each other. Terry, now reinforced by the addition of six companies each of the 5th and 22d Infantry Regiments, boasted a force of some 1,700 men. The combined force, totaling nearly 4,000 men was gigantic, at least by frontier standards. It was the largest gathering of regular army units in an active field campaign since the Civil War. The ponderous size of the combined force positively precluded surprising any Indian encampment.

Subsistence for so large a force was difficult under the best of circumstances and circumstances were seldom favorable. An expedition in the field could sometimes supplement its larder with wild game, but hardtack, coffee, sugar, salt, all had to be brought along with the troops.

The Terry-Crook combine had also to deal with another issue: who was going to command? Both were department heads, but Terry was the senior man, and Sheridan had made it clear that in any combined operation, Terry would call the shots. However, the two commanders favored a different style of campaigning. Terry seemed to favor a little more comfort, preferring a tent to sleep in at the close of day, while Crook, the old seasoned outdoorsman liked the idea of Spartan accommodations. Tents meant wagons, and wagons restricted a column's movements.

The Indian trail seemed to be heading east, but Terry was also fearful that a large portion of those who had killed Custer would escape across the Yellowstone and head north. To counter this possible development, Terry assigned Colonel Miles and his 5th Infantry the job of covering the likely crossings of the Yellowstone. Meanwhile, Terry with the rest of his command, including the greatly diminished 7th Cavalry, joined Crook's ponderous column in following the Indian trail to the east. The weather was foul and wretched in the extreme. Temperatures dropped and rain lashed men and animals alike. By early September the combined forces had reached Glendive Creek not far from the present Montana-North Dakota line. Thus far, the post–Little Bighorn phase of the campaign had accomplished little more than contributing to the exhaustion of men and horses. It now appeared to Terry that any chance of catching the Indians, let alone administering the kind of whipping envisioned at the outset of the campaign, was highly unlikely. Consequently, Terry elected to end his phase of the campaign. Convinced that further pursuit was futile, the Indian allies likewise decided to pull out. The 5th and 22d Infantry under Miles and Lieutenant Colonel Otis respectively, would remain in the Yellowstone Valley with the mission of monitoring Indian movements and building the two new forts for which Sheridan had received recent authorization. The remaining units of Terry's command were directed to return to their permanent duty stations.

If Terry thought it was pointless to continue the campaign the same could not be said for Crook who pressed on. This campaign had been a humbling one for Three Stars and he desperately wanted it to end on a positive note. Downpours continued, turning the ground into mud. Rations were running out. Men shot their gaunt horses for meat, but Crook pressed on toward the Black Hills. Captain Andrew Burt, 9th Infantry described Crook's "Horsemeat March," as it came to be called:

> Our command had marched eighty-three miles and was reduced to horseflesh, but the trail still leading south, threatening the Black Hills and settlements, Crook would not give it up, although opposed by nearly all of his rank officers. In spite of the difficulties appearing, his determination was to keep on and do his imperative duty. The rain beat down each day and night on the unsheltered officers and men. Mud was ankle deep for the plodding, dogged infantry; men going sixty-three miles without wood to cook horseflesh and drinking rain from muddy pools.[37]

The Battle of Slim Buttes

On September 7, Crook detached Captain Anson Mills with 150 men of the 3rd Cavalry on the best of the remaining horses and sent him on to the Black Hills settlements for supplies. Scout Frank Grouard accompanied. Two days later Mills discovered a Lakota camp north of the Black Hills in an area known as Slim Buttes, so named because of the unusual rock formations. Mills sent word back to Crook, then attacked, driving the villagers into the nearby hills. But the Indians regrouped, fought back and kept Mills pinned down until Crook arrived with the main body early in the afternoon of the 9th. Casualties were unusually high given the numbers involved, and included the Lakota chief, American Horse. Later that afternoon, an estimated 200 warriors under Crazy Horse arrived and joined the fight, but were eventually driven off. After helping themselves to the rations left in the village, Crook's men destroyed what remained and pushed on to the Black Hills, where, finally, his hungry, mud-caked, command reached the new boom town of Deadwood, where Crook officially called an end to the summer campaign and sent his units to their respective stations.

Deadwood, Dakota Territory was then about as wild as they came. Indeed, along with Tombstone and Dodge City, it was the most famous—or infamous—of the Wild West boom towns. Deadwood, in that tumultuous summer of 1876, would stand as the last grand gold rush camp in the U.S. until the strike at Tonopah, Nevada, in the early 1900s. Crammed into a ravine-choked piece of real estate the town embodied everything that was wild and woolly about the western frontier. Here, just weeks before Crook's jaded troopers passed through, Broken-Nose Jack McCall murdered James Butler "Wild Bill" Hickok during a poker game in Saloon Number 10. A year later, McCall, tried by a miners' jury was hanged. Hickok would eventually rest not twenty feet from Calamity Jane in Mt. Moriah Cemetery above Deadwood.

So the summer campaign of 1876 was over, but General Philip Sheridan was far from finished. He had plans to resolve the Indian problem permanently and George Crook would play a key role. When Crook returned to Fort Laramie following the Battle of Slim Buttes, he found Sheridan waiting for him, along with Colonel Ranald Mackenzie and his 4th Cavalry. Sheridan already had a strategy in mind and with it as the framework, the trio hammered out an operational plan. Crucial to Sheridan's new strategy was the securing of military authority, viz., control of the reservation agencies, which previously had been under the Indian Bureau, but this control, along with the increased troop buildup and the authorization to construct new forts came at the expense of the Little Bighorn. Custer's demise was the price for this new muscle.

What Sheridan envisioned was first of all keeping the so-called hostiles confined, namely keep them south of the Yellowstone River; Colonel Miles and his infantry would see to that. This, Sheridan hoped, would help contribute to the denouement of the great coalition that had destroyed Custer and made a joke of the summer's efforts. Then, a well organized fall campaign would compel large numbers of Indians to come into the agencies. The reorganized 7th Cavalry would see to the disarmament of Indians who came into the agencies on the Missouri River, while at Spotted Tail and Red Cloud Agencies in Nebraska, Mackenzie's troopers would see to the disarmament of Indians who came into those agencies.

As noted, the Indian victory over Custer had a disastrous fallout for the victors. As a consequence of the Custer disaster, an angry Congress decreed on August 15, that the Indians must surrender all rights to land outside their permanent reservation or risk losing whatever appropriations were due them as a result of previous treaties. This, of course, meant the Black Hills. Early in September a seven-man Congressional committee, headed up by George Manypenny, a former commissioner of Indian Affairs, traveled to the White River Agency in western Nebraska to persuade the Indians to accept. The Indians were between a rock and a hungry place. Times were tough on the reservations and without government support, survival would be even tougher. Consequently, they acquiesced and agreed to surrender title to the Black Hills. The United States Government had ceased making treaties with Indian tribes five years earlier, but as historian Robert Utley observes, the agreement to acquire the Black Hills was in every way a treaty save in name.[38]

Meanwhile, as Sheridan, Crook, and Mackenzie polished the fine points of Sheridan's strategy, up along the Yellowstone, the Army was getting underway with two new military posts. As part of the overall troop buildup, Lieutenant Colonel George Pearson Buell with six companies of the 11th Infantry was assigned the job of building a new post near the junction of the Little Bighorn and Big Horn Rivers, barely a dozen plus miles from the Custer battlefield. Downstream, near the site of present day Miles City, where the Tongue River joins the Yellowstone, Colonel Nelson Miles and his 5th Infantry would construct the second post. Initially, the post was named Cantonment Keogh, to become Fort Keogh once the permanent post was completed.

With the possible exception of Douglas MacArthur, Nelson Appleton Miles may well have been the vainest man ever to wear the uniform of the United States Army, but as an Indian fighter they didn't come much better; some regarded him as the Army's best. Miles and his 5th Infantry foot-sloggers, it will be recalled, had proved their mettle in the Buffalo (or Red River) War of 1874. If ever there was a soldier driven to succeed, it was Nelson Miles. He thumped his own drum ceaselessly; always angling for that next step up the ladder, which at the moment was a brigadier's star and he made it a point to remind General of the Army William T. Sherman of just how much he deserved that star. Of course it didn't hurt that Miles's wife, Mary, was the daughter of Sherman's brother, Senator John Sherman.

When Miles reported to General Terry on the Yellowstone in August he brought with him from Fort Leavenworth, six companies of the 5th Infantry, but was soon reinforced with the remaining six companies of the regiment. Sheridan's evolving plan called for the creation of a new military sphere of jurisdiction to be called the District of the Yellowstone with Miles in overall command. The new district would be part of the Department of Dakota, so Miles would be directly responsible to Terry. In addition to his own 5th Infantry, Miles was also given command of four companies of the 22d Infantry and two of the 17th Infantry under Lieutenant Colonel Elwell S. Otis, which together with Buell's six companies of the 11th Infantry, gave Miles command of nearly 2,000 troops.

When Terry dissolved his expedition in August and Crook marched to the Black Hills, Miles was left behind to begin work on his new fort and prevent any large scale Indian crossings of the Yellowstone. Although it was common knowledge that Sitting Bull and his followers had already crossed the river and moved north into the Upper Missouri River country, Crazy Horse was known to still be south of the river, and it would be Miles's responsibility to prevent any reunion of the two bodies. Although he had a powerful force at his disposal, Miles nevertheless lacked the strength to actively campaign against both Sitting Bull and Crazy Horse. As a consequence, he elected to first focus his attention on Sitting Bull's Hunkpapa and Miniconjous, while keeping an eye on the Oglalas of Crazy Horse south of the river.

As summer in Montana deepens, water levels on the Missouri and Yellowstone Rivers fall off, limiting how far upriver steamboats are able to navigate. Now, as fall approached, steamboats were unable to reach Miles's cantonment at Tongue River and supplies had to be off-loaded at a small depot at the mouth of Glendive Creek. Overseeing this satellite outpost of Miles's new District of the Yellowstone was Lieutenant Colonel Elwell S. Otis, 22d Infantry. Round-featured with a set of mutton chop side whiskers, Otis looked more like a Dickensian uncle than an army officer. From here, Otis would then form a heavily guarded wagon train to haul supplies to Miles at Tongue River and beyond to the site of Fort Custer. The journey to Tongue River could take two weeks, depending on weather and Indians. Like Nelson Miles and Wesley Merritt, Elwell Otis would also eventually rise to the rank of general officer. During the Spanish-American War he would command the Military Department of the Philippines.

When Miles first arrived at Tongue River in August, his primary directive was to resolve the Indian problem. This was not to be accomplished by a single summer campaign, but rather by establishing a permanent presence in the region made possible by the construction of the post at Tongue River. Miles, thus, would be multi-tasking: building the new post while at the same time dealing with the Indian problem.

Miles saw, here, an opportunity to add to his laurels and the way he proposed to go about dealing with the Lakotas and their allies was through a winter campaign, and of course, he did not have to sell Sheridan on that idea. Terry thought it foolish, though, and sought to dissuade Miles from the idea, pointing out that Crook's Powder River effort had hardly been a success, but Miles remained convinced that his philosophy would work. Nelson Miles was nothing if not imaginative and resourceful. He proposed to cover his troops in buffalo robe overcoats, headgear, canvas leggings and either buffalo overshoes or rubber snow pacs. It was a bulky uniform, but did enable the soldiers to function in the snow and biting cold of a Montana winter. The creation of this unique winter uniform the Indians dubbed Bear Coat.

While work continued on Cantonment Keogh, Miles prepared his command to take the field. To support the 5th Infantry, which would do most of the heavy campaigning, Miles assembled an impressive coterie of civilian scouts and Crow Indian auxiliaries. Appointed chief scout for the District of the Yellowstone was twenty-seven-year-old, Luther Sage "Yellowstone" Kelly. Born in the Finger Lakes region of western New York State, the handsome, well educated Kelly, had earlier offered his services to Miles by presenting the forepaw of a large cinnamon bear as a calling card. The two men hit it right off and Kelly would remain a key figure of Miles's team for the next four years. George Crook had his Frank Grouard, and Custer his Lonesome Charley Reynolds, but Miles had his Yellowstone Kelly. Following his discharge from the 10th Infantry in 1868, the youthful Kelly had journeyed west and during the next eight years became one of the most skilled frontiersmen in the Upper Missouri River region and Yellowstone Valley.

Indian presence along the Yellowstone remained strong and from time to time an outpost would be attacked, as was the lumbering supply train plying its way from the Glendive Depot to Tongue River. On October 10, for example, a train of ninety-four wagons, guarded by three companies of the 22d Infantry and one of the 17th Infantry, was attacked in the late morning by a strong war party at Spring Creek, a short distance west of the Glendive Depot. As the day passed, the number of Indians increased until the supply train was under attack by several hundred warriors in what was the first major encounter since the conclusion of the summer campaign. So fierce was this clash that Captain Charles Miner, commanding the train and escort decided to return the train to the Glendive Depot. The Indians were apparently content to know that the wagon train would not get through to Tongue River because they backed off from their attack.

The retreat of Miner's supply train, left Otis with a serious problem: supplies had to be got through to Tongue River, so four days later, a train of eighty-six wagons with Otis himself in command and escorted by 185 men of the 22d Infantry pulled out of the depot. It was the strongest escort Otis could assemble. As it was, he left behind only 97 men under Captain Francis Clarke to protect the Glendive Depot.

On the 15th, Otis reached the vicinity of Spring Creek, near where Miner had been forced to turn back. Meantime, concerned that the Miner train had not reached Tongue River, Miles dispatched a quartet of his scouts to investigate. The scouts met up with Otis just beyond Spring Creek and were lucky to do so, having had their own encounter with the Indians the previous night. The Lakota continued to harass the wagon train, but this time the escort was strong enough to force its way through, although skirmishing continued through the next day as far as Cedar Creek, with Otis suffering three men wounded. On October 16, Otis was approached by an Indian courier bearing a note from none other than Sitting Bull himself. The message was attached to a stake driven in the ground:

> I want to know what you are doing traveling on this road. You scare all the buffalo away. I want to hunt on the place. I want you to turn back from here. If you don't I will fight you again. I want you to leave what you have got here, and turn back from here. I am your friend, Sitting Bull

The message was apparently written for Sitting Bull by a mixed-blood named Johnny "Big Leggins" Bruguier, who was then living with the Sioux. Wanted for murder, Bruguier had fled to the safety of Sitting Bull's camp, where, like Frank Grouard, he had been made welcome by the Hunkpapa leader. Later, Bruguier provided valuable service to Miles as guide and interpreter, and Miles, in turn, helped to clear Bruguier's name of the murder charge.[39]

While Otis pondered the message, the wagon train was approached by three Lakota warriors, bearing a white flag. Otis agreed to parley. Predictably, the Indians asked Otis to turn back. The movement of the supply train was driving off all the game. They also wanted food and ammunition. Otis offered some bacon and hard bread, but refused to give any ammunition. Satisfied, at least for the moment, the Indians moved off and Otis resumed his trek to Tongue River.

Even as Otis was parleying with the Lakotas, Miles, now more than a little concerned, about the absent supply train and fearful that something had happened, formed ten companies of his 5th Infantry, together with a dozen scouts, in all nearly 500 men, plus a 3inch Ordnance Rifle. On the morning of October 17, Miles, no doubt greatly relieved, met the Otis supply train near Custer Creek. Otis reported the incident with the Indians. Knowing that the supply train could now push on to Tongue River with no further interruptions, Miles bivouacked for the night.

According to the most recent information, Sitting Bull and his followers had moved north after buffalo. With this in mind, the 5th Infantry broke camp and marched northeast on a cold 19th day of October. Near Cedar Creek later that morning, Miles was approached by the same messengers that had contacted Otis. Sitting Bull, it seems, wanted to parley. Miles agreed and a nearby site was selected. While several hundred Lakotas looked on from a nearby hilltop, the two leaders confronted one another in the center of a large circle, each with aides and interpreters around them. Watching from a distance, but close enough to respond promptly should the need arise, were Bear Coat's soldiers. Miles later recalled his meeting with the renowned Hunkpapa leader. Sitting Bull was, according to Miles, "a strong, hardy, sturdy looking man of about five feet eleven inches in height, well-built, with strongly-marked features, high cheek bones, prominent nose, straight thin lips, and strong under jaw, indicating determination and force."[40]

It was a dramatic scene under a roiled sky while a ripping wind tore across the prairie. Tension was high as the two leaders exchanged words. Three years earlier General E.R.S. Canby had died from an assassin's bullet while participating in a similar parley during the Modoc War, and some of Miles's staff feared a repeat of that incident, including Miles himself. Interestingly enough, Miles later observed that he could have killed Sitting Bull then and there, and perhaps brought about a quick end to the Indian problem, but Miles respected the rules of negotiations conducted under a flag of truce and could not seriously entertain the idea of doing what Captain Jack had done to General Canby. Honor, it seemed, still ruled in some quarters.

Beneath this chilly, wind-blown autumn setting, the palaver continued for several hours, now and again growing a little heated. But of course there was not the slightest chance that this conference would lead to any real progress toward the resolution of the issues confronting the two parties. Sitting Bull wanted assurance that the soldiers would leave the Yellowstone country. Additionally, he wanted a resumption of trading privileges; essentially a return to the old days. Miles, on the other hand, demanded unconditional surrender, with all the Indians to be temporarily moved to Tongue River. Eventually, as the afternoon deepened Miles concluded further talk was pointless. Sitting Bull and his leaders should ponder what was said here today; they would parley again tomorrow.

Miles was not at all sanguine about reaching a peaceful agreement with the Lakota the next day. Indeed, he was prepared to fight and in the morning the regiment advanced slowly and in line of battle. As the soldiers advanced the Indians fell back. The terrain was rough, composed of hills and high plateaus Small parties of Indians collected on hilltops and ridges, seemingly with the intent to resist. As the soldiers advanced Miles ordered his Rodman, three-inch rifled field piece to the top of a high eminence.

Even as the first shots of battle were about to be fired, Miles and Sitting Bull met again. What Miles did not know was that some Lakotas were not at all anxious to fight again. Ammunition and supplies were running low and of course winter was just around the corner. The setting for this second conference was much like the first. This time, it was Miles who spread out a buffalo robe and Sitting Bull who refused to sit. Nevertheless, talks went forward. Sitting Bull repeated his demands which Miles again rejected, adding that if the Indians failed to comply they could expect immediate military action.

When it became clear to Miles that the times for words had passed he broke off the discussion. Sitting Bull's party retired to their own position, while Miles ordered his companies to advance in line of battle, deploying skirmishers. As the soldiers advance the Indians gradually fell back while others grouped threateningly on the high pieces of ground around the flanks of the soldiers. In terms of numbers, Miles was facing an estimated 800–1,000 Indians, as compared to his own 500, but he had a hole card in the form of the Rodman rifled field piece, which began lobbing shells into the pockets of Indians, scattering them and demonstrating once again the defining power of artillery in the Western Indian wars.

The Indians fell back before the advancing soldiers, galloping about on their ponies, firing at the soldiers whenever an opportunity presented itself and setting fire to the tinder dry grass. Amid the billowing smoke and wind-driven flames the troops pressed on, but it was a dicey situation. Bullets seemed to be zipping around everywhere and one man recalled that thoughts of the "Custer massacre" were on the minds of more than a few of Miles's soldiers.[41]

Miles pressed the pursuit until dark before bivouacking. Through a cold, clear night the sky glowed from the flames of the prairie fire. The following morning Miles resumed the pursuit, following the Indian trail east. En route the soldiers found the detritus of the abandoned Indian camp, including equipage from the 7th Cavalry. On October 24, Miles reached the Yellowstone River, having pursued the Indians for nearly thirty tough miles, only to find that the Indians had already crossed the river. In a report to General Terry,

Miles advised that the Indians were in a difficult way, needing food and ammunition. Then again, Miles needed to replenish his own supplies. To buy a little time while he re-provisioned his regiment, Miles sent a messenger to the Indians suggesting another council.

October 25 was one of those mid-fall days blest with a still warming sun and clear sky, and it was a day that seemed to bode well as a coterie of Lakota leaders splashed across the sparkling waters of the Yellowstone to confer with Bear Coat Miles. Sitting Bull, however, was not among the gathered chiefs. The Hunkpapa leader and an estimated thirty lodges had somehow slipped around the pursuing soldiers and gone north to the Upper Missouri valley to hunt buffalo and trade at Fort Peck.

This council proved little different from the two on Cedar Creek, except of course that Sitting Bull was not present. The headmen essentially adopted the same position taken by Sitting Bull, however, asking that the soldiers return to Tongue River and allow the Indians to hunt without interference. Miles of course said this was unacceptable, and so it went through the course of the conference. At length the council broke up and the Indians retired to decide on a course of action. By the time the council convened the following day the supply train from Glendive Depot had arrived and Miles was able to feed the Indians. Undoubtedly encouraged now by full bellies the chiefs acquiesced and agreed to surrender and return to the agencies.

Miles was obviously pleased, but the surrender also presented an unexpected problem. The quid pro quo here was a real Gordian Knot. If he was to escort these Indians to their agencies it would mean surrendering his pursuit of Sitting Bull. If, on the other hand, he was to take the Indians—estimated at 300–400—to Cantonment Tongue River it meant they would need to be fed from provisions intended for his troops. What to do? The resourceful Miles took a calculated risk. The Indians would conduct themselves to the agency. Miles would provide rations for the journey. To insure that the Indians honored their part of the bargain, several chiefs were sent by steamboat to St. Paul, more or less as hostages. The plan looked good on paper, but failed to work out quite as Miles expected. Some of the Indians slipped away en route so that only about forty or so lodges finally reached Cheyenne River Agency (northwest of present Pierre, South Dakota).

Miles had actually exceeded his authority in making such arrangements with these Lakota, but it seems not to have resulted in any sort of reprimand, and indeed, may have encouraged other bands to come into the agencies. Indeed, General Sherman actually congratulated him "on the prospect of closing this Sioux war." Meanwhile, Miles returned to Tongue River and prepared once more to take the field in search of Sitting Bull, who was still believed to be in the vicinity of Fort Peck on the Upper Missouri River. Colonel William B. Hazen operating out of Fort Buford on the Missouri River had responded to reports of Sitting Bull in the area of Fort Peck, but the wily Hunkpapa leader had slipped away before Hazen reached the area.

Early in November the remaining two companies of the 5th Infantry, under Lieutenant Frank D. Baldwin, arrived at Cantonment Tongue River accompanied by the regimental staff and band. Baldwin, it will be recalled, had served under Miles during the so-called Buffalo War on the Southern Plains, and was probably Miles's most valued and reliable subordinate. A first rate soldier, Baldwin would soon demonstrate once again why Miles valued him so highly.

Weather on the Northern Plains was unpredictable if anything. Spells of unseasonably mild temperatures could quickly be followed by fierce blizzards and sub-zero temperatures. Concerned about the effect of winter weather on his troops, Miles pressed ahead with seeing to it that his men were properly equipped with the necessary cold weather gear. Without proper cold weather clothing, Miles would have been forced to cancel plans for winter operations. Fortunately, the men of the 5th Infantry had campaigned in winter-like conditions during the Red River War in 1874 and that experience would stand them in good stead now.

Early in November, Miles commenced crossing the Yellowstone in phase one of his winter campaign. General Terry was opposed to the idea, but Miles persisted in his belief that it was a workable concept. He had at his disposal ten companies of the 5th Infantry, some 450 men in all, who would be supported by the three-inch ordnance rifle and a twelve-pounder Napoleon gun. A dozen guides and scouts, plus a wagon train, ambulances, pack mules, and a herd of beef cattle rounded out the expedition.

By November 14 Miles had probed the country north as far as Fort Peck on the Missouri River without making contact with Sitting Bull. Here, Miles bivouacked his command on the other side of the partially frozen river. The three-day layover enabled Miles to replenish his supplies and learn something of Indian movements in the area. The Indian agency at Fort Peck served several thousand Indians, and as such was a central collection point for the region. At the agency Miles again met Big Leggins Bruguier who revealed to Miles that he was wanted for murder in Dakota. Miles persuaded the mixed-blood scout/interpreter to join his [Miles's] command, promising to do what he could to aid Bruguier with his legal troubles. Anxious to clear his name, Bruguier agreed to try and persuade Sitting Bull to surrender.

On the 19th, having learned that Sitting Bull's camp was some forty miles south of the Missouri River near an area known as Black Buttes, Miles divided his command taking six companies and a twelve-pounder Napoleon gun with him on a march to Black Buttes while Captain Simon Snyder with the four remaining companies would explore the company around what was called The Big Dry River and rendezvous with Miles at Black Buttes.

By November 25, Miles's battalion had traveled some 100 miles west of Fort Peck, much of it through desert-like country, "as barren as a barn floor," according to Lieutenant Baldwin. Not only was there no Indian sign, there was no sign of any life. One day the command marched through fog, the next enjoying warm, sunny conditions. Daytime temperatures ranged from ten above to near sixty degrees. Captain Andrew Bennett with fifty men of Company B was sent to examine the small river community of Carroll City, which was at the time a key drop-off point for Missouri River steamers. Here freight was off-loaded onto waiting wagons and hauled to Last Chance Gulch (Helena). Miles was concerned that traders here might be stockpiling ammunition to be sold to Indians. If such was found at Carroll, Bennett was to confiscate it.[42]

While Bennett was off on his mission, Miles and the remainder of his command reached a point along the north bank of the Missouri near the Mussellshell River. Here, Miles decided to cross to the south side of the river, but making this happen proved a somewhat tougher challenge than what it appeared. Even though it was late in the season the river was still running fast and choked with ice floes. One wagon was converted into a boat and the troops also constructed an eighty-foot-long log raft. Launched the next morning with Miles, Baldwin and a dozen others on board, the raft snagged in mid-passage, stranding the passengers for most of the day until freed by ropes from the wagon-boat that enabled the raft to finally be pulled to the south shore. Although Miles's predicament was hardly a laughing matter, the men of the 5th had no trouble finding humor in the situation.

Meanwhile, Captain Simon Snyder with his four companies of the 5th Infantry, pursuant to Miles's orders had left the Fort Peck bivouac and reached Black Buttes on November 25 where he expected to rendezvous with Miles and the main body of the regiment. Miles and Baldwin of course were battling the Missouri River and as a consequence failed to reach Black Buttes at the appointed hour. Snyder hung around Black Buttes until December 2, but when Miles failed to show and with his supplies running low, Snyder, guided by scout Yellowstone Kelly, started for Tongue River, arriving on December 10, thoroughly jaded and with little to show for the effort.

On November 29, even as Snyder was waiting, probably somewhat impatiently, for his boss to arrive at Black Buttes, Miles was advised by the Fort Peck Agency that Sitting Bull with 150 plus lodges was preparing to cross to the south side of the Missouri some thirty miles east of Fort Peck. How the Indians had managed to evade him, Miles couldn't say, but he was chagrined to be sure and now had to be concerned that Sitting Bull would attempt to get south of the Yellowstone and join up with Crazy Horse. To try and thwart any such effort, Miles detached Baldwin and three companies and sent them to examine the country east of Fort Peck for any Indian movement. Miles, meantime, pushed his men over rugged terrain, dragging the wagons up rocky slopes and across frozen streams, finally reaching Black Buttes on December 7, only to discover that Snyder's battalion was long gone.

At this juncture, Big Leggins Bruguier brought word from Baldwin, saying that he had reached Fort Peck and Yellowstone Kelly returned from Cantonment Keogh to confirm that Snyder had returned. As well, there was a report that a mixed party of Cheyennes and Lakotas had been raiding the cattle herd around the cantonment. And what may have gladdened Miles's heart was a report that a large party of Crows, said to be eighty in number had enlisted as scouts. Thus far the campaign had accomplished little other than to serve as a winter weather exercise and Miles now concluded to head for Tongue River. On December 12, a fierce blizzard struck. Despite the storm the command slogged its way through, somehow even managing to discover Snyder's trail. Conditions were black as a pit; visibility was limited to thirty feet. Only by using a compass could they manage to stay on course. Finally, on December 14, the hungry, exhausted band of soldiers reached Cantonment Keogh.

In the meantime, Lieutenant Baldwin at the head of his three companies left Miles and the main body on December 2. His route was no less exhausting than Miles's. Learning that a hundred lodges of Hunkpapas were intending to cross the Missouri east of Fort Peck, Baldwin prepared a dispatch for Miles, Led by his scouts, Baldwin headed east, found the Indians and deployed a line of skirmishers along the north bank of the river. Unfortunately for Baldwin, he was not quite in time to interrupt the crossing and was only able to observe the last of the Indians retreating across the ice to the south bank.

After giving his command an opportunity to rest briefly, Baldwin started his command across the river, immediately coming under fire from Indians secreted in the timber that covered the south bank of the river. Deploying a line of skirmishers Baldwin advanced, encountering stiff resistance from a large body of warriors. Having seen to the removal of their non-combatants from harm's way, the Indians now felt free to oppose Baldwin with their entire force. In this they were unexpectedly aided by the appearance of a large body of Yanktonais Indians out of the Fort Peck Agency who had come out to put pressure on Baldwin's reserve company. Although technically, they were not regarded as part of the hostile contingent, Baldwin promptly ordered them to be fired on if they did not retire. Confronted by this, the Yanktonais decided not to become involved.

Baldwin now found himself in a difficult position. The number of Indians seemed to be increasing. He might well be facing Sitting Bull's entire force, estimated to be 600 strong.

In view of this and considering that he had no artillery, he pulled back to the north side of the Missouri, where he decided on a defensive/offensive strategy. At Little Porcupine Creek he created a log barricade, hoping somehow to tempt Sitting Bull into a frontal attack, but the Hunkpapa leader was too cagey to be drawn into such a move, although a few Lakotas crept up close enough to exchange shots with the soldiers. But the position may have served a better purpose for Baldwin's tired soldiers in that it allowed them time to rest, build fires, and prepare a slim repast.

As daylight ebbed on December 7, a fierce blizzard struck, dropping the temperature to minus thirty-five degrees. By full dark, with food gone, Baldwin started his command for the safety of Fort Peck. It may have been the longest night any of the men had ever experienced. Many suffered frostbitten extremities. Baldwin later wrote that the weather was so cold "I had to put 3 old sergeants in the rear with fixed bayonets and strict orders to prick any man who tried to lag or lie down." No man was exempt. Baldwin himself nodded off to sleep, fell off his horse and was prodded to wake up. He later recommended the man for a medal. Baldwin's frost-bitten command finally and mercifully reached Fort Peck on the afternoon of December 8. "I never experienced such suffering," remembered Baldwin.[43]

From Fort Peck Baldwin sent a quick report to both General Terry and Miles. Sitting Bull had boldly let it be known that he would strike Baldwin's command on its journey to Tongue River and then hit Fort Peck. Baldwin suggested to Miles that they try and trap the Indians between them. This done, he began preparing for his return march to Tongue River. The lack of artillery had reduced his effectiveness, and Baldwin now set about trying to remedy that deficiency. Like his boss, Baldwin was a can do officer. He couldn't work miracles, but he was resourceful if nothing else. At Fort Peck he located an old howitzer with a broken wheel and attached it to the front of a wagon, and so provided the expedition with a piece of artillery.

Learning that Sitting Bull might be headed for the Yellowstone, Baldwin sent word to Miles and on December 11—it was a Monday—took the field with his still-jaded command. Three days later they crossed the Missouri and worked their way generally south, but it was tough going through deep snow. On December 15 yet another norther struck. Supplies were running low and the horses were nearly played out; many were unshod. Traveling conditions were almost unimaginably bad. In addition to the bone-numbing cold, much of the country was covered with ice that caused the animals to slip. Nevertheless, Baldwin pressed ahead, and on the 18th found Indian sign not far ahead. Early that afternoon his three companies prepared to attack Sitting Bull's Sioux camp on Ash Creek.

With one company acting as skirmishers and the other two flanked on either side of his wagons, Baldwin struck. The Indians seemed entirely unaware of the soldiers bearing down on them. Baldwin began his attack with a salvo from his jury-rigged howitzer. With each bursting shell, the Indians fled, abandoning their teepees. Wisely, Baldwin elected not to pursue the fleeing Indians; his troops were in no condition to chase after a fleeing enemy, although that would have been the textbook thing to do. Rather his men destroyed most of the village, along with the equipage, save for buffalo meat, blankets and robes which his men put to good use.

That night the Indians fired on the soldier camp, but it was little more than an irritant. In the morning, Baldwin started for Tongue River. Two messengers sent on ahead to inform Miles, arrived at the Cantonment on December 20. A relief column dispatched by Miles met Baldwin on the 21st. The expedition to Fort Peck had failed to bring about the closure that Miles hoped for, but Baldwin's strike on Sitting Bull's village on Ash Creek had worked a real hardship on the Indians. If nothing else, Miles's winter campaign might have given the other hostiles bands reason to think about whether continued resistance was realistic.

Mackenzie's Attack on Dull Knife's Village

Although Miles's campaign north of the Yellowstone had failed to nab Sitting Bull, Sheridan's strategy was nevertheless working. He was keeping the pressure on; giving the Indians no rest. no opportunity to regroup. The blue coats seemed to be everywhere. While Miles was active north of the Yellowstone, south of that river, George Crook had again taken the field with yet another strong column of troops. Dubbed the Powder River Expedition, the column would consist of six companies of the 4th Cavalry, one of the 2d, two of the 3rd, and two of the 5th Cavalry, eleven companies in all, numbering nearly 800 officers and men under Colonel Ranald Mackenzie. Additionally, Colonel Richard Irving Dodge, a grand-nephew of literary giant Washington Irving, commanded a powerful contingent of infantry, eleven companies of the 9th, 14th and 23rd Infantry regiments, plus four batteries of the 4th Artillery, nearly 700 men in all. Altogether Crook would take the field with 1,436 men.

Once again, a large body of Indian auxiliaries would provide additional muscle for Crook. Interestingly, some 150 of these were Lakotas and Cheyennes and some Arapahos who had volunteered from the Red Cloud and Spotted Tail agencies. A second group of Indian scouts was composed of some one hundred Pawnees under the command of the North brothers, Frank and Luther. The North brothers had been responsible for recruiting these Pawnees who had performed valuable service to the Army for several years, including the Battle of Summit Springs which saw the end of Cheyennes Dog Soldier power on the Central Plains.

It will be recalled that the Sioux and Pawnees were fierce enemies of each other.. As the result of a recent directive from Sheridan, authorizing the enlistment of any Lakotas willing to serve as scouts it would shortly determine whether or not Sioux and Pawnee could work together. Frank Grouard again served as Crook's Chief of Scouts, ably assisted by mixed-bloods Baptiste Pourier, Baptiste Garnier—Big and Little Bat, respectively—and Willis Rowland would lend their expertise to the campaign. The expedition staged at Fort Laramie, from which place it took the field and headed north on the morning of November 5. It was another ponderous column with nearly 170 wagons, ambulances, and hundreds of horses and mules.

Crook's objective, once again, was the village of Crazy Horse, believed to be wintering in the Tongue or Powder River Valleys. Perhaps the third effort would bear fruit. Three days after leaving Fort Laramie, the expedition reached Fort Fetterman where final adjustments were made and the troops given a chance to rest before resuming the march on a bitterly cold 14th day of November. The ground was covered with fresh snow, but it was nevertheless "a lovely day," wrote one officer. To those who had marched with Crook back in March and June, the scene must have felt like *de ja vu*.[44]

Neither Crook, his scouts, or his Indian allies seemed aware of the fact that they were moving through Northern Cheyenne territory, which seems odd since Grouard and any of the scouts would have had that knowledge. Apparently, all thoughts were on Crazy Horse, the campaign's primary objective. As it would develop, however, Crook was about to discover that his single achievement during the 1876 campaigns would be against the Northern Cheyennes.

By the middle of the 19th century the Cheyenne nation had split apart. Some bands preferred the territory south of the Arkansas River and accordingly came to be thought of as the Southern Cheyennes, and as we have seen it was these bands who suffered the slaughter at Sand Creek. The remaining Cheyenne bands regarded northern Wyoming and the Powder River basin as their home turf. They were, in fact, occupying territory assigned them by the Laramie Treaty of 1868. Although a numerically smaller tribe than the Lakota, the Northern Cheyenne had played a key role in Red Cloud's War and at Little Bighorn.

By 1876, the two principal leaders of the Northern Cheyennes were Little Wolf and Dull Knife; both were sturdy, dependable and strong traditionalists. Dull Knife's tribal name—Tash-me-la-pash-me—translated in English to Morning Star, perhaps the most beautiful anglicized Indian name ever. An army officer once described Dull Knife as tall, with the appearance of a statesman. Little Wolf, though also a strong leader and renowned as a military tactician, seems to have had a less memorable persona than Dull Knife. In 1878, both Dull Knife and Little Wolf would lead their people from the reservation in Indian Territory, north to their homeland in Montana and the Powder River country; one of the great epics of American history, perhaps rivaled only by the memorable flight of the Nez Perce in 1877. In 1880 Little Wolf, while intoxicated, killed a fellow tribesman in a disagreement over one of his [Little Wolf's] daughters. The incident may have eroded the respect he had previously enjoyed among his people. Shamed by his behavior Little Wolf went into exile for a number of years. Ethnographer George Bird Grinnell thought he was one of the great Indians.

Following the break-up of the big Indian village on the Little Big Horn, some of the Northern Cheyennes, mainly the followers of Dull Knife and Little Wolf elected to head for the Powder River country and the Big Horn Mountains rather than reporting to the Red Cloud Agency. The war of 1876 had begun with Reynolds' attack on what was thought to be the village of Crazy Horse, but which turned out to be a Cheyenne village. Now the final battle of this defining year would again turn out to be against the Cheyennes. Although it had not been planned that way the Cheyennes might be excused for feeling that they had been singled out.

On November 18, The Powder River Expedition reached old Fort Reno. The post had originally been established during General Connor's 1865 campaign, then abandoned and rebuilt during Red Cloud's War and finally abandoned a second time following the closure of the Bozeman Road in 1868. Its location made it ideally suited as a forward base camp for Crook's fall campaign and, accordingly, it had been reactivated to serve the Powder River Expedition. Here Crook's already swollen command was further augmented by ninety-one Shoshones, a dozen Bannacks, and even a Ute and a Nez Perce. All, it seemed were anxious to get back at the Lakotas, who, it was understood they were after.

The expedition awoke on the morning of November 20 to a snow-covered world before them. Barring a dramatic change in the weather it appeared they would be moving through snow when Crook resumed his northward march in twenty-four hours. That Crook was concerned about tribal animosities is evident from the fact that he brought his Indian allies together and made it a point of reminding them that it was important that they put their enmity aside and work together during this campaign. Crook was counting on the fact that most of his allies, anyway, were more interested in whipping the Lakotas—it was not yet evident that they would be attacking a Northern Cheyenne village—and reaping the fruits of plunder from the Indian pony herd, which they had been promised.

The expedition got underway on November 21 with Mackenzie's cavalry taking the lead, followed by Dodge's infantry and the wagons the following day. There had been reason to believe from recent intel that the Sioux were gathering west of the Big Horn Mountains.

However, a party of hungry Black Hills miners had managed to find their way into the cantonment during the snowstorm of the 19th, with a report of heavily traveled Indian trails running between the agencies in Nebraska and Tongue River. This was where Crook had always figured to find Crazy Horse and there the issue would likely have rested had it not been for an unexpected development.

On the afternoon of the 21st a contingent of Crook's Lakota and Arapaho scouts stumbled across a young Cheyenne, Many Beaver Dams by name who informed his captors of the presence of Morning Star's village in the Big Horn Mountains. The youth had been deceived into believing the Lakotas and Arapahos were en route to attack Shoshones. Imagine his surprise when he was suddenly stripped of his weapons, bound up and taken back to meet Three Stars Crook.

Late on the afternoon of November 28 the expedition reached the south fork of Crazy Woman Creek. Here, Crook ordered his supply wagons to be parked and prepared to resume the march against Crazy Horse's village, believed to be farther north along the Rosebud River. The mule pack train would carry rations and extra ammunition to support a ten-day campaign. A reporter accompanying the expedition recalled that "The camp was astir far into the night preparing for the morrow's march."[45]

In the morning, the picture unexpectedly changed once again. Back in October Mackenzie had enlisted the services of a Cheyenne named Sitting Bear and dispatched him on a mission to find out about Crazy Horse and present the Oglala leader with Crook's surrender terms. Now, with the arrival of daylight, Sitting Bear approached the expedition under a white flag. Taken to Crook, the Cheyenne reported that a small band of Cheyennes, Many Beaver Dam's people, had fled toward Crazy Horse, but the much larger village of Dull Knife was camped in the Big Horns. This was an opportunity that could not be ignored and Crook decided to strike the Cheyenne encampment before moving on to deal with Crazy Horse.

Accordingly, at noon on November 23, Mackenzie headed southwest toward the Big Horn Mountains with his powerful cavalry force, together with the Indian scouts; in all 1,100 men. The ten companies of cavalry were organized into two battalions under Major George Gordon and Captain Clarence Mauck. The North brothers (Frank and Luther) had charge of the Pawnees, while Lieutenants William Philo Clark and Hayden De Lany managed the remaining Indian allies. An officer of some significance during the wars on the Northern Plains, William Philo Clark developed a deep interest in Indian language and culture. His published work on Indian sign language was one of the most important works of its kind.

By mid-day of the 24th—it was a Friday—Mackenzie's column had moved into the red sandstone canyon country lying due west of present day Kaycee, Wyoming. Even today it remains a remote region of canyons and buttes. In a small, grassy valley, the cavalry waited, resting and watering horses. Indian scouts confirmed that the Cheyenne camp lay just ahead, though how large was yet to be determined. However, the scouts were able to tell that the pony herd was substantial and that in turn meant an encampment of fairly good size.

Scouts urged a dawn attack and the thirty-six-year-old Mackenzie (who was the same age as Custer) concurred. The afternoon was spent in a cold, cheerless camp; the troopers ate hardtack and cold bacon and checked their carbines. As darkness fell, the troopers mounted and moved forward. It was an arduous climb that took the column higher into the mountains. "We continued our march along into the night [wrote newspaperman Jerry Roche], over jagged hills, through deep ravines, across rapid mountain streams, miry and deep, but the sky was clear and cloudless, and the moon rose to light up our narrow and difficult pathway." By the time the column reached the base of a high hill, first light was moving in, allowing a stunning view of the surrounding country, prompting one trooper to exclaim "What a splendid picture." Unfortunately, there was little time to appreciate the countryside.[46]

The Cheyennes, meanwhile, felt relatively safe in their encampment. Located in a beautiful hidden valley some four miles long, the village was set in an idyllic spot, except for one thing: if it was tough to locate, it was an equally tough place from which to escape. Cheyenne scouts had kept tabs on Crook's advance, at least as far as Fort Fetterman and when the soldiers marched north the Cheyennes concluded that Crazy Horse was the objective. They did not, however, know about the capture of Many Beaver Dams, and, surprisingly, somehow failed to note Mackenzie's march toward their village.

Thus it was that as dawn approached on this Saturday, November 25, Bad Hand Mackenzie's column drew close enough to Dull Knife's village to hear the throbbing of drums from an all-night dance. Clearly, the villagers had no intimation that soldiers were ready to strike. On the other hand, since all were obviously awake, it ruled out the possibility of a full surprise. Notwithstanding, the attack could be launched under cover of the dancing and singing and for that Mackenzie could be grateful.

Cautiously, the cavalry companies moved forward, especially vigilant against making any kind of noise that might betray their presence. Mackenzie had originally planned to encircle the village before launching his attack, but there was no time for that now. The Indian scouts would lead, approaching along the left hand side of the Red Fork of the Powder River, a stream that cut through the encampment. The scouts were not to fire unless fired on; their sole objective was the Cheyenne pony herd and they were only too glad to have been given that assignment, since the captured horses would be divided up among the scouts. The cavalry, meanwhile would proceed along the right side of the Red Fork.

Light began to build in the eastern sky as the scouts first, followed by the cavalry, began their descent toward the valley floor and the unsuspecting village. Reaching the valley floor, Gordon's battalion advanced at a brisk trot, some distance ahead of Mauck's reserve battalion. Out on the left, the Indian scouts followed three parallel routes: the Shoshones on the far left, Arapaho, Lakota, and Cheyenne in the middle, and Luther and Frank North's Pawnees on the right, to the immediate left of Gordon's troopers. Shots now rang out from the left where the Shoshones had opened fire.

The opening shots brought a quick response from the Cheyennes, some of whom began to fire at the attacking soldiers, while others made an effort to see the non-combatants moved to safety. Suddenly all seemed noise and chaos, where just a short time before the peaceful village lay slumbering in the chill autumn pre-dawn. Barking dogs, gunfire, and cries of the Indians permeated the air. Mackenzie's Indian scouts were largely successful in capturing the pony herd, although the Cheyennes strove valiantly to save as many horses as possible, most were lost.

Distressed at the loss of their horses, Dull Knife's warriors, fought back fiercely, taking advantage of the terrain where possible. By mid-morning the fighting was largely over. A number of the villagers had managed to escape from the valley and after a harrowing march would find refuge among Crazy Horse's Oglalas, just as they had done back in March when attacked by Reynolds' troops.

Mackenzie's casualties amounted to six killed and twenty-one wounded. The Cheyennes appear to have lost between twenty and thirty. The troops spent the rest of the day destroying the contents of the village, which included precious quantities of dried meat and hides. The village also contained relics from the Little Bighorn. Fifty pack mules were required to haul away all the buffalo robes. On the 27th, having completed the destruction of the village, Mackenzie began his return march, rejoining Crook on November 30.

Insofar as Sherman, Sheridan, and Crook were concerned, Mackenzie's destruction of the Cheyenne village had been as thorough as could have been hoped for. Indeed, Crook claimed a big victory. And yet, both Mackenzie and Crook were chagrined that Dull Knife and so many of his people had managed to elude the soldiers. For Crook it had to have resurrected memories of Reynolds' attack on another Cheyenne village just eight months earlier. Here the difference was that Mackenzie, unlike Reynolds, remained in control. Nevertheless, a goodly number of Cheyennes had managed to escape and that did not sit well with either Crook or Mackenzie.

What had been a signal victory for Crook had been a disaster for the people of Morning Star's band. If any had been in the village Reynolds attacked they surely must have wondered why the bluecoats seemed to single out their village and strike when the weather was harshest. Those who did manage to escape Mackenzie's troopers, worked their way out of the canyon and probably northeast, reaching the shores of Lake DeSmet and beyond that, the Tongue River. Eventually they were able to unite with the Oglalas of Crazy Horse. The Lakotas had fallen on hard times themselves, but nevertheless welcomed their Cheyenne brethren and provided them with what they could.

The men of the Powder River Expedition might have hoped for a winter-layover in warm quarters and with hot food. Indeed, General Sherman in offering his congratulations, expressed a hope that the men could now be spared the travails of further winter campaigning, but Crook was not about to give up, not when Crazy Horse was still roaming free. Early in December, the expedition returned to old Cantonment Reno, where Crook set about replenishing his supplies, preparatory to taking the field again. Some stocks were available at the cantonment, but grain for the horses was slow and difficult making its way north, first from Cheyenne to Fort Laramie, then from the latter point to Fort Fetterman, and finally Cantonment Reno. From here, some 250 sick and otherwise too ill to continue campaigning, returned to Fort Fetterman.

Notwithstanding his logistical problems, Crook was back in the field by December 3 heading for the northern end of the Black Hills. Forty-eight hours later a winter storm moved in necessitating a layover. Exactly what Crook's plans were seemed a good question. Exasperated at the general's failure to discuss his strategy, Colonel Dodge finally confronted Crook and pinned him down. The expedition would march northeast, following the Belle Fourche River, then north to the Powder and Little Powder Rivers. If they failed to find the village of Crazy Horse, the expedition would turn back to Fort Fetterman. The next three weeks proved a time of misery and discomfort for both men and animals, who suffered unduly from the cold, snow, and poor rations, and all of it for nothing. No Indians were located and finally, mercifully, on December 22, Crook turned back to Fort Fetterman, which place the expedition reached on the 29th, ending the Powder River Expedition.

THE WOLF MOUNTAIN CAMPAIGN

Meantime, even as Mackenzie was in the process of destroying Dull Knife's village, Nelson Miles had not been idle up on the Yellowstone. The union of the survivors of the Cheyenne village with the Oglalas of Crazy Horse in mid–December added to his burden. Exactly when he became aware of this is not clear, but probably soon after the Cheyennes arrived in the region. What Miles did not know, at least immediately, was that there was a growing peace faction among both the Cheyennes and Lakotas. Some had grown weary of fighting and running; of being hungry much of the time. The destruction of Morning Star's village surely reinforced the feeling of futility associated with further resistance. The blue coats, it seemed, were ever present; they never went away.

Back in October, it will be recalled, some Lakota had broached the subject of peace with Miles and now they prepared to take it to the next level. On December 16, a party of Oglala headmen marched down the Tongue, intending to talk to Miles about peace. As the delegation approached the cantonment under a flag of truce, they were approached by some of the Crows camped just outside the cantonment. The Lakotas greeted their old enemies in a spirit of peace, only to have the Crows unexpectedly jerk them from their ponies and proceed to beat and stab them. The rest of the Lakota party quickly withdrew. It was an incident of supreme tragedy and upon learning of it, Miles was irate. He immediately ordered the Crows disarmed He had threatened hanging a Crow who had earlier killed one of his Sioux couriers and probably considered the same punishment for these Crows, but he needed their services

Unfortunately, the incident, rather than serving as a giant step toward a peaceful reconciliation, resulted instead in a prolongation of the conflict. Here might well have been the breakthrough so long sought, but when a council was convened to hear the arguments of the peace faction, Crazy Horse rejected the idea and vowed to fight on. Miles sent messengers to Crazy Horse, but his offers were rebuffed. And so, Miles and his 5th Infantrymen could anticipate another winter campaign.

There was no way to tell exactly how many Lakotas and Cheyennes Miles might have to contend with, but historian Jerome Greene estimates that there may have been as many as 600 lodges, containing perhaps the bulk of the warriors who had defeated Custer. There is some evidence to suggest that Sitting Bull and his followers joined Crazy Horse for a brief time, but if so deep snow and a scarcity of game made it difficult for large bands to remain together for long. By mid–January, Sitting Bull had probably re-crossed the Yellowstone and headed toward the Upper Missouri country.

Angry as he was over the killing of the peace emissaries by the Crows, Miles could ill-afford to do without their services. Accordingly, he requested that the guilty Crows be turned over for punishment and the remaining scouts report for active duty. Work on the cantonment had progress apace and was gradually taking on the appearance of a military post. In late December, Miles was ready to take the field against Crazy Horse, who had by this time become the focus of his attention. The men were now quite fully equipped with buffalo coats, sealskin caps, gauntlets, buffalo overshoes, and face masks.

On a cold, depressing 29th of December Miles left the cantonment and took the field with six companies of the 5th Infantry, three of which were mounted on captured Indian ponies. In all, Miles had 436 men, plus five scouts, including Yellowstone Kelly, Big Leggins Bruguier, and John "Liver-Eating Johnson. A great bear of a man and a veteran frontiersman, Johnson was once accused of eating the liver of an Indian he had killed, hence the sobriquet "Liver-Eating" Johnson.

The 29th was a bitterly cold and somber day, with spitting snow, as Miles marched his command up the Tongue River Valley. That the Lakotas were active of that there was no doubt. On December 18 they attacked a mail party from Glendive and a week later drove off 150 cattle belonging to the cantonment's beef contractor. On January 1, 1877—New Year's Day—conditions changed, as they so often do in this part of the world. The daytime temperature rose; snow changed to rain and the snow cover turned slushy. Indian sign seemed plentiful and Miles advanced cautiously. On the second day of the new year, Scout Kelly found evidence that the Cheyennes who had escaped Mackenzie's attack, had camped in the area.

On January 6, winter weather returned. For the next twenty-four hours a fierce blizzard raged. A dominant feature of the Upper Tongue River Valley is a rugged mountain range known as the Wolf Mountains, the higher points of which were covered with stands of pine. The bluffs rising above the valley floor were composed of shale, coal, and sandstone of varying colors. On a better day, when a man need not be concerned about dodging a bullet or arrow, the mountains were pleasant to gaze upon, but on this particular day the soldiers of the 5th Infantry had to deal with ice and snow, and manhandle their supply wagons over steep, frozen stream banks. Indian sign, meanwhile, grew increasingly plentiful; abandoned camp sites, emaciated ponies too weak to do anything but die.

On the afternoon of the 7th, Kelly and his scouts discovered a party of Lakotas, mostly women, en route to their village. They had been confused by the smoke from Miles's camp, believing it to be their own. Kelly's scouts ushered them back to the army camp where they were fed. Whether Crazy Horse was in the immediate vicinity remained to be seen. That afternoon, the scouts, returning to their original position after escorting the Indians to Miles's camp, suddenly found themselves caught in a cleverly designed ambush. Yes, Crazy Horse was definitely in the area. Hearing the firing, Miles quickly assembled three companies and his three-inch howitzer and started off in relief of his scouts, who suddenly found themselves in a tight fix. A hundred or more warriors closed in from three sides, forcing the scouts to race for the woods, but to do so, recalled Kelly it was necessary to "jump our horses down a rocky shelf five or six feet to rocky ground. All this time the Indians were firing away at us, the bullets, striking the rocks and raising little dust patches from the ground. It was miraculous that no one was seriously hurt."[47]

But Miles was coming on. A mile out, he directed Captain James Casey to take Company A and the field piece and secure a position atop a nearby hill. From here, Casey lobbed shells into the Indian position, causing them to withdraw.

With the arrival of darkness fighting slacked off though there was no sense that it would not be resumed come morning. In the meantime, the temperature dropped to double digits and snow commenced to fall. After breakfast, Miles climbed a prominent hill near his camp and through binoculars, noted hundred of Indians. It was tough country in which to wage war. Timbered slopes rose some 300 feet above the valley floor, through which coursed the Tongue River, frozen over now on this bitterly cold 8th day of January 1877.

The action was quick in developing. The Indians, suddenly appearing on the high ground above the river commenced to taunt the soldiers. Through Yellowstone Kelly who spoke Lakota, Miles challenged the Indians to fight, calling them women, which provoked an advance toward the soldiers. Miles quickly deployed his men and two remaining field pieces. The Indians refused to challenge the soldiers' position directly, however, but rather took up positions on the buttes and along the river bottom, from where they fired on the soldiers, threatening Miles's left flank. The soldiers promptly returned their fire, but it was the artillery, which, as always, compelled the Indians to pull back and away from the exploding shells, communicating with each other through the use of eagle-bone whistles. The soldiers fired plenty, with some reporting that their rifle barrels were hot from the heavy volume of fire.

Unsuccessful in making any headway against Miles's flank on the west side of the river, the Indians, a mixed force of Lakotas and Northern Cheyennes, began to focus their attention on a range of bluffs east of the river. From a high land mass, known today as Battle Butte, the Indians were able to direct a heavy and deadly fire on the troops below. To deal with the threat, Miles now sent Casey and Company A to clear the bluff, and Miles sent a company of the 22d Infantry to protect the backside of his position. At about this time, Big Crow, a Cheyenne medicine man, emerged from the Indian positions all decked out in his warrior uniform, including a full eagle headdress. He danced with impunity until laid low by a bullet.

The fighting was toughest in this sector of the battle. As pressure from the Indians persisted, Miles now directed Butler to take his Company C and clear a high bluff to protect Casey's flank which was up in the air and in danger of being turned. Supported by fire from the three-inch rifled field piece, the troops were finally able to drive the Indians back across a series of ridges. It was now mid-day and as blowing snow moved into the area, the fighting effectively ceased. The Indians withdrew up the Tongue River Valley while Miles's artillery harassed the movement with occasional interdictory fire. The troops pursued only a short distance as Miles concluded it was pointless to continue after mounted Indians with foot soldiers; besides his supplies were running low and there was some concern over the condition of the men who had endured much hardship during the campaign, notwithstanding their new winter gear. One might well imagine that the Indians suffered at least as much. In any case, Miles now began his return march to the cantonment.

Tactically, it could be said that Miles scored a victory at Wolf Mountains. He had driven the Indians off and retained possession of the field. Notwithstanding, Crazy Horse remained at large and so, too, of course, did Sitting Bull. The Army could feel good, too, about having conducted another successful winter campaign, even though that campaign had failed to bring about closure, thus necessitating more campaigning come spring. It had been less than a year since the debacle on the Greasy Grass, but already Congress was beginning to close the purse strings. In response to cutbacks, Terry informed Miles that he would have to get rid of most of his civilian scouts, teamsters, and blacksmiths. Miles was furious. He thought Terry was playing politics and thus compromising his efforts. Bypassing Terry, Miles wrote to Sherman venting his spleen and stating his case for an independent command. Sherman pigeon-holed the request and eventually Miles cooled down.

THE END OF THE GREAT SIOUX WAR

Although the United States Army continued to regard them as a hostile entity still to be reckoned with—and indeed they were still able to respond with plenty of fire and vim—the bands of Lakotas, Northern Cheyennes and Arapahos that had formed the heart of the alliance that destroyed Custer was teetering on the brink of dissolution. Many were tired and not a few were hungry. Resistance that seemed so satisfyingly defiant and the road to follow back when the grass was new and the season young and virile now seemed worn thin and futile to an ever increasing number. While it was true that Crazy Horse and the other recalcitrant leaders still held sway, the hard liners were gradually disappearing. The voice of the discontented was growing ever louder.

Miles was well aware that a peace faction existed; he had already had talks with them and in the weeks after Wolf Mountain sought to try and take advantage of this by sending emissaries among the bands, promoting the idea of surrender. It wasn't so much that Nelson Miles was a peace loving man. In point of fact the effort was fueled mainly by self-interest. As historian Jerome Greene suggests, arranging for the Indians to surrender and thereby bringing about an end to the war would have looked mighty good on Miles's record.

In the immediate aftermath of the Wolf Mountain campaign, Miles rested and refitted his command, and continued work on the cantonment, one day soon to become a full fledged fort. Sheridan, meanwhile, was feeling the pressure of dealing with budget cuts with the arrival of the new fiscal year. Accordingly, he stressed to his department commanders—Terry in St. Paul and Crook in Omaha—that the Sioux war needed to be wrapped up by July 1 because Congress was going to cut the size of the Army.

In late February 1877, Miles received additional reinforcements that included four companies of the 2d Cavalry and two of the 22d Infantry. Sheridan was making sure that that Miles had what he needed to finish the war. Indeed, he would now have 2,000 men at his disposal, more than either Terry or Crook at the outset of the 1876 campaign. Additionally, Lieutenant Colonel George Buell's six companies of the 17th Infantry were constructing Fort Custer near the confluence of the Big Horn River with that of the Little Bighorn.

As the winter progressed, work continued on Cantonment Tongue River. Work parties chopped ice from the river for storage, while other detachments pulled escort duty for supply trains moving back and forth between the cantonment and the Glendive Depot. Miles also dispatched strong patrols to search for Indian sign. Meanwhile, the winter months saw a growing increase in opposition to further resistance. Influential leaders such as the Oglala Lakota, Sword and the Spotted Tail, the fifty-three-year-old Brule headman who had long been a proponent of peace, pressed home the idea of surrender. On February 19, largely through the encouragement of Big Leggins Bruguier, a Lakota-Cheyenne delegation came into the cantonment to talk terms with Miles, who promised to help provided they lay down their arms; they had the option of doing this here or at the agency. Should they fail to do this he would deal with them harshly. Satisfied, the delegation departed having promised to bring their people into the agency.

If Miles had reason to feel optimistic at the conclusion of this council he was soon to be disabused of that notion. After leaving the cantonment the delegation had chanced to meet others who urged the party to return to Miles and negotiate better terms. Politics had been introduced into the equation. Over at Red Cloud Agency and Fort Robinson near present Crawford, Nebraska, George Crook was dangling a more attractive carrot and enticing large numbers of former hostiles to surrender. On March 21 he met again with the same delegation of peace leaders. Miles could only reiterate his terms and ultimately he was successful in persuading some of the Indians to return to the agency, but his numbers could not match those of Crook, who had always been a rival. Miles had wanted the star that Crook got and their relationship had cooled noticeably in the latter weeks of the Great Sioux War.

As it happened, a splinter group of hard line Miniconjou Lakotas, led by Lame Deer, separated from those whom Miles had persuaded to go into the agency. Lame Deer and his followers decided that the old way of life was preferable to life at the agency and presently his original following of perhaps 100–150 was reinforced by small parties of other dissidents. Miles was surprised to learn that Lame Deer was still at large, but at the moment he was unable to do much of anything about it until he built up his supply base and had ample forage for his animals. In the meantime, Lame Deer had good cause to believe in the wisdom of his decision, since, for a few weeks anyway, the Indians lived undisturbed in the Rosebud River country.

It was, relatively speaking, a satisfying if brief hiatus for Lame Deer and his followers, for once he had come to understand that Lame Deer had no intention of surrendering, Miles prepared to go after him. He had learned this through Big Leggins Bruguier whom he had sent to Lame Deer as an emissary, but Bruguier reported back that the Indians had a sizeable pony herd and were reasonably well provisioned and were not at all of a mind to surrender.

On May 1, Miles marched out of the cantonment with nearly 500 men of the 5th and 22d Infantry Regiments plus the usual coterie of white and Indian scouts. Although Miles was fiercely proud of his 5th Infantry, and justifiably so, he had always felt that his field operations had been hampered by the lack of cavalry, so this time his command was equipped with a battalion of the 2d Cavalry, along with a detachment of mounted infantry.

Scouts soon picked up the Indian trail and on May 6 Miles was advised that the village was some sixteen miles up ahead and situated along a branch of the Rosebud. It was a sizeable encampment, with sixty-one lodges, although Miles was at first led to believe it was only half that size. It took the remainder of the day and early evening to get into position, but the troops were able to approach without alerting the Indians and Miles, taking no chances, banned cooking fires. Figuring to strike at dawn, Miles had his men up and moving at 2 a.m. Following a two and a half hour march they were in position and the last major engagement of the Great Sioux War was about to take place.

The rank and file had probably slept fitfully if at all and now in what was stygian darkness with rain pouring down they were marching to battle. It was a miserable approach to Lame Deer's camp, too, over rough ground and swollen creeks, for nearly five miles until at last, about 4:30 they were finally in position. Perhaps it was a good omen that the rain had ceased and a new day was brewing on the eastern horizon. Ahead, smoke curled upward from a few teepees. It gave promise of a pleasant spring morning. New grass was beginning to show and a light breeze swirled through the valley.

Assembling his officers, Miles issued commands. A company of the 2d Cavalry along with the mounted infantry and a detachment of scouts, all under 2d Lieutenant Edward Wanton "Ned" Casey (no relation to James Casey) would charge upstream through the village to secure the pony herd. Only four years out of West Point, Ned Casey had recently served in New Orleans, which was then in the throes of political troubles. Now, leading his troopers upriver toward the Indian horses he led his men across the creek and up the steep bluffs to the herd. His daring here would earn him the sobriquet of Tongue River Casey.

Meanwhile, Miles and the main body struck the village proper, demonstrating yet again how an Indian village could be taken completely by surprise. When the attack broke, Indians tumbled from their lodges, firing, taking pot-shots at the soldiers; there was little time to aim and the soldiers were rather shadowy figures in the not yet full light. Many of the villagers fled. And it then happened that Lame Deer sought an end to the fighting and asked to meet with Miles. Accordingly, the chief and several Lakota leaders, including a nervous and edgy Iron Star, came forward. Lame Deer and Miles shook hands, and Miles told the chief to lay his weapon down. Lame Deer complied. What happened next was one of those accidental moments which sometimes have disastrous if not fatal consequences. Iron Star had not been inclined to lay his weapon down and indeed, edgy as he was, continued to wave the weapon around menacingly. When one of Miles's Indian scouts, White Bull, attempted to wrest the weapon from Iron Star, the gun discharged, narrowly missing Miles but killing the colonel's orderly, Private Charles Shrenger. What had been a peaceful meeting quickly deteriorated into chaos. One soldier reacted by trying to shoot Lame Deer and was himself shot. A few more shots were exchanged, one of which felled Lame Deer; in fact he was hit seventeen times. In the wild melee Lame Deer was also scalped by two of Miles's scouts.

When the firing broke out, the Indians scattered. Most were on foot, but a few were mounted, having kept their ponies nearby rather than in the horse herd. Some took up positions behind boulders and ridge-top west of the village from where they poured a deadly fire down on the troops. Miles formed a skirmish line and advanced, but it took time to mount the steep, timbered ridge. Notwithstanding, the troops inflicted serious casualties on the Indians, and apparently made little distinction between warriors and non combatants. By mid-morning it was all over. The Battle of Muddy Creek, as it would be known, resulted in fourteen Indians killed. Miles's losses amounted to 4 killed and 9 wounded. It had been a sizeable village, containing perhaps 300 inhabitants, most of whom had managed to escape. Working their way through the village the soldiers found much dried buffalo meat, robes, firearms, and blankets, along with a number of 7th Cavalry items. After retrieving anything of value, the troops put the village to the torch. The loss of so much dried meat would work a serious hardship on the Indians, but perhaps not nearly so much as the loss of nearly 500 horses.

Miles remained in the area another day, establishing a defensive perimeter against a possible attempt by the Indians to retrieve some of their horses. On May 8, he sought to mount some of his infantry on captured Indian ponies. The experiment, like Crook's attempt to mount his foot soldiers on mules prior to the Rosebud battle, proved an exercise in comic-relief more than anything else. Most of the horses were distributed among the scouts, but those that were left over were shot. That morning, Miles commenced his return march to the cantonment, which place they reached on May 14.

Although Miles had scored a great victory in destroying Lame Deer's village, Crook claimed Miles had done nothing more than attack a village that was hunting. Neither Crook nor Miles it seems was interested in seeing the other one gain any credit. After his return to the cantonment, Miles remained concerned that a sizeable number of warriors from that encampment were still at large and accordingly sent the 2d Cavalry battalion and four companies of his mounted infantry to search the Tongue and Rosebud River watersheds, but it was a futile gesture. For all intents and purposes, the Great Sioux War was over, but there remained some nasty details to be worked out.

The Surrender and Death of Crazy Horse

In the fall of 1876, as a consequence of the Custer disaster, a committee headed by former Indian Commissioner George Manypenny came west and visited the agencies with the avowed purpose of persuading the Indians to agree to surrender all rights to lands outside the pale of their reservation, and that of course included the Black Hills. Still smarting over the Custer disaster, Congress had declared that if the Indians failed to surrender the territory in question it meant that there would be no issuance of goods and annuities due the Indians as a result of the Laramie Treaty. This was big leverage and the commissioners had little trouble gaining a number of signatures or Xs on the agreement. However the commissioner ignored a key provision from the Laramie Treaty that said the signatures of three-fourths of all adult males were required to validate any agreement and the commission had collected only a fraction of the signatures needed. What the federal government wanted of course was to get these wild bands—especially Crazy Horse and Sitting Bull—ensconced at the agencies and they would agree to almost anything in order to make that happen. If this led to contradictions, that was okay; conflicting details could be worked out later.

Even as Miles was destroying Lame Deer's village at Muddy Creek, Crazy Horse was persuaded by some of the Lakota leaders to turn himself in, but the circumstances surrounding his surrender are confusing and contradictory. When informed that his agency would eventually be located on the Missouri River, Crazy Horse balked at surrendering. Supposedly Crook then promised him an agency in the Powder River country, at least that's what Crazy Horse understood. Satisfied, the Oglala leader then surrendered to Crook at Camp Robinson on May 6.

Through the summer of 1877 Crazy Horse remained a disruptive influence. Although he made no effort to foment trouble, his mere presence was enough to keep the garrison at Camp Robinson edgy and many of his own people found him an unsettling influence as well. Some of the Lakota leaders who had come to terms with living the reservation life were convinced Crazy Horse was preparing to lead a band of warriors on a break out to join Sitting Bull. For his part, Crazy Horse resented the fact that the Army had enlisted Lakotas to serve as scouts on the Nez Perce campaign. In any event there was an undercurrent of fear, distrust, and resentment that hovered around Crazy Horse like a pall. It was astonishing how swiftly loyalty and respect vanished like snow on the buffalo grass when a warming wind swept across the Great Plains. Little more than a year before, Crazy Horse loomed as the symbol of Lakota resistance; the spirit of the old ways. Now, many Lakotas, including some of his own Oglala band saw him as a danger to the accommodation they sought with the white man; his time had passed.

The atmosphere around Camp Robinson was charged with distrust, half truths and lies; there were rumors of plots and back room schemes. It was hard to know who to believe. Ostensibly, there was one plot afoot that called for an Oglala to murder Crazy Horse, for which he would be paid $300 and a fine horse. Yet another plot had Crazy Horse preparing to murder Crook. These were troubled days indeed. Julius Caesar would have understood.

On the morning of September 4, Colonel Luther Bradley, commanding the post at Camp Robinson, sent eight troops of cavalry and some 400 friendly Indian scouts, all decked out in war paint and regalia, to arrest Crazy Horse whose village was located on White River not all that far from Camp Robinson. Although there were a number of loyal followers in the village, the size of the force (and its composition) sent to bring Crazy Horse into the camp speaks volumes about the reputation of the Oglala war chief; he remained a force still to be reckoned with.

After a rather tense and confusing time, Crazy Horse, who had left his village with his sick wife and started for Camp Sheridan outside the Spotted Tail Agency, was finally persuaded to come into Camp Robinson. Apparently Crazy Horse agreed at the urging of Lieutenant Jesse Lee who promised the chief that he would have an opportunity to speak his piece. However, upon arriving at the camp, Colonel Bradley refused to listen to the Oglala leader's entreaties, despite Lee's passionate argument to the contrary and indeed ordered the chief to be incarcerated in the guard house, explaining to Lee that Crook's orders were to confine Crazy Horse and ship him off to Omaha under guard. Lee persisted, but all Bradley would agree to was to promise that Crazy Horse would be protected.

Jesse Matlock Lee was one of the more interesting officers of the frontier army. After his Civil War service he was stationed in the West as both an army officer and Indian agent. In 1879 he acted as recorder for the Army during the famous Reno Court of Inquiry. Rising to the rank of brigadier general he later served in the Philippines. Now, a participant in one of the great moments in American history, Lee shook hands with the chief and remembered him as being slight of stature. Lee sensed, too, that Crazy Horse was a troubled man. As he approached the guardhouse with his escort Crazy Horse seemed to suddenly realize that he was going to be put in jail. Then, with astonishing strength, he tried to wrest himself free from those who were trying to force him into the guard house. The next few moments

Crazy Horse and his band en route to surrender to General Crook (sketch by Mr. Hottes).

were filled with yells and commotion, and in the melee Crazy Horse was stabbed or lunged against a bayonet by one of the guards. The wound was mortal. "I am hurt bad," Crazy Horse said, "Tell the people they cannot depend on me anymore." At 12:15 a.m., on September 6, 1877, Crazy Horse, Tasunka Witko passed into the spirit world and the stuff of legend.[48]

The Army's treatment of Crazy Horse can only be described as shabby. Although tall words were spoken about friendship and peace, there clearly never was any genuine intention to deal with Crazy Horse in an honorable way. Insofar as the military was concerned he posed a threat as long as he remained alive. Although there is no evidence to support a charge that the Army planned to assassinate the Oglala leader, its handling of the chief's surrender was less than honorable and surely contributed to the killing of Crazy Horse. In his final hours, as life seeped out of him, one can only imagine what thoughts were in the mind of the Oglala leader. He has been called a mystic; a visionary and perhaps it was an end he had foreseen.

The Flight of the Nez Perce

As Miles was wrapping up the Great Sioux War with his victory over Lame Deer, a new and unexpected package of trouble was brewing out in Idaho, far removed from his District of the Yellowstone, but soon to become part of his military responsibility.

The genesis of the Nez Perce trouble dates to the 1850s when the aggressive Isaac Stevens was putting together a block of treaties with the tribes of the Pacific Northwest. One such agreement involved the Nez Perce, a tribe that had had an amicable relationship with the U.S. dating back to Lewis and Clark. A people of the Columbia River Plateau, the Nez Perce—the name means pierced noses—were given that name by early French trappers and traders. Like so many indigenous tribes, however, they referred to themselves as Nee Me Poo or the People. The traditional homeland of the Nez Perce included portions of today's northeastern Oregon, southeastern Washington and central Idaho.

In the decades following Lewis and Clark, the Nez Perce had further contact with representatives of the white man's world via French and British trappers and traders, and in the 1840s through Christian missionaries. Although the Christian proselytizers were eminently successful in converting many Nez Perce to Christianity, not all of them, by any means succumbed, to the message of scripture. However, an unanticipated effect of the missionary effort was the birth of a schism that tended to divide Christians from non-Christians through the change it brought about in their traditional way of life. Those Nez Perce who had closer contact with missionaries and the trappings of the white man's world—firearms, cooking utensils, blankets, etc., naturally tended, to be more receptive to the Christian message more readily than those bands who dwelled farther afield from the missions.

By the mid-1850s, with white immigrants moving into the area in growing numbers, federal authorities—in this case Washington Territorial Governor, Isaac Stevens—concluded that the time had come to set aside a reservation for the Nez Perce to insure that there was no conflict or interference with white settlement in the region. Thus was born the Treaty of 1855, which was surprisingly generous in that it set aside most of the traditional Nez Perce land as their reservation. By the terms of this treaty, the Nez Perce were assigned to a reservation that ranged from the Blue Mountains of Oregon, east to the Continental Divide. It was a vast tract covering some five thousand square miles and included much of their traditional homeland. In return, the Nez Perce were to receive certain specified annuities, goods and services.

As generous as the treaty may have seemed on the face of it, the signers of the treaty that included Old Joseph and Looking Glass of whom more will be heard later, discovered that there was a catch, namely that the treaty extinguished Indian ownership of the land. Somehow in the discussions surrounding this treaty that rather key fact was not made clear to the signatories and when they found out what was at stake here they refused to recognize the treaty's legitimacy. Consequences were not immediate, however. For one thing, the treaty did little to disturb the boundaries of the Nez Perce homeland and for another in order for one of these treaties to carry the force of law, they had to be ratified by Congress, which in this case took four years.

The picture began to change by the early 1860s, however, when the discovery of gold within the reservation boundaries resulted in public clamoring for the right to seek fortune where it was found. Once again, as it would so often throughout the Westward movement, Congress could not ignore public outcry for access to this new land of riches. The demand compelled Congress, in 1863, to create a much smaller reservation around the Clearwater River in Idaho. The size of the new reservation reduced the boundaries of the 1855 Treaty by an astonishing 90 percent. Still, some bands of Nez Perce—sometimes called "progressives" and most of whom tended to be Christians—acquiesced and agreed to live on the new reservation. Those who accepted the new terms amounted to about 75 percent of the tribal total. Those who rejected the new treaty and were mostly non-Christians, dwelled along the lower Salmon River and in Oregon's Wallowa Valley and were conveniently known as the "lower bands." Interestingly, Old Joseph, who had originally converted to Christianity renounced that conversion in the wake of the treaty contretemps, and in this he was not alone.

Old Joseph died in 1871 and the reins of leadership passed to Young Joseph—Hinmah-too-yah-lat-kekt—Thunder Rolling Down The Mountain or Thunder Traveling to Higher Areas, or some variation thereof, but for all intents and purposes he would be known to history simply as Joseph. Joseph shared the responsibilities of leading the band with his brother Ollokot who functioned more or less as the military leader.

Joseph inherited a situation ripe to explode. It was inevitable that a confrontation was not far off. As settlers began moving into the Wallowa Valley in steadily increasing numbers the federal government created a commission to determine who had a right to be here. What is surprising is that the commission declared that Joseph's band—which had become the most prominent of the non-treaty bands—had every right to be in the Wallowa Valley as defined by the Treaty of 1855, and since they had not agreed to the 1863 treaty, they were not bound by its provisions. What is not surprising is that the Commissioner of Indian Affairs, the Secretary of the Interior, and President Grant, decreed, however, that while part of the Wallowa Valley should be reserved for the Nez Perce, part should also be opened to settlement. Here was one of those decisions that attempted to satisfy everyone and wound up satisfying no one. Actually, there were settlers already occupying that part of the valley that had been set aside as Indian land, as well as Nez Perce dwelling in the portion that had been thrown open to settlement. It was complicated. And there was yet another factor. Over the years, there had been several instances of Nez Perce being murdered by whites who had never been punished. It was a bone of real contention; a sore that festered.

In November of 1876—about the same time that Mackenzie's command was attacking Morning Star's village on the Red Fork of the Powder River—a new commission, headed by Brigadier General Oliver Otis Howard, commanding the Department of the Columbia, met with the Nez Perce at the Lapwai Agency in Idaho in an effort to resolve the situation. The gathering was notable in that it afforded Joseph a forum to demonstrate his not insignificant oratorical skills. If some individuals are destined to greatness; to somehow make a difference, Joseph was surely one such person. Thirty-six years old, standing six feet tall and straight as an arrow, He was an imposing figure of a man, possessing dignity, clear-headedness and the vision of a true leader, Joseph stands tall in the pantheon of great Native American leaders. The Lapwai council was the first real opportunity for Joseph to demonstrate his leadership skills. All who were present recognized him as a figure of the first rank.

General Howard and the other delegates may have imagined, or at least hoped, that the Nez Perce could be persuaded to accept the new reservation terms, but if so, it was a forlorn hope. Together with his brother Ollokot, Joseph stood firm in refusing to "sell the bones" of their parents. They would not leave the Wallowa Valley. Joseph had also insisted that those responsible for murdering several Nez Perce be punished; and this was a demand that could be met, but there was no fudging on the matter of relinquishing territory. The Nez Perce would have to relocate to the new reservation; that was all there was to it.

In January 1877 the Bureau of Indian Affairs advised Joseph that the non-treaty bands would need to be on the reservation by April 1. To this ultimatum, Joseph could only reiterate his original position, namely that he would not leave the Wallowa Valley. And so now the hour of easy choices had passed. From the Interior Department to Military headquarters San Francisco to General Howard went orders to enforce the Indian Bureau's ruling and see to it that the Nez Perce were removed—albeit peacefully if possible from the Wallowa Valley to their reservation, and Howard proceeded to carry out his orders.

As commander of the U.S. Army's military Department of Columbia, Oliver Otis Howard would figure prominently in the Nez Perce saga about to unfold. Forty-seven-years old in 1877, he was born in Maine, and graduated from West Point in 1854. Like many officers of his antiquity the Seminole and Mexican-American Wars prepared him for service in the Civil War, where he lost an arm at the Battle of Fair Oaks.

General Oliver Otis Howard. His peace treaty with Cochise and his later pursuit of the Nez Perce Indians made him one of the important Army figures during the Indian wars.

A fervent Congregationalist Christian, Howard was often referred to as the Christian General, or somewhat more pejoratively, as Bible-Thumping Howard. Although a devout Christian, those beliefs seem not to have clashed with his soldierly responsibilities. Thus it was that he brought a curious mixture of Christian beliefs to the killing fields of a soldier, and yet he was as dedicated to his military career as he was to his religious beliefs. Howard remains a fascinating if relatively minor figure from history. As a soldier he was solid and able but never quite outstanding. Yet it is interesting that during the course of his career he, should find himself in not one but three crucial situations in American history.

As commander of the Eleventh Corps at Gettysburg Howard was the senior officer on the field during that crucial first day, following the death of General John Reynolds. Whether he was the right man for that critical hour remains debatable. After the war, President Andrew Johnson, recognizing Howard's strong stance in support of Blacks, appointed him to head the Freedmen's Bureau, a position that generated some controversy. In 1872, President Grant sent him off to the Southwest as a Special Indian Commissioner, in which capacity he negotiated what proved to be a temporary peace with the noted Apache leader, Cochise. Now, here in 1877, history, it seemed, was about to thrust him into the forefront of yet another key moment.

In May, a Nez Perce delegation met again with Howard and Agent John Monteith at Fort Lapwai, hoping to somehow persuade them to reconsider, but of course it was an exercise in futility. And so with great reluctance, the various Nez Perce bands returned to their respective areas and prepared to move to the new reservation, while Howard returned to department headquarters. Howard had come away from the final meeting convinced that the Nez Perce would not abide by the ruling. At the same time, he believed that the Nez Perce had been wronged, but orders were orders; they would have thirty days in which to remove to the new reservation.

Following the council at Fort Lapwai each returned to his own territory: Joseph's to the Wallowa Valley, White Bird to the Salmon River, and Looking Glass to the Clearwater River, for example. By early June they were on the move again, however, this time to a place called Tolo Lake on Camas Prairie a few miles west of Grangeville, Idaho. The lake had long been a popular gathering place for the Nez Perce, who came here each summer to greet and mingle with one another and observe their Dreamer ceremonies; in this it was much like the annual Sun Dance ceremony of the Plains tribes. In addition to Joseph's Wallowa band, the gathering included the bands of Looking Glass's, White Bird, the Pikunans of Toohoolhoolzote, and the Palouses. In all, there were some 600 Nez Perce gathered here, of which possibly 100 were warriors. The Wallowa band was the largest of the gathered bands and as the Wallowa leader, Joseph seems to have exerted a little more influence in discussions than the other leaders, but it needs to be understood that he was not recognized as a war leader. In white culture, Joseph would best be described as a civil leader. When it came to military matters, those responsibilities generally devolved to Ollokot or Looking Glass and of the two, Looking Glass would eventually come to be thought of as the principal war chief.

The gathering here at the lake provided the first opportunity since the meeting at Fort Lapwai, for the various bands to discuss their plight. June 14 had been the deadline given by General Howard for moving to the reservation, but since the meeting at Fort Lapwai in May many had begun to second guess their decision to accept the terms of the new (1863) treaty. Confusion and uncertainty abounded. There was still much resentment over the murder of one Nez Perce by white men who had never been punished. In the midst of all this haranguing came word of the killing of four white men by angry and drunken young Nez Perce warriors. Fearful of reprisals from the soldiers, the Nez Perce immediately packed up and moved out of harm's way: the Joseph, Toohoolhoolzote, and White Bird bands moved north to Cottonwood Creek, while the Looking Glass and Palouse bands returned to the Looking Glass campsite on the old reservation. Exactly why the two groups did not remain together is not clear. Both groups were anxious to distance themselves from trouble and evidently each thought safety was to be found in the site of their choosing.

What had happened was much like the flashpoint that ignited the 1862 Minnesota uprising. Even as the two groups were shifting their location to a place of perceived safety, a vengeful war party was already forming up. Roused by a young warrior named Shore Crossing, whose father, Eagle Robe had been murdered by a white man named Larry Ott, the war party set forth on a terror raid. Meantime, both Joseph and Ollokot recognized the killing of the four white men for what it was and were prepared to inform General Howard that this had been an act of individuals and not a tribal matter. Unfortunately, in the rush of things, there would be little opportunity to discuss a reasonable solution. Word reached Fort Lapwai on the 15th, and, by chance as it happened, just as Howard was returning to the fort to oversee the Nez Perce relocation.

The killing alarmed settlers in the area, and since there was no way of knowing whether the killing was a prelude to a full blown uprising, General Howard, to play it safe, sent two companies of the 1st Cavalry under Captain David Perry to reassure and protect settlers. Reaching Grangeville, Idaho, after an all-night march in the rain, Perry learned that there had been more killings. This had been the work of Shore Crossing and his followers. Well liquored-up they launched a two-day rampage of terror, killing another fifteen settlers. Clearly, the trouble here ran deeper than Perry expected. Notwithstanding, reinforced by a dozen civilian volunteers he took off in pursuit. His command was already exhausted, having ridden through a rain-drenched night, but Perry, pressured by angry, fearful citizens, felt compelled to take up the pursuit; it was to prove an unwise decision.

THE BATTLE OF WHITE BIRD CANYON

The Nez Perce, meanwhile, had set up camp along the Salmon River, at the mouth of White Bird Canyon. The village contained several hundred inhabitants, of whom perhaps 125–150 were warriors, including the 17 who had killed the white settlers a few days prior. Just as it happened in Minnesota, the situation quickly escalated out of hand. The actions of a few hot bloods degenerated into a war that neither side really wanted. The Nez Perce leaders sought to talk to Captain Perry to see if a peaceful resolution could not be found, but if that failed they were prepared to fight. Accordingly, on June 27, as Perry's command approached, the Indians came forward under a flag of truce, but a detachment of volunteers in the lead opened fire. Some Nez Perce who had taken up positions on the surrounding hills returned the fire. Indian marksmanship was surprisingly good and Perry quickly found himself in a much tighter situation than expected. Before the troops were able to reach the high ground eighteen soldiers were killed. With half of his force wiped out, Perry was lucky to be able to extricate what remained of his command and make it back to Mount Idaho near Grangeville.

Stunned by what was clearly an inept performance on the part of Perry's command, Howard promptly began calling in reinforcements from his own Columbia Department and the Department of California as well. In addition to what was available to him at Fort Lapwai he could expect six additional companies of cavalry, three companies of regular infantry and five batteries of artillery, with the cannoners acting as infantrymen. Fully assembled, Howard would have nearly a thousand men at his disposal. Over and above this, Major John Green was instructed to march north from Fort Boise to the Wesier Valley. Green's mission was to insure that none of the Indians in that region reinforced the Nez Perce.

For now, though, Howard prepared to take the field immediately with four companies of the 1st Cavalry (including Perry's command—what was left of it) together with six companies of the 21st Infantry and five companies of the 4th Artillery. In all, Howard had at his disposal some 400 men but felt additional support was needed. Accordingly, he requested reinforcements from other departments on top of that. Learning that the village of Looking Glass, leader of the Alpowai band, was close at hand and planned to join the other bands, who were already being referred to as hostiles, Howard dispatched two companies of cavalry and a brace of Gatling Guns to surprise the village and capture Looking Glass. Unfortunately, some volunteers from Mount Idaho attached themselves to Whipple's column. Not since those early days in Oregon and the Rogue River troubles would volunteers cause as much trouble as here against the Nez Perce.

Approaching the Nez Perce village on the morning of July 1, fully intending to talk over matters, Whipple gave the volunteers a free hand; exactly why is not clear, but in any event, they went on a rampage and opened fire, then destroyed the village and captured more than 700 horses, while the Nez Perce fled. It proved the last straw for Looking Glass. Up to this point, he had counseled non-violence, but in light of what had happened of late, he concluded that war was the only option left.

Through the spring and early summer, settlers in the region grew increasingly alarmed, fearing a general uprising. The Nez Perce had assured some settlers that as long as they did not support the soldiers they were not in danger, but this was surely little consolation in the face of the raids that were taking place. Shore Crossing's rampaging party killed, raped and burned ranches, in a reign of terror not unlike what had happened in the Minnesota River Valley back in 1862. What was happening here was the release of pent-up rage over years of injustice, to say nothing of those Nez Perce who had been murdered. One had not to look far for reasons. As historian Jerome Greene points out, the loss of cultural identity, land swindles, and a host of broken promises were the root causes of the trouble.[49]

In retrospect it was never possible for the Nez Perce story to have had any other ending. Indeed, perhaps that could be said about all of history. Only retrospectively can we revise endings. In any event, the final chapter of the Nez Perce saga was written at that very hour when they were presented with the 1863 Treaty; indeed, perhaps even before that moment. In any event, their choice now was either submit or flee and they chose the latter.

As developments unfolded, the objective of the Nez Perce was to avoid contact with the soldiers who they knew were on their trail. However, the long, epic flight to Canada that was soon to capture the nation's attention had not yet become part of the Nez Perce strategy. Howard, meanwhile, was striving to reach the troubled area, but was having difficulty getting his troops across the Salmon River. And even as he was trying to reach the area, the non-treaty bands, viz., Joseph's Wallowas, Toohoolhoolzote's and White Bird's—as they were now calling those Nez Perce who refused to comply with the 1863 agreement—joined those of Looking Glass and the Palouse on the Clearwater River.

Although Howard was having difficulty reaching the scene of action, volunteers were experiencing no trouble at all. On July 7, a party of seventy-five volunteers out of Mount Idaho, under the command of Colonel Edward McConville, located the non-treaty camp and doubtless would have attacked except that the Nez Perce discovered their presence before the volunteers could strike. What followed turned into something of a siege during which the Nez Perce harassed the volunteers through the night and made off with more than forty horses. Pinned down and lacking water the volunteers christened the place "Misery Hill." When at last the Indians withdrew, the sorry lot of volunteers trundled back to Mount Idaho.

Four days later, Howard, quite by accident it seems, found the Nez Perce camp, but he was not of a mind to parley. A canon shell was lobbed into the village and the Battle of Clearwater was underway. The Nez Perce were nothing if not good marksmen and they quickly had the soldiers in a tight position with their accurate firing. In short order, Howard had eight men killed and another twenty-five wounded, as against four Nez Perce killed and a like number wounded. Notwithstanding the fact that they had the better of the situation, apparently not all the Nez Perce warriors were in agreement about the decision to fight and apparently lacking a consensus to continue, the Indians abandoned their camp and moved north. Like Crook at the Rosebud Howard claimed a victory because he now owned the field of battle. After destroying the village, Howard pursued the Nez Perce, but once again was stalled trying to effect a river crossing. Earlier, he had been foiled by the Salmon, now it was the Clearwater. For the moment, the Nez Perce, seeing they had nothing to fear from the soldiers, began their famed crossing of the Lolo Trail on July 16. The epic journey had begun.

Howard, meanwhile, was treading water. He had had a pair of less than satisfactory encounters with the Nez Perce and now, apparently, felt that he lacked the muscle to compel the Nez Perce to move to the new reservation. He was learning a hard truth, namely that the Nez Perce were a tough and determined bunch. Accordingly, while the Nez Perce were climbing the Lolo Trail, Howard awaited reinforcements. It is difficult to say exactly what Howard believed the Nez Perce strength to be, but probably in view of the fact that two of his detachments had been roughly handled, he imagined the Indians to be too strong for him, hence the delay in awaiting reinforcements. Truth be told, however, the two sides were rather equally matched in terms of fighting men. At this juncture, the Nez Perce fighting force numbered around 300, with another 500 non-combatants.

By telegraph Howard also alerted Captain Charles Rawn at the brand new Fort Missoula, requesting him to block the Lolo Trail and delay the Nez Perce while he [Howard] caught up. Rawn had only a small command, but nevertheless assembling twenty-five of his troops along with 150 civilian volunteers, he prepared to comply with Howard's request to block the Lolo Trail. His strategy involved building a sort of log wall across the eastern exit of the Trail, which had shrunk to a narrow gap by that point. Rawn hoped his makeshift fort would delay the Nez Perce long enough for Howard to catch up. Howard's strategy was for the Nez Perce to be held up by Rawn and his makeshift fort long enough for Howard to catch up and end the whole business then and there. The plan might have had some merit if Howard had been close behind the Nez Perce, but as it was he delayed a fortnight for reinforcements and that delay doomed the plan.

Notwithstanding, on July 26, the Nez Perce reached the east end of the Lolo Trail. Approaching Rawn's barricade, they were prepared to negotiate a safe uninterrupted passage through the Valley, but Rawn demanded the surrender of their rifles, which the Nez Perce not surprisingly refused to do. As for the barricade, the Nez Perce simply outflanked it and moved on, and Rawn's log barricade would ever after bear the ignominious sobriquet of Fort Fizzle.

True to their word, the Nez Perce moved on through the Valley, reaffirming their earlier pledge that no settlers would be harmed and no property destroyed. The Nez Perce were no strangers to this valley. Extending some 100 miles from Horse Creek Pass to near Missoula, it is a stunningly beautiful valley featuring with timbered slopes and deep granite canyons. Lewis and Clark had passed through part of this valley on their great adventure and the Nez Perce were frequent travelers through the valley to the buffalo lands beyond. Yet despite their pledge not to harm anyone or anything, settlers were nervous. Word of the troubles at White Bird and Clearwater had filtered into the valley, reinforced by area newspapers, creating an aura of fear throughout the valley.

The Nez Perce moved through the Bitterroot Valley with a sense of assurance. Howard, now with 600 troops was two weeks behind them, and to their knowledge there was no military force ahead to impede their progress, or so they thought. At this juncture there was much discussion and little consensus amongst the leaders as to their objective. Some favored an eastward movement onto buffalo country, but three warriors, recently returned from scouting for the Army against the Lakotas were well aware that there were many soldiers to the east which made a compelling argument for a northward movement. If there was a consensus at this point it favored a movement toward the buffalo country with its promise of meat and hides. Looking Glass favored a movement to the land of their friends, the Crows, going by way of the Big Hole Valley and from there along the Yellowstone River. Joseph apparently felt that since they had left their homeland behind their future destination was of little consequence. At any rate, a decision was finally made to move through the Big Hole Basin.

Unbeknownst to the Nez Perce there were more soldiers in the area than suspected. Up in the Sun River Country near Great Falls were Fort Shaw and the 7th Infantry under Colonel John "No Hip Bone" Gibbon. As word of the Nez Perce trouble reached him, he assembled about 150 men at Fort Missoula and set off in pursuit of the Nez Perce. Along the way Gibbon was joined by some seventy citizen volunteers, about half of whom soon returned home, leaving Gibbon with about 180 men, or roughly half the strength of the Nez Perce fighting command.

Feeling quite safe and secure, the Nez Perce moved leisurely through the Bitterroot Valley, making camp along Ruby Creek, a tributary of the Big Hole River near present day Wisdom, Montana. Their intent was to remain here for a few days, resting and preparing new tepee poles that would be needed when they reached the buffalo country.

Feeling relatively safe, unaware of any soldiers in the area, the Nez Perce did not bother to post guards. With first light on August 9 Gibbon's command launched its attack on the sleeping Nez Perce village. Although taken completely by surprise, the Nez Perce quickly recovered and indeed soon captured the initiative, driving the soldiers back across the Big Hole River and up the hillside, from where they furiously dug rifle pits. While Indian sharpshooters made life miserable for the dug-in troops, Nez Perce women went about dismantling the village and moved on. Once the village was safely on the move, the Indian riflemen withdrew, leaving the soldiers to lick their wounds. Gibbon's attack had not only faltered, it had failed miserably. Army losses totaled some forty wounded—a third of Gibbon's command, and Gibbon himself sustained a severe thigh wound. If there was good news for the Army on this August day it was that Howard was now only two days behind.

Howard reached the battlefield on the morning of August 11, no doubt chagrined to find that the Indians had gotten the better of Gibbon. Fortunately, Howard had the foresight to bring a pair of Army surgeons with him, which was well since Gibbon had no medical personnel with him. Howard had taken a short-cut and in so doing gained three days on the Nez Perce, which must have lifted his flagging spirit somewhat at least.

By this point in time, Joseph's influence as a leader seems to have grown. Increasingly, his words carried more weight. On the other hand, the fact that the soldiers had been able to launch a surprise attack on the village at Big Hole, diminished Looking Glass's reputation as a war leader and he was supplanted by Poker Joe of the Bitterroot band. Although they had turned the tables on the Army at Big Hole in a rather spectacular way, it was now clear that they could no longer afford to travel in a leisurely way.

August 18 found the Nez Perce camped at Camas Meadows, near Spencer, Idaho. This was a traditional gathering place for the Nez Perce who came here every year to harvest the roots of the Camas plant, a principal element of their diet. The area would also later become home to the Camas Prairie Railroad, known lovingly as the "railroad on stilts" owing to the many trestles along its route. Some scenes from the 1975 film, *Breakheart Pass* were filmed on this railroad, which remained active until the 1990s.

The night of their arrival, a warrior named Black Hair dreamed that the Nez Perce captured General Howard's horses. On the day following, the village packed up and resumed its eastward journey, but Black Hair, or at least his dream, had planted a seed in the minds of the other leaders, who decided that they should send a raiding party to capture Howard's horses and thus, make Black Hair's vision a fact. The idea met a warm reception and soon a raiding party was on its way back to Camas Meadows, where Howard was now camped.

Up to this point and beyond, the Nez Perce had been acting on the defensive, reacting to the Army's moves, but on this occasion they seized the initiative, sneaked into Howard's camp and made off with some 150 mules. Three companies of cavalry immediately took up the pursuit, but got separated. One company soon found itself on the defensive for nearly three hours, fighting off Indian snipers until Howard arrived with reinforcements. The attack cost Howard a man killed and another seven wounded. Although the Nez Perce were disappointed to discover that they had run off mules rather than horses, whether they realized it or not, the loss of those mules also created a serious problem for Howard.

Howard's Bannack scouts predicted that the Nez Perce would be aiming for Yellowstone Park, and with this in mind Howard set forth to follow a short-cut that he hoped would help him to cut off the Indians. Reaching Henry's Lake, Idaho, on the northwest fringe of Yellowstone Park, Howard concluded that the pursuit could not be pressed without fresh supplies. Accordingly, a detachment was sent to Virginia City, Montana, seventy miles distant, for supplies. If that wasn't enough, his horses needed to be re-shod and the men needed blankets and shoes. Indeed, it seemed to Howard that he'd done about all he could do and was ready to pack it in, but strong words from General Sherman prompted him to change his mind. Indeed, so bothered was he by Howard's failure to catch and trounce the

Nez Perce that Sherman authorized Lieutenant Colonel Charles Gilbert at Fort Ellis (near Bozeman, Montana) to join Howard's column and take command of same. Sherman sugarcoated a dispatch to Howard by pointing out that he [Howard] had pursued beyond his departmental jurisdiction it might be well to surrender the chase. But the truth was that he did not believe Howard had the stomach to get the job done. Howard, meanwhile, knew nothing of all this and while camped at Henry's Lake moved ahead with preparations to resume the pursuit. Problem was that by the time he got his column re-supplied and squared away, the Nez Perce had gotten the bulge on their pursuers and then some.

It turned out that Sherman just happened to be in Helena at the time and as a result had his finger on the pulse of things more than he would have otherwise. The whole Nez Perce business had really gotten under his hide. As to his reason for being in Montana, he had just days before been looking over the splendor of Yellowstone National Park with a small party of friends. Of course he had no way of knowing it at the time but he and his companions were just days ahead of the Nez Perce. At any rate, what Sherman saw was yet another embarrassment for the Army and the country could ill-afford another mess so soon after the Custer debacle. The whole Nez Perce business was rapidly turning into a sort of comic opera. Twice the Nez Perce had made the Army look like fools and now, Howard seemed incapable of catching them. The whole affair, in point of fact, had become quite a serious mess; no longer was it a local matter. No longer was it the sole responsibility of Howard's Department of the Columbia. Accordingly, orders went out to Terry at St. Paul and Crook at Omaha. Both were instructed to cooperate fully with Howard and never mind departmental boundaries. The object was to catch the Nez Perce; until that was done, procedural niceties were to be ignored.

During the course of their exodus, the Nez Perce had generally conducted themselves with dignity and a respect for private property. But there were incidents that raised genuine alarm among settlers, who banded together in local communities for protection. The fear prompted the creation of local militia companies. A few Nez Perce killed four whites and made off with some 250 horses in Idaho's Lemhi Valley, and on August 15, the Nez Perce attacked eight freight wagons at Birch Creek, Idaho. The wagons loaded with goods and whiskey were a plump target for the Nez Perce who killed five more whites. Yellow Wolf a twenty-one-year-old warrior led the raiding party and later recalled that some of the raiders consumed much whiskey. It was incidents such as these that gave birth to a climate of fear.

On August 22, the Nez Perce entered Yellowstone Park. Created in 1872 as the nation's first national park, the region was sometimes referred to as "Wonderland" in those early days because of the many natural wonders to be found within its more than 3,000 square miles. Although only five years old, the region was already attracting visitors, one of whom we have already seen was none other than William T. Sherman himself, who had been on an inspection tour of western forts. That late summer of 1877 the Park also found a solitary prospector searching for gold, and a touring party of ten from Radersburg, Montana (south of Helena) examining the wonders of this enchanting region. Two days into the Park, all eleven found themselves captives of the Nez Perce. Three of the tourists—a brother and two sisters—were released the following day, but the Nez Perce picked up another lone tourist, James Irwin, recently discharged from the Army. Gradually, however, during the next week all of the captives were either released or managed to escape.

The Radersburg group was not the only such entity to visit the Park that summer. On August 13, a party of ten young men left Helena also bound for the sights of Yellowstone. On the 20th they reached Mammoth Hot Springs and from there moved on to the Falls of the Yellowstone and Sulphur Mountain, from the top of which they spotted the Nez Perce.

This unexpected development prompted the men to seek a safer spot to camp. However, along the way they had met Irwin, who later revealed the Helena group's presence to the Nez Perce. Armed with this information the Nez Perce raided the camp of the Helena party, probably for whatever provisions they might find, and in the process killed Charles Kenck and wounded John Stewart.

Meanwhile, Howard's chief scout, thirty-seven-year-old Stanton Gilbert Fisher had ranged far ahead of the main body of troops with a contingent of Bannack scouts. Not nearly as well known as some of the other frontiersmen who scouted for the Army, S.G. Fisher was as able as any of them and with dogged perseverance stuck to the Nez Perce trail. A man with a varied background, some of it in mining, Fisher had also been a supply contractor for the Union Pacific Railroad. By 1868 he was post trader for the Bannacks, operating out of Fort Hall, Idaho. By the time of the Nez Perce troubles Fisher was well acquainted with the Bannacks and spoke their tongue fluently. His knowledge of both the Bannacks and Nez Perce and the region itself made him an obvious choice for Howard as a chief scout.

On August 31, an advance party of Nez Perce encountered an army patrol under the command of Lieutenant Gustavus Cheney Doane. Unwilling to engage the soldiers, the Nez Perce turned about and headed back to the main band, but en route killed another tourist, one Richard Dietrich, a member of the Helena party at Mammoth Hot Springs. Young Dietrich appears to have been doing nothing more than standing in the doorway of Jim McCartney's cabin—which seems to have doubled as an early day hotel in the Park.

The Nez Perce exited the Park by choosing the toughest course possible, heading due east through the rugged Absaroka Mountains. The Nez Perce had specifically chosen this route, hoping to find support from the Crows whose territory lay just beyond the mountains. It turned out, however, that the Crows had been serving as scouts for the Army in its campaigns against the Lakota and as a consequence were not much inclined to provide aid and comfort to the Nez Perce, although there was great empathy for their position. This turn down by the Crows left the Nez Perce with two options: they could surrender to Howard or press on to Canada and seek help from Sitting Bull. The first choice was no choice at all, leaving Canada as the only viable course of action.

Emerging from the Park, the Nez Perce turned north and crossed the Yellowstone River near present day Laurel, Montana. Continuing downriver, they headed up Canyon Creek. Small parties of raiders, however, managed to find targets of opportunity in local farms and outlying settlements. Near the town of Coulson—today's Billings—they stole horses, torched some buildings and killed two men. To some of the younger warriors at least, the whole business of the tribal flight was a grand lark. At Coulson they captured a stagecoach and, with horses tied behind, drove the thing, lurching and bouncing back to the main body.

Even as their flight continued, forces were mobilizing against them. As previously noted, both Generals Crook and Terry had been directed to cooperate with Howard. Crook obliged by alerting Colonel Wesley Merritt at Camp Brown (later Fort Washakie in present day Lander, Wyoming) to prepare to participate in the chase. Accordingly, on September 9, Merritt marched out of Camp Brown with 500 men and a contingent of Shoshone scouts. Troops from Terry's Dakota Department would also play a very active role in the pursuit of the Nez Perce. The reconstituted 7th Cavalry under fifty-five-year-old Colonel Samuel D. Sturgis had been patrolling north of the Yellowstone all summer, prepared to deal with Sitting Bull's band if and when they came south from Canada. Sturgis had actually been the commander of the 7th Cavalry at the time of the Little Bighorn, but was absent on a special assignment, leaving Custer, the second-in-command in charge of the regiment. Ironically, Sturgis's son, Jack, a recent West Point graduate, had died with Custer, though his remains were never found.

Back on August 12, Miles ordered Sturgis to take up a blocking position in the Judith Gap, an opening between the Big and Little Belt Mountains, through which, Miles conjectured, the Nez Perce were likely to pass on their way to Canada. On August 3, Miles had dispatched Company E, 7th Cavalry, under Lieutenant Doane to look for signs of the Nez Perce and it had been Doane's unit that the Nez Perce met up with at Mammoth Hot Springs earlier.

Howard, meanwhile, elected not to follow the Nez Perce directly through the rugged Absaroka range, but angled instead northeast through a pass in the Absarokas to Clark's Fork on the Yellowstone River, and on to Crandall Creek, where he again picked up the Indian trail, now thirty-six hours old. Advised that Sturgis had been alerted to cooperate with him, Howard, on August 26, fired off a wire to Sturgis saying that the Nez Perce would be moving through Clark's Fork Canyon, and by September 1 Sturgis had his regiment in position to block the Nez Perce route. However, when the Indians failed to show, Sturgis moved south to the Shoshone River, but here, too, he drew a blank and imagining he had been outfoxed, circled around and eventually came up behind Howard; it proved an embarrassing moment for both commanders.

Although short on supplies—his regiment had been in the field all summer—Sturgis pressed on ahead of Howard and caught up with the tail end of the Nez Perce column, some nine miles from the Yellowstone River, along Canyon Creek. Here, on September 13, Sturgis and his 7th Cavalry clashed with the fleeing Nez Perce; as such it was the first major encounter since the Big Hole. And once again, it was the Indians who had the better of things. Nez Perce riflemen, positioned along the hillsides of the Canyon directed accurate fire down on the cavalrymen. Sturgis launched one mounted charge, but it quickly fell apart. Not being an aggressive sort of commander, Sturgis ordered his men to dismount and fight on foot. After a quarter of an hour or so, the Nez Perce withdrew, leaving the soldiers to lick their wounds. The affair had cost Sturgis three killed and a dozen wounded. Three Nez Perce were reportedly wounded.

Sturgis had taken his licks and camp that night was most welcomed. The arrival of several hundred Crows that evening lifted spirits somewhat and they soon took off after the fleeing Nez Perce in the hopes of capturing some of their horses. In the morning, Sturgis resumed his pursuit as far as the Mussellshell River not far from present day Ryegate, Montana. The 7th Cavalry was worn out and Sturgis now elected to await Howard's arrival which happened on September 21.

Howard now made a canny judgment call. If he slowed down, he reasoned, the Nez Perce would also slow down and that might give Miles an opportunity to intercept them before they reached Canada. Meantime, on September 17, Miles received a letter from Howard, bringing him up to date on the Nez Perce situation and requesting support. This was not an unexpected development for Miles, who promptly advised General Terry of his intention to support Howard as best he could. Miles had no trouble imagining a union between the Nez Perce and Sitting Bull and from there it was a short step to another Indian coalition and another bloody war.

In any event, Miles needed little encouragement to act and on September 18 he took the field with part of his own 5th Infantry, those companies of the 7th Cavalry left behind by Sturgis, some artillery, civilian scouts, and a large wagon train, in all more than 500 men. Miles's objective was to reach the junction of the Mussellshell and Missouri Rivers, from which point his future course of action would depend on circumstances. Essential to his plan, though, was that he reached the Missouri before the Nez Perce.

Meanwhile, from Canyon Creek, the Nez Perce pushed on. By this time the strain of their flight was beginning to tell; people and horses were tiring. There had been little letup on the part of their pursuers. Even though the soldiers were usually two to three days behind them, the stress was beginning to tell. Weary but still determined they pushed on, through the Judith Gap, on to the Mussellshell River and finally Cow Island on the Missouri River, an off-loading point for supplies, earmarked for both the military and civilian merchants. Indeed, some fifty tons of supplies and equipment awaited wagons to haul supplies to a variety of locations around the territory.

The Cow Island Landing, where up-river steamboats disgorged their loads, was in a bend of the river known as the Missouri Breaks, an area of steeply eroded badlands; it remains today, one of the most remote areas of Montana. Migratory animals, notably bison, seeking access to the river followed a path down the snake-like Cow Creek to what came to be known as Cow Island (actually two islands). Heavily covered with stands of cottonwood trees, the animals—notably buffalo—liked to gather here thus giving the island its name.

In that eventful August of 1877 it happened that engineers had come down to make the river channel to more accommodating to the steamboats. A detachment of the 7th Infantry out of Fort Benton was sent down to protect the engineers were thus on hand when the Nez Perce appeared on the south side of the river on the afternoon of September 23.

At first pleasantries were exchanged. The sergeant in charge informed the Indians that they would not be allowed to approach the encampment. The Nez Perce then asked for food and some was given, but apparently it did not begin to suffice for the needs of the Indians, who shortly decided to take what they needed and proceeded to attack the engineers and their escort. It proved a surprisingly furious little scrap. The sergeant in charge, William Molchert remembered that "They [the Nez Perce] charged us three times during the night through high willows, impossible to see anyone." Somehow a few Nez Perce managed to sneak into the camp unobserved through a coulee and reached the supply dump where they helped themselves to food and anything else that struck their fancy. This done, they torched the rest, the fire producing a mighty blaze. By mid-morning, the Nez Perce were finished with Cow Island and moved on bound for the Bear's Paw Mountains.[50]

The Nez Perce approach to the Upper Missouri River country had alerted outlying camps of workers and hunters, to say nothing of the military. Forty-eight hours before reaching Cow Island, Major Guido Ilges, a former Prussian soldier who had served in the Union Army during the Civil War and now commanded the post of Fort Benton, learned that the trading post of Fort Clagett—later to be renamed Camp Cooke—was in danger from the Nez Perce. Ilges wasn't in much of a position to help—he had but a single company of infantry at Fort Benton—but he did what he could, which was to send thirteen men, plus a couple of volunteers and a mountain howitzer, down to Clagett on Mackinaw Boats— light water craft, usually with a sail and which was used extensively on inland waterways of North America during the 19th century; it was especially popular on the Upper Missouri River. The origin of the name is unclear, but may have been because of its development for use on the Straits of Mackinaw.

Ilges, meanwhile proceeded overland with but one soldier and thirty-eight citizen volunteers. However, when scouts reported that the Nez Perce had moved on to Cow Island, he started for that place instead, arriving at day's end on September 24, while the flames from the still burning supplies lighting the evening sky. The Nez Perce were long gone by this time, however, and all Ilges could do was to cross the river on the Mackinaw Boats and then take up the pursuit of the Nez Perce with his mounted volunteers.

Around mid-morning on September 25, after following a tortuous route through Cow Creek Canyon, Ilges caught up with the Nez Perce who were then in the act of attacking a small wagon train and a herd of beef cattle, which undoubtedly stood as a most tempting target of opportunity. After killing one of the teamsters the Nez Perce then fired the wagons and prepared to meet the oncoming volunteers. It quickly developed that the Nez Perce had the better position. From the higher ground they fired down on Ilges's command, positioned as it was along the muddy creek bed. The fight lasted some two hours with Ilges suffering the loss of one volunteer before the Nez Perce withdrew. Concerned about his unprotected flanks, Ilges pulled back to Cow Island which place he reached around six that evening.

When the Nez Perce left the Cow Creek Canyon battlefield behind and resumed their northward journey less than a hundred miles separated them from the Canadian line— Land of the Grandmother. They had been on the move now for three months. The suffering and privations it had taken to reach this point may only be imagined. Family members and friends had been lost; food had been in short supply, and the physical toll on bodies, especially on the very young and old had been harsh and demanding. As a people they were nearing the end of themselves. And not surprisingly, leadership was being questioned. True enough, in each encounter with the soldiers they had come out on top, but their resources were finite, while the Army could always replace its losses and bring in more soldiers, if not with ease certainly as needed. War chief Looking Glass, who it will be recalled, had given way to Poker Joe back at Big Hole, now apparently stepped forward and reasserted what he regarded as his rightful role to act as war chief. Beyond this if there was a single guiding spirit that held the people together it was Joseph.

Notwithstanding their near utter exhaustion, the Nez Perce pushed on, slowly to conserve strength. The soldiers were two days behind, however, or so they thought, and on a cold and foggy September 29 the Nee Me Poo at long last reached the Bear's Paw Mountains, ten miles south of present Havre, Montana, some forty miles from the Canadian border.

With Howard forty-eight hours behind, the Nez Perce figured to have some breathing room. They were, however, unaware that Howard was not the only force pursuing them. On September 18, Colonel Nelson Miles had marched out of Fort Keogh and was coming on in hard pursuit. General Howard, although earnest enough, was not an aggressive pursuer; the Nez Perce always seemed to be just beyond his grasp. On the other hand, Miles would not dally; he would press on like the hound after the fox. Had the Nez Perce been aware of this they might well have made one last concerted push to reach the Canadian line, but then had the hound not stopped to hunker, he'd have caught the fox.

As it was the Nez Perce paused here and it proved a deadly hiatus, one that allowed Miles to strike their camp on Snake Creek on September 30. There seems to have been some suspicion that the Nez Perce were aware of soldiers in the immediate area, but for some reason, nothing was done to confirm this, perhaps because the people were simply too tired to be bothered any longer. Evidently some favored pushing on. Knowing Canada was so close must have been a tempting goal, but Looking Glass argued for a halt here to rest and his words ultimately and fatally prevailed.

The Nez Perce had selected a village site that stretched along the grassy bottomland of Snake Creek. Emanating out from three directions were shallow ravines, some of which were filled with heavy brush. As a defensive position it had something to offer, although the Nez Perce seem not to have been overly concerned about an immediate attack. The soldiers, they knew, were gathering, but were not here yet—or so they reckoned. Historian Jerome Greene suggests that as much as anything the position offered protection from the cold winds and also provided a good source of water.

Early on the morning of September 30, indeed in the inky pre-dawn blackness, Miles had his command up and moving, preceded by Yellowstone Kelly and several other civilian scouts who were examining the land to the southwest. There was no question that the Nez Perce camp was in the immediate area, but its exact location needed to be determined before Miles made a move. Meanwhile, a contingent of Cheyenne and Lakota scouts searched off to the northwest. Around eight a.m., under raw, grey skies, scouts reported the village about six miles ahead and Miles unlimbered for action. All the extra ammunition, provisions and equipage were placed under the protection of Miles's 5th Infantry.

The attacking on this day would be carried out by units of the 2d and 7th Cavalry regiments along with a battalion of 5th Infantry mounted on captured Lakota ponies. Overseeing it all was Miles, looking ever like the magnificent soldier. According to his scouts, he appeared "rough, tough, and ready. Weighing nearly two hundred pounds, he sat on his charger like a centaur."[51]

While the soldiers approached and prepared for battle, the Nez Perce were in the process of getting their day underway. Some were having breakfast; others like Joseph and his daughter had gone out to catch horses; later they planned to resume their northward journey. At this point the Indians were seemingly unaware of the proximity of Miles's troops. Insofar as they knew, Howard was two days behind and no other soldiers were known to be in the area. Thus it must have come as a complete surprise when two scouts galloped into the village warning that soldiers were close by.

Forming for his attack, Miles ordered his cavalry into a trot, with the Indian scouts well out in front. The village was believed to be some four to six miles distant, but when it proved farther than that, Miles ordered his horsemen to increase their speed to full gallop. Presently, the Nez Perce horse herd could be seen ahead. Topping the higher ground above the village, Miles paused briefly before ordering the assault. With the 7th Cavalry on the right flank and the 2d Cavalry on the left, and the mounted battalion of the 5th Infantry slightly to the rear, the horsemen began the descent toward the village. The Battle of Bear's Paw was underway.

The Cheyenne scouts, well out ahead, made for the Nez Perce pony herd, followed by some of the cavalry who assumed the main part of the village lay directly ahead, when in fact it was still beyond view in the creek bottom. Miles sensing the situation, directed the 7th Cavalry under Captain Owen Hale to make for the village. Fired up, Hale and his troopers swept on toward the village, but on approaching they encountered withering fire from Nez Perce warriors stationed in the coulees and ravines. Rather stunned by this unexpected reception, the cavalrymen then found themselves confronting a group of warriors who seemingly appeared out of nowhere to deliver a thunderous volley at the charging troopers, stopping them cold. Once again, the Nez Perce had responded to complete surprise with consummate skill and bravery.

Captain Henry Romeyn, a veteran of the Civil War and who had served with Miles on the Southern Plains during the Buffalo War, recalled the initial attack on the Nez Perce camp. He would later be awarded a Medal of Honor for his conduct at Bear's Paw.

> The camp was located on a small stream called Snake Creek, as it proved an excellent position for defense in a kidney shaped depression covering about six acres of ground, along the western side of which the stream ran in a tortuous course, while through it from the steep bluffs

forming its eastern and southern sides, ran coulees from two to six feet in depth and fringed with enough sagebrush to hide the heads of their occupants. Here the Nez Perce chieftain had pitched his camp, and here he now made his last stand for battle.

From the point whence the camp could first be seen, it appeared open to attack from al but its eastern side, and even that was overlooked by bluffs too steep to be readily ascended, and from twenty to thirty feet high. But at the south end of the valley or campground, there was an almost perpendicular bluff that afforded excellent cover for a line firing toward the point from which the attacking force was advancing, and this was instantly occupied by the Nez Perce who, withholding their fire until the 7th [Cavalry] was within 200 yards, then delivered it with murderous effect. Captain Hale and Lieutenant Biddle were killed in the first fire, and Captains Moylan and Godfrey wounded immediately thereafter, thereby leaving but one officer with the three troops.[52]

The Nez Perce response to the initial attack, which had been expected to produce a solid victory over the Indians, was a stunning development. Instead of capturing the village, the troops were forced back. Fighting continued through the day with casualties heavy on both sides. Meantime, the 2d Cavalry battalion was more successful in its attack on the horse herd, capturing some 500 animals. Miles ordered another attack on the village at mid-afternoon, but again, Nez Perce resistance forced the troops to fall back. It was becoming apparent to Miles attempts to force the Nez Perce into surrendering by means of direct assaults was becoming too costly. Gradually, the battle was deteriorating into a siege, with action between the two sides confined to sharp-shooting and the occasional lobbing of shells from the 1.65-inch Hotchkiss Gun into the village. The Hotchkiss Gun was probably an ideal weapon for use in the Western Indian wars. It was light enough to be operated by two men, could be carried on a mule, and fired a two-pound explosive projectile nearly a mile. But perhaps even more demoralizing to the Indians was deadly fire from the infantrymen with their "Long Toms." The 1873 Springfield rifle used by the infantry had a longer barrel than the same model carbine carried by the cavalry, and had proven to be so deadly effective in the Rosebud fight.

Through the next seventy-two hours firing continued, sporadic at times, heavier at others. The exchange of long-range rifle fire was costly to both sides. Yellowstone Kelly's companion on a number of scouting adventures took a bullet in the heart, and an Indian scout named Hump was seriously wounded in a thrilling duel with a Nez Perce warrior. The weather continued to become increasingly winter-like. October 4 dawned a "disagreeable, raw, chilly, cloudy day," wrote Surgeon Henry Tilton.[53]

Joseph Surrenders

Aware that Howard was coming on Miles, on October 1sent an emissary, Lieutenant Lovell Jerome, into the Indian village under a flag of truce to see if the Nez Perce were willing to talk. Some were ready to parley, others such as Looking Glass were not. Joseph, however, was ready and agreed to come over and discuss the situation with Miles. Miles undoubtedly was anxious to wrap things up and claim the kudos for bringing about the surrender of the Nez Perce before Howard arrived on the scene. Joseph was amenable to surrender terms. He was tired, his people were tired, and there seemed little likelihood now of help from Sitting Bull. Then Miles suddenly acting out of character refused to let Joseph return to discuss things with his people. Angered, the Nez Perce then refused to release Lieutenant Jerome; they had called Bearcoat's bluff and Miles was left with no choice but to turn Joseph loose, whereupon the Ne Perce released Jerome.

Meanwhile, and finally, Oliver Otis Howard arrived at the Bear's Paw battlefield at twilight on October 4. Leaving Sturgis behind at Cow Island with the main body of his command, Howard had come on with an escort of twenty-one men, plus some scouts, an interpreter and a pair of elderly Nez Perce, who, presumably, might be effective in persuading their brethren to surrender. Howard might not have been the aggressive commander both Sherman and Sheridan had hoped for, but he was, if nothing else, ever the gentleman. As a department commander and brigadier general, he outranked Miles and could rightfully have insisted on assuming command of the scene; besides he had been chasing these Nez Perce across a huge chunk of the West, but gentleman that he was, Howard graciously deferred to Miles.

If the weather during the course of the five-day siege had been lousy, characterized by biting cold, ominous skies, and just enough rain and snow to make both sides miserable the morning of October 5 dawned clear and beautiful. As the Nez Perce leaders discussed their situation a sniper's bullet struck Looking Glass in the head, killing him. If Joseph had any doubts about surrendering before this morning, the death of Looking Glass surely cinched it. Many of the young men, including his brother Ollokot were also dead. And so, weary and with a heart full of grief. Joseph agreed to surrender.

What has come to be known as Joseph's surrender speech has served as a paradigm of dignity and honor:

> Tell General Howard I know his heart. I am tired of fighting. Our chiefs are killed. Looking Glass is dead. Tu-hul-hul-sote is dead. The old men are all dead. It is the young men who say yes or no. He who led on the young men is dead. It is cold and we have no blankets. The little children are freezing to death. My people, some of them, have run away to the hills, and have no blankets, no food; no one knows where they are—perhaps freezing to death. I want to have time to look for my children and see how many of them I can find. Maybe I shall find them among the dead. Hear me my chiefs. I am tired; my heart is sick and sad. From where the sun now stands I will fight no more forever.[54]

Thus ended a great American epic. Something less than 400 people surrendered with Joseph, of which perhaps 100 were fighting men. Not all of the Nez Perce supported Joseph's decision. Something like 300, or roughly one-half the overall population of those who had fled east, did manage to make it to Canada. The military did not want Joseph and his fol-

Joseph's surrender to General Miles, October 1877 (sketch by G.M. Holland).

lowers returned to Idaho and the Wallowas, and neither were the settlers in that region anxious to see them back. Instead, they were held in custody at Fort Leavenworth for a time, then assigned to a small reservation in Kansas. It was a poor location and many of the people took sick and died. In 1880 the Nez Perce were moved again, this time to Indian Territory, which proved no better than Kansas. In the years that followed, Joseph campaigned for the return of his people to their traditional homeland. He was supported in his effort by both Miles and Howard and finally in 1884 the Nez Perce were returned to the Pacific Northwest where they settled on the Colville Reservation in Washington.

Flight of the Northern Cheyennes, 1878–1879

Barely had news of the Nez Perce flight faded from newspaper headlines than the nation's attention was drawn to yet another instance of Native Americans setting forth on an epic journey to reach their homeland.

The destruction of Dull Knife's village on the Red Fork of the Powder River in November 1876 and the subsequent end of the Great Sioux War, resulted in the Northern Cheyennes being sent from Fort Robinson, Nebraska, to the Cheyenne-Arapaho Agency in Indian Territory the following August. While the Lakota bands essentially remained in the Plains region they had called home for generations, the government chose to relocate the Northern Cheyenne—the *Ohmeseheso*—to this distant inhospitable Indian Territory.

The story of the Cheyennes at Darlington Agency in the "Nations" stands as yet another sad tale of displaced people and their gritty determination to leave this place of "awfulness" behind and somehow return to their beloved Montana and the Powder River country.[55]

How exactly federal authorities, namely General Crook, managed to persuade the Northern Cheyennes to relocate to Indian Territory is not clear and most likely never will be, but probably a distorted image of the advantages offered by Indian Territory, in company with a lie or two here and there, painted a rosy picture that sounded pleasing to a people who had suffered greatly during the past year, beginning with Reynolds' strike on the Powder River and concluding with Mackenzie's attack on Dull Knife's village in November 1876. There may also have been a false promise that if they did not find the new home to their liking they could return to the north country.

If one looks at the Great Sioux War strictly from the white man's perspective there was a certain advantage—almost a bonus, one might say—in that the war created divisions within the Plains tribes that worked to the military's advantage. We have seen how some Lakotas and Cheyennes, who just months before had been fighting the soldiers, were now scouting for the army against the Nez Perce. And it was this same wedge of divisiveness that tended to pull apart the Northern Cheyennes and no doubt contributed to the band's willingness to relocate to Indian Territory.

However it came to pass, more than a thousand Northern Cheyennes, along with a handful of Arapahos trekked south in August 1877. An estimated 35 left the band en route, so that some 900 were finally enumerated on the muster rolls of the Darlington Agency. By actual count there were 235 men, 312 women, and 386 children. The principal leaders of the band were Dull Knife, Little Wolf, and Wild Hog.

Those Cheyennes who may have imagined a good life on this new reservation were soon disabused of that notion. For one thing, relations with the Southern Cheyennes proved rocky, and probably not surprisingly so. The two bands had after all been separated for a dozen years. The Northern band really felt a closer kinship to the Lakotas, while the Southern band had grown closer to the Comanches and Kiowas of the Southern Plains. The northern band was the new kid on the block and they were not welcomed. Then, too, the food rations were not nearly adequate. The Northern Cheyennes, unlike their southern brethren were unaccustomed to the climate of the Indian Territory, so illness was rampant among the people from the north. As the weeks passed, tension between the southern and northern bands increased, and relations between the Northern Cheyennes and John Miles, agent at Darlington, worsened. Insofar as the Northern Cheyennes were concerned this was not the place for them and by the summer of 1878 Little Wolf and Dull Knife were prepared to forsake this God-forsaken place and return to the north country.

Little Wolf seems to have assumed the lead role in vowing to take his people home, though Dull Knife was quick to support him. Little Wolf put the idea to Agent Miles, who summarily rejected it, informing the Cheyenne leaders that they would be required to remain here for at least another year, which was totally unacceptable to the Cheyenne leaders; another year in this wretched place might find them all buried here. And so, determined to put the Indian Territory behind them, some 350 Cheyennes—a third of those who had come south the year before—turned their backs on Darlington Agency on September 9, 1878, and commenced their northward march. Of these, perhaps ninety or so were warriors, the remainder, women and children. It is interesting and perhaps even instructive to note that most of the Northern Cheyennes elected to remain at Darlington, perhaps because they were tired of running and fighting, or were possibly too frightened to take the risk.

Five hours passed before Agent Miles discovered that the Cheyennes had fled the coop. Likely he was not particularly surprised, but in any case, he turned the matter over to the military, thereby beginning yet another desperate flight for freedom. The task of immediate pursuit was given to Captain Joseph Rendlebrock with two companies of the 4th Cavalry. As historian John Monnett points out in his excellent study, the Northern Cheyennes were forced to cross the Great Plains. Their route took them close to settlements and over three railroad lines, whereas the Nez Perce traversed a largely rugged region that was only sparsely settled. And ironically, where the Cheyennes were trying to reach their home country, the Nez Perce were actually fleeing their ancestral homeland.

On the morning of September 13, Rendlebrock caught up with the Cheyennes. Taking up a position several hundred yards from the Indians, he sent an Arapaho scout forward with a message to encourage their surrender, which of course they had no intention of doing. Indeed, through the night they sent scattered shots zinging into the cavalry camp, and set fire to the surrounding grass. With the arrival of morning Rendlebrock found himself pinned down. Needing water he had little choice but to pull back several miles to the Cimarron River, with the Cheyennes sniping at them the entire way. It went down in the books as the Battle of Turkey Springs. The Cheyennes suffered five wounded, the soldiers probably about the same. It would prove to be the last battle between the Army and the Indians in Oklahoma.

The Army was not at all pleased with Turkey Springs; it was one more embarrassment of which the Army had had enough. Rendlebrock and his second-in-command, Captain Sebastian Gunther would eventually be court-martialed. Gunther was eventually restored to active duty. Rendlebrock was dismissed from the service, but by presidential decree was allowed to retire honorably.

Rendlebrock's failure to catch the Cheyennes and return them to Darlington caused fear to ripple through the nearby settlements, just as it had done in Idaho when the Nez Perce exodus began. The Nez Perce had no interest in raiding settlements and neither did the Northern Cheyennes. Both groups wanted nothing more than to reach their objectives: Canada for the Nez Perce, Montana, for the Cheyennes. Settlers and townspeople of course did not think of events in these terms. They judged the unfolding story in light of a settler killed here, a herd of horses stolen there. And in retrospect one can appreciate the fear building in their minds. It was hard to distinguish between a few random acts of violence and a full blown uprising.

On September 17, the Cheyennes crossed the Kansas line. Behind them, meanwhile, were three columns of troops, two under the overall command of Rendlebrock—who was still in the field—and a third force of the 4th Cavalry under Lieutenant William Hemphill which caught up with the Cheyennes just north of the Cimarron River in extreme southwest Kansas, near Bluff Creek. Hemphill dismounted his men and advanced, but once again the Cheyennes had stronger positions and put up a stout resistance. After an hour of fighting, Hemphill withdrew to Fort Dodge.

Hemphill spent little time at Fort Dodge. On the 19th his company and another from the 16th Infantry under Captain Charles Morse took the field again, this time accompanied by twenty cowboys. Altogether there were perhaps a hundred men who boarded a Santa Fe Railroad car and sped west to near Garden City where they hooked up with a small force of the 19th Infantry under Colonel Charles Smith. By this time, the pursuers had lost track of the Indians' whereabouts, so they split up.

On the morning of September 21 Hemphill and Morse were joined by Rendlebrock and the cowboys. Pressing ahead, the cowboys located the Indians on Sand Creek as shadows were lengthening. Shots were exchanged, but not to amount to anything. Rendlebrock bivouacked for the night and sent a rider galloping back to Fort Dodge with a request for ammunition. In the morning, Rendlebrock formed up and advanced against the Cheyennes, who, in the meantime, had fashioned a four-foot-high, forty-foot-long stone fortress of sorts on high ground as their first line of defense. Beyond this they dug a series of rifle pits. Dismounting his command, Rendlebrock moved forward, but with flanker units covering both sides as well as the rear.

With his flankers slowly enveloping the Cheyenne position, the combined force of soldiers and cowboys advanced against the Indian fortification. Outnumbered, and lacking the ammunition reserves of the soldiers, Little Wolf and Dull Knife were finally compelled to fall back to their second line of defense. But the fighting was furious. By late afternoon, Rendlebrock sent a detachment to try and circle round the Indians, but Little Wolf had anticipated just such a move and drove the soldiers back. It was another stand-off and the day ended with Rendlebrock again withdrawing.

The Cheyennes continued their northward march, crossing the Arkansas River on September 23, frequently moving by night to avoid detection. Shortly after crossing the Arkansas they encountered a party of buffalo hunters. They did not harm the hunters, but did take their firearms and ammunition, along with several buffalo cows that were quickly slaughtered and the meat distributed among the people.

Rendlebrock had to be thoroughly disillusioned with lack of success in bringing about an end to the Cheyenne problem, which was rapidly becoming a giant-size headache for the Army. But if Rendlebrock was not disgusted, Lieutenant Colonel William Lewis, post commander at Fort Dodge, was fed up right enough. On the 24th, the forty-nine-year-old Lewis took command of the pursuit, determined to bring about an end to this problem. A West Point graduate, Lewis was no stranger to Indian fighting. He had battled the Seminoles in the 1850s and the Navajos a decade later. Although a Southerner, Lewis did not join the Confederate Army, but remained loyal Yankee soldier. To settle this Cheyenne problem,

Lewis had at his disposal, five companies of the 4th Cavalry and three of the 19th Infantry, some 200 men in all.

Little Wolf and Dull Knife understood perfectly well that the pressure was on and that they would have to demand more from the people than what the people imagined they had to give. And ask they did. By night the *Ohmeseheso* pushed on beyond the Arkansas River and into northwest Kansas. On September 27, the Cheyenne leaders, well aware that their pursuers were closing fast, elected to make a stand along a water course known as Punished Woman's Fork of the Smoky Hill River, in west central Kansas. The site, consisting of bluffs and ravines, was a good choice. Little Wolf and Dull Knife thought to give the soldiers a surprise drubbing here and so had made sure their trail was easy to follow, as indeed it was, and on came the soldiers, preceded by a coterie of experienced scouts.

Once again the Cheyennes built stone breastworks and dug rifle pits. The operational plan was to draw the advancing troops in toward the Cheyenne defenses, and then at an opportune time a party of warriors would charge down from the high ground above the stream bed and cut off the soldiers' retreat. It was a sound plan, too, and would have worked had it not been for one impatient young warrior who gave the whole thing away, alerting the troops before they entered the *cul de sac*. It was not the first time that impatience destroyed an Indian plan.

The shadows were already lengthening on this 27th day of September when the opening shots were echoed through the ravines. Although completely taken by surprise, Colonel Lewis reacted with coolness and soon had his command dismounted and advancing toward the high ground. The Cheyennes offered stout resistance in an effort to slow the advance of the soldiers and protect the villagers, but Colonel Lewis, urging his men forward, joined the skirmish line himself and soon sustained a mortal leg wound that took him out of action. Command now devolved on Captain Clarence Mauck, 4th Cavalry, a veteran officer with plenty of Indian fighting experience. Notwithstanding, Mauck's Indian fighting skills, Lewis's wound slowed the advance. With the advent of night, the troops withdrew to a defensive position inside their wagon train while the Indians stole away to continue their flight north. Although only two Cheyennes had been killed, more importantly they lost perhaps as many as seventy-five horses, the loss of which would work a real hardship on the Indians in days ahead. If the fighting had resulted in only light casualties among both the soldiers and Indians, civilian losses in Kansas amounted to ten killed and five wounded, besides which, ranchers lost more than 600 head of livestock.

On September 28, Colonel Lewis, along with two soldiers who had been wounded in the fight were placed aboard an ambulance and sent to Fort Wallace under escort, but Lewis died en route, probably from loss of blood as the bullet had severed the femoral artery in his leg.

During the three weeks since their departure from Darlington Agency, the Northern Cheyennes had clashed with their army pursuers on four separate occasions, and each time had gotten the better of the troops; indeed casualties among soldiers and civilians were higher than among the Cheyennes. As the future would prove, it would not be the Army that defeated the Cheyennes, rather it was the loss of horses and a shortage of food and other necessities that really crippled the Cheyennes.

As September wound down, the Cheyennes were approaching the Nebraska line in northwestern Kansas. Here, they found cattle herds bound for the market at Kearney and Ogalalla and helped themselves to as much beef as needed. But it didn't end there. The next few days witnessed a minor reign of terror in the area as some forty-one settlers were killed before the Cheyennes crossed the Nebraska line on or about October 2. It has been suggested that the Cheyennes went on their raiding spree in northwest Kansas in order to procure supplies, but, more importantly, it was to replace the horses lost at the Battle of Punished Woman's Fork. Whatever the reason, the raids and the killings aroused public indignation at the Army's failure to prevent such happenings, and certainly cost the Cheyennes whatever sympathy they might otherwise have enjoyed. Communities began organizing militia groups to deal with the threat. If the Army couldn't protect them they would have to protect themselves. It was an all too familiar scenario in the Western Indian wars.

The Kansas raids attracted reporters from major newspapers who arrived in Kansas and Nebraska, smelling another great story like the recently concluded Nez Perce saga. The Northern Cheyennes, meanwhile, reached the North Platte River in western Nebraska on October 4. In an effort to avoid detection they travelled mostly by night and lighted cooking fires sparingly. And they continued their practice of stealing horses and killing when that proved necessary.

Beyond this point, there were few settlements to interfere with the Cheyenne's northward push. The Black Hills and the Powder River country loomed a bit closer every day, but, they knew, the soldiers were never far behind. Captain Mauck was still coming on from Kansas and now, from his department headquarters in Omaha, General Crook dispatched troops under Major Thomas "Tip" Thornburgh (soon to lose his life during Colorado's Meeker Massacre) to take up the pursuit as well. Thornburgh's force was a strong one, too, consisting of four companies of infantry, to which the major added five companies of the 3rd Cavalry under Major Caleb Carleton to march from Fort Robinson and, it was hoped, intercept the Indians in the rugged Sand Hill country of northwest Nebraska. Thornburgh, marching from Sydney Barracks (Nebraska), was just a few hours behind the Cheyennes when he reached Ogallala on October 4. Elsewhere, General Wesley Merritt's 5th Cavalry was watching along the eastern apron of the Big Horn Mountains.

Although he pressed hard, Thornburgh's foot soldiers—they were mounted, by the way—could not quite catch the Cheyennes, despite the fact that they were averaging forty-plus miles a day, and without much food or water. If it was tough campaigning for these soldiers, one wonders how on earth the Cheyennes managed to somehow remain a jump ahead of their pursuers. By October 10, Thornburgh reached the Niobrara River. Here, Thornburgh elected to call it quits. His command was worn out and besides, he knew, elements of the 3rd Cavalry were patrolling this area. The expedition has, "thus far resulted in utter failure," wrote one correspondent.[56]

As the month drew to a close Little Wolf and Dull Knife came to a parting of the ways. Little Wolf wanted to push on to the Powder River country, while Dull Knife opted to settle at Red Cloud Agency where the people of his band had many friends and some relatives among the Lakotas. Unbeknownst to Dull Knife, however, Red Cloud Agency had been closed and the Oglalas who had been located there were moved to the Pine Ridge Agency. The parting of Little Wolf and Dull Knife seems to have been amicable enough, although Little Wolf had urged the two groups to stay together. But when that didn't happen, Little Wolf and his followers headed for the Powder River country and Montana.

On the cold, snowy night of October 23, some seventy miles from Fort Robinson, Nebraska, two companies of the 3rd Cavalry under Captain J.B. Johnson, finally caught up with the Dull Knife band, which with the departure of Little Wolf, now numbered 149, of which 46 were men of warrior age. The Lakotas persuaded the Cheyennes to allow the troops to enter the camp, where the soldiers provided food rations to the hungry Indians. Dull Knife and the other leaders conferred and agreed that it was pointless to resist further.

The next day, Johnson's command, reinforced overnight by additional troops from Fort Robinson, along with artillery, escorted the Cheyennes to Fort Robinson.

What followed was a pitiful tale of woe. At Robinson, the Cheyennes were placed in an army barracks, where, for the next two months they stoutly resisted all entreaties to return to Darlington Agency. Angry and frustrated over their refusal to go south, post commander, Captain Henry W. Wessells sought to force compliance by cutting off their food and water for a week. Finally, unable to deal with the situation in any other way, the Cheyennes forced their way out of the barracks on the frigid night of January 9, 1879. The Cheyenne women had managed to secrete several old weapons on their persons at the time of their surrender, and now, with these, weapons, they shot some of the guards and fled the post. The garrison turned out quickly; they gave chase and were soon on top of the Cheyennes. What followed was a slaughter that resulted in the deaths of nearly half Dull Knife's band. It was not the Army's finest hour. Eventually, these Cheyennes would be settled at Pine Ridge. Little Wolf and his people, meanwhile, reached the Little Missouri River in southeastern Montana, where they would finally surrender to troops from Fort Keogh. Through the intercession of Nelson Miles—by then brigadier general—Dull Knife's people were allowed to join Little Wolf's band at Fort Keogh. Although the events surrounding the capture and subsequent breakout at Fort Robinson captured the nation's headlines for a brief moment, like the Nez Perce story it too would soon fade from the public consciousness.

Sitting Bull Surrenders, 1881

Although officially the Great Sioux War was considered over, unofficially, things were on hold. Some 4,000 Lakotas, representing most of the bands—the Seven Council Fires—resided north of the Canadian border where they still constituted a threat. And it was a hard core group at that. Many of the leading warriors who had whipped Custer were here: Gall, Low Dog, Black Moon and others, but the one figure who towered above them all was Sitting Bull: *Tatanka-Iyotanka*.

The exodus into Canada had begun late in 1876. Sitting Bull and his followers arrived the following spring, and in October 1877 the Lakotas were joined by 150 Nez Perce who had elected not to surrender along with Joseph. The Canadian land had become a refuge of sorts for fleeing Native Americans. Here the Lakotas and Nez Perce found Santees who had fled to Canada in the wake of the Minnesota troubles of 1862. The refugee bands established camps just across the Canadian border, in the area between Wood Mountain on the east and Cypress Hills to the west. Here, in this Land of the Grandmother, they were beyond the reach of the U.S. Army, and, for the moment, anyway, safe. Undoubtedly, it was a great relief to no longer have to worry about soldiers striking the village in some freezing dawn. And yet, there were concerns even here. Buffalo were scarce and those that could be found now had to be shared with Canadian tribes. It was either that or venture south of the Canadian line to hunt buffalo in Montana, where the animals seemed to be more plentiful than in Canada. The territory occupied by these refugee Indians was then considered part of the Northwest Territories, rather than Alberta and Saskatchewan which were not created as such until 1905.

Recognizing that western Canada was growing rapidly, though not perhaps to the extent of the western United States, the Parliament of Canada, in May 1873, authorized the creation of a constabulary force to maintain law and order in the western provinces. Gradually, the unit acquired the name Northwest Mounted Police (NWMP). The following year permanent posts were established at Forts Macleod and Edmonton in Alberta, and Fort Pelly in Saskatchewan. A fourth post, and perhaps the most important because of the role it played in dealing with Native American refugees from the States, was Fort Walsh, located in an area known as the Cypress Hills, Saskatchewan, near the Alberta line and almost directly north of Havre, Montana. On February 1, 1920, the official name was changed to the Royal Canadian Mounted Police. In time, the RCMP would come to be regarded as one of the finest bodies of its kind in the world.

A key figure in dealing with the Lakotas and other bands that had joined them, was thirty-four-year-old superintendent, Major James Morrow Walsh. Walsh soon developed a reputation for being fair but firm in his dealings with the Indians, who in turn responded with generally obedient behavior. Major Walsh assured the refugees that U.S. troops would not be allowed to cross the border in pursuit. On the other hand, the Indians were welcome in Canada so long as they behaved; raids across the border would not be tolerated, nor was it permissible to cross the line into Montana and return to the protection of the scarlet-coated Mounties, but it was clear that survival would leave the Indians little choice except to seek out game—especially buffalo—wherever it was to be found, regardless of boundaries, and that would almost certainly lead to clashes with settlers. It was a touchy situation. Recognizing the potential danger that existed as long as these Indians were free to come and go, prompted both governments to seek a solution whereby the Lakotas could somehow be got onto a reservation in the U.S.

In an effort to promote the idea of persuading the Lakotas and their allies to return to U.S. soil, a joint U.S./Canadian commission was created, with General Alfred Terry representing the administration of President Rutherford B. Hayes. Terry's instructions were two-fold: if upon arriving in Canada he found the Indians to be in the Northwest Territories, he would offer peace terms. If he found them in the U.S. however, he was to conduct military operations against them. Walsh soon developed an amicable rapport with Sitting Bull, indeed to the extent that Prime Minister John McDonald came to question Walsh's lack of forcefulness in trying to persuade the Lakotas to return to the U.S.

In October 1877 the commission convened at Fort Walsh. Terry speaking for the U.S., while Lieutenant Colonel James F. Macleod, Commissioner of the NWMP, spoke for the Canadian government. Getting the Lakotas to participate was no simple task. It was Major Walsh's job to persuade Sitting Bull and other leaders to parley with the commissioners, and the major had to use all of his powers of persuasion to get the Indians to show up, which they finally agreed to do. But the Lakotas harbored much anger and resentment against the U.S., and when the Nez Perce survivors arrived the Lakota were furious at their pitiful condition. Given their bitterness toward the United States it is little wonder that they had no interest in parleying with the commission, but come and listen to the high blown words of the commission they did.

And so Terry made his pitch, saying that the president desired only to make lasting peace; he wanted people to live in harmony. If the Indians would agree to return and refrain from hostile acts, they would receive a full pardon. However, they would be required to surrender their firearms and relocate to their assigned reservation. This was the crux of it. Then it was Sitting Bull's turn. "For sixty-four years you have kept me and my people and treated us bad.... You come here to tell us lies, but we don't want to hear them.... Don't say two more words. Go back where you came from." After others had spoken, and when it appeared that the Indians were ready to leave, Terry inquired if they were refusing the surrender terms, to which Sitting Bull replied that this side of the country—Canada—

belonged to them; the Americans belonged on the other side. They wanted nothing to do with Terry's terms.⁵⁷

Superintendent Macleod informed the Indians that their decision to reject the terms meant that they could never return to the U.S. carrying arms and ammunition and that if any did cross the line with weapons they would automatically become enemies of Canada as well. Rejecting these surrender terms also meant that the Indians would be on their own; they would have to support themselves; there would be no more assistance from the Canadian government. The Canadian government was in a ticklish position here. It was imperative for them to enforce a policy of insuring that these Indians did not feel free to raid across the border and then seek safety in Canada.

His terms firmly rejected, and sensing that nothing further could be accomplished through diplomacy, Terry packed up and left. Unfortunately, the question of what to do about these Indians remained unanswered. The presence of these refugee Indians in Canada was a real Gordian Knot and how to untie same was the question facing U.S. authorities. The problem was one of definition. The United States had yet to clearly define the political status of Native Americans. One view argued that they were political offenders and as such could not legally be extradited, while another view held that they were wards of the federal government and as such had no political status.

Meanwhile, Nelson Miles, ever attentive to the goings-on at Fort Walsh, as understandably he should have been since any returning Indians, peaceful or otherwise, would fall within the jurisdiction of his military department, at least until final disposition was made for their permanent residence. But more than that, when the Indians slipped across the line, it robbed Miles of a chance to score big time by capturing Sitting Bull, and Nelson Miles never saw an opportunity to promote himself that he didn't like.

Upon learning that Terry had given in and gone home, a very frustrated Miles, by-passed the chain of command and wrote directly to Sherman for permission to take the field with a powerful force. The term wasn't in vogue back then, but if it had been Miles would have thought Terry a wimp. On the other hand, if he [Miles] was given the necessary authority he would clear the country north of the Missouri River of all "hostiles." Whether this implied that he would cross the border is not clear, but knowing Miles, the tenor of the letter must have sounded like Thomas Jefferson's "fire bell in the night." to Sherman, who had visions of a major political incident and straight away issued a directive prohibiting all military action north of the Missouri River, unless settlers were in danger.

But Miles wanted closure and, to Sherman's everlasting chagrin he persisted in his arguments for permission to take the field. What Miles wanted in effect, was the same authority Sheridan had given to Mackenzie four years earlier. But Sherman wasn't about to grant *carte blanche* to Miles in this situation. Antagonizing the Mexican government was perhaps one thing, but creating an issue with Canada and, in effect, Great Britain, was quite something else again. "Because [Sherman told Miles] Generals Sheridan and Mackenzie once consented to act unlawfully in defiance of my authority in a certain political contingency is no reason why I should imitate so bad an example."⁵⁸

From the time he arrived in Canada Sitting Bull had envisioned a sort of confederacy of the Plains tribes—on both sides of the border—not unlike that nearly mystical objective pursued by Tecumseh three-quarters of a century earlier. But it was a hard sell and there was little interest. One exception here might have been Louis Riel *de facto* leader of the Red River Métis (or Slotas)—Canadians of mixed-blood ancestry—who promised to intercede with U.S. authorities on Sitting Bull's behalf, but the Hunkpapa leader rejected such overtures. The Lakotas had long enjoyed a trading relationship with the Slotas, but Sitting Bull evidently saw no advantage in establishing a union with them.

On March 20, 1879, Sitting Bull in company with his family and a few followers arrived at Fort Walsh for a conference with Major Walsh, who attempted to convince the Hunkpapa leader of the advantages of returning to the U.S. But Sitting Bull was adamant about remaining north of the border. "I am looking to the north for my life," he said and hope the White Mother will never ask me to look to the country I left, although mine, and not even the dust of it did I sell, but the Americans can have it." Clearly at this juncture, Sitting Bull did not envision returning to the States, a perspective that would change in the coming months.[59]

A partial solution to Sherman's (and Miles's) dilemma presented itself in the summer of 1879. The absence of game north of the border finally compelled some 200 lodges of Lakotas—about third of all the refugee Indians in Canada—to surrender and be placed on the reservation. Other groups of the refugee Indians, however, elected to simply take a chance and slip across the border to hunt buffalo. This did not sit well with the local Indian agent who complained that this unauthorized hunting was thinning out the animals needed to support his charges. In the face of this, Sherman had little choice but to authorize Miles to take action, but it was with the proviso that Miles tread carefully and not create a border incident. Sherman's directive went down the chain of command through Sheridan, who apparently thought the whole business was blown out of proportion. The problem, in Sheridan's view, had been fomented by Montana businessmen and traders. This was nothing new either. Throughout the history of the Indian wars, private interests had always profited by military activity in their region.

So Miles was on a short leash, but at least he was being turned loose. In July he led a strong force along the Milk River in search of the Lakotas. Altogether he had at his disposal nearly 700 men: 7 companies of the 2d Cavalry and a like number of mounted companies from his own 5th Infantry, augmented by 140 Crow and Cheyenne Indian scouts. On the 17th, the Indian scouts, commanded by Lieutenant Philo Clark, chanced upon a hunting party, reportedly led by none other than Sitting Bull. A fight quickly ensued. The Lakotas managed to get their non-combatants across Milk River before turning about and driving back the scouts. Just about this time, Miles arrived with the main body and broke up the Lakota attack with a couple of well-placed shells from his Hotchkiss cannon. Confronted by Miles and his artillery, the Indians retreated to the Canadian line and safety.

The affair resulted in a meeting between Miles and Major Walsh. Present to record a picture of the meeting for posterity was the Chicago newspaperman, John Finerty, whose facile pen, it will be remembered, gave us such an illuminating picture of the General Crook's Big Horn and Yellowstone Expedition:

> Major Walsh came into camp, according to promise, and we had a good time in the general's tent. He was a right pleasant man, with a strong love for Sitting Bull and his tribe. The major did not inflict a red coat upon us, but was dressed in a very handsome buckskin suit. His orderly wore a scarlet arrangement, which looked like a drayman's undershirt, sweaty under the armpits.[60]

Miles wanted something done about Canadian traders who he was convinced were selling arms to the Indians. Walsh did not seem to deny this, but said to Miles "I tell you honestly, General Miles, the Sioux do not want to fight the white people anymore." Miles, however, remained unconvinced and the meeting broke up with the status quo unchanged.[61]

On July 29, Walsh started back for Canada, accompanied by Finerty, "four scarlet-coated policemen, Long Dog, and another Sioux Indian." On the 30th they reached Sitting Bull's camp at Wood Mountain where Finerty hoped for an interview with the Lakota leader. He thought the surrounding country among the finest he had ever seen. Finerty also noted that the Indians appeared to be well armed, but that food was scarce. The visit did not prove fruitful. The Indians, while not outright hostile were not at all friendly toward the newspaperman. Walsh advised him to return and provided Finerty with an escort.

Whether or not the Indians sensed it is uncertain, but it was becoming obvious that Canada could not stand as a permanent home. The problem was food. Buffalo and other wild game had never been bountiful and the situation was getting worse. The winter of 1880–1881 was the beginning of the end. The Lakotas and other refugee bands had managed to survive thus far, but clearly the Indians were coming face to face with a choice of either surrendering or starve.

Although not a chief, Gall was a prominent Hunkpapa Lakota war chief. Staunchly opposed to the white man's take-over of Indian territory, after his surrender Gall, like the Comanche leader, Quanah Parker, eventually embraced the white man's road.

The years 1879–1880 saw a number of bands chose surrender, including even Gall, who at the zenith of Lakota resistance had been as intractable as Sitting Bull. But times change and eventually Gall turned around and became the white man's friend and ally. Finally, on July 19, 1881, Sitting Bull and 185 followers crossed the border and surrendered to Major David Brotherton at Fort Buford, North Dakota.

From the time of his surrender in 1881 until his death nine years later, Sitting Bull continued to stand out as a figure of prominence. If his prestige and influence among his own people was not what it had once been, his presence remained an issue of worry for federal authorities. There were always, it seemed, whisperings of a secret uprising, and of course the old chief was at the root of it all. For two years after his surrender in 1881 he was held prisoner at Fort Randall, South Dakota. Then in

Sitting Bull (left) and his nephew, One Bull.

1883 he was allowed to join Buffalo Bill Cody's wild west show, and for the next two years enjoyed the delights of show business, which he seems to have embraced warmly. Agent James McLaughlin, however, refused to permit the old chief to enjoy another tour, feeling it was in the best interests of the Indian service not to allow further participation; perhaps to do so would somehow set a bad example.

Just as it had been for Crazy Horse, the end for Sitting Bull was an ignominious one. With the spread of the Ghost Dance craze in 1890, Sitting Bull was suspected of being involved in fomenting trouble. It is not clear to what extent he was involved in supporting the movement, but there was little doubt that Sitting Bull remained a hard-liner. It was a touchy situation, but Miles—who was now commander of Sheridan's old Military Division of the Missouri—wanted to take no chances, and ordered Sitting Bull's arrest. During the course of the arrest at Standing Rock Agency, a melee ensued. Sitting Bull was shot and mortally wounded by Lieutenant Bull Head and Sergeant Red Tomahawk of the tribal police.

Crazy Horse was surely the more colorful and mystic warrior of the Plains, but as a visionary leader it is necessary to look beyond the romantic fighter on horseback. With the possible exception of Red Cloud, there was no more influential leader among the tribes of the Northern Plains than *Tatanka-Iyotanka*. During the 1860s Red Cloud was the dominant Lakota, but the Plains were just beginning to feel the pressure of white encroachment, but a decade later his star had begun to wane and as white presence began to increase during the 1870s it was the voice of Sitting Bull that spoke for Lakota resistance.

VII

The Intermountain West

Prologue: The Ute Crisis

> "You, the Mericatz, and Washington you want our land; you want our country. You have tried before to get our country away from us, and us from it. You have tried to get it in pieces; you are now trying to get it all."—Chief Ouray of the Utes in the aftermath of the Meeker Massacre, 1879[1]

Stretching from the Front Range of the Rockies west to, roughly, just beyond Salt Lake City, and south from southern Idaho to the New Mexico line, lies a vast complex region of towering, ermine-capped peaks, semi-arid basins and incredibly rugged canyons. With the exception of southwest Oregon and the Desert Southwest, it is the most difficult of all the varied terrain that witnessed the Indian-white struggles in the Trans-Mississippi West during the last half of the 19th century.

This Intermountain Region, with its vast physiographic variations was home to several tribes of Native Americans. In its northernmost reaches were found the Bannacks and some Paiutes, along with Sheepeaters, a small band of Western Shoshones who had developed a particular skill in hunting the Rocky Mountain sheep, hence their name.

The Upper Colorado River drainage system, south through Colorado's San Luis Valley into northern New Mexico, and including much of the mountainous region of southwestern Colorado, was the homeland of the Utes, a member of the Uto-Aztecan linguistic family. The Ute name, appropriately enough, means "Land of the Sun," or something approximating that idea. Like the Cheyennes, the Utes were composed of a northern and a southern band, which were further divided into still smaller bands. Skilled horsemen and fierce fighters, the Utes shared many characteristics of the Plains tribes, the most prominent of which perhaps was a strong reliance on the buffalo as a staple of life. Hunting parties often ventured out onto the Plains to the east of their traditional homeland to hunt buffalo. Frequently, these forays witnessed clashes between Utes, Arapahos and Comanches. Southern Colorado and northern New Mexico were also the scene of clashes between Utes, Jicarilla Apaches—their sometime allies—and Navajos.

By the late 18th or very early 19th century the Utes had acquired horses through raids and trading with other tribes. As well, the Utes were also in possession of firearms by the time trappers, traders, and explorers began moving into their territory during the early part of the 19th century.

The aftermath of the Mexican-American War introduced a new element to Ute relationships with Americans. In July 1848 U.S. troops attacked a combined force of Utes and Jicarillas around Cumbres Pass, south of Pagosa Springs near the New Mexico line. The following March Utes killed two survivors of John Charles Fremont's exploring expedition.

In 1849, as a belated consequence of the Mexican-American War, a local treaty was signed with the Utes, primarily as a means of addressing relations with the New Mexican population, which had now become the responsibility of the United States Government. New Mexicans had to deal with raids from the Navajos to the west and Utes to the north. The latter tribe was actually as much at home in northern New Mexico, especially around Taos and Abiquiu, as they were in the mountains of Colorado. Despite the treaty, however, there was a persistent recurrence of raids by the Utes, striking ranches and outlying settlements. Prompted by these incidents, the U.S. Army created several outposts in southern Colorado and northern New Mexico in an effort to control Ute mischief.

Mormon Troubles

In July 1847 some 150 Mormon settlers arrived at Great Salt Lake. The old mountain man Jim Bridger warned Brigham Young that the Utes posed a threat, but the Mormons rejected the warning, believing that the Indians would respond to God's word. And initially relations with the Utes was amicable, but as the number of Mormon settlers steadily increased, depleting wild game and altering the land for agricultural purposes, relations gradually deteriorated and clashes inevitably began to occur. Competition for the land was exacerbated by a demographic factor, for even as the Mormon population was swelling, the Ute population was in decline and by 1850 the Mormon population, centered in the Salt Lake City area, but elsewhere as well, had grown to some 11,000 souls.

In 1849, two years after the arrival of the first group of settlers, the Mormons sought to establish their own state, to be called *Deseret* and which initially was envisioned to embrace all the land between the Sierra Nevada Mountains and the Rockies, and from the Mexican border north nearly to the Oregon line. The name *Deseret* had its origins in the Book of Mormons and means "Honeybee." The idea was quickly dismissed by the federal government, but Washington also recognized that some sort of action needed to be taken, hence the creation of Utah Territory in 1850 with Brigham Young as governor.

Determined to spread out and establish new communities, Young, in March 1849, sent a party of 150 to settle the Utah Valley and in November a second group of colonists was dispatched to establish a community in the San Pitch Valley of central Utah. The Utes did not take kindly to these new arrivals. Raids began with thefts of livestock. And tension mounted when a lone Ute was killed for a minor theft. As a consequence of such incidents, Brigham Young decided that military action was justified and accordingly, directed that a war of extermination be carried out in the Utah Valley area. Interestingly enough, the extermination order was to apply only to *select* Indians, although exactly how certain Indians were to be selected was not spelled out. Nevertheless in February 1850 a militia force attacked a Ute encampment near the Provo River. For forty-eight hours the two sides exchanged fire with neither side really gaining the upper hand, although having a cannon gave the militia something of an advantage. By the end of the second day, eight Utes and one militiaman were dead. The remaining Utes slipped away toward the Spanish Fork River. Nearly a month of additional skirmishing followed leaving another seven Utes dead. By month's end both sides, having had enough fighting, agreed to a truce.

A period of relative peace followed the 1850 truce, but trouble always simmered beneath the surface. Almost never were the periods that followed a treaty signing or unofficial truce completely free of incidents. Illustrative of this was an incident when two Utes caught stealing cattle near Utah Lake were caught and killed by a Mormon posse. Such happenings continued to keep emotions riled. Faced with the fear of an Indian incident at any time, Mormon settlers constructed a stockaded fort they dubbed Fort Utah near present Provo. Armed with cannons the post sat on prime Ute land and the Indian reaction may be imagined. The Mormons may have been unaware of this, or perhaps they knew and simply chose to ignore it.

Walkara's War

In the early years of Mormon-Ute relations the most prominent Ute leader was Walkara—or Walker—of the Tumpanawach band. Born around 1815 Walkara was a skilled hunter and horseman. In addition to his native tongue he spoke both English and Spanish and by the time Mormons began moving into the Ute country he was already a noted war leader.

In July 1853, a Ute was killed during a trading dispute near Springville, bringing a militia party to Walkara's village with the intention of calming down the angry Utes. It so happened that the slain Ute was related to Walkara which did not help matters at all and for a time it appeared that angry Utes might well overwhelm the militia company, which however, did manage to extricate itself from harm's way. Whether out of a spirit of retaliation or not is unknown, but a pair of sub-chiefs, Arapeen and Wanship murdered a white man named Alexander Peel in nearby Payson. Although Walkara did indeed seem to want his pound of flesh, he was realist enough to see that Peel's murder would undoubtedly bring on white retaliation. Consequently, he marched his people up into the depths of Payson Canyon, destroying cabins and stealing livestock en route.

Although these isolated incidents were enough to keep both sides on edge, the one single factor that contributed to a deepening rift between Mormons and Utes was the Mormon effort to shut down the Ute slave trade. Over centuries, the Utes had developed channels of trade in horses, silver, and slaves that reached from Mexico to the Columbia River plateau. Mormons believed the slave trade was wrong and sought to shut it down. This hit close to home because Walkara himself was a big trader in slaves.

Amid mounting tensions, Colonel Peter Conover led a 150-man militia expedition into Payson Canyon in pursuit of the Utes. However, Conover's boss, Daniel Wells, commanding the state militia, recalled the bloody clashes of 1849–1850, directed Conover to conduct his expedition in a defensive mode. However, before the directive reached him, Conover had already sent a detachment to attack a village at Pleasant Creek, which resulted in the deaths of six Utes. After Wells's order finally caught up with him Conover returned to Utah Valley.

Confronted by a seemingly never-ending threat of Indian attacks, Brigham Young decided on a defensive policy. Settlers were directed to establish secure defensive forts in the larger communities, which would serve as a safe haven to the more isolated farms and ranches, much like had been done in the east during the colonial period. It looked good on paper, but proved a difficult policy to enforce because settlers were loath to leave their farms and ranches unattended and so the Ute raids continued. Ignoring Young's philosophy, settlers organized their own local militia companies to strike back when the Utes raided, stealing and murdering, and in many cases mutilating settlers. No quarter was given. A militia unit attacked a Ute camp near Goshen, killing five. At Nephi on October 2, 1853, nine Utes were slaughtered by townspeople when they approached the fort, asking for protection.

Settlers were not the only ones to feel the wrath of the Utes either. On October 26, 1853, Captain John Williams Gunnison—for whom the city of Gunnison, Colorado would later be named—of the Corps of Topographical Engineers, surveying the lower Sevier River, was murdered by Utes, along with six other members of his expedition. The killings brought a quick military response in the form of Colonel Edward Steptoe who arrived in the area with 300 cavalry. The presence of the soldiers further infuriated the Utes. The situation turned sticky because Steptoe, a Virginian, was reported to be President Franklin Pierce's favored candidate to replace Brigham Young as governor of Utah Territory, although why is not exactly clear. It was a moot point, however, as Steptoe elected to remain in the army. As things worked out he would later find a different sort of hornet's nest in Oregon four years hence. Meanwhile, though angry the Utes did not cause any further trouble, at least immediately.

In 1854, some Ute leaders, including Walkara, were ready for peace and sought acceptable terms from Brigham Young. The two leaders met at Walkara's camp on Chicken Creek in May. The talks proved fruitful and led to an agreement, bringing the war to a close for the moment anyway.

In the hiatus that followed Walkara's (or Walker's) War a troubled sort of détente existed between Utes and Mormons, but it was inevitable that further troubles were in the offing; inevitable so long as two dissimilar cultures were vying for the same land and its resources, and no agreement or treaty ever struck was going to change that.

Brigham Young, however, believed he had a solution to the Indian problem. Following the end of the Walker War he authorized the creation of a series of farms in key locations. The idea was to repay Utes for lost land and resources by raising crops which would be used to supply the Indians. It was cheaper to feed than fight them, reasoned Young. The idea looked good on paper and at first it seemed to work well. However, Mormon settlers who operated these farms grew tired of laboring for the Indians and the idea gradually faded away.

Conflict in the Mountains

Early in 1855, President Franklin Pierce appointed Garland Hurt to run the Utah Indian Agency. A self-taught physician and former Kentucky legislator, Hurt has been described by historian Will Bagley as "one of the most honorable men ever to serve the federal government." Hurt worked tirelessly to promote peaceful relations between his charges and the Mormons, finding some of the latter group to be little better than common thugs. In 1857 Hurt resigned his post having had enough of what he came to regard as an impossible situation.[2]

It will be recalled that troops operating in Kansas against the Cheyennes had been mobilized and sent to Utah by President James Buchanan to deal with a perceived Mormon uprising. Command of the Utah Expedition, as it was dubbed, had been assigned to Colonel Albert Sidney Johnston. By 1858, Johnston had assembled a force of 2,500 regular army troops (as opposed to volunteers) and set forth to deal with the troublesome Mormons. And there was some reason to believe that things were going to happen. In October 1857, for example, six Californians, east-bound were arrested by Mormons and charged as spies. The six were subsequently released but later murdered in an incident that came to be known as the Aiken Massacre.

On-going events, however, would soon show that the pot was not going to boil over. Ironically, there were no full scale battles between U.S. troops and the Mormon army—called the Nauvoo Legion. Indeed, the Mormons proved less troublesome than the Indians with whom Johnston would focus more attention than the Mormons, although one might point to the Mountain Meadows Massacre as an exception. Far better known than the Aiken Massacre, more than 120 immigrants from Missouri and Arkansas were attacked and murdered by Mormons disguised as Indians.

During the summer and fall of 1861, Colonel Patrick Edward Connor, a fiery, Irishman from County Kerry and a Stockton, California, businessman marched east with a force of California volunteers from California marched across the sun-baked landscape, with an assignment that directed him to protect the Overland Trail route across Utah. Along the way, Connor deposited a company of infantry and another of cavalry to garrison Fort Churchill. Two additional companies were assigned to build a new post to be called Fort Ruby (near present Wells, Nevada), after which Connor continued east to establish Fort Douglas, east of Salt Lake. A bit later, Connor armed with broadened responsibility and authority, would lead a strong punitive expedition against the Lakotas and Cheyennes that would prove a largely futile effort, but for the moment his concern would be the Overland Trail.

Connor Attacks Bear Hunter's Village

If the Mormons had proved less troublesome than the Buchanan administration had anticipated, Patrick Connor like Albert Sidney Johnston found that the Shoshones, Bannacks, and Utes were more troublesome than expected, regularly attacking the Overland Stage line and cutting the telegraph wires. Shoshones and Bannacks were the worst offenders. Connor's first step was to send a company to establish a garrison at Fort Bridger in extreme southwestern Wyoming. Meanwhile, a second company under Major Edward McGarry was directed to secure the release of a white boy held captive by Bear Hunter, a well known Shoshone militant. McGarry made contact and somehow managed to effect the boy's rescue. This was good news, but it also reached Connor with another report to the effect that Bear Hunter was murdering prospectors bound for the Montana "diggings." Connor resolved to act immediately. Mobilizing a strike force of nearly 300 mounted men, he sortied from Camp Douglas in late January 1863. Intelligence had placed Bear Hunter's village on Bear River (near Preston, Idaho), some 140 miles north of Salt Lake.

The village was believed to contain about 300 warriors, roughly equal to Connor's command. The village was set up in a ravine and some care had been given in preparing it defensively. Evidently Bear Hunter anticipated that soldiers would come searching for him and, ingeniously, had directed his warriors to cut steps into the side of the ravine to be used as firing positions.

It was tough campaigning weather; bitterly cold and through deep snow, but Connor was not deterred and hoped to surprise the Shoshones, marching only at night to avoid detection, but somehow Bear Hunter's scouts learned he was on the march and accordingly, were well prepared when Connor arrived at dawn on January 27.

Bear River was filled with ice floes, but Connor managed to get the bulk of his command across. Once on the opposite shore a head-on assault against the village by Major McGarry was thrown back with heavy loss. Connor then divided his force, attacking both flanks of the village while other detachments isolated the ravine and prevented any of the inhabitants from slipping away. Other soldiers, meanwhile, fired down on the village from the rim tops. Hand-to-hand fighting soon followed. Some warriors attempted to escape by plunging into the frigid water, but most were killed before reaching the safety of the opposite shore. By noon, most of the fighting was over. Connor's men counted 224 bodies, including that of Bear Hunter. Additionally, lodges and provisions were also destroyed. The soldiers captured nearly 200 horses and took 160 captives. Connor's losses amounted to 14 dead and some 50 wounded. For the army it had been a costly fight, but a resounding victory, earning Connor a promotion to brigadier general.

Colorado Gold

In July 1858, the discovery of gold on Cherry Creek, near its confluence with the South Platte River, where the city of Denver would soon be born, and elsewhere along the Front Range of the Colorado Rockies, led to a great exodus to the new land of riches; the first real strike since Sutter's Mill. The population swelled quickly and dramatically. By 1860 Colorado's mining camps boasted a population of 35,000. And soon gold hungry Argonauts were crossing the mountains and moving into South Park and elsewhere beyond the Great Divide. The Utes were not happy with this development and their wrath was soon felt by prospectors.

In 1861 Congress authorized the creation of Colorado Territory from western Kansas, plus a chunk from southwestern Nebraska, and a piece of New Mexico as well. Those territorial boundaries would not change when Colorado became a state in 1876. However, new boundaries—Utah and New Mexico had been created a decade earlier—resulted in new policies that affected all of the tribes within the boundaries of all three territories, which were firm enough for the federal government but quite artificial and meaningless to the Indians.

In 1863, Lafayette Head, agent for the Southern Utes, took a party of leaders from all the bands to Washington, D.C., and New York City, hoping to impress them with the white man's power and resources. The visit apparently accomplished its intended purpose which was to persuade the Utes to sign a treaty at Conejos—due south of Alamosa near the New Mexico line. By virtue of this agreement the Utes agreed to surrender all of their land east of the Continental Divide; also in Middle Park. Put another way, it meant that the Utes had to vacate any land currently occupied by whites. The treaty was struck, though not all the bands signed off. One leader who did, however—and it is important to note this—was Ouray, chief of the Uncompahgre band and whose star was then in ascendancy. Born about 1820, Ouray (U-ray) was emerging as perhaps the most influential of Ute leaders. Friendly to the whites early on, he saw resistance to white settlement as futile.

The Blackhawk War

On April 9, 1865, the very day that General Robert E. Lee was surrendering the Army of Northern Virginia to General Ulysses Grant, a minor incident between Mormons and Utes over stolen cattle and perhaps some other things as well, led to the Blackhawk War, reportedly the most destructive in Utah history. The principal Ute leader at this point was a minor chief named Blackhawk, who thus came to lend his name to history, along with an earlier chief of the same name in the Upper Mississippi River Valley.

Ute raids generally concentrated on livestock theft, but sometimes settlers were around when the raids occurred and a skirmish ensued, often with both sides suffering casualties. On May 26, 1865, for example, a settler named John Given, his wife, and three young daughters, ages nine, five, and three were tomahawked to death. Blackhawk himself led some of these raids, reportedly stealing more than 2,000 head of cattle. And the settlers did what settlers had been doing since the first clash between Native Americans and Euro-Americans: they banded together and launched their own raids. In July, a militia unit commanded by Major Warren Snow attacked an Indian village near Burrville, killing a dozen Utes.

Another raid occurred on November 26 at the infant community of Circleville on the Sevier River in southwest Utah. Less than a year old, the community was suddenly attacked by a Ute war party, intent primarily on stealing livestock. The frightened inhabitants of the village attempted to fight back, which may have been a mistake. As it was several of the defenders, including two thirteen-year-old boys lost their lives.

In the spring of 1866, a band of Paiutes—enemies of the Utes and sometimes of the settlers—killed a soldier near Circleville. The shooting led angry citizens to arrest a band of Paiutes camped outside the town. Whether the soldier had been killed by members of this band is not clear, but in any event, the town's relations with Indians—any Indians—were rather tenuous by this time and the killing of the soldier had everybody on edge. Circleville militia went out, arrested the Paiutes and held them under guard. The militia commander asked for instructions. It took time for the communication system to provide needed information, and while everything was on hold, the Paiutes managed to free themselves and made a break for it. A scuffle ensued during which the guards were able to kill the Paiute men, sparing the women and children. But the guards then decided it was necessary to kill the women and children, too, so there would be no witnesses. We don't know how many Indians were in the party altogether, nor do we know the number of men versus women, but in any case, all save two or three very small children were killed. Too late, the militia commander received orders that the prisoners were to be treated kindly; further instructions would be forthcoming. The surviving children would later be adopted by local families. It was yet another brutal story that came to be known as the Circleville Massacre.

As far as the Mormons were concerned a state of war existed between them and the Utes. Forts were built at key locations and militia companies scoured the countryside in search of hostile raiders. As elsewhere in the West it was often impossible to distinguish friendly Indian from those who were hostile. Indeed, one might be hostile this week but friendly the next. In any event, militia companies seldom bothered to determine whether a group of Indians was one or the other. Finally, in 1867, perhaps having grown weary of war, Blackhawk made peace with the Mormons, but what one leader agreed to did not necessarily bind others in his band and spotty raids continued to occur during the next several years. In 1872, U.S. troops brought about an end to the conflict. The war had been costly to both sides. Mormons claimed the war had cost them a million and a half dollars. Insofar as the Utes were concerned the war took the lives of several important leaders. Blackhawk would die of tuberculosis in 1872. The war also altered Ute demographics. As a consequence of the war many Utes moved north to settle with the Uintah band.

By 1865 there were increasing signs of restlessness among the Colorado Utes. Two factors were responsible for this uneasiness. Ute troubles with the Mormons during the past decade had impacted Utes in Colorado, even those who had not been particularly involved in the Mormon troubles. But mainly it was the growing white presence spreading across Colorado Territory. The first permanent white settlement was at San Luis in 1854, soon followed by others at San Pedro, San Acacio, and Guadalupe; and more were springing up overnight, it seemed. Early settlers used their experiences in irrigation to improve farms and ranches, which led to a disruption of the traditional Indian life style. It was an old pattern repeating itself.

In 1868 negotiations were begun with the Utes in an effort to arrive at a permanent solution. That year saw yet another Ute delegation journeying to Washington where President Andrew Johnson conferred silver peace medals to each delegate, in the hope that the Utes would be impressed enough to accept the new treaty terms then being proposed. They did.

Prior to 1868 the only Ute reservation was located in northeastern Utah where the Uintah Agency had been established. In 1868, the Consolidated Ute Reservation was established by treaty. It was a large tract of land, comprising most of western Colorado Territory. Because of his involvement with negotiating the agreement it is sometimes known as Kit Carson's treaty.

The Consolidated Reservation extended from, roughly, the Yampa River on the north to the New Mexico line on the south, and from the Colorado-Utah line on the west to near Aspen, Colorado on the east, embracing most of what is known today as Colorado's Western Slope. Some pockets were excluded, however, namely the North, Middle, and South Parks, along with the San Luis and Yampa Valleys. In exchange for this unusually large tract, the Utes agreed to surrender rights to any other lands, previously considered to be their domain. Like other such agreements—notably the 1868 Laramie Treaty—whites were forbidden from settling on this land. Unlike the Laramie Treaty, however, no whites, other than authorized individuals, were allowed to even *pass through* the reservation.

The treaty also guaranteed the Utes that they would receive annual financial payment, along with the promise of schools, agricultural help, and medical care. To better serve the tribe, two agencies were established; one at Rio de Los Pinos near Conejos in the south, and at White River in the north. The former agency would serve the Tabeguache (Tab uh watch) Muache (Moo ach), Weeminuche (Wee min ooch), and Capote bands, while the White River Agency (near present day Meeker) would see to the needs of the Grand River, Yampa, and Uintah bands. Numerically, the tribe counted about 800 at White River and 2,000 at Los Pinos. The Uintahs were served at both the White River and the Uintah agencies.

The decade following the signing of the 1868 treaty was by no means a trouble-free time of transition. There was much confusion as the Utes attempted to adjust to the new terms imposed by the treaty. Ute bands who had previously resided in northern New Mexico moved into Colorado, while others relocated to White River. One wonders what might have been the outcome if all of the annuities and food rations promised by the treaty (actually, all treaties) had been timely delivered as promised? But the Utes were learning what other tribes had already experienced, namely that rations were usually late, and beef was often spoiled and delivered in insufficient quantities.

In southern Colorado, raids and reprisals—none really on a large scale—persisted. Sometimes Ute bands would raid Navajos, with whom they also traded on occasion. But there were enough minor incidents of this sort to prompt the War Department to establish a post at Pagosa Springs.Initially named Camp Lewis (Durango) (later named Fort Lewis). The 9th Black Cavalry was stationed here to monitor Indian troubles. The garrison also helped construct a road over the rugged San Juan Mountains so as to provide an easier axis of communication between Camp Lewis and Fort Garland in the San Luis Valley.

Meanwhile, pressure on the Southern Utes was also building. Mining and railroad interests lusted after Ute land. *The Denver & Rio Grande Railroad* (later called the Dangerous and Rapidly Growing Worse) would cut right through the heart of Ute territory. Territorial

Governor Edward Moody McCook thought it ridiculous that the U.S. Government had seen fit to set aside a third of the Territory for the exclusive use of the Utes, whom he regarded as lazy savages. But when Indian land was coveted whites paid little attention to treaty stipulations anyway. Agent Jabez Trask at Los Pinos, however, made a serious effort to observe treaty boundaries and wound up being replaced in 1872 by Charles Adams.

The year 1872 saw a mighty gathering in Denver. In August, Governor McCook and several commissioners talked with some 1,500 Utes. Talks focused on the idea of the Utes selling a portion of the reservation that had just been assigned to them four years earlier. Ouray had previously stated that the Utes had no wish to sell any of their lands. The terms of the 1868 Treaty assigned this land to the Utes, said Ouray; it was up to the government to see that those terms were honored.

Tensions were rising. In June 1873 the War Department agreed to send troops into southwestern Colorado to evict miners, who vowed to resist with force of arms. By this time, Samuel Elbert had replaced McCook as governor, and perhaps fearful of repercussions, called off the army, thereby allowing several thousand additional miners to move into the San Juans. It was a scene that would be repeated two years later in the Black Hills of South Dakota.

The upshot of the chaos in the San Juans resulted in yet another agreement, wherein the Utes understood they would only be ceding land presently occupied by miners, but in reality they actually surrendered, without understanding exactly why, nearly all of the San Juans given them by virtue of the 1868 Treaty. In return the Utes were to receive half a million dollars. It was a wearisome tale. Ouray complained because they would be losing sacred hot springs, a favorite haunt. For once the government seemed to actually listen and a small adjustment was made setting this area aside for the Utes.

The decade of the 1870s continued to be an unsettled time, both for the Utes and for Colorado, which was awarded statehood in 1876. Colorado was growing. East of the Continental Divide, on the grasslands of the eastern part of the state, cattle ranches were flourishing, even as the buffalo declined. Along the Front Range, from Fort Collins south the state's economy and population were booming, and west into the mountains, mining interests continued to plumb the depths of Colorado's mineral wealth.

It had taken only ten years for the 1868 Treaty to be modified, and significantly. In August 1878, Congress decreed that the Southern and Tabeguache bands would be moved to White River. Naturally, the Utes balked at the order, but eventually adjustments were made and most of the Ute leaders put their marks on the new agreement. Ouray alone refused to accept the terms and apparently was permitted to remain in the south, at least for the time being.

The Bannack Uprising, 1878

The traditional homeland of the Bannack (sometimes spelled Bannock) branch of the Northern Paiutes ranged primarily from extreme southeastern Oregon to southeastern Idaho, and occasionally parts of western Wyoming and southwestern Montana.

During the summer of 1877, even as the Nez Perce were in flight to Canada, the Bannack, some 600 strong, together with perhaps a 1,000 Shoshones, were assigned to a reservation around Fort Hall, on the Upper Snake River in southwest Idaho. A separate group of Bannacks, known as the Lemhis, shared the Lemhi Reservation north of Fort Hall with a band of western Shoshones led by Chief Tendoy. This particular band of Shoshones had come to be known as "Sheepeaters," owing to their success in hunting the elusive Rocky Mountain sheep. Although not a chief, per se, the Fort Hall Bannacks looked to a young warrior named Buffalo Horn who had served Colonel Nelson Miles as a scout during the Nez Perce and Wolf Mountain Campaigns. The celebrated scout Yellowstone Kelly once referred to Buffalo Horn as one of the bravest Indians he had ever known.

Bannack troubles had been brewing for some time, and the Nez Perce situation added to unrest among the tribesmen. The murder of a white man by a Bannack near Fort Hall in November 1877 precipitated a minor crisis when civil authorities were unable to capture the culprit. As a consequence, three companies of the 14th Infantry came out from Camp Douglas (near Salt Lake) and subsequently were able to capture the guilty party in January 1878. The incident, although minor, aroused the ire of the Bannacks to the extent that it brought Colonel John Smith up from Camp Douglas. Smith aimed to come down hard on the Bannacks before things really got out of hand and arrested fifty-three Bannacks, which fueled further unrest in the tribe.

Since Fort Hall fell within General George Crook's Department of the Platte, the general took it upon himself to visit the scene in April. Crook thought the situation had largely been defused; he could not have been more wrong. Shortly after his visit a group of Bannacks, Lemhi Sheepeaters, Paiutes, and Umatillas gathered at Camas Prairie for the purpose of harvesting the favored camas roots. Through a typographical error the area supposed to have been assigned to the Bannacks by treaty had not been. The Indians, of course, regarded the land as theirs, regardless of what the white man's paper said.

Some of the Indians who had been enjoying the fruits of camas prairie recognized a troublesome situation developing, however, and returned to their agencies. But not Buffalo Horn and his band who, in company with a few Paiutes and Umatillas, perhaps as many as 200, resented the white man's encroaching way and determined to strike back.

After destroying a road station and ferry, the raiders crossed the Snake River and headed west across southern Idaho, killing ten whites along the way. Near Silver City on June 8 they had a run-in with some volunteers. The engagement proved costly in the extreme for the Bannacks in that it took the life of Buffalo Horn. Notwithstanding, the raiders swept on, even adding some 400 Paiutes from the Malheur Reservation.

With the situation rapidly escalating, Captain Reuben Bernard with a troop of the 1st Cavalry left his base at Boise Barracks to go in pursuit. If one was to look for a typical Indian-fighting soldier of the 19th century frontier army it would not be necessary to look further than forty-four-year-old Reuben Bernard. Bernard may well have been the ablest and most experienced officer field officer of his rank at that time. A large beefy man, he weighed one hundred and eighty pounds and stood five feet nine inches tall. Bernard would one day retire as a general officer and write an account of his Indian-fighting experiences which he titled *One Hundred and Three Fights and Scrimmages*.

Once again it seemed that the troubled area crossed the army's departmental boundaries, falling within General Howard's jurisdiction. Howard and his immediate superior, General Irwin McDowell out in San Francisco, began deploying other units to the troubled area, and Howard himself traveled to Boise to get a first hand picture of the situation, arriving on June 12.

Although technically the Camas Prairie area did not belong to the Indians, many, including Generals McDowell, Howard and others, recognized the Indian right to be there and because of this hoped to settle the disagreement without having to escalate military intervention. To achieve this end, Howard authorized Sarah Winnemucca, a literate woman with peaceful visions, and daughter of a highly respected Paiute chief, to try and negotiate a reasonable settlement. However, in visiting the camp of the Bannacks and their allies near Steen's Mountain in southeast Oregon, she discovered that the time for words had passed. Indeed, Sarah and her father—who had accompanied his daughter—and their party were fortunate to escape with their lives. The Indians had been fired-up by a medicine man named Oytes, along with a Paiute chief named Egan, pronounced Ehegante by the Indians but Anglicized to Egan by whites. Egan seems to have agreed to replace the fallen Buffalo Horn, albeit somewhat reluctantly.

Learning of the failed mission Howard now determined to march on Steen's Mountain with three columns of troops to converge on the Indian encampment, which was still believed to be in the area. However, the Indians, it seems, had already moved on to Silver Creek, where hard-driving Reuben Bernard surprised them with three troops of cavalry. Forming his battalion for the attack, Bernard addressed his troopers: "I will say to you men that the enemy is close to us; we came here to whip them and we are going to do it. I want you all to keep good order, and no running. If anyone runs I will have him shot, so he might as well die by the enemy as by friends."[3]

The attack caught the Bannacks by surprise and drove them to the crest of the high bluffs overlooking the camp. Both sides exchanged fire throughout the day, but casualties were light on both sides, except that on the Indian side, the fighting seriously wounded Chief Egan, and Bernard's troopers destroyed the village and its contents, the loss of which would work a real hardship on the Indians.

Meanwhile, out at the Malheur Agency in eastern Oregon, now badly damaged and abandoned by the agent since the outbreak of troubles, Howard, with a mixed force of nearly 500 cavalry and infantry, headed for the valley of the John Day River, where it was reliably reported that the Indians would be reinforced by disaffected Klamaths, Umatillas, and Cayuses. Should this happen it would surely lead to an escalation of the present troubles. Accordingly, Howard alerted his commanders to the north: Colonels Frank Wheaton and Cuvier Grover to prevent any such gathering, while Howard himself struck north in pursuit.

Over the course of the next two weeks, Howard's command worked its way north, crossing various tributaries of the John Day River—named for a Virginia-born frontiersman and trapper who spent a good portion of his life trapping in the Snake River country—through some of the roughest terrain Howard had ever seen. Bernard's cavalry ranged out ahead of the infantry, occasionally skirmishing with the withdrawing Bannacks and their allies. Along the way, though, the Indians still managed to raid and plunder any ranch or farm within reach.

Near Pendleton, Oregon, the arrival of additional units brought the strength of Bernard's command to seven troops; it also brought something of a command dilemma, since the new arrivals included both a colonel and a major, both of whom outranked Bernard. The situation rather resolved itself, however, when the colonel soon departed on another assignment and the major chose not to pull rank on Bernard. Howard, had great faith in Bernard's ability as a field commander and perhaps quietly expressed his wish to have Bernard remain in command.

On July 8, the Indians were located in a strong position near Pilot Butte. Bernard formed his battalion to attack along converging lines. Bernard himself was in the forefront as the attack got underway. General Howard recalled that the slope up which the troops advanced was steeper than what the soldiers had to climb at Missionary Ridge in the Civil War. Despite heavy fire from the Indians that dropped a number of cavalry horses, Bernard pushed on, forcing the Indians to retire to a new position, only to have the soldiers drive them back again and again. As the forward momentum of the troops continued to exert pressure on the Indians, Bernard then launched a flank attack that finally drove the Indians from the field entirely.

Having secured the field, Howard, now believing that the routed Bannacks would be heading south into Idaho organized his pursuit with his own hard-riding troopers out in front. Meanwhile, orders went out to other army units to be on the lookout for the Indians. One of these, a large force consisting of seven companies of the 21st Infantry under Captain Evan Miles—no relation to Nelson—was fortunately, for Howard, in a position to take immediate action when the Bannacks confounded everyone by suddenly reversing course and heading to the Umatilla Agency near Walla Walla. Up to this point the Umatillas had been something of a question mark. Although a few had joined the Bannacks there remained uncertainty as to whether the whole tribe would participate in the uprising. If indeed the Umatilla tribe was to join in it would have given the uprising much more muscle and may have been the reason the Bannacks elected to head for the Umatilla Agency. If such was their intent, the Bannacks were soon disabused of such hope as the Umatillas informed Captain Miles that they had no intention of joining the Bannacks.

On July 13, as the Bannacks approached, Miles deployed his command around the agency. During the next several hours the Indians and soldiers exchanged fire, but when Miles then prepared to advance the Indians fled into the mountains. Two days later, Umatilla scouts found the Bannacks and under the guise of friendship managed to draw the wounded Chief Egan aside and killed him, later presenting his scalp and head to Miles.

On July 14, Lieutenant Colonel James Forsyth, who would later figure prominently in the debacle at Wounded Knee, assumed command of Bernard's cavalry battalion and pressed on in pursuit of the hostiles. The rugged terrain, however, made it difficult to catch up, although Forsyth did have a short scrap with the Bannack rear guard on the 20th.

But the uprising was running short of energy. The coalition split up with the Paiutes fleeing into southeastern Oregon while the Bannacks headed toward Idaho. Howard continued his own pursuit and the Bannacks destroyed whatever property they came across. Some apparently entertained visions of breaking for Canada, following the Nez Perce strategy.

The concluding phase of the Bannack war brought Colonel Nelson Miles into the picture. Miles had been vacationing in Yellowstone Park with family and friends when word of the Bannack trouble reached him. Wasting no time, Miles, in his customary fashion, immediately assembled troops of the 5th Cavalry and surprised the Indians on Clark's Fork of the Yellowstone River on September 4. Eight days later fugitives from the Miles fight were attacked by a company of the 5th Cavalry on the Snake River near Jackson Hole, Wyoming, bringing the Bannack War to a close. The Bannacks were eventually returned to their reservation in Idaho, while the Paiutes were removed to the Yakima Reservation in Washington.

The Ute War and the Meeker Massacre, 1879

In the northern half of Colorado, meanwhile, settlers and prospectors were steadily moving into the region and as their numbers increased, so too did the resentment of the Utes. Middle Park proved an especially touchy locale. Settlers found it attractive, but the Utes also regarded it as prime hunting ground, which led to increasing between the two sides. Insofar as the Utes were concerned they had never surrendered title to this land and so resisted white encroachment. Settlers lobbied for an army post in the area, but the idea was rejected. Given the adversarial nature of Indian-white relations things were not going to improve, either. As the decade of 1870 wound down the discovery of rich silver deposits around Leadville, drew a bevy of prospectors across the Divide and onto Ute lands. Governor Frederick Pitkin vowed that if the Utes did not get out of the way peacefully their land would be taken by force.

The agency that served the Northern Utes was located at White River near the present site of Meeker, but it did not serve the Indians well. Rations were shipped via the Union Pacific Railroad to Rawlins, Wyoming, on the north then hauled overland to White River, but it was a tenuous and unreliable channel of supply. Then in 1878, the Indian Bureau failed to pay freight charges and the rations were held up. The Utes, meanwhile, had no food or blankets to see them through the winter. Some pointed an accusing finger at the Ute agent, the Rev. Edward Danforth, who was actually quite innocent of any wrong-doing. Angry and no doubt embarrassed he resigned.

Danforth's replacement arrived in the spring of 1879 and immediately racked up points with the Utes by seeing to it that their annuities were released and shipped to White River. Thus, did Nathan Meeker's tenure as agent at White River begin on an auspicious note; the ending would not be the same.

In retrospect, Marcus Whitman's life would seem to have been that of an individual born to tragedy. In Pacific Northwest history his name resonates with the memory of the massacre that bears his name. Whitman's counterpart in Colorado would prove to be Nathan Meeker.

Sixty-two years old in 1879, Nathan Cook Meeker was born in Euclid, Ohio. Eighteen of his ancestors had served in the Revolutionary War. Prior to arriving in Colorado Meeker had been a teacher, businessman, and journalist and had become a devoted believer in Fourierism, an early 19th-century philosophy based on the idea that society was best served by being broken up into small, self-sustaining groups. Meeker's higher education had been at Oberlin College, a church-allied institution that was instrumental in shaping the kind of man who arrived at White River. By 1865, Meeker had become an agricultural writer for Horace Greeley's *New York Herald*. Indeed, he had become something of a national authority on agricultural matters. Farmers from all across the nation sought his advice. The publication of two successful books, one on the experimental community at Oneida and another on life in the Mississippi Valley added to his laurels.

In 1869 Meeker headed west to study Mormon agricultural practices in Utah. The weather intervened, however, and his train was stalled by an enormous blizzard at Cheyenne, Wyoming. One could argue that it was destiny then that caused him to turn south toward Denver; destiny or snow. In any case, Meeker was soon intrigued by northeastern Colorado's vast potential. He returned to New York and persuaded Horace Greeley of the need to establish an agricultural community here. Greeley agreed. The site chosen would eventually be called Greeley. Here Meeker and his family remained for eight years. But if the community could be regarded as successful, Meeker's personal life left something to be desired. Heavily in debt, he applied for the agent's position at White River, obviously with the intention of clearing the slate and starting fresh. His application was accepted and he was assigned to White River. Although a religious man, Meeker had not been recommended by any religious denomination.

In retrospect, anyway, one can see how, given his educational background and philosophy of life, Nathan Meeker would soon encounter trouble at White River. Meeker firmly believed he was exactly the right person the assist the Utes in evolving into an agricultural society. Meeker believed that Native Americans needed two things: they needed to be *Chris-*

tianized and *agriculturalized*; the two went hand-in-hand. Indians were savages, and all Euro-Americans approached relations with Indians from that perspective. Nathan Meeker was no exception.

When Meeker started out for White River there was then no direct route across the mountains. Instead, following the route of supplies bound for the agency, he journeyed first to Cheyenne where he boarded a train for Rawlins and from that point by spring wagon to the agency, about 170 miles over extremely rough terrain. Meeker was followed by his sixty-four-year-old wife Arvilla (Arvella in some sources) and their twenty-two-year-old daughter Josephine, called Josie. The ladies were accompanied by Shadrach Price, Meeker's young master farmer and his wife Flora and their two children, Johnny and May. Several other workers from the Union Colony experiment at Greeley also came west to White River.

Slender and white-haired, Nathan Meeker appeared to the Utes as a sort of grandfather, and indeed they soon dubbed him Father Meeker. The new agent arrived at White River determined to turn it into an agricultural paradise. What he did not understand and appreciate at first was that the long, cold winters and short growing season made it tough to produce the kind of bountiful harvest he sought. The agency was located in a high valley through which ran the White River. The lower end of the valley was noticeably lower in elevation, which made it a bit more suitable for growing crops; it was known as Powell Park or Powell Valley, about three miles from the site of Danforth's original agency. The origin of the name Powell Park or Valley is not clear, but may have been in honor of John Wesley Powell. Meeker decided to turn Powell Park into an agricultural area. Irrigation ditches were dug by agency employees with occasional help from the Utes who were able to earn a few dollars for their labors.

Frustration set in early. Although the Utes did participate in spring planting they disappeared on annual summer hunts, leaving agency employees to irrigate and cultivate the crops. This did not sit well with Meeker who wanted to wean the Utes away from the old ways and concentrate on learning how to be farmers. If Meeker was irritated at the behavior of the Utes, many of them were equally annoyed at being forced to change their way of life. The villages of Antelope and Jack were located around the site of the original agency, while those of Douglass and Johnson were in Powell Park, which would soon prove a point of ignition.

The Utes had proved troublesome during the summer of 1878, killing a rancher after erroneously being accused of horse stealing, and now and again they were responsible for mischief in Middle Park, which in turn resulted in the killing of a Ute leader named Tabernash. Subsequently, a council of sorts to mend fences took place at Hot Sulphur Springs. The Utes, led by Douglass, Jack, Colorow, Washington, and Johnson pledged to return stolen property and for the moment anyway peace was restored.

Back at White River, meanwhile, Meeker was growing increasingly frustrated with Ute reaction to his policies, which is to say they mainly disregarded them. By contrast, the Meeker women seemed quite content with their role. Young Josie taught school for the Utes, and Arvilla often cooked meals for those Utes employed by the women to perform domestic chores. The Indians appeared to like and respect the women, but beneath the surface trouble was building. Some Ute leaders took it upon themselves to visit Ouray and complain about Meeker's methods. Knowing of Ouray's influence with the whites they asked him to request Agent J.B. Abbott at Los Pinos to convey their views to Washington, but for whatever reason, Abbott did not see fit to pass on the Ute complaints to higher authorities.

That Nathan Meeker had become more than a little disenchanted with his charges was evident in the articles he wrote criticizing their torpor and lack of morals As the winter of 1878–1879 eased into spring and summer there were increasing incidents of Ute mischief in the White River area, so much so that Meeker requested that a trading post be established on the reservation and asked for federal troops to keep the Indians from wandering off and committing further mischief, but apparently the requests were not judged important enough to be honored.[4]

The very dry summer of 1879 led to outbreaks of wild fires and there were reports of illegal logging in the area as well. To what extent the Utes were responsible for this is impossible to say, but since whites were busy logging and mining, it seems more likely that these activities were responsible for fires and the disappearance of wild game. There were also reports of houses being burned in North and Middle Parks and these were likely attributable to Ute mischief. The quasi truce established the year before had given way to more troubles, compelling settlers to take defensive precautions. In August, Governor Pitkin wrote to the Commissioner of Indian Affairs requesting military assistance, and about the same time another Ute delegation traveled to Denver to urge that Meeker be replaced. Their pleas were turned down.

Undaunted, though, Meeker pressed ahead with his determination to transform the Utes into farmers. Like so many other well-meaning 19th century Americans, Nathan Meeker was blinded with his obsession to turn weapons into ploughshares and this myopic vision would prove his downfall. But things might just have worked out anyway had Meeker not been so obsessed with transforming Powell Park into farm land. From the start, the Utes had resented Meeker's attempts to farm in that area. Chief Johnson's horse pasture was in Powell park and the area was a favorite spot for the Utes to hold horse races. A wiser man might have recognized how important this area was to the Utes and respected their views, but Meeker regarded it as government land and continued to dig irrigation ditches and build fences, thereby continuing to aggravate the Utes.

The sequence of events that opened the door to the Ute War is unclear and contradictory. One account has it that Chief Johnson and Meeker argued over plowing Powell Park and other matters. A fight ensued during which Meeker's arm was injured. Now fearful of trouble escalating, he requested military assistance. Yet another account has Meeker informing the Utes that they were going to be transferred to Utah and consequently no further rations would be issued at White River. In any case, this time Meeker's call for help was answered and resulted in a detachment troops being sent from Fort Fred Steele near Rawlins, under the command of thirty-six-year-old Major Thomas Tipton "Tip" Thornburgh.

Thornburgh, the commander at Fort Steele, left that post on the morning of September 22 with Company E, 4th Infantry, Companies F and D, 5th Cavalry, and E of the 3rd Cavalry, together with some twenty-five civilians who manned the supply wagons. In all, Thornburgh had about 200 men.

An 1863 West Point graduate, Thornburgh had seen action in the Civil War. A fine officer and reportedly a superior marksman, he had once nearly bested the legendary rifleman Doctor Frank Carver—the Spirit Gun of the West—in a shooting contest. Not long before the trouble at White River, Thornburgh had been one of several army detachments that tried to intercept Dull Knife's fleeing Cheyennes but failed to do so.

Thornburgh had received Meeker's initial request on September 16, six days before his departure from Fort Steele. However there had been no further word from the agency since then, so the major was heading into an uncertain situation. Although Thornburgh's orders called for him to provide support for the agency, exactly what that meant was unclear. If the Indians were attacking the agency his mission would be clear, but since that was not the case it was hard to know what he was supposed to do. In an effort to clarify matters, on the 25th he sent a communiqué to Meeker from what was to become the expedition's supply camp on Fortification Creek, asking for an update.

As Thornburgh's command approached the area they encountered a few Utes who inquired as to their purpose. The soldiers thought them friendly and perhaps these particular Utes were friendly, but quite a few Utes were more than a little angry to find soldiers approaching the reservation. Notwithstanding, on the night of September 27, Thornburgh advanced toward the reservation and bivouacked for the night. Here he was visited by Colorow and another Ute named Henry Jim. Accompanying the Utes was one of Meeker's employees with a message advising Thornburgh that the presence of the soldiers was making the Utes nervous, a strange reaction considering that the troops were there at Meeker's request. The agent asked Thornburgh to come in to the agency with just five soldiers, leaving the bulk of his command outside the reservation. Thornburgh may have suspected that Meeker was exaggerating the situation, since those Utes he had encountered seemed quite peaceably inclined.

The major was in an awkward position. His orders were to proceed to the agency, arrest any troublemakers and hold them until an Interior Department investigation could be convened, but Meeker apparently did not want to wait that long; he wanted Thornburgh to convene the inquiry, which was of course beyond the scope of Thornburgh's orders. Meeker might have made an effort to meet Thornburgh outside the reservation to discuss the situation face-to-face, but this seems not to have occurred to him. On the morning of the twenty-eight Thornburgh resumed his advance as far as Deer Creek. As it turned out, Meeker had not been exaggerating about the mood of the Indians; they were pumped up with war dances that lasted through the night of September 28, while the soldiers were bivouacked on Deer Creek.

The Battle of Milk Creek, September 1879

On the morning of September 29, after discussing matters with his staff, Thornburgh decided to ride into the agency with a small detachment. As the major and his detachment approached Milk Creek, not far ahead, and just outside the reservation boundary they were attacked by a Ute war party led by Colorow and Jack. The Utes opened fire on the soldiers from the hills and ridges overlooking Thornburgh's line of advance. The major himself was killed almost immediately. The remainder of the expedition fell back and formed a breastwork out of their wagons and horses that had already been killed. Caught in a position from which they could neither advance or retreat, the troops were pinned down here for six days while scout Joe Rankin rode the 160 miles back to Fort Steele for help.

The first relief reached Thornburgh's command in the form of a company of the 9th Cavalry under Captain Francis Dodge and welcome though they were, the addition of Dodge's troopers was not enough to break the siege. However, on October 5, Colonel Wesley Merritt reached the scene with five companies of the 5th Cavalry. Whether the Utes decided there were now simply too many soldiers to handle, or whether they were tired of fighting is not known, but in any case they produced a white flag and the siege was ended. The fight had cost the lives of Thornburgh and ten of his men. It had been a costly siege for the Utes who lost thirty-seven warriors.

With the siege ended, Merritt proceeded on to the agency. What he expected to find upon arrival is not known. The fight at Milk Creek and the death of Major Thornburgh had been completely unexpected, but the Utes fortunately elected to surrender, so Merritt had no reason to suspect anything was amiss. He must have been shocked when he reached the agency and found the dead, mutilated bodies of Nathan Meeker, nine employees and that of a visiting merchant. As had happened at Waiilatpu the pent-up anger that had been building in these Utes for months finally spewed forth in horrendous fashion. As for the women, it was soon learned that Arvilla and Josie, along with Flora Ellen and her children had been taken captive by Chief Douglass and were currently being held near the present site of Mesa, Colorado.

Faced with a serious hostage crisis, Merritt backed off on his pursuit of the Utes. Efforts to secure the release of the hostages began almost immediately. Charles Adams newly appointed special agent met with Douglass on October 21 and persuaded him to release the captives. It should be noted that not all the Utes supported the White River uprising; Ouray in particular was strongly opposed. When the captives were finally released they spent some time in Ouray's home, where they were well cared for by the chief and his wife Chipeta. Part of the lore that surrounds the Meeker Massacre includes the story that Ouray's sister, Susan, the wife of Chief Johnson, persuaded her husband to treat the captives kindly. Another story is that the Ute Persune had a crush on Josie and kept the women from being killed.

With the fight at Milk Creek over and the hostages returned it might seem as though there was nothing more to the Ute War, but in fact there was a great deal more. Reports of what had happened at White River spread quickly and fears of an Indian uprising filled the air. Settlers clamored for military protection and reinforcements were rushed to the area. Down from Wyoming came the balance of Merritt's 5th Cavalry. Up from New Mexico came General Edward Hatch with the 9th Cavalry, marching by way of Fort Lewis and taking up station at Animas City. And that was not all. Colonel Ranald Mackenzie leading six companies of his 4th Cavalry marched from Fort Clark, Texas, to Fort Garland. Over and above this, Governor Pitkin mobilized three regiments of state militia.

Especially in the aftermath of the Meeker tragedy most whites in Colorado viewed all Utes as dangerous. Many were of the opinion that the state would never be truly safe until all Indians had been exterminated or at least removed to some area where they posed no threat to the white way of life. It was a common reaction, one that typically followed in the wake of Indian troubles. It was, of course, an exaggerated reaction. The Southern Ute bands had not been at all involved. Ouray told the Uncompahgres to stay where they were and to not become involved, and most did just that. A few fled, however, to avoid fighting the soldiers which they were certain would happen. Most of the Northern Utes who had been involved in the Meeker tragedy disappeared like dry leaves in a strong autumn wind.

Anytime there was an event such as Sand Creek and White River it could be expected that the federal government would launch an investigation and they did exactly that in the wake of White River. Secretary of the Interior, Carl Schurz named General Edward Hatch, Special Agent, Charles Adams, and, interestingly enough, Ouray himself to investigate and report on the tragedy. Born in Germany the thirty-nine-year-old Adams' original name was Schwanbeck, which he changed at the time of his marriage in 1870. At the time of his appointment as special agent, Adams was an active duty army officer. A fair-minded man he cultivated a warm relationship with Ouray and Chipeta. Adams would later serve as United States Minister to Bolivia.

The new commission convened at the Los Pinos Agency in November 1879. Unfortunately, Ouray's deteriorating health prevented him from attending all sessions. As it should have been the commission's focus was on the massacre itself and not on the fight at Milk Creek. Thus, Colorow and Jack who had led the fight at Milk Creek were not charged with any part of the massacre events. Twenty-five Utes gave testimony, including Douglass, Johnson, Colorow, and others, while another fifty acted as policemen. A dozen Utes were singled out as perpetrators of the massacre, chief of whom was Douglass, who had personally held Arvilla prisoner. There was some evidence that two brothers, Antelope and Pauvitz had murdered Meeker, but the evidence against them was slim. The women captives could likely have said who killed Meeker, but tempers flared when the commission wanted the women to testify. This, said the Utes, was unacceptable. Ouray stood firm on the issue, too, even going so far as to say that Adams was no longer his friend. General Hatch then threatened to send soldiers to arrest Antelope and Pauvitz, but again the Utes, led by Ouray, drew a line that Hatch was finally reluctant to cross. Meanwhile, Douglass slipped away, to where no one knew and Ouray asked for a hearing in Washington where his friend Secretary Schurz would listen to the Ute words and respond fairly.

Meanwhile, the general public was ever loud in its declaration that the Utes needed to be removed, an attitude that was largely echoed by local newspapers and Senator Henry Moore Teller. Perhaps not surprisingly Meeker was lauded for his work. It would be too strong a statement to say that he was elevated to martyr status, but his murder served as leverage against the Utes. Despite the public outcry and the support of at least one United States Senator, a hearing was ordered to determine not only the guilty parties and their fate, but the ultimate disposition of the Ute tribe. Accordingly, in October 1879, Ouray, Chipeta and eight other Utes, in company with their agent, set out for Washington. En route they were threatened by lynch mobs at Alamosa and Pueblo. Clearly the Colorado populace was angry. Notwithstanding, the Ute party reached Washington safely and without further incident.

On the 15th, the hearing got underway. Testimony was taken from Josie Meeker and others, but it provided little additional information that would change the picture of what was already known about the tragedy. The commission decided that all twelve of the Utes charged with criminal behavior should appear before the commission and accordingly, Charles Adams was directed to bring those Utes to Washington. However, only seven of the dozen could be found, or perhaps the other five simply refused to go. Douglass was one of the seven, but owing to his culpability in holding the Meeker women hostage, Adams arranged for him to be imprisoned at Leavenworth en route to the capital.

The fact that the whole Meeker business was given a hearing in Washington is interesting in and of itself. Ordinarily, such an event would have resulted first in military action, followed by punishment to guilty parties, and lastly by removal to a new location that would not interfere with white settlement, and indeed all of the above did happen with the Meeker tragedy, but what set it apart was the federal government's agreeing to hold hearings in Washington to investigate the causes of the tragedy and then decide on an appropriate course of action.

While in Washington, the Utes shopped, visited important sights, and Ouray received medical attention. He was afflicted with kidney disease and was told he had not long to live. By March the commission, composed of George Manypenny, former Commissioner of Indian Affairs, Alfred B. Meacham, John Bowman, and the influential Colorado railroad builder, Otto Mears, had completed its hearings and on the 6th Ute leaders agreed to a major shift of their tribe. The White River band would remove to the Unitah Reservation in Utah. The Uncompahgre band would move to an area along the Grand River, while the Southern Utes would relocate to an area along the La Plata River in Colorado. The Utes were to receive annuities for a period of twenty years. The captives and families of the White River victims were also to be compensated. The agreement was ratified by Congress on June 1, 1880. Four months later, on October 24, Ouray succumbed to the ravages of kidney disease.

Sporadic clashes between Utes and Coloradans continued for the next two years, but the serious trouble was over. The relocation of the Utes did not happen immediately, but finally in late summer 1881 the Commissioner of Indian Affairs decreed that the time had come for the Utes to begin their removal to Utah. And so the removal began in a long march reminiscent of the Navajos "Long Walk" to the Bosque Redondo.

The Ute War of 1879, while far from being as costly as other Indian-white conflicts, resulted in freeing Colorado's high country and Western Slope from further interruption of the development of its rich mineral resources. For Coloradans it was a win-win situation; it was not so for the Utes. The Unitah Reservation did not prove to be a happy location for the White River Utes. Today, the Southern Utes and the Ute Mountain band occupy small reservations in extreme southwestern Colorado, a far cry from the vast area they once called home.

The Sheepeater War, 1879

Although the war with the Bannacks and their allies had technically ended, trouble developed up in central Idaho in 1879 with the band of Western Shoshones called Sheepeaters who had been allied with the Bannacks in that conflict. The Sheepeaters were a small band, numbering only 300 at best, and as previously noted, they had earned their sobriquet because of their proficiency in hunting Rocky Mountain Sheep.

As so often happened, trouble developed in 1878 when settlers accused the Sheepeaters of stealing horses in Indian Valley and killing three settlers near present day Cascade, Idaho, during the settlers' pursuit to recover stolen horses. In August the Indians were accused of killing two prospectors in an ambush at Pearsall Creek, five miles from Cascade. And the incidents continued. In February 1879 the Sheepeaters were accused of murdering five Chinese miners at Oro Grande, and committing another murder at Loon Creek. As winter turned to spring, two ranchers were killed on the South Fork of the Salmon River. Although there was no evidence to support the allegations, Sheepeaters were implicated in all these killings and once again it brought forth the Army to settle matters.

Two detachments were ordered into the field with instructions to rendezvous at Payette Lake, near present day McCall. The principal unit was once again led by Captain Reuben Bernard who marched north from Boise Barracks with G Troop, 1st Cavalry. Meanwhile, a detachment of Company K, 2d Infantry under 1st Lieutenant Henry Catley, meanwhile, marched south from Camp Howard. Twenty Indian scouts commanded by Lieutenant Edward Farrow, 21st Infantry headed east from the Umatilla Agency.

From June to September the troops pursued the Sheepeaters through the incredibly rough terrain of the Salmon River country and with little success. On August 20 a dozen or so Sheepeaters attacked a pack train escort on Big Creek. The defenders managed to drive off the raiders, suffering only one casualty in the skirmish. The short-lived campaign ended in October when Lieutenants W.C. Brown and Edward Farrow negotiated the surrender of the Sheepeaters, who had gained little but made some noise.

VIII

The Desert Southwest

Prologue: West of South and South of West

The late novelist Jack Schaefer once described the American Southwest as being west of south and south of west, and if such a definition leaves something to be desired in terms of accuracy the simple beauty of the expression more than suffices for any lack of geographical precision.

Indian-white conflicts in this harsh, arid land "south of west and west of south," occurred for the most part in what was called Apacheria, domain of the several bands of Apaches who dwelled in the rugged mountains and desert of southern Arizona and southwestern New Mexico. True enough, the fingers of the Apache domain reached eastward across southern New Mexico and beyond to the banks of the legendary Rio Bravo, but with the exception of the escapades of Victorio, Apacheria, at least for the purposes of this book, will essentially consist of southern Arizona and that part of southwestern New Mexico, along the headwaters of the Gila River.

Although the scope of this narrative primarily concerns itself with Indian-white clashes that occurred within the forty-eight contiguous states, one cannot write about the Apache wars without at least some reference to clashes south of the border, notably in the states of Chihuahua and Sonora. Indeed, one cannot even possibly hope to understand the challenges involved in campaigning against the Apaches without an appreciation of the incredibly rugged and tortuous terrain of the Sierra Madres: at once remote and forbidding, composed of steep, nearly impassable (except for an Apache) canyons (called *barrancas*), high peaks, and a lunar-like landscape. Of all the western Indian wars, the ongoing effort to subdue Apache raiders—mainly the Chiricahua band, of which more in a moment—this was the only Indian-white conflict that involved two countries.

True it was that the mid–1870s saw Colonel Ranald Mackenzie cross the Mexican border on his campaign of retaliation against Lipan Apache raiders, but these were isolated campaigns, whereas the U.S. Army's efforts to control Apache raiders in the desert southwest often found U.S. troops operating below the border for extended periods, sometimes with the tacit approval of Mexican authorities, but not always. And here it should be noted that U.S. efforts to end the Apache menace—as many locals viewed it—involved more U.S. troops against fewer Indians than in any of the other Indian wars of the West.

Farther west, beyond the boundary of Apacheria, where the Yuma and Colorado Rivers joined forces, there was trouble with the Yuma and Mojave tribes, and while some of these disagreements could be nasty affairs they paled in comparison to those with the Apaches.

Outposts on the Colorado: Clashes with the Yumas and Mojaves, 1849–1858

In the extreme western part of present Arizona, the desert dwelling Yumas and Mojaves proved more than a little troublesome to California bound travelers. After the discovery of gold in 1849, the Yuma crossing at the confluence of the Gila and Colorado Rivers became especially important as the gateway to southern California.

The Yumas who could muster no more than 300 warriors on a good day were an enterprising lot if nothing else. When Argonauts came trudging across the desert, bound for California, the Yumas, seeing a good thing, opened a ferry across the Colorado River. Unfortunately for them, some white men also recognized the potential here drove the Yumas off and took over the operation. But turnabout is fair play and in due course the Yumas struck back, wiped out all but three of the white men and reclaimed their operation.[1]

When news of the Yuma attack reached San Diego, Governor Peter Burnett directed Major General Joshua Bean [older brother of the infamous Judge Roy Bean, law west of the Pecos] commanding the state militia to assemble a force and punish the Yumas. Accordingly, a company of 60 [one report says 150] from San Diego and Los Angeles Counties under Quartermaster J.C. Morehead reached the river crossing in July 1850.

The volunteers were spoiling for a fight. Although the situation had quieted down by the time Morehead arrived, they did manage to kill one Yuma and destroy Indian crops. Morehead let it be known that he was interested in parleying, but the Yumas had something else in mind. Shortly, 150 of them attacked Morehead's camp with bows and arrows. Twenty Indians lost their lives in the attack, while inflicting little damage on the volunteers who quickly sought refuge in a stockade built by the second owners. The Yuma leader reportedly put in an appearance the following day and looked things over, but no words were exchanged with Morehead, and shortly the Yumas retired, apparently not interested in continuing hostilities. Although it hardly deserved to be called such, the action here cost the state $76,000 and came to be known as Morehead's War.[2]

Meanwhile, a decision had been made to establish a permanent post at the river crossing and in October 1850, Major Samuel P. Heintzelman left San Diego to carry out that order. En route, Heintzelman met Morehead and his volunteers returning to San Diego. Heintzelman's column reached the crossing in December and set up camp. The men were quartered in brush *jacales* while building a permanent post on a nearby high point. Called Camp Yuma at first, the name was later changed to Fort Yuma after the permanent post was completed in June 1851, at which time Heintzelman returned to San Diego, leaving one-armed Lieutenant Thomas Sweeney in command. If it was nothing else, Fort Yuma was difficult to supply. Due to the long trek across the desert, overland supply was not feasible, leaving the river as the only practical way, but this, too, presented difficulties and in a few months the army decided it wasn't worth the candle, abandoned the post, and the garrison returned to San Diego. However, Indians continued to molest travelers, prompting Heintzelman to have another try at re-establishing Fort Yuma. The previous garrisons had lacked sufficient manpower to take action against the Indians, but this time Heintzelman was determined to take enough men to put an end to the problem. If the Indian problem could not be resolved, travelers would be denied the use of this river crossing and that was simply unacceptable. So Heintzelman faced two challenges: controlling the Indians meant maintaining Fort Yuma, which in turn required development of a river-supply system.

By spring 1852, Heintzelman had two companies of the 1st Dragoons under Major

Edward Fitzgerald on station, along with Sweeney and his command, reportedly an unruly lot and no doubt made all the more so by having to return to the hated post on the Colorado River. But at least, it appeared they would have supplies if nothing else. Fitzgerald, with a detachment of forty dragoons marched downstream to open communication with the steamer *Sierra Nevada*, which had come down from San Francisco with supplies but the closest it could get to the post was seventy miles. It was a two-day trek for the dragoons, during the course of which they were attacked by an estimated 200 Yumas. The command was forced to dig in and fought through the night, losing the horse guard, consisting of a sergeant and eight men. Once more the Yumas disappeared and Fitzgerald returned to Fort Yuma, where Heintzelman added another seventy men to his [Fitzgerald's] command, which immediately returned to the scene of the fight, buried their dead comrades and moved on to rendezvous with the *Sierra Nevada*.

In March 1852, Heintzelman organized a three-pronged punitive expedition. Number one column of forty men composed of Fitzgerald's dragoons and number two column under Captain Delozier Davidson, who had a like number of men in his command, was to examine the country between the Colorado and Gila Rivers, while column number three marched up the right bank of the Colorado and intercepted any Indians that the first two columns might drive their way. It was all pretty much an exercise in futility. Lieutenant Sweeney later wrote that they went where no white men had ever been and perhaps that counted for something. Despite their efforts, the Indians had little trouble avoiding the soldiers, mainly because the troops had no idea as to where they were going. Notwithstanding, they did manage to burn a couple of villages and destroy some planting ground. Eventually, a shortage of supplies compelled all three columns to return to Fort Yuma, where sporadic Indian troubles managed to occasionally occupy the troops through the remainder of 1852, but it mostly was a hated duty post: isolated, boring and humid along the river bottom, prompting more than a few desertions.

In the wake of another campaign, with the Yumas pressed hard by the soldiers, a council was convened at the fort on October 2, during the course of which the Indians, weary of being harassed by the soldiers agreed to coexist peacefully with the whites. They had been led astray, they claimed, by the bad leadership of Pascual I, a notoriously recalcitrant head man, killed by a gunshot wound. He was succeeded by Pascual II, who appeared more kindly disposed toward whites. On October 11, Major Heintzelman officially proclaimed hostilities with the Yumas to be at an end.

But life at Fort Yuma wasn't altogether boring, even when they weren't chasing Indians across the desert. Two weeks after Henitzelman declared hostilities at an end, a fire destroyed the post commissary, which included ammunition for the rifles and pistols, and powder for the cannon. After that episode it was decided that a brush *jacale* was probably not a reliable structure for storage and it was replaced by a stout, new adobe structure. This was not good news to a garrison still waiting for a steamboat load of supplies. Fortunately, a wagon train from San Diego brought some relief, and on December 3, a steamboat finally put in an appearance. Scarcely a month after the commissary fire a powerful earthquake shook the area, frightening the soldiers more than boredom, hunger, or Indians. The Yumas, for their part, shrugged it off and assured the soldiers that this sort of event happened frequently.

Meanwhile, 150 crow-flight miles upstream from Fort Yuma, were the Mojaves, the most powerful and war-like of the river dwelling tribes, numbering perhaps 1,500 souls. The Mojaves claimed a cultural affinity to their downstream cousins, belonging to the Yuman language family. Historically, they were called "people by the water." As far as is known, the missionary Fray Francisco Garces was the first white man to establish contact with the Mojaves in 1775. The good padre called them Jamajab and thought them a handsome and healthy people. In 1781 Garces would be murdered by those loving souls and afterward, canonized by the Roman Catholic Church. Half a century later mountain men Jedediah Smith and James Ohio Pattie made contact with the Mojaves and the meetings were not cordial. A failure to understand the Mojave concept of life and plain rudeness on the part of the trappers led to stiff fights with heavy casualties on both sides. Because of their geographical location, the Mojaves escaped the initial pressure of west-bound travelers during the gold rush period. Then, in 1851 Captain Lorenzo Sitgreaves reached Mojave country on an exploring expedition, followed three years later by Lieutenant Amie Whipple, whose expedition mapped a railroad route from Arkansas to the Pacific. Whipple seems to have established a rapport with the Mojaves, whom he thought a genial folk. Others, however, claimed they were head-hunters who prized girls and young women as captives.

The so called Mormon War of 1857 affected Fort Yuma peripherally in two ways: first, although the navigability of the Colorado River along its northern reaches was questionable, it was nevertheless viewed as a possible conduit for funneling troops and supplies upstream, as close as possible to Utah. Secondly, it was believed by some that Mormon agitators were trying to foment trouble with the river tribes as a means of disrupting U.S. efforts to establish order among the tribes, so here again, just as in the Pacific Northwest were rumors of Mormons stirring up trouble.

By 1858, it looked as though there might be a second crossing site of the Colorado River when Lieutenant Edward Beale (a former naval officer, oddly enough) having followed Whipple's old trail, explored a route across northern New Mexico, eventually reaching a point on the river just north of present Needles, California. Interestingly enough, on his trek, Beale employed a dozen camels that then Secretary of War Jefferson Davis had imported to the Southwest on an experimental basis. An energetic and able man, Beale had been appointed Indian agent for California back in 1852 during the Mariposa troubles. Beale's Crossing or Beale's Route, as it came to be called, did experience some emigrant traffic, but most of these trains found that when they reached the Colorado River, the lay of the land compelled them to strike south anyway and cross the river at Yuma Crossing. In the spring of 1858, the first train to try Beale's Route was subsequently attacked by a large party of Mojaves, and endured a lengthy siege before finally retreating all the way to Albuquerque.

Beale had recommended that a fort be built at this point on the river, and now, as a result of the attack on the wagon train and pursuant to Secretary of War John Floyd's directive, Camp Colorado was founded at Beale's Crossing. Accordingly, in December 1858, Colonel William Hoffman, with a company of dragoons set out from Los Angeles on a reconnaissance mission. The aggressive Mojaves sniped at the column along the way and in a fight on January 9, lost a dozen warriors. After returning to Los Angeles, Hoffman, under orders from his department command, General Newman Clarke, assembled a force of seven hundred, part of which went overland and part by water. Rendezvousing at Fort Yuma, the combined force then marched upstream to establish a new post to be called Fort Mojave. According to historian Robert Utley, after seeing the size of Hoffman's force, the Mojaves quickly agreed to behave and thereafter proved tractable.

In April 1852, Congress managed to set aside funds to provide for a permanent Indian agent in California and appointed Edward F. Beale to the post. Beale, recommended that Congress set aside five separate areas for Indian use. Beale envisioned a plan whereby the Indians would be placed on federal land there to take up farming. These areas would not be permanent as under the terms of a treaty, but would be rather temporary. Under this arrangement the government could feel free to shift the occupants to another site as needs dictated. The plan was first approved, then rejected, then finally authorized in a modified form that created four permanent reservations by 1856.

Apacheria

> *In the days of their hostility the Apache Indians were the most expert thieves in the world, and in waylaying a miner, ranchman, or traveler they had few equals and no superiors.*[3]

Apacheria! None of the other locales in the Western Indian wars was christened with its own sobriquet. If it is no less important to have an appreciation of Apacheria's topography it is no less important to understand the hatred—indeed the loathing—that Apaches felt for Mexicans, especially the Sonorans. This animosity had been fueled by generations of savage and brutal raids and betrayals. And in fairness, it should be noted that Mexicans held a deep and abiding fear of Apache raiders, who struck their villages like a thunderclap in the night to plunder, rape, and take captives. Hatred walked both sides of the street.

And what of these people we call Apaches? Anthropologists classify them as the southern branch of the Athapascan linguistic family, the other two being the northern and Pacific Coast branches. Apaches were linguistically related to the Navajos and at some far distant time, the two may have been as one. It has been suggested that the name "Apache" comes from a Zuni Indian word meaning enemy, which, considering their war-like nature, is probably a fitting appellation. Like other North American tribes, however, Apaches tended to call themselves "dine" or "inde," meaning man, or some variant of that word. There is no real consensus as to when the Apaches arrived in the American southwest, but in any case they were well established in the region by the time the Spanish arrived in the 16th century.

Seven major divisions make up the Apache nation. The Jicarilla (Hik a ree ah), Lipan, and Kiowa Apaches comprise the easternmost tribes. Navajo, Mescalero, Western Apaches (sometimes referred to as Coyoteros) and Chiricahuas making up the western branch. Of these, it was the Chiricahua tribe that was best known and the one that was most actively engaged in warring with the Mexican states of Sonora and Chihuahua and later North Americans, although from time to time the others were also active against both sides.

The White Mountain tribe, whose territory embraced most of northeastern Arizona, was the largest of the Western Apache groups. Four other tribes were found within the larger Western grouping: the San Carlos, Cibicue (Seeb-a-q), the Southern Tontos, and the Northern Tontos. To the east, the Mescaleros occupied the Sierra Blanca Mountains of southern New Mexico, while the Jicarillas were found in the northern reaches of New Mexico.

As noted earlier, the Chiricahua—known locally by whites as Cheery-cows—was the most prominent of the Apache tribes and the one that was by far the most aggressive in its dealings with both the U.S. and Mexico. It was composed of four bands: the Chihenne (Chee-hennie); also known as the Red Paint people, who lived in the rugged fastnesses of the Mogollon (Muggy-own) Mountains of southwestern New Mexico. Within the Chihenne structure were four sub-bands: Warm Springs, Copper Mine, and Mogollon were so named because of the particular locale where they lived. The second of the Chiricahua tribes was the Chokonen (Cho-ko-nen) whose territory was southeastern Arizona, in the Dragoon Mountains—this was the band of Cochise. The third and smallest of the Chiricahua bands was the Bedonkohe (Bee-don-ko-hee), Geronimo's people. Finally, the fourth band of Chiricahuas was the Nednhi (Ned-knee) who mostly lived in the rugged Sierra Madre Mountains of northern Mexico.

The best known—and feared—Apache leaders were from the Chiricahua tribe: Mangas Coloradas, Cochise, Juh (pronounced Who by most whites), Victorio, and of course, Geronimo, who historian/biographer, Robert M. Utley argues is the best known of all North American Indian leaders, despite the fact that Geronimo was never actually a leader, but rather a warrior who somehow seemed to attract a following.[4]

Military operations against the Apaches were not quite the same as conducting campaigns against other tribes. With one or two possible exceptions there was never any real coalition of the Apache bands comparable, for example, to what confronted Custer on the Little Bighorn. The U.S. Army's operations against the Apaches tended to consist of small detachments, often accompanied by friendly Indian scouts, heading off in pursuit of a raiding band of Apaches.

It is more than a little important to bear in mind that Apache raids and depredations were usually committed by a particular band that followed the leadership of one chief or renowned warrior, and names quickly become confusing when attempting to identify exactly which Apaches were involved in what incident.

Apaches conducted raids for one of two reasons: first to plunder; to replenish supplies: food, weapons, ammunition. Horses were always needed, and captives seized in these raids were kept as slaves. Such raids as these were usually carried out by smaller parties. If an attack was a reprisal to avenge some wrong the attacking party tended to be much larger and perhaps composed of warriors from more thanone band.

It has been said that Apache men were born to war; from childhood they learned the skills necessary to survive in the harsh environment of Apacheria, and they learned the ways of fighting; of war. Whether they were born to be warriors more so than any other group of Native Americans is arguable. What is not debatable is that they were fierce fighters, superb horsemen, and pre-eminent raiders.

THE APACHE VERSUS THE SPANISH

Hostilities between Apaches and Spaniards began with the Spanish arrival in the region in the late 16th century. Early on Spanish livestock became a tempting target for Apache raiders, and as the Spanish responded, enmity grew and hostilities increased. During the next 130 years or so raids and retaliations mounted in intensity, with neither side gaining an upper hand, though Spain had rather come to recognize a hard truth, namely that complete subjugation of the Apaches was an exercise in futility. This realization prompted Spanish officials to consider a more humane approach, resulting in what was known as the Regulation of 1729, and which remained the de facto policy for the next four decades. Notwithstanding Spain's efforts to make the new policy work, it never took hold, mainly because the Apaches had by this time come to neither fear the Spanish, or more importantly, trust them.

By the middle of the 18th century, however, Spain was compelled to face the truth and issued a revised policy, this one dubbed the Regulation of 1772. The new policy, strangely ambivalent in design, sought to wage total war on the one hand, while clinging to some aspect of its earlier humane approach on the other. The Regulation of 1772 left a great deal to be desired, and actually resulted in an increase in hostilities. With the proclamation of the new policy, Spain came out swinging in its war against the Apaches and as the century drew to a close, many of the Apache bands had come to see some wisdom in submitting to Spanish demands, and so in 1790, both sides agreed to a truce that lasted for the next three decades.

If the truce of 1790 suggests a period of peace and quiet in Apacheria, let it be noted that during the first two decades of the 19th century there were, nevertheless, moments of fierceness and dread among both Apaches and Spaniards, for there were always incidents to remind all parties that serious outbreaks always lurked just below the surface.

About 1803 Spain established copper mines at Santa Rita del Cobre in southwestern New Mexico. Located in the heart of Chihenne territory, this area was to become a trouble spot in the years ahead. Although the Spanish, recognizing that their intrusion into this area would prove prickly, made a strong effort to appease the Apaches, and although the Chihennes were somewhat pacified by Spanish efforts they never truly accepted the Spanish intrusion here.

Indeed, within four years a large war party attacked the copper mine operation, killed several workers and ran off Spanish livestock. Indian reaction to the mines reflected Apache discontent with the activity generated by the mines. For the Apaches there was a basic economic concern here. The mining activity resulted in competition for the natural resources of the area. Spanish presence, for example, impacted the local game population. The Spanish presence at Santa Rita also heralded an increase in raids south into Sonora. Meanwhile, periodic raids against Santa Rita persisted.

Notwithstanding the raids and counter-strikes the relationship between Spanish and Apaches was often a curious one. The states of Chihuahua and Sonora, particularly the former sometimes traded rations to the Apaches in exchange for protection. In other words we feed you and you leave us alone. At times the Apaches rather forced this arrangement when they were short on food and other provisions the villages might be able to supply. Call it a form of protection. However even after agreeing to a quasi-peace with one village, the Apaches were not above turning around raiding another village on the other side of the mountain.

Despite the fact that Apaches raided Santa Rita del Cobre during the early part of the 19th century, the Chihennes asked the Spanish for permission to live in the area. Of course this had been Chihenne country long before the Spanish arrived on the scene, but the Spanish now regarded the territory as theirs. Regardless, the Spanish saw a certain benefit here. Spanish authorities were attracted to the proposal because it meant they would no longer have to issue rations, so they agreed, to the request providing the Indians set up their *rancherias*—what Apaches called their villages—along the Gila River and not around Santa Rita itself. However, the notion of not having to issue rations fell apart soon enough and Spanish commanders soon found themselves issuing rations anyway. Another factor influencing the picture was the Mexican Revolution which was gaining momentum, forcing Spain to withdraw its garrisons from the north to combat the revolution; as a consequence, Spain had fewer rations to issue to the Apaches.

The Apache versus Mexico

In 1821, the revolution that had been ongoing for a decade finally achieved success when Mexico gained its independence from Spain, but Mexico's new found freedom changed little in terms of its relationship with Apaches. For one thing, the cost of the revolution had drained most of the treasury, forcing the new government to cut back drastically, and that included rations to Apaches. Mexico also relaxed rules about foreigners—namely *Norte Americanos* (North Americans)—from entering the country (namely the present day American Southwest), which naturally led to an increase in the arrival of trappers and opportunists seeking the perceived riches of Apacheria. Not surprisingly, the combination of reduced rations and more whites entering the southwest desert region, led to an increase in friction between Apaches and Mexicans.

The decade of 1820 saw an outbreak of Apache resistance that bordered on a full scale war. Recognizing the threat, Mexico dispatched troops into southern Arizona and for the time being anyway that tended to quell the Apache taste for battle. By 1826, however, Chiricahuas were back attacking Santa Rita, practically laying siege to the place. Despite the fact that they loathed both Spanish and Mexicans, the Apaches, as we have seen, continued to transact business with them. The Apaches possessed enough street smarts to not dismiss this opportunity out of hand, but there had been too many betrayals to believe the Mexicans were truly trustworthy; indeed each side was fully wary of the other.

The decade of 1830 brought with it yet another change of policy. No longer would the Mexican government provide rations and assistance to the Apaches. As a consequence Indian raids intensified in Sonora and Chihuahua. Within the Chiricahua tribe itself, a change was taking place as well. Some leaders eschewed the life of raiding, preferring a style of living based on a peaceful co-existence with the Mexicans, accepting their largesse whenever available. It was a position that seemed to disregard the emerging Mexican policy. But as always, a younger faction which continued to view Mexicans with loathing, favored a tougher stance.

Throughout the 1830s it was always chancy to say whether Apache-Mexican relations were truly peaceful, but one could fairly safely predict that if things were quiet today, a change would arrive tomorrow. Frustration over repeated killings and livestock thefts, prompted strong from both Chihuahua and Sonora sent strong retaliatory columns into southern Arizona and New Mexico. These counter-measures proved effective enough to bring about truce negotiations at Santa Rita in August 1832. An agreement was subsequently reached, but of course it failed to hold up and soon it was business as usual. Raids resumed and provoked counter-strikes, but it was nearly impossible to implement a system of defense that effectively thwarted the Apache menace.

Three years later another attempt to establish peace occurred at Santa Rita in 1835. A Chiricahua peace faction led by Juan José Compá, whom the Mexicans perceived as having more influence than he actually possessed, agreed to terms, but the faction was unsuccessful in persuading the hard-liners led by Mangas Coloradas—about whom more later—and others, to agree.

Accordingly, raids and retaliations continued until, finally, in 1835, the Sonoran government, no doubt frustrated in the extreme, decided to take things to the next level by offering a bounty for Apache scalps: one hundred pesos—roughly the equivalent of $100—for every Apache scalp over the age of fourteen; how exactly the age was to be determined was not specified. The same autumn that saw the installation of the bounty system, found a strong column of Mexican troops moving north into Arizona where it located and routed a large party of Apaches, reportedly killing as many as fifteen.

In 1837, one John Johnson, a white man living in Sonora, was authorized by Governor Escalante y Arvizu to hunt down and kill Apaches; hostile Apaches it was specified. It was an under-the-table arrangement. Johnson was a mercenary and what other assignments of a similar nature he had undertaken is not known, but reportedly his payment was to consist of one-half of whatever was taken from the Apaches his men killed, and no doubt included scalp bounties as well.

In April 1837, Johnson, leading a party of seventeen whites and five Mexicans set out on their deadly mission and quite by accident met up with Juan José Compá's band of Apaches in the mountains of southwestern New Mexico. Two days of trading and hail fellowship followed, but on the morning of the third day when the Apaches entered Johnson's camp for more trading they were greeted by a fusillade from a small cannon. Several Indians were immediately killed, and more followed when the traders opened fire with rifles. The five Mexicans who had accompanied Johnson's party had apparently pulled out earlier, wanting nothing to do with the betrayal. When the last shot had been fired, some twenty Apaches, including Juan José Compá himself lay dead. Governor Escalante y Arvizu would rue the day he ever contracted with John Johnson.

The Chiricahua response to this act of unbridled treachery was predictable. If the Sonoran government expected that the Johnson massacre would compel the Apaches to cease and desist from raiding and plundering they were soon disabused of that notion. Treachery was nothing new to the Apaches, but this seemed beyond the pale of the usual brand of treachery, and they retaliated with a vengeance, wiping out a wagon train of trappers and killing Mexicans wherever they found them.

Mangas Coloradas

The great Chiricahua chief Mangas Coloradas may have been present at the Johnson Massacre but in any event his wives seem to have been victims of Johnson's treachery. In any event, Mangas—he was as probably called Fuerte by the Mexicans—now approaching fifty years of age, had risen to the top level of leadership among the Chiricahua tribe; his name began to appear ever more frequently now in clashes with Mexicans and later, with Americans as well.

Mangas Coloradas would have been a giant in any era. Standing six foot five inches and weighing some 200 pounds it is easy to see how awesome he must have appeared to all who saw him, when a man six foot tall was considered above average height. But it wasn't just his huge physical stature that set him apart. Mangas was shrewd, intelligent, and a dynamic leader. He was unquestionably the mightiest Apache of his era. Born into the Bedonkohe band of the Chiricahuas, he later married a Chihenne woman, thereby expanding his sphere of influence within the greater Chiricahua band, and when his daughter later married Cochise he had familial ties to the Chokonens as well.

Not long after the Johnson Massacre, Mangas and his band wiped out a party of trappers led by a man named Kemp, following which Fuerte seems to have acquired a shirt with red sleeves, perhaps taken from one of the trappers in the party, and from this, insofar as we are able to determine, he acquired the name Red Sleeves, by which name he is best remembered to history, although some Mexicans at least probably continued to call him Fuerte.

By the end of 1837, the Chiricahuas were in full retaliation mode, wreaking havoc on both Sonora and Chihuahua. So fierce were the Apache onslaughts that the governors of the two states elected to strike Apache rancherias with all the force they could muster, using Santa Rita as a base of operations. So many things look so terribly promising on paper, as did this one, but like so many other well crafted plans this one, too, fell apart due to political issues and lack of money.

The Apaches, meantime, had been busy formulating plans of their own. It was, they decided, time to kick the Mexicans out of Santa Rita and reclaim that part of their traditional homeland. One very large party led by the noted war leader, Tapilá, would sweep down into Sonora to continue on the vengeance trail for the Johnson Massacre, while a second group led by Mangas and Pisago Cabezón planned to cut off the flow of supplies into Santa Rita, thereby forcing closure of the mines.

On March 30, 1838, Mangas and Pisago's party, judged to be some 400 strong, ran off the cattle attached to a supply train at Carrizalillo Springs in the Florida Mountains, near present Deming, New Mexico. The train had a strong guard and a furious fight soon developed with neither side gaining the upper hand, and the next day, following strained truce talks, the Mexicans agreed to abandon their wagons and return to Janos.

A widely circulated story had the Apaches investing Santa Rita and massacring the inhabitants, thereby compelling the Mexicans to abandon the mines. In fact, while the Apaches certainly killed some of the inhabitants it was only necessary to shut down the flow of supplies to achieve their objective. Meanwhile, the Apaches continued raiding down into Chihuahua and Sonora. Mexican regular army troops did enjoy some success against the raiders, but they were generally much too elusive to get pinned down. Then in 1839, Chihuahua decided to hire professional scalp hunters just as Sonora had done with John Johnson. The figure appointed to form a band of mercenaries was James Kirker, a veteran frontiersman who was familiar with Apaches; knew their ways. In December, Kirker's scalp hunters pulled out of Chihuahua City and a month later struck an Apache rancheria north of Janos, killing fifteen and capturing twenty others.

The Apaches then living around Janos had been led to believe that if they remained peaceful they need not fear reprisals. Now this, and more would follow. Indeed, during the next two years Kirker's bloody handed hunters, reinforced by more thugs—many from different nations—plus a few Shawnee Indians struck unsuspecting Apache camps, looting; and killing men, and capturing women and children.

But the Chiricahuas were not idle. A powerful war party led by Mangas swept down into Chihuahua, reportedly killing twenty-seven, wounding a number of others, and carrying off captives as well. But Chihuahua now had a new governor, one Francisco Conde who saw this as a road to nowhere policy. He ended the reign of Kirker's scalp hunters and decided to seek peace with the Chiricahuas. Mangas, however, scorned any such efforts, remaining bitter and vengeful over the deaths of his wives at the hands of John Johnson's mercenaries.

Some Apaches, weary of war, liked the sound of peace, even if Mangas did not. Meanwhile, raids against Sonora persisted and Mangas remained at the forefront of Apache leaders. Indeed, at this point there was no one who could eclipse him; he was the symbol of Apache resistance. Mangas, however, was not beyond reach. In 1843, a peace-maker named Lieutenant Antonio Sanchez Vegara, an officer of integrity and a man trusted by the Chiricahuas began to lay the groundwork for a new peace accord to which Mangas agreed that spring.

But this agreement, too, was destined to fall apart. Mangas made a concerted effort to live up to the terms of this latest accord, but other Apache leaders refused to honor the agreement and continued raiding as usual. An attack near Fronteras that resulted in the death of two men and the wounding of another, who happened to be a soldier, brought swift reprisal. The Mexicans struck back killing several Chiricahuas and even some Chokonens, neither band of which had been involved in the raid.

Although he had gone along with it, Mangas had never really been content with any of the peace agreements and terminated the most recent one in the summer of 1843, and by 1844 the Chiricahuas were raiding Sonora once again. Thus, the decade of the 1840s would become known to history as the bloody 40s. It is ironic that during these final years of the 1840s, even as they plundered Sonora, the Apaches continued to draw rations from what had become something of a sanctuary around Janos in Chihuahua. Following their raids elsewhere the Chiricahuas either retired to their rancherias around Janos, or headed north to the relative safe haven in the Mogollon Mountains in southwestern New Mexico.

The Norte Americanos

During the early part of the 19th century small groups of North American trappers began filtering into the southwest in search of beaver and other fur bearing mammals, but their numbers were too small to pose a threat to Native American tribes of the region, except as occasional targets of opportunity for Indian raiders.

The arrival in Santa Fe in August 1846 of General Stephen Watts Kearny with a 1,500-man column of troops from Fort Leavenworth, Kansas, marked the first real introduction to the American military for many Apaches, including Mangas Coloradas. The Apaches were also, unfortunately, introduced to measles, which assaulted U.S. soldiers as well.

The Mexican-American War of 1846–1848 and the discovery of gold in California shortly thereafter introduced a change in the region's demographics, bringing more people into Apacheria, but mostly there were travelers passing through, en route to somewhere else, at least at first. The Apaches of course, had already experienced Anglo scalp hunters such as John Johnson, which tended to make them leery of all *Norte Americanos*. At first, however, U.S. soldiers were here to fight Mexicans, which was just fine with Apaches. Eventually, of course, that picture would change dramatically, but for now Apaches need not be overly concerned with the blue coats.

As we have seen, the Mexican states of Sonora and Chihuahua, generally speaking, had different philosophies about dealing with Apaches. The former tended to pursue a more aggressive, hard-line policy, while Chihuahua leaned more toward appeasement.

Throughout this period, Mangas Coloradas remained the dominant Apache leader, strong, forceful and physically imposing. Preoccupied with the invasion of Mexico, the Mexican military leaders offered little opposition to Apache raiders, though there were occasions when a Mexican force would move into southern Arizona with retribution on its mind, as one such force did in September 1847 when it attacked a Chokonen rancheria in the Chiricahua Mountains.

On February 2, 1848, the United States and Mexico signed the Treaty of Guadalupe Hidalgo, which dramatically altered the ground rules governing Apache behavior. Essentially, the terms of the treaty granted to the U.S. all of present day New Mexico and nearly all of Arizona, plus Utah, California, and parts of Colorado and Wyoming. Only the southernmost strip of Arizona and extreme southwest New Mexico remained a part of Mexico, and that, too, would be added a few years hence with the Gadsden Purchase of 1854. The Treaty of Guadalupe Hidalgo and the Gadsden Purchase represented the final land acquisition that created forty-eight contiguous states of the Union.

The change of land ownership meant very little to the Native American tribes who inhabited the region. What did matter of course was how the policies of the new owner would affect them. We have seen what effect American ownership had in New Mexico, but to those Apache bands who dwelled in southwestern New Mexico and Arizona, and whose life style was so closely tied to the Mexican states of Sonora and Chihuahua, U.S. policy was going to have a very serious impact.

An important caveat of the Guadalupe agreement, at least insofar as the Mexicans were concerned, was that the Americans would assume responsibility for controlling the Apaches who lived north of the new boundary, and put an end to their raiding down into Sonora and Chihuahua. The Americans agreed to honor this, but with tongue in cheek, one imagines, since they knew full well the impossibility of keeping the Apaches out of Mexico, and of course they could not and did not.

In the dozen years between the end of the Mexican-American War and the Civil War, Apache raids into Mexico continued unabated. Initially, relations between Mangas and other Apache leaders and General Kearny were amicable enough, but as the rush to California got underway in 1849 it saw more Americans pouring through Apacheria, with many greedy and indifferent enough to Apache ways to create a basis for distrust, particularly when some Anglo Americans sought to reopen the long closed mines at Santa Rita del Cobre. However, most encounters between Apaches and Americans at this juncture tended to be non violent, but there were moments when blood was spilled. On August 16, 1849, for example, a company of the 1st Dragoons under Captain Enoch Steen had a sharp encounter with Apaches near Santa Rosa. The dragoons were successful in driving off the Apaches, but not before Steen himself was seriously wounded, reportedly by a white man who had gone over to the Apaches.

JOHN RUSSELL BARTLETT AND THE MEXICAN BOUNDARY SURVEY

In 1850, John Russell Bartlett, Canadian born, and a former New York bookseller who had written *Progress in Ethnology*, along with several other works of note, and who apparently had political connections, was appointed to head up a commission to establish the official boundary between the U.S. and Mexico. An honorable man who, like many 19th century Americans from the east Bartlett tended to view Native Americans through rose-colored glasses.

Bartlett's commission was to be a joint endeavor with a Mexican group. Bartlett and his team began work at El Paso, Texas, in November 1850 and arrived at Santa Rita del Cobre on May 13, 1851. With more than a hundred on his official staff, plus an army escort of around eighty-five, this represented a major invasion of the Santa Rita area, whose mines had been shut down since 1838. To say that the Apaches found this more than a little disturbing would be a decided understatement.

Bartlett held several meetings with the Apaches, including Mangas. It was during one of these gatherings that Mangas learned, probably for the first time, that Americans were now obligated to prevent the Apaches from raiding in Mexico. It is questionable to what extent Mangas understood the agreement though it seems likely he at least grasped the essence of it. Initially at least, Mangas appeared to be not overly concerned with Bartlett's words, and indeed even promised not to interfere with the Mexican commission that would be surveying the boundary from their side. Mangas seems to have developed a liking for Bartlett and agreed to some sort of truce. However, given his deep seated hatred of Sonora it is difficult to imagine Mangas agreeing to permanently ceasing all raids into Mexico.

In an effort to make the arrangement a little more palatable, Bartlett issued presents, including a handsome frock coat lined with scarlet to Mangas, along with a white shirt and red silk sash. Historian Edwin Sweeney, biographer of Mangas, tells us that the Apache leader wore the coat with great pride for a week until he lost it through gambling, a favorite Apache pastime.

The decade of the 1850s continued to be a time of uncertainty and high tension.

Notwithstanding their promise to Bartlett, the Apaches continued raiding down into Mexico, Sonora in particular. And there were incidents that always stood in the shadow of trouble, as for example when a party of New Mexicans arrived in Santa Rita with a Mexican girl who had been taken captive by some Western Apaches a year earlier and eventually wound up in the hands of these New Mexicans. Bartlett immediately turned to the army and demanded she be turned over to his commission. Surprisingly, the New Mexicans complied without a whimper, and Bartlett eventually saw the girl returned to her home. In yet another incident, two Mexican boys taken captive by the Chiricahuas appealed to Bartlett for sanctuary, to which Bartlett agreed. Angry, the Apaches insisted the boys be returned. Bartlett refused and tension rose, but eventually an arrangement was worked out whereby their freedom was purchased. Either incident could well have led to a serious confrontation. Fortunately, Bartlett's negotiating skills made it possible to avoid trouble.

Life in the southwest in the years following the Mexican-American War was a three-part arrangement between Mexicans, Americans, and Apaches, notably the Chokonen, Chihenne, and Bedonkohe bands of Chiricahuas. Depending on which band and whether it was Sonora or Chihuahua, the Apaches had one arrangement with the Mexicans and another with Americans. At any given moment the Apaches might be at war with either or both. It was complicated and confusing but necessary for American military commanders, Indian agents, and territorial officials to understand and appreciate the fluidity of the situation if they hoped to be effective in their respective roles, which unfortunately was often not the case.

Peace talks were frequent and sometimes bore fruit, but just as often did not and when they did tended to be of brief duration. In 1851, talks between Chokonens and Sonoran officials fell apart when it became clear to the Apaches that there would be no return of captive Indians. This, in turn, led to a large campaign in which some 300 Sonoran troops moved against Apaches at Apache Pass, a name that would later resonate during the Apache wars with the United States. During the course of this particular campaign, waged during the autumn of 1851, a number of Apaches were killed in surprise attacks and a number were taken captive. But each of these clashes always produced a counter-strike. Enraged, a large Apache war party, said to have numbered 200 or more, and probably led by Mangas, swept down into Hermosillo, Sonora and killed 30 Mexicans. Such incidents tended to fuel an environment of fear. One never knew whether the new day would usher in another bloody attack.

The Acoma Peace Agreement

There had been clashes between Apaches and the U.S. Army in New Mexico during the '50s, but in Arizona and around the headwaters of the Gila River in southwestern New Mexico, army relations with Chiricahua and Chokonens remained mostly amicable because the area was just beginning to be developed. Nevertheless, there were incidents from time to time that compelled the Americans to wave the flag and remind Apaches that they would not be leaving.

By 1852, Chiricahua losses to Sonorans made peace with the Americans highly desirable, and on July 11, Mangas signed a peace accord with General Edwin "Bull" Sumner at Acoma. Although Mangas was the only Chiricahua leader to sign the treaty, he was the most important. His willingness to do this demonstrated his strong desire to have peace with the Americans.

The Acoma agreement was important for a pair of reasons: first, the Americans demanded no land, which as we might imagine, appealed mightily to Mangas. After all, when was the last time Americans proposed a treaty that did not demand land ... or more land? There was a rub, however, and it called for a cessation of raiding south of the border. Here was that old chestnut again. This was unacceptable and of course, U.S. officials recognized the near impossibility of enforcing such a ban. However, Sumner's first responsibility was to ensure protection of the territory under his jurisdiction, and he may have whispered to Mangas that he would look the other way in the event Apache raiders slipped down into Sonora or Chihuahua.

On May 31, 1852, Sumner ordered the old Spanish presidio at Santa Rita del Cobre abandoned and moved to the Mimbres Valley. The new location offered a better source for water and communications; supposedly it would also enable the military to better monitor Apache activities along the Mimbres River. Whatever the reasons, Mangas approved of seeing soldiers depart from Santa Rita del Cobre.

As the 1850s progressed, Americans continued to arrive in ever increasing numbers, with farmers and ranchers settling along the Mimbres and Gila Rivers. Other Americans were employed by the Butterfield Overland Stage Company. If the Apaches were cognizant of such details, they would surely have been alarmed to learn that even as the number of Americans was on the rise, their own population was shrinking. Notwithstanding the increasing number of Americans, their presence had yet to really impact the Apache way of life and for this reason Mangas Coloradas continued to seek peace. However, as the decade deepened, Mangas grew increasingly disillusioned with American failure to deliver on the promises made at Acoma.

Although the Gadsden Purchase was signed in 1854, it was not until late 1856 that U.S. troops arrived in southern Arizona to replace Mexican troops who had returned to Sonora. This first contingent of U.S. troops was commanded by Major Enoch Steen, who, it will be recalled, as then Captain Steen had had a sharp encounter with Apaches near Santa Rosa back in 1849. Steen, an officer of long frontier experience, departed from Fort Thorn, north of present day Hatch, New Mexico, with four companies of the 1st Dragoons, in all some 300 officers and men, plus a number of civilian employees. Steen's orders were to construct a new military post at Tucson to be named Fort Buchanan in honor of the current president. Steen proceeded without, apparently, ever intending to construct a post at Tucson. Instead, he selected a site near Calabasas, only a few miles north of the border. His decision, it might be noted, did not sit well with the Tucson citizenry who had counted on the economic benefit to be derived from a local army post.

The Butterfield Overland Mail Route

In September 1858, the Butterfield Overland Mail Route began operations, replacing the San Antonio to San Diego Mail Company. Relay stations were established 20 miles apart. Overall, 141 stations were built along the company's 2,800-mile route. Recognizing that much of its route ran through hostile Indian country, Butterfield promoted a realistic Indian policy: stay away from the Indians if at all possible, but be prepared to defend the relay stations if attacked.

Mangas was not anxious to go to war with the Americans. By this time, too, Cochise had reached a level of some prominence as a leader and he was not interested in seeking war, either. Both leaders were well aware of the U.S. Army's ability to respond to Apache mischief with more vigor than the Mexicans.

In June 1858, a heavily armed American party, numbering a dozen, and led by a man with the most unusual name of Phocion Way was en route from El Paso to the Santa Rita mining region when it encountered an estimated 100 Apaches at a place with the foreboding name of Doubtful Canyon just west of Stein's Peak. Way recorded his impressions of the moment:

> They were truly a wild and fierce looking race [he said of the Apaches]. The men were almost entirely naked and the women not much better.... The old chief came after our wagon on his horse with his long lance in his hand. He shook hands with some of our party and appeared to be very friendly. He told us where we could get water and rode alongside of our wagon some distance.[5]

Historian Edwin Sweeney believes the old chief alluded to was Mangas and if so, it serves as a good illustration of Mangas's efforts to be friendly with Americans, though to be sure his rage against Mexicans, particularly Sonorans had not lessened. Indeed, there seemed to always be another incident to fan the coals of anger. In that same summer of 1858, for example, an Apache woman of the Chokonen band appeared at Fronteras, Sonora, asking for peace. Whether she had been selected as an emissary of some sort is not clear. In any case, discussions apparently followed, resulting in an understanding that Cochise and other leaders would return to finalize an agreement of sorts. What happened next is conjectural. Mexican sources claim that when the Apaches arrived a week later they were drunk and in a fighting mood. Other sources say the Mexicans furnished the Apaches with plenty of mescal; got them drunk, then proceeded to slaughter twenty-three.

The attack called for retaliation and accordingly, in September Mangas and Cochise assembled a war party that may have contained as many as 200 warriors, and around nine a.m. on the 15th struck Fronteras like a thunderclap. Mexican soldiers who were caught outside the presidio fled into the surrounding hills from where they managed to give a good account of themselves. Fortunately for Fronteras a small canon mounted atop the presidio wall served to help keep the Apaches honest and eventually force them to withdraw. Mangas returned to Arizona while Cochise remained in the area seeking less well defended targets of opportunity.

If Mangas made a genuine effort to avoid confrontations with Americans, and had been largely successful in doing so, a pair of events a year apart transpired to make it nearly impossible for him—and Cochise—to remain on quasi-friendly terms with the *Norte Americanos*. The first event occurred in the summer of 1860 with the discovery of gold at Pinos Altos near Silver City in southwestern New Mexico. The discovery brought a fresh rush of prospectors into the region. Mangas appears to have recognized potential trouble brewing and sought to keep his people from having any more contact with the Americans than necessary, but he was swimming upstream. As historian Edwin Sweeney points out, the increasing white presence altered the Apache way of life forever.

While many of the Americans began moving into the Santa Rita area to farm and ranch there was also the usual collection of adventurers, gamblers, and opportunists who tended to be rough, noisy, and at times troublesome, and it was the likes of these that tended to disturb amicable relations with the Apaches. Miners, in particular had a far greater impact on the region than the farmers and ranchers. In order to work the ground for precious minerals it was necessary to cut down trees and scare off the wildlife on which the Apaches depended for their livelihood.

Michael Steck

It will be recalled that the agent for the Mescalero Apaches (also the Gilas) was one Michael Steck. Fair-minded and hard working, Steck has to be regarded as one of the best

Indian agents on the Western frontier. During the summer of 1860, he journeyed to Washington on official agency business. Steck had long nurtured a dream of creating a reservation for Cochise and his Chokonens at Santa Lucia Springs, New Mexico, not far from Pinos Altos. Whether Cochise looked favorably on such an idea is not known, but it seems unlikely since the traditional Chokonen home was in the Dragoon Mountains of southern Arizona. Nevertheless, Steck appears to have clung to this dream and when he returned from Washington and broached the subject to Colonel Richard—Dick—Ewell, now in command at Fort Buchanan, he discovered that he had Old Baldy's—the sobriquet by which Ewell was known, and a future Confederate luminary—complete backing, probably because if should such a move actually take place, it would be easier to monitor Apache behavior.

Steck was pleased, of course, to know he had Ewell's backing, but he ran into trouble from an unexpected quarter. The swarming miners at Pinos Altos reacted vehemently to the idea of an Apache agency in their midst. Steck was stunned; this he had not anticipated. The miners petitioned him to cease and desist. Angry himself, Steck sent off a fiery letter to Superintendent James Collins, whose meek response was to take legal action; let the courts sort it out. Until then it was business as usual. The whole affair seems to have disgusted Steck who shortly resigned his position to enter the political arena where he became Arizona's territorial delegate to Congress. And so faded the Santa Lucia dream.

Superintendent Collins was not happy with Steck's abrupt departure, and the former agent, now *sans portfolio*, had made no arrangements for an interim replacement. Who would administer to the Apaches now? Who indeed? And there was mischief brewing, too. In December 1860, Chihennes living along the Mimbres River were suddenly attacked by a group of miners, angry over the continued presence of Indians in their mining region, never mind that the Indians had at least as much right to be there as the miners. Four Apaches died in the attack, several others were wounded, and a dozen women and children were taken captive. The unprovoked assault brought a quick response from Mangas who assembled a large war party and prepared to seek revenge.

Meanwhile, Major Isaac Lynde, who had been ordered to build a new post along the Mimbres River, had selected a site east of Pinos Altos which he called Fort Floyd (later Fort McLane). Lynde received word of the December 4 attack and, anticipating an Apache response, sent Lieutenant John Sappington Marmaduke to provide protection for local settlers. Marmaduke, who had studied at both Harvard and Yale before entering West Point, would soon cast his lot with the Confederacy and serve with distinction in the Trans-Mississippi theatre. In 1887, he would die as Governor of Missouri. In any event, at the same time he dispatched Marmaduke Lynde sent word to Agent Steck in Mesilla, but for some reason, Steck failed to take action, perhaps because this was about the time he was preparing to head off to Washington.

As it worked out, Marmaduke happened to encounter the miners with their Apache captives. Ordered to turn over their captives, the miners quickly complied. However, James Henry Tevis, instigator of the unprovoked attack, refused to return captured livestock, which, they claimed, had been stolen by the Indians. Marmaduke seemed uninterested in pressing the thing then and there and returned to Fort Floyd with eleven Apache prisoners; two of whom were children who were subsequently returned to their families. The Apaches were charged with thievery, the miners with nothing.

Meanwhile, newly arrived at Fort Floyd was Captain Matthew R. Stevenson, sent by Lynde to hold talks with the Apaches, of whom Mangas was the most prominent. The Apaches denied having any stolen property, but who could say what belonged to who when it came to horses. The Apaches had their own gripes. Mangas claimed that Agent Steck failed to live up to his promises, although it was not clear which promises he alluded to. In any event the matter rested there with nothing really accomplished in the way of resolution.

By 1860, Mangas was sixty-five, give or take, depending on what one accepts as his birth year. Although still a powerful force in the Chiricahua tribe, he found himself turning more and more to his son-in-law, Cochise. If Mangas's star was waning, that of Cochise was rising.

Although the discovery of gold at Pinos Altos was a pivotal event in Apache-American relations, the event that really incurred the wrath of the Apaches, especially Cochise, and insured that the two cultures would be at war for the next two decades, occurred in 1861.

War with the Americans: The Bascom Affair

If ever a single incident could be said to have triggered an Indian war it was one that occurred early in 1861. Ironically perhaps, as a divided nation was about to embark on a cataclysmic four-year struggle, out beyond the Mississippi, a smaller war, yet one no less brutal was about to commence in the far off desert southwest. The irony lies in the fact that this territory acquired as a result of the Mexican-American War became a hot button topic during the 1850s. The South felt the new territory should be open to the expansion of slavery, while Northerners—especially abolitionists—were exposed to such expansion, and thus did a nation go to war. Of course there was more to it than that, but how to admit the new territory acquired from Mexico was the major issue of the day.

The Bascom Affair—known to the Apaches as the cut-the-tent incident, the meaning of which will be made apparent shortly—had its origin on January 27 when raiding Apaches struck the ranch of one John Ward, a dozen miles south of Fort Buchanan. In addition to stealing a few head of cattle, the raiders grabbed a twelve-year-old boy named Felix, the son of a widowed Mexican woman living on the ranch. After her husband's death, Felix's mother lived with Ward, who may or may not have actually adopted Felix. In any event, the boy was taken in to the Apache band and became an Apache in spirit if not in name. Years later, he would work as a scout for the army, by which time he had come to be known as Mickey Free, but all of that was yet to come.

The following day, January 28, the commander at Fort Buchanan sent Lieutenant George Nicholas Bascom with a mixed force of infantry and dragoons in pursuit of the raiders. After some searching, Bascom located a trail that seemed to lead into Chokonen territory, which immediately cast suspicion on Cochise. who Ward was convinced had carried out the raid. Cochise, however, had nothing to do with the raid, let alone the abduction of Felix. Historian Edwin Sweeney believes the raiders were probably from one of the Western Apache bands.

By way of background, Arizona was then still part of the Military Department of New Mexico with headquarters in Santa Fe and the department's standing orders stipulated that Indian raiding parties should be pursued and punished. But the picture had gotten complicated with the outbreak of the Civil War and General Henry Sibley's invasion of New Mexico early in 1862. Sibley's invasion, coupled with Captain Sherod Hunter's attempted takeover of the motley collection of adobe structures called Tucson, prompted President Lincoln to send a force of volunteer troops from California to the southwest as a means of discouraging further Confederate designs on the region. Entrusted with this command was

Colonel James Carleton, who was destined to become the driving force behind the subjugation of the Navajos.

Thus was the stage set. Lieutenant Bascom's commanding officer at Fort Buchanan was Lieutenant Colonel Pitcairn Morrison. Morrison's whose orders to the young Bascom—he was totally without experience in dealing with Indians—were to follow the trail and recover stolen property, including the boy. If necessary, Bascom was to employ all the force at his disposal to execute his orders. It was an example of extraordinarily poor judgment on the part of the post commander to entrust such a mission to a young and inexperienced subaltern. The southwest would pay a fearsome price for Morrison's poor judgment. The Chiricahuas seldom took white captives; this was more a trademark of the Western Apache bands, a fact that Colonel Morrison ought to have been aware of.

In any case, as the poet says, "The moving finger writes," and Bascom's column reached Apache Pass around noon on Sunday, February 3. Here, they were joined by a second column of troops returning to Fort Buchanan from escort duty. The united column then proceeded to the Butterfield Stage Station, where they found two employees and a pair of Apache women. When questioned, the women claimed to know nothing about the boy and suggested the lieutenant go to Cochise's camp, then in Cochise Canyon.

Bascom then moved about a mile beyond the stage station, set up camp, and sent a messenger to the Apache rancheria, requesting that Cochise come in for a parley. Apparently the request also inquired as to the Ward boy, about whom Cochise had no knowledge whatever. When the chief did not immediately respond to Bascom's invitation a second messenger was sent. This time, Cochise did respond and came in to the army camp with his wife, two children, a brother, Coyuntura and a couple of warriors who may have been nephews. Obviously, Cochise anticipated no trouble.

Bascom invited the Apaches to dine with him and of course inquired about the Ward boy. Cochise replied that he did not have the boy, who he suspected was being held by Western Apaches, and asked for ten days in which to recover the boy. Bascom later claimed he agreed to this. There is, however, ample reason to believe that Bascom lied because rancher Ward testified that Cochise was informed that he and his party would be held as hostages until the boy was returned. The Apaches were then confined to tents, from which Cochise cut his way out by slicing through the tent and escaping. Soldiers fired at him as he ran and may possibly have wounded the chief as he ran up the hill. Thus, did the affair come to be known among Apaches as Cut the tent incident.

It would not be unreasonable to propose that Bascom likely believed at the outset that the Chokonens were guilty because popular opinion had already judged them so, and Bascom was too naive to have as yet formed any experienced-based opinion. Chokonens had after all been involved in any number of raids, so it was natural to see them as the ones who had made off with the Ward boy.

At any rate, in the immediate aftermath of Cochise's escape, the Chokonen leader appeared on high ground above the army position and asked to speak with his brother. At this juncture, Bascom still had an opportunity to mend some fences. Instead, his response was to unleash a volley of fire at Cochise who quickly disappeared but not before vowing revenge. Following this, Bascom withdrew to the stage station.

On the following morning, February 5, a Chokonen emissary appeared bearing a flag of truce. Cochise wished to parley with Bascom. The lieutenant agreed, and in company with a pair of sergeants and the rancher Ward, he met with Cochise and three Apaches a hundred yards or so from the station. One of the sergeants, Smith by name, was carrying a white flag. Cochise reiterated his earlier position that he did not have the Ward boy and pleaded for the release of the hostages. Bascom, however, insisted that the other Apaches would continue to be held as hostages until the boy was returned. Cochise again insisted that he was not holding the boy.

At this point, three Butterfield employees decided on their own that if Bascom was unable to resolve the crisis they would and accordingly moved toward the Apaches aiming to broker some sort of deal. Angry, Bascom ordered them back, but as they were not soldiers under his command he had no authority over them and they paid him no heed.

The three employees evidently had it in mind to arrange a hostage exchange, although exactly how they thought this might be pulled off is unclear, since Bascom had made it clear he would honor no such agreement unless the Ward boy was returned. What followed is a confusing chain of events. As the three men—Wallace, Culver, and Welch—entered a ravine they were attacked by Apaches. Welch and Culver managed to break free and return to the station. Wallace, however, was taken prisoner. Meanwhile, the Apaches also opened fire on Bascom's party. The soldiers fired back and intermittent exchanges continued on into the evening.

For a few hours the status quo remained unchanged, but then early on the afternoon of the 6th, Cochise again appeared on a hill above the station. With the chief, was Wallace his hands bound and a rope around his neck. Thus far, Cochise had made no effort to attack the station, which he easily could have destroyed and wiped out Bascom's entire command, but he was undoubtedly thinking about the hostages and much preferred to make the whole episode disappear without a fight if at all possible.

Cochise now offered to exchange Wallace together with a herd of government mules in return for the Apache hostages. Historian Edwin Sweeney suggests that Bascom was more than a little angry at Wallace and his companions for creating the present situation and in any event held a hard line, refusing to release the Apache hostages until the Ward boy was returned. And there the matter stood until mid-afternoon of February 6—it was a Wednesday. To further complicate matter, at this point the east-bound stage and an east-bound wagon train entered the picture and prepared to play a role in the unfolding drama.

The wagon train, operated by one José Montoya was loaded with flour and bound for Las Cruces. Ordinarily, Montoya's trains passed over Apache Pass with no trouble from the Apaches who usually did nothing more than ask for hand-outs. Today was different. This time the Apaches surrounded the train, captured nine Mexicans and three Americans. The Mexicans were tied to the wagon wheels, tortured and killed, while the three Americans now became hostages. With four Americans, Cochise now figured to have enough leverage to bargain for the release of the Apache hostages.

Ahead of schedule by several hours, the east-bound stage had left Tucson the morning of February 5. No word of the Bascom affair had yet reached Tucson, so for all intents the passengers anticipated nothing more than a hot, dusty, and bumpy ride. Nearing the crest of Apache Pass in the mid-winter darkness the driver and passengers were jolted out of whatever sleep they may have been enjoying by the sound of gunfire which wounded the driver and killed a mule. As it happened, line superintendent, William Buckley, was one of the passengers. Helping the wounded driver into the stage and cutting away the dead mules from its traces, he climbed up onto the seat and urged the one-mule-short team onward. At one point he pushed the team to jump a gap in the trail created when the Apaches removed a small stone bridge. Lurching on through the darkness, punctuated now by Apache gunfire the stage finally rattled into the station three miles away and just ahead of the dawn's early light.

Bascom's party expected an Apache attack the next day, but it was not forthcoming.

As we have seen, Cochise was now in a strong bargaining position, but for some reason seemed uninterested in a prisoner exchange. It may be that as Historian Sweeney conjectures, he may have regarded any further attempt to negotiate with Bascom as futile, since the lieutenant seemed absolutely unwilling to consider any arrangement without first having the Ward boy. Geronimo later claimed that the four Americans had already been tortured and killed, which if true meant that Cochise no longer had a bargaining chip anyway.

During the evening of the 7th a small party of soldiers and one civilian, just arrived from the east, volunteered to go for help and reached Fort Buchanan late on the 8th. Their timing was good, too, as the Apaches had withdrawn from their position above the stage station, but Cochise was already making plans with Mangas about organizing a war party to rescue the Apache captives.

Indeed, on Friday, February 8, a large war party attacked Bascom's water detail at Apache Springs. The lieutenant had few men to spare, but he sent a small relief party under the command of Lieutenant John Cooke who had arrived with the east-bound stage. The Apaches were quick to run off the horses, leaving the men afoot. Meantime, another part of Apaches made a demonstration against the station itself but were driven off. Bascom's casualties were one killed and another wounded. The defenders reported killing five Apaches. Cochise and Mangas—if he was present—were probably reluctant to press the attack out of concern for the hostages and indeed withdrew from the area entirely.

The Bascom party, however, considered themselves surrounded for the next three days, totally unaware that the Apaches had departed. Bascom of course had no idea whether the men he sent to Fort Buchanan had gotten through, but he must have hoped they made it, and they had because finally on February 14 two companies of dragoons under Lieutenant Isiah Moore arrived and probably informed Bascom that they had encountered no Indians along the way.

Two days later a search of the surrounding hills was made, and found were the badly mutilated bodies of the four Americans. After burying the remains the search party returned to the station. Given what they had found, most of the Bascom party believed the Apache hostages should be executed by hanging. The newly arrived Lieutenant Moore then volunteered to carry out the execution. Searching the surrounding hills Moore located four oak trees from which Cochise's two nephews and his brother Coyuntura were hung. One hostage reportedly pleaded for his life but the others ended their lives singing the Apache death song. Bascom returned to Fort Buchanan on February 23, probably with no real comprehension of what terrible consequences his obstinacy was to bring about. Notwithstanding, he received a commendation from department headquarters.

Meanwhile, the looming Civil War was casting its long shadow across Arizona. By March 1861 the Butterfield Stage had ceased operations and Apaches were much in evidence. In the months preceding the Bascom Affair, Cochise's animosity toward Americans had grown as a result of several incidents in which Chokonens were killed for stealing livestock. They were small things in a sense, but each added to a growing resentment Apaches had come to feel about these new intruders. Of course Americans harbored the same resentment as a result of whites murdered by Apaches. It was hard to point a finger at one without pointing a finger at the other.

It is inviting to speculate about what Apache-American relations might have been like had there been no Bascom Affair, but history is replete with "ifs" and to pursue that line of questioning leads nowhere. All we can safely say is that it would have had an impact, but how much we shall never know. What we do know is that the southwest paid a fearsome price because of George Nicholas Bascom.

One can only imagine the wrath Cochise must have felt in the aftermath of the Bascom Affair, and in the months that followed the Chokonen leader expressed that wrath against Americans wherever he found them. As far as Cochise was concerned he had made a genuine effort at conciliation, but the Americans—specifically the army—had failed to keep the faith time and again, and the flash point had been the Bascom Affair. To soldier and civilian alike, if you were an Arizona resident during these times the name Cochise was one to be reckoned with. As John C. Cremony wrote, "Cochise has been one of the most bitter, most active, and unrelenting of foes, losing no opportunity to destroy life and property."[6]

In the aftermath of the Bascom Affair, Cochise and Mangas laid plans for their future course of action. The Apaches became more aggressive, and by June, Butterfield felt compelled to abandon its Overland Mail Route. For all intents and purposes, the road between Mesilla, New Mexico, and Tucson was shut down. Indeed, the war caused Americans to abandon virtually all military posts and stage stations in Apacheria. Cochise and Mangas—now in the seventh decade of his life—combined their bands in an effort to drive out those soldiers who remained, following the eastward movement of troops as a result of the Civil War and the closure of the Butterfield Trail.

The impact of the Civil War and the Bascom Affair conspired to attract warriors from the four Chiricahua bands: Chokonens (Cochise) Bedonkohes (Mangas) Chihennes (Nana), and Nednis (Juh). It seems a curious thing but even as the Americans were mobilizing their forces in the East, so, too, were the Apaches. A new era had dawned for the Chiricahuas.

Although Mangas worked in close concert with his son-in-law he was also weary. He did remain committed to driving the whites from Pinos Altos, but the idea of driving the Americans out of all Apacheria was not a prospect that aroused him, as it once might have. Still, he felt he had little choice. Cochise had assumed the dominant role as leader of the Chiricahuas and Mangas felt obliged to support his son-in-law.

About 1859, or possibly 1860, an incident occurred in which Mangas was ostensibly tricked by some miners from Pinos Altos. Taken unawares, he was bound to a tree and whipped. Had such an event actually taken place it would surely have been sufficient cause for Mangas to declare war on the Americans. The incident seems to have had its origin in the writings of a former Boston journalist named John C. Cremony who had been on the staff of Bartlett's boundary commission and was later an officer in Carleton's California volunteers. Cremony's account seems to have been picked up by others, until the incident of Mangas being whipped by a group of burly miners has nearly attained the status of legend. However, careful research by historian Edwin Sweeney makes it abundantly clear that Cremony's account lacks sufficient credibility to be taken seriously.

In an effort to deal with the Apache vengeance that followed the Bascom Affair, the army prepared to launch a two-pronged campaign against Chiricahuas and Mescaleros. Charged with conducting this offensive was Major Isaac Lynde, whose track record as an aggressive field commander left something to be desired. In the final analysis, however, it mattered little for when the Apaches melted away into the mountains or crossed the border the campaign fizzled regardless of who was in command.

Cochise Takes the Offensive

For his part, Cochise crossed the border into Sonora where he assembled a war party of about sixty and prepared to make the Americans feel the heavy hand of his wrath. And the hand struck a party of freighters near the Stein's Peak Station in April. Nine white men died and five others wounded who were then tortured and burned to death.

And not long after this, a train of army wagons with a forty-man escort pulled out of Fort Buchanan for the Rio Grande. On May 3, while camped near San Simon they were attacked by a Cochise-led war party that succeeded in running off most of the livestock. Several of the defenders pursued the raiders and after a brisk fight managed to recover some of the stolen livestock. Reportedly, three Apaches were killed. A fortnight later, another raiding party struck an army patrol out of Fort Buchanan.

The army sought permission to pursue Apache raiders down into Sonora, but Mexican authorities refused. Although they, too were troubled by Apache mischief they were also reluctant to trust the American military who they feared would not respect Mexican rights and property.

Throughout June 1861, Cochise leading a large war party, variously estimated to number 100–150, raided across the Santa Cruz Valley, running off livestock and reportedly killing four men. At one point, a party of soldiers out of Fort Buchanan and led by none other than Lieutenant Bascom, caught up with the raiders. A brisk fight ensued, during which Cochise supposedly recognized his old enemy and filled the air with taunts, before the Apaches were finally compelled to withdraw. Four Apaches were killed and several others wounded. Bascom returned with one wounded man

It was tough to be a rancher, freighter, or much of anything else for that matter during the reign of Cochise. Apache raids on livestock, stage coaches, freight wagons and even army patrols made existence in Apacheria a chancy proposition, but there were those who endured: the army because it had to and others out of pure grit and determination. There stands no better example of the latter than cattleman Peter "Pete" Kitchen.

Born in Kentucky in 1819 Kitchen's family later removed to Tennessee. During the Mexican-American War, Kitchen was an army teamster. Later, he was a member of the Mounted Rifles that marched from Fort Leavenworth to Fort Vancouver in 1849. By 1854 he was established as a rancher in the Santa Cruz Valley, probably about as dangerous a spot as one could then find in southern Arizona. As a supplier of beef to the army, Kitchen's herds were frequent targets of Apache raids. In 1868, he built a fortress-like structure that inevitably came to be known for its hospitality and equally for its impregnability. Although seven of his employees were killed by Apache raiders, Kitchen himself survived to be remembered as a real Arizona legend.

Although Cochise had made his presence felt time and again, it had not been without losses that were more difficult for the Chiricahuas to replace. There was a war of attrition going on here, a war that the Cochise could not hope to win. Probably at some level he was aware of this, but Cochise was not yet ready to surrender to that realization.

By the summer of 1861, Cochise and Mangas had established a headquarters of sorts at Cooke's Peak, just north of present Deming, New Mexico, where the Overland Trail wound across southwest New Mexico. From here they prepared to harass travelers both east and west who were fearless enough to attempt the passage.

Strategically located, the route through Cooke's Canyon was the shortest route across that stretch of country and was the mail carriers route of choice; fresh water was available at Cooke's Spring. The route was not without drawbacks however; in spots it was narrow and confining; ideally suited for ambush. Indeed, Colonel James Carleton, for one, regarded it as the most dangerous in New Mexico and Arizona. The peak and the canyon were named for Colonel Phillip St. George Cooke, who it will be recalled, served in New Mexico Territory during the 1850s and would later command of the Mountain District, Department of the Platte at the time of the Fetterman disaster in 1866.

Between 1861 and 1863 Apaches reportedly killed a hundred whites. On July 20, 1861, a well-armed, seven-man party who had volunteered to carry the mail from Mesilla to San Diego was attacked by 200 warriors led by Mangas and Cochise. The seven who were northern sympathizers and feared retribution from pro-Confederates in Mesilla, had hoped to escape trouble by moving to San Diego. Although heavily outnumbered, the seven men gave an excellent account of themselves, killing several Apaches and possibly wounding both Cochise and his son Taza, but in the end the numbers were against them and all were killed.

Later that summer, another party another party led by one Felix Grundy Ake, leading a small wagon train and several hundred head of livestock, east from southern Arizona, were attacked in Cooke's Canyon by another large war party again led by Cochise and Mangas. A fierce fight ensued with the Apaches capturing the livestock, after which they broke off the battle, satisfied to have captured the livestock. The affair rapidly turned into a sniping match, that kept the whites pinned down. Both sides exchanged deadly sniper fire until relieved by the Arizona Guards who had come on from Pinos Altos and eventually drove off the Apaches.

An avowed Indian-hater, Lieutenant Colonel John Baylor had created the Arizona Guards as a Confederate military unit during those heady early days of the Civil War when all looked so bright for the South. Baylor created the Guards—they only numbered thirty-forty, but were men familiar with the terrain and fighting Apaches—to reestablish the road between Mesilla and Tucson, which in effect meant fighting Apaches, and fight they did. Indeed, late that same summer they managed to surprise a Chiricahua rancheria of Cochise and Mangas in the foothills of Arizona's Florida Mountains and send the Apaches scurrying into the hills.

Baylor had counted on the Arizona Guards to keep open the road from Mesilla to Tucson, but despite some successes, Apache aggressiveness made this an impossability. Baylor's attitude proved his own undoing. In March 1862, he informed Captain Thomas Helm of the Arizona Guards that Confederate policy called for the extermination of all Indians, which of course was patently untrue. Fortunately, however, before this policy could be put into practice, the Confederacy was forced to withdraw from Arizona and indeed the Southwest. And as for Baylor, he was subsequently relieved of his command for his harsh Indian policy.

On September 27, 1861, a large Apache war party struck the mining camps around Pinos Altos. The attack came as a surprise. The miners suffered heavy losses, but the Apaches did not escape unscathed. When it was over, five whites lay dead, including one Tom Mastin, captain of the Arizona Guards. Reportedly, ten Apaches lost their lives. Interestingly, part of fight centered around the general store of the Bean brothers, Roy and Sam, the former being the noted Judge Roy Bean, who was considered the law west of the Pecos.

Colonel James Henry Carleton

Although General Henry Hopkins Sibley's invasion of New Mexico had run aground with twin defeats at Valverde and Glorietta Pass, sending his once proud command fleeing back to Texas in disarray, the mere fact that the Confederacy had even launched an invasion served as a wake-up call to reinforce Canby's New Mexico department, particularly the southwestern sector. Accordingly, in the spring of 1862 a column of California volunteers numbering about 2,300, under the command of Colonel James Henry Carleton, who, it will be recalled, had earlier seen service in New Mexico, headed east to reestablish federal rule in southern Arizona and re-open the road from Tucson to Mesilla. En route

Carleton learned, no doubt with much satisfaction, that he had been promoted to brigadier general.

On or about April 16, an advance element of the California column clashed with a Confederate detachment belonging to Major Sherod Hunter's command at Picacho Pass north of Tucson. The affair wasn't much as these things go; more of a skirmish than an actual fight, but the Californians had the best of it, and most importantly, signaled an end to Confederate presence in Arizona.

Carleton himself reached Tucson in June. The Confederates no longer posed a serious threat, but there were still the Apaches to be dealt with if southern Arizona and the Mesilla Valley were to be made safe. Insofar as the Apaches were concerned there was little to choose between Baylor and Carleton; it was hard to say who hated Indians more.

Carleton's grasp of conditions in the Southwest was less than up-to-date. Evidently, he had not as yet received reports of Sibley's defeat, and he seems not to have been acquainted with the Apache problem, which seems strange considering his past service in New Mexico. However, he was quickly brought up to speed when two of the three messengers he dispatched to inform Canby of his arrival in Arizona were killed by Chokonens near Apache Pass. The third messenger, however, managed to get through and deliver Carleton's message.

The Battle of Apache Pass

On June 17 Carleton decided to make a reconnaissance in force along the trail to Mesilla. The mission was assigned to Lieutenant Colonel Edward Eyre with 140 men from the 1st California Cavalry. Predictably, Eyre found Cochise and a party of warriors numbering nearly a hundred. Having been cautioned about avoiding conflict with the Apaches if at all possible, the colonel assured Cochise of his intention to be friendly, but also reminded the Apache leader that there were many more soldiers in Tucson, and that the great chief, Carleton, was anxious to speak with all the Apaches.

Cochise was undoubtedly well aware that there were more soldiers in Tucson and whether it was his intent to deceive Eyre into believing that the Apaches would not bother troops moving through Apache Pass is not clear. Perhaps he imagined that by not attacking Eyre's column, Carleton would be lulled into thinking he could anticipate safe passage. In any case, Eyre was allowed to proceed undisturbed.

On July 4, Carleton ordered a celebratory dress parade down the main street of Tucson. The temperature was likely in triple digits; not an ideal day for parading, but perhaps offset by the news that the California column would shortly be heading east. And so it was. In the early morning hours of July 10, Captain Thomas Roberts, 1st California Infantry, a former Sacramento, California, bookkeeper, led a mixed command of 126 men from his own 1st California, plus a detachment from the 2d California Cavalry under Captain John Cremony (originator of the whipping incident of Mangas Coloradas). A wagon train managed by some two dozen teamsters and a large herd of cattle rounded out the column. As he had done with Eyre, Carleton specifically instructed Roberts to avoid any clash of arms with the Apaches if at all possible. Nevertheless, should the Apaches choose to fight, Roberts had a pair of howitzers to provide extra firepower.

En route to Apache Pass, Roberts divided his command, leaving a portion under Captain Cremony with the wagons and cattle at Dragoon Springs, while Roberts himself pushed on to the Pass, some forty miles east, with about ninety men. Through the night they tramped across the hot, dry desert, following the Butterfield Overland Stage route. Dawn found them twenty miles from the Pass, which place they reached at mid-morning, exhausted, hungry, and most of all thirsty.

Roberts and his tired, footsore soldiers undoubtedly anticipated a most welcome rest here, but that expectation was quickly put to rest. Mangas and Cochise were waiting and ready. Roberts, with the main portion of his command had passed beyond the currently unoccupied stage station, and as the rear elements numbering perhaps twenty men, approached the station the Apaches cut loose with a furious burst of fire killing one man and wounding another. The Apaches then charged down from their hillside positions to attack the somewhat demoralized soldiers. It was hand-to-hand, and had it not been for the timely return of Roberts and the rest of his command, the rear guard would likely have been wiped out. As it was, the soldiers drove the attackers back into the hills above the station. Unlimbering his artillery, Roberts sent a few shells at the Apache positions, which at least temporarily discouraged further assaults, but the battle was far from over.

As meridian neared, Roberts regrouped around the stage station, but now of increasing concern was the fact that the fresh water his men needed was at the spring, some seven hundred yards away and the Apaches had positioned themselves behind boulders and rock outcroppings, ready to make any attempt at getting water dangerous in the extreme. Moreover, the Apaches outnumbered Roberts by something like two-to-one.

Roberts had to do something. He was not an experienced Indian-fighting officer, though his actions on this day would suggest otherwise. Dividing his command into two sections, he sent one forward to the spring, while the other, with the howitzers, provided covering fire. From their strong defensive positions, the Apaches poured a heavy fire down on the soldiers. Fortunately for the troops, however, the Apaches, overshot their targets. When it appeared that Sergeant Albert Fountain's detachment might reach the spring, the Indians let loose with another volley and evidently adjusted their marksmanship because this torrent of fire compelled Fountain to pull back.

In the brief lull that followed, jeers and taunts were exchanged by both sides. Roberts had hoped to soften up the Indian positions with his howitzers before attempting another attack but both pieces had become damaged with broken trails (legs) and were unable to elevate their tubes so as to fire on the higher Apache positions. So, once again, Sergeant Fountain leading twenty volunteers worked his way up to the crest of a hill above the spring. Here the Chiricahuas had taken up a strong defensive position. Under heavy fire from the top, Fountain leap-froged his command upward and in a final grand bayonet charge drove the Apaches from their position. The position, Overlook Ridge as it would come to be called, was the commanding height and from its eminence the troops could now fire on the Apache positions. More importantly, the troops now had access to precious water. Having gained higher ground Roberts managed to jury-rig his howitzers into firing position. As the howitzer shells began dropping on their position the Apaches were driven back. Thanks to the gallantry of Fountain and his men, the inexperienced Roberts had won a key victory here at Apache Pass. Fountain would later be commissioned a second lieutenant. In the post Civil War years he would go on to be an influential figure in New Mexico politics.

Although Roberts had won a victory at the Pass, the Apaches still posed an immediate threat. A detachment of six men was sent back to alert Captain Cremony not to enter the Pass with the wagons. As the detachment started out they were observed by a party of Apaches. Sergeant Fountain, who had noted this development from his position on Overlook Ridge, reported to Captain Roberts. Meanwhile, The Chiricahuas attacked the six-man detachment under Sergeant Titus Mitchell. One soldier was wounded, but the entire party, save one who had been unhorsed, was able to outrun the Indians to reach Cremony's camp.

Unbelievably, the fourth man in Mitchell's detachment, one John Teal, although cut off and without a horse, managed to defend himself quite admirably. Armed with a Sharps repeating carbine, Teal kept kept the Apaches at a distance and indeed, may have wounded none other than Mangas himself. Whether it was by Teal or someone else, Mangas was wounded and later taken to Janos, Chihuahua for medical treatment. On foot, Teal managed to reach Captain Cremony's camp around midnight, probably surprising his three comrades who had likely given him up for dead.

The following day, Roberts and Cremony rendezvoused at the latter's camp, then formed up and carefully approached the Pass once more ready for another fight. With the howitzers zeroing in on the Apache positions and supplemented by fire from the infantry's rifles, the troops moved on through the Pass encountering little resistance as most of the Apaches had already left the area. The Battle of Apache Pass was a watershed event in the Apache wars. It marked the first real clash of arms between Apaches and U.S. troops, and, as a consequence, it brought to light the strategic importance of the Pass. Indeed, Captain Roberts who distinguished himself in this action recommended to Carleton that a military post be established here and Carleton agreed. A detachment of troops was immediately deployed for duty here and a proper site was selected. The post was named for Colonel George Bowie. Initially it was Camp Bowie until the permanent post was built. Fort Bowie would prove the pivotal point on which turned the Army's operational strategy for campaigns against the Apaches. General Carleton considered it one of the most important military post in the Southwest.

The Death of Mangas Coloradas

In mid-September, Mangas, now well past seventy, sent out peace feelers which found their way into the hands of Colonel Joseph Rodman West, commanding the District of Arizona, and also crossed Carleton's desk; what would come of this remained to be seen. Outspoken and impertinent, West would prove a pivotal figure in the final hours of Mangas's life. Born in New Orleans but raised in Philadelphia, West saw service in the Mexican-American War, following which he removed to California, where, as a newspaperman, he acquired the sobriquet "Dandy" [someone fastidious in dress and appearance] while attempting to deal with vigilante action in the San Francisco area. At the outbreak of the Civil War he was mustered into the 1st California Volunteer Infantry and led the advance of Carleton's California column into Tucson. In October 1862 he was promoted to brigadier general of volunteers and assigned to command the District of Arizona with headquarters in Mesilla, The Arizona district was a sprawling one, with boundaries that extended from the Colorado River on the west to the Rio Grande on the east. Argumentative and insubordinate West clashed often with Carleton and the adjutant general over an issue of taxes. West left the service in 1866 and was later elected to the U.S. Senate from Louisiana.

Carleton had no interest in discussing peace terms with Mangas or any other Apache leader. When West reported Indian troubles in the Pinos Altos area, Carleton automatically assumed Mangas was responsible, but in a sense, all Apaches were guilty insofar as Carleton was concerned. As Edwin Sweeney points out, Carleton's strategy for dealing with Apaches was simple and brutal: extermination.[7]

In the fall of 1862, Carleton issued his first general order that directed West to build a post near Santa Lucia to be called Fort West. The second part of General Order Number 1 directed West to begin plans for a campaign against Mangas, who had now become fully committed to the idea of peace. Whether Carleton or West had any knowledge or even suspicion of how Mangas felt seems unlikely since they were preparing for military action. Meanwhile, in council, the Chiricahuas discussed the notion of seeking a peace accord. Mangas pushed hard for the idea. Notwithstanding the Bascom incident and the fight at Apache Pass, Mangas seemed to feel the Apaches could know peace with the Americans. We might wonder whether the old chief's desire for peace would have been as strong twenty or thirty years earlier. In any event, he now appeared ready to trust Americans even if others—Geronimo for example—did not.

About this same time Mangas sought counsel at Pinos Altos from thirty-one-year-old Jack Swilling, one of those colorful characters one finds spread across the tableau of the Old West. Swilling introduced the first modern irrigation system to the Salt River Valley and is thus credited with being the founder of Phoenix. It is said that no one in Arizona's history had more lies told about them than Jack Swilling.

Born in South Carolina, Swilling made his way to Arizona via Texas. A former employee of the Butterfield Overland Stage Company, Swilling had become an officer in the 2d Texas Mounted Rifles. It was Swilling's detachment, incidentally, that had defeated the Union force at Picacho Pass the previous April. Swilling appears to have been a fair-weather soldier because when the Confederates were forced to abandon the Southwest Swilling deserted and became an express messenger. His career embraced a variety of occupations ranging from teamster and prospector to dance hall impresario. Some said he even scouted occasionally for the Union after the departure of Confederate forces. A steady hand when sober he was the polar opposite when in his cups, which was often. Exactly when Swilling and Mangas met is not known, but Mangas apparently trusted him enough to discuss how he (Mangas) might seek peace. At this meeting, reportedly, Swilling was drunk and threatened to kill Mangas, who, however, seems not to have taken the threat seriously.

The council finally decided that Mangas would take half of the Bedonkohes and Chihennes to Pinos Altos to see if the peace accord would work. If all went well, viz., if the Americans welcomed them and provided rations the remainder of the Apaches would join them. It should be noted here that this involved only the two bands of Chiricahuas. This was the plan. Victorio, Nana, and probably Geronimo—who was not yet the voice of influence he was to become—attempted to dissuade Mangas from the idea, but the old chief was determined.

In mid–January 1863, General West set out from his headquarters in Mesilla with an expedition numbering some 250 men. The first step in his campaign was to establish a field headquarters at the now abandoned Fort McLane near Santa Rita del Cobre. Learning that Mangas was in the Pinos Altos area, West sent a small detachment under Captain Edmund Shirland to investigate. Pointing the way for Shirland's party were three of the best scouts around, including Juan Arroyo, Felipe Gonzalez, and Merejildo Grijalva. From here on the this point the plot begins to get complicated.

Upon reaching Fort McLane, Shirland's detachment found a party of prospectors led by the famous mountain man, Joseph Reddeford Walker. Jack Swilling was also a member, in fact had been named leader of the group. Traveling through Apache country was always a chancy dodge and between the two of them Walker and Swilling decided that their best insurance would be to hold an important Apache leader as hostage until they had passed through the danger zone. When their plan was unveiled, Shirland evidently agreed to support it. On the morning of January 16, the combined party headed to Pinos Altos and, with a white flag plainly visible, waited for Mangas to appear. We have to believe that Mangas regarded Swilling's earlier threat as nothing more than whiskey talk because he seems to have trusted Swilling enough to come into Pinos Altos.

It took twenty-four hours but the next day Mangas surrounded by a dozen warriors, put in an appearance. The crafty Swilling had directed Shirland's troops to take cover. When Swilling then approached Mangas the soldiers appeared, rifles leveled. If Mangas had not suspected entrapment beforehand he surely did now. Recognizing the futility of resistance, he dismissed his escort and turned himself over to Captain Shirland. When they reached Fort McLane on the 18th Shirland turned the chief over to General West who had followed Shirland's detachment to Fort McLane where he established temporary headquarters.

West, whose attitude toward Indians was on a par with that of Carleton and Baylor informed Mangas he would spend the rest of his days as a prisoner, though he would be treated kindly. The old chief was told that if he attempted to escape he would be shot. West allegedly told the guards that he wanted Mangas dead by morning. The mid–January night was bitterly cold. Mangas had but a single blanket that was not quite large enough to cover his massive body. To amuse themselves, the guards began putting the points of their bayonets into the warming fire, then torturing Mangas by touching their heated bayonets to feet. When Mangas, angry at being tormented, shouted at his tormentors, they shot him, apparently more than once. And so Mangas Coloradas, perhaps the greatest of all Apache leaders was gone. Shot while trying to escape was the official version, which satisfied West and which Carleton did not question. The body was scalped, the head removed and sent to an eastern museum for examination. The remainder of the great chief's body was wrapped in a blanket and dumped in a hole and covered up.

In the aftermath of the Mangas murder, West, imagining that word of Mangas's death had not reached the general Apache population, hoped to take advantage of the situation by sending patrols out to scour the countryside and attack any Apaches they found, and so they did. Both Captain William McCleave and Captain Edmund Shirland killed several Apaches in surprise attacks. Indeed, some of the troopers returned displaying scalps they had taken.

But if Carleton and West imagined they had taken the sting out of Apache resistance they were soon to be disabused of that notion. Unfortunately, all too often military commanders in the West tended to be hard-liners where Indians were concerned. One has only to begin with Sherman and Sheridan to understand how policies were carried out, and nowhere did one find a better exponent of this attitude than James Henry Carleton. As historian Edwin Sweeney has suggested, if only Carleton had made an effort to meet Mangas half way it might well have resulted in a genuine effort to reach a peaceable agreement with the Chiricahuas, but this would have been akin to asking Carleton to grow another inch. Instead, by driving the hardest sort of bargain with the Apaches, Carleton insured the perpetuation of hostilities for another two decades.

The Rise of Cochise

With the death of Mangas, Cochise assumed the role of the foremost Chiricahua leader. After the demise of Mangas, the Bedonkohes, always the smallest of the Chiricahua groups, joined Cochise's Chokonens. A skilled warrior and a more than able leader of his band, Cochise was surely the best known Apache of his time. Today, only the name Geronimo has a higher name recognition. Although a head shorter than his father-in-law, Mangas, Cochise was nevertheless a fine physical specimen. His straight-as-an-arrow posture made him seem taller than he actually was. A fearless fighter and a no-quarters opponent, Cochise possessed the gift of leadership. If Mangas had been the preeminent Chiricahua leader during his lifetime, Cochise was "the man" for the decade that followed Mangas's murder.

The murder of Mangas incensed Cochise who was already filled with a deep hatred of Americans as a consequence of the Bascom Affair. Following his July 15 fight with Captain Roberts at Apache Pass, Cochise took his Chokonens down to Fronteras to regroup and trade for guns, ammunition, horses, and anything else that might aid his prosecution of the war against the Americans. The surprising defense of the Americans at Apache Pass was probably surprising to Cochise, but he was by no means discouraged from waging war against the Americans.

Apparently, Carleton seems not to have regarded Cochise on the same level as Mangas, and would quickly learn how formidable an adversary Cochise could be. The murder of Mangas cried out for vengeance and accordingly, during summer of 1863, a large war party released their anger on a number of Americans, mutilating their bodies in response to what had been done to Mangas. And throughout 1863–1864 Apache raids were plentiful all across southern New Mexico and Arizona. But the Apaches were again feeling pressure from two fronts. North of the border, it was the U.S. Army and during the fall and winter of 1863–1864, Mexican forces, too, were on the move, often compelling the Apaches to scatter from their hideouts.

In February 1865, a mixed force of Bedonkohes and Chokonens set out with the avowed intention of raiding the mining camps around Pinos Altos. This particular party seems to have been led by a Bedonkohe named Luis (or Louis), who may possibly have been a son of Mangas. Unbeknownst to the Apaches, word had filtered through to the army, prompting Captain James Whitlock to head for Pinos Altos with a detachment of twenty-one, that seems to have included several Mexicans. Whitlock reached Pinos Altos on the 24th, in advance of the raiders, so that when Luis (or Louis) and his warriors arrived they encountered some unexpected resistance. Whitlock's troopers practically wiped out the war party, killing thirteen of the eighteen. Reportedly, the Mexicans took Apache scalps which they later took back to Mexico for the bounty.

A month later, the Indians retaliated by stealing mules from a government wagon train at Camp Mimbres, north of present Deming and of course the army then struck back when Whitlock led a devastating attack on an Apache rancheria in the Graham Mountains, killing twenty-one.

On May 5, 1864, Cochise was back in the picture. With a war party estimated to contain as many as 200 warriors, he ambushed a 60-man army detachment under Lieutenant Henry Stevens in the deadly confines of Doubtful Canyon. The fight was a fierce one. Apparently, short of firearms, the Apaches rained volleys of arrows down on the defenders, but the soldiers gave a good account of themselves. Finally, after nearly an hour the Indians withdrew. Lieutenant Stevens judged that they had killed 10 and wounded perhaps as many as 20. Four soldiers were wounded, one of which would die later and yet another was reported missing.

This scrap at Doubtful Canyon earned Stevens many points with Carleton, who, having now disposed of the Navajo problem prepared to go all out against the Apaches, and judging from the local media it was high time he did so, too, as, for all intents and purposes, Apaches controlled Arizona. Carleton's plan was ambitious and international in scope; you had to give him credit for that. From throughout his department units were concentrated north of the Gila River, believing this would compel the Apaches to seek safety south of the border. Provincial governors in Sonora and Chihuahua were asked to cooperate by assembling their troops near the border. Thus, caught between U.S. troops on one side and Mexican forces on the other, the Apaches would be crushed and defeated by Christmas. Throughout U.S. history there seems to have been a fixation with ending wars by Christmas: Europe in the fall of 1944; Korea, in the fall of 1950, or here in the Southwest circa 1864.

In July, Major Nelson Davis with an infantry detachment attacked an Apache rancheria along the Gila River, killing forty-nine, or so it was reported, but Cochise had little difficulty avoiding foot soldiers. Meanwhile, other units from Fort Bowie searched through the mountains and valleys of southeast Arizona with only minor success and certainly far from the results anticipated by Carleton.

As summer pressed on Carleton concluded that the Apaches had largely vacated the area and crossed the border. Thus far, his grand scheme seemed not to be reaping dividends, but Carleton still believed that a December victory was within reach. How, one wonders, did Carleton manage to conclude that the Apaches had pulled out of southwest New Mexico and southern Arizona when in fact war parties, sometimes numbering 200 or more continued to raid livestock herds. Army patrols operating out of Fort Bowie pursued the raiders with mixed results. However, a large Mexican force scored big time when it slipped across the border and surprised an Apache rancheria in the Animas Mountains of southwestern New Mexico, killing 39 and capturing nearly as many.

Early in 1865, Chihenne Apaches under Victorio and Nana let it be known they were tired of fighting and wanted peace, but on what terms? There was a kerfuffle of sorts over who had the authority to dictate terms: the military or the Indian bureau. Carleton won out and his terms were that all Indians would be confined to the Bosque Redondo, perhaps the most hated reservation in the West, with the possible exception of San Carlos.

Thus, even as the Civil War was winding down, two powerful Apache war leaders turned themselves in and agreed to live in peace, providing, however, they be allowed to live along either the Mimbres or Gila Rivers. Carleton, of course, had no intention of acquiescing to Victorio's demands and for the moment must have felt like a strutting turkey, but he had yet to account for Cochise.

If Victorio had forsaken the warpath, at least for the time being, Cochise was making his presence felt more strongly than ever. The decade following the Civil War was to witness Cochise reach the zenith of his power. His resistance to the Americans during these years would enshrine him in the pantheon of notable Indian leaders. Apache raids were unrelenting. In the fall of 1865, for example, Cochise leading a party of some eighty warriors attacked several miners near Santa Rita del Cobre killing two. Later that day he struck an army station, stealing horses, weapons, and ammunition.

Cochise continued to wage war on two fronts. In April 1865, he and Juh organized a large war party said to number 200 for a retaliation raid against the Mexicans, probably in pay-back for family members killed by Mexican forces the previous December.

During 1866–1867 there just enough encounters with the Chiricahuas to keep the Army alert and responsive. Cochise remained dedicated to the proposition of striking the Americans whenever the opportunity presented itself, and when resources were available, namely manpower, weapons and ammunition. To what extent Cochise thought about this we cannot say, but able leader that he was Cochise surely recognized that his resources were limited and needed to be used wisely.

Had they even known about it, or understood the significance of it, the Apaches might have celebrated the Army's realignment of departmental boundaries. In January 1865 the District of Arizona was transferred from Carleton's department to the Department of Pacific. Appointed to command the new district was one Brigadier General John Mason who held forth the view that Cochise was the worst Indian on the continent. Thus Cochise became the object of Mason's attention. How or if the change in command would affect the Apaches remained to be seen.

Following a personal inspection tour of his department which had to have been discouraging, as he lacked nearly everything needed to meet his responsibilities, from troops and horses to equipment and supplies. The territory for which he now found himself responsible was vast, hot and unforgiving. Under these conditions, bringing about peace with the Apaches seemed quite impossible. Notwithstanding, Mason approached the challenge with a two-point philosophy. Those Indians who sought peace would be confined to a reservation where they would be cared for by the army. Those who refused to walk that road would face the consequences of army campaigns that would seek them out on search and destroy missions.

Insofar as Cochise was concerned, the answer to this was to simply re-locate south of the border, from where he could dash into Arizona, conduct a raid and retired to Sonora or Chihuahua, as he did during the summer of 1865 when he launched several stinging attacks on ranches and army patrols in southern Arizona.

Meanwhile, during this same summer of 1865, forty-five-year-old Hiram Starrs Washburn, Vermont-born and a surveyor by trade, was given a commission to enlist new men for the Arizona Volunteers. It will be recalled that the volunteers had come into being during the early years of the Civil War to hunt Apaches. Back in February, Washburn, along with Lieutenant Manuel Gallegos, leading a forty-man patrol of Arizona Volunteers attacked an Apache camp under the Mogollon (Muggy own) Rim, killing thirty and capturing a dozen women and children. Seven volunteers were wounded.

Washburn took to his new assignment enthusiastically and by September was writing to territorial governor, Tom Goodwin, reporting that he had enlisted eighty new men— mostly Mexicans who were unprincipled when it came to fighting Apaches. As far as Washburn was concerned, the end justified the means. Then, too, Washburn was taken with the idea of enlisting Mexicans, thinking that to do so would promote harmony with Mexico.

Washburn set his sights on capturing (or killing) Cochise, whom he believed to be around Fronteras. Once Cochise was erased from the picture, the other Apache leaders could easily be persuaded to quit the warpath and the Apache problem would be no more. Whether Washburn was aware of it is not clear, but apparently Cochise had advised Mexican authorities at Fronteras that he and several other leaders were willing to come in and talk about peace. But it wasn't quite that simple because Mexican national authorities could not count on support from their provincial counterparts who had been driven into exile by the French forces of Napoleon Bonaparte III.

Even as Washburn sought Cochise, in August 1865, the Chokonen leader appeared at Fort Bowie quite unexpectedly to discuss peace. A trifle flustered at this Major James Gorman, commanding the post directed Cochise to return in a fortnight, by which time the major would have received instructions from topside, but Gorman, no Indian lover, apparently did not take Cochise seriously and prepared to find and attack the Apaches who obviously were in the area. Assembling a detachment, he concealed them in wagons ordinarily used to haul wood. Knowing what the wagons were used for, the Apaches paid them little mind. Moving into the Chiricahua Mountains, Gorman found a camp and attacked, killing seven. The soldiers also found considerable loot taken on various raids.

Meanwhile, since Major Gorman had worked through the Chiricahuas, General Mason planned a major campaign, using two columns of troops to scour the country east and west of those mountains. The campaign yielded little, reinforcing the general public's poor impression of the general for his failure to put an end to the Apache menace.

Nothing seemed to come out of Cochise's peace-feeler and in the spring of 1866 he raided down into Mexico, killing several ranch hands and making off with cattle. Interestingly enough, this particular raid angered some of the normally non-warlike Apaches who had lost some of their own to these raiders and decided to take action. Accordingly, a group followed Cochise's trail, located his rancheria and killed several, although Cochise himself managed to escape. The attack, however, had little effect on Cochise, who struck the new Camp Waller, near Babocomari Creek a month later. A fifty-man detachment came on from Fort Mason two days later, by which time the Apaches were of course long gone.

Hiram Washburn's Arizona Volunteers continued their search and destroy operations. On March 31, 1866, the volunteers located a rancheria in the Pinal Mountains near Globe and devastated the camp, reportedly killing twenty-five.

Continued dissatisfaction with the Army's efforts to put an end to the Apache problem led, in mid–January 1867, to the formation of another volunteer force organized at Prescott and calling itself the Yavapai Rangers, who pursued Indians into the rugged country northwest of Prescott where they attacked an Apache camp, killing twenty.

Notwithstanding the dissatisfaction of the Arizona citizenry, the army had been busy in its own right. Early in April, Captain James Williams with two companies of the 8th Cavalry left Fort Whipple near Prescott in search of Apaches said to be camped northeast of the fort. For a solid week, Williams pursued the Apaches, destroying three rancherias and killing as many as fifty.

Although the decade of the 1860s found the army predominantly occupied with raiding Apaches, most of whom were Chiricahuas, there were clashes with other tribes as well. These years found detachments of the 1st and 8th Cavalry and 14th Infantry almost constantly in the field in pursuit of Hualapai raiders. Mostly these campaigns were conducted in northwest Arizona, often in the Hualapai Mountains near Kingman. An example of these clashes took place on January 14, 1868, when a company of the 8th Cavalry under Captain Samuel Baldwin Marks Young had a brisk fight with some of these raiders in Hualapai Canyon. Both Young and the Hualapai chief, Scherum were wounded. Young would recover and go on to serve as a general officer in the Spanish-American War.

Early in October 1869 Cochise attacked a stagecoach near Douglas, Arizona, and the next day stole a herd of cattle and attacked a government train. This brought Lieutenant William Winters and twenty-five men of the 1st Cavalry out from Fort Bowie in pursuit. On the 8th of the month Winters located Cochise's camp in the Pedregosa Mountains of Cochise County, Arizona. Although exhausted from their tough, exhausting three-day pursuit, Winters attacked and killed three. Some of the Apaches, Cochise included, happened to be mounted at the time of the attack, perhaps returning from yet another foray, and managed to escape. Nevertheless, it was brisk ninety-minute fight.

Back at Fort Bowie, Captain Reuben Bernard learned of Winters' fight and assembled a detachment from the 1st and 8th Cavalry and set out to try and pick up Cochise's trail. Bernard managed to locate the trail, but soon found himself under attack by an estimated 150 Apaches. The fight continued through most of the 19th. Unsuccessful in trying to outflank the Apaches, Bernard elected to withdraw, lacking sufficient strength to force the Apaches out of their position.

The Pinal Apaches also proved troublesome from time to time. On May 26, 1870, the Israel-Kennedy supply train bound for Camp Grant left Tucson with an escort of twenty-one men. Incredible as it may seem, only four of the men were armed. Near Oracle, Arizona, they were attacked by fifty Pinal Apaches. The four men who were armed, fought back as best they could but died by the time a relief party arrived from Camp Grant.

On June 5, a mixed force from the 1st and 3rd Cavalry under Lieutenant Howard Bass Cushing left Camp Grant in pursuit of the Pinal raiders. After following a torturous trail Cushing located the Indian camp near Signal Peak (present Globe) and attacked in the darkness, killing thirty Apaches, while suffering no casualties himself.

Howard Bass Cushing was one of those fiery, energetic young officers who seemed destined for the battlefield. His was a military family with three brothers who served in the Union Army or Navy. Brother William is said to have sunk the Confederate Ironclad *Albermarle* and another brother Alonzo died at Gettysburg. Howard himself served in the Union artillery, earning a commission. A lean five-foot seven inches with green eyes, he was sometimes called the Custer of Arizona for his vigorous, determined pursuit of Apaches.

On August 1, 1870, Cushing led two companies of the 1st and 3rd Cavalry in pursuit of raiding Pinals. Locating a rancheria near present Miami, Arizona, Cushing attacked, killing six Pinals and capturing two women who agreed to lead the soldiers to a second camp. Wary but willing Cushing followed the women, but sensed an ambush in time. The troops exchanged long distance fire with the Indians until the latter pulled out abandoning their camp, which Cushing then proceeded to destroy before returning to Camp Grant.

At this time, another War Department shuffle affected the army's command structure in the Southwest. On April 15, 1870, the District of Arizona became the Department of Arizona, within the Division of the Pacific. New Mexico, however, remained a military district within General John Pope's Department of Missouri. Brevet Major General George Stoneman was appointed to command the newly created Department of Arizona. A cavalry officer with a somewhat checkered Civil War career, Stoneman, for some odd reason, established his department headquarters on the Southern California coast, rather than in southern Arizona where the heart of his command responsibilities were located. Nevertheless, Stoneman sought to comply with the directives (and philosophy) of Grant's peace policy by establishing a series of stations where the Apaches could be fed and their behavior monitored. One such station was Camp Grant on the lower San Pedro River. And there may have been no better illustration of the failure of President Grant's Peace Policy than what happened at Camp Grant on April 30, 1871; it could well be likened to Sand Creek.

The Camp Grant Massacre

At Camp Grant some 500 Pinal and Aravaipa Apaches, mainly under the leadership of Eskiminzin (Old Skinny, as he was known), had been moved onto reservations where they could be fed and encouraged to take up farming. Some of these Apaches took advantage of government largesse, while others continued to raid at will. Angry citizens saw the reservation program as nothing more than a disguise that allowed the Apaches to feed off the government on the one hand and raid off the other.

Responsible for the Apaches at Camp Grant was thirty-eight-year-old Lieutenant Royal Emerson Whitman, 3rd Cavalry. Sympathetic to the needs of the Indians, Whitman had developed a good rapport with them. Born in Maine, Whitman had served with distinction in the Civil War. Residents of Tucson and environs, however, held Whitman responsible for the raids and murders that were committed off the reservation. "Whitman's Indians," they were called. Early in April, Captain Frank Stanton was appointed to command at Camp Grant. However, as the end of the month of April drew near, Stanton took the bulk of his troops on a scouting expedition, leaving Whitman in charge of the post.

The raids led to the creation of a mixed force of some 90 Mexicans, six Americans, and some Papago Indians, traditional enemies of the Apaches. It was purely a vigilante force that left Tucson on April 28, 1871, and struck the unsuspecting Apaches on the reservation two days later. Depending on the source consulted, 125 to 140 Apaches were brutally murdered. In addition, two dozen children were sold into slavery in Mexico. Among those killed were the four wives of Eskiminzin and five of his children. Notwithstanding the massacre, the surviving Apaches stood by Whitman, who arrived on the scene too late to prevent the killing. Later, a sham trial was held in Tucson, but those charged were acquitted.

Whitman, meanwhile, was censured for creating a safe haven for raiding Apaches. A court-martial followed, but Whitman was cleared of any wrong-doing. Crook, appointed department commander shortly before the incident, came to scorn Whitman, and to many local citizens his name would be anathema forever more.

As a consequence of Camp Grant massacre, President Grant was on the verge of establishing martial law in Arizona, but the Board of Indian Commissioners, after considering the matter, decided that secretary, Vincent Colyer, a solid humanitarian should visit Arizona and see if there wasn't an opportunity to establish peaceful relations with the Apaches. The consensus among the humanitarian crowd was that, in view of the Camp Grant tragedy, the army had been unable to achieve anything resembling peaceful relations. The announcement of Colyer's appointment angered the Arizona citizenry, who were furious that an easterner should be sent to make peace with bandits and killers.

Crook Arrives in Arizona

The plan to send Colyer to Arizona was only one part of a new strategy for dealing with the Apaches. Part two had its origin in territorial governor Anson Safford who augured for the replacement of Stoneman with George Crook. The governor was convinced that Stoneman was responsible for the Camp Grant tragedy and truth to tell, Grant had been impressed with Crook's work against the Paiutes, though it should be noted that Crook did not want the assignment; he saw Arizona as a dead end, but was persuaded to take the job on a temporary basis.

There was a sticking point, however, in that the billet actually called for a general officer (or at least a full colonel) and Crook was only a lieutenant colonel. The way around that was to promote Crook, despite the fact that he was well down the line in rank and seniority. Sherman and Sheridan were opposed (as were a number of ranking colonels who had been passed over). Nevertheless, two years later, in 1873, Crook received the coveted star of a brigadier general.

If most attention seemed to be riveted on the episode at Camp Grant, during this spring of 1871, not all eyes were thinking of that tragedy. For one, Lieutenant Howard Cushing remained determined to find Cochise and bring about an end to the Apache war. On May 5, 1871, at the head of a small detachment of nineteen men from the 3rd Cavalry, Cushing sortied from Fort Lowell (present Phoenix) with exactly that objective in mind. Picking up an Apache trail Cushing followed it into the Whetstone Mountains of southern Arizona. A tough fight soon followed with what was probably Juh's band of Nednhi Chiricahuas. Three troopers were killed, including the gallant and aggressive Cushing, who somehow seemed like one of those figures destined to surrender his life on a battlefield.

When Crook arrived in Arizona in June 1871, he faced a delicate political situation. The local citizenry wanted—indeed, demanded—that he take a hard line with the Apaches, but Crook had to balance this against that bloc of Easterners who believed in and supported the president's peace policy. Despite this, Crook wasted no time laying out plans for an offensive designed to force the Apaches onto reservations. And Crook soon found another reason to be disturbed. As it had played out, Colyer's mission was less than successful, in view of which, President Grant appointed Brigadier General Oliver Otis Howard to also investigate the situation in Arizona and see if a peaceful settlement could not be reached. Half a dozen years later, Howard would play a key role in the Nez Perce story. Owing to his strong humanitarian stance, President Grant thought he would be the right individual to bring about peace in embattled Arizona. Crook thought otherwise but had no voice in the matter.

During that first summer of his tenure in Arizona, Crook took five companies of the 3rd Cavalry on a reconnaissance mission from Camp Lowell (Tucson) to Camp Bowie. It was of course at the peak of the hot season, but the expedition gave Crook an opportunity to get a feeling for the country. It was probably this outing that enabled him to see the great value of employing Indian scouts. He was not exactly a stranger to employing Indians as scouts and guides, but in dealing with Apaches, he would soon come to see how invaluable it would be to use friendly Apaches to track the hostiles. Throughout the remainder of his frontier service, Crook would come to rely on the use of Indian scouts. The idea of using indigenous peoples in military operations did not originate with Crook, but he relied on the use of Indian scouts to probably a greater extent than any other commander in the West, and considering the terrain over which military operations against the Apaches were conducted it made perfectly good sense. In this, Crook did not have the blessing of General Sheridan, and many Arizona locals who believed one could not trust the Apaches, but Crook was willing to take the chance, believing that the potential gain outweighed the risk.

On July 1, Captain Guy Vernor Henry with three companies of the 3rd Cavalry surprised an Apache band on the Salt River, killing seven and atoning to some extent for the loss of Cushing. Elsewhere, in November, Apache-Yumas and Apache-Mojaves, living on the Date Creek Reservation northwest of Wickenburg, raided a stagecoach, killing six. Two passengers—a man and woman managed to return to town with the news.

Crook himself took the field from Camp Verde on August 15, following an Apache trail into the rugged Tonto Basin, an area much favored by the Apaches and understandably so as it contained ample water and grass, to say nothing of wild game. As the troops moved into the Basin, they were showered with arrows by the Apaches, who evidently were short on firearms just then. The Apaches soon disappeared and Crook returned to Camp Verde. His expedition to Camp Bowie in July and this one into the Tonto Basin had given Crook a first-hand look at the tough nature of the area for which he was now responsible.

It seemed clear enough to Crook that the only way to control the Apaches was to put them all on reservations and see to it they stayed there. His grand offensive, therefore, would sweep throughout the realm of Apacheria (or at least that part of it where Apaches proved the most troublesome) and compel the Apaches to seek the safety of the reservation, for only here would they be free from the relentless pressure of Crook's field columns, or so the general imagined.

Crook soon found his strategy hampered, however. General Howard arrived in April and although he made no effort to assume military command (he outranked Crook) his presence understandably made Crook uncomfortable. Still, relations between the two men seemed cordial enough, although there was an undercurrent of animosity, at least on Crook's part. Notwithstanding, the two officers did see eye-to-eye on one major point: Howard agreed that military force should be used to deal with Apaches who proved intractable, and he encouraged Crook to proceed accordingly. Howard also supported the notion of using Indian scouts. Overall, Howard appears to have been a better choice as an emissary of peace than Vincent Colyer whom Crook sarcastically referred to as "Vincent the Good." In comparing Colyer and Howard, the historian Hubert Howe Bancroft said that Howard's visions of peace were touched with common sense.

But more than anything else, though, it was Howard's buddy-buddy attitude toward Lieutenant Whitman that really got under Crook's hide. Howard and Whitman were friends of long standing and indeed related, albeit distantly, by marriage. But that aside, Whitman had been a frequent letter-writer to the Indian Bureau about the mistreatment of Apaches and as historian Charles M. Robinson III points out Howard was obligated to investigate as part of his mission, so on that basis alone he could hardly not have paid attention to the lieutenant.

A month after his arrival, Howard convened a council near Camp Grant. Large numbers of Apaches were in attendance, along with Pimas and Papagos. Unfortunately for Howard, Cochise was not present. Howard, Crook, Governor Anson Safford, a number of prominent Tucsonans represented the U.S. Government. Numbered among the gathered throng was Lieutenant Whitman who seems to have been the only army officer whom the Indians trusted, and which must have rankled Crook no end. It was a tense gathering. A number of the Apaches were armed and surly-looking. Crook feared an attempt on their lives.

Notwithstanding, the council proved fruitful. Howard listened and appreciated the long standing enmity between the Apaches and the Pimas and Papagos. To resolve this, he moved the Camp Grant reservation to the Gila River and closed those at McDowell, Date Creek, and Beale Spring. President Grant subsequently created two huge new reservations, the one on the Gila to be called San Carlos and the second the White Mountain or Fort Apache Reservation.

Following the San Pedro Council, Howard took a group of Arizona Indians to Washington for a face-to-face with President Grant, and there were interviews with the media and others as well. The delegation left the capitol on July 10, stopping en route to visit Vincent Colyer and the Dutch Reformed Society of New York.

When he first arrived in Arizona Howard asked Crook for a meeting with Cochise, but the Chiricahua leader was unavailable at that time. However, recognizing the importance of meeting with Cochise, Howard intended try again, and when he returned from Washington resumed his efforts to set up a meeting.

As a result of the San Pedro council, a new reservation was to be established at Tularosa, just across the New Mexico line, east of Fort Apache. In his effort to find a way to meet with Cochise, Howard learned of a white man who was on friendly terms with the Chiricahua leader and might be willing to carry a message to him. The man was Thomas Jonathan Jeffords, who was to figure prominently in Southwestern history.

Thomas Jeffords

Forty years old, Jeffords hailed from New York. He was an educated man, read law, and may actually have practiced some in Denver. Reportedly, he had also spent time as a Great Lakes sailor, eventually becoming captain, a name by which he was often referred to the rest of his life. By all accounts, Howard seems to have reached New Mexico by 1859, driving a stage for the Butterfield Overland Stage Company. Later, he prospected for gold in Colorado. During the Civil War he served with General Canby's forces that repelled the

Confederate invasion of New Mexico. The war's end again found him employed as a stage driver along the route from Mesilla to Tucson, and later served as mail superintendent. Concerned over the loss of so many of his drivers to Apache attacks, Jeffords rode alone into the Dragoon Mountains hoping to meet with Cochise. Impressed by this white man's bravery, Cochise promised that the drivers would heretofore not be molested. The meeting led to a deep and abiding friendship between the two men. Indeed, Jeffords was thereafter known to the Apaches as brother.

Jeffords proved willing to take Howard to Cochise, providing that the general was willing to go without an escort. Howard wasted little time in agreeing to this proviso and so plans were promptly laid for one of the most significant meetings in Western history. Before setting out on his mission Howard apologized to Crook for complicating matters in his military department; notwithstanding, the apology did not sit well with Crook who resented Howard's interference in any event and considered him a nuisance at best.

HOWARD MEETS COCHISE

In preparation for what he hoped would prove a fruitful rendezvous, Howard set about laying some groundwork that would demonstrate the sincerity of his intentions to Cochise. Perhaps the most important step was to cancel the Tularosa Reservation and designate instead Cañada Alamosa between Tularosa and the Rio Grande, a site much preferred by the Apaches. Howard's second step was to appoint Tom Jeffords as agent for the new Apache reservation.

On September 18, Howard started out with a small party that included Jeffords, two Apache guides named Che and Ponce along with Howard's long time assistant, a young officer named Lieutenant Joseph Alton Sladen who would later write an account of Howard's efforts to negotiate a peace agreement with Cochise.

The journey proved long and circuitous, and without any assurance that Cochise would meet with them, but the effort was to prove worthwhile. On October 1, Howard and Jeffords, accompanied by Sladen and the two Apaches, met with Cochise in the camp of Tygee in southeast Arizona's remote Dragoon Mountains. Lieutenant Sladen described the setting:

> The sun had set before we entered this valley, but the long twilight enabled us to form some idea of our environment. The place seemed the center of a natural fortification. In extent it seemed some 40 to 50 acres, flanked on either hand with precipitous bluffs 300 or 400 feet in height. Through the center ran a stream of water coming from a large spring nearby.[8]

Joseph Sladen had served as Howard's aide and confidant since the Civil War. When Howard was assigned to command the Department of the Columbia, two years later, Sladen accompanied him. In 1875, Sladen broke his right leg in a fall from his horse. Complications ensued, necessitating amputation. Remarkably, however, the devoted aide remained on active duty, serving his general throughout the Nez Perce and Bannack uprisings. After two decades, the two men were finally separated in 1885. Four years later, Sladen was promoted to captain and retirement soon followed. For the remainder of their lives, general and aide remained close friends. Howard died in 1909, Sladen two years later.

For the next two weeks Howard and Cochise discussed the particulars of a peace accord. Finally, on October 12, 1872, an agreement was struck. General Oliver Otis Howard, the one-armed Christian general and Cochise, the magnificent Chiricahua leader together brought the first peace in the Southwest in a decade. Runners were dispatched to the various Apache camps, notifying them of the new peace agreement. Lamentably, it would not prove a lasting peace. Cochise would honor this agreement with Howard for the remainder of his life, which unfortunately for Americans and Apaches alike was to end in two years. For now, though, Americans were free to travel through Apacheria without fear. Cochise agreed to keep the Apaches on the reservation and protect the Tucson road to Mesilla.

The story of the Howard/Jeffords/Cochise relationship was brought to life in Elliott Arnold's novel, *Blood Brother*, later adapted for the screen in a film titled *Broken Arrow* starring James Stewart as Tom Jeffords, Jeff Chandler as Cochise, and Basil Ruysdael as General Howard.

The new reservation—called appropriately enough the Chiricahua Reservation—was not as it turned out *Cañada Alamosa* after all, but was instead set in the southeast corner of Arizona, extending from the Dragoon Mountains to Stein's Peak, thence south to the Mexico line, and west again back to Dragoon Springs.

It should be understood here that Cochise made peace with the Americans, *not* the Mexicans. Apaches would continue to raid to raid into Sonora, eliciting loud protests from below the border. Howard, who had not been treated kindly by the local press prior to the agreement with Cochise, was now being applauded (though that too would prove short lived). However, if some regarded Howard's achievement as being of the first rank, not all were ready to heap praise on the one-armed general, namely, George Crook.

The importance of the Howard-Cochise peace agreement cannot be overstated, both for what it achieved and what it did not. Arizona knew peace for the first time in a decade. The failure of the agreement to shut down cross-border raids left a volatile situation unchanged. And remember, too, that by virtue of the Treaty of Guadalupe Hidalgo the United States had agreed to see that these raids would end, but no one with any understanding of life in the Southwest knew that this would ever happen and so it did not.

Cochise freely admitted that he had not made peace with the Mexicans, and Howard, it seems, had but a limited understanding of the deep and abiding hatred Apaches held for Mexicans, and of all the Apache bands, none had suffered at the hands of the Mexicans more than the Chiricahuas. Cochise understood that the Americans wanted him to cease raiding into Mexico, but he had no intention of ending that practice, at least not immediately. He probably understood that day was coming, but he may not have imagined it would arrive in his life time, and he very likely did not recognize what was liable to happen if he failed to end the raids immediately. In retrospect, one is tempted to ask why a man of Jeffords' experience failed to make that clear to Howard, whose ear he certainly had. The answer may lie in Jeffords' own bias. Jeffords was very much pro–Apache; he understood the enmity the Apaches felt Sonorans and sympathized with them. During his tenure as agent he did little to try and discourage raids into Sonora. Indeed, critics of the new Chiricahua Reservation (including Crook) argued that the reservation was ideally situated for raiding parties to strike across the border and return.

In any event, it did not take long for the agreement to show signs of weakening, and it was not surprising, either. Howard, after all, was a kindly man; his heart was in the right place, and he was full of sincerity. Cochise, too, wanted peace, but he was aging and not in the best of health. So, looking at it retrospectively, one can see that it was an agreement built on a shaky foundation.

To begin with, Jeffords soon learned that he was to be answerable to Herman Bendell, Superintendent of Indian Affairs in Arizona. Bendell, a typical bureaucrat was a stickler for proper procedure, which frustrated Jeffords no end. Indian rations were also maddeningly slow to arrive and sometimes short. Jeffords complained loudly and frequently to Bendell, to no avail, but the superintendent had his own problems, not the least of which were budgetary constraints, and there was little sympathy from Washington. Jeffords finally complained to Howard and that resulted in a little action, but not nearly enough. But Tom Jeffords wasn't the only one who was frustrated, however. On March 24, 1873, Bendell resigned.

As Sonoran raids continued through the remainder of 1872 and on into 1873, Cochise was blamed for all, even though he had not been personally involved. Sonoran officials complained to the U.S. that General Howard had given Cochise permission to raid across the border, a ludicrous charge, but it had an effect. Insofar as George Crook was concerned he welcomed these complaints against Howard whom he regarded as entirely too naive to be formulating Indian policy in the Southwest (or anywhere for that matter). Crook thought Howard had a rose colored vision of the Apaches.

Crook hungered for more freedom to punish raiders, but in this he was hampered by Howard's treaty. Crook believed the Apaches would have to be whipped before they would comply. In this, he seems to have overlooked or ignored the fact that the treaty had brought peace to southern Arizona. Granted, the cross border raids were continuing and one could be critical of the treaty for not addressing that issue, but this in no way diminished what Howard and Cochise had achieved insofar as Arizona was concerned.

But Crook saw a way around the restraints imposed by the treaty. It was simple: enforce General Order Number Ten. Any Indians caught off the reservation, such as those heading for or returning from Mexico would be subject to chastisement. And it should be noted that although the Howard-Cochise agreement resulted in many Apaches moving to the new reservation, a good many remained in the wild and therefore subject to attack by the army.

Although the Howard/Cochise agreement did bring peace to southern Arizona for a time, it needs to be remembered that Cochise did not exercise iron and unconditional control over all Apaches. A great many respected his decision and removed to the reservation; but not all did so. There were a number of wild bands who chose to ignore Cochise's order, if in fact it may be thought of as such, and it was these bands that Crook sought to locate and move onto their reservation.

Crook's Grand Offensive

The council on the San Pedro calmed the turbulent political waters for the moment, allowing Crook to again focus his energies on the Grand Offensive. As noted, his first step was to resurrect the old General Order Number 10, which basically directed all Indians to report to their reservation or be considered hostile. It was exactly the same approach that the president, supported by Generals Sheridan, Terry, and Crook would implement four years later against the hostile Lakota and Cheyenne on the Northern Plains. Crook's orders to his field commanders stressed that Indians should be given every chance to surrender, but if they refused, to bring the hammer down hard. Crook took the position that if fighting proved necessary his commanders should not hold back.

Crook proposed to start things off by traveling to Date Creek Reservation some sixty miles south of Prescott. Word had it that Yavapai-Apaches living on that reservation were the ones who had attacked the Wickenburg Stage back in July. Additionally, the unexpected death of the post commander at Date Creek provided more incentive for Crook to put in a personal appearance here. From Hualapai scouts came word of a plot brought to assassinate Crook adding a sense of drama to the impending visit. With this as background,

Crook set out with an escort and on September 8 met with Ochocama and a council of Yavapais to discuss matters. During the course of the negotiations Ochocama himself attempted to shoot Crook, but an aide managed to deflect the shot. A fight promptly followed in which seven Apaches were killed and four whites wounded. Several Apaches, including Ochocama managed to escape into the mountains.

On September 25, a fortnight after the Date Creek meeting, thirty-seven-year-old Captain Julius Wilmot Mason, a former engineer on the Brooklyn Water Works, with three companies of the 5th Cavalry and a contingent of Hualapai scouts led by the celebrated scout Al Sieber attacked Ochocama and his followers along the Santa Maria River, killing about forty, while suffering no army casualties. This attack sent a strong message and henceforth there was little trouble with the Yavapai and Yuma Apaches.

Farther south, on September 30, Apache raiders struck a ranch near Camp Crittenden (the successor to old Fort Buchanan). Upon learning of the attack, twenty-four-year-old Lieutenant William Preble Hall, who would one day rise to the rank of brigadier general and serve as the army's acting adjutant general, took a dozen 5th Cavalry troopers in pursuit. Picking up the trail, Hall determined that the raiders numbered sixty. Heavily outnumbered, Hall wisely elected to return to Crittenden, but detached a patrol of five to alert other ranches in the area. While returning to camp, the patrol was attacked, losing three of the original five members. The remaining two men managed to reach the safety of the camp.

One prong of Crook's grand offensive consisted of Company C, 5th Cavalry, supported by a contingent of Paiute scouts, all under forty-one-year-old, Bavarian born Captain Emil Adams. A lithographer by trade, Adams had served in the Civil War. After assignment to the 5th Cavalry in 1870, Adams went on to see considerable service on the Western frontier. In 1874, while commanding the post at San Carlos, Adams created something of a stir when he refused to fire on Indians who had attacked a wagon train stranded on the Gila River. Adams argued that he could not legally fire on Indians while they were on their reservation. Nevertheless, charges were preferred and Adams was suspended for six months. Crook felt the penalty was insufficient, but accepted it. Two years later, Adams would serve under Crook during the Big Horn and Yellowstone Expedition. Now, here in November 1872, Adams left Camp Hualapai and followed a trail into Chino Valley and Hell's Canyon where he attacked an Apache camp on the 25th, killing eleven and capturing three women. One soldier lost his life.

Through that autumn of 1872 and on into the winter, Crook continued to apply pressure on the Indians. By mid-month, he had nine expeditions in the field. On the 7th, a mixed detachment of the 23rd Infantry and 5th Cavalry moved into the Tonto Basin, where they attacked an Apache camp near Prescott, killing a dozen and burning the camp. A few days later, another column under Captain George "Blackjack" Randall with two companies of the 5th Cavalry and 23rd Infantry headed into the Mazatzals, a rugged mountain range in south central Arizona, some forty miles northeast of present Phoenix. "Jack" Randall, as he was sometimes known, sported a huge black mustache that was said to captivate an Apache. Randall had a distinguished record as a scouting commander; indeed, he was said to be the best of his rank when it came to leading a field command. Here in the Mazatzals a detachment under Galway born Lieutenant Thomas Garvey attacked the camp of Delshay, one of the toughest and most militant of Apache leaders, killing fourteen Apaches in a two-hour fight on the 11th. In 1888 Garvey would be court-martialed for drunkenness while commanding an escort for the paymaster.

The Salt River Cave Fight

Meanwhile, Delshay and some of his band who had managed to escape Garvey's attack were cornered near Tortilla Flat (currently said to be Arizona's smallest community with a population of six) near Apache Junction. The place is said to owe its name to inebriated cowboys who failed to purchase enough supplies and were forced to make tortillas using only flour. The Apaches had taken a strong position in a cave along the heights above the Salt River. Two columns of the 5th Cavalry, supported by 30 Apache and 100 Pima scouts, under the command of Major William Henry Brown and Captain Jim Burns, rendezvoused and attacked the Apaches, said to be of the Yavapai band. Lieutenant John Gregory Bourke, Crook's right-hand man was with the troops and later described the scene in his diary. It was December 28. These troopers had spent Christmas in the field on a grueling campaign.

> Upon the crest of the bluffs which here enclose the Rio Salado was a small cave or depression in the rocks which overhung this nook by at least five hundred feet, the bluffs mentioned being one thousand or twelve hundred feet above the Rio Salado. In front of the cave, a natural rampart of sandstone ten feet high afforded ample protection to the Indians, although the great number of boulders scattered in every direction screened our men in turn from the fire of the besieged.
>
> Our policy was obvious—the incorrigible Apaches, at least a portion of them, were now entrapped beyond possibility of escape, and in justice to our men, whose lives should not be rashly imperiled, orders were made to make no charge upon the works, to pick off every Indian showing his head, to spare every woman and child, but to kill every man. Twice the besieged were asked to surrender their families, promises being given that no harm should befall them but, confident in their ability to repel us, their only answers were yells of defiance. These shouts of scorn were soon changed into groans of despair as our shots began to fall with deadly accuracy about them, reckless attempts at escape being made but in each case resulting in the death of those of those who tried to run our gauntlet of fire. One splendid-looking Indian over six feet, most beautifully proportioned but with a very savage countenance, did indeed succeed in breaking through our front line and making his way down the arroyo full of large rocks, upon one of which he sprang with a yell of defiance, bravado, or joy, I cannot say which. Twelve of us concealed at this point, leveled our rifles and fired. Every shot must have hit him as he fell dead, riddled from head to foot.
>
> A volley was now directed upon the mouth of the cave, and for three minutes every man in the command opened and closed the breechblock of his carbine as rapidly as his hands could move. Never have I seen such a hellish spot as was the narrow little space in which the hostiles were crowded. To borrow the expression employed by a brother officer, the bullets striking against the mouth of the cave seemed like drops of rain pattering upon the surface of a lake.
>
> A charge was now ordered and the men rushed forward; upon entering the enclosure a horrible spectacle was disclosed to view—in one corner eleven dead bodies were huddled, in another four, and in different crevices they were piled to the extent of the little cave and to the total number of fifty-seven (seventy-six altogether were killed in this fight and twenty women and children were taken prisoner).[9]

A fortnight after the Salt River cave fight (sometimes called the Battle of Skull Cave), Brown, leading six companies of the 5th Cavalry followed an Apache trail into the Superstition Mountains, where he surprised a rancheria, though most of the inhabitants managed to escape. For his work in Arizona, Brown would later be recommended by Crook for promotion to brigadier general. However, the captain would never wear the stars of a brigadier. In 1875 he took his own life, ostensibly because the woman he loved married, instead, General Phil Sheridan.

Throughout 1873, Crook's columns were constantly in the field, pressuring non-compliance Apaches. Virtually every month found units seeking out and attacking rancherias with varying degrees of success. Crook's winter campaign through the Tonto Basin and surrounding mountains was, as historian Robert Utley points out, was soldiering of the toughest sort. Some years later, Lieutenant Britton Davis would write: "Those who today ride over this country on well-built auto roads; who drive easily from Phoenix to Payson, under the rim, in six hours, can have little real appreciation of the difficult task these army men faced in 1882." Thanks to field commanders like William Brown, Crook's Tonto Basin campaign was a resounding success. If the Indian wars of the West are thought of as guerrilla warfare, then this campaign of Crook's would have to be regarded as a textbook example. Interestingly enough, this Tonto Basin area would one day see the construction of the Theodore Roosevelt Dam, which would be built in large part by Apache labor.[10]

The Death of Cochise

In late March 1873, at the urging of the post trader, Sidney Delong, Cochise made the first of several visits to Fort Bowie, where he was treated courteously and made it a point of saying how pleased he was with the new peace. It is interesting to note that Delong was a man who had participated in the Camp Grant Massacre and who later is said to have regretted his part in that infamous affair. Now the trader at Fort Bowie, Delong was convinced that the Howard/Cochise peace agreement was really working, and he was anxious for Cochise to visit the post. But the Chiricahua leader's health was deteriorating and we suspect he probably felt poorly much of the time. Given the same set of circumstances, one wonders whether he would have embraced peace with the same fervor a decade earlier.

On June 8, 1874, Cochise died. He apparently had been suffering from stomach problems and historian Edwin Sweeney conjectures that cancer may have been the cause. As an indication of the depth of their friendship, Tom Jeffords was the only white man present at the Chiricahua leader's last rites. Cochise was buried in a deep crevice somewhere in the East Stronghold of the Chiricahua Mountains. His final resting place remains a secret to this day. Jeffords knew the location but he honored the memory of his friend by never revealing its location through the remainder of his own life.[11]

Although the Howard-Cochise peace agreement ushered in a new era of peace in Arizona it did not mean a total absence of Apache troubles. The difference was that prior to the peace accord, Cochise regarded the Chiricahuas, and his Chokonen band in particular, to be at war with the Americans. In the years following the agreement, however, there were still occasional incidents, and, as previously noted, not all Apaches respected Cochise's promise to remove to the reservation, as Crook's Tonto Basin campaigns illustrated.

Even as Cochise's life was ebbing, Crook's troops were hard at it. In January 1874, Lieutenant Walter Schuyler, 5th Cavalry attacked the rancheria of Natotel on the Verde River. Two months later, on March 8, Blackjack Randall with six companies of the 23rd Infantry and a detachment of friendly Apache scouts led by Archie McIntosh attacked the rancheria of Cochinay, killing a dozen and capturing twice that number. Randall earned a brevet for his service on this campaign.

In April, another detachment of the 5th Cavalry struck an Apache camp near present Miami, Arizona, killing thirty. Later that month, Lieutenant Schuyler, guided by Al Sieber with a hundred Apache scouts struck a rancheria in the Aravaipa Mountains near old Camp Grant. Walter Schuyler was another of those young officers who served in the frontier army and would go on to have a distinguished career, serving in Puerto Rico and the Philippines.

In 1904 he was sent to Manchuria as military attaché and observer with the Russian army. In September, when Indians murdered a prospector and sheep herder on the Agua Fria River a detachment of the 5th Cavalry led by Sieber and a contingent of friendly Apache scouts responded, attacking the perpetrators (who turned out to be Apache-Mojaves) on the 17th at Cave Creek, killing fourteen.

In November, Tonto Apaches killed a mail carrier on the rugged Mogollon (Muggy Own) Plateau. In response, Lieutenants Charles King and George Eaton, 5th Cavalry, with the usual complement of Indian scouts, were ambushed near Winslow, Arizona. King was badly wounded and the Tontos escaped. Three weeks later a second expedition led by Eaton, with Sieber accompanying set out from the Verde River, and quite by accident, ran into a band of Tontos. A fight ensued in which all the Apaches were killed save for six women and some children who were taken captive.

Charles King, it might be noted, went on to become something of a celebrated literary figure within the old frontier army, later reaching the rank of general. King would eventually write a number of novels of the Western frontier and army life and Lieutenant Eaton would later serve as the model officer in King's novel *The Colonel's Daughter*.

In March 1875 Crook was reassigned to take command of the Military Department of the Platte with headquarters in Omaha. During his tenure in Arizona, Crook's campaigns had been as successful as could have been hoped for. Campaigning in Apacheria was a tough, dirty, and dangerous business, but Crook approached his task with the vision of a hard-eyed realist. Despite opposition from General Sheridan and others, Crook championed the use of Apache scouts. Who better to find the Apaches than other Apaches? Crook also developed the use of pack mules to provide the necessary logistical support for his columns, a practice he would take north with him. In his new command Crook would face a different sort of adversary and with mixed results. His replacement Brigadier General August Valentine Kautz, a German-born veteran of the Civil War, soon proved to be a cautious commander, quite disinclined to take the field without specific orders from higher authority.

It should not come as any particular surprise that in June 1876 the powers in Washington decided that the Chiricahua Reservation should be closed and the Apaches relocated to the hated and dreadful San Carlos Reservation near present Globe, Arizona. The so-called Chiricahua reservation set aside by the Howard-Cochise agreement had never been a popular choice. Crook didn't approve of the location and neither did the southern Arizona citizenry. Thus, it was inevitable that a change was almost certain to take place.

The end of the reservation came about through a series of unfortunate incidents. It all began in March 1876 when a Sulphur Springs rancher, Nicholas Rogers by name sold some whiskey to a pair of Chiricahuas, Pionsenay and Piarhel, recently returned from a Sonoran raid, flush with booty. Rogers meanwhile had been joined by his partner, Orizoba Spence. The following day the two Apaches returned to buy more whiskey, but this time Rogers refused to sell them any. Angry, Pionsenay then shot and killed both men, in an act reminiscent of the start of the 1862 Minnesota uprising. After murdering the two ranchers, the Apaches looted the house, taking whiskey, and ammunition before heading back to their camp in the Dragoon Mountains.

The word spread. Agent Tom Jeffords requested help from Fort Bowie, which in turn resulted in a forty-man detachment of the 6th Cavalry under Lieutenant Austin Henely being sent to the area. The guilty Apaches were evidently from the band led by Skinya, but Jeffords was concerned that Henely might mistake Cochise's old band, now led by his son Taza, as the guilty group. Using his powers of persuasion and relying on the trust Taza, like his father before him, placed on the agent, Jeffords was able to convince Taza to remain where he was; not to flee. Henely seems likewise to have relied on Jeffords' judgment.

The chain of events continued. It was then learned that Pionsenay and Nazaree, quite likely still liquored-up, had killed yet another man. When Skinya learned what had happened and knowing the repercussions that were sure to follow, he prepared to head for Sonora forthwith. However, Pionsenay with half a dozen followers elected to make a side trip. To the ranch of one Gideon Lewis they went, killing Lewis and wounded a Mexican boy who managed to escape. The raiders then went on to wound yet another nearby rancher. When word of this latest attack reached Henely he immediately decided to go after Skinya, with Taza as a guide. Taza's instincts as to which route Skinya would take were spot on. The problem, as it turned out, was that Skinya had ensconced his band on top of a high peak in the Mule Mountains. Using their position to great advantage, Skinya's warriors opened a furious fire on Henely's men. The soldiers returned the fire, but there was little to be done at this point save for a suicidal charge and Henely elected to return to Fort Bowie. Skinya, meanwhile easily slipped across the border into Sonora. Henely, a hard-working, courageous young officer would lose his life in a flash flood two years hence.

It is important here to recognize that the Pionsenay incident (and others like it) was not representative of all Chiricahuas. The Howard-Cochise agreement did indeed bring peace to southern Arizona, but troublemakers are with us always and such was the case with Pionsenay, who in the best of times seems to have been a dour, mean-spirited individual. In the aftermath of the killings of Rogers and Spence, Taza, who apparently inherited his father's wisdom, made a concerted effort to assist in bringing to an end the mischief of Pionensay and his followers. None of the Chiricahuas on the reservation participated in these incidents.

It is not clear exactly how long Skinya remained in Mexico, but apparently not long, as he was soon back on the reservation. His stay at San Carlos seems to have been brief, however, as he soon left there for Ojo Caliente. The numbers who left San Carlos are confusing but apparently there were about 200 under Skinya's leadership, who stole whatever they came across en route. Ojo Caliente, however, did not prove to be the haven they sought; for one thing rations at the agency were low and insufficient to feed those Apaches already there. Then, too, squabbles broke out between bands, so that all in all things were quite unsettled. Colonel Edward Hatch, commanding the Military District of New Mexico rushed down from Santa Fe to see about soothing jangled nerves.

John Clum

The upshot of all this was that with serious trouble apparently looming, Governor Safford and John Philip Clum, agent at San Carlos, agreed that the Chiricahua Reservation should be closed and the Apaches living there removed to San Carlos. Clum, something of a controversial figure in Southwest history had long argued for a centralization of the reservation system, an idea that seemed to find great favor in Washington. If all Apaches were brought together in one location it would simplify managing and caring for them. The philosophy was embraced by Washington bureaucrats who of course possessed little understanding of the situation, but the idea looked good on paper so that was that. Of course, knowledgeable people in Arizona such as Tom Jeffords knew better. For one thing not all Apaches were friendly with other Apaches and secondly those Apaches sent to San Carlos despised the place, and for good reason; it was an unhealthful arm pit of a location. The army's medical director at Whipple Barracks (Prescott) noted that here the Indians were subject to malarial fevers, dysentery, and diarrhea. Clum, Governor Safford and a handful of others supported the idea because it was in their best interests. John Clum would later leave the Indian Bureau and move to Tombstone where he again gained a measure of prominence as publisher of the *Tombstone Epitaph*.

Tom Jeffords' days as agent were numbered, and more than likely he could see the end approaching. For one thing, the local press blamed him for the troubles caused by Pionsenay and others. As noted, Jeffords, actually, was in sympathy with the Apaches who raided south of the border. When he inadvertently let it be known that he was in sympathy with the Apaches he drove another nail in his coffin. In any event, on June 5, 1876, Jeffords was relieved of duty. Officially, the term was suspended, but there was no disguising the fact that he was fired.

And so, the Chiricahua Apaches—four bands of them, numbering just under 1,300, removed to the San Carlos Agency. But understand that Apache resistance was by no means at an end; the blood, sweat and hardships that would follow in the decade to come would suggest in the strongest way that relocating the Chiricahuas to San Carlos was indeed shortsighted wisdom.

As for Jeffords, his work went largely unappreciated. Unlike so many agents, Tom Jeffords was honest. Not one iota of evidence was ever found to suggest graft on his part. If Jeffords had a failing it was probably that he was too sympathetic toward the Apaches. He could certainly have pressed a little harder to discourage cross-border raids, which might have served the Apaches' best interests later on. During the two decades of his life that remained, Jeffords was a stagecoach driver, prospector and homesteader. He died on February 21, 1914, and rests today in Tucson.

The Emergence of Victorio

The decade of the 1870s saw the emergence of the Apache war chief Victorio as New Mexico's principal Indian threat. Following their confinement at the hated San Carlos Reservation the Warm Springs band, some 300 strong and led by Victorio, bolted the reservation but were quickly cornered and induced to surrender at Fort Wingate. The Apaches requested they be allowed to return to their traditional homeland around the warm springs near present Truth or Consequences, New Mexico. After considering the matter, however, the Indian Bureau decided they must return to San Carlos. To this ultimatum, Victorio said no and with eighty of his followers broke free.

During the next two years Victorio's band was constantly on the move, ever raiding always a threat. In 1876, Colonel Edward Hatch was appointed military commander of the District of New Mexico (In 1871 the Department of New Mexico became the District of New Mexico within the larger Division of the Missouri). The fall of 1879 saw Victorio at the head of a mixed band of disaffected Warm Springs, Mescaleros, and some Chiricahuas, raising havoc across southwest New Mexico, raiding, plundering, and crossing the border with impunity, knowing full well U.S. troops were forbidden from following.

In February 1880, Hatch put nearly all of the 9th Cavalry in the field to try and corner the elusive Apache leader, who was certainly one of the best. Mexico who had suffered about as much at the hands of the Apaches as had the U.S. agreed to allow U.S. troops to pursue the raiders across the border. Additional army units from Texas and Arizona supported Hatch's effort, along with some 1,000 Mexican regulars. However, Colonel Joaquin

Terrazas, who had been ill-inclined to cooperate from the start, ordered American units back across the border. On October 15, Terrazas managed to trap Victorio in the Tres Castillos Mountains, killing the Apache chief and some sixty of his warriors.

The Rise of Geronimo

The death of Cochise created a cavity in Apache leadership. For the first time, there was no one dominant leader of the Chiricahuas. When Americans first arrived in the Southwest there was Mangas Coloradas, then Cochise, and for a time, the pair stood as a dynamic force with which to be reckoned. Both were extraordinary leaders and their like would not be seen again. True enough, Victorio had been a fearsome raider, but with the passing of Cochise, Geronimo would soon rise to the fore. Juh and Nana would also continue to plague the Americans, but none would rise to the level of leadership provided by Cochise and his father-in-law.

His Chiricahua name was Goyaalé, but it was his Mexican sobriquet, Geronimo, by which he would be remembered to history. His biographer, Robert M. Utley suggests that so deeply entrenched is the name Geronimo in the public consciousness that it rises above other Indian leaders, even those of Sitting Bull and Crazy Horse. A squat fireplug of a man with hard, scowling features suggesting he was born to be feared, Geronimo first saw light in the Valley of the Upper Gila River about 1823. He was born into the Bedonkohe band, smallest of the Chiricahua groups.[12]

Through his youth and early manhood, Geronimo learned the Apache way of war, developing his skills as a warrior to a high degree. Mean, harsh, and truculent, he became an incorrigible opponent of all whites. Geronimo was not born to inherit the role of chief, but he seems to have been one of those individuals who were born to be a leader, and in the years following the death of Cochise Geronimo increasingly moved to the forefront of Apache resistance.

In the void left by the death of Cochise, Taza, who had inherited the mantle of chief from his father, found himself embroiled in a power struggle with Skinya who had grown increasingly incorrigible. Strong words were exchanged when Skinya tried to induce Taza to bring his people to Mexico, but Taza who respected and honored his father's promises rejected Skinya's argument and chose to remain at San Carlos.

During the summer of 1876, Geronimo raided across southern Arizona nearly at will. The halcyon days of the Howard-Cochise peace accord seemed like something from the distant past. Livestock was always a tempting target: horses because they provided mobility and cattle because they provided meat when the agency beef rations were slim or late. Such raids did not stand as an outright declaration of war from the Apache perspective, but to area ranchers and stagecoach drivers alike this was perhaps too subtle a distinction.

On September 26, Taza, who had picked up a bug at the unhealthful San Carlos, died of pneumonia, elevating a younger brother, Naiche to the role of chief. A well-liked young man, Naiche nevertheless lacked the skills and wisdom to replace Taza, who had been well educated to the responsibilities of chief by Cochise.

Unlike Taza, neither Geronimo nor Juh (leader of the Nedni band of Chiricahuas), would accept San Carlos with its hostile environment and headed across the border. Mexico, however, had one big disadvantage: there was no way for the people to survive, other than by raiding the local villages, which had little to offer at any rate, so in November 1876, Geronimo elected to leave Juh and return to the U.S. The locale he chose was in the Animas

Mountains of southwestern New Mexico. En route, Geronimo raided targets of opportunity that presented themselves.

The army's job of course was to pursue these raiders and, if possible, recover stolen property; in a sense it could almost be thought of as police duty. On January 4, 1877, Lieutenant John Anthony Rucker left Fort Bowie with a detachment of seventeen men from the 6th Cavalry supported by thirty-four Apache scouts in pursuit of Geronimo's band who had stolen horses. For three days Rucker and his men trailed the raiders into the mountains near Lordsburg, New Mexico. Carefully, Rucker surrounded the camp at night and prepared to attack at first light on the 9th. Unfortunately, the Apache scouts opened fire prematurely, allowing the raiders an opportunity to organize a defense of sorts. Twice the soldiers were driven, but after a two-hour fight the Apaches were withdrew. Geronimo led the rest of his people to Ojo Caliente. Ten of the raiders lay dead. Rucker was of the opinion that this marked the first time that the Chiricahuas had really felt the heavy hand of the army, but it was a questionable claim at best.

John Rucker, known as Tony, was the son of General David Rucker and the great grandson of Captain John Whistler, who had established Fort Dearborn (now Chicago). Tony's sister Irene later married General Phil Sheridan. Some considered Tony Rucker the ablest Apache fighter since George Crook.

A week later, Captain George Mitchell Brayton, leading a detachment of the 8th Cavalry and aided by Al Sieber and a contingent of Apache scouts, took the field in search of some Tonto Apaches who had broken out of San Carlos. Cornered in a cave, the Apache leader, Eskeltsettle refused to surrender, leading to a siege amid snow and bitter temperatures. After three days the Apaches finally yielded having lost three killed. Through the remainder of the month, Brayton and Sieber were in the field in pursuit of raiders who had stolen livestock.

Through the spring of 1877 Geronimo continued to raid across southern Arizona. The Sonoita and Sulphur Springs Valleys seemed to provide favorite targets. However, in April, when he appeared at the Ojo Caliente Agency to draw rations he was arrested by Apache police, shackled, taken to San Carlos and put in jail.

In March 1878, General Kautz was replaced by fifty-five-year-old Colonel Orlando Bolivar Willcox. A West Point graduate and an officer of wide experience, who had seen extensive combat during the Civil War. Since George Crook's departure, the Department of Arizona had been poorly managed under General Kautz; there would be little change during Willcox's tenure.

A favorite Apache beverage was a concoction made from fermented corn called tiswin. In August 1878, during a "tiswin drunk" Geronimo harangued one of his nephews to such a degree that the young man committed suicide. Fearful of the consequences, and perhaps somewhat remorseful after sobering up, Geronimo gathered his immediate family and struck out for Old Mexico, where he again joined forces with his old friend Juh. It was Geronimo's first break-out from San Carlos; it would not be his last.

Generally, Apaches tended to feel secure in the mountains of Mexico, but that sense of security needed to be taken with a grain of alertness, which seems not to have happened in November when Sonoran troops surprised Geronimo's camp, killing a dozen before they withdrew. Later that month Geronimo and Juh moved their combined camps to a new location in the mountains near Janos. While here they received an emissary from Arizona encouraging them to return to San Carlos. The promise of rations, as always, was a powerful inducement, and the bearer of this message, a minor Bedonkohe sub-chief named Gordo promised Geronimo he would not be hanged, nor punished for the suicide of his nephew.

It took a good deal of patience, but through the combined efforts of Tom Jeffords and Lieutenant Henry Leland "Harry" Haskell, but by the end of the year Geronimo and Juh were both back at San Carlos. Forty-year-old Harry Haskell had served as an enlisted man during the Civil War before accepting a commission. In 1878 he was appointed aide to General Willcox and charged with the unenviable task of seeing to it that the two Apache leaders returned to San Carlos. An able officer, Haskell would go on to see service in Cuba and the Philippines, eventually rising to the rank of brigadier general.

Through 1879, raiding parties persisted in sneaking out of San Carlos to create a little mischief. Partially this was to relieve the ennui of reservation life and party out of anger and frustration.

The Cibecue (Cibicue) Affair, August 1881

General Crook's relentless campaigns against the White Mountain Apaches had mostly taken them out of the picture as serious adversaries, but then came Cibecue (Cibicue) Creek, forty some miles northwest of Fort Apache. Here was located a sub-agency to serve some of the White Mountain tribe. Leader of the Cibecue band was one Nock-ay-det-klinne, who seems to have been something of a holy man as well. Through special dances, ceremonies and incantations, Nock-ay-det-klinne claimed to have the power to raise two dead Apache leaders from the dead. Like Isatai of the Comanches and Wovoka still to come, Nock-ay-det-klinne promised that he would lead Apaches to victory over the white man.

As a serious threat, Nock-ay-det-klinne's prophecies were not taken seriously at first, but as his preaching and prophesying attracted an increasing number of Apaches with this messianic message, Joseph Tiffany, the agent at Cibecue began to grow concerned and requested military support, which soon materialized in the form of Major Eugene A. Carr with eighty men of the 6th Cavalry from Fort Apache, supported by two dozen friendly Apache scouts. Carr, it will be remembered had ended the Cheyenne Dog Soldier threat at Summit Springs back in 1869.

Even as Nock-ay-det-klinne's message was attracting a wider audience, an eighty-year-old Chihenne war leader named Nana set off on a mighty raid from his camp high in the Sierra Madres. Striking east, Nana raided and looted through Texas and New Mexico on a month long foray during which he killed an estimated fifty whites and captured a number of others, to say nothing of livestock before returning to Mexico.

Meantime, Colonel Carr arrived at Cibecue on August 30 carrying orders to take Nock-ay-det-klinne into custody. The Apache leader surrendered easily; that was no problem, but his followers quickly swarmed around Carr's troopers. A fight unexpectedly erupted. Suddenly, the Apache scouts revolted and turned on the soldiers, who were undoubtedly stunned at this turn-about. Two Apaches attempted to rescue Nock-ay-det-klinne, but he was killed by the soldiers. An officer and six soldiers were killed in the melee and two others were wounded before Carr wisely withdrew to Fort Apache on August 31. Angered over the killing of Nock-ay-det-klinne, Apaches attacked Fort Apache but were quickly repulsed, though they managed to kill several whites in the area.

Although Carr would later come under much criticism for his handling of that moment at Cibecue, his men thought their bearded colonel's behavior was all that it should have been and indeed more. If he had not enjoyed the respect of his troopers before Cibecue, he certainly did afterward.

John Finerty, "The Fighting Irish Pencil-Pusher," reported on Cibecue for the *Chicago Times*. His facile pen, it will be recalled, had earlier described General Crook's Rosebud Campaign. and here described Carr's actions at Cibecue:

> Talking of Carr, his conduct at Cibicue [wrote Finerty] has won for him the lasting respect of his soldiers. He never took cover, and when a sergeant called out "For God's sake, General, get under cover or you'll be killed sure," the gallant old chief replied coolly: "Oh, God damn these whelps, they can't hit me, God damn 'em." And they couldn't.[13]

In response to Cibecue General Willcox set up a field headquarters at Fort Thomas on the Gila River southeast of San Carlos where he proposed to respond to this latest outburst of trouble big time. His first step was to issue orders for the arrest of the Cibecue leaders. It did not take long for that word to reach San Carlos, and when they learned that large numbers of soldiers were even then gathering at Cibecue and would soon be at San Carlos, Geronimo and Juh gather their families and followers—about 400 in all—and cloaked by the darkness of September 30, once again headed south to Mexico. Along the way they availed themselves of the opportunity to steal a mixed herd of horses and mules. At a point along the Gila River, Juh—who appears to have taken charge of the breakout—divided the group into four parties so as to confuse the soldiers they knew would soon be following. On September 30, the four groups came together again at Black Rock. On October 1 they attacked a large Mexican wagon train under the command of one Mariano Samaniego. Here was a prize they ill afford to resist: a dozen wagons carrying 14,000 pounds of provisions for San Carlos, to say nothing of more than a hundred mules. For a time the teamsters held off their attackers, but eventually all were killed, and the Apaches made off with nearly all the mules (several had been killed in the fight) before pursuing troops dictated a hasty withdrawal. John Finerty who accompanied the army patrol that discovered the remains of the wagon train fight, described the scene:

> I had an opportunity of seeing, near Cedar Springs, the riddled wagons of Samaniego's ill-fated train. The Indian fire directed against the half dozen brave and unfortunate Mexicans, headed by the teamster's younger brother, must have been simply infernal. The number of bullet holes in the vehicles is enormous. It is wonderful, contemplating this fact, how the doomed half dozen held their own against seventy-five Apaches for upward of two hours. The bodies found beside the wagons were full of lead. These men died hard, and the rude cross in front of "Shotgun Smith's" ranch that marks the common grave of five of them throws its sacred shadow on the dust of heroes.[14]

From here Geronimo and Juh moved into the Pinaleño Mountains where they ambushed their pursuers at Cedar Springs in a furious six-hour fight before resuming their southward trek.

It seemed the route to the border might be wide open. However, on October 3, while pausing to butcher some stolen cattle in the Dragoon Mountains the Apaches suddenly came under attack by a mixed detachment of soldiers and Indian scouts. The attack caught the usually alert Geronimo and Juh quite by surprise. Still they managed to recover their composure enough to respond with vigor, and by the 5th had given the soldiers the slip and continued on to Mexico where they joined forces with Nana's band now back from its New Mexico raids.

If nothing else Mexico meant safety from U.S. troops, or so Geronimo and Juh thought, but there was also a need to survive. The two leaders had in excess of 400 mouths to feed, which, in turn, led to efforts to negotiate an arrangement of sorts with the authorities in Mexico, but it never got any further than words. The failure of such talks to produce solid results led to a resumption of raids, mainly in Sonora. Mangas and Cochise had both despised Sonora and Geronimo, it seems was no different.

The departure of Geronimo and Juh from San Carlos meant that the only sizeable body of Chiricahuas remaining at that despised place was the Warm Springs band of Chihennes led by Loco and a handful of others. It did not sit well with those Chiricahuas struggling to survive in the Carcay Mountains of Mexico, to know that their brethren in San Carlos were enjoying government rations. In any event, between them, Geronimo and Juh concluded that the presence of Loco's band would give them more muscle with which to fend off attacks by Mexican troops, which was a growing threat.

With this in mind, Geronimo assembled a party of some sixty warriors and brazenly prepared to head up to San Carlos, there to persuade (by force if necessary) Loco to join them in Mexico. Juh elected not to participate in this mission, possibly believing it too risky. In advance of his departure, Geronimo sent a Chiricahua named Bonito to apprise Loco of the plan. In January 1882, Bonito reached San Carlos and informed Loco that Geronimo would arrive in a month.

A fifty-eight-year-old Mimbres leader of some stature, Loco had been a fiery warrior in his younger days. He had lost an eye reportedly in a scuffle with a grizzly bear. For a time Loco had shared the duties of chief of the Warm Springs band with Victorio. As he advanced in age, Loco had grown more inclined toward peace, which likely explains why he had had no interest in leaving the reservation in the first place.

Not only did Loco have no desire to take his people to Mexico, once he learned of Geronimo's plan, he made it a point to alert the San Carlos agent and General Willcox. The latter moved promptly to throw up a screen of patrols to watch for Geronimo, but as the days passed with no sign of the recalcitrant Chiricahua leader, Willcox began to sense that perhaps his informant had been mistaken.

Then on April 19, 1882, Geronimo and his followers suddenly appeared in Loco's camp. The army, meanwhile, had learned what was happening and rather stumbled about in an effort to organize a pursuit, but they were a day late and a dollar short. At any rate, they were here and confusion reigned. Issuing orders like fiats, Geronimo directed that all were to accompany him; any who resisted or refused were to be summarily shot. Loco attempted to argue, but finally gave in when they threatened to shoot him. All together the forced break-out resulted in some 400 Apaches heading for Mexico. Geronimo had really gotten the bulge on Willcox, who we might imagine was a trifle upset when he learned what had happened. Wasting no time, he soon took the field with a mixed force of the 1st and 6th Cavalry, 8th and 12th Infantry and a contingent of scouts.

Geronimo's break-out quickly stirred the army to action, but the fact that two military departments were involved (Arizona and New Mexico) complicated matters insofar as any organized pursuit was concerned. General Willcox assigned the responsibility for southern Arizona to Major David Perry, who, it will be recalled, had suffered the ignominy of that opening defeat by the Nez Perce at White Bird Canyon, Idaho, back in 1877.

When Perry, an able officer, notwithstanding White Bird Canyon, learned early on that the Chiricahuas were seen in the vicinity of Gayleyville, he immediately sent Captain Tullius Cicero Tupper with a company of the 6th Cavalry and some scouts to the area. Tupper had first served as an enlisted man during the Civil War and was then commissioned a second lieutenant. He won a brevet at Gettysburg and went on to see extensive service in the West. Near San Simon on the Southern Pacific Railroad, Tupper was reinforced by Captain William Rafferty's company from Fort Bowie. With Al Sieber as guide the combined force picked up the Apache trail and followed it toward the border.

Meanwhile, unknown to Willcox, Lieutenant Colonel George Alexander "Sandy" Forsyth hero of the Beecher Island fight, operating out of the Department of New Mexico with a detachment of the 4th Cavalry picked up Geronimo's trail and followed it into the Peloncillo Mountains. In a place called Horseshoe Canyon, Geronimo ambushed Forsyth's advance element under Lieutenant David McDonald. McDonald managed to get word back to Forsyth, who came on in relief. The Apaches fired the grass, then climbed high into the rocks, where Forsyth soon decided they would be impossible to dislodge and called off the pursuit, having lost two killed and five wounded.

In the aftermath of Horseshoe Canyon, Geronimo cannily pulled out under cover of darkness and resumed his march to Mexico. As historian Robert M. Utley points out Geronimo had conducted a masterly withdrawal, and as the end of April neared, all the Chiricahuas were across the border. Loco had finally and reluctantly given in and now considered himself a true hostile.

The Apaches were soon to learn, however, that Old Mexico was not quite the safe haven they had imagined. On April 28, the combined force of Captains Tupper and Rafferty, who had ignored the boundary located the rancheria and prepared to attack at dawn. Captain Rafferty later wrote an account of the fight that appeared in the Tucson *Arizona Daily Star*:

> The signal for the charge was to be a volley from the scouts as soon as they could see well. About 4:45 a.m. a blaze of fire from the mountains announced the beginning of the fight. At the same instant the cavalry sprang on their horses and with a yell charged into the basin fronting the camp, and within one hundred yards of the rocks lay camped the Indians. They then jumped from their horses and began firing rapidly at the Indians, who were running for the rocks. As soon as they got in the rocks they made it very warm for us, we were so close. We then scooped in the greater part of their herd and returned at a walk to a great distance. Goodrich of my company was killed and Miller badly wounded at this place. We then formed a dismounted skirmish line on the plain and kept up a good fire till 11:30 a.m.
>
> By that time we were satisfied that we could not get the savages out of the rocks and that no good could result from further firing, which would reduce our supply of ammunition, and hence we concluded to withdraw, which was done slowly, one company holding the skirmish line at a time.[15]

The plan of attack was sound and went south only when one of the scouts opened fire prematurely. In any case, a furious fight followed before the Chiricahuas were able to withdraw. With, with ammunition running low, Tupper and Rafferty turned about for the border.

Pursuing U.S. soldiers, it soon developed, were not the only reason to remain alert. Early on the 29th, the Apaches, having managed to withdraw and move on after yesterday's surprise attack, made their way through the foothills of the Sierra Madres and paused to refresh mind and body at a place called Alisos Creek, unaware of the ambush prepared by Colonel Lorenzo Garcia and his Mexican regulars. When the Apaches, strung out as they were in a long column reached the trigger point, the Mexicans opened fire. The Chiricahuas assumed that any trouble was most likely to strike from the rear, consequently, Geronimo and Chihuahua rode at the tail end of the column in charge of the rear guard.

The Mexican attack was brutal. Women and children in the forefront of column were hit hard; dead and wounded lay everywhere. Geronimo and Chihuahua rushed forward at the sound of the firing. Fighting was furious; much of it hand-to-hand. Finally, Garcia launched a bayonet charge, but the Apaches were able to unleash a furious fusillade that broke the charge. By noon the heaviest fighting had ended. Fresh Mexican troops arrived on the scene and resumed the attack, but they too were beaten back. As the Mexicans withdrew the Apache leaders discussed their options. They needed to leave this place and someone, it is not clear who, set the grass on fire to cover their withdrawal. It was later reported that Geronimo suggested abandoning the non-combatants so as to allow the warriors to escape. As well, there was a rumor that Geronimo behaved in a cowardly fashion, but as Robert Utley points out in his biography of Geronimo, there is virtually no evidence to support either allegation. Moreover, it would seem totally out of character for Geronimo to behave in a cowardly way; it was not at all like him.

The repercussions from Cibecue continued to resonate long after the event itself. A small band of believers who followed a minor leader named Natiotish and had refused to surrender after Cibecue caused a new ruckus to unfold in July 1882 when they killed a San Carlos Apache policeman. About sixty of them then commenced raiding through the Tonto Basin. The raids brought forth the army in some strength: a mixed force of fourteen troops of cavalry from the 3rd and 6th regiments took up the chase. One troop, commanded by Captain Adna R. Chaffee, located the Apaches and prepared to dry gulch them. Presently, Chaffee was reinforced by Major Andrew "Beans" Evans with a squadron of the 3rd Cavalry. The troops also had the advantage of the expertise of scout Al Sieber. Evans graciously deferred to Chaffee his junior, who cannily positioned his forces so as to trap the Apaches in a canyon, while other units struck them on the flanks. Masterfully conducted the attack was pressed home. Indian casualties were reported to range from a dozen to nearly thirty. At any rate, those who survived what came to be called the Battle of the Big Dry Wash scampered back to the reservation. Chaffee had done a 4-0 job. Adna Ronanza Chaffee would later rise to the rank of lieutenant general and would see service in the Spanish-American War, and would later command the American relief expedition to China during the Boxer Rebellion of 1900.

Writing about the battle many years later, Arizona historian Will Barnes wrote about an extraordinarily courageous young Apache woman.

> Early the next morning, July 18, Hodgson's men heard groans as from a wounded man. A wounded Apache at bay is a dangerous person. The men cautiously investigated the vicinity from which the groans seemed to come. While they were doing this a shot came from some sort of breastwork of rocks on the edge of the canyon. They hunted cover and locating the point by the rising powder smoke (there was no smokeless powder then), they fired at the rocks. Two or three more shots came from the nest, then ceased.
>
> The troopers blazed away at it for some minutes, then charged. Curled up behind it they found a young Apache squaw—the hostiles had but five or six women with them—with a young baby by her side, together with a very old woman who seemingly had taken no part in the firing.
>
> The girl pulled a knife from her belt and attacked the soldiers fiercely. When she was overpowered and disarmed she had a rifle. The three shots she fired were her last cartridges. She proved to have a bullet through her leg above the knee which had broken and shattered the bone.
>
> The men rigged up a rough litter of pine saplings, and with a soldier carrying the baby, got the poor thing down the rough trail to the bottom and up and out the other side to the camp. It must have been a terrible ordeal but she stood it without a groan.
>
> The following day, September [sic] 19, the army surgeons amputated her leg close to the thigh, doing it without anesthetics or stimulants of any kind. The soldiers who helped in the operation said they never saw such fortitude and apparent indifference to pain as that young Apache squaw displayed.
>
> The column from Fort Apache took a gentle saddle mule, covered the army saddle with many folds of blankets, making a sort of broad seat, on which they placed the wounded woman. With a soldier to lead the mule, her baby at her breast, she rode for seven long, hot days across those rough mountains to Fort Apache.

The writer saw her not so long afterward hobbling around the post with a crutch. Eventually, they fitted her up with a peg leg, with which she got about nicely.¹⁶

The Return of General Crook

The late summer and fall of 1882 had left the army with more than a little egg on its face, at least at the higher levels of command. To further complicate matters, the political climate in Arizona was unsettled and confrontational. The local press and citizenry complained loudly and vociferously about the Apache problem, and bickering between the Indian Bureau and the War Department was never-ending. And within the Army itself there was dissatisfaction. Sherman himself came out for a personal look-see not long after Cibecue and just missed the Loco abduction, the Cibecue Affair, and Geronimo's breakout Acrimonious charges and counter charges between Willcox and Carr kept the telegraph wires humming. Back in Washington, Sherman, weary of the bickering and very much dissatisfied with the army's handling of affairs in Arizona, elected to change pitchers. In September, Willcox was replaced by George Crook, who was expected to set things right. If Orlando Willcox left Arizona under something of a cloud he could at least take pride in knowing that a railroad stop on the Southern Pacific would later bear his name. Originally, the stop was named Maley and would be changed in 1889 to honor the general.

Throughout 1882 Geronimo and Juh remained in Mexico mainly raiding and consuming copious quantities of mescal—an alcoholic beverage distilled from the maguey plant. On mornings when they were hung over from too much partying they were vulnerable, as on May 25 when Lieutenant Colonel Lorenzo Garcia who had commanded the Mexican force at Alisos Creek back in April, surprised the rancheria, killing ten and capturing two dozen. Somehow, though, Geronimo always managed to avoid being killed or seriously wounded in these affairs.

George Crook officially assumed command of the Department of Arizona on September 4, 1882. After five years on the Northern Plains Crook was, in effect, re-assuming command of an area where he had enjoyed a greater measure of success than he had in the north country. Crook was, arguably, the U.S. Army's premier expert on waging guerrilla warfare in the 19th century. His Tonto Basin campaigns during the 1870s testified to the effectiveness of his philosophy. Crook believed, unreservedly, in the use of Apache scouts to catch other Apaches, and unlike his predecessors in the southwest, he relished being in the field.

But if Crook returned to Arizona bearing a tried and true philosophy for subjugating the Apaches, he also returned under a cloud of resentment on the part of many of his brother officers who felt betrayed by his promotion from lieutenant colonel to brigadier general over the heads of a number of full colonels. And now, as he was being considered for a second star, an anonymously written letter to the president let it be known that Crook's advancement in rank was unfair and a violation of army protocol Such complaints, however, never accomplish anything more than allowing the writer (s) to speak their piece. And so it was in this instance.

EMMET CRAWFORD AND CHARLES GATEWOOD

Two young officers who were to play a pivotal role in Crook's forthcoming Apache campaigns were Captain Emmet Crawford and Lieutenant Charles Gatewood, the former at San Carlos, the latter at Fort Apache. Crook's instructions to these two young officers who would each command a detachment of Apache scouts, was to recruit new men; they were to live with their scouts; develop a rapport with them, quite unlike other officers who had worked with Apache scouts in the past. Their immediate and only superior was to be Crook himself. Crook was eminently fortunate in his selection of these two officers. Both men came to be highly respected by the scouts they commanded and both were blessed with strong constitutions that enabled them to function in the harshest terrain.

Born in Woodstock, Virginia, in 1853, Charles Bare Gatewood graduated from West Point in 1877, joining the 6th Cavalry regiment in Arizona the following year. During the next eight years, he was almost constantly in the field, mostly as commander of a company of Apache scouts at Fort Apache, first under General Crook and later under General Nelson Miles. Stationed at Fort Apache, Gatewood was assisted by Lieutenant Hampton Mitchell Roach, who was awarded a Medal of Honor for his behavior at the Battle of Milk Creek during the Meeker Massacre. Charles Gatewood would prove instrumental in negotiating Geronimo's final surrender; tall and slim, he was absolutely devoted to duty.

Nine years older than Gatewood, Emmet Crawford was born in Philadelphia in 1844. He served in the Civil War, first as an enlisted man and later as a commissioned officer, earning two brevets for meritorious service. In 1871 he joined the 3rd Cavalry in Arizona. In 1876 his regiment was part of Crook's Big Horn and Yellowstone Expedition during the Great Sioux War. John Finerty once described him as "Over six feet high, with a genuine military face and a spare but athletic form."[17]

Still another young officer who would play an important role in Crook's Apache campaigns was twenty-two-year-old Britton Davis, who functioned as Crawford's second at San Carlos. An 1881 graduate of West Point, Davis had arrived in Arizona with the 3rd Cavalry regiment the following year. Later, Davis would pen an account of Crook's Apache campaigns with *The Truth About Geronimo*, which was destined to become a classic.

Back in Arizona Crook prepared to deal with the Apache threat, which these days primarily meant Geronimo. Of course one could hardly ignore the likes of Juh, Nana and others, but Geronimo was the headliner. If Crook was not appreciated by many of the army's senior officers, it seems not a few young officers also found him cold and aloof. On the other hand, he was quick to spot young officers who demonstrated an aptness for getting the job done; in other words, can-do officers.

Until now, American conflicts with Apaches had largely, indeed, almost exclusively been concentrated in Arizona and New Mexico. True enough, there were occasional troubles elsewhere in the region, but mainly the scene of action was in southern Arizona and southwestern New Mexico. By the early 1880s, however, Mexico had become the focal point of Crook's efforts to end the Apache problem once and for all. As he prepared for a campaign into Mexico's Sierra Madres, Crook must have been pleased to receive a directive from General of the Army William T. Sherman, advising him not to worry about crossing the border. Then, on July 29, Mexican President Porfirio Diaz renewed the cross-border agreement initially signed in 1882. And that wasn't all. Both the governors of Chihuahua and Sonora welcomed the prospect of U.S. troops entering their country; whether in so-called "hot pursuit" or otherwise. They, too, it seems were weary of having to suffer from Apache depredations.

The McComas Murders

Although by the time Crook resumed command in Arizona the focus of the Apache war had largely shifted to Mexico, incidents north of the border continued to happen, probably the most prominent of which was that of the McComas murders. In the spring of 1883, a raiding party under the dual leadership of Chatto (Chato) and Bonito chanced upon the family of Judge Hamilton McComas, his wife Juniata and their seven-year-old son, Charles (or Charley), as they traveled the lonely road between Silver City and Lordsburg, New Mexico, on a fine spring day. The date was March 28, 1883. As the family stopped for a picnic lunch, the Apaches seemingly materialized out of nowhere. The judge and Juniata were both killed and little Charley was taken captive.

The massacre of the McComas family was one of those incidents that managed to get under the hide of just about every white person (and perhaps others as well) in the region. It was just the sort of incident that brought forth cries for justice and revenge; the cry to rescue poor Charley was loud and clear. Crook, in the midst of preparing his Sierra Madre campaign, vowed to use every means at his disposal to rescue the lad.

Three days after the McComas murders, Lieutenant Britton Davis met a discontented refugee from Chatto's band named Tzoe at San Carlos. Owing to his lighter than usual complexion, whites dubbed Tzoe "Peaches." Peaches knew the Sierra Madres like the back of his hand and was easily persuaded to guide Crook's troops. Here was a break that Crook would use to good advantage as we shall see. The story of Tzoe aka Peaches is an interesting one and became the subject of a 1972 Will Henry novel entitled *Chiricahua*.

The winter of 1882–1883 found Apaches raiding heavily in Chihuahua. With the arrival of spring, four major war parties prepared to strike out in search of plunder. While Geronimo and Chihuahua worked south of the border, a second party led by Chato and Bonito brazenly swept up into Arizona and east into New Mexico, looting and killing a dozen or more before returning to the Sierra Madres. The entire region was in an uproar. The army pursued but to no avail at all. The twenty-nine-year-old Chato, a passionate and able war leader, had been responsible for slaying of the McComas family. Directed by Sherman to pull out all stops in pursuing these raiders, Crook obliged. His well conceived plan was coordinated with his New Mexico counterpart, Colonel Ranald Mackenzie, and the governors of Sonora and Chihuahua.

On May 1, Crook assembled a powerful striking force on the border. Much of his cavalry, under Colonel Carr, was distributed at key locations along the border with instructions to block any Apache efforts to escape to the north. It was expected, or at least intended, that Crook would flush the Apaches out of their mountain hideaways and some would attempt to flee across the border.

Crook, meanwhile, with a single troop of cavalry under Captain Adna Chaffee and nearly 200 Apache scouts under Crawford and Gatewood, together with a huge pack train containing more than 300 mules, plus Crook and his staff, scouts Al Sieber, Archie McIntosh and Mickey Free, figured to penetrate the Sierra Madres, and with the help of Peaches, find the hostile Chiricahuas. Mickey Free, it will be recalled, was the Ward boy who had been captured by (probably) White Mountain Apaches, and had become the underlying cause of the Bascom Affair.

Led by Peaches Crook's column pushed on over tortuous terrain, through steep-sided *barrancas* and over lofty ridges. The heat was enervating; the terrain so rough and treacherous that even the normally sure-footed mules had difficulty.

On May 15, near a place called Bugatseka, a pair of Crook's Apache scouts stumbled on some Chiricahuas belonging to the rancheria of Chato and Bonito. A fire fight ensued, but as most of the warriors were off on a raid, the defenders were quickly overcome. Seven were killed and four were taken prisoner. It happened, by way of good fortune that one of the leaders, Chihuahua, was present when the attack took place.

Fort Bowie, Arizona. The key Army post during the Apache wars.

What happened next was a sequence of events that led to the sort of unfortunate consequences that sometimes occur in the midst of tense moments. When the scouts opened fire on the rancheria Chihuahua's aunt was among those slain. The killing of Chihuahua's aunt reportedly led to the woman's angry son killing little Charley McComas in retribution. This was one account of Charley's fate, but there were others, and what really happened to the boy will forever remain a mystery. Notwithstanding, Chihuahua was willing to talk to Crook, and sent a woman envoy to convey that message. Crook eagerly replied with the assurance that he did not come to make war, only to see that the Apaches returned to San Carlos.

On May 18, Chihuahua appeared in person to meet with Crook. The fact that their rancheria in the Sierra Madres had been discovered by other Apache s working with the soldiers proved disconcerting. Mexico had always proved a safe haven from the pursuing troops. Perhaps it was time to consider returning to San Carlos? This appears to have been the case as it did not take long for Chihuahua to agree to surrender and return to San Carlos. Shortly thereafter, Geronimo and others came in and also agreed to surrender.

When Crook returned to Arizona he did so with the assumption that the Chiricahuas would be following directly, but when that failed to happen, he was scorned by the press who believed he had been duped. Indeed, in June 1885, citizens of Cochise County, Arizona, adopted a resolution stating that they believed that the Apaches should be removed "from this territory to some region where it will be impossible for them to continue the outbreaks which result in sacrificing the lives and property of our people, prohibiting all immigration and continuously preventing the growth and property of the territory."[18]

Between the time of their meeting with Crook and their return to San Carlos, the Chiricahuas had also met with Mexican leaders to discuss terms of peace. Apparently, however, Juh, while drunk, fell to his death and that seemed to end those discussions. By the spring of 1884, those who believed that Crook had been played for a fool by the Apaches now had to eat their words of scorn when all the Chiricahuas who had surrendered were finally back at San Carlos.

For Crook, it appeared that his Sierra Madre campaign had achieved its desired objective, and if he felt a measure of satisfaction in this, he soon felt differently. It turned out that finding the Apaches and bringing them back to the reservation was not nearly as challenging as administering to them on the reservation. The San Carlos agent, Philip Wilcox, as it turned out, was staunchly opposed to having the hostile Chiricahuas as his chargés. Called to Washington to testify before Secretary of the Interior, Henry Teller and the Commissioner of Indian Affairs, Crook stated his case and was subsequently given full responsibility for the San Carlos Indians. Crook, in turn, delegated this responsibility to Captain Crawford.

By 1880 the reservation system all across the Trans-Mississippi West could unreservedly be counted as an abysmal failure and San Carlos did nothing to change that picture. Oh, San Carlos was a perfectly dreadful location; everyone thought so, or nearly everyone. Lieutenant Britton Davis called it "Hell's Forty Acres." But there were some who rather liked the locale. In 1905, for example, the former frontiersman and army scout on the Northern Plains, Yellowstone Kelly, was appointed agent at San Carlos and called it a fine, hot old country. But it wasn't only the location of San Carlos; that was just the face of it. Another issue was the tension between the White Mountain Apaches and the Chiricahuas; relations between the two groups were lousy. But the overarching problem was expecting one culture to surrender its traditions in exchange for another that was totally alien. It was a process that had been ongoing since the formation of the Union, and one could say it was still not working. And truth be told, it was never going to work, at least not in the way the original designers conceived it working.

Adjusting to reservation life proved a challenge of the first order for most Apaches. On top of that strong disagreements between Captain Crawford and Agent Wilcox created a serious issue at San Carlos. Divided authority seldom works; almost always it is an invitation to trouble, and so it was with Crawford, the dedicated, hard-working soldier doing his duty, and Philip Wilcox the corrupt agent. Both men wound up frustrated. Crawford requested a transfer and was soon on his way to a new assignment in Texas. His role at San Carlos would be filled by Captain Francis Pierce. Wilcox, for his part, was fed up and resigned to be replaced by one Charles Ford.

Angered by what he regarded as interference in his official jurisdiction, Crook laid down an ultimatum: give him more authority; widen the army's role, or release him from all responsibility for the reservation Indians. Crook's immediate superior, General Irwin McDowell, commanding the Department of California, backed him, but Sheridan (who had now replaced Sherman as General of the Army) was not particularly keen on the idea. In any event, with an upcoming change in the administration in Washington, the idea was pigeon-holed.

Problems in managing the Chiricahuas surfaced quickly. Hardly any of them took a liking to the farming life. The Apaches were hunters and raiders; that had been their life for generations; not tilling the land behind a plow. That said, quite a few did make a serious effort. But many were restless and restless souls become troublesome souls. Then, too, one of the hard-line rules laid down by Crook absolutely prohibited wife-beating and brewing tiswin. In the white man's culture, wife-beating was not tolerated, but in the Apache world it was a common thing, and to expect them to change overnight was simply unreasonable. Notwithstanding, when a fiery young leader named Kaytennae broke these rules he was arrested and sent to Alcatraz for safe keeping.

It was probably inevitable then that the constraints imposed on them would ultimately lead to a confrontation, and so it did. On May 15, 1885, a group of well-armed, hung-over, and moody Chiricahua leaders approached Lieutenant Britton Davis, confessed to a "tiswin drunk," and brazenly demanded to know what the army intended to do about it. Most of the prominent leaders were present, including Geronimo, Loco, and Chihuahua. It was a cheeky move and caught Lieutenant Davis quite by surprise. He said the idea would need to be kicked upstairs and that's where matters stood for the moment. Davis meanwhile promptly sent a wire to Crook:

> There was an extensive tiswin drunk here last night and this morning the following chiefs came up and said they with their bands were all concerned in it: Geronimo, Chihuahua, Mangas, Naiche, Fele and Loco. The whole business is a put-up job to save those who were drunk. In regard to the others I request instructions. The guardhouse here is not large enough to hold them all, and the arrest of so many prominent men will probably cause trouble. Have told the Indians I would lay the matter before the general, requesting, at the same time, that their captives in Mexico be withheld.[19]

Presumably, the Apaches imagined that such a straight forward demand might compel the army to soften its stance, at least on the troublesome issue of tiswin. However, when no resolution was forthcoming, some 150 Chiricahuas, including perhaps fifty warriors, led by Geronimo, Nachez, Chihuahua, and Nana broke out of San Carlos and headed for Mexico.

And so once again the wily Apaches struck south and with great cunning avoided contact with nearly a thousand cavalry troops and Apache scouts. Not only that, but the Chiricahuas also managed to raid en route, weaving a trail of burning and looting before crossing the border nearly a month after the breakout.

George Crook wasted no time in preparing a response. One of the first things he did was to recall Emmet Crawford from Texas. In order to roust out these Apaches from hideouts in the forbidding Sierra Madres, Crook was going to need his scouts and their commanders.

Meanwhile, up at Fort Apache, Lieutenant Gatewood's continuing demands, regarding what he considered the needs of his charges, were beginning to rub Crook the wrong way. Crook's attention was focused on the recalcitrant Chiricahuas. At the moment, Fort Apache was pretty much off his radar. Finally, exasperated, Crook opted to replace Gatewood who would not as a consequence, participate in the second Sierra Madres campaign.

With Gatewood out of the picture, Britton Davis joined Emmet Crawford. Their flying column consisted of a troop of the 6th Cavalry and some ninety scouts. Crook's second field force was headed by Captain Wirt Davis (no relation to Britton) and Lieutenant Matthias Walter Day, with a troop of the 4th Cavalry and a like number of scouts. Wirt Davis was another Civil War veteran, while thirty-two-year-old Matthias Day was an 1877 graduate of West Point and would later be awarded the Medal of Honor for service at Las Animas Canyon in 1879. Day seems to have been a gutsy sort of officer. Britton Davis would later recall how Day crossed the Sierra Madres with badly swollen feet wrapped in bandages torn from his shirt. Day would go on to see varied and at time hazardous duty that included supervising a census of the Philippine Island in 1901 and chasing pirates in the Sulu Sea in 1907.

Although Crook's two columns located and struck the Apache rancherias several times during the course of that summer of 1885 they were never able to inflict anything resembling a decisive victory, nor was Crook's rather elaborately conceived border defense any more effective. Indeed, in September, Chihuahua's brother Josanie aka Ulzana disrupted southern

Arizona and southwestern New Mexico on a savage raid that covered some 1,200 miles and killed 38. Crook's second campaign across the border accomplished little and was mainly a struggle against heat, hunger, thirst, and exhaustion. Frustrated, Crook pulled his forces back to Fort Bowie to refit.

Crook was fighting a war on two fronts. The Apache problem had become a sore point, not just in Arizona, but in Washington as well; so much so that it brought General Sheridan himself out to discuss matters with Crook, whose position, politically speaking, was weakening. Although he and Crook had known each other for thirty-five years, Crook's star was no longer in its ascendancy; he had not covered himself with any laurels during the Great Sioux War, and now there was a growing sense that he couldn't quite get a handle on the Apache situation either. A major rubbing point was Crook's heavy reliance on the use of Apache scouts. At best Sheridan was lukewarm about the idea; he felt they could not be trusted: witness what had happened at Cibecue! Notwithstanding, Crook had demonstrated that his strategy worked, but Sheridan seems not to have quite grasped what it took to run down these Apaches who knew virtually every rock in the Sierras, and without the expertise of the Apache scouts, locating the hostile rancherias would be nearly impossible.

Over and above Sheridan's objection to the reliance on Apache scouts, there was a movement afoot in Washington to remove the Apaches from the southwest entirely, and not surprisingly the idea found favor with the Arizona citizenry. Crook was staunchly opposed to any such plan and in this he was supported by Emmet Crawford. Sheridan at least had the good sense to recognize that enforcement of such a plan on the eve of Crook's second campaign was a bad idea and backed down, at least for the moment.

Fending off arguments to relocate the Apaches was not all Crook had on his plate as he prepared to resume his Sierra Madre campaign. He was also nervous about rumors that Nelson Miles was after his job. The two were long time competitors, and Crook, well aware of Miles's insatiable appetite for advancement, saw no reason to doubt the rumor.

Notwithstanding the political issues, in December 1885, Crook's columns took the field once again. Regular troops were deployed at key locations along the International Boundary, while the hard work of locating and rounding up the Apaches would be done by Emmet Crawford who took with him two companies Apache scouts under Lieutenants Marion Maus and William Ewen Shipp who would lose his life on San Juan Hill thirteen years later.

On January 9, 1886, Crawford with Wirt Davis's mixed company of White Mountain and Chiricahua scouts located the Apache rancheria on an escarpment in what was known as Espinosa del Diablo (the Devil's Backbone) near the Aros River in Sonora, some 200 miles south of the border. Crawford's scouts included the soon-to-be-notorious Tom Horn.

Tom Horn

Crawford figured to make a dawn strike on the rancheria, but to do so would require a rugged night march. With Wirt Davis left behind to guard the pack train, Crawford, took Maus, Shipp and seventy scouts, plus a hospital steward and two others and set out on their trek. And a brutal march it was, over towering mountains and steep-sided canyons. Lieutenant Maus, who at forty-one was the oldest man present, and who had served through the tough winter campaigns against the Lakotas on the Northern Plains had never experienced anything like this.

Lieutenant Shipp later described the experience:

During all this dark night we climbed steep mountains covered with loose stones, or struggled through gloomy canyons, following our Chiricahua guides, who seemed perfectly at home. Sometimes we almost despaired and felt like succumbing to the fatigue that nearly overpowered us, but at such moments the thought of what dawn should bring buoyed us up and revived our drooping spirits.[20]

In that eerie sort of pre-dawn half light, Crawford met Tom Horn and two Apache scouts who had been reconnoitering the trail ahead. Based on their intel and his own intuition, Crawford elected to continue with his original plan to surround the camp and strike at dawn. Although the approach continued with due caution, something, a displaced rock, a cough; it was hard to say what exactly, but in any event one or more of the mules in the herd located several hundred yards from the sleeping camp commenced braying and alerted the Apaches.

Shots rang out. Geronimo and the other leaders quickly took charge of the situation, responding to the attack while women and children fled, with Geronimo and his warriors following. Crawford's scouts pursued, though not with any alacrity it seems, probably because of the confusion; it was hard to tell who was who. As fights went it didn't amount to much and Crawford's carefully laid plan was sent south by the braying of a mule.

All was not lost, however, as Geronimo and the other leaders, now feeling uncomfortably vulnerable, sent a runner to Crawford requesting a parley, which sounded promising, but an unsuspecting problem was about to surface. On the morning of January 11 a Mexican force unexpectedly arrived on the scene. Crawford had had no intimation that a Mexican unit was operating in the area. The Mexicans, it seems, guided by their Tarahumara Indian scouts had trailed the Apaches to this spot and now without warning opened fire on the Americans. Crawford, Maus, and Shipp, in company with Tom Horn, headed out to alert the Mexicans to the presence of an American unit in the area. As it happened, the Mexican force was commanded by Major Mauricio Corredor, reportedly the killer of Victorio at Tres Castillos in 1879.

Tom Horn took the point as Crawford and Maus advanced. As they approached the Mexicans, Maus pointed out that they were Americans. But Corredor was on a mission of annihilation; he was prepared to wipe out both Apaches and Americans; a scalp is a scalp, after all. However, he seemed to back down a bit in confronting Maus and Crawford, perhaps realizing that the American force was larger than he had initially thought.

Meantime, the Chiricahuas had withdrawn some distance, but were still within eyesight of the drama then unfolding between the Americans and Mexicans. Bitter and long time enemies the Chiricahuas and Tarahumaras faced each other threateningly. It was a tense moment. Angry rhetoric flowed back and forth; taunting, jeering. Anxious to avoid a confrontation, Crawford climbed atop a large rock and began waving a white cloth. One member of Corredor's party, having taken up a position behind a nearby tree, took aim and fired at Crawford, the bullet striking him in the head. It was a mortal wound.

Immediately a fierce fight erupted with Crawford's scouts making a sterling defense. The Chokonen scout known as Dutchy, who had served as Crawford's orderly got his pound of flesh by killing the sniper who had shot Crawford. Nine of Corredor's party died in the fight, though the major himself managed to escape. Aside from Crawford and one of the scouts, only Horn received an arm wound.

All the while, Geronimo and his band had observed the fighting from a distance. They were still much interested in discussing peace, but not while the Tarahumaras were around. Ordinarily, it would have been Crawford's job to try and work out something with the Tarahumaras, but that responsibility now devolved to Lieutenant Maus, who after considerable haggling was able to persuade the Tarahumaras to depart in exchange for half a dozen mules. Low on ammunition, the Mexican troops also withdrew.

On the morning of January 14, Maus, Tom Horn and four scouts met with two Chiricahua emissaries who agreed to bring Geronimo the next day. Accordingly, on the 15th, Geronimo, Naiche, Chihuahua, and Nana appeared as promised. After some discussion, Geronimo agreed to meet with Crook near San Bernadino in one month.

CROOK MEETS WITH GERONIMO

Things were looking up. After meeting with the Apaches, Maus promptly sent a dispatch to Crook by courier, and started back for the border himself. En route, they had a near run-in with another Mexican force, which fortunately had a commander wise enough to prevent an incident, and Maus himself was able to defuse a touch situation between the White Mountain and Chiricahua scouts.

Back in December, before the breakout, that quintessential raider, Ulzana, set forth on yet another reign of terror that took him up into the Mogollon Mountains of southwestern New Mexico with a party of ten. Ulzana struck outlying ranches and stage stations, murdering, burning, and stealing livestock, particularly horses. Over the next two months the raiders captured two women and a boy from the Fort Apache reservation. Ulzana's path of destruction had reawakened the great fear of Apaches throughout Arizona and New Mexico. As historian Edwin Sweeney points out, it was this raid that ultimately brought about a harsh revision of U.S. Indian policy, primarily against the Chiricahuas. The story of Ulzana's raid was brought to the silver screen in a 1972 film, *Ulzana's Raid*. In the film version, Burt Lancaster portrays Archie McIntosh, one of Crook's favorite scouts.[21]

On March 25, 1886, Crook and his staff met with Geronimo and several other Chiricahua leaders at Cañon de los Embudos (Canyon of the Funnels), a dozen miles south of the border. Crook wasted few pleasantries in two separate meetings with the Apaches. Accompanying Crook was his omni-present aide, Lieutenant John Gregory Bourke, a renowned anthropologist in his own right. Bourke counted twenty-four warriors present, each armed with a Winchester or Springfield rifle. To Crook, these Apaches appeared as fierce tigers. Like Grant in the Civil War, Crook's terms were unconditional surrender. If the Apaches rejected that offer, he promised to hunt them down if it took fifty years. Crook's terms were that the Apaches would be confined to some as yet undisclosed eastern location for two years after which they would be allowed to return to San Carlos. Crook of course did not suspect that his terms would be rejected by Washington.

At length, after considerable haggling the Apaches agreed and Crook figured he had finally finished the thing, but then the Apaches managed to find some whiskey from a passing trader named Charles Tribolet, and after a wild night of drinking apparently thought better of surrendering and scattered into the fastness of the Sierra Madres. Unfortunately, Crook had already sent Maus on ahead to Fort Bowie with instructions to send a telegram to Sheridan with the good news.

MILES REPLACES CROOK

Even as Crook was counseling with the Apaches, Washington was already taking a harder look at the Chiricahua problem, thanks in good part to the terror unleashed by Ulzana's raid. And when Sheridan learned that the Apaches had surrendered, then bolted again, he was furious. He had had it with Crook. Insofar as Little Phil was concerned,

Crook had had ample troops available to finish the job. But here was a perfect illustration of the man at the top having an unrealistic grasp of the actual situation. Crook, wizened old warrior that he was, could sense this and asked to be replaced. Sheridan wasted no time in signing off on the request and indeed, within twenty-four hours General Nelson Miles received orders to assume command of the Department of Arizona. The order must have brought a glib smile of satisfaction to Miles's countenance; for once he had gotten the best of his old nemesis.

On April 2, 1886, the first contingent of Chiricahuas arrived at Fort Bowie, from where they would entrain for their long journey to Fort Marion, Florida. Nine days later, Miles arrived at Fort Bowie with a dictum from Sheridan decrying the expanded use of Apache scouts. George Crook, meanwhile, began his return to Omaha and command of the Department of the Platte.

With the equivalent of nearly twelve regiments, Sheridan saw no reason why the border could not be sealed off like a tight-fitting drum. That's what the army was for after all. Had the combative Sheridan anything resembling a literary bent in his character, he might have prefaced Winston Churchill by quipping that never had so many been sent to catch so few.

Miles agreed, or at least paid lip service to Sheridan's argument about the use of Apache scouts, but, as it turned out, he proposed a strategy not all that dissimilar to Crook's. Apache scouts would still play a role, but the core of his flying columns would be composed of regular troops. Miles also introduced the heliograph as a tool for monitoring Apache movements; it was ideally suited for use in the southwest with its abundant sunshine and clear air. Stations were set up on high peaks at key locations, from which a system of mirrors could be used to flash messages as far as thirty miles, thereby keeping Miles and his field commanders apprised of developing situations. One of the soldiers who participated in operating the heliograph system later wrote "From the peak in that clear atmosphere we had an interesting view that covered many miles, even beyond the international border. Nogales, fifty miles away was plainly visible, and away to the eastward one could see a surprisingly long distance."[22]

How effective the heliograph would prove remained to be seen. However, even before it had a chance to become operational an Apache raiding party ripped through the Santa Cruz Valley of southern Arizona, doing what Apache raiders had always done before slipping back across the border to their hideaways in the Sierra Madres.

Crook had relied on Crawford, Gatewood and their Apache scout companies, but then Gatewood departed and Emmet Crawford left his soul behind in the Sierra Madres. For his own man, Miles chose forty-three-year-old, six foot, three inch Captain Henry Ware Lawton, who had served under Miles in the Red River War of 1874. Looking every inch like a wild Norse berserker, Lawton was a two-fisted, hard driving, hard drinking soldier. He was also, unfortunately, a mean drunk when in his cups. A brother officer once described Lawton as not a pretty man whose hair stands up like bristles. A major general by 1899, Lawton would die from a sniper's bullet during the Battle of San Mateo, Philippine Islands.

Lawton's colleague was an army surgeon named Leonard Wood, who would later command the famed Rough Riders during the Spanish-American War and become a confidante of Theodore Roosevelt. Despite the fact that he was a medical officer, Wood had a hankering to be a front line soldier.

On May 5, 1886, Lawton led a mixed force composed of the 4th Cavalry, 8th Infantry, altogether numbering fifty-five, plus twenty White Mountain and San Carlos Apache scouts. Supplies were hauled on 100 pack mules. From May until September, Lawton doggedly kept his column in the field, constantly pressuring the Apaches, though without actually whipping them or bringing them in under unconditional surrender terms. It was campaigning of the toughest sort. As Leonard Wood later wrote,

> One who does not know this country cannot realize what this kind of service means—marching every day in the intense heat, the rocks and earth being so torrid that the feet are blistered and everything metallic being so hot that the hand cannot touch them without getting burnt. It is a country rough beyond description, covered everywhere with cactus and full of rattlesnakes and other undesirable companions of that sort.[23]

While Lawton and Wood were working their way through the Sierra Madres, Miles, back in Arizona, oversaw the removal of all remaining Chiricahuas to Fort Marion. So long as they remained at San Carlos they were in a position to provide support for their brethren in Mexico.

Miles Meets with Geronimo

Miles was thinking outside the box as well. He selected two Chiricahuas who were on good terms with Geronimo and sent them off to present a peace offering to the hostiles. To carry out such a mission he needed an experienced, steady hand and reached out to Charles Gatewood. Crook's old scout commander was in lousy health but he could not resist the call and came on to serve Miles. It took Gatewood and his companions two weeks of hard riding before they were finally able to rendezvous with Lawton. In their pursuit, Lawton and Gatewood had somehow lost track of Geronimo because fresh intel now reached them, revealing that Geronimo was far to the north near Fronteras attempting to make peace with the Mexicans. Lawton and Gatewood then turned about and rushed north, where, on August 24, Gatewood managed to arrange for a meeting with Geronimo. We might well imagine a tense gathering. Here was Gatewood, tall and spare, his gaunt features

A scene in Geronimo's camp prior to the surrender.

somewhat hidden in the shadow of his great broad sombrero. Then there was the tall, wild looking Lawton and the squat, ugly-as-a-mud fence figure of Geronimo. Gatewood laid it on the table and essentially told the Chiricahua leader that if they surrendered they would be able to rejoin their families and would be sent to Fort Marion with all of the other Chiricahuas; essentially it was reiterating Crook's ultimatum.

Miles had not wanted the Apaches to know the other Chiricahuas were already on their way to Florida until after the surrender, but the cat was now out of the bag. Gatewood's poor health did not prevent him from spending long, trying hours attempting to induce Geronimo to surrender; this in itself was tough enough, but the chemistry between Gatewood and Lawton was poor at best. Lawton argued that he had orders directly from President Cleveland directing him to kill Geronimo, which was not true of course. True enough the president wanted Geronimo out of the picture, but his orders went down the chain of command from the White House to Miles, *thence* to Lawton. In any event, Lawton refused to countenance all of this talk about peace; his orders were to kill Geronimo. And, truth be told, Miles's orders were ambiguous enough to be taken either way.

Notwithstanding Lawton's argument, Gatewood persisted in his efforts to get Geronimo to surrender and it took all of his powers of persuasion to do so and in the end, Geronimo and the other leaders finally agreed to surrender, but it remained a delicate situation, one that was nearly shattered because of Miles's insistence that they surrender to Lawton. This was ego at work. Lawton was Miles's man and for the record it would look better for Miles if the Apaches surrendered to his lieutenant. Lamentably, in the end Charles Gatewood who had done so much to bring an end to this business was shoved into the shadows, while Henry Ware Lawton basked in the sunny glow of triumph.

On September 4, 1886, Miles and his aides met with the Chiricahuas at Skeleton Canyon, sixty-five miles southwest of Fort Bowie. When the final words were spoken, the Apaches were marched back to Fort Bowie from which place they were placed on board a Southern Pacific train for the journey to Florida. Actually, President Cleveland had wanted the Chiricahuas turned over to civil authorities for trial, but Gatewood and Miles stood up for what they had promised the Apaches and the president backed off until he had a chance to learn the detail of the surrender. After familiarizing himself with the terms, he ultimately agreed that the provisions of the surrender pact would indeed prohibit any transfer to civil authorities.

And so it was over; essentially over at any rate. Americans had been fightingApaches since Stephen Watts Kearny rode into the Southwest four decades earlier; nearly as long as the U.S. had been in conflict with the indigenous tribes of the Trans-Mississippi West. In a very real sense, the Apache wars were the most difficult—and took the longest—to prosecute, but now the conflict was at an end. There were shots still to be fired; bodies to be placed in a mass grave at a place called Wounded Knee, but here in the Desert Southwest residents could at last begin to conduct their lives without fear of Apache raids.

Epilogue

Wounded Knee, South Dakota, December 1890

"It was a good winter day when all this happened."[1]

They called it the Ghost Dance. It was not an uprising, regardless of what was feared at the time. It was a religious revival—a reaching out by a people who saw in this messianic craze one last opportunity to grasp for a way of life already vanished, but still near enough in memory to feel within reach.

There had been earlier manifestations of such movements, which powered a belief that white interlopers would be expelled; the buffalo would return, and the good times would again roll. This time his name was Wovoka, a member of the Nevada Paiute tribe. In terms of physical appearance there was nothing much about Wovoka to capture the eye, but he carried within his soul a living coal; the ember of spiritual renewal. When hope vanishes, desperation sets in, and so the door opens to welcome promises to restore the flagging spirit. It is not difficult to see how such promises rekindled hope through the Ghost Dance.

By 1883, as General William T. Sherman declared, the Indians had been eliminated as an obstacle to the settlement of the West. The Indians had no place to turn except capitulation. The old ways were now a distant memory. True, Geronimo and a handful of Apaches were still holding forth, but soon, they, too, would succumb. The fight was over; there was no alternative but the reservation. And as the realization of that reality began to sink in we can only try and imagine the sense of dejection that must have settled over many Indians.

The Indians had initially resisted the reservation concept, but in the end had been compelled to accept it; there was no other option. Now the Great Father was putting the squeeze on them again with the allotment plan. It was like being squeezed in a vise. Once they had challenged and fought the Long Knives, but this time there was no recourse; the days of fighting were past; the only recourse left was the Great Spirit.

Not only were the reservations a form of prison, but tribes often found themselves now engaged in a sort of inter-tribal war: one side favored a sort of reform stance while others tended toward a more traditionalist point of view.

A key factor in Indian-white relations as the 19th century drew to a close was the passage of the Dawes Act of 1887. By virtue of this law Indian reservations were divided into individual allotments, which meant that instead of a reservation being home to one or more tribes, the land was now divided in such a way so as to give each Indian or Indian family a piece of land. What was left of the original reservation was then put up for sale as surplus land.

Although the Ghost Dance gospel preached non-violence, among the Lakota that gospel had begun to turn increasingly militant, causing concern among white authorities to grow. In March 1890, Major General Nelson Miles, now commanding the Military Division of the Missouri, was responsible for maintaining order on the reservations.

By 1890 the Lakotas were located on four major reservations: Standing Rock, Cheyenne River, Pine Ridge, and Rosebud. There was also a fifth smaller, Lower Brulé Reservation. All were located in South Dakota, except that the tip of Standing Rock extended into North Dakota.

Nearly intolerable conditions at the reservations had caused much unrest among the Lakotas, and to nearby white communities serious trouble began to look imminent. The agent at Pine Ridge, Daniel Royer asked for military assistance. President Benjamin Harrison complied. From the Secretary of War to General Miles went orders directing units of the 2d and 8th Inf. and 9th Cavalry to take up station at the troubled area. In all, some 600 men were assigned to monitor conditions at the several reservations. Brigadier General John Rutter Brooke, who now commanded the Department of Platte set up headquarters at Pine Ridge.

The arrival of the troops caused the Indians to split off into two groups: those who wanted to avoid conflict with the soldiers came in to the agency while their recalcitrant brethren removed to the isolated parts of the reservation. During the war years the army had classified Indians as hostile and friendly and now used those same terms to define the present Lakotas.

Tension on the part of the Lakotas continued to rise and by December 1890 a faction of Oglala and Brulé Lakotas—some 600 lodges under Little Wound and Two Strike—had gathered on high ground between the White and Cheyenne Rivers in the northwest corner of Pine Ridge, which came to be known as the Stronghold where the Ghost Dances were held.

While Brooke worked to quiet the Indians under his command, General Miles was up at Standing Rock, where Sitting Bull was located. Still a force to be reckoned with, Sitting Bull, who was still an influential and charismatic leader, was Miles's big concern. The Ghost Dance craze had taken hold among Sitting Bull's Hunkpapas along the Grand River and the wily old leader saw this as an opportunity to gain leverage with the white man.

Meanwhile, down at the Cheyenne River Reservation the principal Miniconjou leaders were Hump and Big Foot. The latter's village was located" near the forks of the Cheyenne River." Although army officers had enjoyed some success in calming down these leaders, Hump and Sitting Bull remained a concern for Miles and he ordered them both arrested.

A key figure in the events to unfold, agent James McLaughlin had long wanted Sitting Bull arrested, but believed it ought to be done with Indian police not soldiers. McLaughlin was supported in this by Lieutenant Colonel William Drum, commanding Fort Yates at the Standing Rock Agency. Miles, however, preferred the use of soldiers. Notwithstanding Miles's preference, McLaughlin and Drum proceeded with Indian police. Accordingly, at dawn on December 15, forty-three Indian policemen prepared to arrest Sitting Bull, with soldiers standing by if needed. Probably McLaughlin and Drum did not anticipate the strong reaction that followed, but in any event, Sitting Bull's angry followers reacted violently. A fight ensued, in which Sitting Bull was killed along with six policemen. A number of Ghost Dancers were wounded before the soldiers were able to disperse the mob.

Sitting Bull's death was big news. Recognized as the spirit of Indian resistance he had also gained a measure of fame through participation in Buffalo Bill's Wild West Show. It is important to understand that by 1890 a new generation of Americans had reached adulthood and tended to view the Indian in a more sympathetic light than many of their predecessors. The death of Sitting Bull also reawakened an old feud between the War Department and the Indian Bureau over who was responsible for the chief's death.

In the aftermath of Sitting Bull's death, army officers, supported by Hump managed to persuade most of the Hunkpapas to turn themselves in at the Cheyenne River Agency, but some thirty-eight fled south to join Big Foot's band.

Insofar as federal authorities were concerned, the principal remaining threat now appeared to be Big Foot and the job of arresting him fell to Lieutenant Colonel Edwin Vose Sumner, who had previously been directed to establish what was called "a camp of observation" on the Cheyenne River. A veteran officer who had seen much service in the Civil War and on the frontier, Sumner was a volatile individual not known for his negotiating skills and would seem to have been a poor choice for such a delicate job. By contrast, Big Foot was known to be a peacemaker and had been asked to come down to Pine Ridge to calm the people, who were nervous and excitable, made all the more so by the presence of the soldiers.

Unknown to white observers, on the night of December 23 Big Foot and his Miniconjous, along with the Hunkpapas who had joined them, left Big Foot's camp and headed south to Pine Ridge. Learning of this, Miles, who meanwhile had established his headquarters at Rapid City, was furious and was determined to prevent Big Foot and his contingent from reaching the stronghold. As it turned out, Miles's assumption that Big Foot and his followers were aiming for the Stronghold was wrong. Nevertheless, with this in mind, Colonel Eugene Carr's 6th Cavalry and Major Guy Henry with a squadron of the 9th Cavalry were ordered to block Big Foot's route. Unknown to Miles and his officers, however, Big Foot was not aiming for the stronghold, but rather for Pine Ridge and by moving through the Badlands he was able to avoid the troops. En route to the stronghold, Big Foot came down with pneumonia and had to continue the journey in a wagon.

Turn about is fair play and it happened that 7th Cavalry, now commanded by Colonel James W. Forsyth was now directed to intercept the fleeing Miniconjous. Accordingly, a battalion of the 7th under Major Samuel Whiteside did just that. There was a tense standoff before the Indians agreed to let the soldiers escort them to Wounded Knee. Some twenty miles from Wounded Knee the two bodies set up camp .That night Colonel Forsyth arrived with the remainder of his regiment plus a battery of artillery.

As darkness settled in on December 28, the Miniconjous felt relatively safe, but when the cold dawn of the 29th arrived they were more than a little surprised to find some 500 soldiers surrounding their camp. Not only that, but on a high point just to the north were positioned four Hotchkiss cannons that appeared ready to open fire at any minute.

In retrospect anyway, it would seem that Forsyth's next move was not very carefully thought out. He now ordered that all the Indian men, about 120 in all, were to gather in front of the tent where Big Foot lay dying from pneumonia. Some 230 women and children then commenced packing for the day's journey to Pine Ridge.

Forsyth also ordered the Indians to surrender *all* firearms. It was an invitation to trouble. The order added to tension of the moment. Many Miniconjous did not want to give up their prized Winchester repeating rifles. Although Forsyth, understandably, felt that he was defusing a potentially deadly situation, one wonders whether awaiting a calmer moment might not have made more sense. At any rate, the soldiers were ordered to conduct a search, even looking beneath the blankets of both women and men.

Tension mounted as the soldiers went about their work. The incantations of a medicine man, Yellow Bird, did not help matters either. There was a confrontation between a soldier and a brave; a rifle was fired, from who it is not known, but it didn't matter as the shot ignited the fuse. The young warriors cast their blankets aside and unleashed a volley into the soldier ranks. A furious hand-to-hand frenzy followed. The non combatants scattered; firing was everywhere and random.

Then the Hotchkiss guns opened up; shells burst throughout the village. The Indians sought shelter in a ravine. By the time the firing stopped a few minutes later, more than 150 Indians lay dead, including Big Foot and Yellow Bird; another 50 Lakotas were wounded. A storm moved in covering dead bodies with snow, where they would lay in the grotesque positions of death until, on New Years Day, wagons arrived and carted them off to a mass grave.

On December 30 a few shots were exchanged at Drexel Mission Church some four miles from the agency. A detachment of the 7th Cavalry was sent to see what it was all about, but got caught in a cross fire. Major Henry's squadron of the 9th Cavalry was ordered to reinforce Forsyth and drive off the Indians. Once again, it seems the 7th Cavalry had been bested by the Indians, leaving Forsyth mightily chagrined. His whole handling of this affair did nothing to earn Miles's support.

Wounded Knee was a completely unnecessary tragedy. Miles was furious and charged Forsyth with incompetence, and removed him from command, but the Secretary of War and General of the Army John M. Schofield disagreed and ordered Forsyth reinstated.

Despite the endorsement from the Secretary of War and the General of the Army, one cannot help but question Forsyth's judgment. Certainly he must have realized that he confronted a volatile situation, yet his decisions seem not to have reflected that realization. An otherwise able enough officer, Forsyth appears to have lacked the kind of tactful touch later demonstrated by Miles.

Wounded Knee was over and so was the Ghost Dance, but the problem that underlay the trouble was yet to be resolved. There remained what was regarded as a hostile village of some 4,000 people, including perhaps as many as a thousand men of fighting age. Miles approached the problem with great shrewdness and an understanding of the Indian mind set. With a combination of tact, supported by a low key threat of force he succeeded in defusing a tense situation and on January 15, 1891, the Indians surrendered.

Wounded Knee represented the last gasp of a culture that had fought to survive. In retrospect it had been a losing effort from the start, but also in retrospect one can see that it was a war—perhaps a series of wars more accurately—that had to be waged; it was destined to be fought and lost. Whether it was a war that one side won with class and the other lost with dignity will forever be argued.

As a postscript, eighty-three years later, in February 1973 members of the American Indian Movement, having chosen the original site of Wounded Knee as a symbolic gesture, held off a force of U.S. Marshalls, FBI and other law enforcement agencies for seventy-one days.

The past was prologue, or perhaps as the poet T.S. Eliot says, past, present and future are all but one.

Notes

Introduction

1. For an excellent introduction to America's role as an expansionist nation see Walter Nugent's *Habits of Empire*. Bernard De Voto's *1846: The Year of Decision* is an excellent look at Westering America in the mid-nineteenth century.

2. In *Counting Coup and Cutting Horses: Intertribal Warfare on the Northern Great Plains, 1738-1889*, Anthony McGinnis paints an excellent picture of intertribal warfare.

3. See *Citizen Explorer: The Life of Zebulon Pike* by Jared Orsi.

4. See *Washington: A Life* by Ron Chernow.

5. See *Jefferson's Lost Cause: Land, Farmers, Slavery, and the Louisiana Purchase* by Roger G. Kennedy.

6. The best single volume work on treaties is *American Indian Treaties: The History of a Political Anamoly* by Francis Paul Prucha. *Great Father* is a more detailed study of the subject by the same author.

7. See Robert M. Utley, *The Indian Frontier, 1846-1890*.

8. Letter from Nathaniel Taylor, Commissioner of Indian Affairs to Secretary of the Interior.

9. Ibid.

10. Finerty, *War-Path and the Bivouac: or, The Conquest of the Sioux*, p. 49.

11. *The Natural West Environmental History in the Great Plains and Rocky Mountains* by Dan Flores is an excellent study that should be read by anyone attempting to arrive at a more complete understanding of the role the environment played in the Indian-white conflicts on the Plains.

Part I: The Pacific Northwest

1. For personal information on the Whitmans see Jeffrey, *Converting the West*, Morrison, *Outpost John McLoughlin and the Far Northwest*, and Josephy, *The Nez Perce and the Opening of the Northwest*.

2. An excellent summary of the Whitmans overland journey is found in the *Rocky Mountain Fur Trade Journal* Volume 8 (2014): 62-81.

3. *Outpost John McLoughlin and the Far Northwest*, by Dorothy Nafus Morrison is a well written account of Hudson's Bay role in the Pacific Northwest, and provides a background for the Whitman story from that perspective. See also Jeffrey, *Converting the West* and Josephy, *The Nez Perce and the Opening of the Northwest*.

4. For an understanding of the Indian reaction to the missionaries see Burns, *The Jesuits and the Indian Wars of the Far Northwest*, Josephy, *The Nez Perce and the Opening of the Northwest*.

5. Burns, *The Jesuits and the Indian Wars of the Far Northwest*, p. 62.

6. A good, solid explanation of the Trade and Intercourse Act may be found in *The Rise and Fall of Indian Country, 1825-1855* by William E. Unrau.

7. The trial that resulted in the execution of those who participated in the massacre is an interesting, though little known postscript to the Whitman tragedy. See Ronald B. Lansing, *Juggernaut: The Whitman Massacre Trial, 1850*. See also Josephy, *The Nez Perce and the Opening of the Northwest*, pp. 284-286; Keenan, *The Great Sioux Uprising Rebellion on the Plains*, p. 80, and *38 Nooses: Lincoln, Little Crow, and the Beginning of the Frontier's End* by Scott W. Berg.

8. For a discussion of Isaac Stevens and his role in the development of the early Northwest see Josephy, *The Nez Perce and the Opening of the Northwest*; Burns, *The Jesuits and the Indian Wars of the Northwest*, and Prucha, *American Indian Treaties*.

9. For a description of the Rogue River country, its early history, and the indigenous people of the region see Beckham, *Requiem for a People*.

10. A good summary of the indigenous people of this region will be found in Schwartz, *The Rogue River Indian War and Its Aftermath, 1850-1980*; Beckham, *Requiem for a People*, and *Uncertain Encounters: Indians and Whites at Peace and War in Southern Oregon* by Nathan Douthit.

11. Beckham, *Requiem for a People*, pp. 143-144, and Douthit, *Uncertain Encounters*, pp. 108-109.

12. Beckham, *Requiem for a People*, pp. 60-62; Douthit, *Uncertain Encounters*, pp. 117-118.

13. Beckham, *Requiem for a People*, p. 115.

14. *Ibid.*, p. 116.
15. *Ibid.*, p. 122.
16. Douthit, *Uncertain Encounters*, p. 156.
17. Schwartz, *The Rogue Indian War*, p. xii.
18. Letter from Gen. John Wool to T.J. Henley.
19. Letter from Joel Palmer to Commissioner George Manypenny, October 9 and 16, 1855. House Executive Document 93, 34th Congress, 1st Session.
20. Adj. Gen., E.M. Barnum, General Order Number 10, October 20, 1855, pp. 5–6.
21. Letter from Joel Palmer to George Manypenny, October 1855.
22. Letter from Sub-Agent Edward Geary to Joel Palmer.
23. Harvey Robbins, Journal of Rogue River War.
24. Letter from Lieut. John Withers to Adj. Gen. Samuel Cooper.
25. Schmitt, Martin, General George Crook His Autobiography, p. 26.
26. Letter from Joel Palmer to Gen. John Wool, December 1, 1855. House Executive Document 93, 34th Congress, 1st Session, pp. 23, 87.
27. Letter from Joel Palmer to Commissioner of Indian Affairs, George Manypenny, November 12, 1855. House Executive Document 93, 34th Congress, 1st Session, p. 87.
28. Letter from Gen. John Wool to the Adj. Gen., Lorenzo Thomas, March 5, 1856. House Executive Document 93, 34th Congress, 1st Session.
29. Although there is no biography of Kamiakin as such, insightful accounts of his life will be found in Josephy, *The Nez Perce and the Opening of the Northwest*; Glassley, *Pacific Northwest Indian Wars*; Burns, *The Jesuits and the Indian Wars of the Northwest*, and Utley, *Frontiersmen in Blue*.
30. Nelson, *Fighting for Paradise: A Military History of the Pacific Northwest*, p. 134; Guie, *Bugles in the Valley: Garrett's Fort Simcoe*, p. 179, Utley, *Frontiersmen In Blue*, p. 195.
31. Burns, *The Jesuits and the Indian Wars of the Northwest*, p. 204.
32. Kip, *Indian War in the Pacific Northwest*, p. 55.

Part II: California and Nevada

1. Schmitt, ed., *General George Crook: His Autobiography*, p. 16.
2. "California and the Indian Wars," The Mariposa War of 1850–1851, www.militarymuseum.org/HistoryIW.html.
3. Crampton, C. Gregory, Ed., *The Mariposa Indian War, 1850–1851*, p. 69.
4. *Ibid.*
5. *Ibid.*
6. "California and the Indian Wars," The Mendocino War of 1859–1860, www.militarymuseum.org/HistoryIW.html
7. *Ibid.*
8. *Ibid.*
9. *Ibid.*
10. *Ibid.*

11. Hoxie, *Encyclopedia of North American Indians*, pp. 458–459.
12. A good account of the Pony Express story may be found in *Saddles and Spurs: The Pony Express Saga* by Raymond W. and Mary Lund Settle.
13. *Ibid.*, p. 140.
14. Settle, *Saddles and Spurs*, p. 149.
15. *Ibid.*
16. Utley, *Lone Star Justice*, Volume 1, p. 5.
17. The best account of the Owens Valley War will be found in *The Boys in Sky-Blue Pants* by Dorothy Clora Cragen. Also useful are Ella M. Cain's *The Story of Early Mono County*, and *The Expedition of Captain J.W. Davidson: From Fort Tejon to the Owens Valley in 1859*, Philip J. Wilkie and Harry W. Lawton, eds.
18. Schmitt, *General George Crook: His Autobiography*, p. 144.
19. *Ibid.*
20. Cozzens, *Eyewitnesses to the Indian Wars, 1865–1890. Vol. 2 The Wars for the Pacific Northwest*, p. 72.
21. *Ibid.*, pp. 69–70, 84–85.
22. *Ibid.*
23. Michno, *The Deadliest Indian War in the West*, p. 349.
24. Downey, Fairfax, *Indian Fighting Army*, p. 151.
25. The best account of this gritty conflict is *The Modocs and Their War* by Keith A. Murray. Arthur Quinn's *Hell with the Fire Out* is also a good source. Modoc The Tribe That Wouldn't Die by Cheewa James is a good account of those troubled times during the Modoc War from the Indian point of view.
26. Murray, *The Modoc War*, pp. 244–245.

Part III: New Mexico Territory

1. McNitt, *Navajo Wars*, p. 124.
2. Meriwether, *My Life in the Mountains and on the Plains*, pp. 227–228.
3. McNitt, *Navajo Wars*, p. 253.
4. *Ibid.*, p. 228. This is the best and most complete account of the Navajo-American conflicts. *Blood and Thunder: An Epic of the American West* by Hampton Sides is excellent, as is *Kit Carson and the Indians* by Tom Dunlay. Lawrence C. Kelly's *Navajo Roundup: Selected Correspondence of Kit Carson's Expedition Against the Navajo, 1863–1865* is an excellent reference source.
5. *Ibid.*, p. 275.
6. Utley, *Frontiersmen in Blue*, p. 156.
7. McNitt, *Navajo Wars*, p. 341.
8. *Ibid.*, p. 367.
9. *Ibid.*, p. 367.

Part IV: The Central Plains

1. Prucha, *American Indian Treaties*, pp. 237–239; McChristian, *Fort Laramie*, pp. 51–59. The importance of the 1851 Horse Creek Treaty, along with the Treaties

of Medicine Lodge (1867) and Fort Laramie (1868) cannot be overstated.

2. The best accounts of the Indian-white troubles on the Central Plains following the signing of the Horse Creek Treaty will be found in McChristian, *Fort Laramie*, Paul, *Blue Water Creek and the First Sioux War, 1854–1856*, and Utley, *Frontiersmen In Blue*.

3. McChristian, *Fort Laramie*, p. 86.
4. Utley, *Frontiersmen in Blue*, p. 115.
5. Commissioner of Indian Affairs, "Annual Report, 1861."
6. Gary Roberts, *Sand Creek: Tragedy and Symbol*, Vol. I, p. 219.
7. *Ibid.*, p. 232.
8. *Ibid.*, p. 242.
9. *Ibid.*, p. 250.
10. *Ibid.*, p. 251.
11. There is a rich body of source materials for anyone wishing to study the Sand Creek tragedy in depth. The most complete account of the massacre will be found in the two volume work, *Sand Creek: Tragedy and Symbol* by Gary Lela Roberts. Other useful studies include Gregory F. Michno's *Battle at Sand Creek: The Military Perspective*, Stan Hoig's *The Sand Creek Massacre*, and *Frontiersmen in Blue* by Robert M. Utley.
12. Roberts, *Sand Creek*, Vol. I, pp. 304–313.
13. Utley, *Frontiersmen in Blue*, p. 292.
14. Roberts, *Sand Creek*, p. 427.
15. *Ibid.*, Vol. II, pp. 431, 489–490.
16. Linda Womack, "Sand Creek: Battle or Massacre?" http://sandcreekmassacre.homestead.com/TheworksofLindaWommack.html.
17. Roberts, *Sand Creek*, Vol. I, p. 438.
18. *Ibid.*, p. 442.
19. *Ibid.*, p. 444.
20. *Ibid.*, p. 445.
21. *Ibid.*, p. 457.
22. Letter from Commissioner of Indian Affairs N.G. Taylor to Secretary of the Interior.
23. Roberts, *Sand Creek*, Vol. I, p. 475.
24. *Thomas Merton Journal*, Vol. 4, p. 301.
25. Roberts, *Sand Creek*, Vol. I, pp. 497–498.
26. *Ibid.*, Vol. II, pp. 502–504.
27. *Ibid.*, pp. 500–502, 512–514; Vol. I, pp. 474–475.
28. Roberts, *Sand Creek*, Vol. II, p. 503.
29. A military division constitutes the largest sphere of jurisdiction. Within a given military division are one or more departments. Each department in turn consists of one or more districts, which may contain sub-districts.
30. Utley, *Frontiersmen in Blue*, pp. 300–301.
31. The best coverage of the conflicts following Sand Creek is found in *The Circle of Fire* by John D. McDermott.
32. Utley, *Frontiersmen in Blue*, pp. 301–302.
33. McDermott, *Circle of Fire*, p. 40.
34. *Ibid.*, p. 41.
35. *Ibid.*, p. 44.
36. White, ed., *Chronicle of a Congressional Journey*, p. 3.
37. The best account of Connor's 1865 Expedition is David Wagner's two volume *Powder River Odyssey* and *Patrick Connor's War*. McDermott's *Circle of Fire* is also an excellent source.
38. McDermott, *Circle of Fire*, p. 113.
39. *Ibid.*, pp. 134–135.
40. Utley, *Frontier Regulars*, p. 115.
41. *Ibid.*, p. 118.
42. *Hancock's War* by William Chalfant is a thorough and excellent account of this campaign.
43. *Ibid.*, pp. 105–108.
44. *Ibid.*, p. 118.
45. *Ibid.*, p. 128.
46. *Ibid.*, pp. 142–143.
47. *Ibid.*, p. 159.
48. *Ibid.*, pp. 163–164.
49. *Ibid.*, pp. 171–172.
50. An excellent account of the famed Beecher Island Fight will be found in *The Battle of Beecher Island and the Indian War of 1867–1869* by John H. Monnett.

Part V: The Southern Plains

1. Dunlay, *Kit Carson and the Indians*, p. 332.
2. Morris, *El Lano Estacado*, pp. 7, 162–163, 179.
3. Utley, *Lone Star Rangers*, Vol. I, pp. 23–24.
4. Utley, *Frontiersmen in Blue*, p. 135.
5. *Ibid.*, p. 137.
6. Utley, *Lone Star Rangers*, Vol. I, pp. 130–131.
7. Utley, *Frontier Regulars*, pp. 147–149.
8. Thrapp, *Encyclopedia of Frontier Biography*, Vol. I, p. 472.
9. Utley, *Cavalier in Buckskin*, p. 68 To clarify a distinction in military terminology, infantry units were called companies, while an artillery unit of a similar size was called a battery. Prior to 1883, cavalry units were called companies and troops, but the designation "troop" did not become official until that year. Six years later, in 1889, cavalry battalions were re-designated squadrons, a squadron nominally consisting of two or more troops. A grouping of, say, as many as seven troops could still constitute a squadron, but the number of troops in a given squadron could not exceed twelve which made it regimental size. In practice, however, the designation troop and company were often used interchangeably.
10. An excellent account of the Red River War (sometimes called the Buffalo War) will be found in James L. Haley's *The Buffalo War*. Another excellent source is *Battles of the Red River War: Archaeological Perspectives* by J. Brett Cruse.
11. Haley, *The Buffalo War*, p. 38.
12. *Ibid.*, p. 177.

Part VI: Iowa, Minnesota and the Northern Plains

1. Nester, *The Arikara War*, p. 157.
2. One source says the origin of the name is traced back to excessive bleeding that occurred during circumcision. See Beck, *Inkpaduta*, p. 5.
3. Carley, *The Sioux Uprising*, p. 71.

4. Anderson, *Little Crow*, p. 4.
5. The story of the Minnesota uprising is well covered in works such as *38 Nooses: Lincoln, Little Crow and the Beginning of the Frontier's End* by Scott W. Berg; *The Sioux Uprising of 1862*, by Kenneth Carley; *The Great Sioux Uprising* by Jerry Keenan, *Birch Coulee: The Epic Battle of the Dakota War* by John Christgau, and *Soldier, Settler and Sioux* by Paul Beck.
6. Anderson, *Through Dakota Eyes*, p. 161.
7. Ibid., pp. 83–84.
8. Keenan, *The Great Sioux Uprising*, p. 73.
9. Ibid., p. 74.
10. Carley, *The Sioux Uprising*, p. 87.
11. An excellent study of the Dakota Campaigns will be found in Clodfelter's *The Dakota War: The United States Army Versus the Sioux, 1862–1865*.
12. Report of Major Albert House, *Official Records of the War of the Rebellion*, Series I, Part IV, pp. 564–565.
13. "The Letters of Private Milton Spencer, 1862–1865," *North Dakota History* (Fall 1970): 255.
14. Clodfelter, *The Dakota War*, p. 165.
15. "The Letters of Private Milton Spencer, 1862–1865," *North Dakota History* (Fall 1970): 261.
16. Clodfelter, *The Dakota War*, p. 180.
17. The Most complete account of the Bozeman Trail story and Red Cloud's War will be found in John D. McDermott's two volume study, *Red Cloud's War*: *The Bozeman Trail* by Grace Hebard and E.A. Brininstool remains a useful if somewhat dated account. Margaret Carrington's *Absaraka* provides a view of those tragic weeks at Fort Phil Kearny, along with a woman's perspective of life on a frontier army post.
18. McFarling, *Exploring the Northern Plains*, p. 215.
19. The best account of the Fetterman Disaster will be found in John H. Monnett's *Where a Hundred Soldiers Were Killed*. *Give Me Eighty Men* by Shannon Smith is also an excellent account of the disaster.
20. Hagan, *Exactly in the Right Place*, p. 120.
21. Cozzens, *Eyewitnesses to the Indian Wars: The Long War For The Northern Plains*, Vol. IV, p. 137.
22. Ibid., p. 183.
23. Ibid., pp. 206–207.
24. Ibid., p. 234.
25. Ibid., p. 652.
26. Ibid., p. 262.
27. The best accounts of the Battle of the Rosebud are J.W. Vaughn's *With Crook at the Rosebud* and Neil C. Mangum's *The Battle of the Rosebud*.
28. The literature on the Little Bighorn is vast and selecting two or three studies is anything but easy. That said, I offer these: John Gray's *Centennial Campaign* and *Custer's Last Campaign*; *Custer's Last Fight* by David Evans, James Donovan's *A Terrible Glory*, and *Archaeology, History, and Custer's Last Battle* by Richard Fox are all worthy of reading for those with a serious interest in the Little Bighorn story. One final suggestion: For a fascinating collection of "then and now" photographs, together with an excellent summary of the battle, see *Where Custer Fell: Photographs of the Little Big Horn Battlefield Then and Now* by James S. Brust, Brian C. Pohanka and Sandy Barnard.
29. Utley, *Frontier Regulars*, p. 261; Utley, *Cavalier in Buckskin*, p. 179.
30. Gibbon, *Adventures on the Western Frontier*, p. 131.
31. An. interesting discussion regarding the difference between a "Letter of Advice" and a direct order will be found in *Legend Into History* and *Did Custer Disobey Orders* by Charles Kuhlman.
32. Evans, *Custer's Last Fight*, p. 185; Gray, *Centennial Campaign*, p. 168.
33. For a kinder defense of Reno, see Ronald H. Nichols, *In Custer's Shadow*.
34. Utley, *Cavalier In Buckskin*, pp. 197–199.
35. Finerty, *War Path and the Bivouac*, pp. 113–121.
36. Hedren, *First Scalp for Custer*, pp. 63–64.
37. Cozzens, *Eyewitnesses to the Indian Wars: The Long War for the Northern Plains*, Vol. IV, p. 376.
38. Utley, *The Indian Frontier 1846–1890*, p. 178.
39. Greene, *Yellowstone Command*, p. 94.
40. Ibid., p. 103.
41. Ibid., p. 115.
42. Ibid., pp. 124–125.
43. Ibid., p. 138–139.
44. Greene, *Morning Star Dawn*, pp. 42–44.
45. Cozzens, *Eyewitnesses to the Indian Wars: The Long War for the Northern Plains*, Vol. IV, p. 415.
46. Ibid., p. 417.
47. Keenan, *The Life of Yellowstone Kelly*, p.170.
48. Powers, *The Killing of Crazy Horse*, p. 422.
49. Greene, *Nez Perce Summer*, p. 33. Although there are several fine studies of the Nez Perce War (if indeed it deserves to be called a war), Greene's work, in my opinion, is the best overall account.
50. Ibid., p. 237.
51. Ibid., pp. 261–263.
52. Cozzens, *Eyewitnesses to the Indian Wars: The Long War for the Northern Plains*, Vol. II, p. 563.
53. Greene,. *Nez Perce Summer*, p. 306.
54. Ibid., p. 309.
55. The definitive account of the odyssey of the Northern Cheyennes is told in *Tell Them We Are Going Home* by John H. Monnett.
56. Ibid., p. 109.
57. Manzione, *I Am Looking to the North for My Life*, p. 103.
58. Utley, *Frontier Regulars*, p. 295.
59. Manzione, *I Am Looking to the North for My Life*, p. 133.
60. Finerty, *War Path and the Bivouac*, p. 264.
61. Ibid., p. 265.

Part VII: The Intermountain West

1. Emmitt, *The Last War Trail*, p. 281.
2. Bagley, *Blood of the Prophets*, p. 46.
3. Bernard, *One Hundred and Twenty-three Fights and Scrimmages*, p. 125.
4. The best accounts of the Ute War of 1879 will be found in *The Last War Trail* by Robert Emmitt and

Hollow Victory and the White River Expedition of 1879 by Mark Miller.

Part VIII: The Desert Southwest

1. Apparently for a time there were two ferries. One was originally built by a man bound for California who was angry over the rates charged by the other ferrymen and established his own operation. Later, he seems to have turned his ferry over to the Indians, and it was this ferry that was in turn appropriated by whites, headed up by notorious scalp hunter from Texas named John Glanton who viewed this as a more profitable operation. In any event, it was this party that was attacked by angry Yumas in April 1850. See *Feud on the Colorado*.
2. The best account of the clashes with the Yumas and Mojaves will be found in Woodward, *Feud on the Colorado*.
3. Azor H. Nickerson, *Harper's Weekly*, July 10, 1897.
4. Utley, *Geronimo*, p. x.
5. Sweeney, *Mangas Coloradas*, p. 367.
6. Cremony, "Some Savages," *Overland Monthly*, March 1872, p. 201.
7. Sweeney, *Cochise: Chiricahua Apache Chief*, p. 203.
8. Sladen, *Making Peace with Cochise*, p. 62.
9. Cozzens, *Eyewitnesses to the Indian Wars: The Struggle for Apacheria*, Vol. I, p. 150.
10. *Ibid.*, p. 268.
11. Sweeney, *Cochise*, p. 395.
12. Utley, *Geronimo*, p .x.
13. Cozzens, *Eyewitnesses to the Indian Wars: The Struggle for Apacheria*, Vol. I, p. 248.
14. *Ibid.*, pp. 256–257.
15. *Ibid.*, p. 287.
16. *Ibid.*, p. 275.
17. Altschuler, *Cavalry Yellow and Infantry Blue*, p. 84.
18. Cozzens, *Eyewitnesses to the Indian Wars: The Struggle for Apacheria*, Vol. I, p. 414.
19. *Ibid.*, p. 428.
20. *Ibid.*, p. 524.
21. Sweeney, *From Cochise to Geronimo*, p. 522.
22. Cozzens, *Eyewitnesses to the Indian Wars: The Struggle for Apacheria*, Vol. I, p. 559.
23. Utley, *Frontier Regulars*, p. 398.

Epilogue

1. Neihardt, *Black Elk Speaks*, p. 201.

Recommended Reading

This following is not a comprehensive listing of all available sources relevant to the Western Indian wars, but is rather intended as a guide to selected sources, most of which were used in the creation of this volume. The works cited below will in turn provide the reader with additional sources to pursue in the quest for a more complete understanding of the subject. The reader will also find listed below some sources not found in the endnotes.

Altschuler, Constance Wynn. *Cavalry Yellow and Infantry Blue.* Tucson: The Arizona Historical Society, 1991.

Anderson, Gary Clayton. *Kinsmen of Another Kind Dakota: White Relations in the Upper Mississippi Valley, 1650–1862.* Lincoln: University of Nebraska Press, 1984.

———. *Little Crow: Spokesman for the Sioux.* St. Paul: Minnesota Historical Society Press, 1986.

Anderson, Gary Clayton, and Alan R. Woolworth. *Through Dakota Eyes: Narrative Accounts of the Minnesota Indian War of 1862.* St. Paul: Minnesota Historical Society Press, 1988.

Bagley, Will. *Blood of the Prophets: Brigham Young and the Massacre at Mountain Meadows.* Norman: University of Oklahoma Press, 2002.

Beck, Paul N. *Inkpaduta Dakota Leader.* Norman: University of Oklahoma Press, 2008.

———. *Soldier, Settler, and Sioux: Fort Ridgely and the Minnesota River Valley, 1853–1867.* Sioux Falls, SD: Center For Western Studies, 2000.

Beck, Warren, and Ynez D. Hasse. "The Mariposa Indian War, 1850–1851. http://www.militarymuseum.org/mariposa1.html.

Beckham, Stephen Dow. *Requiem for a People.* Corvallis: Oregon State University Press, 1996.

Berg, Scott W. *38 Nooses: Lincoln, Little Crow, and the Beginning of the Frontier's End.* New York: Vintage Books, 2012.

Bigelow, Ed. "White Man's Cattle, Red Man's Game: Issues in the Mendocino War, http://www.militarymuseum.org/historyiw.html.

Bledsoe, A.J. *Indian Wars of the Northwest.* San Francisco, CA: Bacon & Co., 1885.

Bray, Kingsley M. *Crazy Horse: A Lakota Life.* Norman: University of Oklahoma Press, 2006.

Brust, James S., Brian C. Pohanka, and Sandy Bernard. *Where Custer Fell: Photographs of the Little Big Horn Battlefield Then and Now.* Norman: University of Oklahoma Press, 2005.

Burns, Robert Ignatius, S.J. *The Jesuits and the Indian Wars of the Northwest.* New Haven, CT: Yale University Press, 1966.

Cain, Ella M. *The Story of Early Mono County.* San Francisco, CA: Fearon Publishers, 1961.

California State Military Museum: California and the Indian Wars:
http://www.militarymuseum.org/historyiw.html.
http://www.militarymuseum.org/mariposa1.html.
http://www.militarymuseum.org/mendocino%20war.html.
http://www.militarymuseum.org/owensvalley.html.

Calloway, Colin G. *One Vast Winter Count: The Native American West Before Lewis and Clark*, Lincoln: University of Nebraska Press, 2003.

Carley, Kenneth. *The Sioux Uprising of 1862.* St. Paul, MN: Minnesota Historical Society, 1976.

Carlson, Paul H. *The Plains Indians.* College Station: Texas A&M University Press, 1998.

Carrington, Frances C. *My Army Life: A Soldier's Wife at Fort Phil Kearny.* Boulder, CO: Pruett Publishing, 1990.

Carrington, Margaret Irvin. *Absaraka: Home of the Crows.* Lincoln: University of Nebraska Press, 1983.

Chalfant, William Y. *Cheyennes and Horse Soldiers: The 1857 Expedition and the Battle of Solomon's Fork.* Norman: University of Oklahoma Press, 1989.

_____. *Dangerous Passage: The Santa Fe Trail and the Mexican War*. Norman: University of Oklahoma Press, 1994.

_____. *Cheyennes at Dark Water Creek: The Last Fight of the Red River War*. Norman: University of Oklahoma Press, 1997.

_____. *Hancock's War: Conflict on the Southern Plains*. Norman, OK: Arthur H. Clark Co., 2010.

_____. *Without Quarter: The Wichita Expedition and the Fight on Crooked Creek*. Norman: University of Oklahoma Press, 1991.

Chernow, Ron. *Washington: A Life*. NY: Penguin Press, 2010.

Christgau, John. *Birch Coulee: The Epic Battle of the Dakota War*. Lincoln: University of Nebraska Press, 2012.

Clodfelter, Michael. *The Dakota War: The United States Army Versus the Sioux, 1862–1865*. Jefferson, NC: McFarland, 1998.

Cook, S.F. *The Conflict Between the California Indian and White Civilization*, Vol. I. Berkeley: University of California Press, 1943.

Cozzens, Peter. *Eyewitnesses to the Indian Wars, 1865–1890. Volume One: The Struggle for Apacheria*, Mechanicsburg, PA: Stackpole Books, 2001; *Volume Two: The Wars for the Pacific Northwest*, Stackpole, 2002; *Volume Three: Conquering the Southern Plains*, Stackpole, 2003; *Volume Four: The Long War for the Northern Plains*, Stackpole, 2004; *Volume Five: The Army and the Indian*, Stackpole, 2005.

Cragen, Dorothy Clora. *The Boys in Sky-Blue Pants: The Men and Events at Camp Independence and Forts of Eastern California, Nevada and Utah, 1862–1877*. Independence, CA: Dorothy Cragen,1975.

Crampton, C. Gregory, ed. *The Mariposa Indian War, 1850–1851: Diaries of Robert Eccleston: The California Gold Rush, Yosemite, and the High Sierra*. Salt Lake City: University of Utah Press, 1957.

Cruse, J. Brett. *Battles of the Red River War*. College Station, TX: Texas A&M University Press, 2008.

Davidson, Homer K. *Blackjack Davidson, a Cavalry Commander on the Western Frontier: The Life of General John W. Davidson*. Glendale, CA: The Arthur H. Clark Co., 1974.

Devoto, Bernard. *The Year of Decision, 1846*. Boston, MA: Houghton Mifflin, 1943.

Dietrich, William. *Northwest Passage: The Great Columbia River*. NY: Simon & Schuster, 1995.

Donovan, James. *A Terrible Glory*. Boston, MA: Little Brown, 2008.

Douthit, Nathan. *Uncertain Encounters: Indians and Whites at Peace and War in Southern Oregon, 1820s–1860s*. Corvallis: Oregon State University Press, 2002.

Downey, Fairfax. *Indian Fighting Army*. NY: Harper, 1941.

Dunlay, Tom. *Kit Carson and the Indians*. Lincoln: University of Nebraska Press, 2000.

Emmitt, Robert. *The Last War Trail: The Utes and the Settlement of Colorado*. Boulder: University Press of Colorado, 2000.

Evans, David C. *Custer's Last Fight: The Story of the Battle of the Little Big Horn*. El Segundo, CA: Upton & Sons Publishers, 1999.

Finch, L. Boyd. *Confederate Pathway to the Pacific: Major Sherod Hunter and Arizona Territory, C.S.A.* Tucson, AZ: The Arizona Historical Society, 1996.

Finerty, John F. *War-Path and Bivouac, or The Conquest of the Sioux*. Norman: University of Oklahoma Press, 1961.

Flores, Dan. *The Natural West Environmental History in the Great Plains and Rocky Mountains*. Norman: University of Oklahoma Press, 2003.

Fox, Richard Allan, Jr. *Archaeology, History, and Custer's Last Battle*. Norman: University of Oklahoma Press, 1993.

Gaff, Alan, and Maureen Gaff, eds. *Adventures on the Western Frontier: Major General John Gibbon*. Blomington: Indiana University Press, 1994.

Glassley, Ray Hoard. *Pacific Northwest Indian Wars*, Portland, OR: Binfords & Mort, 1953.

Gray, John S. *Centennial Campaign the Sioux War of 1876*. Fort Collins, CO: The Old Army Press, 1976.

_____. *Custer's Last Campaign: Mitch Boyer and the Little Bighorn Reconstructed*. Lincoln: University of Nebraska Press, 1991.

Greene, Jerome A. *American Carnage: Wounded Knee, 1890*. Norman, OK: Oklahoma University Press, 2014.

_____. *Morning Star Dawn: The Powder River Expedition and the Northern Cheyennes, 1876*. Norman: University of Oklahoma Press, 2003.

_____. *Nez Perce Summer: The U.S. Army and the Nee-Me-Poo Crisis*. Helena, MT: Montana Historical Society Press, 2000.

_____. *Slim Buttes, 1876: An Episode of the Great Sioux War*. Norman: University of Oklahoma Press, 1992.

_____. *Yellowstone Command: Colonel Nelson A. Miles and the Great Sioux War of 1876–1877*. Norman: University of Oklahoma Press, 1991.

Guie, H. Dean. *Bugles in the Valley: Garnett's Fort Simcoe*. Portland, OR: Oregon Historical Society, 1977.

Hagan, Barry J., C.S.C. *"Exactly in the Right Place": A History of Fort C.F. Smith, Montana Territory, 1866–1868*. El Segundo, CA: Upton & Sons Publishers, 1999.

Haley, James L. *The Buffalo War*. Austin, TX: State House Press, 1998.

Hart, Herbert M. *Tour Guide to Old Western Forts*. Boulder/Fort Collins, CO: Pruett Publishing Co., Old Army Press.

Hebard, Grace Raymond, and E.A. Brininstool. *The Bozeman Trail*, two volumes. Lincoln: University of Nebraska Press, 1990.

Hedren, Paul L. *First Scalp for Custer: The Skirmish at Warbonnet Creek, Nebraska, July 17, 1876*. Lincoln: University of Nebraska Press, 1980.

Hoig, Stan. *The Sand Creek Massacre*. Norman: University of Oklahoma Press, 1963.

Hoxie, Frederick E., Jr. *Encyclopedia of North American Indians*. Boston: Houghton-Mifflin, Co, 1996.

Jeffrey, Julie Roy. *Converting the West: A Biography of Narcissa Whitman*. Norman: University of Oklahoma Press, 1991.

Josephy, Alvin M. *The Nez Perce and the Opening of the Northwest*. New Haven, CT: Yale University Press, 1965.

Keenan, Jerry. *The Great Sioux Uprising Rebellion on the Plains, 1862*. Cambridge, MA: DaCapo Press, 2003.

———. *The Life of Yellowstone Kelly*. Albuquerque: University of New Mexico Press, 2006.

Kelly, Lawrence C. *Navajo Roundup: Selected Correspondence of Kit Carson's Expedition Against the Navajo, 1863–1865*. Boulder, CO: Pruett Publishing, 1970.

Kennedy, Roger G. *Jefferson's Lost Cause: Land, Farmers, Slavery, and the Louisiana Purchase*. New York: Oxford University Press, 2003.

Key, Capt. John W.V., U.S. Army Reserve. "The Owens Valley Indian War, 1861–1865. www.militarmuseum.org/owensvalley.html.

Kip, Lieutenant Lawrence. *Indian War in the Pacific Northwest*. Lincoln: University of Nebraska Press, 1999.

Knight, Oliver. *Following the Indian Wars: The Story of the Newspaper Correspondents Among the Indian Campaigners*. Norman: University of Oklahoma Press, 1993.

Kuhlman, Charles. *Legend into History: And, Did Custer Disobey Orders at the Battle of the Little Big Horn?* Mechanicsburg, PA: Stackpole Books, 1994.

McChristian, Douglas C. *Fort Laramie: Military Bastion of the High Plains*. Norman, OK: The Arthur H. Clark Co., 2008.

McDermott, John D. *Circle of Fire: The Indian War of 1865*. Mechanicsburg, PA: Stackpole Books, 2003.

———. *Red Cloud's War: The Bozeman Trail, 1866–1868*, two volumes. Norman, OK: The Arthur H. Clark Company, 2010.

McFarling, Lloyd. *Exploring the Northern Plains*. Caldwell, ID: Caxton Printers, 1955.

McGinnis, Anthony. *Counting Coup and Cutting Horses: Intertribal Warfare on the Northern Great Plains, 1738–1889*. Evergreen, CO: Cordillera Press, 1990.

McNitt, Frank. *Navajo Wars: Military Campaigns, Slave Raids, and Reprisals*. Albuquerque, NM: University of New Mexico Press, 1990.

Madley, Benjamin. "The Yuki Case, 1851–1910." http://www.militarymuseum.org/historyiw.html.

Mangum, Neil C. *Battle of the Rosebud: Prelude to the Little Bighorn*. El Segundo, CA: Upton & Sons, 1987.

Manring, B.F. *The Conquest of the Coeur d'Alenes, Spokanes, and Palouses: The Expeditions of Colonels E.J. Steptoe and George Wright Against the Northern Indians in 1858*. Spokane, WA: Inland Print. Co., 1912.

Manzione, Joseph. *"I Am Looking to the North for My Life": Sitting Bull, 1876–1881*. Salt Lake City: University of Utah Press, 1991.

Meriwether, David. *My Life in the Mountains and on the Plains*. Norman: University of Oklahoma Press, 1965.

Merton Thomas. *Turning Toward the World: The Journals of Thomas Merton, Volume Four, 1960–1963*. San Francisco, CA: Harper, 1996.

Michno, Gregory F. *Battle at Sand Creek: The Military Perspective*. El Segundo, CA: Upton and Sons Publishers, 2004.

———. *The Deadliest Indian War in the West*. Caldwell, ID: Caxton Press, 2007.

———. *Lakota Noon: The Indian Narrative of Custer's Defeat*. Missoula, MT: Mountain Press Publishing Co., 1997.

Miller, Mark E. *Hollow Victory: The White River Expedition of 1879 and the Battle of Milk Creek*. Boulder, CO: University Press of Colorado, 1997.

Monnett, John H. *The Battle of Beecher Island and the Indian War of 1867–1869*. Boulder, CO: The University Press of Colorado, 1992.

———. *Tell Them We Are Going Home: The Odyssey of the Northern Cheyennes*. Norman: University of Oklahoma Press, 2001.

———. *Where a Hundred Soldiers Were Killed: The Struggle for the Powder River Country in 1866 and the Making of the Fetterman Myth*. Albuquerque, NM: University of New Mexico Press, 2008.

Morris, John Miller. *El Llano Estacado Exploration and Imagination on the High Plains of Texas*. Austin: Texas State Historical Association, 1997.

Morrison, Dorothy Nafus. *Outpost John McLoughlin and the Far Northwest*. Portland, OR: Oregon Historical Society Press, 2004.

Murray, Keith A. *The Modocs and Their War*. Norman: University of Oklahoma Press, 1959.

Neihardt, John G. *Black Elk Speaks: Being the Life Story of a Holy Man of the Oglala Sioux*. Lincoln: University of Nebraska Press, 2000.

Nelson, Kurt R. *Fighting for Paradise: A Military History of the Pacific Northwest*. Yardley, PA: Westholme Publishing, 2007.

Nesmith, James W. "A Reminiscence of the Indian War, 1853." *Oregon Historical Society Quarterly* Vol. 7, (1906).

Nester, William R. *The Arikara War: The First Plains Indian War, 1823*. Missoula, MT: Mountain Press, 2001.

Nichols, Ronald H. *In Custer's Shadow: Major Marcus Reno*. Fort Collins, CO: The Old Army Press, 1999.

Nugent, Walter. *Habits of Empire: A History of American Expansion*. New York: Alfred Knopf, 2008.

O'Donnell, Terence. *An Arrow in the Earth: General Joel Palmer and the Indians of Oregon*. Portland: Oregon Historical Society, 1992.

Orsi, Jared. *Citizen Explorer: The Life of Zebulon Pike*. New York: Oxford University Press, 2014.

Paul, R. Eli. *Blue Water Creek and the First Sioux War, 1854–1856*. Norman: University of Oklahoma Press, 2004.

Powell, Fr. Peter J. *Sweet Medicine*. Norman: University of Oklahoma Press, 1998.

Powers, Thomas. *The Killing of Crazy Horse*. New York: Alfred Knopf, 2010.

Prucha, Fr. Francis Paul. *American Indian Treaties: The History of a Political Anomaly*. Berkeley: University of California Press, 1994.

_____. *Great Father: The United States Government and the American Indians.* Lincoln: University of Nebraska Press, 2 volumes, 1984.

Quinn, Arthur. *Hell with the Fire Out: A History of the Modoc War.* Boston, MA: Faber & Faber, 1997.

Robbins, Harvey. "Journal of the Rogue River War, 1855." *Oregon Historical Quarterly* Vol. 34 (December 1933).

Roberts, Gary Lela. *Sand Creek: Tragedy and Symbol.* Ann Arbor, MI: University Microfilms, 1996.

Russell, Don. *One Hundred and Three Fights and Scrimmages: The Story of General Reuben F. Bernard.* Mechanicsburg, PA: Stackpole Books, 2003.

Schmitt, Martin, ed. *General George Crook: His Autobiography.* Norman: University of Oklahoma Press, 1946.

Schwartz, E.A. *The Rogue River Indian War and Its Aftermath, 1850–1980.* Norman: University of Oklahoma Press, 1997.

Settle, Raymond W. and Mary Lund Settle. *Saddles and Spurs: The Pony Express Saga.* Lincoln: University of Nebraska Press, 1989.

Sides, Hampton. *Blood and Thunder: An Epic of the American West.* New York: Doubleday, 2006.

Simmons, Marc. *The Little Lion of the Southwest: A Life of Manuel Antonio Chavez.* Chicago, IL: Swallow Press, 1973.

Smith, David A. "The Mariposa War." http://www.militarymuseum.org/Mariposa1.html.

Smith, Shannon D. *Give Me Eighty Men: Women and the Myth of the Fetterman Fight.* Lincoln: University of Nebraska Press, 2008.

Strobridge, Truman R. and Bernard C. Nalty. "And Down Came the Indians: The Defense of Seattle." *Pacific Northwest Quarterly* 55 (1964).

Sweeney, Edwin R. *Cochise: Chiricahua Apache Chief.* Norman: University of Oklahoma Press, 1991.

_____. *From Cochise to Geronimo: The Chiricahua Apaches, 1874–1886.* Norman: University of Oklahoma Press, 2010.

_____. *Mangas Coloradas: Chief of the Chiricahua Apaches.* Norman: University of Oklahoma Press, 1998.

_____, ed. *Making Peace with Cochise: The 1872 Journal of Captain Joseph Alton Sladen.* Norman: University of Oklahoma Press, 1997.

Thrapp, Dan L. *Encyclopedia of Frontier Biography in Three Volumes.* Glendale, CA: Arthur H. Clark Co., 1988.

Unrau, William E. *The Rise and Fall of Indian Country.* Lawrence: University Press of Kansas, 2007.

Unruh, John D., Jr. *The Plains Across: The Overland Emigrants and the Trans-Mississippi West, 1840–1860.* Urbana: University of Illinois Press, 1993.

Utley, Robert M. *Cavalier in Buckskin: George Armstrong Custer and the Western Military Frontier.* Norman: University of Oklahoma Press, 1988.

_____. *Frontier Regulars: The United States Army and the Indian, 1866–1890.* New York: Macmillan, 1973.

_____. *Frontiersmen in Blue: The United States Army and the Indian, 1848–1865.* New York: Macmillan, 1967.

_____. *Geronimo.* New Haven, CT. Yale University Press, 2012.

_____. *The Indian Frontier, 1846–1890.* Albuquerque: University of New Mexico Press, Revised, 2003.

_____. *Lone Star Rangers: The First Century of the Texas Rangers,* Volume I. New York: Oxford University Press, 2002.

Vaughn, J.W. *With Crook at the Rosebud.* Norman: University of Oklahoma Press, 1956.

Victor, Francis Fuller. *The Early Wars of Oregon: Volume One: The Cayuse War.* Corvallis, OR: Taxus Baccata, 2006.

Wagner, David. *Patrick Connor's War: The 1865 Powder River Indian Expedition.* Norman, OK: The Arthur H. Clark Company, 2010.

_____. *Powder River Odyssey: Nelson Cole's Western Campaign of 1865 the Journals of Lyman G. Bennett and Other Eyewitness Accounts.* Norman, OK: The Arthur H. Clark Company, 2009.

"War in the Redwoods." http://www.militarymuseum.org/Mendocino%20War.html.

White, Lonnie J., ed. *Chronicle of a Congressional Journey: The Doolottle Committee in the Southwest, 1865.* Boulder, CO: Pruett Publishing Co., 1975.

_____. *Hostiles and Horse Soldiers: Indian Battles and Campaigns in the West.* Boulder, CO: Pruett Publishing Co., 1972.

Wilke, Philip J. and Harry W. Lawton. *The Expedition of Capt. J.W. Davidson: From Fort Tejon to the Owens Valley in 1859.* Socorro, NM: Ballena Press, 1976.

Womack, Linda. "Sand Creek: Battle or Massacre?" sandcreekmassacre.homestead.com/theworksoflindawommack.html.

Woodward, Arthur. *Feud on the Colorado.* Los Angeles: Westernlore Press, 1975.

Index

Abbott, J.B. 389
ABCFM (American Board of Commissions of Foreign Missions) 16
Abernathy, Gov. George 19
Absaroka Home of the Crows 287, 293
Absaroka Mountains, MT 358–359
Acton Township, MN 251
Adams, Charles (Ute agent) 384, 392–393
Adams, Capt. Emil 434
Adams, Mary (Custer's cook) 301
Adobe Walls, TX: first fight at 217–218, 235; second fight at 142, 235
Agua Fria River, AZ 7, 437
Ahwahnee *see* Yosemite National Park
Aiken Massacre 379–380
AIM *see* American Indian Movement
Ake, Felix Grundy 419
Alabama Hills, CA 72–73
Alamagordo, NM 108
Alaska 7, 92
Albermarle (Confederate ironclad) 427
Alberta, Canada 370
Alcatraz Island 451
Alden, Lt. Bradford 27–28
Alder Gulch, MT 285–286
Alexander, Lt. Col. Edmund Brooke 97
Alisos Creek, Sierra Madres. Mexican regulars ambush Chiricahuas 445
Allegheny Mountains 7
Allen, Lt. Jesse 47
Allen, William 67
Alpowai (Nez Perce band) 353
Alta *see* San Diego
Ambrose, Dr. George 31

American Horse (Lakota chief) 292, 327
American Indian Movement (AIM) 462
Anadarko, OK 214, 233, 237
Anderson, Gary Clayton (historian) 254
Anderson, Capt. Joseph 261
Anderson, Maj. Martin 176
Anglo-European 2
Animas Mountains, NM 441
Antelope (Ute warrior) 389, 393
Antelope Hills, TX, fight at 213
Anthony, Maj. Scott 153, 156–159, 160, 163, 165, 170
Antietam, Civil War battle at 146, 251
Apache Cañon, NM, Civil War Battle at 128
Apache Indians 13, 76, 107, 120–121, 208, 395, 399–458
Apache Nation 427
Apache Pass, AZ 413–423; Apaches led by Cochise and Mangas attack 419; Mangas wounded, taken to Janos 420; Sgt. Albert Fountain leads detachment to spring 419–420; Sgt. Fountain later commissioned lieutenant as a result of conduct at Apache Pass 419–420
Apache scouts 435, 456
Apache Springs 414
Apacheria 395, 399, 432
Appalachian Mountains 7
Apple River 272
Applegate, Ivan 81–82
Applegate, Jesse 29, 85
Applegate, Oliver 82–83
Applegate Cut-Off 21, 25, 28, 80
Applegate River 27, 33, 38
Apserkahar (chief) 22
Arapaho Indians 132–133, 136, 141, 144, 160, 165, 170, 172, 180, 182, 189, 202, 208, 218–219,

222, 224–226, 234, 270, 284, 336, 339, 341, 376
Arapeen (Ute sub-chief) 378
Aravaipa Mountains, AZ 436
Archuleta (Navajo headman) 103
Argonauts 50
Arickara Indians 13, 133, 248, 270, 304, 318
Arickaras, War with 248–249
Arizona 92, 107, 197, 215, 405, 424
Arizona Guards 417
Arizona Territory 92, 129
Arizona Volunteers 424, 426
Arkansas River 132, 141, 145, 149, 152–153, 160, 170, 183, 207–208, 216, 219, 233, 337, 367
Arkansas Territory 10
Armijo (Navajo chief) 121
Armstrong, Capt. Pleasant 28
Army, U.S.: charged with difficult responsibility for protecting Trans-Mississippi West 289–290
Arnold, Elliott (novelist) 432
Aros River, Sonora, Mexico 453
Arroyo, Juan (Mexican scout) 421
Arthur, Jean (actress) 193
Ash Hollow, NE 139
Ashland, OR 27
Ashley, William Henry 133, 248
Assiniboine (Indians) 133
Astoria, OR 22
Atchison, KS 166
Atlanta, Civil War battle of 1864 283
Atwood, KS 244
Augur, Gen. Christopher C. 39, 196, 206, 228, 235, 245
Auguste, Lucien 136
Aurora, NV 70
The Avengers 26, 63
Averell, Lt. William Woods 114–115

473

Baca, Capt. Francisco 201
Backus, Maj. Electus 101, 117, 119
Bacon, Capt. John 219
Bad Hand Mackenzie *see* Mackenzie, Col. Ranald
Badlands (Dakota) 461; Suilly's 1864 fight at 283
Bagley, Will (historian) 379
Baird, Agent Spruce 102
Baker, Maj. Eugene 300
Baker, Col. James 272
Baker Massacre 8, 164, 300
Bakersfield, CA 69
Baldwin, Lt. Frank Dwight: 238, 243, 332–334; attacks Sitting Bull's camp at Ash Creek, MT 334–336
Bancroft, Hubert Howe (historian) 430
Bancroft, Samuel 166
Bannack, MT 285–286
Bannack (Bannock) Indians 68, 74, 337, 356, 358, 376, 380, 384–387
Bannack War, 1878 384–387
Barboncito (Navajo headman) 104, 118–119, 122, 129
Barnes, Will (historian) 446
Barnitz, Capt. Albert 197
Bartlett, John Russell: 406–407; appointed to head commission to establish Mexican-American boundary 406; arrives Santa Rita del Cobre May, 1851 406; begins work at El Paso, TX November, 1850 406
Bascom, Lt. George Nicholas 411–416
Bascom Affair, 1861 411–415, 423, 449
Battalie, Lawrence 59
Battle Butte, MT 342
Battle Rock, OR 22
Baumer, Lt.-Col. William 172
Baylor, Lt. Col. John Robert 127, 214–215, 417–418
Beale, Lt. Edward: appointed as Indian agent in California 398; uses camels in desert 398
Beale Spring, AZ 430
Beale's Crossing (of the Colorado River) 398
Bean, Maj. Gen. Joshua 395
Bean, Judge Roy 395, 417
Bear Butte, SD 174
Bear Coat *see* Miles, Col. Nelson
Bear Creek Massacre 164
Bear Hunter (Shoshone chief) 74
Bear River, ID 380
Bear's Paw Mountains, MT, Battle of 361–363

Beaumont, Capt. Eugene Beauharnais 240–242
Beautiful Mountain, NM 96, 118
Beaver Creek Valley, KS 199
Beck, Paul (historian) 250
Beckham, Stephen Dow (historian) 27
Beckwourth, Jim 157
Bedonkohe (Chiricahua band) 400, 407, 415, 421, 440
Bee, Capt. Bernard 250
Beecher, Lt. Frederick H. 202
Beecher, Henry Ward 202
Beecher Island, Battle of 203–205, 304, 445
Beeson, John 39
Belknap, Sec. of War William 219, 245, 306
Bell, Lt. David 105
Belle Fourche River, SD 340
Bendell, Herman (Superintendent of Indian Affairs in AZ) 432–433
Beni, Jules 166
Bennett, Capt. Andrew 333
Bennett's Peak, NM 118
Bent, Charley 94–95, 166, 197, 201–202
Bent, George 159–160, 165–167, 169, 179, 197, 202, 222
Bent, Robert 158, 197
Bent, William 94, 144, 151, 158–159, 165, 197, 216
Benteen, Capt. Frederick 222, 302, 319–324
Bent's Fort on the Arkansas 94, 126, 142, 145, 216; *see also* Bent's New Fort
Bent's New Fort 144–145, 216
Bernard, Capt. Reuben 83–84, 89, 385, 394, 426
Big Belt Mountains, MT 359
Big Crow (Cheyenne) 171
Big Dry River, MT 333
Big Eagle (Santee chief) 258, 260
Big Foot (Miniconjou) 460–462
Big George (Paiute chief) 72–73
Big Goose Creek, WY 316
Big Head (Lakota chief) 277
Big Hole River, MT, Battle of 355–356, 361
Big Horn and Yellowstone Expedition 308, 313–314, 434, 448; reinforced by Crow and Shoshone allies 315
Big Horn Mountains, WY 175, 286, 337, 369
Big Horn River 179, 180–181
Big Mound, ND, Battle of, 1863 270–271
Big Sand Butte, CA 90
Big Stone Lake, MN 252
Big Thunder (Santee chief) 254
Big Wolf (Cheyenne chief) 155

Billings, MT 358
Billy the Kid 129, 231
Bingham, Lt. Horatio 291
Birch Coulee, MN, Battle of 262–253, 265–266
Bishop, Samuel 69, 70
Bishop, CA 69
Bismarck, ND 300
Bismarck Tribune 304, 313
Bitterroot Valley, ID 355
Black Bear (Arapaho chief) 178
Black Butte, MT 333–334
Black Hair (Nez Perce warrior) 356
Black Hills, SD 135, 141, 177, 179, 181–182, 284, 303–307, 324, 326, 327–328; Army attempts to prevent miners from entering 306; miners 314–315; U.S. government attempts to purchase from Indians 306
Black Horse, Cheyenne 244
Black Jim 80, 82, 88, 114–116, 119
Black Kettle (Cheyenne chief) 147, 153, 156, 158, 221–222, 224, 287
Black Mesa, NM 124
Black Moon (Lakota warrior) 370
Blackfeet Indians 133, 248, 284
Blackfoot (Lakota Indians) 284
Blackhawk (Sac & Fox chief) 285
Blackhawk (Ute chief) 381; dies of tuberculosis (1872) 382; leads raids 381–382
Blackhawk (CO) *Mining Journal* 162
Blackhawk War, IA/WI 102, 104, 137, 285
Blackhawk War, Utah 381–383
Blanket Indians 253
Blood Brother (novel) 432
Bloodless Third's attack on Cheyenne camp at Valley Station *see* 3rd Colorado Cavalry
Bloody Knife (Arikara scout) 302, 318
Bloody Point, CA Massacre 80
Blue Mountains, OR 349
Blue Water, Battle of 139, 161; Indian reaction to Harney's attack 139
Bluff Creek, KS 376
Blunt, Gen. James Gilpatrick 152–153, 155; assigned to command District of Upper Arkansas 152
Bogart, Humphrey (actor) 69
Bogus Charley 88
Boise, ID 8
Boise Barracks 385
Boling, Capt. John 54–56
Bonaparte, Napoleon, III 425

Bonito (Apache chief) 449
Bonito (Chiricahua messenger) 385
Bonneville, Col. Benjamin L.E. 111, 114, 116–117, 119, 120–121
Bordeaux, James (trader) 135–136
Bosque Redondo (Navajo Long Walk) 100, 125, 129–130, 394, 424
Bourke, Lt. John Gregory 435, 455
Boutelle, Lt. Frazier Augustus 82–83
Bouyer, Minton (Mitch) 318–319
Bowen, Lt. Col. Leavitt 160
Bowie, Col. George 420
Bowman, John 393
Boxer Rebellion 237, 446
Bozeman, John 393
Bozeman Trail (Road) 177–178, 284, 285–288, 308, 314, 337; Laramie Treaty closes 289
Bozeman, MT 357
Brackett, Maj. Alfred Gallatin 279–281
Brackettville, TX 245
Braden, Lt. Charles 302
Bradley, Lt. James 323
Bradley, Col. Luther Prentice 295, 347
Brady, Cyrus Townsend 2
Brayton, Capt. George Mitchell 441
Brazos River, TX 208, 211; Bacon's fight on 219
Breaking-Up (Santee warrior) 251
Brewer, Lt. John 166
Bridger, James (Jim) 172, 286, 288, 294, 318, 377
Bridger Trail 286
Brisbin, Maj. James (Grasshopper Jim) 318
Brisbois, Louis 263
Broken Arrow (movie) 432
Brooke, Brig. Gen. John Rutter 460
Brooks, Maj. William 114–117
Brotherton, Maj. David 374
Brown, Capt. Albert 180–181
Brown, Dee 2
Brown, Capt. Fred 291–292
Brown, John 163, 215
Brown, Maj. Joseph Renshaw 261–262
Brown, Samuel 267
Brown, Lt. W.C. 394
Brown, Maj. William Henry 435–436
Brown Wing (Santee warrior) 251
Bruguier, John "Big Leggins 329, 333–334, 341, 344

Brule (Lakota Indians) 137, 165, 284, 460
Buchanan, Pres. James 379
Buchanan, Secretary of State James 95
Bucklands, NV 62
Buckley, Superintendent William 413
Buell, Lt. Col. George Pearson 236, 242, 328, 344
Buffalo, WY 179
Buffalo Bill's Wild West Show 461
Buffalo (bison) herds 232–233, 233
Buffalo Calf Woman (Cheyenne) 239
Buffalo hides, commercial exploitation of 232
Buffalo Horn (Bannack warrior) 385
Buffalo Hump (Comanche chief) 213
Buffalo hunters 233
Buffalo Soldiers *see* 9th and 10th Cavalry
Buffalo War *see* Red River War
Buford, Lt. John 98, 141
Bugatseka, Mexico 449
Bull Bear (Dog Soldier chief) 153, 188, 191–192
Bull Head, Lt. 375
Bullis, Lt. John Lapham 246
Bunker Hill, Battle of 315
Bunnell, Dr. Lafayette 55
Buoy, Capt. Laban 34
Burnett, Gov. Peter 52, 395
Burney, Sheriff James 53
Burns, Capt. Jim 435
Burt, Capt. Andrew 326
Bushy, Michael 65
Butterfield Overland Stage Co. 97, 197, 408, 414–415, 418, 421, 430

Cabrillo, Juan Rodriguez 50
Cache La Poudre River 150
Calamity Jane 327
Calhoun, Lt. James "Jimmi" 321
Calhoun, James S. (Indian agent and governor) 97–99, 101–102
California 7; volunteers 83
California Indians, treaties with 54–59
California Trail 62
Camas Meadows, ID 356
Camas Prairie, ID 351, 385
Camas Prairie Railroad 356
Camp Alden, OR 29
Camp Allaston, OR 35
Camp Atchison, ND 270
Camp Bidwell, NV 77
Camp Brown, WY 358
Camp Buchanan 142, 166
Camp C.F. Smith, OR 77–78

Camp Colorado 398
Camp Cooke, MT 360
Camp Crittenden, AZ 434
Camp Douglas, UT 385
Camp Floyd, UT 68
Camp Fremont, CA 54
Camp Grant, AZ 427–428; 1871 massacre 8, 426–428, 430, 436
Camp Hualapai, AZ 434
Camp Independence, Owens Valley, CA 72
Camp Latham, CA 72
Camp Lewis, CO 383
Camp Lyon, ID 74–75, 77
Camp McClellan, ISA 268
Camp McDermitt, NV 77
Camp Pope, MN 270
Camp Radziminski, TX 213–214
Camp Release, MN 267
Camp Sanborn, CO 150
Camp Stuart, OR 27–28, 34, 36
Camp Supply, OK 221, 226–227, 238
Camp Verde, AZ 429
Camp Waller, AZ 426
Camp Warner, OR 77–78
Camp Watson, NY 77
Camp Weld, CO 150
Camp Winfield Scott, NY 77
Camp Winthrop, OR 77
Camp Yuma, AZ 396
Campbell, Robert 134
Canada 359, 372
Cañada Alamosa, NM 431
Canadian border 367, 370
Canadian River 207, 214, 217, 220, 233–234
Canby, Col./Gen. Edward Richard Spriggs 232, 330–331, 417–418, 430; appointed to command Department of New Mexico 1861, 126–127; campaign against Navajos, Sept.–Oct. 1860 123, 125–126; deals with Confederate invasion 128; Mescalero Apache attacks and Confederate invasion 126; Modoc War 81–91; murder 88, 192
Cañon de los Embudos (Canyon of the Funnels) 455
Cantonment Keogh *see* Cantonment Tongue River
Cantonment Reno, WY 340
Cantonment Tongue River, MT 332, 344
Canyon Creek, MT, fight at 358–360
Canyon de Chelly, AZ 94–95, 100–101, 104, 117–118, 120, 124, 129–130
Cap Rock, TX 237, 240
Capitan Mountain, NM 107
Capote Band of Ute Indians 91, 121, 383

Capt. George (Paiute chief) 72–73
Capt. Jack (Modoc chief) 80–91, 331
Capt. Soo (Paiute chief) 62
Carcay Mountains, Mexico 444
Carleton, Maj. Caleb 369
Carleton, Maj. James 100, 105–106, 128–130, 217, 220, 411, 418–424
Carpenter, Capt. Louis 205
Carr, Col. Eugene Asa 205–206, 219–220, 220, 324, 442–443, 447, 449, 461
Carrington, Col. Henry B. 287–294; builds Bozeman Trail forts 288–289; issues orders to Fetterman 291
Carrington, Margaret Irwin McDowell 287, 291, 293
Carrizalillo Springs, NM 404
Carroll City, MT 333
Carson, Christopher Kit 98, 103, 105–106, 114, 121, 126, 128–129, 207, 217; 1864 Campaign to Canyon de Chelly ends Navajo War 129–130
Carson City, NV 63, 68
Carson District, NV 61
Carson Rangers 65
Carson River, NV 60
Carson Valley, NV 65
Carson Valley Expedition 65
Carter, Lt. Robert 245
Carver, Dr. Frank 390
Cascade Mountains 20, 41, 43
Case, Acting Indian Agent Samuel 85
Casey, Lt. Edward Wanton 345
Casey, Capt. James 342–343
Casey, Lt.-Col. Silas 25, 39, 43
Casper, WY *see* Upper Platte Bridge Station
Castro, Gen. Jose 80
Catley, Lt. Henry 394
Cavalry 12
Cave Creek, AZ: 5th Cavalry attacks Apache-Mojave camp 118, 347
Cayetano (Navajo headman) 103, 116–117, 121
Cayuse Indians 17–18, 40, 43, 45, 386
Cayuse War 15, 43
Cedar Creek, MT, fight at 329, 331
Cedar Springs, AZ, fight at 443
Central City *Miners Register* 160
Central Plains 132, 219, 298
Chaco Canyon 97
Chacón (Jicarilla Apache leader) 105
Chaffee, Capt. Adna Ronanza 237, 446, 449

Chalfant, William (historian) 188, 192, 196
Chandler, Lt. Col. David 56, 110–111
Chandler, Jeff (actor) 432
Chandler, Secretary of the Interior Zachariah 307
Chantilly, VA (Battle of) 20, 23, 288
Chapman, Amos 234
Chapultepec 111
Chatto (Apache chief) 449
Chavez, Lt. Col. J. Francisco 129
Chavez, Capt. Manuel 111–112, 122–123, 125–127
Chavez, Manuel Antonio 99
Che (Apache guide) 431
Chelmsford, Lord 293
Chenowith (Chinook chief) 44
Cherry Creek, CO 165, 167
Cheyenne Indians 107, 133, 136, 141, 144, 147, 165–167, 170, 172, 179, 182, 187, 189, 201, 218–219, 221–222, 224–226, 228, 234, 236–237, 270, 286, 295, 303, 310, 314, 334, 336, 341, 362, 373, 376, 379, 433
Cheyenne River, SD 460
Cheyenne village at Sand Creek *see* Sand Creek Massacre
Chicago Inter-Ocean 304, 313
Chicago Times 313, 433
Chickamauga, Civil War Battle of 149–150
Chihenne (Chiricahua Apache band) 401, 407, 410, 415, 421, 424
Chihuahua (Apache chief) 445, 449, 452, 455
Chihuahua, Mexico 395, 401–408, 423–424; establishes bounty for Apache scalps 416, 448–449
Chinese Massacre 75
Chino Valley, AZ 434
Chinook Indians 43
Chipeta (wife of Ouray) 392
Chippewa Indians *see* Ojibway
Chiricahua (Apache band) 395, 399, 400, 407–408, 412, 415, 426, 436, 439, 444, 451, 453, 455–456
Chiricahua (novel) 449
Chivington, Col. John Milton 148, 164, 179, 215, 217; attitude toward Indians 27, 148; called the "Fighting Parson" 148; commands Military District of Colorado 149; erroneously judges Sand Creek encampment hostile 157; leads parade through Denver after Sand Creek 160–161; officers in Chivington's command opposed to plan 157; physical de-

scription 148; plans major attack on Cheyennes on Republican River 156; plans secret campaign to Sand Creek 157; political ambition 148; resigns command 160; victorious at Apache Cañon and Glorietta Pass 128, 148
Choctaw Indians 213
Chokonen (band of Chiricahua) 400, 405–406, 409–411, 415, 418, 423, 436
Chookchancie Indians 53
Chowchilla Indians 53, 55–56
Churchill, Gen. Sylvester 67
Chuska Valley, AZ 96–97, 117, 120–121, 124
Cibecue, fight at 442–443, 446–447
Cibicue Apaches 442, 452
Cimarron Crossing of Santa Fe Trail 153
Circleville, UT 382
Claiborne, Capt. Thomas 124
Clark, Watson (teamster) 157
Clark, Lt. William Philo 338, 373
Clarke, Capt. Francis 329
Clarke, Gen. Newman 46–47, 398
Clark's Fork Canyon, MT 359
Clearwater, ID, battle of 354–355
Clearwater River, ID 348, 351
Cleveland, Pres. Grover 173, 458
Clitz, Lt. Henry 113–114
Clum, John Philip 438–439
Clymer, Sen. Heister 312
Coast Range Mountains 21, 30
Coates, Dr. Isaac (Hancock expedition surgeon) 189, 191, 196
Cochinay (Apache chief) 436
Cochise (Chiricahua chief) 10, 230, 351, 400, 409, 411–415, 418–420, 422, 427, 430–433, 437, 440, 444; ambushes Army detachment in Doubtful Canyon 405, 409, 423; assumes dominant role as leader of Chiricahuas 422; attacks stagecoach near Douglas, AZ, October, 1869 426; death 436; described by John Cremony 415; discusses peace at Fort Bowie 425; illness 436; incensed by murder of Mangas Coloradas 423; marries daughter of Mangas Coloradas 403; physical description 422–423; wages war on two fronts 424
Cochise County, AZ 450
Cody, William F. "Buffalo Bill"

206, 220, 325, 375, 461; claims first scalp for Custer 325
Coeur d'Alene Indians 48
Cole, Col. Nelson 173
Colley, Dexter 157
Colley, Sam (agent) 157, 161
Collins, Lt. Caspar 170, 176, 179
Collins, Superintendent James 97, 113–114, 116, 119–120, 418
Collins, Col. William O. 150, 153, 168–169
The Colonel's Daughter 437
Colorado 92, 132, 146, 170, 197, 405
Colorado River 47, 211, 219, 393, 397
Colorado Volunteers 149
Colorow (Ute chief) 389, 391, 393
Columbia River 15–16, 21–22, 26, 44, 248
Columbia River Basin 20, 41, 79
Columbia River Plateau 348
Colville, WA 40, 46
Colyer, Vincent (secretary, Board of Indian Commissioners) 428–430
Comanche (horse) 323
Comanche Indians 93, 107, 143–145, 147, 153, 161, 189, 207, 209, 213–214, 216, 218–219, 222, 224, 225–226, 228, 234, 237, 241, 376, 442
Comancheria 208–209
Comancheros 208, 217, 231
Comes-in-Sight 315
Commissioner of Indian Affairs, U.S. 350
Compa, Juan José 402
Compromise of 1850 99
Condon, Capt. Thomas 66
Confederate deserters 163
Conklin, James 97
Connell's Prairie, fight at 42
Connelly, Henry 119–120
Connor, Gen. Patrick Edward 154, 173–174, 174, 180–181, 183, 284, 288, 337, 380; asks Chivington's cooperation in protecting overland trails 155; attacks Bear Hunter's village, 1863 74, 161, 380–381; attacks Black Bear's Arapahoi village, 1865 178, 287; creates District of the Plains 170; launches 1865 Campaign 170; ordered to protect Overland Trail 170
Conover, Col. Peter 378
Conquering Bear (Brule Lakota leader) 135–136
Conrad, Secretary of War Charles 100
Continental Divide 16
Cooke, Jay 300–301
Cooke, Lt. John 414

Cooke, Col. Philip St. George 68, 105, 139, 143, 293
Cooke, Lt. William Winer 197
Cooke's Canyon, NM 416; Cochise and Mangas attack Felix Grundy Ake's wagon train 416–417
Cooke's Peak, NM 416
Cooke's Spring, NM 416
Cooper, Gary (actor) 193
Cooper, Adj. Gen. Samuel 34
Cooper, Maj. Wyckliff 195
Copper Mine Apaches *see* Chihenne
Coquille Indians 20
Coquille Massacre 24–25
Coquille River, OR 20, 24
Coronado 207
Corredor, Maj. Mauricio 454
Coteau des Missouri, ND 270
Cottonwood Springs, NE 167
Coulson, MT *see* Billings
Council House, TX, fight at 210
Coursolle, Corp. Joseph 261–262
Cow Creek Canyon, MT 361
Cow Island Landing, Missouri River: fight with Nez Perce 360
Cowart, Robert (Navajo agent) 119
Cox, Lt. Charles 199
Coyotero (Apaches) 110, 112–113, 116, 399
Coyuntura (brother of Cochise) 412, 414
Cradlebaugh, Judge John 63
Cramer, Lt. Joseph 157, 162
Crater Lake, OR 20
Crawford, Capt. Emmet 447–458
Crawford, Samuel (Kansas governor) 201, 218, 220
Crawford, NE 344
Crazy Horse 230, 284, 291, 310, 322, 327, 336–338, 341, 347–348, 348, 375, 440; death 348; possible presence at Fetterman Fight 291
Crazy Woman Creek, WY 338; attack on wagon train 289
Cremony, Capt. John 418
Crescent City, CA 33
Crescent City Guards 29
Cromwell, Oliver 18
Crook, Gen. George 12, 30, 35, 39, 47, 76–79, 81, 247, 306, 308, 308–309, 313, 316–317, 325, 327–329, 336–340, 344, 358, 365, 369, 385, 428–437, 447–455; attacks Cheyenne village on Powder River 310–311; at Battle of Rosebud 314–316; deals with political situation in AZ 428–429; promoted

to Brig. Gen. 308, 428; replaces Stoneman as commander of AZ Dept. 428; replaces Willcox as commander of AZ Dept. 447
Crooked Creek, TX fight at 214
Crooks, Col. William 261
Crossen, Yank 70
Crow Indians 150, 284, 286, 315, 318, 334, 341, 355, 373
Crows Nest, MT 318
Cuba 7
Cuchillo Negro (Black Knife) 112
Cullen, Maj. William 251, 261
Cullen Frontier Guards 261
Culver (Butterfield employee at Bascom affair) 413
Culver, Agent Samuel 29
Cumbres Pass, CO, fight at 377
Cummings, Alexander (Colorado governor; replaces John Evans) 171
Curly (Crow scout) 323
Curly-Headed Doctor (Modoc) 80, 85, 87
Curry, Gov. George 29, 33, 38, 41–43
Curtis, Gen. Samuel Ryan 149, 150, 152–153, 155–156, 160, 162, 165; creates District of Upper Arkansas 152; issues directive to Chivington 156; launches campaign through Kansas and Colorado 153
Cushing, Lt. Howard Bass 130, 427–428; attacks Apache camp near Signal Peak, AZ, 1870 427; attacks Nednhi camp in Whetstone Mountains, 1871 427; attacks Pinal Apache camp near Miami, AZ, 1870 427; called Custer of AZ 427; killed in action, May, 1871 428
Custard, Sgt. Amos 176–177
Custer, Boston 304, 321
Custer, Elizabeth Bacon (Libbie) 194, 197, 313
Custer, Lt. Col. George A. 8, 185, 187, 189, 191–193, 196, 198–201, 220–221, 222, 224, 228, 276, 301–309, 305, 317–324, 325–326, 370, 400; articles for *Turf, Field and Farm* 201; ceremonial ashes 226; court-martialed for absence 200; critical of Grant administration 311–312; divides regiment at Little Bighorn 319; fight on the Yellowstone, 1873 302–303; at Gettysburg 175; given command of 7th Cavalry 185; killed at Little Bighorn 316; leads expedition to Black Hills 303–306; misses Libby 194,

198; restored to active duty 219
Custer, Tom 196, 222, 304, 321
Cut-the-tent Incident *see* Bascom Affair
Cypress Hills, Saskatchewan, Canada 370–371

Dakota Columns 270, 309, 313
Dakota Indians *see* Santee
Dakota Territory 134, 173, 269–270
Dalles, OR 18, 40, 43–45
Danforth, the Rev. Edward (Ute agent) 388
Dark (Cheyenne medicine man) 142
Darlington, Brinton (agent) 227, 233, 243–244, 366
Darragh, John. 77
Dart, Anson 22, 24–25
Date Creek, AZ 430
Davenport, IA 268
Davidson, Capt. Delozier 397
Davidson, Lt. Col. John Wynn (Blackjack) 69, 105, 236, 242
Davis, Lt. Britton 436, 448–449, 451–452
Davis, Edmund 230
Davis, Secretary of War Jefferson 45, 137, 139–140, 142, 212, 398
Davis, Maj. Gen. Jefferson Columbus 89–91
Davis, Maj. Nelson 424
Davis, Lt. S.R. 72
Davis, Theodore (artist) 191–192, 197, 199
Davis, Capt. Wirt 452–453
Dawes Act, 1887 459
Day, Lt. Matthias Walter 452
Dayton, WA 19
Dead Buffalo Lake, ND: 1863 fight at 272
Dead Canyon at the Rosebud 316
Deadwood, SD 327
Death on the Rye Grass *see* Whitman Massacre
Death Valley 50
Decatur (sloop) 42
Deer Rocks, MT 317
Delano, Columbus (Indian commissioner) 85–86, 234
De Lany, Lt. Hayden 338
Delaware Indian scouts 143, 185, 192, 216
Delgadito, Navajo headman 124
Delong, Sidney 436
Delshay (Apache chief) 434–435
DeMille, C.B. 193
Deming, Dexter F. 61
Deming, NM 416, 423
Democratic Review 9
Dent, Capt. Frederick 48

Denver, James (Indian commissioner) 251
Denver & Rio Grande Railroad 383
Department of the Interior 307
Deschute Indians 45
Deseret 377
Desert Southwest 10, 376
De Smet, Father Pierre-John 179, 279–280, 286
Devil's Lake, ND 270, 278
Devil's Tower, WY 181
Diaz, Porfirio (Mexican president) 246–247, 448
Dietrich, Richard 358
Dill, Capt. William 53, 55, 279
Dillon, Lt. Edward 58
Dixon, Billy 234
Dixon, Daniel 293
Doane, Lt. Gustavus Cheney 358–359
Dodge, Capt. Francis 391
Dodge, Frederick 68
Dodge, Gen. Grenville 165, 170–171
Dodge, Capt. Henry Lafayette 97, 102–106, 109–111, 113
Dodge, Col. Richard Irving 336
Dodge City, KS 144–145, 234, 327
Dog Soldiers (Cheyennes) 146–147, 150, 182, 188–191, 194, 201–202, 205–206, 219, 226, 325, 336
Dole, William P. (Commissioner of Indian Affairs) 60, 161, 264
Donation Land Law, OR 22, 24
Doniphan, Col. Alexander 94, 96, 119
Doolittle, Sen. James R. 173, 184
Dorris, Pressly 85
Doubtful Canyon, NM 409
Douglas, James 18
Douglas, AZ{e}426
Douglass (Ute chief) 389, 392–393
Dove Creek, TX 217
Downing, Maj. Jacob 148, 150–151
Dragoon Mountains, AZ 400, 410, 431–432, 437, 443
Dragoon Springs, AZ 418, 432
Drake, Sir Francis 50
Dreamer Ceremony 351
Drexel Mission Church 462
Drum, Lt. Col. William 460
Dry Lake, CA, fight at 90
Dubois, Lt. John van D. 120
Dull Knife (Cheyenne chief) 179, 295, 337–340, 365–370, 390
Dunn, Lt. Clark 150
Dutch Phil 62
Dutchy (Chokonen scout) 454

Dyar, L.S. (Klamath Indian agent) 87–88

Eagan, Capt. James "Teddy" 310
Eagle Robe (Nez Perce) 352
Eastlick, John 260
Eastlick, Johnny 260
Eastlick, Lavinia 260
Eastlick, Merton 260
Eaton, Lt. George 437
Eaton, Lt. Col. John 110
Eayre, Lt. George 150
Edmund, Gov. Newton 277
Eel River Rangers 59
Egan (Paiute chief) 386–387
18th U.S. Infantry 287, 293
8th Minnesota Infantry 278, 280
8th U.S. Cavalry 235, 426, 441–444
8th U.S. Infantry 111, 456, 460
El Gordo (The Fat One) 113
Elbert, Gov. Samuel 384
Eldorado of the North *see* Colville
11th Kansas Cavalry 170–171, 176
11th Ohio Cavalry 168, 172, 176, 178
11th U.S. Infantry 242, 338
Ellendale, ND 275
Ellen's Man (Modoc) 90
Elliott, Maj. Joel 196–197, 222, 321
Ellsworth, Lt. William 168
Emory, William H. 168
Eskeltsetle (Apache chief) 441
Eskiminzin (Apache chief) 427
Espinosa del Diablo (The Devil's Backbone, Sonora) 453
Estherville, IA 250
Eubank, Lucinda 172
Eugene, OR 33
Evans, Maj. Andrew "Beans" 220, 225, 446
Evans, Col. George 70
Evans, Gov. John 147, 149, 151–154, 161–163, 171
Evans Creek, OR 27–28
Ewell, Col. Richard Dick 103–104, 107, 410
expansion of slavery into Western Territories 99
Eyre, Lt. Col. Edward 418

Fairchild, John 85
Far West (steamboat) 316–317, 323
Farmington, NM 96
Farrow, Lt. Edward 394
Fauntleroy, Col. Thomas T. 121–122, 125
Felner, Capt. John 279
Fetterman, Capt. William Judd 290–292
Fetterman Fight 8, 177, 184, 290–294, 292

Index

15th Kansas Cavalry 174
5th Minnesota Infantry 255, 265
5th U.S. Cavalry 205, 220, 227, 314, 324–325, 336, 369, 387, 390–391, 434–435, 437
5th U.S. Infantry 126, 211, 236, 325–326, 333, 340–346, 359, 362, 373
Fighting Irish Pencil Pusher *see* Finerty, John
Fillmore, Pres. Millard 24, 102
Finerty, John 220, 313, 325, 373–374, 443, 448
1st California Cavalry 418
1st California Infantry 217, 418, 420
1st Colorado Infantry 153, 156–159, 163
1st Dragoons 23, 27, 41, 46, 69, 103–104, 106, 110–111, 144, 396, 406
1st Nebraska Cavalry 153, 167
1st New Mexico Volunteer Cavalry 128–129, 217
1st U.S. Cavalry 74, 77–78, 81–82, 84, 90, 141, 214, 216, 352–353, 385, 394, 426–427, 444
1st U.S. Infantry 213, 215
1st Washington Territorial Infantry 74
Fischer, Waldmar 106
Fischer's Peak, CO, fight at 106
Fisher, Isaac 292
Fisher, Stanton Gilbert 358
Fisk, Capt. James L. 283
Fitzgerald, Maj. Edward 397
Fitzpatrick, Thomas "Broken Hand" 133, 136, 138, 210
Flandrau, Judge Charles 250–251, 258–261, 264
Flathead Indians 20
Fleming, 2d Lt. Hugh Brady 135–137
Fleming, James 62
Flipper, Lt. Henry 246
Florida (State of) 7
Floyd, John (Secretary of War) 122–123, 142, 398
Flynn, Errol (actor) 322
Foote, Capt. Rennselaer 145–146
Ford, Charles 451
Ford, Gen. James 170, 173
Ford, Capt. John "Rip" 213
Forest City, MN 263
Forsyth, Col. James 202, 387, 461–462
Forsyth, Maj. George A. "Sandy" 202, 304–305, 445; conducts defense of Beecher Island 203–205, 304, 445; forms company of scouts 202
Fort Abercrombie, MN 265, 270, 278

Fort Abraham Lincoln, ND 300, 303, 308, 313
Fort Alcatraz, CA 65
Fort Apache, AZ 442
Fort Arbuckle, OK 213–214
Fort Atkinson, KS 144
Fort Atkinson, NE 249
Fort Atkinson, TX 144
Fort Bailey, OR 34
Fort Bascom, NM 217, 219–220, 225
Fort Belknap, MT 213
Fort Bennett, OR 43
Fort Benton, MT 285, 360
Fort Berthold, ND 280
Fort Birdseye, OR 33
Fort Bliss, TX 107
Fort Boise, ID 74, 77, 353
Fort Bowie, AZ 420, 424, 426, 436–438, 441, 444, 450, 455
Fort Breckenridge, NM 127
Fort Bridger, WY 211
Fort Buchanan, AZ 127, 408, 411, 414, 416, 434
Fort Buford, ND 332, 374
Fort Caspar, WY 293
Fort C.F. Smith, MT 288–289, 294–295
Fort Churchill, NV 68, 71, 380
Fort Clagett, MT 360
Fort Clark, TX 245, 392
Fort Cobb, OK 214, 216, 221, 224–225
Fort Collins, CO 384
Fort Concho, TX 219, 231, 236
Fort Connor, WY 179–180; *see also* Fort Reno
Fort Conrad, NM 107
Fort Craig, NM 110, 122, 124
Fort Custer, MT 329, 344
Fort Dalles, OR 41, 43–44
Fort Defiance, NM 100–101, 104, 106, 108–109, 111–117, 119–123, 125–126, 129
Fort Davis, TX 107
Fort Dodge, KS 187, 205, 221, 232, 237–238, 367
Fort Douglas, UT 380
Fort Edmonton, Alberta, Canada 371
Fort Ellis, MT 308–309, 357
Fort Ellsworth, KS 183, 186
Fort Fauntleroy, NM 123, 126
Fort Fetterman, WY 308, 311, 314, 336, 340
Fort Fillmore, NM 103, 107, 127
Fort Fizzle, MT 355
Fort Floyd, NM *see* Fort McLane
Fort Fred Steele, WY 390
Fort Garland, CO 383, 392
Fort Gary Manitoba, Canada 272
Fort Gibson, Indian Territory 103, 215

Fort Griffin, TX 242
Fort Hall, ID 73, 285, 358, 384–385
Fort Halleck, WY 170
Fort Harker, KS 185–186, 193, 196, 199, 205, 221
Fort Harney, OR 79
Fort Haven, NV 67
Fort Hays, KS 193, 197, 226, 232
Fort Jones, CA 27, 30
Fort Kearny, NE 138, 142, 146, 153, 170–171, 288
Fort Keogh, MT 328, 370
Fort Klamath, OR 81, 91
Fort Lane, CA 30, 34, 37–38
Fort Lapwai, ID 351–353
Fort Laramie, WY 16, 133, 135–140, 142, 144–145, 150, 182, 165, 168, 171, 173–176, 179, 182, 286–288, 304, 306, 325, 327, 336, 340
Fort Larned, KS 146, 151–152, 161, 183, 185, 187, 188, 190, 193, 219
Fort Leavenworth, KS 96, 98, 100, 140–141, 145–146, 152, 172, 174, 185, 199, 210, 325, 416
Fort Lewis, CO 383
Fort Lowell, AZ 428–429
Fort Lupton, CO 150
Fort Lyon, CO 147, 149–151, 153, 156, 160, 162, 165, 206, 220
Fort Lyon, NM 126
Fort Macleod, Alberta, Canada 371
Fort Marion, FL 456–458
Fort McLane, NM 410, 421
Fort McPherson, NE 194–195, 199, 201, 206
Fort Miller, CA 57
Fort Missoula, MT 354–355
Fort Mitchell, NE 168
Fort Morgan, CO 194
Fort Mojave, CA 398
Fort Naches, WA 44
Fort Orford, OR 24, 29–30, 34
Fort Osage, OK 111
Fort Peck, MT 332–335
Fort Pelly, Saskatchewan, Canada 371
Fort Phil Kearny, WY 105, 287–298, 314
Fort Pierre, SD 139–140, 274, 277
Fort Pitt, PA 9
Fort Pueblo, CO 142
Fort Rains, OR 43
Fort Randall, SD 277
Fort Rankin, CO 166–167
Fort Reno, WY 179, 288–289, 337, 340
Fort Rice, ND 279–280, 283, 301
Fort Richardson, TX 228–229, 231

Index

Fort Ridgely, MN 250, 252, 256–267, 278–279
Fort Riley, KS 137, 152, 185, 210, 216
Fort Ripley, MN 210, 264–265, 278
Fort Robinson, NE 325, 344, 347–348, 365, 370
Fort Ross, CA 50
Fort Ruby, NV 380
Fort St. Vrain, CO 138, 142, 145
Fort Sedgwick, CO 178, 194–195, 198
Fort Selden, NM 130
Fort Shaw, MT 300, 308–310, 355
Fort Sill, Indian Territory 211, 225–226, 229–231, 236, 238
Fort Simcoe, WA 44, 48
Fort Smith, AR 211
Fort Snelling, MN 252, 257, 259, 268
Fort Stanton, NM 128, 130
Fort Steilacoom, WA 40, 42–43
Fort Sully, SD 277–278
Fort Sumner, NM 129, 207, 231
Fort Tejon, CA 69–70, 236
Fort Thomas, AZ 443
Fort Thorn, NM 108, 408
Fort Union, NM 100, 105, 128, 216
Fort Union, NDF 283, 286
Fort Utah (near Provo) 378
Fort Vancouver, WA 16, 18, 23, 29, 34, 43, 47, 416
Fort Walla Walla, WA 16, 45, 47–48
Fort Wallace, KS 194, 196–199, 202, 206, 368
Fort Walsh, Saskatchewan, Canada 371, 373
Fort Waters, WA 19
Fort West, NM 420
Fort Whipple, AZ 426, 439
Fort Wingate, NM 123, 129, 439
Fort Wise *see* Fort Lyon
Fort Wright, CA 58
Fort Yates, SD 460
Fort Yuma, AZ 47, 396–398
Fort Zarah, KS 187
Fortification Creek, CO 391
Forty Mile Desert, NV 62
Forty-ninth Parallel 15
The Forty Thieves 31
14th U.S. Infantry 74, 336, 426
4th U.S. Artillery 89–90, 336, 353
4th U.S. Cavalry 130, 219, 228, 236, 240, 245, 247, 325, 327, 336, 366–367, 392, 445, 452, 456
4th U.S. Infantry 40, 42–43, 313, 390
Fouts, Capt. William 169, 172
France 141

Franklin, Civil War battle of 301
Fraser River 40
Frazier, Lt. William 59
Free, Mickey 411, 449
Fremont, John Charles 80, 133, 377
Fremont's California Battalion 52
French, Lt. George 71
French Pete *see* Gasseau, Pierre
Fresno Crossing, California 53
Front Range of Colorado 376
Fronteras, Sonora Mexico 404, 409, 423, 425
Fuerte *see* Mangas Coloradas
Furnas, Robert 276

Gadsden Purchase 13, 15, 92, 106, 405, 408
Gaines, Gov. John 22, 24–25
Galbraith, Thomas (agent) 253
Gall (Hunkpapa Lakota warrior) 280, 370, 374
Gallegos, Jesus 123
Gallegos, Lt. Manuel 424
Galvanized Yankees 171–172
Garces, Fray Francisco 398
Garcia, Col. Lorenzo 445, 447
Garden City, KS 367
Garland, Brig. Gen. John 103–117
Garnett, Lt. Richard 44, 48, 134
Garnier, Baptiste (Little Bat) 336
Garryowen (song) 221
Garvey, Lt. Thomas 434
Gasseau, Pierre 288
Gatewood, Lt. Charles Bare 447–458
Gatling Guns 237, 244, 304, 313, 318, 353
Gayleyville, AZ 444
General Order No. 1 420–421
General Order Number 10 433
Genoa, NV *see* Mormon Station
George, Lt. Col. Milo 170
Gerard (Girard), Fred 320
Gere, Lt. Thomas 255; assumes command of Fort Ridgely 257
German, Adelaide 239, 243
German, Catherine 239, 243
German, Joanna 239
German, John 239
German, Julia 239, 243
German, Lydia 239
German, Rebecca 239
German, Sophia 239, 243
Geronimo (Bedonkohe Apache leader) 230, 400, 421–422, 440–443, 459
Gettysburg, Civil War Battle of 129, 183, 252
Ghent, Treaty of 248
Ghost Dance 235, 375, 459–462

Gibbon, Col. John 308–309, 311, 316–318, 323, 355–356
Gila Apaches 93, 110
Gila Expedition 111
Gila River, NM 99, 112, 397, 400, 423; Maj. Nelson Davis attacks Apache camp 1864 429
Gilbert, Lt. Col. Charles 56, 357
Gillem, Col. Alvin Cullem 84, 87–90
Gilliam, Cornelius 18
Gilpin, Maj. William 94, 147
The Girl I Left Behind Me 221
Glendive, MT, supply depot 302, 328–329, 331, 344
Globe, AZ 437
Glorieta Pass, NM, Civil War battle at 128, 155, 417
Glover, Ridgway 289
gold: discovered in Black Hills, 1874 232, 299, 305; discovered in California, 1848 7, 9, 60, 132, 211; discovered in Colorado, 1858 9, 381; discovered in Montana, 1862 248, 278, 285
Gold Canyon, NV 61, 65
Gold Hill, NV 63
Gonzalez, Felipe (Mexican scout) 421
Goodall, James 28
Goose Creek, WY 316, 325
Gordon, Maj. George 338–339
Gordon, Capt. William 98, 113
Gorman, Maj. James 425
Goshen, UT 378
Goshute Indians *see* Western Shoshone
Graham, Wilson 189
Graham Mountains 423
Grand Offensive (Gen. Crook's) 429, 433
Grand River (Ute band) 383
Grand River, SD 383
Grande Ronde Reservation, OR 39
Grande Ronde Valley, CA 45
Grangeville, ID 351
Granite Falls, MN 252
Grant, Col. Fred 301, 304
Grant, Capt. Hiram 261–262
Grant, Orvil 312
Grant, Pres. Ulysses S. 11, 48, 80, 86, 165, 184, 189, 226, 304, 306, 307, 311, 350, 381, 430
Grant's Pass, OR 32
Grasshoppers 283
Gratiot House 135–136
Grattan, Lt. John Lawrence 136–137
Grattan Massacre 136–137, 139, 177
Gray, John 322
Gray, William 16
Gray Bird (Santee leader) 262

Greasy Grass *see* Little Bighorn, Battle of
Great American Desert 9
Great Basin 60
Great Britain 11, 13, 372
Great Overland Trail 10
Great Plains 10, 12, 132
Great Sioux Reservation 202, 304, 307
Great Sioux War 8, 348, 370, 448, 453
Great Spokane Plain 48
Greeley, Horace 388
Greeley, CO 142, 388
Green, Maj. John (Uncle Johnny) 81–84, 89, 353
Green River, WA, fight at 42
Greene, Jerome (historian) 343
Gregg, Lt. David McMurtrie 47
Grey Beard (Cheyenne chief) 243
Grey Eagle (Santee chief) 272
Grierson, Col. Benjamin 225, 225, 228–229, 232
Grijalva, Merejildo (Mexican scout) 421
Grinnell, George Bird 337
Gros Ventre Indians 133
Grouard, Frank 77, 310, 325–326, 329–330, 336
Grover, Abner Sharp 202
Grover, Cuvier 386
Grummond, Frances Courtney 290, 293
Grummond, Lt. George W. 290–292
Guadalupe Hidalgo, Treaty of 13, 15, 92
Guam Island 7
Guerrier, Edmund 165, 191–192
Gunnison, Capt. John Williams 379
Gunther, Capt. Sebastian 366

Hagan, J.F. 66
Hale, Capt. Owen 362
Haley, James (historian) 239
Hall, H.L. 59
Hall, Lt. William Preble 434
Halleck, Maj. Gen. Henry 74, 154, 162, 170, 269
Haller, Maj. Granville 40–41
Halsey, Adm. William F. 100
Hämäläinen Pekka (historian) 208
Hamilton, Capt. Louis 196, 222
Hancock, Gen. Winfield Scott 184, 183–197, 202, 301; confrontation with Roman Nose 192; parleys with Dog Soldiers 192
Hancock's War 183, 217, 322
Hardee, Gen. William J. 212
Harding, Judge Stephen 161

Harley, William (Navajo agent) 113
Harney, Gen. William S. 137–138, 140–143, 145–146, 161, 305
Harpers Ferry, VA 103, 163, 215
Harper's Weekly 189, 199
Harrisburg, OR 33
Harrison, Pres. Benjamin 460
Hartwell, Capt. Charles 243
Harvey, Thomas J. 61
Harvey, Walter 57
Hasbrouck, Capt. Henry 90–91
Haskell, Harry 442
Hat Creek, NE *see* War Bonnet Creek
Hatch, Gen. Edward 392–393, 437, 439
Hatch, Capt. John 113, 117
Hated Post on the Piney *see* Fort Phil Kearny
Hawaiian Islands 7, 92
Haworth, James M. 237
Hayes, Pres. Rutherford B. 246–247, 371
Hays, Col. John Coffee "Jack" 65, 67
Hazen, Gen. William Babcock 219–221, 224, 289, 332
He-Dog (Oglala warrior) 310
Head, Lafayette 381
Heart River, ND 282
Heavy Runner (Piegan chief) 300
Heintzelman, Maj. Samuel P. 396–397
Helena, MT 333, 357
Heliograph 456
Hell's Forty Acres, AZ 451
Hell's Gate *see* Fort Defiance
Helm, Capt. Thomas 417
Hemphill, Lt. William 367
Henderson, Sen. John Brooks 202
Henely, Lt. Austin 244, 437–438
Henning, Maj. Benjamin 155–156, 160
Henry Jim (Ute warrior) 391
Henry, Capt. Guy Verner 170, 315, 429, 461
Henry, Will (author) 449
Henry repeating carbine 324
Henry's Lake, ID 356
Heth, Capt. Henry 141
Hickok, James Butler (Wild Bill) 185, 192–193, 215
High Sierra (Movie) 69
Highland Rangers 65
Hildt, Lt. John 121
Hill, Gen. A.P. 141
Hitchcock, Brig. Gen. Ethan Allen 24–25
Hoffman, Maj. William 137, 140, 398
Hole-in-the-Day (Chippewa chief) 264–265

Holladay, Ben (Overland Stage owner) 154, 166
Holt, Judge Advocate General Joseph 163
Holt, Secretary of War Joseph 124
Homestead Act, 1862 10, 253, 278
Honey Lake, CA 61–62
Honeybee *see* Deseret
Hood, Gen. John Bell 212
Hooker, Jim (Modoc) 80, 82–83, 87, 91
Hopi Indians 92, 116, 119, 129
Horn, Tom 453–455
Horse Creek Pass, MT 355
Horsemeat March 326
horses: effect of on Indian warfare 12–13
Horseshoe Canyon, AZ, fight at 445
Horseshoe Creek, WY, telegraph station 293
hostages 257
Hot Sulphur Springs, CO 389
Hotchkiss Gun 364, 373, 461–462
House, Maj. Albert 274–277
Howard, Gen. Oliver O. 350–352, 351, 352–365, 361, 363–365, 386, 429–433; hampers Crooks strategy 429–430; negotiates peace agreement with Cochise 431–433, 436–438, 440; sent to AZ as peace emissary 429
Howard Lake, MN 269
Hualapai Canyon, AZ 426
Hualapai Scouts 433
Hudson's Bay 16
Huggan, Nancy Fairibault 263, 267
Humboldt River, NV 60
Humbug Creek, OR 31
Hump (Lakota warrior) 363, 460
Humpy (Crow scout) 315
Humpy Joe (Modoc warrior) 80
Hundred Dazers *see* 3rd Colorado Cavalry
Hundred in the Hands, victory of *see* Fetterman Fight
Hungate Massacre 151–152, 155
Hungerford, Dan 65
Hunkpapa (Lakota) 181, 284, 328, 461
Hunt, Alexander (Colorado territorial governor) 195
Hunter, Capt. Sherod 411, 418
Huntington, J.W. (Superintendent of Indian Affairs) 74
Hurt, Garland (Ute agent) 379
Hutchinson, MN 263

Ice (Cheyenne medicine man) 142

Idaho (state) 68, 348, 365
Idaho Territory 73, 285
Ilges, Maj. Guido 360–361
Illinois River, OR 30
Indian agencies and reservations: Brazos, TX 215; Cheyenne-Arapaho 233; Cheyenne River Agency, SD 332, 460; Chiricahua, AZ 432, 437; Consolidated Ute Reservation 383; Crow Wing, MN Agency 264; Darlington Agency 243–244, 365, 370; Date Creek, AZ 429, 433; Fort Apache, AZ 430, 447–448; Klamath Lake, OR 74; Lapwai Agency, ID 350–351; Lemhi Reservation, ID 384; Los Pinos Agency, CO 383–384, 392; Lower Sioux Agency, MN 252–255–256, 259, 267; Malheur Reservation, OR 386; Mendocino Reservation, CA 58; Pine Ridge, SD 369, 370, 460; *see also under* Ghost Dance; Red Cloud 304, 306, 325, 327, 336, 344, 369; Rosebud, SD 460; San Carlos, AZ 424, 430, 437–442, 444, 447–448, 450–453, 455; Standing Rock, SD 375, 460; Taos, NM, 105; Tularosa, NM 430; Uintah, UT, 383, 394; Umatilla Agency, OR 387, 394; Upper Platte Agency, WY 138; Upper Sioux Agency, MN 252–253, 256, 264, 266–267; White Mountain, AZ *see* Fort Apache; White River Agency, CO 327, 383; Yainax, OR 81–83
Indian Bureau 22, 80, 136, 138, 184, 187, 214, 280, 307, 327, 350, 388, 424, 430, 439, 447, 461
Indian Removal Act 10
Indian Territory 202, 207–208, 233
Indian Trade and Intercourse Act, 1834 19, 210
Indian Tribes *see* specific tribes or bands
Indian War Expenses, OR & WA 39
Inkpaduta (Santee renegade) 249, 271–272, 275, 280–281
Intermountain Region 376
Interstate Highway 25 286
Interstate Highway 90 286
Intertribal Warfare 114, 149, 176, 213
Inyan Kara (Black Hills, SD) 305
Iowa (state) 173
Iowa Northern Border Brigade 264

Iron Brigade (Civil War) 309
Iron Horse *see* Union Pacific Railroad
Irwin, James 257
Isatai (Comanche prophet) 235, 442
Israel-Kennedy Supply Train 426

Jack (Ute chief) 389, 393
Jackson, Pres. Andrew 11, 189
Jackson, Lt. Col. Cosgrove 94
Jackson, Capt. James 82–83
Jackson Creek, OR 26
Jacksonville, OR, fight near 27, 33, 38, 85
Jake's Village (Rogue Indians) 32
James River, ND 274, 278
Janos (Chihuahua, Mexico) 441
Jarboe, Walter 58–59
Jefferson, Pres. Thomas 10, 15, 372
Jeffords, Thomas Jonathan 430–433, 436–439, 442
Jenness, Lt. John 296
Jennings, Isaac 76
Jenny, Walter Proctor 306
Jerome, Lt. Lovell 363
Jicarilla Apaches 92–93, 105–107, 116, 121, 377, 399
Jilla Apaches 107
Joaquin Jim 70
John Day River, OR 386
Johnson (Ute chief) 389, 393
Johnson, Pres. Andrew 84, 184, 202, 351, 383
Johnson, Col. J. Neely 54
Johnson, Capt. J.B. 369
Johnson, John 402–404
Johnson, John Liver-Eating 341
Johnston, Col. Adam 52
Johnston, Gen. Albert Sidney 142, 212–213, 379
Johnston, Lt. Col. Joseph Eggleston 141–142
Jones, Capt. John 279–280, 283
Jones, Sgt. John 259–260
Jones, Robinson 251
Jordan, Capt. David Starr 289
Jornado del Muerto 100, 107, 128
Josanie *see* Ulzana
Joseph (Old Nez Perce chief) 349–350
Joseph (Young Nez Perce chief) 350, 352, 362–363; surrender speech 364, 364
Juarez, Chief Jose 51, 53
Judah, Lt. Henry 31, 36
Judith Gap, MT 359–360
Juh (Chiricahua chief) 400, 415, 440–448, 450
Julesburg, CO 153, 165–167, 170, 179, 197
Jump-Jo Creek, OR 35
Jupes (Comanche band) 208

Kahwah Indians 53
Kamiakin (Yakima leader) 39–41, 43–44, 47, 49
Kaneatchi (Ute chief) 118
Kanipe, Sgt. Daniel 321
Kansas (state) 132, 141, 146, 149, 173, 197, 202, 367
Karok Indians 50
Kautz, Brig. Gen. August V. 24–25, 29, 34, 39, 437, 441
Kaycee, WY 177, 338
Kaytennae (Chiricahua leader) 451
Kearny, Maj. Philip 23, 39, 288
Kearny, Gen. Stephen Watts 23, 93–94, 132, 210, 405–406, 458
Kelley, Sgt. Matthew 43
Kellogg, John 71
Kellogg, Mark 313
Kelly, Luther Sage Yellowstone 329, 334, 341–342, 362–363, 385, 451
Kemp 403
Kenck, Charles 358
Kendrick Maj. Henry 102–104, 106, 109–110, 112–114
Kendrick, Silas (Navajo agent) 120, 122
Keogh, Capt. Myles 194, 197, 322–323
Ker, Capt. Croghan 98–99
Kerbyville, OR 31
Ketcham, L.R. 69–70
Keyes, Capt. Erasmus 54
Kickapoo Indians 216–217, 245
Kicking Bird (Kiowa leader) 229
Kidd, Col. James H. 173, 177, 179
Kidder, Lt. Lyman 198–199
Killdeer Mountain: 1864 battle 280–282
Killing Ghost (Santee warrior) 251
King, Lt. Charles 437
King Phillip's War 8, 285
King's River, CA 55
Kinney, Capt. Nathaniel 394
Kintpuash *see* Capt. Jack
Kiowa Apaches 208, 399
Kiowa Indians 143–144, 153, 161, 189, 207, 209, 216, 218–219, 222, 224, 226, 228, 234
Kip, Lt. Lawrence 48
Kit Carson of the Northwest *see* Northrup, George
Kitchen, Peter 416
Klamath Falls, OR 81
Klamath Indians 21, 50, 74, 79–80, 386
Klamath River, OR 31
Klickitat Indians 22, 40, 42–43
"Knits make lice" 27, 282
Know Nothing Party 38
Knox, Secretary of War Henry 9
Kotsoteka (Comanche band) 208

Kuykendall, Capt. John 53–55
Kwahadi (Quahadi) (Comanche band) 208

La Junta, CO 163
La Framboise, Frank (scout) 274–275, 279–280
Laguna Negra, NM 109, 123
Lake Abert, OR 76
Lake Coeur d'Alene, ID 47
Lake DeSmet, WY 179, 314, 340
Lake Shetek, MN 259
Lakota *see* Teton Lakota
Lamar, Mirabeau 208
Lame Deer (Miniconjou chief) 344–346
Lamerick, John 27
Lamson, Chauncey 269
Lamson, Nathan 269
Lana, Ramon (Navajo agent) 126
Lancaster, Burt (actor) 455
Land of the Sun *see* Utes
Lane, Joseph 21, 23, 28
Lane, William Carr 102–104
Lane County, OR 33
Lapwai, ID 16
LaRamee, Jacques 134
Laramie Loafers 171
Las Cruces, NM 107, 413
Las Vegas, NM 94
Lassen, Peter 61
Last Chance Gulch *see* Helena, MT
Lava Beds, CA 83
Lawrence, KS 163
Lawton, Capt. Henry Ware 240, 456–458
Leavenworth, Col. Henry 249
Leavenworth, Jesse (agent) 161, 185, 187–188, 193
Lee, Lt. Jesse Matlock 347
Lee, Gen. Robert E. 129, 188, 212, 215, 381; surrenders at Appomattox 171
Left Hand (Arapaho chief) 158
Leg-in-the-Water (Cheyenne chief) 165
Lemhi Indians (Bannack band) 384
Lemhi Valley, ID 357
Leschi (Nesqually chief) 42
Lewis, Gideon 438
Lewis, Lt. Col. William 367–368
Lewis and Clark 7, 248, 348
Lincoln, Pres. Abraham 125, 129, 162, 264
Lindsay, Capt. Andrew 117
Lipan Apaches 209, 245, 395, 399
Litchfield, MN 263
Little Belt Mountains, MT 359
Little Bighorn River, MT 317, 328
Little Bighorn, Battle of 8, 164, 177, 182, 222, 251, 275–276, 309, 317–324, 337, 343, 400; Lone Tepee 319; news reaches Sherman and Sheridan 324; Reno's valley fight 320
Little Blue River, KS, fight on 153
Little Brave (Miniconjou chief) 135
Little Bull, leads band of Cheyennes in escape from Darlington 244
Little Cheyenne River, Dakota Territory 274, 279
Little Colorado River, CA 120, 125
Little Crow (Santee chief) 146, 251, 255, 258–260, 263, 265, 267, 269; fights brothers for right to leadership 254; volunteers to find Inkpaduta 251
Little Dried River *see* Sand Creek
Little Missouri River Badlands 280, 282–283
Little Mountain (Kiowa chief) 217
Little Priest (Winnebago chief) 177
Little Raven (Arapaho chief) 117, 160, 193
Little Robe (Cheyenne warrior) 226
Little Soldier (Lakota chief) 276
Little Thunder (Brule leader) 138–139
Little Trout Creek, battle of 79
Little Turtle (Miami chief) 285
Little Wolf (Cheyenne chief) 325, 337, 365–370
Little Wound (Oglala Lakota) 460
Livingston, Dr. David 185–186
Livingston, Col. Robert 153, 167, 170
El Llano Estacado 207
Lobo Blanco (White Wolf; Jicarilla Apache leader) 105
Lockhart, Matilda 210
Loco (Apache chief) 444, 447, 452
Lodge Trail Ridge, WY 291, 314
Lolo Trail, ID 354–355
Lone Bear (Cheyenne chief) 150, 158
Lone Teepee *see* Little Bighorn
Lone Tree Lake, MN 266, 269
Lone Wolf (Kiowa chief) 224, 230
Long, Stephen Harriman 9
Long Chin (Brule chief) 140
Long Walk *see* Bosque Redondo
Longstreet, Maj. James 107
Looking Glass (Nez Perce chief) 349, 352–353, 355–356, 361, 363–364
Looking Glass Prairie, OR 33
Loon Creek, ID 394
Lords of the Southern Plains *see* Comanches
Loring, Col. William Wing 111, 113, 115, 126
Los Lunas, NM 107
Lost River, OR 79, 82, 87
Louderback, David 157
Louisiana Purchase 209
Loup River, NE 141, 174
Low Dog (Lakota warrior) 370
Lowe Percival 144–145
Lucero, Blas 116–118, 124
Lugenbeel, Maj. Pinkney 74
Luna, Ramon 99
Lupton, James 32
Lupton's Exterminators 38
Lyman, Capt. Wyllys 238
Lynde, Maj. Isaac 127, 410
Lyon, Gov. Caleb 75
Lyon, Capt. Robert 67

MacArthur, Gen. Douglas 328
Mackenzie, Alexander Slidell 241
Mackenzie, Col. Ranald 228, 231, 236–237, 240–247, 325, 328, 336–340, 372, 395, 449; assumes command of 4th Cavalry 228; attacks Dull Knife's village 338–340; destroys Comanche village in Palo Duro Canyon 112, 241–242; raids into Mexico 245–246
Mackinaw Boats 360
Macleod, Lt. Col. James F. 371–372
Makhpiya Luta *see* Red Cloud
Maley, AZ *see* Willcox, AZ
Maloney, Capt. Maurice 41
Maman-ti (Kiowa prophet) 240
Mandan Indians 133, 270
Mangas Coloradas 110, 400, 403–411, 414–415, 418–423, 440–444; murder of 422; myth surrounding alleged whipping 415; prowess as warrior 403–404; signs Acoma Peace Agreement 407
Manifest Destiny 2, 132, 308
Mankato (Santee chief) 258, 260, 266
Mankato, MN 260; hanging of condemned Santees 268
Manuelito (Navajo leader) 108–109, 113, 115, 118
Many Beaver Dams (Cheyenne informant) 338–339
Manypenny, George (Commissioner of Indian Affairs) 33, 38, 327, 346, 393

Marcy, Gen. Randolph Barnes 46, 211, 212, 228
Mare Island, CA 42
Mariano (Navajo headman) 97
Marias River, MT 300
Maricopa County, CA 69
Mariposa Battalion 56–57
Mariposa Creek, California 51, 54, 56
Mariposa War 51
Marmaduke, Lt. John Sappington 410
Marsh, Capt. John 255–257
Marsh Pass, NM 124
Marshall, Maj. Louis 74–75
Martin, Trumpeter John 321
Martin, Ramon 102
Martin, Maj. William J. 33, 36
Mason, Acting Gov. Charles 41
Mason, Maj. Edwin Cooley 89, 91
Mason, Brig. Gen. John 425
Mason, Capt. Julius Wilmot 434
Massacre on the Marias *see* Baker Massacre
Masterson, William Barclay "Bat" 234
Mauck, Capt. Clarence 338, 368
Maus, Lt. Marion 454–455
May, Col. Charles 98
Mayfield, Colonel 71
Mazatzal Mountains, AZ 434
McCall, Broken-Nose Jack 327
McCartney, Jim 358
McChristian, Douglas C. (historian) 136
McClellan, Lt. Gen. George B. 97, 211
McComas, Charley 449–450
McComas, Judge Hamilton 449
McComas, Juniata 449
McComas Murders 449
McConville, Col. Edward 354
McCook, Gov. Edward Moody 384
McDermott, John D. (historian) 180, 182
McDonald, Lt. David 445
McDonald, Prime Minister John 371
McDougal, California Gov. John 53–54
McDougall, Capt. Thomas 319
McDowell, Gen. Irwin 385, 451
McGarry, Maj. Edward 380
McIntosh, Archie 77, 449, 455
McKay, Alexander 77
McKay, Donald (scout) 77, 89–90
McKay, Dr. William "Billy" 77
McKee, Redick 53
McLane, Capt. George 115–117
McLaughlin, James (Indian agent) 460
McLaughlin, Capt. Moses 73

McLaughlin. Capt. Napoleon Bonaparte 240–242
McLaws, Capt. Lafayette 124–125
McLeave, Capt. William 128
McLoughlin, John 16, 77
McPhail, Col. Samuel 261–262, 271
Mdewakanton (Santee) 252, 254
Meacham, Alfred Benjamin (Modoc agent) 80–81, 85–88, 393
Mears, Otto 393
Medford, OR 23
Medicine Arrows (Cheyenne chief) 226
Medicine Bottle (Santee chief) 268
Medicine Tail Coulee, MT 322
Medicine Water (Cheyenne warrior) 239
Meek, Joe 19
Meeker, Arvilla 389, 392, 393
Meeker, Josephine (Josie) 389, 392, 393
Meeker, Nathan Cook 388–393
Meeker County, MN 263
Meeker Massacre 392, 448
Mendocino County, CA 59
Mendocino War 57
Meotzi *see* Monahsetah
Merced River, CA 51
Meriwether, Gov. David 103–104, 108–109, 112–113
Merritt, Col. Wesley 324–325, 329, 358, 369, 391–392
Mescalero Apaches 92, 103, 107–108, 126, 128, 130, 245, 399, 439
Mesilla Guard 114
Mesilla, NM 100, 107, 416
Metcalf, Robert 30
Métis or Slotas I *see* Red River traders
Mexican-American War 20–21, 30, 103, 137, 210, 376, 405, 416
Mexican Border Crisis 244
Mexican Cession 92
Mexico 13; gains independence from Spain 15, 92, 209, 401
Meyers, Capt. Edward 197
Michno, Gregory (historian) 79
Middle Park, CO 383, 387, 390
Midway Island 7
Miles, Lt. Col. Dixon Stansbury 103–104, 107–108, 111–112, 116–119
Miles, Capt. Evan 387
Miles, John (Cheyenne agent at Darlington) 227, 366
Miles, Col. Nelson A. 234–236, 236, 237–245, 325–336, 340–346, 359, 361, 372–373, 385, 387, 453, 455–458, 460–462; describes Sitting Bull 330–331; ends Great Sioux War 345–

346; fight with Bannacks on Clark's Fork 387; meets with Sitting Bull 330–331; nicknamed Bear Coat 329; prepares troops for winter campaigning 329; promoted to general 247; Red River Campaign 237–244
Miles City, MT 302, 328
Military Department of Arizona 79, 427, 441, 456
Military Department of California 74, 353, 451
Military Department of Dakota 106, 201, 312
Military Department of Kansas 149, 165
Military Department of New Mexico 96, 104, 127, 411, 439, 445
Military Department of Texas 107, 211–212
Military Department of the Columbia 74, 77, 81, 350, 357
Military Department of the Northwest 165, 264, 269
Military Department of the Pacific 71, 424
Military Department of the Platte 196, 206, 247, 285
Military District of Arizona 127–128, 424, 427
Military District of Boise 77
Military District of Nebraska 150
Military District of New Mexico 437
Military District of Owyhee 77
Military District of the Black Hills 325
Military District of the Plains 182
Military District of the Upper Arkansas 152, 160, 191, 221
Military District of Utah 182
Military Division of the Mississippi 173, 195
Military Division of the Missouri 159, 165, 170, 173, 375, 460
Military Road, KS 185, 187
Milk Creek, CO 448; battle of 391–392
Milk River, MT 373
Miller, John 28
Miller, Robert (agent for Upper Arkansas tribes) 144–145, 213
Mills, Capt. Anson 311, 316, 326
Mimbres (Apache band) 108
Mimbres River, NM 408
Mimbres Valley, NM 408
Miner, Capt. Charles 329
Miniconjou (Lakota) 135–136, 165, 284, 328
Minnemocker (Paiute chief) 64

Minnesota River 251
Minnesota River Valley 251, 258–259, 264, 278
Minnesota Territory created 252
Minnesota Uprising 8, 11, 146–147, 181, 198, 220, 248, 252, 277, 352; atrocities 267–269
Minnesota 9, 173, 252
Minor, Capt. Nelson 279
Misery Hill, Nez Perce fight at 354
Missouri (state) 141, 149, 202
Missouri Democrat 185
Missouri Fur Company 249
Missouri River 248, 252, 272–273, 278, 284–285, 300, 328, 333, 347, 359
Missouri Volunteers 94–95
Mitchell, Gen. Robert Byington 149–150, 153, 167
Mitchell, Sgt. Titus 419
Mix, Charles E. (U.S. Commissioner of Indian Affairs) 116
Moache (band of Utes) 92, 117
Mochi *see* Buffalo Calf Woman
Modoc Indians 13, 50, 74, 78–79
Mogoannoga *see* Soo, Capt.
Mogollon Apaches *see* Chihenne
Mogollon Mountains, NM 110, 399
Mogollon Rim, AZ 424, 437
Mojave Indians 395–399
Molchert, William 360
Monnett, John (historian) 366
Mono (Paiute) Indians 69
Montana (state) 367
Montana and Idaho Expedition *see* Fisk, Capt. James
Montana Column 311
The Montana Press 164
Montana Road *see* Bozeman Trail
Montieth, John (agent) 351
Montoya, José 413
Monument Valley, AZ 120
Mooar, John 232
Mooar, Josiah 232
Mooers, Surgeon J.H. 204
Moonlight, Col. Thomas 162, 164, 171–173
Moore, Lt. Isiah 414
Moore, Col. John 210
Moore, Tom 313
Moore, Lt. Treadwell 57
Moore and Kelly's Stage Station 150–151
Morehead, Quartermaster J.C. 396
Morgan, Anna Belle Brewster 226
Mormon Station, NV 60–61
Mormons 109, 142, 377–380
Morning Star *see* Dull Knife
Morrison, Lt. Col. Pitcairn 412

Morse, Capt. Charles 367
Mt. Graham, AZ 112
Mt. Idaho, ID 353–354
Mt. McLoughlin, OR 20
Mt. Moriah Cemetery, SD 327
Mt. Whitney, CA 50, 69
Mountain Chief (Piegan chief) 300
Mountain Meadows Massacre 380
Moylan, Capt. Myles 302
Muache (Ute band) 121, 383
Mud Springs, NE, siege of 168–170
Mule Mountains, AZ 438
Müller, Mrs. Eliza 260
Mullin Road 285
Munroe, Col. John 98–101
Murray, Keith (historian) 90
Mussellshell River, MT 359–360
My Army Life and the Fort Phil Kearny Massacre 294
Myer, Maj. Albert 125
Myers, A.C. 234
Myers, Capt. Edward 222
Myrick, Andrew (trader) 255

Naches Pass 45
Naches River, WA 44
Nahondzod (The Fearing Time) 125
Naiche (Chiricahua chief) 440, 455
Nakota (Sioux) 252
Nana (Chiricahua chief) 415, 421, 424, 440, 442, 448, 452, 455
Napoleon Gun 333
Narbona (Navajo chief) 97
Natrona County, WY 286
Nauvoo Legion 380
Navajos 92–131, 208, 399
Nazaree (Apache warrior) 438
Nebraska 132, 134, 141, 170, 173, 284, 368
Nednhi (Chiricahua band) 415, 440
Nee Me Poo *see* Nez Perce
Neighbors, Robert (agent) 214–215
Nephi, UT 378
Nesmith, Col. James 41, 43, 46
Nesqually Indians 42
Nevada (state) 74, 92, 133, 210
Nevada Rifles 65
New Mexico (state) 92, 132–133, 144, 154, 197, 207–210, 220, 395, 405, 424, 442
New Mexico Territory 92, 107, 121, 125
New Ulm, MN 250, 252, 256, 258–261, 263, 268
New York Herald 313, 388
New York Tribune 164, 167
New York World 304

Newby, Col. Edwin 96
Nez Perce Indians 13, 16, 20, 40, 77, 133, 236, 348–365, 367, 370, 444; non treaty bands 353–365
Nez Perce War 8, 40, 348–365, 385
19th Kansas Cavalry 220–221, 224, 226
9th Minnesota Infantry 265
9th U.S. Cavalry 219, 242, 383, 391–392, 439, 460–462
9th U.S. Infantry 42–44, 48, 74, 313, 326, 336
Niobrara River, NE 179, 369
No Hip Bone *see* Gibbon, Col. John
Noble, Lt. Herman 71–73
Nocy-ay-det-Klinne (Cibecue chief) 442
Nome Cult Farm, CA 59
Nootchus Indians 53, 55–56
Norte Americanos 405–406, 409
North, Frank 141, 171, 175, 182, 206, 336, 339
North, Luther 141, 336, 339
North Canadian River, OK 244
North Dakota (state) 265
North Park, CO 383, 390
North Platte River 286, 369
Norther (storm) 182, 243
Northern Cheyennes, flight of 208, 284, 343, 365, 370
Northern Pacific Railroad 248, 299–301, 306
Northern Paiute Indians 60, 74, 78, 309, 384
Northern Paiute War 73
Northern Plains 248, 433, 451
Northrup, George 281
Northwest Mounted Police 371
Northwest Territory 370
Northwestern Indian Expedition, 1864 278
Noyes, Capt. Henry 311
Numaga (Paiute chief) 62
Nye, Gov. James W. 69, 71

O'Brien, Capt. Nicholas 166–167, 178
O'Brien, OR 30
Ochocana (Yavapai chief) 434
Odeneal, Thomas (Modoc agent) 81–82
Ogallala, NE 369
Ogden, Peter Skene 18, 21
Oglala (Lakota) 165, 192, 201, 284, 340–341, 460
Ojibway Indians 252, 254, 264, 286
Ojo Caliente, NM 438, 441
Oklahoma (state) 207
Old Blizzards *see* Loring, Col. William
Old Pawn (Santee) 260

Old Tipsey's Band (Rogue Indians) 30
Ollokot (Nez Perce war chief) 350, 352
Omaha scouts 175, 178, 180
On the Border with Mackenzie 245
One-Eye *see* Lone Bear
One Hundred and Three Fights and Scrimmages 385
One-Stab (Lakota headman) 304
Ord, Gen. Edward Otho Cresap 39, 246–247
Oregon (state) 7, 13, 68, 210, 285, 376
Oregon-California Trail 21, 34, 73, 132, 167, 210, 285
Oregon City, OR 21
Oregon Country 13, 15
Oregon Mounted Volunteers 74, 43, 83
Oregon Statesman 32
Oregon Territory 20–21, 23, 26, 74
Oregon Trail 23, 46, 145–146
Oregonian 38
Ormsby, Maj. William 63–68
Orofino, ID Mining District 73
Osage Indians 226
O'Sullivan, John L. 9
Other Day, John 256, 266
Otis, Lt. Col. Elwell 325–326, 328–330
Ott, Larry 352
Ouray (Ute chief) 381, 392–394
Overland Stage Line 166, 170
Overland Trail 141, 168, 172, 175, 181, 380
Owens, Capt. Elias 29
Owens, Richard 69
Owens Lake, CA 69
Owens Valley, CA 79, 237
Owens Valley War 69
Owyhee, ID, mining district 73, 78
Owyhee River, ID 75
Oytes (Bannack medicine man) 386

Pacific Northwest 10, 13, 20, 133, 154
Pacific Steamship Line 22
Pagosa Springs, CO 383
Paiute Indians 61, 68, 70, 76, 376, 382, 385, 460
Paiute scouts 434
Paiute War, 1861 59
Palmer, Capt. Henry 175
Palmer, Col. Innis 293
Palmer, Joel 20, 26, 29, 32, 37–38, 40
Palo Duro Canyon, TX, fight at 240–242
Palouse Indians 40, 43, 46, 48, 352

Papago Indians 430
Parker, Cynthia Ann 230
Parker, Quanah (Comanche chief) 230, 230, 235, 242–243
Parrish, Josiah 24
Parrott, R.P. 167
Parrott Gun 167
Pascual I (Yuma chief) 397
Pascual II (Yuma chief) 397
Pattee, Col. John 279, 280
Patten, Capt. George Waynefleet 30
Pattie, James Ohi 398
Patton, Lt. Rober 169
Paulina (Snake Indian chief) 74, 76, 79
Paulina Creek 74
Pauvits 393
Pawnee Battalion 141, 171, 175, 178, 206, 336, 339
Pawnee Fork of the Arkansas 190, 192, 201
Pawnee Indians 132, 141–142, 146, 171
Pawnee Killer (Lakota war chief) 190, 195–196, 202
Payette Lake, ID 394
Pawnee Rock, KS 187
Payson Canyon 378
Peace Policy, Pres. U.S. Grant's 80, 88–89, 227–228, 427
Peaches *see* Tzoe
Peanuts (Comanche boy; brother of Quanah Parker) 231
Pearsall Creek, ID 394
Pease River, TX, battle at 231
Pecos River 107
Pedregosa Mountains 426
Peel, Alexander 378
Peloncillo Mountains, AZ 445
Penateka 208
Pend d'Orielles 48
Pendleton, OR 386
Peo-peo-mox-mox (Yellow Serpent; Walla Walla chief) 43
Pepoon, Lt. Silas 75
Peralta, NM, Navaho raid at 108
Perry, Capt. David 91, 352, 444
Peta Nocona (Comanche chief) 230
Pfeiffer, Capt. Albert 129
Philippine Islands 7
Phillips, John Portugee 292–293
Piarhel (Apache scout) 437
Picacho Pass, AZ, Civil War battle of 418, 421
Piegan Indians 300
Pierce, Capt. Francis 451
Pierce, Pres. Franklin 379
Pike, Zebulon Montgomery 9
Pike's Pead or Bust 146
Pilcher, Joshua 249
Pima Indians 430
Pima scouts 435
Pinal Apaches 426–427

Pinaleño Mountains, AZ 443
Piney Creek, WY 295
Pino, Col. Miguel 126
Pinos Altos 409, 415, 417, 421, 423
Pionsenay (Apache scout) 437–438
Pisago Cabezón (Chiricahua war leader) 404
Pit River 50
Pit River Indians 79
Pitkin, Gov. Frederick 387, 390
Piute Indians *see* Northern Paiutes
Place of the Rye Grass *see* Waiilatpu
Plains Apaches 144, 187, 218
The Plainsman (movie) 193
Platte Bridge Station 172, 175; battle of 176, 182
Platte River 132, 135, 140–141, 149, 152, 169, 174, 183, 194, 208, 219, 248, 284
Plumb, Lt. Col. Preston 170
Plummer, Capt. Joseph Benne 215
Point of Rocks, NM, wagon attacked at 98
Poker Joe (Nez Perce war chief) 356, 361
Polk, Pres. James K. 15, 19, 21, 132
Pollock, Lt. Col. Samuel McLean 279–280
Ponce (Apache guide) 431
Ponoeohe *see* Sand Creek
Pontiac's War 8, 285
Pony Express 59, 68
Pope, Maj. Gen. John 170–171, 235, 237, 244, 264, 268–270, 274, 277–278, 427; appointed to command new Military Department of the Northwest 165, 264
Pope, Capt. Nathaniel 279, 281
Pork Barrel War *see* Rogue War, 1855
Port Orford, OR 24
Potencie Indians 53
Pourier, Baptiste "Big Bat" 325, 336
Powder River, WY 181, 284, 310, 318, 340
Powder River Country 172, 286, 369
Powder River drainage system 316, 336–337
Powder River Expedition 173, 181, 183, 185, 336–337
Powder River, Red Fork of 350, 365
Powell, Capt. James 291, 294–297
Powell, John Wesley 389
Powell Park, CO 389–390

Powell Valley, CO *see* Powell Park
Prairie Flower (Comanche girl; sister of Quanah Parker) 231
Prairie Traveler 211
Preston, UT 74
Price, Flora 389, 392
Price, Johnny 389, 392
Price, May 389, 392
Price, Shadrach 389
Price, Col. Sterling 95, 155
Price, Maj. William Redwood 236, 243
Prince of Dragoons *see* Harney, William S.
Provo River 377
Pueblo Indians 129
Pueblo Revolt 92
Puerto Rico 7
Puget Sound, WA 20, 41–43
Pumpkin Buttes, WY 179
Punished Woman's Fork of Smoky Hill River, KS, fight at 368–369
Putnam, Charles 69
Putnam's Trading Post, Owens Valley, CA 69
Pyramid Lake, NV, Battle of 64

Quakers *see* Society of Friends
Qualchim 47, 49
Quinn, Scout James 105–106

Radersburg, MT 357
Rafferty, Capt. William 444–445
railroads *see* specific lines
Rains, Maj Gabriel 41
Ramsey, Gov. Alexander 257, 259, 261, 265, 269
Ranchester, WY 178
Randall, Capt. George Blackjack 434, 436
Rankin, Joe, scout 391
Ransom, Lt. Robert 103–104
Rapid City, SD 461
Raton Peak, NM *see* Fischer's Peak
Rawlins, WY 388–389
Rawn, Capt. Charles 354–355
Red Beard 198
Red Cloud (Oglala chief) 284–285, 287, 289, 297, 375
Red Cloud's War 285–298, 337
Red Iron (Wahpeton chief) 266
Red Leaf (Brule chief) 140
Red Paint Apaches *see* Chihenne
Red River, TX 211, 213, 237, 241, 242, 372
Red River War of 1874 8, 232, 328, 333
Red Shirt *see* Dodge, Henry
Red Sleeves *see* Mangas Coloradas

Red Tomahawk, Sgt. 375
Redwood Falls, MN 252
Redwood Ferry, MN 256
Reed, Autie 321
Reed's Station, NV 65
Regulation of 1729 400
Regulation of 1772 400
Rencher, Abraham 113, 122, 124–125
Rendlebrock, Capt. Joseph 366–367
Reno, Gen. Jesse Lee 288
Reno, Maj. Marcus 316–317, 319–324, 347
Reno Court of Inquiry 347
Renville Rangers 258
Republican River Valley, CO 142, 149, 153, 167, 194, 202, 205, 227
reservation system, failure of 227–228
Rey, Chief Jose 53–54
Reynolds, Gen. John 39, 351
Reynolds, Col. Joseph J. 310–311, 315, 317, 337
Reynolds, Lonesome Charley 305, 318, 329
Riddle, Frank 87
Riel, Louis 372
Riggs, the Rev. Stephen 267
Riley, Bart 64
Riley, J.W. 53
Rio Caliente, NM, fight at 105
Rio Grande River 92, 107, 208, 395
Rio Grande Valley 128
Ripley, W.D. 150
Roach, Lt. Hampton, 448
Robbins, Harvey 31, 33
Roberts, Gary (historian) 155, 161, 164
Roberts, Capt. Thomas 128, 418–420, 423
Rock Springs, WY 169
Rocky Mountain News 160–163–164, 175, 313
Rodman field piece 301, 304, 331
Rogers, Nicholas 437–438
Rogue Indians 21
Rogue River, OR 20, 22, 37
Rogue River, Big Bend of 39
Rogue River wars 20
Roman Nose (Cheyenne warrior) 190–192, 201–202, 204
Romeyn, Capt. Henry 362
Roop, Gov. Isaac 61, 65, 68
Roosevelt, Theodore 456
Ropes, Capt. James 72
Rosebud River, MT, Battle of 178, 309, 315–317, 346
Roseburg, OR 33
Ross, Horatio 305
Ross, John 28, 33, 35
Rosser, Tom 301
Roth, Charles 187

Rough Riders 456
Round Valley, CA 57–58
Rowe, Capt. Edwin 71–72
Rowland, Willis 336
Royall, Col. William Bedford, fight with dog soldiers, Oct. 1867 205, 315
Royer, Daniel (agent at Pine Ridge) 460
Rucker, Lt. John Anthony 441
Ruff, Maj. Charles Frederick 121
Ruidoso, NM 107
Runs Against Something When Crawling (Santee warrior) 251
Rush Creek, NE, siege at 170
Rush Springs, TX, fight at 213
Russell, Majors and Waddell 68, 166
Russia 50
Ruysdael, Basil 432

Sacramento Mountains, NM 108
Sacramento Union 58
Safford, Gov. Anson 430, 438–439
Safford, AZ 112
St. Croix River, MN 254, 264
St. Francis Ranch, CA 70
St. Peter, MN 258
St. Vrain, Col. Ceran 126
Saline River, KS 143, 152, 205, 224
Salmon River, ID 349, 351–352, 394
Salt Lake City, UT 68, 166–167
Salt River, AZ 429; fight at 435–436
Salt River Valley, AZ 435–436
Samaniego, Mariano 443
Samoa Island 7
San Antonio, TX 210, 214, 244–245
San Antonio to San Diego Mail Co. 408
San Bernardino, Mexico 455
San Diego, CA 47, 50, 395
San Francisco, CA 22
San Francisco Alta 313
San Francisco Bulletin 58
San Jacinto, TX 209
San Joaquin Valley, California 54, 57
San Juan Rifles 65
San Luis Valley, CO 376, 383
San Mateo, Philippine Islands, Battle of 456
San Pedro, AZ Council at 430
San Saba River, TX 210
San Simon, AZ, Cochise attacks Army wagon train, May 1861 416
San Ysidro, NM 117
Sand Creek, KS, fight at 367
Sand Creek Massacre 27, 154–164, 183, 189, 217, 221–223, 287

Sand Hill (Arapahoe chief) 158
Sand Hill Country 369
Sandia Mountains, NM 92
Sandoval 98, 102, 104, 114, 119
Sanford, Gen. John Benjamin 173
Sangre de Cristo, NM 92
Sans Arc (Lakota) 165, 284
Santa Anna 107
Santa Cruz Valley, AZ 416, 456
Santa Fe, NM 92, 107, 211
Santa Fe Railroal 367
Santa Fe Trail 93, 144, 209, 216–218
Santa Fe Weekly Gazette 114
Santa Maria River, AZ, fight at 434
Santa Rita del Cobre 100, 401–402, 405, 421; Gen. Sumner orders site abandoned 408; Spain establishes copper mine at 400
Santa Rosa, NM, Steen's fight at 406
Santees (Dakota Sioux) 146, 249, 270, 278; hanging of at Mankato, MN 268
Santo Domingo Pueblo 100
Sappa Creek, KS *see* Dark Water Creek
Saskatchewan, Canada 370
Satank (Kiowa chief) 229–230
Satanta (Kiowa chief) 193, 217, 224, 229, 229, 231
Satus Creek 43
Saunders, Lt. Col. 65
Sawyer, James Alexander 178–179, 181
Savage, James D. 52, 54–55, 57
Scar-faced Charley (Modoc warrior) 80, 82–83, 87–88
Scarlet Point/Red Cap/Red End *see* Inkpaduta
Schaefer, Jack (novelist) 395
Scherum (Hualapai chief) 420
Schofield, Gen. John M. 462
Schonchin, John (Modoc) 80
Schoolcraft, Henry 110
Schroeder, Capt. Henry 120
Schurz, Sec. of the Interior Carl 80, 392–393
Schuyler, Lt. Walter 436
Schwartz, E.A. (historian) 31
Scorpion Point, CA 84, 90
Scott, William 59
Scott, Winfield (General of the Army) 42, 137, 214
Scott Valley, CA 27, 31
SeaGull 23
Seattle, WA 42
2d Artillery 100, 104
2d California Infantry 57
2d California Cavalry 70–73, 175, 178, 180, 418
2d Colorado Cavalry 150, 162

2d Dragoons 98, 105, 124, 141, 216
Second Manassas, Civil War Battle of 165
2d Minnesota Cavalry 278, 280, 282
2d Missouri Light Artillery 175
2d Nebraska Cavalry 276
2d Texas Mounted Rifles 215, 421
2d U.S. Cavalry 212–213, 215, 293, 308–309, 313, 318, 326, 336, 344–345, 362–363, 73
2d U.S. Infantry 394, 460
Secretary of the Interior 350
Sedgwick, Maj. John 141–142, 145, 166, 216
Selden, Capt. Henry 123
Seminole Indians 241
Seminole Wars 103–104, 111, 137, 309, 367
Sequoia National Park, California 54
Serra, Father Junipero 50
17th U.S. Infantry 313, 329, 344
7th Iowa Cavalry 153, 166–167, 169, 172, 175, 178, 274, 276, 279–280, 346
7th Minnesota Infantry 266, 271–272
7th U.S. Cavalry 185, 192, 194, 196, 199, 202, 205, 220, 224, 226, 301–304, 313, 317–327, 358, 362, 461–462
7th U.S. Infantry 123, 309, 355
Sevier, John, Gov. of Tennessee 159
Shacknasty, Jim 83
Shafter, Col. William R. (Pecos Bill) 231, 146–147
Shakopee, Santee leader 268
Shasta Indians 21, 27, 31, 50, 79
Shaw, Lt. Col. Benjamin Franklin 45
Sheehan, Lt. Timothy 256, 258, 262
Sheepeater Indians 376, 385, 394
Shelby, MT 300
Shepherd, Maj. Oliver 120–123
Shepherd Wagon Train Raid 73
Sheridan, Gen. Philip 41, 43, 159, 202, 218–220, 224, 226, 232, 235, 245, 247, 304, 306, 327–328, 364, 372–372, 375, 422, 429, 433, 441, 451, 453, 455–456; creates Military District of the Yellowstone 328; named to command Missouri Department 202; plans campaign for Great Sioux 308; plans Washita campaign 221; pleads for Custer's return 219; strategy for dealing with discovery of gold in Black Hills 306

Sheridan, WY 286, 314
Sherman, Sen. John 236
Sherman, Gen. William T. 86–87, 89, 183, 187, 189, 193, 195–196, 201, 218–219, 226, 229, 232, 235–236, 245, 247, 287, 301, 306, 317, 328, 332, 340, 356, 364, 372, 422, 447–448, 451, 459; appointed General of the Army 226; says "no peace should be shown these Indians" 184; tours Southern Plains 228–229; tours Yellowstone Park 357
Sheyenne River, ND 270
Shipley, Lt. Alexander 122
Shipp, Lt. William Ewen 454
Shiprock, NM 103
Shirland, Capt. Edmund 421–422
Shore Crossing (Nez Perce warrior) 352
Shoshone Indians 74, 207, 337, 339, 380
Shoshone River, WY 359
Shoup, Lt. George L. 153, 158, 160
Shrenger, Private Charlie 345
Shurly, Lt. Edward Richard Pitman 297
Sibley, Lt. Frederick 325
Sibley, Gen. Henry 123, 128, 259–263, 266–267, 270–271, 273–274, 278, 325, 411, 417
Sidney, MT 283
Sieber, Al 77, 310, 434, 436–437, 441, 444, 449
Sierra Blanca Mountains, NM 399
Sierra Guards 65
Sierra Madre Mountains., Mexico 395, 442, 445, 449–450, 452, 456
Sierra Nevada (steamer) 397
Siletz, Samuel 85
Siletz Reservation, OR 39
Sill, Gen. Joshua 225
Silver City, ID 385
Silver City, NM 409
Silver City Guards 65
Silver Creek, OR 386
Simonson, Maj. John 107, 119–121
Simpson, Lt. James 97
Sioux City, IA 274
Sioux Indians *see* Lakota bands
Siskiyou Mountains, CA 20, 30
Sisseton Indians (band of Santee) 252, 264
Sitgreaves, Capt. Lorenzo 398
Sitting Bear (Cheyenne informant) 338
Sitting Bull (Hunkpapa Lakota leader) 10, 230, 245, 280, 284, 307, 324, 328–329, 331–334,

336, 358–359, 363, 370–375, 374, 440, 460; harasses Army's supply trains 330–334; surrenders 371; vision of great victory 317
Six-Bit House, OR 33–34
16th Kansas Cavalry 153, 174
16th U.S. Infantry 367
6th Iowa Cavalry 274, 276, 279–281
6th Michigan Cavalry 175, 180
6th Minnesota Infantry 261, 266, 271–272
6th U.S. Cavalry 235, 244, 437, 442, 444, 446, 448, 452, 461
6th U.S. Infantry 58, 139, 145, 248, 313
Skeleton Canyon 458
Skinner, Alonzo 24, 26
Skinya (Apache chief) 437–438, 440
Skullcave fight *see* Salt River Cave
Slade, John (Jack) 166
Sladen, Lt. Joseph Alton 431
Slaughter, Lt. William 40–42
Slaughter Slough 260
Slim Buttes, SD, fight at 327
Small, Lt. John 76
Smith, Capt. A.J. 29–30, 35, 39, 185, 186, 196, 199
Smith, Gen. Andrew Jackson 189
Smith, Maj. Benjamin 294, 297
Smith, Col. Charles 367
Smith, Gen. Charles Ferguson 288
Smith, Gen. Edmund Kirby 212
Smith, Jedediah (Jed) 398
Smith, John (scout for Chivington) 157
Smith, Col. John Eugene 294, 297, 385
Smith, Joseph 94
Smith, Gen. Persifor Frazier 141, 212
Smith, Shotgun 443
Smith's Creek, CA 64
Smoky Hill River, KS 143, 152, 173, 194
Smoky Hill Trail 152, 160, 183, 187, 194, 196, 201, 210
Snake Creek, MT, fight at 361–363
Snake Indians *see* Northern Paiutes
Snake River 46, 48, 74
Snyder, Capt. Simon 333–334
Sobeta (Ute chief) 118
Society of Friends 11, 227, 232
Socorro, NM 107, 110, 122
Soldier Creek, TX, Evans' fight at 225
Solomon River, KS 152–153, 205, 224

Solomon River Valley, KS 142
Solomon's Fork, TX, fight at 216
Sonoita Valley, AZ 441
Sonora, Mexican state 395, 401, 408, 416, 423, 433, 438, 444, 448–449; offers bounty for Apache scalps 402–403
Soo, Capt. 62
Soule, Capt. Silas 157, 159; murder of 162
South Dakota (state) 11
South Park, CO 383
South Pass, WY 16
South Platte Corridor *see* South Platte River
South Platte River, CO 149, 152, 165–167, 179
Southern Cheyenne Indians 132, 208, 337, 365
Southern Pacific RR 444
Southern Plains 207, 219, 248
Southern Ute band 384
Spain 13, 141
Spalding, Eliza 16
Spalding, Henry 16, 25
Spanish 208
Spanish-American War 325
Spence, Orizoba 437–438
Spencer repeating carbines 169, 182, 203, 290
Spirit Gun of the West *see* Carver, Dr. Frank
Spirit Lake, IA, Massacre 249–251, 264, 272, 275
Spokane Gary (Indian chief) 46
Spokane Indians 48
Spokane Plain, battle of 49
Spotted Tail (Brule chief) 140, 285, 344
Spottsylvania Courthouse, VA, Civil War Battle at 142
Sprague, Capt. Franklin 76
Springfield breech-loader 294
Springfield carbine 324
Springfield muzzle-loader 261, 290
Springfield rifle 363
Spy Co 65
Squier, Charles 163
Staked Plains *see* Llano Estacado
Stanard, Lt. A.W. 34
Standing Buffalo 271
Standing in Water (Cheyenne chief) 159
Stanley, Gen. David Sloan 193, 301–303
Stanley, Henry M. (correspondent) 185, 218
Stanley's Stockade, MT 302
Stanton, Secretary of War Edwin M. 147, 170, 172, 201
Stanton, Capt. Frank 427
Stanton, Capt. Henry 107
Stanton, Maj. Thaddeus 311

Steck, Michael 114, 409–411
Steele, Elisha 26
Steele, Maj. Gen. Frederic 74, 76
Steen, Capt. Enoch 406, 408
Steen's Mountain, OR 78, 386
Stein's Peak, NM 409, 432
Steptoe, Col. Edward 44–47, 379
Sternberg, Lt. Sigismund 295–296
Sterrett, Commander Isaac 42
Stevens, Lt. Henry 423
Stevens, Isaac Ingalls 20, 40–41, 45, 49, 77, 348–349
Stevenson, Capt. Matthew R. 40
Stewart, Capt. George 141
Stewart, James (actor) 432
Stewart, John 358
Stewart, Capt. Joseph 65, 67–68
Stone Calf (Cheyenne chief) 243
Stoneman, Gen. George 25, 39, 427
Stone's River, TN, Civil War Battle of 225
Stony Lake, ND 272
Storey, Capt. E.F. 66
Stout, Capt. Richard 263
Strahorn, Robert 310
The Stronghold 460–461
Stuart, Capt. James 23
Stuart, J.E.B. 105, 143, 175, 216
Stufft, Capt. Christian 279
Sturgis, Lt. Jack 359
Sturgis, Capt. Samuel 105, 107, 145, 216, 358–359, 364
Sturgis, Private William 257
Sublette, William 134
Sullivan, Samuel 62
Sully, Gen. Alfred 170, 181, 185, 205, 220–221, 270, 273–285
Sully-Sibley campaigns in Dakota 269–284
Sulphur Springs Valley, AZ 441
Summers, Jesse 70
Summers, Col. Samuel 153
Summit Springs, CO, Battle at, July 1867 206, 219, 325, 336, 442
Sumner, Col. Edwin Vose "Bull" 94, 100, 102–103, 141–145, 142, 166, 187, 407–408
Sun Dance, Plains Indian ritual 314, 317
Sun River Country, MT 309
Superstition Mountains, AZ 435
Susan (wife of Ute chief Johnson) 392
Susanville, CA 61
Sutaio band of Cheyennes 183, 190
Sutter's Mill 146
Sweeney, Edwin (historian/biographer) 406, 411
Sweeney, Lt. Thomas 396, 409, 413–414, 420, 422

Sweet Medicine (Cheyenne peace prophet) 305
Sweetwater Station, WY 175
Swilling, Jack, involved in death of Mangas Coloradas 421–422
Sword (Lakota chief) 344
Sydney Barracks, NE 369
Sykes, Capt. George 105

Tabeguache band of Utes 383, 384
Tabernash, Ute leader 389
Table Rock, OR 23, 27, 28
Tafoya, José 240
Tahchakuty Mountain *see* Killdeer Mountain
Talking Wire *see* telegraph
Tall Bull (Dog Soldier chief) 188–189, 206
Ta-Ma-has (Cayuse chief) 17
Tammutsa (Nez Perce chief) 46
Taos Pueblo Indians 95
Taoyateduta *see* Little Crow
Tappan, Lt. Col. Samuel 162
Tappan Commission investigates Sand Creek 162–163
Tarahumara Indians (Mexico) 454
Tashunka Witko *see* Crazy Horse
Tatum, Lawrie 227–228, 232
Taylor, Nathaniel G. (Commissioner of Indian Affairs) 12, 161
Taza (Apache chief) 417, 437–438, 440
Teal, John 420
Tecumtum (Rogue chief) 34
Telegraph, U.S. connected by 132
Teller, Sec. of Interior Henry 451
Templeton, Lt. George 289
Tendoy (Shoshone chief) 384
Ten Eyck, Capt. Tenodor 292
Tenieya (Tenaya; chief) 55–57
Tennessee (state) 416
10th U.S. Cavalry 202, 205, 220, 225, 236–237, 242
Terrazas, Col. Joaquin 439–440
Territorial Enterprise, Virginia City, NV 61, 63
Terry, Gen. Alfred Howe 301, 312–313, 316–318, 323, 328, 333, 335, 344, 358, 371–372, 432
Terry, MT 286
Terry-Crook combine 325–326
Teton Lakota Indians 132–133, 139, 141, 150, 165–166, 170, 172, 179, 182, 189, 192, 202, 219, 236, 258, 252, 271, 272, 275, 280, 284, 286–287, 295, 301–303–334, 336, 339, 341, 347–348, 362, 370, 433, 453
Tevis, James Henry 410

Texas (state) 7, 92, 99, 209, 211, 442
Texas Panhandle 207
Texas Rangers 209, 213, 216, 219, 231
Theodore Roosevelt Dam, AZ 434
They Died with Their Boots On (movie) 322
3rd Colorado Cavalry 155–157, 160
3rd Minnesota Battery 278
3rd Minnesota Infantry 265–266
3rd U.S. Artillery 54, 96–97
3rd U.S. Cavalry 187, 220, 308, 313, 336, 369, 390, 427–428, 446, 449
3rd U.S. Infantry 97–98, 100, 104, 107, 111, 113, 120, 176, 205
35th Wisconsin Infantry 279
37th U.S. Infantry 130, 185, 193, 220
Thomas, the Rev. Eleasa 87–88
Thomas, Capt. Evan 89
Thomas, Maj./Gen. George H. 212, 215–216
Thomas, Col. Minor 278, 283
Thompson, Al 70
Thompson. Lt. William 241
Thornburgh, Maj. Thomas Tip 369, 390–392
Thunder Bear 140
Thunder Rolling Down The Mountains *see* Young Joseph
Tierra Blanco 105
Tiffany, Joseph, agent 442
Tilokaikt 17
Tilton, Surgeon Henry 363
Tiswin 441
Tohtseeah *see* Prairie Flower
Tolo Lake 351
Tolowa Indians 50
Tombstone, AZ 327, 439
Tombstone Epitaph 439
Tongue River, MT 178, 302, 316, 325, 328–329, 331, 334, 336
Tonkawa Indian 209, 219, 242
Tonopah, NV 327
Tonto Apaches 437, 441
Tonto Basin, AZ 429, 434, 436, 446–447
Toohoolhoolzote (Pikunan leader) 352
Toppenish Creek, fight at 41
Tortilla Flat, AZ 435
Touchet River, WA 19
Trail of Tears 10
Trans-Mississippi West 7, 8, 106, 127, 139, 183, 217, 451
Transcontinental Railroad 20
Trask, Jabez (agent) 384
treaties and agreements: Acoma Peace Agreement, 1852 407–408; Col. Doniphan's Treaty

with Navajos 1846, 95, 118; Collins/Yost treaty with Navajos, 1858 377; Fort Atkinson, Treaty of 1853 210; Fort Wise treaty, 1861 147; Guadalupe Hidalgo, 1848 13, 15, 211, 405; Harney treaty with Lakotas 1856, 140; Horse Creek Treaty 133–136, 140, 202, 284, 286–287; Laramie treaty, 1868 202–298–299, 306, 337, 346, 383; Little Arkansas treaty 183, 189; Medicine Lodge, KS, treaty 201, 218–219, 224, 232–234; Mendota, MN treaty, 1851 252–253; Meriweather's treaties with Navajos 108; Sumner/Calhoun agreement with Navajos, 1851 101; Table Rock, 1853 29; Traverse des Sioux, 1851 249, 252–253; treaty with Navajos, 1861 126; treaty with Nez Perce, 1855 348; treaty with Nez Perce, 1863 350, 354; truce between Mormons and Utes, 1850 377; truce between Mormons and Utes, 1854 379; Ute Treaty at Conejos, 1863 381; Ute Treaty of 1868 384
Tres Castillos, Mexico 440
Tribolet, Charles 455
Trinity River, TX 50, 211
Truckee Rangers 65
Truckee River, NV, battle at 63, 67
The Truth About Geronimo 448
Truth or Consequences, NM 439
Tucson, AZ 408, 413, 416, 418
Tucumcari, NM 207, 217
Tulare Valley, CA 55
Tularenos Indians 51
Tule Canyon (Staked Plains), TX 240–242
Tule Lake, CA 80, 84
Tupper, Capt. Tullius Cicero 444–445
Turkey Leg (Cheyenne chief) 195
Turkey Springs, OK 366
Turner, Nat (revolt) 161
Tutt, Lt. J.W. 61
T'Vault, William 24
12th U.S. Infantry 89, 444
20th U.S. Infantry 313
21st U.S. Infantry 81, 89, 353, 387, 394
24th U.S. Infantry 219, 246
22d U.S. Infantry 325–326, 329, 343, 345
27th U.S. Infantry 293–294
23rd U.S. Infantry 76, 78, 336, 434
Twiggs, Gen. David 212–213

Twiss, Thomas (agent at Upper Platte Agency) 138–141
Two Kettles (Lakota) 284
Two Moons (Cheyenne chief) 295
Two Strike (Brulé Lakota) 460
Tzoe (Apache scout) 449

Uintah band of Utes 383
Ulzana 452
Ulzana's Raid (movie) 452
Umatilla Indians 40–43, 45, 385–387
Umpqua Canyon 23, 26
Umpqua County, OR 33
Umpqua Indians 21
Umpqua Massacre 21
Umpqua Mountains, OR 20, 23
Umpqua River, OR 20–22
Uncompahgre band of Utes 381, 392–393
Underground Railroad 163
U.P. (Union Pacific Railroad) 195, 289, 298, 358, 388
U.P.E.D. (Union Pacific Eastern Division) 197
Upper Agency, MN 252
Upper Cascades 44
Upper Colorado River Drainage System 376
Upper Mississippi River Valley 210, 248, 256, 264
Upper Missouri River 248, 324, 332, 360
Upper Platte Bridge Station 141, 286
Upper Republican river 198
Upper Snake River 384
Upper Sonoran Desert, NM 92
Utah (state) 92, 142, 170, 212–213
Utah Expedition 142, 379
Utah Valley, UT 377
Ute Indians 13, 92–92, 105–108, 114, 116, 129, 132, 208, 217, 376–378, 382–384
Utley, Robert M. (historian) 2, 65, 93, 156, 214, 217, 227, 306, 317, 319, 328, 398, 400, 436, 440, 445–446
Utter-Van Ornum wagon train raid 73

Valdez, Capt. Jose 117–118
Valley Station, CO 156
Valverde, Civil War battle of 128, 417
Van der Horck, Capt. John 265
Van Doen, Maj. Earl 213–214, 216
Van Fleet, Allen 69
Van Moll, Sgt. 315
Varnum, Lt. Charles 319
Vaughn, Jesse W. (historian) 311
Vegara, Lt. Antonio Sanchez 404

Vicksburg, Civil War battle of 129, 225
Victorio (Warm Springs chief) 395, 400, 421, 424, 439–440, 444
Virginia City, MT 285–286, 356
Virginia City, NV 75
Virginia Dale, CO 175
Virginia Rifles 65–66
Visalia, CA 53, 70

Wabash College 293
Wabasha (Santee chief) 260
Wagner (Waggner), Jacob 32
Wagon Box fight, WY 180, 294–297
Wagon Mound, NM 98
Wagon train out of Fort Wallace attacked June 26, 1867, 197
Wahe (chief) 68
Wahpekute (band of Santees) 249, 251–252, 272
Wahpeton (band of Santees) 249, 252, 264
Waiilatpu 17–19, 392
Wake Island 7
Walker (Ute chief) 378–379
Walker, Capt. John 120
Walker, Joseph Reddeford 421
Walker, Maj. Lucius 264
Walker, Maj. Robert 95
Walker, Lt. Col. Samuel 173–183
Walker-Among-Sacred-Stones (Santee leader) 263
Walker River, NV 68
Walker's and Cole's columns rendezvous at Devil's Tower, August 18, 1865, 181
Walker's War 378–379
Walla Walla Council 20
Walla Walla Indians 20, 40, 43, 45
Walla Walla River 16
Wallace (Butterfield employee at Bascom Affair) 413
Wallace, Maj. Andrew Wallace 220
Wallowa Valley, OR 349,–351, 365
Walnut Creek, KS 145
Walsh, Maj. James Morrow 371, 373
Wamdesapa (Santee warrior) 249
Wanship (Ute sub-chief) 378
War Bonnet Creek, NE, fight at 325
War Department, U.S. 86, 140, 165, 170, 184, 210–211, 214, 216, 222, 268, 278, 307, 447, 461
War Path and Bivouac or the Conquest of the Sioux 313
Ward, Felix 411
Ward, John 411–412

Ward Wagon Train Massacre 8, 73
Ware, Lt. Eugene 166
Warm Springs (Apache band) 439, 444
Warm Springs Scouts 77–79
Washburn, Hiram Starrs 425–426
Washington (state) 15, 285
Washington (Ute chief) 389
Washington, Pres. George 9
Washington, Lt. Col. John Macrae 96–97, 102
Washington Pass 118
Washington Territory 20, 26, 38
Washita, battle of 221, 223, 223, 226, 321
Washita River 213–214, 226, 237
Washoe Indians 60–61
Wasson, Joseph 78–79
Wasson, Agent Warren 65–66, 68, 71–72
Watkins, Capt. R.G. 64–65
Wawona, CA 55
Way, Phocion 408–409
Wayne, Gen. Anthony 249
Wayne, John (actor) 245
Weatherlow, Capt. William 61, 68
Weawea (Snake chief) 79
Webster, Ben 67
Weeminuche band of Utes 383
Weiser, Dr. Josiah 271, 273
Welch (Butterfield employee at Bascom affair) 413
Weller, Gov. Joh 58
Wellman, Paul 2
Wells, Danie 378
Wesier Valley 353
Wessells, Lt. Col. Henry 293, 370
West, Col. Joseph Rodman 420–421
West Point (U.S. Military Academy) 20
West Texas 207
Western Apaches *see* Coyotero, Tonto, White Mountain
Western Shoshone Indians 74
Western Slope of CO 383
Wharton, Capt. Henry 139
Wheatley, James 292
Wheaton, Col. Frank 81, 83–85, 89, 386
Whetstone Mountains, AZ 428
Whipple, Lt. Amie 353, 398
Whipple, Bishop Henry 251
Whiskey Creek, OR 26, 37
White, David 289
White, Sarah Catherine 461
White Antelope (Cheyenne chief) 147, 156, 158
White Bird Canyon, battle of 352–353, 355, 444
White Bull 345

White Earth *see* Tierra Blanca
White Mountain Apaches 442, 229, 251, 455–456
White River, CO 388–394
White River, NE 41, 306, 460
White Wolf *see* Lobo Blanco
Whitestone Hill, Dakota, Battle of 251, 275–277, 280
Whitfield, John 138
Whitman, Alice Clarissa 17
Whitman, Marcus 16–17, 132, 388
Whitman, Narcissa 16–17, 132
Whitman, Lt. Royal Emerson 427–428, 430
Whitman Massacre 8, 18–19
Wichita Expedition 213
Wickenburg, AZ 429, 433
Wilcox, Agent Philip 451
Wild Hog (Cheyenne chief) 365
Willamette Valley 18, 22–23
Willamette Valley Treaty Commission 19
Willcox, Gen. Orlando 441, 443, 445
Willcox, AZ 447
Williams, Calvin 62
Williams, David 62
Williams, Cpt. James 426
Williams, James O. 62
Williams, Oscar 62
Williams, Capt. Robert 35
Williams Station, NV 62
Williamson, Pvt. James 162
Williford, Capt. George 178
Willow Creek, CA 91
Wilson, Col. David 274, 276
Wilson, Isaac 78
Wilson-Graham Circus 189
Wilson's Creek, Civil War battle of 149
Winchester Repeating Rifles 461
Wind River Valley, WY 172
Window Rock, NM 101

Winder, Capt. Charles 46
Winema (Toby) 87–88
Wingfield, Edward H 110.
Winnebago Scouts 175, 180, 282
Winnemucca (chief) 60–62
Winnemucca, Sarah 60, 385
Winnipeg, Manitoba, Canada, *see* Fort Gary
Winslow, AZ 437
Winters, Lt. William 426
Wintun Indians 50
Wisconsin (state) 9, 173
Wisdom, MT 355
Withers, Lt. John 34
Wolf Mountain Campaign 341–343, 385
Wood, Charles 250
Wood, George 250
Wood, Col. Leonard 456–457
Wood, William 250
Wood Mountain 370, 374
Woods Lake, *see* Lone Tree Lake, MN
Wool, Gen. John 31, 37–39, 42–43
Wounded Knee, SD 142, 387, 460
Wovoka 235, 459
Wowinape 268
Wozencraft, Oliver 53
Wright, Ben 80
Wright, Gen. George 43, 46, 49, 71–72
Wright, Lt. Thomas 25, 89
Wrinkled Hand Chase 239
Wynkoop, Maj. Edward 153, 155–157, 162, 183, 185, 187–188, 190, 193
Wyoming 92, 132, 134, 405

Yakima and Coastal Wars 39
Yakima Indians 20, 40, 43
Yakima Valley 41, 43
Yampa Band, Utes 383

Yampa Valley, CO 383
Yamparikas 208
Yankton, Nakota 252, 278
Yanktonai, Nakota 252, 272, 278, 280
Yates, Capt. George 322
Yavapai (Apaches) 426, 433–434
Yellow Bear, Arapaho 226
Yellow Bird (medicine man) 462
Yellow Hair (Cheyenne warrior) 325
Yellow Medicine River, MN 252
Yellow Wolf (Cheyenne chief) 159, 357
Yellowstone National Park 356–357
Yellowstone River, MT 284, 286, 316–317, 324, 327, 333, 336, 355
Yellowstone Valley 356–357
Yerba Buena 50
Yosemite Indians 53, 55–56
Yosemite National Park, CA 51, 55
Yosemite Valley, CA 57
Yost, Acting Superintendent Sam 114–116, 119
Young, Brigham 61, 377–379
Young, Capt. Samuel Baldwin Marks 426
Yreka, CA 23, 27, 33, 80
Yreka Union 32
Yuki Indians 57, 59
Yuma (Apaches) 395, 396–399, 429
Yuma Crossing of Colorado River 395–396
Yuma River, AZ 395
Yurok Indians 50

Zarcillos Largos (Navajo headman) 104, 115, 117, 119
Zulu 64
Zuni Indians 92, 116–119, 129